CENSUS OF INDIA 1891

Census of India 1871-1951, 9 Sets In 384 Bindings (9788121258876) Rs. 700000

Census of India 1891, 28 Vols. In 49 Bindings (978-81-212-7129-5) Rs. 125000

1. General Report (9788121269834) Rs. 1450
2. General Tables For British Provinces And Feudatory States (9788121269810) Rs. 2710 (Vol. I)
3. General Tables For British Provinces And Feudatory States (9788121269797) Rs. 950 (Vol. II)
4. Assam - Report (9788121269773) Rs. 2390 (Vol. I, V.1)
5. Assam - Tables (9788121269759) Rs. 2210 (Vol. II, V.2)
6. Assam - Provincial Tables (9788121269735) Rs. 1310 (Vol. II, V.3)
7. The Lower Provinces of Bengal and their Feudatories - The Report (9788121269711) Rs. 1660 (Vol. III)
8. The Lower Provinces of Bengal and their feudatories - The Administrative Tables (9788121269698) Rs. 4200 (Vol. IV)
9. The Lower Provinces of Bengal and their feudatories - The Caste Tables (9788121269674) Rs. 2600 (Vol. V, Pt. 1)
10. Lower Provinces of Bengal - The Provincial Tables (9788121269650) Rs. 1980 (Vol. V, Pt. 2)
11. Berar or the Hyderabad Assigned Districts (9788121269636) Rs. 3360 (Vol. VI)
12. Bombay and Its Feudatories - Report (9788121269612) Rs. 4010 (Vol. VII, Pt. 1)
13. Bombay And Its Feudatories - Imperial Tables (9788121269599) Rs. 790 (Vol. VIII, Pt. 2)
14. Imperial Series - Burma Report (9788121269575) Rs. 2320 (Vol. IX-V.1)
15. Imperial Tables - Burma Report (9788121269551) Rs. 3360 (Vol. X-V.2)
16. Provincial Tables Burma Report (9788121269537) Rs. 3510 (Vol. X-V.3)
17. Provincial Tables Burma Report (9788121269513) Rs. 3630 (Vol. X-V.4)
18. The Central Provinces And Feudatories - The Report (9788121269490) Rs. 2290 (Vol. XI, Pt. 1)
19. The Central Provinces And Feudatories - Imperial tables and supplementary returns (9788121268936) Rs. 2010 (Vol. XII)
20. Madras The Report On The Census (9788121269476) Rs. 2870 (Vol. XIII)
21. Madras - Tables I to XVII-C, British Territory (9788121269452) Rs. 3490 (Vol. XIV)
22. Madras - Tables A TO E, British Territory. Tables for feudatory States and A Caste Index (9788121269438) Rs. 2820 (Vol. XV)
23. The North Western Provinces and Outh - Report and Provincial Tables (9788121268912) Rs. 3100 (Vol. XVI, Pt. 1)
24. The North - Western Provinces and Oudh- Imperial Tables (9788121269414) Rs. 2000 (Vol. XVII, Pt. 2)
25. The North - Western Provinces and Oudh- Imperial Caste Tables (9788121269391) Rs. 3020 (Vol. XVIII, Pt. 3)
26. Punjab and Its Feudatories - The Report on the Census (9788121269377) Rs. 2710 (Vol. XIX, Pt. 1)
27. Punjab and Its Feudatories - Imperial Tables and Supplementary Returns for the British Territory (9788121269353) Rs. 1370 (Vol. XX, Pt. 2)
28. Punjab and Its Feudatories - Imperial Tables and Supplementary Returns for the Native States, Together With A Caste Index (9788121269339) Rs. 4910 (Vol. XXI, Pt. 3)
29. Report on The Census of The Districts of Ajmere-Merwara (9788121269056) Rs. 720 (Vol. XXII)
30. His Highness The Nizam's Dominions - Report (9788121269315) Rs. 2240 (Vol. XXIII, Pt. 1)
31. His Highness The Nizam's Dominions - Report (9788121269292) Rs. 2410 (Vol. XXIII, Pt. 2)
32. His Highness The Nizam's Dominions - Imperial And Supplementry Tables and Caste Index (9788121269278) Rs. 3390 (Vol. XXIII, Pt. 3)
33. Baroda - Report (9788121269254) Rs. 3810 (Vol. XXIV, Pt. 1)
34. Baroda - Tables (9788121269230) Rs. 2620 (Vol. XXIV, Pt. 2)
35. Mysore - Report (9788121269216) Rs. 2590 (Vol. XXV, Pt. 1)
36. Mysore - Imperial Tables (9788121269193) Rs. 1600 (Vol. XXV, Pt. 2)
37. Mysore - Tables (9788121269179) Rs. 5320 (Vol. XXV, Pt. 3)
38. Mysore - Supplementary Tables (9788121269155) Rs. 3590 (Vol. XXV, Pt. 4)
39. Mysore- Supplement to the Mysore census report of 1891 being a list of villages in the Mysore province and : comparing the population as per Censuses of 1891, 1881 & 1871 (9788121279024) Rs. 5350 (Vol. XXV, Pt. 5)
40. Rajputana - The Report, Imperial Tables And Supplementary Returns (9788121269131) Rs. 2330 (Vol. XXVI, Pt. 1)
41. Rajputna - The Provincial Tables and Remarks (9788121269117) Rs. 550 (Vol. XXVI, Pt. 2)
42. Central India (9788121269094) Rs. 2000 (Vol. XXVII)
43. Kashmir State - The Report on the census and Imperial and supplementary Tables (9788121269070) Rs. 2290 (Vol. XXVIII)
44. The Census of Calcutta (9788121269032) Rs. 890
45. Report on the census of Cochin (9788121269018) Rs. 790 (Pt. 1)
46. Report on the census of Cochin - The Final Census Tables with Appendices (9788121268998) Rs. 910 (Pt. 2)
47. Report on the Census of Coorg (9788121268974) Rs. 730
48. Report on the census of Travancore -Report (9788121274029) Rs. 4220 (Vol. I)
49. Report on the census of Travancore -Appendix (9788121268950) Rs. 5300 (Vol. II)

Owing to the antiquity and rarity of this book, certain pages are regrettably absent, and readability is compromised due to the blurring of the original text. If you possess any insights regarding the availability of these missing sections, kindly inform us. Your assistance is crucial in ensuring the completion of this significant work for the benefit of future generations.

CENSUS OF INDIA, 1891

BOOK-18: VOL. XI

THE CENTRAL PROVINCES AND FEUDATORIES

PART - I

THE REPORT

B. ROBERTSON

GYAN

Published by

Gyan Publishing House
5, Ansari Road
Daryaganj, New Delhi-110002
Phone: 011-47034999, 9811692060
E-mail: books@gyanbooks.com

Distribution Network
gyanbooks.com
India, USA, Canada, UK, Australia

ISBN: 978-81-212-7129-5 (Set) 28 Vols. In 49 Bindings
978-81-212-6949-0 (PB) Book-18, Vol. XI, Pt. I

First Published, 1893

2nd Impression 2024

Printed at: Gyan Press, Delhi.

CENSUS OF INDIA 1891

CENSUS OF INDIA, 1891.

VOLUME XI.

THE CENTRAL PROVINCES AND FEUDATORIES.

PART I.

THE REPORT.

BY

B. ROBERTSON,

OF THE INDIAN CIVIL SERVICE,

PROVINCIAL SUPERINTENDENT OF CENSUS OPERATONS.

CALCUTTA:

OFFICE OF THE SUPERINTENDENT OF GOVERNMENT PRINTING, INDIA.

1893.

ERRATA.—Vol. XI.

Page 232, in column 3 of table, *for* "Perso" *read* "personal and".
„ 244, line 14 from top, *for* "term" *read* "terms".
„ 249, line 16 from bottom, *after* "hundred" *add* "and".
„ 258, line 3 from top, *for* "9" *read* "·9".
„ 259, line 6 from top, *for* "36·7" *read* "39·2".
„ „ in column 4 of table, last line, *insert* "65·14".
„ 290, line 23 from bottom, *for* "Kidnepped" *read* "Kidnapped".
„ 299, line 3 from top, *for* "time sulted" *read* "time resulted".
„ line 5 from top, *for* "T religion" *read* "The religion".

CENSUS OF 1881.

CENTRAL PROVINCES REPORT.

INDEX.

Part I.—THE RESULTS OF THE CENSUS.

Part II.—THE OPERATIONS OF THE CENSUS.

APPENDICES.

CONTENTS.

Part I.—THE RESULTS OF THE CENSUS.

CHAPTER I.—GENERAL.

CHAPTER II.—FLUCTUATIONS OF THE POPULATION.

CHAPTER III.—RELIGION AND SECT.

CHAPTER IV.—SEX AND AGE.

CHAPTER V.—CIVIL CONDITION.

CHAPTER VI.—INFIRMITIES.

CHTPTER VII.—EDUCATION.

CHAPTER VIII.—LANGUAGES.

CHAPTER IX.—BIRTH-PLACE.

CHAPTER X.—CASTES, TRIBES, AND RACES.

CHAPTER X.—CASTES, TRIBES AND RACES—*contd.*

CHAPTER XI.—OCCUPATION.

CHAPTER XI.—OCCUPATION—*contd.*

PART II.—THE OPERATIONS OF THE CENSUS.

CHAPTER I.—PRELIMINARY MEASURES.

CHAPTER II.—THE ENUMERATION.

CHAPTER III.—SPECIAL AND SUBSIDIARY MATTERS.

CHAPTER IV.—THE PREPARATION OF THE RESULTS.

CHAPTER IV.—THE PREPARATION OF THE RESULTS—*contd.*

CHAPTER V.—PRINTING.

CHAPTER VI.—THE LAST.

APPENDICES.

APPENDIX A.—CENSUS CIRCULARS AND INSTRUCTIONS.

APPENDIX B.—VILLAGES CONTAINING OVER 3,000 POPULATION.

APPENDIX C.—PROPORTIONAL TABLES OF AGE AND SEX.

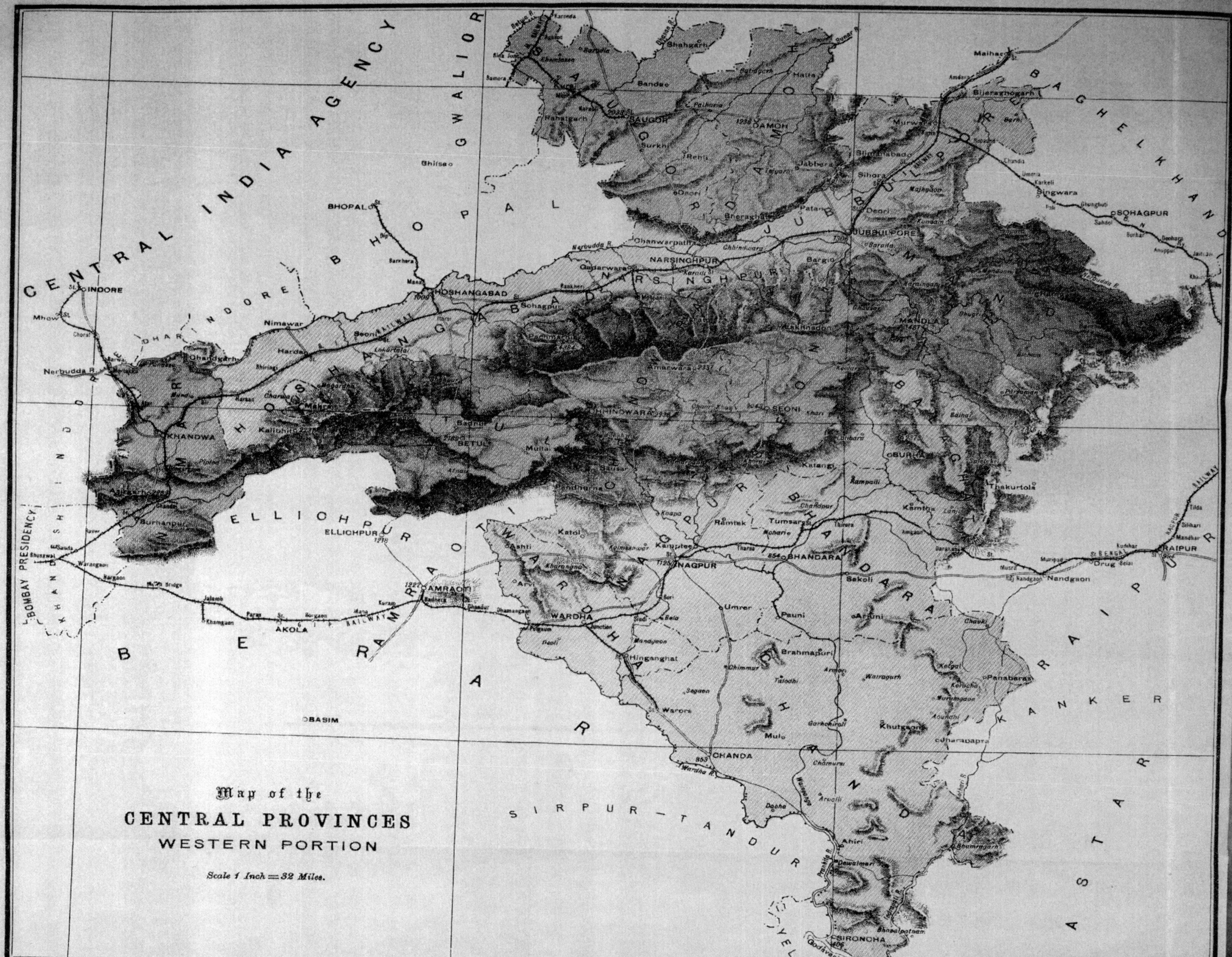

Reg. No. 381, Sup., Census C. P.—Jan. 95—610.

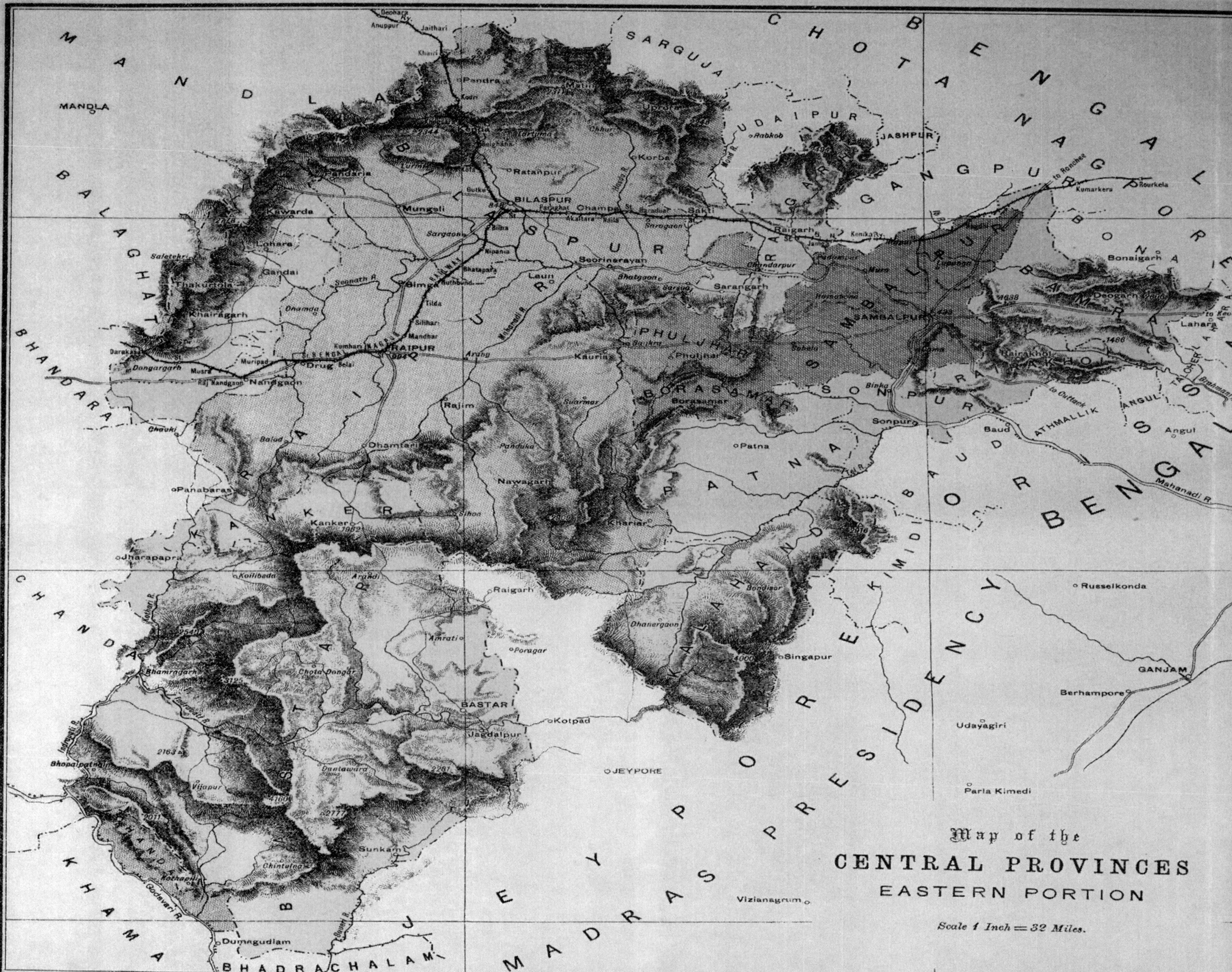

Map of the
CENTRAL PROVINCES
EASTERN PORTION

Scale 1 Inch = 32 Miles.

CENSUS OF 1891.

PART I.

THE RESULTS OF THE CENSUS.

PART I.

THE RESULTS OF THE CENSUS.

CHAPTER I.

GENERAL DESCRIPTION, PHYSICAL AND CLIMATIC DIVISIONS, AREA, DENSITY, RURAL AND URBAN POPULATION.

1. The fourth general Census of the Central Provinces was taken on the night of the 26th of February 1891. With the results thus disclosed the present Report will deal. But before entering on the task I propose giving a short account of the main physical features of the country, and of such events in its history as have a more direct bearing on the questions regarding its population, which are to be discussed.

2. **Historical retrospect.**—Of the history of the tracts which were in 1861 combined to form the Central Provinces, we have excellent summaries in the Introduction to the Gazetteer published in 1870, and in Chapter I of the second part of the Annual Administration Report. From both I shall freely quote for the purpose of the slight sketch which will be here given.

Gond rule.—I pass over the period when the Rajput Princes established themselves in the Nerbada valley, extending their power to the Nagpur country and Chhatisgarh. With the exception of the Haihaibansis who ruled at Ratanpur in Chhatisgarh until overthrown by the Marathas in the eighteenth century, all traces of the other Aryan kingdoms early disappeared. "The conquerors were swallowed up by the conquered, the lower race assimilated to itself the superior element, for as time goes on certain Gond kingdoms replace all other dynasties and divide between them the whole of Gondwána." Coming to the sixteenth century we find the Gond Chief of Garha Mandla ruling over Saugor and Damoh on the Vindhyan plateau, Hoshangabad, Narsinghpur, and Jubbulpore in the Nerbada valley, and Mandla and Seoni in the Satpura highlands. The succeeding century saw the rise of the Gond house of Deogarh with possessions above and below the Southern Satpuras. The remaining Gond kingdoms were those of Kherla and Chanda, the former of which became extinct as early as A. D. 1433. "The other kingdoms flourished, or perhaps it may be more correct to say, existed, for a longer period. Garha Mandla acknowledged the supremacy of the Moghal Emperors, and Deogarh and Chanda also tendered their submission to the imperial power, but they all remained practically independent, their remoteness and inaccessibility doubtless preventing anything like interference in their affairs. Eventually the Deogarh Prince turned Mahomedan, taking his independence, which was threatened, as the reward of his conversion, and it was not till the advent of the Marathas that the Gond rule came to an end. It must not, however, be supposed that the whole of the present area of the Central Provinces was parcelled out among these Gond Chiefs, and that the limits of their kingdoms remained for long fixed or unchanged. The Mahomedan Princes and Generals settled in Malwa occupied at times some of the finest parts of the Nerbada valley, chiefly in the Hoshangabad district. It could not but be that, with an imperial seat of Government at Burhanpur, the country within a considerable radius was entirely under the Imperial Government; but in reality until the Marathas came the Gond Kings or petty local Chiefs alternately relaxed and tightened their hold on these territories, and there was no other settled or recognized government."

Maratha rule.—In 1737 Raghoji Bhonsla, the founder of the Bhonsla State, received an order from the Peshwa directing him to collect the chouth of Berar and Gondwána, and in the following year he came to Nagpur. Finding a feud raging as to the succession to the Gond principality of Deogarh, the Maratha leader interfered in the quarrel and was not long in usurping the whole territory of the Prince whom he had offered to support. By 1743 he had acquired the Deogarh kingdom, and had penetrated into Chhatisgarh and rendered it tributary. Within the next ten years Chhatisgarh, Sambalpur, and even Cuttack, were added to the Bhonsla State, in which the kingdom of Chanda was also merged. The Marathas had meantime also gained a footing in the Saugor country in the north. On the decline of the Moghal power, Chhatra Sál, the powerful Chief of Panna, took the opportunity to overrun the greater part of Saugor and Damoh and add them to his territory; but in 1733, finding himself hard-pressed by the Mahomedan Governor of Allahabad and Malwa, he called in the help of the Peshwa. On Chhatra Sál's death in 1735, he left one-third of his kingdom to the Peshwa, who sent an agent to take charge of his heritage, and thus founded the rule of the Maratha Subas of Saugor. Continuing to hold office hereditarily, they in time began to take possession of the territories of the Gond Kings of Garha Mandla. The crushing disaster of Pánipat in 1761 for a time stopped the Maratha encroachments, but in 1781 the independence of the Gonds was completely overthrown, and their possessions became part of the Maratha principality of Saugor. Ten years later the Bhonsla Raja of Nagpur expelled the Saugor Marathas from the greater part of the Nerbada valley; in 1799 he also gained possession of Mandla. The twenty years that elapsed before the coming of British rule were troublous times for the Nerbada valley. There was constant warring between Bhopal and the Maratha Generals; in 1805 Scindia invaded Hoshangabad, and for some time held part of the district, and lastly came the scourge of the Pindharis who for several years devastated the country. In 1818 the overthrow of the Peshwa gave the British all the territories in Saugor and the Nerbada valley, which were nominally his. The same year also saw the disturbances in Nagpur and the flight of Appa Sahib. By treaty all the Bhonsla possessions about the Nerbada were ceded to the British, and what remained of the Bhonsla State was taken under management during the minority of the young Raja who had been placed upon the throne. In 1830 the government was assumed by the Raja himself, but on his death, without heirs in 1853, the State lapsed to the British.

British rule.—Previous to the formation of the Central Provinces, British rule had thus been established in the Saugor and Nerbada territories from the year 1818, and in the Nagpur Province from 1853. In 1861 both were united, and the administration of the Central Provinces established. Sambalpur, which had passed into the possession of the British Government in 1849 and had formerly been governed from Hazaribagh or Cuttack, was incorporated with the Provinces in 1862, and in 1864 the new administration received a fresh accession of territory by the addition to it of the Nimar district in the Nerbada and Tapti valleys.

3. **Aryan colonization.**—*The Nerbada Valley.*—The earliest influx of Hindu settlers into the Nerbada country is believed to have taken place about the time of the Emperor Akbar. In 1564 Asaf Khan, the Imperial Viceroy at Kara Manikpur on the Ganges, invaded Gondwána at the head of a considerable force and took the fortress of Chauragarh, securing an immense booty. "This invasion is remarkable as probably having opened out the valley for the first time to the foreign immigration which has been the means of reclaiming it from barbarism. Asaf Khan held Garha for some years as an independent principality, and there are various circumstances which indicate an incursion of northern settlers nearly contemporaneous with his epoch. Tradition is almost silent now with regard to ages so remote, but Sleeman says that in his time (1825) it spoke of an intercourse with Delhi and a subjection, nominal or real, to its sovereigns from Akbar downwards, but that no mention was ever made of any such connection before Akbar's reign. He adds that the oldest rupees found in the earth along the line of the Nerbada were of the reign of Akbar. The mass of the Hindu population is probably, however, of later date, and counting by the number of generations may be referred to the time of Aurangzeb." The establishment of the Maratha administration at Saugor also at a later period made way for a considerable influx of Hindu immigrants from the north. As the settlers spread over the low country, the Gonds retired before them to the hills or remained behind as drudges of the soil, becoming gradually absorbed, though never so completely as to obtain equality with the people who had overrun them.

The Nagpur country.—The colonization of the Nagpur country took place in much the same manner, but in this case the settlers were Marathas from the Deccan. The immigration commences about the year 1700, when Bakht Buland, the founder of the city of Nagpur, was Raja of Deogarh. His rule was an era of great improvement in the country which he governed. He employed Mahomedans and Hindus of ability to introduce order and regularity into his immediate domain, industrious settlers were attracted from all quarters, and agriculture and manufactures made some progress. Under his son, who succeeded him, immigration continued to receive encouragement. It was on the death of the latter in 1739 that arose the quarrels which ended in the transfer of the Deogarh kingdom to the Marathas. With Raghoji, the founder of the Bhonsla State, occurred the great influx of Marathas, which resulted in the spread of the Kunbis and cognate Maratha tribes over the Nagpur plain; from this time the vernacular in every village became Marathi.

Chhatisgarh.—Chhatisgarh had for centuries been in the possession of the line of Haihaibansi Chiefs, whose rule extended down to the year 1740, when it was first assailed by the Marathas. Under the Haihaibansis the country had at an early date been peopled by settlers from the north and west. The strongest body of these, the Chamárs, have been so long settled in Chhatisgarh that they seem to have no kind of tradition, even in the remote past, of any other home. Many of the other Hindu castes were also settlers in Chhatisgarh when the country was still a wilderness; they are known as Jharias or forest people, to distinguish them from later immigrations which took place two or three hundred years ago.

Nimar.—The outlying districts of Nimar on the west and Sambalpur on the east have also long possessed a resident Hindu population. Lying, as it does, on the high road between Hindustan and the Deccan, Nimar has been frequently overrun by northern races. Before the middle of the fourteenth century it had been held by Rajput Chiefs; but that any considerable numbers of pure blooded Aryans had then settled in the district is highly improbable. In 1310 the Mahomedans conquered Malwa and subsequently extended their authority over Northern Nimar; during their rule took place a second influx of Rajputs into the country, many of the chief Nimar families tracing back the establishment of their Watans to the time of the Ghori Sultans. In 1600 Akbar invaded the Deccan.

"The conquest by Akbar was certainly an era in the history of Nimar; an immense impulse was given to the population and agriculture of the district. Burhanpur became an important city and the seat of the viceroyalty of the Deccan. Immense armies marched through the district between Hindustan and the Deccan. The demand for food-grains must have been enormous, and the culturable land of Nimar acquired a high value. But neither the proud and lazy Rajputs nor the feeble aborigines could provide the labour to bring forth its treasures, and a large influx of the best agricultural races took place. Kunbis of different classes came from the Deccan and Gujerat, and Gujars, Mális, and other industrious classes from Hindustan" (*Nimar Settlement Report*, page 60).

The Uria country.—Sambalpur and the Eastern Feudatories were peopled at an early date by Urias from Orissa; in all there is besides a large aboriginal population.

4. **Boundaries and physical divisions of the Province.**—The Central Provinces lie, as their name implies, about the centre of the Indian Peninsula, and cover an area of 115,936 square miles. Their greatest length is about 500 miles and their extreme breadth 600 miles. They are bounded on the north by the Central India States, which comprise the tracts of Baghelkhand and Bundelkhand, and by the district of Jhansi belonging to the North-West Provinces. On the north-west lie Gwalior, Bhopal, and Indore. To the west and south the Provinces are bounded by the Khandesh district of the Bombay Presidency, by Berar and the Nizam's Dominions. On the east come the Godavery district of Madras, the Agency tracts of Vizagapatam and Ganjam, and the Feudatory Mahals of Orissa. Along the north-east border lie the Native States of Chhota-Nagpur. The Central Provinces are thus almost completely surrounded by foreign territory.

Physical divisions.—Most prominent among the physical features of the Province is the range of the Satpuras, which, crossing it from east to west, divides the country of the Nerbada valley in the north from the plains of Nagpur and Chhatisgarh in the south. Beyond the Nerbada valley and separated from it by the range of the Vindhyas lie the districts of Saugor and Damoh; the streams that drain these districts run north to join the Jumna. The tehsil of Murwára, which belongs to the Jubbulpore district, though lying below the Vindhyan escarpment, also sends its surplus waters not to the Nerbada, but to the Ganges. Properly speaking, Murwára should, therefore, have been classed with Saugor and Damoh in what may be called the Vindhyan division, but the inconvenience of splitting up the returns for districts, which alone appear in the published Census Tables, induces me to include it with the rest of the Jubbulpore district in the next physical division—that of the Nerbada valley. This comprises the districts of Jubbulpore, Narsinghpur, and Hoshangabad, and the Native State of Makrai, lying along the course of the Nerbada, between the Vindhyas and the Satpuras. To these might be added the northern part of Nimar which slopes from the Satpuras towards the Nerbada; the rest of the district falls within the Tapti valley and forms the commencement of the fertile plain of Khandesh. It is, however, perhaps preferable to keep the district as a division by itself; it has a distinct history, and its people are to a certain extent different from those of the Nerbada valley and talk a different dialect. Next in order comes the hill country of the Satpuras, consisting of the districts of Mandla, Seoni, Chhindwara, and Betul. Here again has been included a tract of country comprising the greater part of the Sausar tehsil of the Chhindwara district, which lying below the ghats should properly have been classed with the plain country which it adjoins. The fifth division is made up of the districts of Wardha, Nagpur, Chanda, Bhandara, and Balaghat, lying in the valleys of the

Wardha and Wainganga rivers, both of which flow towards the Godavery. The district of Balaghat again presents a difficulty; part of it situated above the ghats belongs to the Satpura plateau rather than to the Nagpur plain. The Burha tehsil, however, which is the best part of the district, lies in the Wainganga valley and closely resembles the neighbouring district of Bhandara; and Balaghat has, therefore, been classed among the plains districts. To the east of the Nagpur conntry, from which it is divided by a range of hills running south from the main chain of the Satpuras, is the great plain of Chhatisgarh forming the upper basin of the Mahanadi. It comprises the districts of Raipur and Bilaspur, and the Native States of Kanker, Nandgaon, Khairagarh, Chhuikhadan, Kawardha, and Sakti. With these may be included also the dependency of Bastar, which lies to the south of the Chhatisgarh plain proper. Separated from the latter by a low range of hills is the Sambalpur country which forms the central basin of the Mahanadi. This forms the seventh and last division of the Province; it is made up of the British district of Sambalpur and the Feudatory States of Raigarh, Sarangarh, Bamra, Rairakhol, Sonpur, Patna, and Kalahandi.

As has been remarked, the arrangement of the Province into these seven physical divisions is in some degree defective, but it appears the best that can be made without breaking up districts and States. In dealing with the results of the Census, it will frequently be of advantage to view them in the light of the racial and physical distinctions which these divisions represent, rather than in connection with the territorial units which have been adopted for administrative purposes.

5. Physical Aspect,* Climate, Crops, etc.—A statement is appended which shows the cultivated and uncultivated area in each district, the main crops grown, and the average rainfall for the past twentyfour years. The figures for cultivation in the khalsa of British districts have been taken from the Revenue Reports for the season 1890-91; for the zemindaris, full details are not available. The latest information with regard to the latter, which can be looked upon as at all complete, is given in a statement published by the Settlement Department in 1886; from this the areas have been calculated both for zemindaris and Native States. The proportions of the area of each district under the different kinds of crops have been taken from Tabular Statement I appended to the Annual Administration Report for 1890-91. Except in Bhandara, they refer only to the khalsa, no details being forthcoming for zemindaris. The remeasurement that is taking place in connection with the present Settlement proves the old statistics to be, in many cases, untrustworthy; where, as in the zemindaris and Feudatory States, these are alone available, it is probable that the figures I have given are frequently wide of the mark. The same must be said of the returns for Betul, Chanda, Balaghat, Bhandara, and Seoni, which have been compiled according to the records of the old survey. The remarks of the last Administration Report on the subject may be quoted:

"As an instance of the extent to which the Provincial area statistics are affected by the remeasurement operation which is concluded or is in progress, it may be observed that the area returned this year as under crop exceeds that so returned in the previous year by nearly 10 per cent., the area under current fallow also being in excess. It is of course impossible that so large an increase in cultivation could have taken place in a single year."

The appended table can, therefore, in many cases, be looked upon as only an approximation to the actual state of cultivation in the Province, but it is near enough the truth to exhibit what are the most marked distinctions in this respect between the different districts and physical divisions.

* The descriptions are taken mainly from the published Settlement Reports.

Statement showing Cultivation, Crops, *and* Rainfall *for Districts and States.*

Districts and States.	Area in Square Miles.				Percentage of Cropped Area under					Average rainfall of the past 24 years.
	Total.	Uncultivated.	Cultivated.	Percentage of cultivated area on total area.	Wheat.	Rice.	Other food-grains.	Cotton.	Other crops.	
1	2	3	4	5	6	7	8	9	10	11
Saugor	4,007	2,406	1,601	40	59	2	25	4	10	46·9
Damoh	2,831	1,867	964	34	43	10	32	1	14	49·6
Total Vindhyan Districts	*6,838*	*4,273*	*2,565*	*38*	*53*	*5*	*28*	*3*	*11*	...
Jubbulpore	3,948	1,821	2,127	54	46	11	29	2	12	57·1
Narsinghpur	1,916	856	1,060	55	38	4	27	6	25	53·6
Hoshangabad	4,594	2,860	1,734	38	57	1	21	2	19	47·1
Makrai	155	107	48	31	...	...	...	...	...	...
Total Nerbada Valley	*10,613*	*5,644*	*4,969*	*47*	*48*	*6*	*25*	*3*	*18*	...
Nimar	*3,357*	*2,614*	*743*	*22*	*6*	*1*	*61*	*18*	*14*	*32·8*
Mandla	5,056	4,153	903	18	24	14	44	...	18	52·3
Seoni	3,198	1,875	1,323	41	35	13	34	1	17	51·7
Chhindwara	4,630	3,229	1,401	30	28	1	46	9	16	44·2
Betul	3,824	2,659	1,165	31	19	1	43	1	36	44·0
Total Satpura Districts	*16,708*	*11,916*	*4,792*	*29*	*26*	*7*	*42*	*3*	*22*	...
Nagpur	3,843	1,805	2,038	53	30	3	35	12	20	46·2
Wardha	2,428	810	1,618	67	19	...	28	30	23	40·9
Chanda	10,749	9,402	1,347	13	14	28	37	3	18	50·4
Bhandara	3,968	2,504	1,464	37	14	53	23	...	10	54·7
Balaghat	3,139	2,530	609	19	6	62	25	...	7	67·0
Total Nagpur Plain	*24,127*	*17,051*	*7,076*	*29*	*19*	*24*	*30*	*10*	*17*	...
Raipur	11,724	7,525	4,199	36	7	47	25	1	20	51·5
Bilaspur	8,341	5,872	2,469	30	7	51	25	1	16	46·2
Chhatisgarh Feudatories	4,321	2,908	1,413	33	...	...	...	...	...	...
Total Chhatisgarh	*24,386*	*16,305*	*8,081*	*33*	...	...	...	...	...	..
Bastar	13,062	...	...	...	...	...	...	...	...	...
Sambalpur	4,948	3,205	1,743	35	1	76	13	3	7	77·1
Uria Feudatories	11,897	8,841	3,056	26	...	...	...	...	...	...
Total Uria Country	*16,845*	*12,046*	*4,799*	*29*	...	...	...	...	...	...

Note.—In column 4 current fallows have been included. In Jubbulpore 460 square miles or more than one-fifth of the cultivated area has been thus returned. In the rest of the Province the proportion shown as fallow is about one acre in every twelve.

Vindhyan Division.—The districts of Saugor and Damoh, which are situated on the Vindhyan plateau, form a hilly and undulating country. Saugor may be described as an elevated plain sloping to the north-east, broken in places by low hills of sandstone; the soil of the south and centre is black soil formed by the decaying trap, and to the north and east is a reddish-brown alluvium. In Damoh the parts to the south and east are hilly and wooded; the rest of the district consists of open plains of varying degrees of fertility interspersed with detached hills and low ranges, the richest tracts lying in the centre. As might be expected from their elevated position—the hills attain in places a height of 2,500 feet—the climate of both districts is salubrious, and the temperature is lower than in the districts of the Nerbada valley. The staple crop of the country is wheat, which in Saugor is grown in 59 per cent. of the cultivated area, and in Damoh in 43 per cent. Gram and other food-grains are extensively produced. The Vindhyan division covers about a sixteenth part of the total area of the Province, and next to the Nerbada valley it contains the largest proportion of cultivation.

The Nerbada Valley.—The valley of the Nerbada is a long narrow plain of alluvial soil sloping gently to the south-west. In Jubbulpore and in parts of Narsinghpur, the valley extends on both sides of the Nerbada, but along the entire length of the Hoshangabad district the plain lies on the left bank of the river, which throughout forms the northern boundary of the district. On both sides the valley is shut in by hills, on the north by the steep bluffs of the Vindhyan range, and on the south by the Satpuras. The northern part of the Jubbulpore district lies within the Bhanrer and Kaimur hills, off-shoots of the Vindhyas, and thus forms no part of the Nerbada valley proper, the streams which drain it flowing north to join the Jumna and the Ganges. The soil of the valley varies in places with the nature of the rocks of which the adjoining hill ranges are composed. In general, the black soil prevails, but in the north where small ranges of sandstone occur the soil is light, while lower down the valley where the hills that bound it on the south are also of sandstone, the surface is again largely mixed with sand. The valley is, perhaps, the most fertile tract in the Province; it has been described as in the cold weather "green from end to end with wheat." This is its staple product, more specially in Jubbulpore and Hoshangabad, where 46 and 57 per cent. respectively of the cultivated area is under wheat. In Jubbulpore there is also a considerable amount of rice cultivation and gram, and other food-grains as well as oil-seeds are extensively grown. Narsinghpur produces, besides wheat, sugarcane, cotton, gram, and the minor cereals; in Hoshangabad the crops are similar, but amongst oil-seeds til is largely cultivated. In length the valley is about 300 miles, and in average breadth 30. Its elevation above the sea is 1,400 feet at Jubbulpore and 1,100 at Hoshangabad, the average fall being about twenty feet in seven miles. The districts possess a regular rainfall; in Hoshangabad there is a local proverb that there have been famines from too much rain, but never any from drought. Jubbulpore from its elevated situation has a generally lower temperature and more salubrious climate than either Hoshangabad or Narsinghpur. The combined area of the three districts and the Makrai State is 10,613 square miles, being about an eleventh of the total area of the Province.

Nimar.—The northern part of the district in the Nerbada valley is much broken by low irregular hills, and is in consequence sparsely cultivated. The southern part in the Tapti valley is more open and cultivated, especially towards the west where commences the rich alluvial plain that stretches into Khandesh. Between the Tapti and Nerbada valleys runs the range of the Satpuras, here narrowed down to an average width of about 15 miles; the ridge is very irregular and broken, and is for the most part unculturable. About its centre for a short space the hills almost altogether disappear, "causing in Nimar," as Captain Forsyth has described, "a gap through the long unbroken barrier of the Satpuras which has for ages made it the natural highway, and now the railway line between Hindustan and the Deccan, and has given to the district the eventful history it possesses. Right in the gap too stands the fortress of Asirgarh on a scarped inaccessible rock, commanding the pass below, a spot marked out by nature as one of the centres of events." The average elevation of the northern part of Nimar is about 1,000 feet above sea-level; that of the Tapti valley is 850 feet. The rainfall is considerably lighter than further up the Nerbada. The heat in the valleys of the Tapti and Nerbada is severe during April and May; but at other seasons the air is cool and clear, and the climate salubrious, except in the jungle parts which are malarious during the latter part of the year. The chief crops grown in Nimar are jowar and other cereals; they are for the most part kharif or monsoon crops, the lighter soil of the district being less adapted for the growing of winter wheat than the richer lands of the higher Nerbada valley. Cotton and til occupy 18 and 9 per cent. of the cultivated area respectively.

The Satpura Districts.—Of these the most northerly is Mandla, which may be described as a mountainous tract comprising the valleys of many rivers. These valleys are extremely rich, containing frequently large tracts of fine black soil, but the inaccessibility of the country and its known unhealthiness have somewhat deterred settlers from entering the district. The population is largely aboriginal, and a great part of the cultivation is of the rudest possible description. The main crops are wheat, rice, kodo, kudki, and other grains. Five-sixths of the area of the district is waste and forest land. South-west of Mandla lies the district of Seoni consisting to a great extent of finely-cultivated plateaus and fertile valleys. The tablelands of Seoni and Lakhnadown have a varying height of from 1,800 to 2,200 feet; they are well cultivated, clear of jungle, and their temperature is always moderate. The soil of two-thirds of the cultivated area of the district, including all the loftier plateaus, is black soil; towards the south the surface contains a large proportion of clay, and rice is the crop mostly grown; but in the rest of the district the chief produce is wheat. Other cereals and pulses are also grown in large quantities; they represent about a third of the total cultivation of the district. To the east of Seoni comes the Chhindwara district. It has two distinct natural sub-divisions, the hill country above the slope of the Satpuras and a tract of low land beneath them to the south. The north of the district is occupied by zemindaris covering an area of 1,597 square miles; the whole of this part is mountainous and very sparsely cultivated. The remainder of the part above the ghats consists of a regular succession of hill and fertile valley, formed by the small ranges which cross its surface in a general direction east and west. The slopes of the Satpuras which intervene between the high lands and low lands of the district are for the most part covered with forest; below them lies a well-cultivated tract resembling the plain of Nagpur and Berar on which it borders. The climate above the ghats is temperate and healthy, the elevation being in parts very considerable. The highest uplands are 2,500 feet above sea-level, but there are many points much higher; Chhindwara on the second level is 2,200 feet, and the third step above the ghats is about 1,900 feet, or 800 feet above Nagpur. The crops grown are wheat, jowar, and other grains; cotton occupies 9 and oilseeds 14 per cent. of the cultivated area. Betul comprises the western part of the Satpura plateau. The district has a mean elevation of 2,000 feet and possesses in the open and cultivated parts a salubrious climate: but in the denser jungles malaria is prevalent after the rains. The richest tract is the part in which the chief town of Betul stands. To the south lies an undulating plateau, extending over the whole of the southern face of the district, and finally merging into the wild and broken line of ghats, which lead down to the lower country of the plains. To the north and west the country is poor and little cultivated, the western portion specially being a mass of hill and jungle inhabited by Gonds and Korkus. The principal agricultural staples of the district are wheat and pulses, but sugarcane is also an important product. The large proportion of "other crops" shown in the statement is due mainly to the great extent of area entered in the agricultural returns as under fodder crops.

Of the Satpura country the best part has been seen to be the open table-lands of Seoni, Chhindwara, and Betul. Of the rest the greater portion consists of hill and forest, and the population, except in the richer valleys, is scanty and backward. The combined area of the hill districts is 16,708 square miles, or one-seventh of the area of the Province.

The **Nagpur plain** has been already described as consisting of the basins of the Wardha and Wainganga and of the country which lies between them. The districts situated in this tract are Wardha in the valley of the river Wardha, Balaghat and Bhandara in the valley of the Wainganga, Nagpur situated in the north between the two river systems, and Chanda in the south, where both meet and form the Pranhita which flows on to join the Godavery. The tract thus formed has an area of 24,127 square miles; in population and language it forms a distinct part of the Province, its inhabitants being mostly Marathas from the Deccan and Berar. The extreme western portion of this Maratha country, comprising the northern part of Wardha and the western part of Nagpur, is broken and hilly, being intersected by spurs running out from the range of the Satpuras. The surface of these hills is in general rugged and stony, but the valleys and low lands intersecting and adjoining them are extremely fertile and are rich with corn and garden cultivation. Further down the Wardha valley, along the left bank of the river, lies a rich cotton producing country, comprising the whole southern portion of the Wardha district, and extending east across the border of Nagpur and south into the north-west corner of Chanda. Of the whole cultivated area of Wardha, a third is sown with cotton, the other chief crops being jowar, wheat, and linseed, comprising a fourth, a fifth, and a seventh respectively of the total cultivation of the district. Next to Wardha comes the district of Nagpur. Hilly in the north and west, the centre and east of the district is a vast cultivated expanse; even here, however, its surface is hardly ever level, low detached hills and ridges jutting up in places above the plain. The drainage of this tract finds its way into the Wainganga, while the streams that drain the more broken country to the west of the district run to the Wardha. The mean elevation above the sea of the plain country is 1,000 feet in its central portion, lessening to below 900 feet towards the Wardha and Wainganga. The prevailing soil of the Nagpur district is the black cotton soil, and the principal crops grown are wheat, occupying 30 per cent., jowar 25, cotton 12, linseed 10, and other grains and pulses 10 per cent., of the cultivated area. In point of climate Nagpur and Wardha resemble one another; Nagpur, as will be seen, receives a slightly higher rainfall. The cold of the winter season is never severe, and in the hot weather, which lasts from April until about the middle of June, the heat during the day is excessive; the mean temperature is therefore higher than in many other parts of India of the same height above the sea-level, but the climate of the districts is not considered unhealthy.

Passing east into the district of Bhandara in the valley of the Wainganga, we enter what has been called the Lake region of Nagpur. The surface of the district is diversified; in the west and north-west it is comparatively open, but in the interior the low country is crossed by several small ranges, branches of the Satpuras, running generally in a southerly direction and thickly covered with forest. To the east lies a belt of hill and jungle which, fringing the open lands of Chhatisgarh, separates the valley of the Mahanadi from the basin of the Godavery and its affluents. Lakes and tanks are numerous all through the district, but the chief exist in the southern tracts, scattered about wherever spurs of ranges, slopes, streams, or even inequalities of the ground render their formation possible. With the extensive irrigation thus available, the staple produce of the country is rice, with which 53 per cent. of the cultivated area is sown. Other crops are wheat, gram, and other cereals, besides linseed and sugarcane. The open country to the west of the Wainganga is comparatively healthy, but to the south and east fever prevails during the closing months of the year, as might be expected in a damp country where the numerous hills and rivers attract rain, where the jungles are still extensive, and where so much of the area is down with rice cultivation. To the north of Bhandara is situated the district of Balaghat, containing two well marked natural divisions, the first forming the eastern part of the central plateau of the Satpuras, the second consisting of a rich low-land tract lying along the south of the district in the valley of the Wainganga. The first of these tracts is a vast undulating tableland broken into numerous valleys by irregular ranges of hills. The general height of these valleys is about 800 or 900 feet above the plains below and nearly 2,000 feet above the sea. By far the greater part of these highlands is covered with dense jungle, and there is a sparse population, consisting largely of Gonds and Baigas. The low-land portion of Balaghat is a fertile well-watered country, closely resembling the district of Bhandara which it adjoins. Rice is the principal product. Malaria is rife in the upland parts of the district for a considerable portion of the year.

The fifth and largest of the districts of the Nagpur plain is Chanda, covering an area of 10,749 square miles. Through the centre of the district from north to south flows the Wainganga; half-way down the southern border of the district it meets the river Wardha, which, up to this point, has formed the southern limit of Chanda. Below the confluence the united stream is known as the Pranhita, which continues to be the district boundary, until near Sironcha its waters join the Godavery. A little below this a portion of the Bastar State abuts on the Godavery and cuts off from the rest of the district the narrow strip of country which forms the southern portion of the Sironcha tehsil. The latter was originally part of the Upper Godavery district abolished in 1874, when the lower taluks were transferred to the Madras Presidency. Up to where the Pranhita commences, Chanda mainly consists of a great central valley, the southern portion of the basin of the Wainganga. Below this point, the Pranhita valley—a prolongation of that of the Wainganga—begins and has the southern part of the district on its eastern face. Of the remainder of the district the north-west corner forms the left slope of the lower Wardha basin, while the portion to the south-east drains into the Indrávati, a tributary of the Godavery. Except in the extreme west hills are thickly dotted over the whole face of the country, sometimes in detached ranges, sometimes rising isolated from the plain; east of the Wainganga they increase in height and form a broad tableland some 2,000 feet above the sea at the highest point. The district is thickly wooded. The soil over the greater portion of Chanda is red or sandy; as the Wardha and Wainganga are neared it changes to belts of heavy black loam and of yellow loam on the left bank of the Pranhita. Rice is the chief product, more specially in the southern part of the district; wheat, jowar, cotton, and pulses are also grown. The climate differs little from that of the Nagpur country, but in the fall of the year fever of a malarious type is prevalent all over the district.

The Nagpur plain which has been described may, therefore, be looked upon as containing two well-defined tracts, the first comprising the districts of Wardha, Nagpur, and the north-west corner of Chanda, being essentially a dry crop country, while Bhandara, Balaghat, and the remainder of Chanda, which form the second tract, are in the main rice-producing. In population, with one exception, they differ but little, though in the last three districts the proportion of aborigines is greater than in the other two. In the south of Chanda the Telugu element preponderates.

Chhatisgarh.—The sixth division of the Province is the plain of Chhatisgarh, forming the upper basin of the Mahanadi and its tributaries. The whole of this tract is surrounded by ranges of hills, off-shoots of the great central chain which, in the extensive zemindaries of Bilaspur, skirts the plain country on the north. Below the hills to the west and south there is a broad belt of fertile black soil, embracing the western portion of the Bilaspur district, the Feudatory States of Kawardha, Chhuikhadan, Khairagarh, and Nandgaon, and the southern border of Raipur. The centre of Chhatisgarh is an undulating cultivated plain intersected by numerous streams and copiously supplied with tanks. In this tract lies the greater portion of the khalsa or Government lands of the Raipur and Bilaspur districts. The Mahanadi flows along its eastern border, pursuing a north-easterly direction; on the right bank the hills come close to the stream, leaving but a small share of fertile plain between them and the river. Further to the east the whole country, comprising the southern and eastern zemindaris of Raipur, is hilly and covered with jungle. South of the Chhatisgarh plain lie the Feudatory States of Kankar and Bastar, both of them mountainous and sparsely inhabited by aboriginal races. The best parts of the latter dependency are those to the north-east and south-west, where the country is less hilly than in the north and centre. Of the immense tract that has just been described, covering an area of 37,448 square miles, it is only the great central plain that is thickly peopled and highly cultivated. The combined area of the districts of Raipur and Bilaspur—omitting the Raipur and Bilaspur tehsil zemindaris—and of the five States of Nandgaon, Khairagarh, Chhuikhadan, Kawardha, and Sakti, which form the central plain, amounts to 15,514 square miles, out of which 7,410 or about 47·8 per cent. are under cultivation. Rice is the staple produce of the greater part of the country, but wheat, kodo, and other food-grains and pulses are also grown. Linseed is another important staple; cotton is confined to the black soil tract to the west of Chhatisgarh, but its cultivation has of late years decreased, the little of it that is produced coming chiefly from the Native States. The average rainfall is 51 inches in Raipur and 46 in Bilaspur. The hills encircling the country generally ensure an adequate or nearly adequate supply of water, which is readily stored in the numberless tanks which are scattered over Chhatisgarh, so that a season of scarcity is very seldom known. Cholera and fever are the great scourges of the plain, the former frequently occurring in the hot weather, while fever is very prevalent towards the close of the rains. In the great hill tracts to the north and south the malaria at this season is of a virulent type.

The Uria Country.—The last division of the Province occupies the basin of the Central Mahanadi and of the streams, which, taking their rise in the hilly barrier which separates the Uria country from Chhatisgarh, flow east into the main river. In the north-west corner of the tract, on the left bank of the Mahanadi, lies the Native State of Raigarh; the southern portion towards the river is fertile and well cultivated, but the northern and eastern parts are a mass of hill and jungle. Across the Mahanadi is Sarangarh; the State, except in the south and east, is generally level and well cultivated. Lower down the river which divides it in two, lies the district of Sambalpur, the greater part of which is an undulating plain, out of which in places rise low ranges of hills. More than half the area of Sambalpur is occupied by zemindaris, the most important of which, Borasambhar and Phuljhar, situated on its eastern border, contain large tracts of forest. The khalsa is generally well cultivated; more especially in the portion that lies to the south of the Mahanadi, the jungle has been almost completely cleared, and the country presents a well settled appearance. Leaving Sambalpur the Mahanadi enters Sonpur, rather more than half of which is situated on its right or southern bank. The surface of the State is for the most part flat and more than three-fifths of the total area is under cultivation. The north-eastern corner of the Uria country is occupied by the States of Bamra and Rairakhol. The southern portion of the Bamra State is covered with hill and forest, but in the north-west and centre the land is fertile and well cultivated. To the south of Sambalpur situated in the valley of the Tel, a tributary of the Mahanadi, are the important States of Patna and Kalahandi. In both there are extensive level tracts, but a large proportion of the land is waste, the wildest part being the eastern half of Kalahandi, which lies along the range of the Eastern Ghats. Throughout the country which has been described the main crop grown is rice; in the khalsa portion of Sambalpur, for which alone returns are available, it occupies more than three-fourths of the total cultivated land. On the higher grounds, pulses, til and cotton are grown. Sambalpur possesses an abundant rainfall, the registered average being the highest in the Province. The Uria country has the reputation of being unhealthy; fever is prevalent from September to November, and as in Chhatisgarh cholera frequently makes its appearance.

6. **Area and Administrative Divisions.**—The area of the Central Provinces has been given as 115,936 square miles. At the Census of 1881, it was taken as 113,279 square miles. There has been no change in the limits of the Province, but the figures given show an increase of 2,657 square miles, according to the corrected area statement issued by the Revenue Department in 1886. Of this difference the greater part, 2,056 square miles, has taken place in the area of the British districts, the remainder, 601 square miles, occurring in that of the Native States. As the figures now stand the area of the British territory is 86,501 square miles, and of the Feudatory States 29,435 square miles. The British districts of the Central Provinces thus cover an area which is only 2,100 square miles less than the combined area of England, Scotland and Wales. Amongst European countries the whole Province compares in point of extent most nearly with Austria excluding Hungary, the area of which is 115,903 square miles, or 33 less than that of the Central Provinces.

Administrative Divisions.—The British part of the Province has been for administrative purposes divided into eighteen districts, which again are grouped into four divisional commissionerships as shown below:—

JUBBULPORE DIVISION	Saugor, Damoh, Jubbulpore, Mandla, and Seoni.
NERBADA "	Hoshangabad, Narsinghpur, Nimar, Betul, and Chhindwara.
NAGPUR "	Nagpur, Wardha, Chanda, Bhandara, and Balaghat.
CHHATISGARH "	Raipur, Bilaspur, and Sambalpur.

The Native State of Makrai is politically attached to the Nerbada Division and the fourteen Eastern States to Chhatisgarh. The area of each division, both with and without Feudatory territory, is shown in the margin. For purposes of comparison, I have added the areas of European countries which more closely approach the commissionerships in size, as in this way one is better able to realise the enormous extent of country which Indian officials are called upon to administer. To take a more familiar standard in the case of the first two divisions, the Commissioner of Jubbulpore has under his control an area

Division.	Area in square miles. Total including Feudatory States.	British Territory.	European Countries of corresponding area.	Area in square miles.
Jubbulpore	19,040	19,040	Servia	19,050
Nerbada	18,476	18,321		
Nagpur	24,127	24,127	Holland and Belgium.	24,021
Chhatisgarh	54,293	25,013	Greece	25,041

which is very nearly one-third the size of England and Wales, while the Nerbada division is equal in extent to three-fifths the area of Scotland. If to the area directly administered by the Commissioner of Chhatisgarh, we add the Feudatory country over which he exercises political control, the extent of his charge falls only some 4,000 miles, or about one-fifteenth, short of the area of England and Wales.

Of the districts the largest are Raipur, Chanda, Bilaspur, Mandla, and Sambalpur. All of these, with the exception of Mandla, contain a large zemindari area. The average size of the district is 4,806 square miles, an area equal in extent, if we take a home standard of comparison, to the combined area of the five midland counties of Northampton, Leicester, Stafford, Derby, and Nottingham.

British Districts arranged in order of magnitude.

District.	Area in Square Miles.		Total Area.
	Khalsa.	Zemindaris.	
Raipur	6,848	4,876	11,724
Chanda	5,899	4,850	10,749
Bilaspur	3,872	4,469	8,341
Mandla	5,056	...	5,056
Sambalpur	1,955	2,993	4,948
Chhindwara	3,033	1,597	4,630
Hoshangabad	4,421	173	4,594
Saugor	4,007	...	4,007
Bhandara	2,489	1,479	3,968
Jubbulpore	3,948	...	3,948
Nagpur	3,843	...	3,843
Betul	3,824	...	3,824
Nimar	3,357	...	3,357
Seoni	3,198	...	3,198
Balaghat	2,179	960	3,139
Damoh	2,831	...	2,831
Wardha	2,428	...	2,428
Narsinghpur	1,916	...	1,916

The most extensive of the Feudatory States is Bastar, with an area of 13,062 square miles; next in order come Kalahandi 3,745, Patna 2,399, Bamra 1,988, Raigarh 1,486, and Kanker 1,429 sqaure miles. The remaining ten States are all under 1,000 miles in extent, the smallest being Sakti with an area of 138 square miles.

7. **The population of the Province.**—The total number of persons enumerated at the Census was 12,944,805, of whom 10,784,294 were resident in British Territory and 2,160,511 in the Feudatory States. Apportioning the population and area between these two units, it will be seen that the British districts, while comprising only 75 per cent. of the total area of the Province, contain more than 83 per cent. of the population. In 1881 over 85 per cent. of the people were enumerated in British districts, the drop in the percentage being due to the remarkable increase exhibited by the present Census returns in the population of the Native States. The ratio of population to area is in British districts 124·7 persons, and in the Feudatories 73·4 persons per square mile: for the whole Province the ratio is 111·7 persons per mile. Before noticing the density of the population in further detail, it will

Countries and Provinces arranged in order of Density of Population

Country.	Density.	Province.	Density.
Belgium	536	Oudh	522
England and Wales	498	North-West Provinces	419
Italy	249	Bengal	399
Germany	222	Madras	261
		Punjab	168
Austria	191	Berar	163
France	186	Bombay	139
Ireland	159	Central Provinces, British Districts.	125
Scotland	132	Assam	112
Hungary	125	Central Provinces Total.	112
Servia	110	Bengal Feudatories	91
Spain	89	Central Provinces Feudatories.	73
Greece	87	Burma	48
Sweden	27		

NOTE.—The figures for European countries are taken from the Census Commissioner's Note U., dated 16th July 1891. Those for the Provinces of Assam, Berar, Bombay, and Madras are from the final Census Tables: for the other Provinces the preliminary Census returns have been made use of.

be of interest to see how the Province stands when compared in this respect with some of the chief States of Europe and with other Indian Provinces. From the figures given in the margin, it will be noticed that in the Central Provinces the population is more scantily distributed over the surface of the country than in any other part of the mainland of British India. The proportion of persons to the square mile in the British districts is exactly one-fourth of the average density of England and Wales. In the Feudatories the density is considerably less than in the Tributary States of Bengal, the great bulk of which lie along the Central Provinces border.

8. **District and State Population.**—*Density.*—The accompanying abstract has been drawn up to show the population and its average density in the several districts of the Province. It will be seen that a distinction has been preserved between Total and Rural* population. In dealing with scattered units, such as districts, tehsils or zemindaris, the distinction is of considerable importance, as the figures themselves sufficiently show. Taking for instance the district of Nagpur which includes within its limits the important towns of Nagpur and Kampti, we find that in respect of density of total population it stands at the head of British districts. Omitting the inhabitants of its towns, and looking only at the compactness of the rural population, it will be observed that there are five other districts in the Province more densely peopled than Nagpur. With more minute divisions, such as tehsils, the difference arising from the inclusion of a large town population will be still more marked. The result, it might be added, will be proportionately devoid of meaning, for what we most want to know for administrative purposes is the way in which the population has spread over the general surface of the country, exclusive of the groups gathered together in the larger towns. The latter are in themselves definite units, admitting of separate examination and comparison. The density of the rural population is therefore the chief matter of interest in contrasting the distribution of the people in different parts of the Province. For purposes of comparision, I have added figures showing the percentage of cultivated area in each district, so far as statistics can be at present ascertained, and from these has been calculated the extent of cultivation per head of the population.

Statement showing density *of* Total *and* Rural *Population.*

Districts and States.	1891.									1881.	
	Population.		Number of persons per square mile.		Percentage of cultivation on Total area.	Average number of cultivated acres per head of		Serial order in respect of density of		Number of persons per square mile.	
	Total.	Rural.	Total Population.	Rural Population.		Total Population.	Rural Population.	Total Population.	Rural Population.	Total Population.	Rural Population.
1	2	3	4	5	6	7	8	9	10	11	12
Saugor	591,743	*524,966*	147·7	*131·0*	40	1·7	*2·0*	7	*10*	141	*122·6*
Damoh	325,613	*308,059*	115·0	*108·8*	34	1·9	*2·0*	15	*14*	110·5	*105·3*
Total Vindhyan Districts	*917,356*	*833,025*	*134·2*	*121·8*	*38*	*1·8*	*2·0*	*III*	*III*	*128·4*	*115·4*
Jubbulpore	748,146	*648,407*	189·5	*164·2*	54	1·8	*2·0*	3	*3*	174·1	*131·2*
Narsinghpur	367,026	*347,991*	191·6	*181·6*	55	1·8	*1·9*	2	*1*	190·6	*181·0*
Hoshangabad	529,945	*488,809*	115·4	*106·4*	38	2·0	*2·3*	14	*15*	106·4	*97·4*
Makrai	18,549	*18,549*	119·7	*119·7*	31	1·6	*1·6*	12	*12*	108·2	*108·2*
Total Nerbada Valley	*1,663,666*	*1,503,756*	*156·8*	*141·7*	*47*	*1·9*	*2·1*	*I*	*I*	*146·8*	*132·7*

* For the definition of Town and Rural Population, see para. 10.

Statement showing density *of* Total *and* Rural *Population*—contd.

Districts and States.	1891. Population. Total.	Rural.	Number of persons per square mile. Total Population.	Rural Population.	Percentage of cultivation on Total area.	Average number of cultivated acres per head of Total Population.	Rural Population.	Serial order in respect of density of Total Population.	Rural Population.	1881. Number of persons per square mile. Total Population.	Rural Population.
1	2	3	4	5	6	7	8	9	10	11	12
Nimar	253,486	205,645	75·5	61·3	22	1·9	2·3	19	21	68·9	55·4
Mandla	339,373	334,316	67·1	66·1	18	1·7	1·7	20	19	59·7	59·7
Seoni	370,767	358,791	115·9	112·2	41	2·3	2·4	13	13	104·7	101·5
Chhindwara	407,494	379,624	88·0	82·0	30	2·2	2·4	17	17	80·5	76·0
Betul	323,196	312,922	84·5	81·8	31	2·3	2·4	18	18	79·7	79·7
Total Satpura Districts	*1,440,830*	*1,385,653*	*86·2*	*82·9*	*29*	*2·1*	*2·2*	*VI*	*VI*	*78·7*	*76·8*
Nagpur	757,862	540,172	197·2	140·6	53	1·7	2·4	1	6	181·5	126·7
Wardha	400,854	356,142	165·1	146·7	67	2·6	2·9	5	5	159·4	145·8
Chanda	697,610	671,417	64·9	62·5	13	1·2	1·3	21	20	60·4	57·6
Bhandara	742,850	712,067	187·2	179·5	37	1·3	1·3	4	2	172·3	163·9
Balaghat	383,331	378,193	122·1	120·5	19	1·0	1·0	11	11	108·4	108·4
Total Nagpur Plain	*2,982,507*	*2,657,991*	*123·6*	*110·2*	*29*	*1·5*	*1·7*	*IV*	*V*	*114·3*	*101·9*
Raipur	1,584,427	1,548,692	135·1	132·1	36	1·7	1·7	10	9	119·9	117·2
Bilaspur	1,164,158	1,146,647	139·6	137·5	30	1·4	1·4	8	7	122·0	120·4
Chhatisgarh States	600,904	581,030	139·0	134·5	33	1·5	1·6	9	8	124·1	120·1
Total Chattisgarh	*3,349,489*	*3,276,369*	*137·4*	*134·4*	*33*	*1·5*	*1·6*	*II*	*II*	*121·3*	*118·8*
Bastar	310,884	305,840	23·8	23·4	...	...	...	22	22	15·0	15·0
Sambalpur	796,413	781,842	161·0	158·0	35	1·4	1·4	6	4	140·2	137·3
Uria States	1,230,174	1,216,436	103·4	102·2	26	1·6	1·6	16	16	80·7	80·1
Total Uria Country	*2,026,587*	*1,998,278*	*120·3*	*118·6*	*29*	*1·5*	*1·5*	*V*	*IV*	*98·2*	*96·9*

NOTE.—The figures for 1881 have been corrected in accordance with the revised areas given for districts and States in 1886.

Density of Population in Zemindari Districts.

Districts.	Population. Khalsa. Total.	Khalsa. Rural.	Zemindaris.	Density. Khalsa. Total Population.	Khalsa. Rural Population.	Zemindaris.
Hoshangabad	525,276	484,140	4,669	118·8	109·5	27·0
Chhindwara	339,443	311,573	68,051	111·9	102·7	42·6
Chanda	561,099	534,906	136,511	95·1	90·7	28·1
Bhandara	510,028	479,245	232,822	204·9	192·5	157·4
Balaghat	285,432	280,294	97,899	131·0	128·6	102·0
Raipur	1,255,698	1,219,963	328,729	183·4	178·1	67·4
Bilaspur	827,433	809,922	336,725	213·7	209·2	75·3
Sambalpur	388,205	373,634	408,208	198·6	191·1	136·4

Considerations affecting Density.—Coming next to a consid eration of the figures, it may be remarked that what will in the main determine the density of the population, and more especially the rural population, in one district as compared with another is the extent of culturable soil that each possesses in proportion to its total area. Where, as in Mandla, the physical conformation of the country renders cultivation to any great extent impossible, the population will necessarily be less dense than in parts, such as the Nerbada valley, where no such obstacles to agriculture exist. Again, were other conditions equal, the specific population of a district will ordinarily be high in proportion as the cultivated area nearly approaches the arable limit. Of the latter we have, however, such an uncertain record and so much do important factors vary, such as the intrinsic fertility of the soil, superior or inferior methods of husbandry, facility of carriage enabling the produce of the fields to find a ready market, that any rule of general application will hardly be found to bear upon the averages that have been given.

The Nerbada Valley and Chhatisgarh.—Of the physical divisions into which the Province has been divided, the most thickly peopled is the Nerbada valley, where taking only the rural population there are 141·7 persons per square mile. This cannot, however, compare in point of density with the Chhatisgarh plain proper. Taking this to exclude the Native State of Kanker and the jungle zemindaris of the Raipur and Bilaspur tehsils (see page 11), we find that in Chhatisgarh the density of the rural population is 182 persons per square mile. Both in the Nerbada valley and in Chhatisgarh, as thus defined, we get about the same proportion of land under the plough, 47 per cent. of the total area. In the latter it is possible that the extent of cultivation in the States and Zemindaris is under-stated, but any variation there may be in this respect is hardly sufficient to account for the very considerable difference which is observed in the specific population of the two tracts. This difference is to be referred rather to the exceptionally easy conditions of life which obtain in Chhatisgarh. For long the Chhatisgarh plain has lain in comparative isolation from the outside world. It is only within the last few years that its western border has been tapped by a line of railway, now extended towards Bengal; formerly, besides a good road to Nagpur, almost its sole communications were the Banjara routes over which salt and the few external necessaries or luxuries of the ryot were brought within his reach and grain taken away in exchange. The facilities for import or export being thus so small, the standard of comfort was low and food was plentiful and cheap. The surplus produce of the soil, which with improved communications would have left the country, was here available for the support of an ever-increasing population. Added to this, Chhatisgarh possesses a fertile soil and a constant rainfall, and the land produces in abundance the great staple of the country,—rice. If we refer to column 8 of the table, which has been given at the head of this paragraph, we shall see that in the rice districts of the south and east of the Province, each head of the population is supported on about an acre and a half of cultivated land. Elsewhere the proportion rises to two acres and over. The presence in some of the former districts of a large aboriginal population, that can hardly be said to have properly taken to agriculture, no doubt tends to reduce the average cultivation per individual. Account must also be taken of the fact that the rice districts have been, perhaps, specially backward in point of communications, so that there has been a large surplus produce available for home consumption. But the inference remains that generally in tracts where rice is the staple crop, the soil supports a proportionately larger population than in places where other produce is grown. To a combination of all the influences detailed above may, therefore, be assigned the high density of population which we find in Chhatisgarh.

SHEWING INHABITANTS PER SQ. MILE.

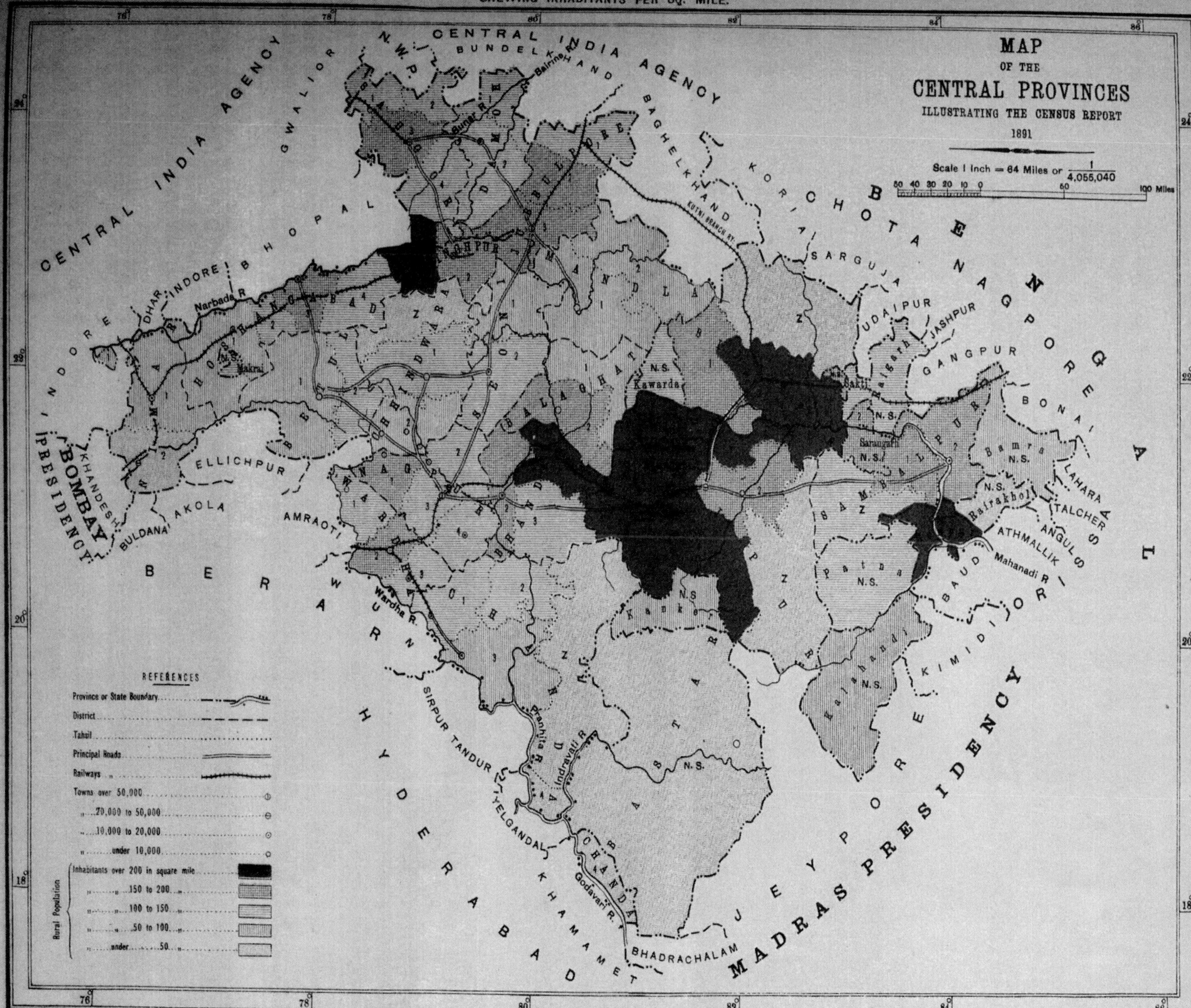

Reg. No. 38, C. P., Census—Mar. 93.—615

Photo S. I. O., Calcutta.

REFERENCES

No	TAHSIL	DISTRICT
1 2 3 4	Khurai Banda Saugor Rehli	SAUGOR
1 2	Hatta Damoh	DAMOH
1 2 3	Murwara Sihora Jubbulpore	JUBBULPORE
1 2	Gadarwara Narsinghpur	NARSINGHPUR
1 2 3 4	Harda Seoni Hoshangabad Sohagpur	HOSHANGABAD
1 2	Khandwa Burhanpur	NIMAR
1 2	Betul Multai	BETUL
1 2	Chhindwara Sausar	CHHINDWARA
1 2	Lakhnadon Seoni	SEONI
1 2	Behar Burha	BALAGHAT
1 2 3	Tirora Bhandara Sakoli	BHANDARA
1 2 3 4	Katol Ramtek Nagpur Umrer	NAGPUR
1 2 3	Arvi Wardha Hinganghat	WARDHA
1 2 3 4	Warora Brahmapuri Mul Sironcha	CHANDA
1 2 3 4	Drug Raipur Simga Dhamtari	RAIPUR
1 2	Bargarh Sambalpur	SAMBALPUR
1 2 3	Mungeli Bilaspur Seorinarain	BILASPUR
1 2	Mandla Ramgarh	MANDLA

Z. .... Zamindari
N. S. ..... Native State

Sambalpur.—Without attempting to discuss in such detail the averages that result for each division or district, I shall pass on to notice only some of the more salient features that present themselves. To take first of all Sambalpur, it will be observed that the district possesses a high density of rural population, in the khalsa amounting to 191·1 persons per square mile. That the land is able to support so thickly-distributed a population would appear to be due to the superior husbandry of the Uria cultivator.

"The fact remains that the cultivated land of Sambalpur supports a large number of people. This is possible not because the soil is more fertile, but because it is better worked. In intrinsic fertility the soil is indeed rather below than above the average of the Provinces. Rice is, *par excellence*, the crop of the district and occupies over 90 per cent. of the total cropped area; its cultivation is much more carefully conducted than in the adjacent districts of Raipur and Bilaspur. Irrigation too plays an important part in the agriculture of Sambalpur."—Paragraph 4 of Despatch of Central Provinces Administration, No. 226, dated 12th June 1884, to Government of India, Department of Revenue and Agriculture, published in the Sambalpur Settlement Report.

The Nagpur Plain.—Coming next to the Nagpur plain, it will appear that in point of density the tract would stand high, but for the inclusion of Chanda, which with its immense stretches of waste and forest, is the most thinly peopled district in the Province. Wardha contains a larger average of cultivation than any other district, but as at least a third of this is under a non-food crop—cotton—its actual capability for carrying a heavy population would appear to be diminished. In the Hinganghat tehsil, which is the finest part of the cotton field, over 69 per cent. of the total area is cultivated, yet the average density of the rural population is only 137·9 persons per square mile. In the tehsil of Wardha the ratio of cultivation is about the same, 71 per cent., but the density amounts to 171·7. Bhandara, essentially a rice-growing country with a fair proportion of its total area under the plough, possesses a high rate of village population; in the khalsa it rises to 192·5, being greatest in the Tirora tehsil where the density is 273·5 persons per square mile. In Balaghat the difference between the high lands and low lands of the district is most marked; excluding Zemindaris there are 202·5 persons per mile in the Burha tehsil, and only 63·7 in Behir.

The Satpura districts.—Of the Satpura districts the most thickly peopled is Seoni, but the population in all the districts is necessarily sparse on account of the large extent of unculturable area which these hills contain. The best parts are the tehsils of Seoni and Multai, with an average density of 126·4 and 121·6 persons per square mile, respectively, and the worst the tehsils of Betul and Ramgarh, where the density sinks to 66·6 and 57·6.

The Nerbada districts.—Nimar stands lowest among British districts as regards the density of its village population, a great part of the district being barren waste; in the Burhanpur tehsil, if the town is left out of account, there are only 43·2 persons to the square mile. To the Nerabada districts reference has already been made; the most thickly peopled part of the valley is the Gadarwara tehsil of the Narsinghpur district, with a density of 212·1 persons per mile, while the lowest density, 82·1, is found in the Harda tehsil of Hoshangabad, which includes the sparsely populated Charwa tract and the Kalibhit forest range. Of the Vindhyan districts Saugor with a larger proportion of cultivation possesses also a higher rate of population than Damoh.

The Feudatory States.—Amongst the Feudatory States the most thickly populated are Chhuikhadan with 235·6 inhabitants per mile, Nandgaon with 200·9, Sonpur with 200·3, Khairagarh with 188·5, and Sakti with 183·9. The figures refer to rural population only; including towns, Sonpur stands first with a density of 215·5 persons per square mile, and Nandgaon next with 211. Both States are highly cultivated, in Sonpur close on two-thirds of the total area being cropped. At the other end of the scale come Kanker, Bamra, Rairakhol, and Bastar with 57·6, 52·5, 24·4 and 23·8 persons per mile respectively. The last is, considering its size, the most thinly peopled tract in the Province, its immense area of 13,062 square miles carrying a population of only 310,884 persons.

Special Tracts.—The following statement exhibits in detail some of the district sub-divisions in which the density is very much above or below the mean. The tehsil figures are for the rural population of the khalsa only :—

HIGH.				LOW.			
District.	Tehsil or Zemindari. Name.	Tehsil or Zemindari. Area.	Persons per square mile.	District.	Tehsil or Zemindari. Name.	Tehsil or Zemindari. Area.	Persons per square mile.
Bhandara	Kamptha, Z.	275	338·9	Chanda	Muramgaon, Z.	149	8·7
Raipur	Gondardehi, Z.	83	277·3		Ahiri, Z.	2,600	10·3
Bhandara	Tirora	559	273·5	Bilaspur	Uprora, Z.	448	12·8
Sambalpur	Chandarpur and Padampur, Zs.	304	266·0		Matin, Z.	544	18·5
Raipur	Drug	1,139	246·2		Lapha, Z.	359	26·7
Bilaspur	Seorinarain	1,129	223·1	Raipur	Bindra Nawagarh, Z.	1,559	32·9
Narsinghpur	Gadarwara	874	212·1	Chanda	Sironcha	1,085	38·7
Bilaspur	Bilaspur	1,460	211·2	Nimar	Burhanpur	1,138	43·2
Raipur	Simga	1,469	206·6	Mandla	Ramgarh	2,524	57·6
Balaghat	Burha	1,019	202·5	Balaghat	Behir	1,160	63·7

The most notable feature in the above is the extreme scantiness of the population in the great Ahiri Zemindari of the Chanda district. The area of the zemindari extends to 2,600 square miles, yet its population is only 26,703. In 1881 the density was 10·0 persons per mile, regarding which the Census Report notes that the enumeration was conducted in the most careful manner, and that no ground existed for supposing that any omissions had taken place. On the present occasion also the Census operations in Ahiri were well carried out, and the very slight increase that has resulted in the past ten years goes to confirm the view expressed by the local officers in 1881, that the reason of the zemindari being so badly populated is its notorious natural unhealthiness. Of the Bilaspur Zemindaris Matin and Uprora show the sparsest population; in Uprora the number of persons per square mile is now 12·8 against 10·6 in 1881, while Matin now shows a density of 18·5, as compared with 10·9 at the last Census. The increased density in these zemindari tracts will be further noted on in the chapter dealing with the variations in the population.

9. **Statistics of Houses.**—*Definition.*—At paragraph 7 of chapter I of the second part of the Report, reference will be found to the definition of a house adopted at the present Census. In 1881 the huts that comprise the enclosures, which are the common dwellings of the people in the eastern portion of the Province, and to a small extent in other parts as well, were treated as separate houses; in order to retain the means of comparison with the figures of last Census, a system of sub-numbers for such houses was adopted on the present occasion. Each enclosure was, in the first place, to bear a serial number; from this the sum total of esclosures, independent of the number of houses each contained, could be calculated. In this way comparison could be effected with the returns of neighbouring Provinces, where such enclosures were treated as single dwellings, but none could be made with the Census results of ten years ago. To provide for the latter, it was proposed to sub-number each hut in an

enclosure, so that by counting up the sub-numbers another total would be arrived at, which would admit of such comparison. The double system led to ceaseless trouble and in the end had to be practically abandoned. In nearly every district the use of sub-numbers was abolished, and the building or buildings occupied by each separate family living in an enclosure reckoned as a single house. Thus what we have really got must be looked upon as in part a record of families as well as of houses. Uniformity, besides, was not everywhere attained, so that the results can hardly be regarded as possessing much statistical value.

Statistics.—Compared with 1881 the number of persons per house has, of course, risen; in British Districts it is now 5·00 against 4·21, and in the Feudatory States 5·28 against 4·56; the figures for the whole Province being 5·04 in 1891 as against 4·26 in 1881. The abstract in the margin contrasts the proportion of persons per house for each district and for ten of the chief towns of the Province. In some cases it is hardly worth while to discuss the variations that are disclosed, as these are occasionally due to different treatment of the subject in different districts at the enumeration, rather than to actually existing divergences in the housing of the population. Generally speaking, however, the numbering was fairly uniform in the northern and western districts of the Province, where the difficulty about enclosures was hardly experienced. Comparing these it will be noticed that the number of persons in each house is small in the Vindhyan and Nerbada districts, while on the Satpura Range the ratio rises to 5·18, the district with the highest house-population being Mandla. Coming to the Nagpur Division we find a marked difference between the districts of Wardha and Nagpur on the one hand, and Balaghat, Bhandara and Chanda on the other, while in Chhatisgarh and the Uria country the proportion of inhabitants per house is considerably higher than the average of the Province. Here, however, some notable exceptions crop up, the most marked being Bilaspur, with a ratio of 4·47, Kanker 4·04, and Kalahandi 5·01 persons per house. The sole reason for these discrepancies is the fact that the system of sub-numbering was carried to a further extent in Bilaspur and the two States mentioned than in the rest of Chhatisgarh. Thus in Raipur, if an enclosure contained 4 huts occupied by 2 separate families, the residence of each of the latter was counted a house, and the enclosure thus contained only 2 houses. In Bilaspur each of the 4 huts in such an enclosure would have been separately listed and the number of houses would thus be doubled. In the latter district the preliminaries of the Census had been carried out expeditiously and were early completed, so that alteration in the system of numbering would have caused great inconvenience and confusion. In many cases,

Number of persons per house.

(*a*) Districts.

District.	No. of persons per house.	District.	No. of persons per house.
Saugor	4·88	Wardha	4·70
Damoh	4·63	Nagpur	5·03
Jubbulpore	4·70	Chanda	5·30
Narsinghpur	4·54	Bhandara	5·33
Hoshangabad	5·00	Balaghat	5·34
Nimar	4·97	Raipur	5·27
		Bilaspur	4·47
Mandla	5·46	Sambalpur	5·22
Seoni	4·99	British Districts	5·00
Chhindwara	5·13	Feudatory States	5·28
Betul	5·18	Total C. P.	5·04

(*b*) Principal Towns.

Town.	No. of persons per house.	Town.	No. of persons per house.
Nagpur	4·66	Raipur	4·08
Jubbulpore	4·34	Chanda	4·35
Saugor	4·92	Khandwa	4·33
Kampti	4·44	Umrer	4·98
Burhanpur	4·72	Sambalpur	4·85

therefore, the rule as to sub-numbering, as it originally stood, was allowed to remain, and the amendment as to grouping huts by families was only partially carried out. In both districts the number of houses has considerably decreased since last Census, but in Raipur where the method of counting each hut in an enclosure as a separate house was severely followed in 1881, but in great part abandoned on the present occasion, the fall has been nearly 33 per cent., whereas in Bilaspur the decrease is only 8 per cent. on the figures of ten years ago. Something of the same kind happened in Kanker and Kalahandi. Nowhere, perhaps, has there been exact uniformity, but in the other districts and States the divergence from the ordinary practice adopted elsewhere in the Province has not been so marked.

Considerations affecting the House-room.—In the margin I have given a statement which throws considerable light on the results that have been obtained. It will be seen that generally where there is a large proportion of young children, the number of persons per house is also large. The figures possess only a relative value, but they are of some use as explaining the variations prevailing in different parts of the Province. They do not, however, constitute the only explanation available. Had we more exact statistics for the eastern districts and States, it would be seen that the number of persons per house or joint family—the distinction, as I have noted, can scarcely be preserved in dealing with enclosures—would be considerably larger than the results of the present Census show. In the part of the Report which discusses the operations of the Census, I have quoted at paragraph 8, Chapter I, an excellent description of the constitution of the Chhatisgarh enclosure. The prevailing custom of the country is for the family to stick to the common homestead so long as the members can be housed within its bounds; as the married members of the family increase, it becomes necessary to increase the number of sleeping places, and the number of huts in the enclosure thus tends to multiply. The facilities for such expansion that the enclosure affords is an important factor in determining the strength of the household. In Chhatisgarh, therefore, the number of persons per house or cluster of confocal dwellings is ordinarily largely in excess of similar proportions in other parts of the Province, where the family when pressed for room overflows into distinct houses and where the tendency is thus for its members to separate. At another Census I have suggested the counting of the people in enclosures by households and taking no notice of the number of huts they occupy. The attempt to take both into account on the present occasion ended in failure and has to a large extent destroyed the value of the figures we have got.

Division.	Average number of persons per house.	Percentage of children, aged 0—4, on Total Population.
Vindhyan Division	4·79	13·3
Nerbada valley	4·76	14·0
Nimar	4·97	14·4
Satpuras	5·18	15·5
Nagpur Plain—		
Nagpur and Wardha	4·91	13·1
Chanda, Bhandara, Balaghat	5·32	15·5
*Chhatisgarh	5·30	16·8
Uria country	5·30	15·8

* Exclusive of Bilaspur and Kanker.

Towns.—The density per house in towns, it will be noticed, is generally less than is the case in the districts in which they are situated. The result is probably to be attributed to the tendency to separation which want of space must necessarily entail on the poorer part of the population.

At the present Census no record was made of unoccupied houses.

10. **Rural and Urban Population**.—Having discussed the distribution of the population by houses, we now come to consider its distribution over the groups of these, which are shown in the Census returns as towns and villages. But

first it will be necessary to explain the sense in which these terms have been used.

Definition of Town.—Only those places have been reckoned as towns which fulfil the two following conditions :—

(*a*) The population should be not less than 5,000, residing in houses more or less contiguous, not in scattered collections, as hamlets, etc.

(*b*) The place, though containing the above population, should not be merely a large village, but should have some distinctly urban character, as that of a market town.

The Census Commissioner in his circular note L, dated 18th July 1890, had allowed for places with under 5,000 population being counted as towns, provided they were under the operation of some Municipal or Chaukidari Act, but on the analogy of the last Census 5,000 was taken as the lowest group unit of population, which might be considered to be urban. The standard is necessarily an arbitrary one. If the definition of a town turns upon the comparative strength of the industrial and commercial, and the absence of the agricultural element in its population, there must be not a few places which merit the appellation perhaps more than some of the over-grown villages which have been included in the Census Tables. Some of the settlements which, for instance, have grown up in proximity to railway stations—occasionally they are of considerable size—are, as commercial centres, more urban in character than the rural municipalities or pergannah head-quarter towns which fall within the Census definition. Under the circumstances, it is hardly possible to avoid the adoption of an arbitrary limit, and the one that has been chosen is perhaps as suitable as any other. I may add that places have been omitted from the list of towns which, though containing a population above this limit, have no municipal form of government or are otherwise wanting in town characteristics.

Definition of Village.—The word village in the Census returns has been taken to include the population living within the *mauza*, the well defined area, which, administratively as well as in the opinion of the people, is recognized as the ordinary village unit. Within this area the population is usually collected together in a single group of houses, but occasionally hamlets have been thrown off from the main group and set down in the outlying fields; these are inhabited sometimes by cultivators from the principal village, who have for convenience sake or otherwise built themselves a separate habitation, but more frequently by aboriginal or outcaste tribes, the drudges of the village whom custom has compelled to live apart from the better classes of the community. In both cases, however, close relationships, social or industrial, exist between the inhabitants of the main village and its dependent hamlets, and it is impossible to look upon them as anything but one and the same. As the enumeration deals with the population only, no account, it may be added, is taken of uninhabited mauzas. In jungle tracts the ordinary village as above described can hardly be said to exist; here we find only scattered clusters of huts inhabited by aborigines, with no compact block of land to form a connecting link between the different clusters. Each of the latter has therefore to be separately taken into account. The same is also the case in many of the Zemindaris and Feudatory States, where the mauzawar system is practically non-existent; in these it has not always been possible to draw a distinction between main villages and subordinate hamlets, so that the latter have sometimes been shown separately when otherwise they would have been included in the parent stock.

11. **Distribution of the Population over Towns and Villages.**—This will appear from the abstracts that are subjoined. The first gives the ratio of the rural and urban to the total population.

Proportion of Rural *and* Urban *to Total Population.*

Population.		British Districts.			Feudatory States.			Central Provinces.		
		Total.	Males.	Females.	Total.	Males.	Females.	Total.	Males.	Females.
Rural		10,044,702	5,017,576	5,027,126	2,121,855	1,068,845	1,053,010	12,166,557	6,086,421	6,080,136
Urban		739,592	379,728	359,864	38,656	20,166	18,490	778,248	399,894	378,354
Total		*10,784,294*	*5,397,304*	*5,386,990*	*2,160,511*	*1,089,011*	*1,071,500*	*12,944,805*	*6,486,315*	*6,458,490*
Percentage on Total of	Rural	93·1	93·0	93·3	98·2	98·1	98·3	94·0	93·8	94·1
	Urban	6·9	7·0	6·7	1·8	1·9	1·7	6·0	6·2	5·9

The proportions that have been here brought out will be discussed in further detail, when the figures for individual districts and States are considered. Meanwhile two points are worthy of note; first, that both in British and Feudatory territory the towns contain a larger share of the male than of the female population, and second, that the strength of the urban population in districts is on an average four times as high as in the Native States. In the whole Province 6 per cent. of the total population is returned as living in towns, the same proportion as resulted in 1881. Of the neighbouring Provinces, for which returns have been as yet received, Bombay stands highest in point of urban population, 17·2 per cent. of the inhabitants of the Presidency being so returned. Berar shows 12·4 and Madras 9·1 per cent. of town population.

The second statement given indicates how the people are distributed over the different classes of towns and villages distinguished in the Census returns.

Proportion of Total Population living in towns and villages of each size.

Villages or Towns.		British Districts.		Feudatory States.		Central Provinces.	
		Number of persons.	Proportion on total population.	Number of persons.	Proportion on total population.	Number of persons.	Proportion on total population.
Villages.	1—199	1,734,904	16·1	595,152	27·6	2,330,056	18·0
	200—499	3,792,632	35·2	886,641	41·0	4,679,273	36·2
	500—999	2,740,609	25·4	436,425	20·2	3,177,034	24·5
	1,000—1,999	1,182,127	10·9	135,600	6·3	1,317,727	10·2
	2,000—2,999	320,324	3·0	34,838	1·6	355,162	2·7
	3,000—4,999	237,360	2·2	33,199	1·5	270,559	2·1
	5,000—9,999	36,746	0·3	...	...	36,746	0·3
Total Villages		*10,044,702*	*93·1*	*2,121,855*	*98·2*	*12,166,557*	*94·0*
Towns.	5,000—9,999	226,286	2·1	38,656	1·8	264,942	2·0
	10,000—14,999	121,023	1·1	...	...	121,023	0·9
	15,000—19,999	46,944	0·5	...	...	46,944	0·4
	20,000—49,999	143,844	1·3	...	...	143,844	1·1
	50,000 and over	201,495	1·9	...	...	201,495	1·6
Total Towns		*739,592*	*6·9*	*38,656*	*1·8*	*778,248*	*6·0*

More than two-thirds of the persons living in the Feudatory States are shown as residing in villages of less than 500 inhabitants, as compared with half the population, so returned in British Districts.

12. Variations in villages since 1881.—The number of villages has decreased since 1881 by 261 in British Districts and 837 in the Feudatory States. Were it possible to obtain accurate mauzawar returns, it is probable that such differences would not arise. As the population increases changes will, no doubt, be observable in the numbers of villages of each class; villages which ten years before were in the lowest class would tend to move into the one next higher, but the actual number of mauzas being fairly constant, the total returned should scarcely be affected thereby. At the present Census the decrease has been wholly in villages of the smallest size; in nearly every district these have declined, and the better classes of villages have gone up in consequence. But the change that has taken place cannot be looked upon as normal, for the increase in the better classes does not balance the decrease in the lowest class, and in some districts there are considerably fewer villages now in existence than there were in 1881. In Chhindwara the total number of villages has declined by 89, in Chanda by 52, in Balaghat by 110, and in Sambalpur by 405. The difference is to be accounted for by the inclusion of hamlets in main villages being more carefully carried out at the present Census than was the case in 1881; in Sambalpur the re-settlement that has taken place has materially contributed to this result. Raipur is the only district where the number of villages has largely increased, a possible explanation being that the village returns for zemindaris were not compiled strictly according to the mauzawar rule, as in many cases the requisite information was not forthcoming from the Census papers. Amongst the Feudatories, there has been little variation in the returns for the Chhatisgarh States, accurate village statistics being available. In Bastar the number of villages has increased, due probably to new settlements and to more correct enumeration than in 1881. The figures for the Uria States show most divergence from the results of the previous Census; in Sonpur the number of villages has sunk from 868 to 703, in Patna from 1,591 to 1,157, and in Kalahandi from 2,461 to 1,989. The result is to be set down to more careful compilation. In 1881 the Uria statistics were worked out at Sambalpur, and it would appear that by taking separate account of every hamlet that bore a name of its own, the number of villages was unduly increased. The results, as noticed by Mr. Drysdale, at pages 154-6 of his review, were out of all proportion to the returns of the Census of 1872. To these the figures of the present Census more closely approximate, though in the course of twenty years a very considerable rise is observable in some of the States to which new settlers have more particularly been attracted. In Patna there are now 264 more villages than there were in 1872, and in Kalhandi the number has risen by over 500.

Variation *in the* number *of* villages *since last Census.*

Villages.	British Districts.			Feudatory States.			Central Provinces.		
	1881.	1891.	Increase or Decrease.	1881.	1891.	Increase or Decrease.	1881.	1891.	Increase or Decrease.
With less than 200 inhabitants	19,076	17,179	−1,897	8,540	6,810	−1,730	27,616	23,989	−3,627
With 200 and less than 500 inhabitants.	11,231	11,946	+715	2,257	2,812	+555	13,488	14,758	+1,270
With 500 and less than 1,000 inhabitants.	3,379	4,073	+694	385	649	+264	3,764	4,722	+958
With 1,000 and less than 2,000 inhabitants.	694	901	+207	42	106	+64	736	1,007	+271
With 2,000 and less than 3,000 inhabitants.	121	134	+13	9	15	+6	130	149	+19
With 3,000 and less than 5,000 inhabitants.	63	63	...	5	9	+4	68	72	+4
With 5,000 and less than 10,000 inhabitants.	...	7	+7	...	...	...	...	7	+7
Total Villages.	34,564	34,303	−261	11,238	10,401	−837	45,802	44,704	−1,098

13. **Statistics of villages.**—In columns 6 to 15 of the appended statement is given the number of villages of each class, and the proportion they bear to the total villages of the district. Villages of the lowest class are, of course, most common in those districts which contain a large extent of forest and waste. Such are Mandla, where 65·4 per cent. of the villages contain under 200 inhabitants, Chhindwara, where the proportion is 63 per cent., and Chanda, 64·5 per cent. In Chhindwara most of the small villages are situated in the jaghirs in the north of the district, where the population is almost entirely aboriginal. In Bastar, and generally in the Uria States, the nnmber of villages of the smallest size is very high; in Rairakhol they form 90·6 per cent. of the total, in Bastar, 83·9, and in Kalahandi, 75·6 per cent. The places with the lowest proportion of small villages are Bhandara, where they are 32·7, Khairagarh, 30·4, and Chhuikhadan, 25·2 per cent. of the whole. Villages of the next class, containing between 200 and 500 inhabitants, are most numerous in Chhatisgarh, where they are nearly as common as ones of the smallest size, which predominate in other parts of the Province. On the two following classes, with a population of between 500 and 1,000, and between 1,000 and 2,000, it is hardly necessary to remark. It will be noticed that they drop off in strength in the Satpura districts and in the Uria States, in all of which small villages are the rule.

Statistics of Villages.

Districts.	Average number of inhabitants per village.		Total number of villages.		Number of Villages of each kind and percentage on total villages—1891.									
					1—199.		200—499.		500—999.		1,000-1,999		2,000 and above.	
	1881.	1891.	1881.	1891.	No.	Percentage.	No.	Percentage.	No.	Percentage.	No.	Percentage.	No.	Percentage.
1	2	3	4	5	6	7	8	9	10	11	12	13	14	15
Saugor	267	287	1,837	1,829	969	53·0	595	32·5	195	10·6	58	3·2	12	·7
Damoh	260	271	1,144	1,136	633	55·7	346	30·5	114	10·0	35	3·1	8	·7
Vindhyan Districts	*265*	*281*	*2,981*	*2,966*	*1,602*	*54·0*	*941*	*31·8*	*309*	*10·4*	*93*	*3·1*	*20*	*·7*
Jubbulpore	259	280	2,307	2,313	1,195	51·7	803	34·7	254	11·0	49	2·1	12	·5
Narsinghpur	352	345	985	1,010	486	48·1	329	32·6	136	13·5	45	4·4	14	1·4
Hoshangabad	292	309	1,532	1,579	772	48·9	533	33·8	209	13·2	53	3·4	12	·7
Makrai	284	330	59	56	25	44·6	24	42·9	3	5·4	3	5·3	1	1·8
Nerbada Valley	*288*	*303*	*4,883*	*4,958*	*2,478*	*50·0*	*1,689*	*34·1*	*602*	*12·1*	*150*	*3·0*	*39*	*·8*
Nimar	337	347	625	592	255	43·1	230	38·9	75	12·7	22	3·7	10	1·6
Mandla	172	190	1,751	1,756	1,148	65·4	543	30·9	55	3·1	8	·5	2	·1
Seoni	222	256	1,162	1,401	751	53·6	517	36·9	109	7·8	22	1·5	2	·2
Chhindwara	192	218	1,830	1,741	1,097	63·0	529	30·4	79	4·6	30	1·7	6	·3
Betul	260	271	1,172	1,154	600	52·0	408	35·3	113	9·8	30	2·6	3	·3
Satpura Districts	*187*	*229*	*6,215*	*6,052*	*3,596*	*59·4*	*1,997*	*33·0*	*356*	*5·9*	*90*	*1·5*	*13*	*·2*
Nagpur	296	321	1,673	1,682	830	49·3	613	36·4	169	10·1	42	2·5	28	1·7
Wardha	392	392	903	908	346	38·1	348	38·3	157	17·3	41	4·5	16	1·8
Bhandara	403	440	1,612	1,617	528	32·7	577	35·7	378	23·4	114	7·0	20	1·2
Balaghat	281	343	1,211	1,101	462	42·0	380	34·5	216	19·6	36	3·3	7	·6
Chanda	221	244	2,801	2,749	1,772	64·5	646	23·5	242	8·8	66	2·4	23	·8
Nagpur Plain	*300*	*330*	*8,200*	*8,057*	*3,938*	*48·9*	*2,564*	*31·8*	*1,162*	*14·4*	*299*	*3·7*	*94*	*1·2*
Raipur	290	305	4,741	5,080	2,202	43·4	2,001	39·4	754	14·8	114	2·2	9	·2
Bilaspur	270	301	3,722	3,804	1,738	45·7	1,485	39·0	483	12·7	86	2·3	12	·3
Chhatisgarh States	247	281	2,101	2,065	904	43·8	904	43·8	228	11·0	25	1·2	4	·2
Chhatisgarh	*274*	*299*	*10,564*	*10,949*	*4,844*	*44·2*	*4,390*	*40·1*	*1,465*	*13·4*	*225*	*2·1*	*25*	*·2*
Bastar	89	123	2,204	2,479	2,080	83·9	328	13·2	62	2·5	8	·3	1	·1
Sambalpur	209	274	3,256	2,851	1,395	48·9	1,063	37·3	335	11·8	50	1·7	8	·3
Uria States	139	209	6,874	5,801	3,801	65·5	1,556	26·8	356	6·2	70	1·2	18	·3
Uria Country	*161*	*231*	*10,130*	*8,652*	*5,196*	*60·0*	*2,619*	*30·3*	*691*	*8·0*	*120*	*1·4*	*26*	*·3*
Total British Districts	265	293	34,564	34,303	17,179	50·1	11,946	34·8	4,073	11·9	901	2·6	204	·6
Total Feudatory States	150	204	11,238	10,401	6,810	65·5	2,812	27·0	649	6·3	106	1·0	24	·2
Total Central Provinces	237	272	45,802	44,704	23,989	53·7	14,758	33·0	4,722	10·6	1,007	2·2	228	·5

Large villages.—The most important type of village is that which forms the last class, *viz.*, whose population is over 2,000 persons. Such villages are of importance not only on account of their size, but also as indicating by their prevalence in any particular tract a commercial and industrial development which is wanting in places where the villages are small. In whatever manner they may have arisen, trade is ordinarily attracted to these large villages, and they thus tend to become the nucleus of towns. In many cases their origin is to be looked for in the days when might was right, when the people banded together for purposes of mutual protection. In more settled times the tendency has been for large communities thus formed to break up, except where a thriving population has necessitated their continuance as market towns or where they have been rendered of importance as centres of the Administrative Government. Their numbers are greatest in the Nagpur plain and the Nerbada valley, while they are less frequently met with in the Satpura districts and in the eastern districts and States of the Province. Wardha and Nagpur, it will be seen from the next paragraph, besides containing the highest proportion of large villages, are also the districts with the greatest number of towns; in Wardha there are six towns and in Nagpur nine. The reasons for the high rate of towns and large villages have been discussed in the Settlement Reports of the two districts, from which I quote.

Wardha.—"To each circle of ten or twelve villages, forming their common centre, is some place of rather higher pretensions than its neighbours, at which the weekly market is held. This is called the kasba, and as some small amount of trade is carried on here, the population, not being limited to agriculturists, is more numerous than that of the adjoining villages. In the same proportion to the kasba as the kasba is to the smaller village is the town, the old pergannah head-quarters, which, from associations, has still some importance in the eyes of the inhabitants, and generally boasts of an old mud fort in which the deshmukhs or deshpandias of the pergannah reside. But apparently the pergannah towns and the kasbas have for many years past been falling off in importance, and as they decline the adjacent villages improve, so that village, kasba, and pergannah town are, by degrees, approaching one level, the villages profiting by the decline in the towns, the one rising in proportion as the other falls. This is to be attributed to the change in the times. The kasba originally did not owe its importance to the small amount of trade carried on there, so much perhaps as to some advantage of position which constituted it a convenient place of rendezvous in troublous times. In days when a visit from the Pindharis or some other lawless band from across the river was no very extraordinary occurrence, the agriculturists were obliged to flock together for purposes of mutual protection and defence, and sacrificing convenience to safety to take up their quarters at some central spot, at perhaps a considerable distance from their fields. Thus large gatherings together of agriculturists, deserving the name of town, became dotted at considerable intervals over the district. The villages were comparatively few, and the country indeed was a country of towns, traces of the importance of many of which are still to be seen. But times being now peaceful, the necessity for crowding together no longer exists, the large gatherings of agriculturists are breaking up, and the cultivators are taking to living as near as possible to their fields, and what were once small hamlets are now flourishing villages."

Nagpur.—"The size, population and importance of the larger towns, when compared to the total district population and area, are remarkable. The circumstance is, in some measure, to be accounted for by the system under the Maratha Government, which made the Kamaishdar or head administrative official of each pergannah reside at the head-quarters of the pergannah. The pergannahs were small and many. The Kamaishdar brought in his train a numerous retinue for whose food, lodging and clothing arrangements had to be made on the spot and thus the nucleus of something like a town was commenced at once by the drawing together of a body of artizans, grain-sellers and others, who were required to provide for the wants of the officials and their followers. The cloth trade again, which is so largely followed and so widely dispersed over the district, must have done much to increase the towns. There may be other special causes on which it would be out of place to speculate. At all events to whatever cause ascribable, the preponderance in number of the rural over the urban population is here much smaller than in most other districts of India."

The process of disintegration to which the Wardha report refers has long been a thing of the past, but of the old order traces remain in the large number of populous villages and towns which are still a distinguishing feature of the district. The commercial development, moreover, which Wardha has witnessed during the past twenty years, has helped to increase the size and importance of its large villages and to check any tendency to decline which might otherwise have existed. Nagpur from its proximity to the seat of the former ruling power, and Chanda and Bhandara from their greater inaccessibility, were less exposed to the raids of free-booters than the border tract of the Wardha valley. The growth of the pergannah towns in their case has therefore probably taken place in the more peaceful manner described in the second extract that has been given. In the Nerbada districts and in Nimar, as in Wardha, it is likely that many of the larger villages* trace their origin to the close of the last and the early years of the present century, when the valley was the scene of constant warfare and plunder. That more of these have not remained is probably due to the utter devastation that had been wrought. The land had been laid wholly waste and trade there was none, so that the larger communities which had been formed for purposes of protection, were necessarily compelled to break up in order to obtain the means of support. The scarcity of large villages and towns in Chhatisgarh, so noticeable a feature in the Census returns, has been thus accounted for in the Bilaspur Settlement Report.

"It is the marked absence of towns which soon strikes a visitor to Chhatisgarh, a matter for the more surprise when the entire plain is seen covered with hamlets. It arises from the fact that the people are a simple agricultural community requiring few of the luxuries which have become necessities in more advanced localities. The tract too possesses but little amassed wealth, having lain for so long a period distant and remote from all the regular channels of trade. All the demands of the people are fully satisfied by the weekly markets which are very common all over the district."

A list of all the more important villages in each district containing 3,000 of a population and over has been prepared for reference, and is published as Appendix B of this report.

14. **Statistics of Town Population.**—In the accompanying abstract is set forth the proportion of urban to the total population in each district, the latter being arranged in the order in which they stand as regards the strength of their town population. Columns have been added to show the relative proportion of the followers of each religion who are resident in towns.

Percentage *of* Urban *on* Total Population *of each district in detail of* Religion.

District.	Number of towns.	All Religions.	Hindus.	Mussulmans.	Christians.	Jains.	Animistic.
1	2	3	4	5	6	7	8
Nagpur	9	28·7	26·6	72·2	99·6	52·2	4·3
Nimar	2	18·9	14·1	55·5	84·1	36·9	·7
Jubbulpore	3	13·3	12·2	56·4	99·0	23·6	·6
Saugor	4	11·3	9·6	44·1	80·1	15·3	·7
Wardha	6	11·2	10·8	35·4	79·3	39·6	2·0
Hoshangabad	4	7·8	7·0	37·5	84·8	41·0	·5
Chhindwara	4	6·8	9·6	28·5	78·8	30·9	·3
Damoh	2	5·4	4·9	22·0	100·0	10·5	·3
Narsinghpur	2	5·2	4·9	22·6	68·0	26·5	·7
Bhandara	3	4·1	4·3	23·1	73·6	17·7	·2
Chanda	2	3·8	4·4	20·8	55·5	40·0	·5
Seoni	1	3·2	3·9	21·1	98·0	28·8	·4
Betul	2	3·2	4·3	22·6	53·0	10·7	·3
Raipur	3	2·3	2·2	26·5	24·9	52·1	·6

*Cf. Nimar Settlement Report, para. 86, and Hoshangabad Settlement Report, para. 27.

Percentage *of* Urban *on* Total Population *of each district in detail of* Religion—*contd.*

District.	Number of towns.	All Religions.	Hindus.	Mussalmans.	Christians.	Jains.	Animistic.
1	2	3	4	5	6	7	8
Sambalpur	1	1·8	1·6	35·9	58·2	...	3·8
Bilaspur	2	1·5	1·5	16·7	27·5	5·0	·1
Mandla	1	1·5	2·7	19·4	41·9	5·4	...
Balaghat	1	1·3	1·5	10·2	97·1	9·3	·2
Total British Districts	**52**	**6·9**	**6·6**	**40·9**	**84·5**	**23·0**	**·6**
Total Feudatory States	*6*	*1·8*	*2·1*	*21·4*	*79·3*	*69·2*	*·1*
Total Central Provinces	**58**	**6·0**	**5·9**	**40·2**	**84·4**	**23·6**	**·5**

The number of towns returned is 52 in British Districts and 6 in Feudatory States against 48 and 4, respectively, at the previous Census. There has been some slight variation in the standard adopted, as in 1881 every place with over 5,000 population was counted a town, whereas on the present occasion seven such have been included among villages for reasons already noted. On the other hand, three places which were reckoned towns in 1881, Armori, Rehli and Mohari, have similarly been classed as villages, as their population has decreased below 5,000, or because they are not urban in character; while again some places on account of their growing importance are now for the first time put among towns. Comparison of the figures for town population with those of the last Census is therefore hardly possible, unless we take only the towns which are common to both enumerations. In these it will be found that the population has increased by 6·9 per cent., a rate which is considerably less than that which obtains for the total population. The latter has increased by 9·6 per cent. in British territory, in which nearly all the towns are situated. Allowing for the fact that the excess of births over deaths is probably less amongst the urban than amongst the rural population, and that the natural increase in towns is therefore slow, yet it would appear from the proportions that have been given that there is no general movement of the people towards the towns. The Province, it has been seen, possesses a high rate of village population, and agriculture is therefore the mainstay of the great mass of its inhabitants. To force the villager to migrate to the town, either new industries must have sprung up to attract the surplus peasantry from their fields, or the pressure of the people on the land must have reached such a high pitch that support for part of them must be looked for elsewhere. Neither of these conditions exist to any extent in the Central Provinces. In only two or three towns do we find important manufactures, and these are scarcely yet so far developed as to give employment to a large number of persons. On the other hand, the native weaving industry in many towns has declined or has become so unprofitable, that, instead of newcomers being attracted to the weaving centres, the latter are actually breaking up, and many of the poorer classes, finding it impossible to live by the produce of their looms, are taking to other avocations. Nor can the pressure of the village population on the land be yet considered to be excessive. In most parts of the Province land still remains to be taken up, and there is no lack of room for the cultivating classes to spread. But even where the culturable margin is lowest, the soil with careful husbandry will support a much larger population than it at present bears. In proof of this may be noted the low density of the population in even the most fertile tracts as compared with the high rate prevalent over Northern India. The immense export of agricultural produce, which takes place from the Nerbada valley and which the new line of railway is beginning to foster in Chhatisgarh, is also sufficient evidence that in the Central Provinces at least the expansion of the rural population is far from having reached its furthest limit.

15. **Religions in Towns.**—Coming next to the religions of the urban population, it will be noticed that the great mass of the people of the Province being Hindus, the proportion of Hindus who live in towns closely approximates the general average of town population, about 6 per cent. It is only in other religions that significant variations are observable. Of Mussalmans over 40 per cent. live in towns, the districts which contain the highest averages in this respect being Nagpur, Jubbulpore, Nimar and Saugor, that is, in which the largest towns of the Province are situated. To these Mahomedans have been most attracted, but in the northern districts as well as in the Nerbada valley and Seoni, there is also a considerable Mussalman population settled in the country. Of Christians 84 per cent. are found in towns, specially in the large cantonments which are garrisoned by European troops. Jains are a much more scattered community in the northern districts, where they chiefly reside, than in the south and west of the Province, where a large proportion of their number is confined to towns. In the latter parts they are for the most part strangers engaged in trade, and they have therefore established themselves mainly at places which are commercial centres. Persons whose religion has been recorded as Animistic are necessarily scarce amongst the urban population. Members of the forest or hill tribes, who have actually come to live in towns, will almost all return themselves as Hindus, and that the record contains so many persons who have been otherwise returned is probably to be put down, as remarked in 1881, to the caprice of the enumerator rather than to the will of the enumerated.

16. **Notices of Towns.**—Reference has been made above only to the general preponderance of towns-people in different parts of the Province or among different sections of the community. I shall now note upon the distinguishing features of some of the more important towns.

Proportion of males per 1,000 of both sexes in certain Towns.

Males more.			Males less.		
Town.	District.	Per 1,000 of Population.	Town.	District.	Per 1,000 of Population.
1	2	3	4	5	6
Warora	Chanda	564	Mohpa	Nagpur	492
Wardha	Wardha	551	Pandhurna	Chhindwara	489
Murwara	Jubbulpore	546	Umrer	Nagpur	487
Harda	Hoshangabad	533	Chhindwara	Chhindwara	485
Khandwa	Nimar	533	Chanda	Chanda	484
Jubbulpore	Jubbulpore	532	Tumsar	Bhandara	484
Saugor	Saugor	531	Mohgaon	Chhindwara	483
Arvi	Wardha	529	Ramtek	Nagpur	479
Kampti	Nagpur	525	Betul	Betul	478
Hoshangabad	Hoshangabad	524	Arang	Raipur	475
Gadarwara	Narsinghpur	522	Ratanpur	Bilaspur	470
Nagpur	Nagpur	518	Dhamtari	Raipur	468

Proportions of the Sexes in Towns.—I take first the proportion of the sexes, figures for which in those towns which show most inequality in this respect are given in the margin. The towns in which the number of males is much in excess of females are generally the trading centres to which a large floating population of labourers and others is attracted during the busy season. Wardha, Murwara and Harda are conspicuous examples of this. The workmen employed in the coal mines at Warora raise the average for that town, while in Saugor, Jubbulpore and Kampti the presence of troops considerably affects the proportions between the sexes. In the quiet country towns which contain no foreign element, females are nearly always more numerous than males.

Hindus and Mussalmans in twenty chief towns.—The relative strength of the two main religions in 20 of the chief towns of the Province will appear from the statement which is here given. The fact that Nimar was for long the seat of Mahomedan power may be taken to account for the high proportion of Mussalmans returned from Burhanpur and Khandwa. The former also contains an important colony of Shiah Bohras from Gujerat. In Kampti the presence of a Madras Cavalry regiment, in which most of the troopers were Mahomedans, has had an appreciable effect upon the high average shown for the cantonment. Seoni has always possessed a considerable Mussalman population.

Percentage of Hindus and Mussalmans on Total Population in certain Towns.

Town.	District.	Religion.	
		Hindu.	Mussalman.
1	2	3	4
Nagpur	Nagpur	80·8	14·0
Jubbulpore	Jubbulpore	72·1	23·0
Saugor	Saugor	75·0	20·2
Kampti	Nagpur	66·0	26·8
Burhanpur	Nimar	66·6	32·5
Raipur	Raipur	80·0	15·2
Chanda	Chanda	90·3	6·8
Khandwa	Nimar	64·0	30·7
Umrer	Nagpur	94·5	4·7
Sambalpur	Sambalpur	83·5	8·7
Harda	Hoshangabad	73·8	20·2
Hoshangabad	Hoshangabad	73·4	22·0
Bhandara	Bhandara	86·2	12·4
Seoni	Seoni	64·1	26·5
Damoh	Damoh	80·1	14·5
Bilaspur	Bilaspur	85·3	13·0
Hinganghat	Wardha	85·4	11·1
Narsinghpur	Narsinghpur	74·6	19·1
Warora	Chanda	80·5	12·3
Chhindwara	Chhindwara	70·9	21·6

Variations in Town Population since last Census.—The next statement given exhibits the most notable variations that have taken place in the towns of the Province during the last ten years. The increase or decrease in all towns containing over 10,000 inhabitants has been set down; among the smaller towns only those are mentioned in which there has been a marked change in the population.

Increase *and* Decrease *in* Town Population.

Town.	District.	Population.			
		1881.	1891.	Difference.	Increase or Decrease per cent.
1	2	3	4	5	6
Nagpur	Nagpur	98,299	117,014	+18,715	+19·0
Jubbulpore	Jubbulpore	75,705	84,481	+8,776	+11·6
Saugor	Saugor	44,416	44,674	+258	+·6
Kampti	Nagpur	50,987	43,159	−7,828	−15·4
Burhanpur	Nimar	30,017	32,252	+2,235	+7·4
Raipur	Raipur	24,948	23,759	−1,189	−4·8
Chanda	Chanda	16,137	16,175	+38	+·2
Khandwa	Nimar	15,142	15,589	+447	+·3
Umrer	Nagpur	14,247	15,180	+933	+6·5
Sambalpur	Sambalpur	13,939	14,571	+632	+4·5
Harda	Hoshangabad	11,203	13,556	+2,353	+21·0

Increase *and* Decrease *in* Town Population—*contd.*

Town.	District.	Population. 1881.	1891.	Difference.	Increase or Decrease per cent.
1	2	3	4	5	6
Hoshangabad	Hoshangabad	15,863	13,495	−2,368	−14·9
Bhandara	Bhandara	11,150	13,348	+2,198	+19·7
Seoni	Seoni	10,203	11,976	+1,773	+17·4
Damoh	Damoh	8,665	11,753	+3,088	+35·6
Bilaspur	Bilaspur	7,775	11,122	+3,347	+43·0
Hinganghat	Wardha	9,000	10,964	+1,964	+21·8
Narsinghpur	Narsinghpur	10,222	10,220	−2	−·0
Warora	Chanda	8,022	10,018	+1,996	+24·9
Garhakota	Saugor	11,414	9,525	−1,889	−16·5
Wardha	Wardha	5,816	8,322	+2,506	+43·1
Narkher	Nagpur	7,061	8,256	+1,195	+16·9
Ramtek	Nagpur	7,814	7,584	−230	−2·9
Seoni	Hoshangabad	6,998	6,779	−219	−3·1
Deori	Saugor	7,414	6,306	−1,108	−14·9
Khurai	Saugor	5,370	6,272	+902	+16·8
Hatta	Damoh	6,325	5,801	−524	−8·3
Sindi	Wardha	4,644	5,463	+819	+17·6
Burha	Balaghat	4,136	5,138	+1,002	+24·2
Badnur	Betul	2,881	5,014	+2,133	+74·0

Nagpur, the chief city of the Province, has increased 19·0 per cent. since the Census of 1881, its population now amounting to 117,014 souls. The opening of the Nagpur-Chhatisgarh Railway for traffic in 1882 brought a large accession of trade to Nagpur. In 1887 the conversion of the narrow gauge line and its extension to Assensole on the East Indian Railway was undertaken; at the time of the Census the new line had been opened up to the border of the Province, and a considerable trade established with the eastern parts of Chhatisgarh. The presence of the head-quarters of the Railway which are stationed at Nagpur has also materially added to the population.

Jubbulpore, population 84,481, has grown by 11·6 per cent. due mainly to its importance as a commercial centre.

Saugor, population 44,674, shows hardly any increase on the Census of 1881. It is now connected by a branch with the main line of the Indian Midland Railway, and some development in its trade has no doubt taken place in consequence; but against any increase in population that may have resulted from this, must be set a considerable falling off due to the military station being no longer garrisoned by Madras troops. In 1881 the number of persons resident in Saugor who were born in Madras was 1,750; there are now only 103 so returned. The Bengal troops now cantoned in Saugor do not make up for this decline. The Madrasi sepoy moves about with his wife and family and freely spends his pay, so that his presence implies a well populated bazaar. The Bengal soldier is usually a single man; he lives on the plainest of food and likes to hoard up his few rupees. The petty vendor of the bazaar, therefore, tends to disappear with the Madras troops who were his customers. The difference produced by the change of garrison is illustrated by the fact that while males have increased by 1,169, the female population of Saugor has fallen off by 911.

Kampti has decreased by 7,828 persons of whom 4,144 are females. The withdrawal of the Madras garrison and the consequent decline in the bazaar population would appear to be the principal reason for the decrease. The number of Madras-born alone in the Nagpur district has fallen by over 2,000 persons, the greater part of whom have probably gone from Kampti. The place has also lost much of the importance as a trade centre which it formerly possessed. The days are now past when "during the Maratha rule traders flocked to Kampti on account of the immunity which they enjoyed within the cantonment from the taxation to which they would have been subjected anywhere else in the Nagpur Province."

Burhanpur, population 32,252 or 2,235 more than in 1881. The town is said to be decaying, but the Census returns show no indication of this. At the time of the enumeration new water-works were in progress; the inclusion of the labourers on the works may have helped to swell the return. The opening of new cotton-ginning factories has also had a similar effect.

Raipur, population 23,759, has declined by 1,189 persons of whom 725 are females. The chief cause seems to be the withdrawal of Madras troops. Madras-born in the district have fallen from 2,717 to 698, for which the presence of a wing of a Bombay Regiment does not compensate Something also is to be set down to Raj-Nandgaon having been for years the terminus of the line of Railway and trade being attracted thither from Raipur.

Chanda, 16,175, has remained almost stationary. The Deputy Commissioner writes that the populaton of the town might have been expected to have declined—the Census of 1881 showed that it had fallen since 1872. He attributes the fact that no decrease has taken place to the better circumstances of the weaving and labouring classes, more especially the Mahars and Beldars, who used to leave their homes in search of employment for months together, but who now seldom do so.

Khandwa, 15,589, shows hardly any increase: it has little trade.

Harda, 13,556, a centre of the wheat trade, has increased by 2,353 persons.

Hoshangabad, 13,495, has declined considerably since 1881. At the time of the former Census the Bhopal State Railway was under construction, and there was consequently a large floating population of workmen and traders in the town, which then showed an increase of 4,250 persons on the figures of 1872. Of this increase more than half, 2,368, has disappeared at the present Census. The place is not of commercial importance.

Bhandara, 13,348. The increase of 2,198 is partly due to inclusion of suburbs.

Seoni, 11,976, has grown by 1,773 persons. It is the head-quarters town of the Seoni district, and is the chief commercial town above the ghats.

Damoh, 11,753, has largely increased since 1881. Improved communications and the opening of the Railway to Saugor have helped to bring about this result. It is the only town with any trade in the district.

Bilaspur.—The opening of the Bengal-Nagpur Railway has raised the population of Bilaspur to 11,122. This does not include the Railway Settlement, which lies at a distance from the town and which at the time of the Census numbered 957 persons. Situated as it is at the junction of the Katni branch with the main line of Railway, Bilaspur may be expected to develop into an important commercial and railway centre.

Hinganghat, 10,964, the centre of the Wardha cotton trade, is a growing town.

Narsinghpur, 10,220, has not advanced since 1881; it has little trade.

Warora, 10,018, has increased by 1,996 persons, due to development of the coal-mining industry. The output of coal in 1890-91 was 142,673 tons as compared with 68,156 tons in 1881-82.

Garhakota, 9,525, has declined by 1,889 persons, due chiefly to the breaking up on account of cholera of the annual fair, which is held in the month of February. In 1881 the population included 2,611 persons attending the fair. The town is also reported to be declining; the poorer classes, especially the weavers, are gradually leaving the place in search of employment elsewhere.

Wardha now contains 8,322 inhabitants or 2,506 more than in 1881. The town is growing in importance; it is the head-quarters of the district and is an important cotton mart.

Deori, 6,306, has decreased by 1,108 persons. The opening of the Saugor Railway branch has completely cut off the through traffic between Saugor and Kareli on the Great Indian Peninsula Railway. This accounts for the deterioration of Deori which is situated on the high road.

Hatta has fallen from 6,325 to 5,801, mainly owing to the decline in the weaving trade.

Khurai, 6,272, has benefited by the opening of the Bina-Saugor Railway.

Sindi, 5,463, is a growing town conveniently situated on the Great Indian Peninsula Railway in a rich agricultural country.

Burha, 5,138, is the head-quarters of the Balaghat district. Part of the recorded increase appears to be due to inclusion of neighbouring hamlets.

Badnur, 5,014, the Civil Station of Betul, has increased by 2,133 persons. It is now connected by a good road with the Railway at Itarsi, which has largely helped to its development.

17. Cantonments.—For convenient reference, the following additional details are furnished with regard to the Civil Station of Sitabuldi and cantonments other than Kampti:—

DISTRICT.	Suburb or Cantonment.	TOTAL POPULATION.			Hindus.	Mussalmans.	Christians.	Jains.	Sikhs.	Others.
		Total.	Males.	Females.						
1	2	3	4	5	6	7	8	9	10	11
Nagpur	Sitabuldi	24,019	13,340	10,679	16,905	3,157	2,721	130	138	968
Jubbulpore	Jubbulpore	11,326	6,674	4,652	7,523	2,275	1,270	56	...	202
Saugor	Saugor	11,938	7,156	4,782	7,652	3,549	665	10	17	45
Hoshangabad	Pachmarhi	1,823	1,023	800	1,271	493	24	14	...	21
Nimar	Asirgarh	1,740	909	831	968	584	14	174	...	...
Raipur	Raipur	2,090	1,192	898	1,337	640	92	...	...	21
Sambalpur	Sambalpur	1,415	886	529	1,001	355	59	...	...	...

As regards Sitabuldi and the cantonments of Jubbulpore, Saugor, Raipur and Sambalpur, the population has in each case been included in the general population of the town to which the suburb or cantonment is attached.

CHAPTER II.

FLUCTUATIONS OF THE POPULATION.

18. The variation that has taken place in the enumerated population since last Census is set forth in Table II. Proportionate figures are given in the statement on the next page. Comparison with the census results of 1872 shows that the population has grown enormously during the last two decades. Large allowances must, however, be made for deficiencies in the enumeration of 1872, which was admittedly incorrect in Mandla and in parts of the Chhatisgarh and Uria districts and states. But for the present we are concerned only with the fluctuations that are apparent since the last Census was taken ten years ago. Throughout the Province, these, as will be seen, result in an increase which in British districts amounts to 9·6, in Feudatory States to 26·4 and for the whole of the Central Provinces to 12·1 per cent. on the population of 1881. The reasons for this increase, and the causes which have led it to vary in one district as compared with another, are what we have now to consider.

Variation since 1872.

	Population.			Increase per cent. in 19 years.
	1872.	1881.	1891.	
British districts .	8,173,824	9,838,791	10,784,294	31·9
Feudatory States .	1,049,710	1,709,720	2,160,511	105·8
Total Central Provinces .	9,223,534	11,548,511	12,944,805	40·3

As noted by Mr. Ibbetson in the Punjab Census Report of 1881, the increase or decrease of the population of a given tract of country during the interval between any two enumerations, as shown by a comparison of the figures of the one with those of the other, may be due to any combination of the following causes :—

(1) greater accuracy of enumeration on the one occasion than on the other ;

(2) movement of population into or out of the tract during the interval ;

(3) actual increase or decrease of resident population owing to the number of births during the interval having been greater or less than the number of deaths.

19. **Increased accuracy of the enumeration.**—*Proportion between the sexes a test.*—Of the operation of the first cause we shall find evidence when we come to examine the figures for some of the more remote and jungle tracts, specially among the Native States in the south and east of the Province. Something too may be said for the greater accuracy of the present Census, from a consideration of the proportion between the sexes. It is well known that among certain classes there exists or did exist an objection to disclose information about their women. As the Census becomes more familiar to the people at each successive enumeration, it is likely that such prejudices will disappear, and we may expect the number of females to rise in proportion to the number of males. This we find to be the case, as is shown by columns 8 and 9 of the statement which is given. In British districts the sexes very nearly balance one another, there being now about 1,002 males to every 1,000 females ; in the Feudatory States the proportion has fallen from 1,030 to 1,016 and in the whole Province from 1,018 to 1,004. In 1872 for every 1,000 females there were 1,036 males. It is difficult to say whether the female population is really increasing to the extent which these figures indicate, or whether some part at least of this may not be set down to the gradual

Statement showing Variation in the Population since last Census.

District.	Population.		Increase per cent.			Serial order of districts, etc., in respect of column 4.	Males per 1,000 Females.	
	1881.	1891.	Total.	Males.	Females.		1881.	1891.
1	2	3	4	5	6	7	8	9
Saugor	564,950	591,743	4·7	4·7	5·9	15	1,091	1,068
Damoh	312,957	325,613	4·0	2·9	5·3	16	1,081	1,057
Total Vindhyan Districts	877,907	917,356	4·5	3·4	5·7	VI	1,088	1,065
Jubbulpore	687,233	748,146	8·8	7·6	10·1	9	1,033	1,010
Narsinghpur	365,173	367,026	·5	−1·4	2·5	18	1,045	1,005
Hoshangabad	488,787	529,945	8·4	7·2	9·7	12	1,068	1,043
Makrai	16,764	18,549	10·6	9·6	11·7	...	1,033	1,014
Total Nerbada valley	1,557,957	1,663,666	6·8	5·4	8·2	V	1,047	1,020
Nimar	231,341	253,486	9·5	8·4	10·8	7	1,096	1,073
Mandla	300,496	339,373	12·9	12·0	13·9	3	1,036	1,019
Seoni	335,997	370,767	10·4	9·7	11·0	6	1,007	994
Chhindwara	372,899	407,494	9·2	8·6	10·0	8	997	984
Betul	304,905	323,196	5·9	5·3	6·7	14	1,026	1,013
Total Satpura Districts	1,314,297	1,440,830	9·6	8·9	10·4	III	1,015	1,001
Wardha	387,221	400,854	3·5	3·9	3·1	17	1,020	1,028
Nagpur	697,356	757,862	8·6	8·8	8·5	10	1,017	1,021
Chanda	649,146	697,610	7·5	7·8	7·1	13	1,014	1,020
Bhandara	683,779	742,850	8·6	7·6	9·7	11	993	974
Balaghat	340,554	383,331	12·5	12·9	12·2	5	983	989
Total Nagpur Plain	2,758,056	2,982,507	8·1	8·1	8·2	IV	1,007	1,006
Raipur	1,405,171	1,584,427	12·7	11·4	14·1	4	982	959
Bilaspur	1,017,327	1,164,158	14·4	13·7	15·2	2	982	969
Chhatisgarh States	536,247	600,904	12·1	11·8	12·3	...	991	985
Total Chhatisgarh	2,938,745	3,349,489	13·2	11·6	14·1	II	984	967
Bastar	196,248	310,884	58·4	54·9	62·3	...	1,105	1,055
Sambalpur	693,499	796,413	14·8	14·5	15·2	1	998	993
Uria States	960,461	1,230,174	28·1	27·1	29·1	...	1,038	1,021
Total Uria country	1,653,960	2,026,587	22·5	21·9	23·2	I	1,022	1,011
British Districts	**9,838,791**	**10,784,294**	**9·6**	**8·8**	**10·4**	...	**1,016**	**1,002**
Feudatory States	**1,709,720**	**2,160,511**	**26·4**	**25·5**	**27·3**	...	**1,030**	**1,016**
Total Central Provinces	**11,548,511**	**12,944,805**	**12·1**	**11·3**	**12·9**	...	**1,018**	**1,004**

disappearance of the prejudice to which I have referred. Without for the present entering upon a discussion of the prevalence of one or other of the sexes in different districts, it may be remarked that divergences in respect of males being much in excess of females may be looked for more in the northern than in the southern districts of the Province. In the former the seclusion of women is carried to a further excess, and among some of the immigrant castes from northern India and Rajputana, who form the great bulk of the population of these districts, there are probably to be found more pretentious ideas of the honour of women than among the cultivating classes of the Maratha country and Chhatisgarh. This is certainly borne out by the proportions which have been given for these districts; and if the prejudice be taken to exist, its strongholds would appear to be the districts of Saugor, Damoh, Hoshangabad and Nimar.

20. *Less distrust of the Census.*—Another ground of inaccuracy which it would seem must occasionally have some effect upon the Census returns, is the absurd stories which get about among the hill people as to the intention of Government in making the enumeration. In no other way that I can think of can some of the variations that are apparent in the rate of increase among the sexes be explained. To take, for instance, the case of Kawardha; while the male population of the state has increased by 7·9 per cent., the female population has grown only 4·7. This is the more to be wondered at, when the adjoining disfrict of Bilaspur exhibits an increase among females which is 1·5 per cent. greater than among males, and the states of Chhuikhadan and Khairagarh, which lie to the south, show a similar preponderance, amounting to 2·8 and 2·7, respectively. Turning to page 105 of Appendix A of the Census Report of 1881 we find the following extract from the Bilaspur District Report:—

"Among the most ignorant, and especially the hill tribes, the belief was that it was intended to carry off a portion of the male population for fighting purposes."

From the results now disclosed it would appear as if the superstition had the effect of considerably reducing the number of enumerated males in Kawardha, where, owing to the remoteness of the state, the rumour stood perhaps less chance of contradiction than in the khalsa portion of Bilaspur. The instance is rather an exaggerated one, but it shows that after all we must sometimes take into account the fears of the aborigines about their young men being carried off for war, or what is more common, their young women being taken to replenish imaginary zenanas.

21. **Fluctuations due to migrations of the people.**—The figures for immigration and emigration will be found discussed in Chapter IX, which deals with the birth-places of the people. Two difficulties present themselves in connection with any attempt which may be made to explain variation in the population of a district in the light of these returns. The first is that as the migration figures refer to movements throughout the lifetime of the present generation, we cannot be sure what part has taken place during the past ten years and what took place previous to the last enumeration. It is of course only the former which will affect the increase or decrease of the population as compared with the Census of 1881. Again, even could we obtain a fair index of, say, the immigration into a district within the last ten years, the effect upon the enumerated population will vary greatly according as the immigration took place at the beginning or end of the decade. If the former, the number of persons in the district will be increased not only by the immigrants themselves, but by the children who have been born to them in the meantime, and whose birth-place will be recorded as the district where their parents have come to reside. If the immigration has taken place at the end of the decade, no such natural increase will have accrued. The second difficulty in connection with the emigration returns is that,—as explained in the chapter on place of birth,—we possess full information of the num-

ber of persons who have entered each district from outside, but we have no record of the number of persons who have left each district, unless they are still resident within the Province. For persons who have gone to other parts of India and who have been enumerated there, in most cases no account has been kept of the districts of the Central Provinces from which they have come. It is thus impossible to contrast immigration with emigration for any particular district, as in the one case we have figures for all immigrants from whatever part of the world, in the other we have returns of emigrants only to other parts of the Province. Movements which are entirely confined to the Central Provinces can, it is true, be compared, and the gain or loss which thereby results to each district can be estimated. This has been done in Statement C at Chapter IX; but all that we gather from such a return is an indication of the general tendencies which during the lifetime of the present generation have served to attract or repel people differently to or from different districts.

22. *Inferences to be drawn from the migration returns.*—When we come to gauge the strength of such movements within a particular period of time, figures, as we have seen, are not so readily available. Something may, however, be judged of the extent of migration that has taken place in the interval between 1881 and 1891, by comparing the birth-place returns for the two enumerations. Comparative figures for the whole Province are given opposite; they will be found also in somewhat greater detail in Chapter IX. The number of immigrants from other parts of India is 528,407 as against 546,644 in 1881,—a decrease of 18,237. If allowance is made for possible incorrectness in the record of some of the Feudatory States at the last Census, it is probable that the decrease should be even greater. The figures, as they stand, show that there has been increased immigration from Bengal, Oudh, the Punjab and Rajputana; for Berar, Bombay, and Madras, the returns of the two enumerations are almost equal, while for the North-West Provinces, Hyderabad and Central India, the Census of 1891 shows a distinct falling off. Now, in the course of ten years, there have no doubt been decided changes among the individuals returning themselves as born beyond the Province; many have gone back to their homes, but so long as their places are taken by others, no gain or loss results from the movement as far as the enumerated population is concerned. The only matter which affects the inferences to be drawn from the birth-place returns would thus appear to be the following.

Supposing the immigration to have remained constant since the last Census, that is, assuming that there have been no new immigrants, or that any such have merely taken the place of others who have gone away, the number of foreign-born enumerated in 1891 will be less than the number enumerated in 1881 by the portion that has died in the interval. To estimate what this portion may be is almost out of the question, so much do the circumstances vary on which it depends; but generally the following rule may be deduced from the proposition set forth above. If the number of immigrants into any tract, according to the Census of 1891, considerably exceeds the number enumerated in 1881, the tract has largely gained in population in the interval; if the numbers of the two enumerations are about equal, there has still been a gain by immigration about equal to the portion of the former immigrants who have died; if the 1891 census shows considerable decrease on the figures of 1881, there has either been no gain or the tract has lost by some of the former immigrants returning to their country, without others arriving to take their place. Thus the population of the Province has been increased in the last ten years by immigration from all the places mentioned, except the North-West Provinces, Hyderabad and Central India, the increase being greatest in the case of immigrants from Bengal, Oudh, the Punjab and Rajputana, and slight from Berar, Madras and Bombay.

Statement showing the rise or fall in migration between the Province and other parts of India during the last ten years.

A.—Immigration into the Central Provinces from the places mentioned in column 2.

	Province or State.	1881.	1891.	Difference.	Remarks.
Increased immigration.	Oudh	17,048	32,966	+ 15,918	The Province has gained by fresh immigration from these parts.
	Bengal and States	51,709	55,741	+ 4,032	
	Punjab and States	2,834	6,541	+ 3,707	
	Rajputana	19,300	22,042	+ 2,742	
	Other parts of India	679	3,147	+ 2,468	
Decreased immigration.	Berar	52,311	52,110	— 201	
	Madras and States	28,419	26,795	— 1,624	
	Bombay and States	26,510	24,554	— 1,956	
	Hyderabad	28,033	21,885	— 6,148	
	N.-W. P. and States	105,590	90,043	— 15,547	
	Central India States	214,211	192,583	— 21,628	
	Total	546,644	528,407	— 18,237	

B.—Emigration from the Central Provinces to the places mentioned in column 2.

	Province or State.	1881.	1891.	Difference.	Remarks.
Increased emigration.	Bengal and States	40,486	85,742	+ 45,256	By the emigration to all of these places the Province has lost in population. The figures for Bengal, Central India and Madras are, however, doubtful.
	Central India States	78,258	117,878	+ 39,620	
	Berar	185,142	216,488	+ 31,346	
	Madras and States	4,936	16,253	+ 11,317	
	Assam	825	3,844	+ 3,019	
	Mysore	1,063	2,016	+ 953	
	Burma	310	527	+ 217	
Decreased emigration.	Bombay and States	10,537	10,494	— 43	
	Punjab and States	1,441	1,095	— 346	
	Hyderabad	13,287	6,782	— 6,505	
	N.-W. P., Oudh, and States	29,361	12,179	— 17,182	
	Total	365,646	473,298	+ 107,652	

23. The same principle also applies to the statistics for emigration, figures for which for the most important Provinces and States are given above. The Province has largely lost by increased emigration to Assam, Berar, Madras, Bengal and Central India, while some of the emigrants of 1881 to the North-West Provinces would seem since then to have returned to the Central Provinces; in hardly any other way can the fall from 29,361 persons in 1881 to 12,179 at the present Census be accounted for. The emigration figures for 1881 may also be open to doubt in some cases, owing to the birth-place return having been incomplete in some of the more backward of the Native States which border on the Province. In 1881 there were only 4,936 persons in Madras who returned the Central Provinces as their place of birth; in 1891 the number has risen to 16,253, mainly owing to more complete enumeration in the Agency Tracts of the northern districts of the Presidency. So in Bengal in 1881 only 40,486 emigrants from the Central Provinces were enumerated; there are now 85,742, of whom no less than 62,402 are found in the Chhota-Nagpur and Orissa Tributary States. The

figures for 1881 would seem to be far under the mark. The emigration to the Central Indian States has increased from 78,258 in 1881 to 117,878 in 1891; here also improved or more extended enumeration may probably account for part, at least, of the increase. The emigration to all parts of India, for which figures have reached me, amounts to 473,298 persons as against 365,646 who had gone from the Central Provinces to the same places previous to the last census; there is thus a difference of 107,652 persons lost to the Province, plus a further number necessary to cover the losses by death among former emigrants since 1881. Though these figures are, no doubt, for the reasons above given, to a considerable extent erroneous, yet there would appear to have been a very marked outgoing movement specially towards Berar and Central India, and its effect will be noticed when we come to consider the variations int he districts which border on these territories.

24. **Births and Deaths.**—*General considerations.*—The circumstances which in this country combine to stimulate multiplication of the race have frequently been discussed. In the Bombay Census Report of 1881, page 29, they have been classed as physical and social, and are thus described by Mr. Baines:—

> "There is first the tropical climate with its accompaniment of a low standard of requirements in the way of food and clothing and an equality of temperature that admits of an outdoor life to an extent that alone renders habitable the ordinary style of dwelling. There is then the extent of arable soil, most of which yields to a comparatively simple cultivation the amount of food that suffices for the wants of the family, whether of two or half a dozen members. Strongest of all is the religious sanction, or the social influence, that contains within itself all the vitality of the popular belief of the masses, and according to which the want of a male heir leads to difficulties as regards inheritance of property, as well as to the omission of ceremonial observances of the utmost importance after death. There is, lastly, the stereotyped structure and want of elasticity inherent in the form of Indian society, which retards to an indefinite degree the development of a standard of comfort in advance of that of the preceding generation, and has thus the effect of discouraging that foresight which, originating in the desire of rising in the social scale, has an enduring effect on the marriage relations of the class which has once acquired it."

Against these influences, all tending to foster the production of children, is to be set the natural check which consists in the condition of comparative want which is to be found among the great mass of the population. Among people living from hand to mouth and depending for their existence almost solely on the produce of the fields, the effect of a bad season speedily makes itself felt, and insufficiency of food intensifies the liability to disease of the poorer classes of the community. There is further the prevalence of epidemics, such as cholera and small-pox, of which, as the figures in the next paragraph will show, there are not infrequent severe visitations. Though during the five years preceding the Census, the operation of the former check was also to some extent manifest, yet from their situation and soil these Provinces are much less liable to suffer from shortness of rainfall than most other parts of India. Owing possibly to the hills and forests, which cover some 45 per cent. of the surface, the rainfall is less liable to fluctuation than in more open tracts, and the black soil, which constitutes the greater part of the cultivated area, is so retentive of moisture as to yield a crop, when lighter land would be dry and barren.

25. **Vital Statistics of the past ten years.**—A statement has been prepared which exhibits the number of births and deaths in the British districts of the Province during the ten years, 1881 to 1890. The figures are taken from the Vital Statistics Tables, published in the Annual Reports of the Sanitary Commissioner. I have added a summary of the conditions of these years, as regards the health of the people, which have had a more direct bearing upon the returns that are

given. The birth and death ratios are calculated per mille of the total population under registration.

1881. **Births, 48·94; Deaths, 32·58; Excess of births over deaths, 16·36.**—The rainfall was heavy. Cholera, 9,140 deaths, visited nearly every district, but not with severity. Mortality was not excessive, and the condition of the people was in most districts good. Prices of staple food rose in the northern districts of the Province, but were low in Nagpur and Chhatisgarh.

1882. **Births, 41·73; Deaths, 29·98; Excess of births over deaths, 11·75.**—The rainfall was again heavy, but it was not favourably distributed; the kharif harvest was therefore poor. Cholera, 11,932 deaths, was general, but was most severe in Damoh, Narsinghpur, Seoni, and Bilaspur. Food was abundant and fairly cheap. The opening of the Nagpur-Chhatisgarh Railway tended to raise the price of rice in the eastern districts.

1883. **Births, 40·59; Deaths, 34·56; Excess of births over deaths, 6·03.**—In the four northern districts and in Chhatisgarh the rainfall was below the average. The year was an unhealthy one. Cholera, 16,235 deaths, was severe in the Satpura districts, and specially so in Wardha, Nagpur and Bhandara. Small-pox was also prevalent. Food was cheap and abundant.

1884. **Births, 41·75; Deaths, 27·30; Excess of births over deaths, 14·45.**—The rainfall was excessive, 67·4 inches. The year was generally a healthy one and there was no outbreak of cholera. Small-pox visited every district. The harvest of the year was not good, but prices fell owing to the abundance of stock in hand, and the decrease of the general export demand.

1885. **Births, 45·36; Deaths, 34·21; Excess of births over deaths, 11·15.**—The rainfall was considerably below the average in all districts, except Saugor, Mandla, Chanda, and Sambalpur. Cholera, 21,868 deaths, and fever of a severe type, prevailed; the former was specially fatal in Jubbulpore, Mandla, Hoshangabad, Raipur, and Bilaspur, while the central hill districts suffered most from fever. Prices rose during the year. The rice crop was only a fairly good one and its price ruled high.

1886. **Births, 37·79; Deaths, 33·24; Excess of births over deaths, 4·55.**—The rainfall was everywhere below the average. The year was unhealthy. Cholera, 16,679 deaths, was very severe in Balaghat and in Raipur and Bilaspur, and fever was more fatal than in the previous year. The season was favourable to cotton and juari, the staple crops of Wardha and Nagpur, but unfavourable to rice. The crop was a failure in Chhatisgarh. Prices were very high. There was a good deal of distress among the poorer classes, and relief works had to be started in one or two places. Throughout the Province prices generally were higher than in the previous year.

1887. **Births, 40·20; Deaths, 32·70; Excess of births over deaths, 7·50.**—The rainfall was above the average. The year was one in which the poorest classes suffered from the continued pressure of high prices, and in some districts insufficiency of food tended to produce a low condition of health among these classes. Cholera was prevalent, but was specially severe in Damoh, Narsinghpur, Wardha, and Sambalpur. Towards the end of the year rice and wheat declined in price, the outturn of both being above the average. The autumn crops had however been poor.

1888. **Births, 41·52; Deaths, 28·70; Excess of births over deaths, 12·82.**—The rainfall was generally below the average. The health of the population was better than in the previous year. Small-pox caused 10,729 deaths, of which 7,419 were in Raipur and Bilaspur. The wheat harvest in the spring had been good, but most of the other crops suffered from drought. The effect of the short rainfall showed itself in the price of food-grains, which everywhere rose, with the exception of juari, which fell from the high standard of the previous year.

1889. **Births, 39·30; Deaths, 43·79; Excess of deaths over births, 4·49.**—The rainfall was above the average in 12 out of the 18 districts. The year was a most unhealthy one.

"Every district had the same tale to tell of severe suffering from epidemic and endemic disease. The registration returns everywhere afford evidence of depressed vitality, originating in previous bad harvests and the continued

Vital Statistics, 1881—1890, according to the Registration Returns.

District and Population under Registration.	Births or Deaths.	Number of Births and Deaths. 1881-85.	1886-90.	Proportion of births or deaths of males per 100 females.	Average annual rate per mille.	Serial order in respect of magnitude of Birth-rate.	Death-rate.	Net Increase, 1881-90. Total.	Males.	Females.	Increase per cent. on population under Registration.	Remarks.
1	2	3	4	5	6	7	8	9	10	11	12	13
Saugor, 564,950	Births *Deaths*	134,903 *96,627*	112,229 *120,165*	108·2 *116·4*	43·7 *38·4*	1	2	30,340	11,793	18,547	5·4	
Damoh, 312,957	Births *Deaths*	74,490 *54,793*	60,441 *64,995*	111·0 *117·3*	43·1 *38·3*	2	3	15,143	6,342	8,801	4·8	
Jubbulpore, 686,606	Births *Deaths*	151,069 *117,527*	130,220 *125,499*	109·2 *116·3*	41·0 *35·4*	9	5	38,263	16,188	22,075	5·6	
Narsinghpur, 365,173	Births *Deaths*	80,558 *68,264*	70,563 *74,493*	108·9 *117·8*	41·4 *39·1*	8	1	8,364	1,563	6,801	2·3	
Hoshangabad, 488,594	Births *Deaths*	93,135 *77,745*	96,004 *87,600*	112·5 *120·9*	38·7 *33·8*	17	8	23,794	9,619	14,175	4·9	
Nimar, 231,123	Births *Deaths*	48,551 *39,690*	49,335 *43,817*	107·5 *117·7*	42·4 *36·1*	4	4	14,379	5,576	8,803	6·2	
Mandla, 301,760	Births *Deaths*	60,092 *40,765*	58,481 *49,857*	107·2 *118·5*	39·3 *30·0*	14	16	27,951	12,205	15,746	9·3	
Seoni, 334,733	Births *Deaths*	69,551 *55,251*	64,228 *53,926*	103·6 *120·0*	40·0 *32·6*	13	9	24,602	8,517	16,085	7·3	
Chhindwara, 308,388	Births *Deaths*	67,001 *55,817*	63,442 *49,094*	107·2 *117·9*	42·3 *34·0*	5	6	25,532	10,735	14,797	6·8	

Vital Statistics, 1881—1890, according to the Registration Returns—*continued.*

District and Population under Registration.	Births or Deaths.	Number of Births and Deaths.		Proportion of births or deaths of males per 100 females.	Average annual rate per mille.	Serial order in respect of magnitude of		Net Increase, 1881-90.			Increase per cent. on population under Registration.	Remarks.
		1881-85.	1886-90.			Birth-rate.	Death-rate.	Total.	Males.	Females.		
1	2	3	4	5	6	7	8	9	10	11	12	13
Betul, 304,905	Births	67,381	60,002	104·1	41·8	6	7	23,592	10,278	13,314	7·7	
	Deaths	*50,040*	*53,751*	*111·3*	*34·0*							
Wardha, 387,221	Births	75,746	73,093	107·5	38·4	18	10	24,207	11,081	13,126	6·3	
	Deaths	*57,868*	*66,764*	*112·7*	*32·2*							
Nagpur, 697,356	Births	151,960	137,338	109·0	41·5	7	11	66,494	33,391	33,103	9·5	
	Deaths	*109,646*	*113,158*	*111·5*	*31·9*							
Chanda, 534,245	Births	108,800	100,209	105·4	39·1	15	12	42,704	20,878	21,826	8·0	
	Deaths	*76,272*	*90,033*	*108·1*	*31·1*							
Bhandara, 683,779	Births	150,130	142,165	104·9	42·7	3	14	86,448	43,711	42,737	12·6	
	Deaths	*101,258*	*104,589*	*106·1*	*30·1*							
Balaghat, 340,554	Births	70,648	68,157	105·2	40·8	10	15	36,809	17,765	19,044	10·8	
	Deaths	*48,020*	*53,976*	*109·9*	*30·0*							
Raipur, 1,141,882	Births	225,258	234,552	105·9	40·3	11	13	115,285	52,649	62,636	10·1	
	Deaths	*157,981*	*186,544*	*114·5*	*30·2*							
Bilaspur, 761,468	Births	153,802	141,732	106·4	38·8	16	17	83,024	39,509	43,515	10·9	
	Deaths	*100,823*	*111,687*	*113·2*	*27·9*							
Sambalpur, 371,491	Births	72,918	76,689	104·6	40·3	12	18	48,042	23,424	24,618	12·9	
	Deaths	*44,109*	*57,456*	*109·4*	*27·3*							
Total Population under Registration, 8,817,185	Births	1,855,993	1,738,880	107·1	40·8	IXa	IXa	734,973	335,224	399,749	8·3	
	Deaths	*1,352,496*	*1,507,404*	*114·0*	*32·4*							

prevalence of high prices of food, which made the people exceptionally susceptible to the inroads of disease. The excessive unhealthiness of the year seems to have been due to two main causes. The first was excessive heat and drought, owing to the early cessation of the rains of 1888. Over large tracts of country the water-supply was accordingly deficient and exceptionally foul. Cholera became epidemic and raged throughout the year. The second cause was the heavy rainfall which followed on the drought. There was no winter rain, and the hot sun acting on a saturated soil appears to have given to malarious fever and all cognate diseases an exceptional virulence."

Cholera caused 52,588 deaths and small-pox 17,529. Cholera was specially severe in Chanda and the three eastern districts. The spring harvests of the year were poor, causing a rise in the price of wheat, and there was some privation among the poor in Saugor and Damoh and in the districts of the Nerbada valley. The juari and rice harvests were generally good.

1890. **Births, 38·41; Deaths, 32·52; Excess of births over deaths, 5·89.**—The rainfall was above the average in nearly all districts. The birth-rate fell considerably, the effect of the unusual sickness in the preceding year. The general health was good. Cholera visited almost every district, but was severe only in Narsinghpur. The wheat harvest in the beginning of the year was better than in 1889, and the price of the grain declined. There was no real scarcity in any part of the Province; the crops were better and the conditions of life easier than in the preceding year. The improvement was most marked in Chhatisgarh.

26. *Summary.*—Roughly speaking the Province has had since 1881 five years of comparative plenty and immunity from excessive sickness, followed by five of general scarcity and high prices, coupled with a very unhealthy season in 1889. As a consequence, assuming the value of the registration statistics to be the same throughout, we find that in every district of the Province except four—Hoshangabad, Nimar, Raipur and Sambalpur—there has been a decline in the birth-rate during the last half of the decade. On the other hand, the number of deaths has largely increased, except in the two districts of Chhindwara and Seoni, which were visited by a severe epidemic of fever in 1885. Without attaching to these returns more value than they perhaps possess, we may nevertheless draw from them the following conclusions.

Vindhyan and Nerbada districts.—The effect of the bad times would appear to have made itself most felt in the northern districts of the Province. In Saugor, Damoh and Jubbulpore the birth-rate has regularly declined since 1885. In the latter year the births in these districts were 28,446, 15,204 and 32,214, respectively; they gradually get less until in 1890 they are 18,709, 10,000 and 22,585. The case of Narsinghpur has been somewhat similar. Again, in Saugor, Damoh and Narsinghpur the mortality in these five years has been excessive; they are the only districts where the deaths are more than the births. In 1887 and again in 1890 Narsinghpur has lost heavily from cholera. Hoshangabad and Nimar, from whatever cause, have fared better than the districts higher up the Nerbada; in both, as has been noticed, the number of births registered during the last five years is greater than during the first half of the decade.

Satpura districts.—The districts in the Satpuras have not suffered so severely as those in the plains. The birth-rate in 1888 was high, possibly due to the excellent harvests of the previous year; and except in Mandla and Betul, which were visited by cholera, the bad season of 1889 seems to have been less felt than in most other places. In Seoni and Chhindwara the death-rate was only 34·5 per mille, while the average for the Province was 43·8.

Nagpur plain.—In 1883 the districts of the Nagpur plain suffered severely from cholera, which again visited Wardha in 1887. The sickness of 1889 proved most fatal in Chanda and least so in Bhandara and Balaghat. In the latter district the death-rate did not exceed 32·7 per thousand, while in Chanda it rose to 51·1. The excess of births over deaths is, it will be observed, most marked in Bhandara.

Chhatisgarh.—In the Chhatisgarh districts and in Sambalpur the population keeps steadily growing despite an unhealthy climate and frequent attacks of small-pox and cholera.

Two further points deserve to be noticed in connection with the registration returns. First, the number of females appears to be in most districts increasing at a faster rate than the number of males, in which respect they to some extent bear out the Census results. In both the Nagpur plain is an exception, though the excess of male increase over female is not found in quite the same districts. The second point is that according to the Vital Statistics Table there are on an average 107 males born for every 100 females, while 114 males die according to a like proportion. The subject will be referred to in the chapter dealing with the age and sex of the population to which it properly belongs.

27. **Subsidiary considerations.**—Though the growth of the population is directly due to the three causes which have been alluded to above, there is still to be considered why it is that the third cause, the excess of births over deaths, varies so much in one part of the country as compared with another.

Variation in the death-rate.—I think I need hardly further notice the variations in the death-rate; the abstract of the conditions of the past ten years, which has been given in the last paragraph, shows sufficiently for the purpose of this review in what places the general health has suffered most. In the introductory chapter I have also noted upon the salubrity or insalubrity of different parts of the Province, though I hardly know that the registration statistics which have been given quite bear out the ordinarily accepted views on this subject. The districts with the lowest average death-rate for the last ten years are the reputedly unhealthy districts of Mandla, Bhandara, Raipur, Bilaspur, and Sambalpur, while the highest rate is found in the Vindhyan and Nerbada districts, most of which have the name of being comparatively healthy. This is the more to be wondered at considering that specially in the case of the Chhatisgarh districts and Sambalpur, epidemic diseases commit greater ravages than perhaps anywhere else.

Variation in the birth-rate.—The causes which lead the birth-rate to vary in one district as compared with another are so complex, and it is so difficult to judge of their operation from any figures which can be given, that I approach the matter with some amount of hesitation, the more so as the results of the Census are in many cases at variance with those which are exhibited in the vital statistics returns. The matter belongs properly to the fourth chapter of the report, as there statistics will be given showing that—

(1) in certain districts of the Province, particularly those on the Satpuras, the three districts of Chanda, Bhandara and Balaghat in the Maratha country, and the three eastern districts, the number of young children is very much greater than elsewhere in the Province; and

(2) that among the aboriginal tribes a like excess of children results as compared with other races (Appendix C, Parts III and IV).

In nine districts, according to the Sanitary Commissioner's returns, the average birth-rate for the ten years is above the mean; these are Saugor, Damoh, Jubbulpore, Narsinghpur, Nimar, Betul, Chhindwara, Nagpur, and Bhandara. In the first four of these the number of births must have been excessive during the first half of the decade, as during the latter half, as we have seen, there has been an immense fall in the number of children born. Turning to the Census figures we find that out of the nine districts whose names have just been given, only three, Betul, Chhindwara and Bhandara, and to a less extent Nimar, show a high proportion of children to correspond with the large number of births which have taken place. Mandla, Balaghat, Chanda, the Chhatisgarh districts, and Sambalpur have returned a very great number of small children at the enumeration, but the vital statistics of the past ten years fail to show that children have been born to the extent which the Census returns indicate. Thus we have, according to the annual Registration tables, a comparatively high birth-rate in districts like Saugor, Damoh, Jubbulpore, Narsinghpur and Nagpur, all of which the Census shows to contain few young children, and a low birth-rate in other districts, where, according to the Census, the number of children is very great. The only inferences possible are that in the former districts the infant mortality must be severe, or that in the latter registration is not so complete as it might be.

28. **Percentages bearing on the birth-rate.**—Anticipating the results which will be found discussed in succeeding chapters, I on the next page present in tabular form some of the percentages which are worth noting as casting a side-light on the varying rate of increase that has taken place in the population of the several districts since 1881.

The figures for the most part speak for themselves; but it may be remarked how very generally the causes which might be expected to lead to a rapid increase in the population are found in the districts on the Satpuras and in those of the south and east as compared with the other districts of the Province. In the second statement which has been given I have arranged the districts roughly according to these two divisions, giving to each serial numbers as it exhibits the conditions which are favourable to propagation of the race; and it will be seen how with comparatively few exceptions the districts above the dividing line have single numbers opposite their names, while those beneath that mark of division have almost a monopoly of the double figures. The following points are worthy of notice in connection with the proportions which are shown.

Column 2.—The figures in this column are affected by migration, so that in several cases they are at variance with those in column 3 and with the general tendency of the percentages given.

Column 3.—The high position occupied by the Nagpur district in respect of excess of births over deaths cannot be readily explained. There has been a good deal of immigration into the district, so that we might expect the Census increase to be considerably ahead of the natural growth of the population, but the opposite is the case. I have referred to the matter further in paragraph 41; the number of young children in the district is, it will be seen, exceedingly low.

Column 4.—Though the figures for age given at the Census cannot of course be regarded as strictly accurate, yet, assuming the amount of mis-statement to be constant throughout the Province, the proportions which this column contains are very significant, as showing that in the first ten districts more children are born—or, if we rely on the Registration returns, survive their immediate infancy—than is the case in the remaining eight. I have already mentioned that a high average of young children is almost invariably found among the aboriginal tribes,* so that the position which the Satpura districts occupy in this respect is easily accounted for. In Chhatisgarh the number of young children to be seen in the villages has always been a matter of common remark.

---

* The tables in Appendix C must be referred to. The proportion of children, aged 0—9, per 10,000 of the total population is as follows for the different religions:—

Animistic	3,218
All religions	3,069
Hindus	3,060
Mussalmans	2,669

A.—Statement showing certain percentages relating to variations in the district population.

District.	Increase per cent.		Proportion of children 0—9 per 1,000 of total population.	Females per 1,000 males, aged 15 and over.	Proportion of widows aged 15—39, per 1,000 of total females of that age.	Percentage of aboriginal population on total population.	Percentage of area under rice to total cultivated area.
	According to Census.	Excess of births over deaths (Registration returns).					
1	2	3	4	5	6	7	8
Saugor	4·7	5·4	287	943	144	8·3	2
Damoh	4·0	4·8	289	966	121	11·4	10
Jubbulpore	8·8	5·6	295	1,016	107	24·9	11
Narsinghpur	·5	2·3	287	1,034	107	13·2	4
Hoshangabad	8·4	4·9	276	969	95	20·1	1
Nimar	9·5	6·2	278	911	92	14·5	1
Mandla	12·9	9·3	341	1,000	68	60·3	14
Seoni	10·4	7·3	304	1,022	74	43·4	13
Chhindwara	9·2	6·8	308	1,034	71	40·3	1
Betul	5·9	7·7	306	982	70	39·5	1
Wardha	3·5	6·3	265	960	72	11·3	...
Nagpur	8·6	9·5	263	983	65	6·3	3
Chanda	7·5	8·0*	305	989	88	25·2	28
Bhandara	8·6	12·6	315	1,058	62	15·1	53
Balaghat	12·5	10·8	308	1,034	58	26·7	62
Raipur	12·7	10·1*	339	1,096	56	20·7	47
Bilaspur	14·4	10·9*	338	1,067	73	17·8	51
Sambalpur	14·8	12·9*	312	1,029	70	30·3	76

* Does not include zemindari area.

B.—Districts arranged serially as noted below.

District	2	3	4	5	6	7	8
Sambalpur	1	1	5	7	7	5	1
Bilaspur	2	3	3	2	10	11	4
Raipur	4	5	2	1	1	9	5
Balaghat	5	4	6	4	2	6	2
Bhandara	11	2	4	3	3	12	3
Chanda	13	8	9	11	12	7	6
Mandla	3	7	1	10	5	1	7
Seoni	6	10	10	8	11	2	8
Chhindwara	8	11	7	5	8	3	16
Betul	14	9	8	13	6	4	17
Nagpur	10	6	18	12	4	18	12
Wardha	17	12	17	16	9	16	18
Nimar	7	13	15	18	13	13	15
Hoshangabad	12	16	16	14	14	10	14
Narsinghpur	18	18	14	6	16	14	11
Jubbulpore	9	14	11	9	15	8	9
Damoh	16	17	12	15	17	15	10
Saugor	15	15	13	17	18	17	13

NOTE.—In columns 2, 3, 4, 5, 7, and 8 the districts are arranged according to the magnitude of the items given in Statement A; in column 6 the reverse is the case.

Column 5.—The question of the proportion of females to males is perhaps too slight to have much effect upon the growth of the population. Figures showing the ratio between the sexes of all ages have already been given at paragraph 19; here the number of adults of each sex is similarly compared. With the exception of Jubbulpore and Narsinghpur, children are generally few in the northern districts, where also grown-up women are few, and numerous in those places where there are many adult females.

Column 6.—Here again details are given of a circumstance which can have but a very slight effect upon the variation in the population, but if we take it that a like standard of virtue prevails in all parts of the Province among the widowed of the female sex, it must follow that in Raipur, where there are only 56 widows amongst every thousand females of what may be taken to be the child-bearing age, the number of children born must be appreciably greater than in Saugor, where there are 144 on a like proportion. Nagpur and Wardha are however, an exception to the rule, which cannot therefore be too strictly interpreted.

Column 7.—To the fact of the reproduction of the species taking place more rapidly among the aboriginal tribes, reference has already been made. The point has an important bearing on the high rate of increase observable in the districts where aborigines are numerous, and to it may in part be ascribed the phenomenal growth which will be seen to have taken place in the population of some of the remoter Native States.

Column 8.—In this column has been given the proportion of cultivated land under rice in each district of the Province. It is most noticeable that generally the districts where rice is the staple crop are those which show the largest percentage of children; Betul and Chindwara we must except, but here we find a numerous aboriginal population to account at least in part for the high average of children they contain. Mr. Fuller, Commissioner of Settlements and Agriculture, who first called my attention to the point, has referred me for an explanation to the crop outturn statistics for the Central Provinces, published in

Crop outturns in lbs. per acre.

Wheat.		Juari.		Rice.	
District.	lbs per acre.	District.	lbs per acre.	District.	lbs per acre.
Saugor . .	640	Nimar . .	600	Chanda . .	2,000
Damoh . .	640	Wardha . .	750	Bhandara . .	1,500
Jubbulpore .	700	Nagpur . .	750	Balaghat . .	1,500
Narsinghpur .	740			Raipur . .	1,000
Hoshangabad .	740			Bilaspur . .	1,000
				Sambalpur .	1,500

1889,* from which I take the figures for three of the chief crops in some of the districts where they are principally grown. From the statement given it will be seen that in the rice districts the average outturn runs from 1,000 to 2,000 lbs of unhusked rice per acre. Assuming that 100 lbs of unhusked rice yields 60 lbs of

* Note on Crop Experiments made in the Central Provinces during the four years 1884-85 to 1887-88, appended to Revenue Book Circular, No. III—25, dated 20th September 1889.

husked rice, the average outturn becomes 600 to 1,200lbs against an outturn of 640 to 740 lbs of wheat per acre and 600 to 750 lbs of juari. If to the greater yield which the soil makes in the case of rice, we add the fact that the districts where it is grown are those where, through lack of communications, the surplus produce has been less able to find a market and has thus been made available for home consumption, and where, therefore, food has always been abundant and cheap, we can better understand the rapid growth of the population in these parts of the Province.

29. I now come to notice the variations that have taken place in the population of the individual districts of the Province. My remarks will have reference principally to the extent of the variation which may be put down to movements among the people. Of the other causes which have led to a more rapid growth in the population of one district as compared with another, sufficient mention has already been made, but for purposes of comparison it will be necessary to bear them in mind in discussing the fluctuations which the Census results exhibit. Of these causes I have taken the percentage of increase which is due to excess of births over deaths—what may be called the natural increase—to be an approximate index, but before leaving the subject it is as well to state that the rate of increase deducible from the vital statistics returns can hardly in every case be relied on. The whole tendency of the proportional figures which have just been examined goes to contradict the low proportion of births which are registered in some of the southern and eastern districts as compared with those in the north and west. In the former there can be hardly a doubt that registration has been imperfect during some part of the decade.

30. **Saugor.**—*Census increase, 4·7 : natural increase, 5·4.*—In 1877-78 a large number of famine refugees came into the district from Gwalior and the north and many remained on as labourers, etc. In 1881 the number of persons enumerated in the district, who gave their place of birth as the Central India States, was 45,696; at the present Census they have dropped to 33,924. It is possible that some of the refugees have gone back to their homes since 1881, as the difference is too large to account for by deaths among their numbers within the district.

Year.	Immigrants.	Emigrants.
1881 . . .	92,399	27,212
1891 . . .	76,646	26,836
	Less 15,753	Less 376

There has been a slight gain by increased immigration from the Punjab, the North-West Provinces and Oudh during the last ten years, but from other parts of India there has been hardly any fresh immigration since 1881. Of the increased emigration to the Central India States, which has been noticed at paragraph 23, part has certainly taken place from Saugor.

Colonel Hogg writes :—

"It appears that a good number of the inhabitants of the Saugor and Banda tehsils have emigrated into Panna and other adjoining Native States, some for employment on the railway, and others in hopes of bettering themselves elsewhere or for other reasons. As an instance, it has been reported that several families of Lohars in villages of the Banda tehsil have gone to live in the Panna State, the reason given being the high charges realized by the Forest Department for charcoal largely used by blacksmiths."

To other parts of the Central Provinces there has been little fresh emigration. The part of the district which has increased most is the Khurai tehsil, 7·9 per cent., and least the Rehli tehsil, 1·3 per cent. The low rate of increase in the Saugor district may therefore be attributed to a reduced birth-rate and high mortality, due to the late bad seasons, and to people having left the district from the same causes.

31. **Damoh.**—*Census increase, 4·0 : natural increase 4·8.*—The circumstances of Damoh are very much similar to those of Saugor. Previous to the last Census there had been a large inflow of famine refugees from Central India. The number of persons born in the Central India States was, in 1881, 26,211; it is now 23,222. There is thus no sign of the previous settlers returning to their homes, as would seem to be the case in Saugor, as the decrease of 2,989 is sufficiently accounted for by death. The district has gained nothing by fresh immigration; the facts point rather the other way. Emigration, on the other hand, has largely increased, mainly to the Jubbulpore district. At the present Census 11,761 persons in Jubbulpore returned Damoh as their place of birth, against 7,788 in 1881.

Year.	Immigrants.	Emigrants.
1881 . . .	50,895	18,483
1891 . . .	44,836	21,759
	Less 6,059	More 3,276

Colonel Lugard assigns, as a reason, that a great number of people had left the district for the harvest in Sehora and Jubbulpore. "They do so every year in much larger numbers, I should say fifteen or twenty thousand, but in 1881 the imigration had not commenced, and in 1891 it had taken place, but many came back to be enumerated in their own homes. I am even surprised that the number of absentees was not much larger, as I know from personal knowledge that in the southern part of the district whole villages are fairly deserted, a few old men and women being left to look after the horses and cattle. I think there can be no doubt that this is the real cause of the apparent decrease on the vital statistics returns."

The Central India States have also probably attracted emigrants from Damoh. The increase in population has been 3·7 per cent. in the Hatta tehsil and 4·3 in Damoh. As most of the people who had left the district for the harvesting had gone from the Damoh tehsil, it is evident that the increase in the actual population of the latter has been considerably larger than what has been given; it probably amounts to over 6 per cent.

32. **Jubbulpore.**—*Census increase 8·8 : natural increase 5·6.*—The number of persons who, in 1891, have returned themselves as born beyond the district is slightly less than the number so recorded in 1881, but the difference is slight in comparison with the total number of immigrants. There has, therefore, been a considerable amount of fresh immigration into the district to keep the numbers of foreign-born up to their former strength. About the time of the Census, Damoh and the Central India States sent large numbers of labourers into Jubbulpore for the winter harvest. There has thus been no falling-off in the figures for immigrants from Central India, as was the case in Saugor and Damoh, and as otherwise there would have been also in Jubbulpore; the number returned in 1891 is 56,748 against 56,008 at the enumeration of 1881. The number of Madras-born has fallen from 2,742 to 498, due to garrison changes. This is about the only instance in which there has been a distinct decline in immigration. The district has not lost by emigration. The tehsil which exhibits the highest rate of increase is Sehora, 10·5 per cent., while the lowest 6·5, occurs among the rural population of the Jubbulpore tehsil. Generally speaking it may be said that the Jubbulpore district would have shown a much smaller variation from the Census of 1881, had it not been for the temporary influx of large numbers of labourers, just previous to the enumeration, from Central India and the surrounding districts. It is on this account that the rate of

Year.	Immigrants.	Emigrants.
1881 . . .	118,415	33,585
1891 . . .	117,797	30,537
	Less 618	Less 3,048

SHEWING INCREASE IN POPULATION.

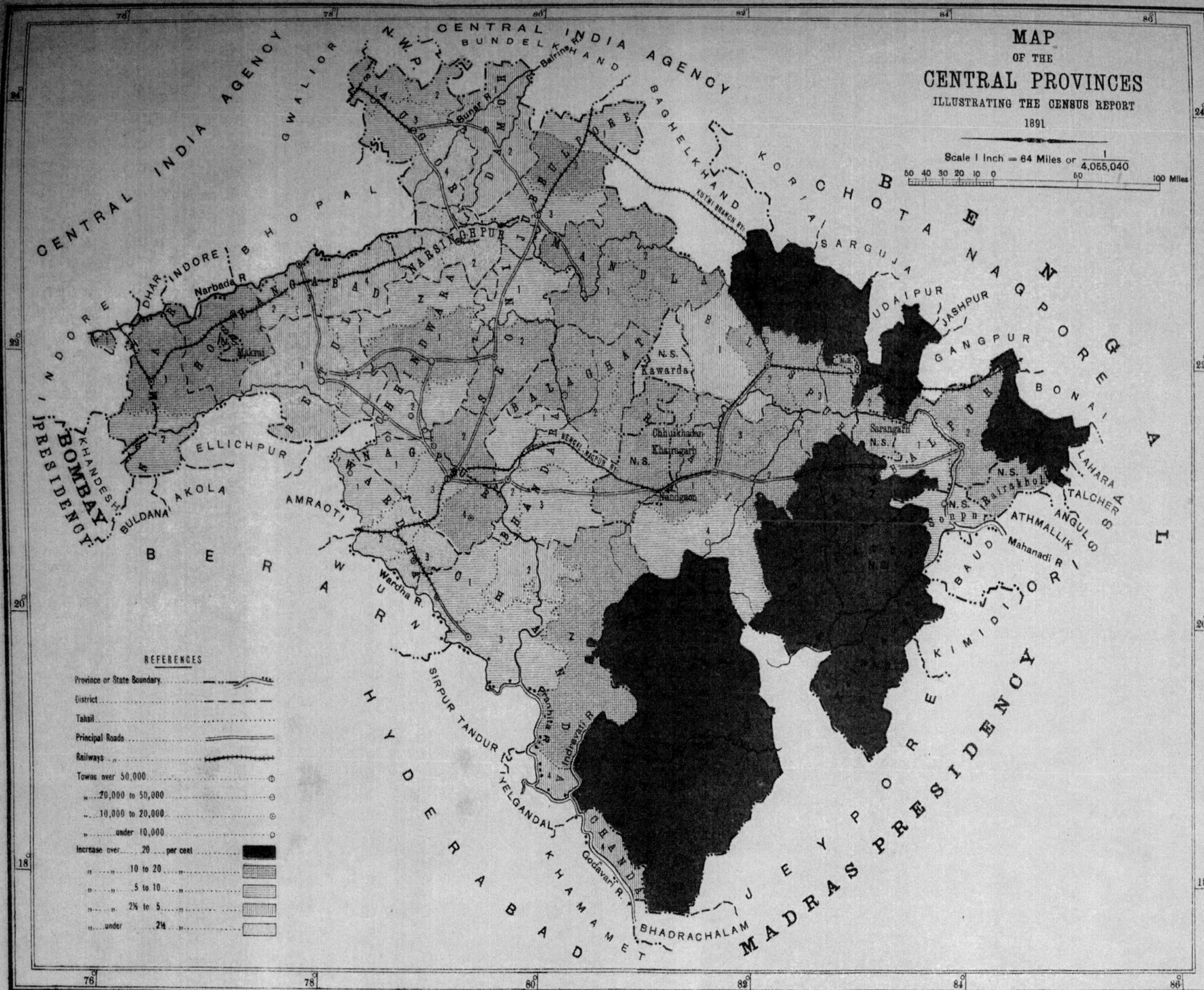

No.	TAHSIL	DISTRICT
1	Khurai	SAUGOR
2	Banda	
3	Saugor	
4	Rehli	
1	Hatta	DAMOH
2	Damoh	
1	Murwara	JUBBULPORE
2	Sihora	
3	Jubbulpore	
1	Gadarwara	NARSINGHPUR
2	Narsinghpur	
1	Harda	HOSHANGABAD
2	Seoni	
3	Hoshangabad	
4	Sohagpur	
1	Khandwa	NIMAR
2	Burhanpur	
1	Betul	BETUL
2	Multai	
1	Chhindwara	CHHINDWARA
2	Sausar	
1	Lakhnadon	SEONI
2	Seoni	
1	Behar	BALAGHAT
2	Burha	
1	Tirora	BHANDARA
2	Bhandara	
3	Sakoli	
1	Katol	NAGPUR
2	Ramtek	
3	Nagpur	
4	Umrer	
1	Arvi	WARDHA
2	Wardha	
3	Hinganghat	
1	Warora	CHANDA
2	Brahmapuri	
3	Mul	
4	Sironcha	
1	Drug	RAIPUR
2	Raipur	
3	Simga	
4	Dhamtari	
1	Bargarh	SAMBALPUR
2	Sambalpur	
1	Mungeli	BILASPUR
2	Bilaspur	
3	Seorinarain	
1	Mandla	MANDLA
2	Ramgarh	

Z. ....Zamindari
N. S. .....Native State

Reg. No. 38, C. P., Census—Mar 9? —645

Photo S I O., Calcutta.

increase according to the Census is so much higher than that which is furnished by the Registration returns. The actual resident population of the district may be taken to be probably considerably lower than what the Census figures show.

33. **Narsinghpur.**—*Census increase, 0·5: natural increase, 2·3.*—The district has gained by slightly increased immigration from Saugor, Damoh, Jubbulpore and Hoshangabad; from the Satpura districts and from Central India there has been no accession of population since 1881, while in the latter year there were in Narsinghpur 4,940 persons born in the North-West Provinces and Oudh as against only 3,410 at the present enumeration. On the whole, there has been hardly any gain to the district by immigration; neither has it lost to any extent by emigration to districts within the Province. The only supposition that can be put forward to account for the extremely low rate of increase, shown by the Census, is that Narsinghpur must, within the last ten years, have contributed considerably to the extensive emigration which has taken place from the Province to the Central India States. The people of the district are known to be deeply indebted and the adjoining state of Bhopal probably furnishes a safe refuge from the moneylender's toils. In the Narsinghpur tehsil the population has decreased by 1·4 per cent.; in Gadarwara there has been an increase of 2·3. The district, as has been already seen, has suffered from bad seasons, resulting in a very low birth-rate and greatly increased mortality.

Year.	Immigrants.	Emigrants.
1881 . . .	36,209	28,457
1891 . . .	33,751	26,269
	Less 2,458	Less 2,188

34. **Hoshangabad.**—*Census increase, 8·4: natural increase, 4·9.*—In 1881 the Bhopal State Railway was under construction, and the presence of workmen from other places thus helped to swell the immigration returns. At the present Census the figures are somewhat less, but not so much so as to preclude some margin of gain having resulted from the fresh immigration that has occurred since 1881. The district has had an accession of population chiefly from Nimar, Betul, Bombay, and Central India; from elsewhere any increase there has been is slight. The emigration figures have gone down by nearly 4,000. Hoshangabad has been returned as the birthplace of about 2,847 persons in the Makrai State against 6,000 at the last Census. The report of 1881 doubts the figures then given, as the name of the district is sometimes returned in place of the Feudatory State politically attached to it. Makrai is also described as a harbour of refuge for Gonds and Korkus dissatisfied with the forest rules, and for debtors and accused persons seeking to avoid legal process. Whether recent events in Makrai—the Raja was, in 1890, deprived of his powers for maladministration—may not have had the effect of causing many of the refugees to return to British territory, it is difficult to say, but the figures given seem to point to this result. The distribution of the increase in the population has taken place most unequally over the district. In the northern tehsils the variation from the returns of 1881 is very small. In Sohagpur the increase has been 3 per cent.; in Hoshangabad 3·2; in Seoni 6·9; while the population of the Harda tehsil has grown by 19·5 per cent. There are now in Harda 28,606 more persons than there were in 1881; of these 2,353 represent the increase in the population of Harda town, 10,855 the increase in the newly-settled Charwa tract, and 15,398 that in the remainder of the tehsil; or to give proportional figures, the town of Harda has grown by 21 per cent., Charwa by 42·3 and the rest of the tehsil by 14·0 per cent. The population of the Charwa tract amounts to 36,520 persons against 25,665 at the last enumer-

Year.	Immigrants.	Emigrants.
1881 . . .	70,196	27,160
1891 . . .	65,431	23,296
	Less 4,765	Less 3,864

ation. Thus while the northern part of Hoshangabad has, like the adjoining district of Narsinghpur, advanced but slowly during the past ten years, the south of the district has largely gained by new settlements that have taken place.

35. **Nimar.**—*Census increase, 9·5: natural increase 6·2.*—For the high rate of increase in Nimar shown by the Census it is difficult to account; the Registration figures are more than 3 per cent. lower, while the migration returns would seem to indicate, if anything, rather a decline in the population. The rise has been chiefly in the Khandwa tehsil, which contains about two-thirds of the inhabitants of the district; here the increase amounts to 11·8 per cent., while the small tehsil of Burhanpur has advanced only 5·5, most of the increase moreover taking place in the Burhanpur town. The falling-off in the immigration figures at the present Census may possibly be due to persons born in Holkar's Nimar being recorded as born in *Nimar,* without any indication of whether foreign territory was meant. The number of persons born in the Central India States has fallen from 9,699 at the last enumeration to 7,991 at the present one, whereas, as a matter of fact, immigration is reported to have increased and persons from Holkar's Nimar are taking to settling in the British district. The fact that the increase in the population of Nimar is so largely confined to the Khandwa tehsil goes far to support this view.

Year.	Immigrants.	Emigrants.
1881 . . .	42,424	2,371
1891 . . .	36,425	3,541
	Less 5,999	More 1,170

36. **Mandla.**—*Census increase, 12·9: natural increase, 9·3.*—At the enumeration of 1881 there was extensive immigration from Central India, 13,523 persons being recorded as born in the states that adjoin the district. There are now only 8,091 persons so returned. The difference of 5,432 is more than can be accounted for by deaths among the immigrants of 1881; many of the latter must, therefore, it would appear, have left the district in the interval. Though it can hardly thus be said that Mandla has gained by new immigration within the past ten years, it would seem as if it had received some accession of population by the return of natives of the district who were residents beyond its limits in 1881. The large decrease in emigration at least points to this conclusion. The unstable movements of the jungle tribes on the Seoni and Bilaspur border are sufficient to account for the variations that are apparent. It is likely, also, that some part of the increase in the population of the district is due to better enumeration on the present occasion. In 1881 the preparatory measures for taking the Census were greatly delayed, and the work had to be hurriedly pushed through at the last moment, and it is therefore highly probable that the returns of the more difficult tracts were not quite accurate. The Mandla tehsil shows an increase of 13·7 per cent. and Ramgarh, 11·9.

Year.	Immigrants.	Emigrants.
1881 . . .	43,881	23,578
1891 . . .	37,467	17,206
	Less 6,414	Less 6,372

37. **Seoni.**—*Census increase, 10·4: natural increase, 7·3.*—The great extent of the immigration which is shown by the figures in the margin took place prior to 1881. In the interval Seoni has gained by immigration from Narsinghpur, Saugor, Nagpur, the North-West Provinces, and the Central India States, but there has been no marked movement into the district from the neighbouring Satpura districts or from

Year.	Immigrants.	Emigrants.
1881 . . .	61,784	36,420
1891 . . .	55,875	35,233
	Less 5,909	Less 1,187

Bhandara. There has been some emigration from Seoni to Balaghat, which now returns 12,513 persons born in the former district as against 10,447 in 1881. The Deputy Commissioner attributes the increase in the population to persons being attracted to the district as traders or labourers rather than as agricultural settlers, and the Census figures, which show most of the new-comers during the last ten years to be fortune-seekers from Northern and Central India, certainly confirm this opinion. The increase in the population of the Seoni tehsil has been 11·9, and in that of Lakhnadown 8·2 per cent.

38. **Chhindwara.**—*Census increase, 9·2 : natural increase, 6·8.*—The increase in the population of the district is distributed as follows; Chhindwara tehsil exclusive of zemindaris, 10·6 per cent., zemindaris 5·5; Sausar tehsil 9·1. There has been increased immigration into Chhindwara from most of the surrounding districts, as well as from Berar, the North-Western Provinces and the Central India States. The district has lost by emigration into Nagpur, there being in the latter district 7,426 persons born in Chhindwara as against 6,777 at the previous Census.

Year.	Immigrants.	Emigrants.
1881 . . .	41,849	24,691
1891 . . .	43,874	22,269
	More 2,025	Less 2,422

39. **Betul.**—*Census increase, 5·9 : natural increase, 7·7.*—The increase has been mainly in the Multai tehsil, 9·3 per cent.; in Betul the population has advanced only 3·9. At the time of the Census a survey party was employed in the district; the operators and khalasis were chiefly men from Northern India, as will be seen from the fact that 1,317 persons have returned Oudh as their place of birth against 540 in 1881. From elsewhere there has been no increase in immigration since the last enumeration, whilst emigration from the district has risen. Berar returns 8,799 persons as born in Betul; it is probable that, as in the case of the next district Wardha, there was a considerable outflow of labourers for the harvest in the low country at the time the Census was taken. It has already been seen that emigration from the Central Provinces to Berar has largely increased since 1881, and to this the Betul district has, in all likelihood, contributed.

Year.	Immigrants.	Emigrants.
1881 . . .	19,950	14,165
1891 . . .	17,943	14,368
	Less 2,007	More 203

40. **Wardha.**—*Census increase, 3·5 : natural increase, 6·3.*—The increase is thus distributed: Wardha tehsil 1·8 per cent., Hinganghat 0·8 and Arvi 8·3. The increase in the Wardha and Hinganghat tehsils is wholly due to growth of the town population; in the country there is a falling off equal to 0·7 and 1·0 per cent., respectively. The district has gained by increased immigration from Chanda, Bhandara and Berar and also from Northern and Central India and from Rajputana. In 1881 Sambalpur was recorded as the birth-place of 1,512 persons in the Wardha district; now there are only 3. Emigration to Nagpur has grown considerably during the last ten years, but the main reason for the low increase in the population of the district is the following given by the Deputy Commissioner, Mr. Drysdale:—

Year.	Immigrants.	Emigrants.
1881 . . .	88,388	15,211
1891 . . .	87,237	16,443
	Less 1,151	More 1,232

"The decrease in the rural population of the Wardha and Hinganghat tehsils is probably due chiefly to increase in the number of labourers who annually leave this district temporarily to work as shearers of the rabi harvest in Berar. The shearing was still going on when the Census was taken, and the cold weather harvest in Wardha being a poor one, the numbers who left the district for Berar were much larger than usual. The Census Superintendent of Berar has informed me that the Wardha district was recorded as the birth-place of 39,922 persons enumerated in Berar. This is 12,873 more than the corresponding figure, 27,049, at the Census of 1881, and suffices to account for a decline of over 5 per cent. in the village population of Wardha and Hinganghat."

41. **Nagpur.**—*Census increase, 8·6: natural increase, 9·5.*—The two percentages present a divergence for which it is difficult to account. Considering the large amount of immigration that has taken place into the district since last Census, the increase in the enumerated population might be expected to be much in excess of the increase shown by the preponderance of births over deaths. The opposite is, however, the case. The high rate of natural increase is further contradicted by the age figures to which reference will be found in Chapter IV. Taking the percentage on the total population, of the children under 10 years of age, *i.e.*, the children born within the decade, we find it to be lower in Nagpur than in any other part of the Province. This would seem to point either to a low birth-rate for the district or to great mortality among children; in either case a low rate of natural increase would result. The highest variation from the Census of 1881 is to be found in the tehsils of Umrer and Katol, where the population has advanced 11·4 and 10·7 per cent., respectively. In Ramtek the increase has been only 6·6 and in the Nagpur tehsil 7·3 among the rural, and 7·4 among the urban population. The exchange of population between Nagpur and the surrounding districts is worthy of note. From Bhandara, Chanda, Wardha and Chhindwara there has been increased immigration since last Census, while emigration to these districts has either declined or remained almost stationary. From Bhandara the number of immigrants into Nagpur has risen from 17,554 to 20,030, from Wardha the figures are 10,069 against 8,924 in 1881, from Chanda 9,170 against 5,800, and from Chhindwara 7,426 against 6,777. On the other hand from Seoni and Balaghat there is hardly any immigration, whilst both have drawn additional settlers from Nagpur. The city of Nagpur has probably attracted few of the incomers from the surrounding districts; most of these have spread themselves over the villages, chiefly it appears to the north and south of the district, in the directions from which they have come. The immigrants from Bhandara and Chanda are many of them labourers who had crossed the border for the wheat harvest in the Umrer tehsīl. From outside the Province there has been a considerable inflow of settlers from Berar, Bombay, Rajputana, and the North-West Provinces and Oudh; the number of persons who have returned themselves as born in the latter now amounts to 12,499 against 9,852 at the last Census. The immigration from these outside sources chiefly affects the town population. The decline of immigration from the Madras Presidency has already been noticed in connection with the large decrease in the population of the Kampti cantonment. From Berar details are not forthcoming of the number of persons enumerated there who have returned Nagpur as their birth-place; but probably the district has, like Wardha, contributed largely to the increased emigration from the Central Provinces to the Berars. This alone can be suggested as a possible explanation of the Census increase falling short of the natural one, despite the considerable accession of population the district has received from elsewhere.

Year.	Immigrants.	Emigrants.
1881 . . .	82,388	85,596
1891 . . .	92,095	76.747
	More 9,707	Less 8,849

42. **Chanda.**—*Census increase, 7·5: natural increase, 8·0.*—The increase is distributed as under. In Warora it amounts to 6·1 per cent.; in the khalsa portions of Brahmapuri and Mul to 3·1 and 6·7, and in the zemindari portions to 21·8 and 6·4, respectively; in Sironcha the population has grown

Year.	Immigrants.	Emmigrant.
1881 . . .	70,294	26,970
1891 . . .	69,989	33.591
	Less 305	More 6,621

by 4·8 per cent. The large increase in the Brahmapuri zemindaris may be set down partly to more correct enumeration at the present Census and partly to increased immigration from Raipur, on the border of which district they are situated. In 1881 the number of persons in Chanda, who returned Raipur as their place of birth, was 13,760; they now number 20,445, 19,338 of whom are found in the Brahmapuri zemindaris. The rest of the birth-place returns present little that is noticeable except as regards emigration, which has risen considerably within the last ten years. Natives of Chanda have been drawn in increasing numbers to Wardha, Bhandara and Nagpur. The emigration to the Nizam's Diminions may be also conveniently referred to here. In 1881, 13,287 persons in Hyderabad Territory returned themselves as born within the Central Provinces as against 6,782 on the present occasion; most of the people so recorded are presumably natives of Chanda. The large fall in their number is probably to be assigned to change in the designation of the place of birth of those of them who came from the southern taluks of the Sironcha tehsil. In 1881 many of the latter who had crossed into the Nizam's Diminions previous to the transfer of the taluks to Madras were no doubt returned as born in Chanda; all such would now be entered as natives of the Godaveri district. There has thus been no return movement to the Province of former emigrants who had left it, as the variation between the figures for the enumerations might tend to suggest.

43. **Bhandara.**—*Census increase, 8·6 : natural increase, 12·6.*—The large difference between the two percentages is certainly not accounted for by the migration figures. At the time of the last Census the Nagpur Chhatisgarh Railway was under construction and there were large numbers of workmen from up-country and Bombay in the district. These have all disappeared, causing a considerable decline in the figures for persons born beyond the Province, who number only 4,706 against 9,092 in 1881. Bhandara has a large interchange of population with the surrounding districts, gaining by increased immigration within the last ten years from Raipur, Balaghat and Chanda, and losing by increased emigration to Wardha and Nagpur. But the variations from this source seem hardly sufficient to explain the falling-off exhibited by the Census increase as compared with that due to excess of births over deaths.

Year.	Immigrants.	Emigrants.
1881 . . .	57,679	83,892
1891 . . .	53,360	77,369
	Less 4,319	Less 6,523

44. **Balaghat.**—*Census increase, 12·5 : natural increase, 10·8.*—The district has gained by immigration from Seoni and from Chhatisgarh. The presence in the district of an increased number of persons from Chhatisgarh is accounted for by the Deputy Commissioner, by the fact that about February—the time of the enumeration—there was a steady flow of Banjaras through the north of the district from Raipur and Bilaspur. To this may be referred part of the increase in the Behir tehsil, which amounts to 14·2 per cent. on the population of 1881. The spread of cultivation has apparently done little to attract immigration within the last decade; the great number of the settlers from the surrounding districts had presumably entered Balaghat previous to the Census of 1881.

Year.	Immigrants.	Emigrants.
1881 . . .	60,594	53,264
1891 . . .	60,103	50,949
	Less 491	Less 2,315

45. **Raipur.**—*Census increase, 12·7 : natural increase, 10·1.*—Registration of births and deaths is carried out only in the khalsa; here the Census increase amounts to 10·0 per cent. distributed as follows; the khalsa portion of the Raipur tehsil has increased by 10·8 per cent., Simga by 10·1, the khalsa of

Dhamtari by 7·1, and of Drug by 12·0. In Chapter IX I have noted how little immigration there is from outside into Chhatisgarh. It has also been pointed out that the interchange of population between the Chhatisgarh districts and states cannot, in every case, be definitely ascertained as in the birth-place returns the latter have sometimes been confused with the districts to which they were formerly attached. The movements that are taking place appear to be, however, from the more thickly populated plain country to the sparsely inhabited tracts which compose the southern and eastern states. Thus, with no immigration to speak of, the variation in the enumerated population of the khalsa closely corresponds with the natural increase, the only exception being the Dhamtari tehsil, whence the people who have gone to settle in the southern Feudatories are chiefly drawn. The increased emigration from the district into Chanda must also have been derived in great part from the Dhamtari tehsil, which adjoins the Brahmapuri zemindaris where nearly all the emigrants are found. Dissatisfaction with the forest rules has been assigned as a reason for numbers of the jungle tribes leaving this part of the district. To this we may add the spread of cultivation in the southern states. Bastar now shows 7,106 persons born in Raipur against 445 in 1881,—but the latter figures are probably short, as may be judged from paragraph 50,—and Kalahandi 3,580 against 1,828.

In the zemindaris the population has increased by 24·9 per cent. since the last Census was taken, the large estates attached to the Raipur tehsil presenting the greatest variation from the figures of that enumeration. The population of these now amounts to 189,985 against 136,892 in 1881, an increase of 38·8 per cent.; Khariar, the largest of the zemindaris, has advanced 39·8 per cent.; Bindra Nawagarh 38·4, Fingeshwar 30·3, and Kauria 47·9. To the Dhamtari tehsil there is only one zemindari attached, Dondi Lohara; it shows 10·8 per cent. of increase on the population it possessed in 1881. In the zemindaris of the Drug tehsil, the chief of which occupy the north-west corner of the district, the increase has been 9·5 per cent. The growth of the population thus appears abnormal only in the zemindaris of the Raipur tehsil, the reasons given being greater correctness of the enumeration at the present Census, and probable immigration from the khalsa. Of the difficulties which were encountered in carrying out the Census operations in these remote tracts in 1881 an account has been given at page 11 of Appendix A of the Census Report of that year. In 1891 several of the estates were under management and generally there was no such trouble experienced as appears to have then been the case.

46. **Bilaspur.**—*Census increase, 14·4: natural increase, 10·9.*—The latter percentage is exactly the same as the Census increase in the khalsa, to which and one or two of the zemindaris the registration of births and deaths has alone been extended. In the zemindaris of the district the increase according to the Census has been 24·2. Like Raipur, Bilaspur has received no great accession of population from outside Chhatisgarh. The construction of the Bengal-Nagpur Railway had brought into the district a number of labourers and railway employés from other parts, but the increase on this account has not been large, as the figures for immigration from beyond the Province are only 2,807 more than they were in 1881. From Raipur there has been a considerable outflow of population to the south, but in Bilaspur hardly any such emigration would appear to have taken place. The only Feudatories which attract natives of the district are Raigarh and Sarangarh; in the former there are found 5,930 persons born in Bilaspur against 4,871 in 1881 and in the latter 5,427 against 4,816. The excess is slight and may in great part be referred to better counting. On the whole, therefore, migration has had little to do with the variation in the population of the district.

The most noticeable feature in connection with the latter is the high rate of increase in the northern zemindaris; the population of those attached to the Bilaspur tehsil is now 180,806 against 132,067 in 1881, representing an advance of 36·9 per cent. The zemindaris extend over an area of 3,619 square miles, most of which is covered with hill and forest. At the present Census the utmost pains was taken to secure accurate enumeration, a force of patwaris having been for months employed upon the preliminary operations; to the thoroughness with which the work was done, the greater part of the increase may therefore be ascribed. The figures for the various zemindaris are given in the margin. The khalsa portion of the Bilaspur tehsil has grown by 13·7 per cent. In Seori Narain the increase has been 16·5 in the khalsa and 13·9 in the zemindaris, while in Mungeli, situated in the extreme west of the district, we find the rate to be only 2·6 in the khalsa portion of the tehsil and 10·7 in the zemindari part. A reference to the table given at paragraph 48 will show that in the Feudatory States which adjoin Mungeli the increase is also small, though not to such an extent as is exhibited in the British tehsil; in Kawardha it amounts to 6·3 per cent., in Chhuikhadan to 10·0 and in Khairagarh to 9·1, all of which are comparatively low figures for this part of the Province. The only way in which we can account for this result is the marked physical difference between the western portion of Chhatisgarh and the rest of the plain country, to which reference will be found at page 11. Here we have a black soil tract where the staple grown is wheat, while throughout the centre and east of Chhatisgarh almost the only crop produced is rice. Thus we find exemplified the general tendency which seems to run through these returns, of the greater capability of a rice country to support a large and growing population, than is the case in tracts where other food-grains are grown.

Increase in population of the Zemindaris of Bilaspur tehsil.

Zemindari.	Population.			
	1881.	1891.	Actual variation.	Variation per cent.
Pendra	43,868	54,891	+11,023	25·1
Korba	42,122	62,724	+20,602	48·9
Chhuri	16,088	22,240	+ 6,152	38·2
Kenda	12,252	15,576	+ 3,324	27·1
Lapha	7,044	9,593	+ 2,549	36·2
Mátin	5,950	10,043	+ 4,093	68·8
Uprora	4,743	5,739	+ 996	21·0

47. **Sambalpur.**—*Census increase, 14·8: natural increase, 12·9.*—The percentage of natural increase applies only to the khalsa part of the district; here the Census increase has been 9·3 per cent., being 12·1 in the Sambalpur tehsil and 6·9 in Bargarh. In the Sambalpur zemindaris the population has advanced 20·3 per cent. and in those attached to Bargarh 21·2. Again, there can be hardly a doubt that better enumeration has had to do with such abnormal variations, which in Chandarpur zemindari result in as high a divergence as 28·3 per cent., in Phuljhar 33·0, and in Borasambhar 27·3 from the Census of 1881. The comparatively low increase in the khalsa population, especially of Bargarh, is to be accounted for by enhanced emigration to the surrounding zemindaris and states. The figures, with regard to the latter, are not very reliable in every case for reasons already noted, but to the following no suspicion seems to attach; in Bamra there are now 9,784 persons born in Sambalpur against 7,086 at the previous Census; in Kalahandi 1,143 against 441; in Patna 21,057 against 17,628. To the other states there has no doubt been similar emigration, which, to judge from the smallness of the increase in the number of its inhabitants, has evidently been drawn principally from the Bargarh tehsil. The construction of the Bengal-Nagpur Railway which was in progress at the time of the Census has added somewhat to the population of the Sambalpur tehsil, immigration from Raipur, Bilaspur, Nagpur, and from Bombay and Northern India having grown since 1881.

48. **Variations in the population.—Feudatory States.**—These are exhibited in the following abstract:—

Statement showing Variation in the Population since last Census—Feudatory States.

STATE.	POPULATION.		INCREASE PER CENT.			Serial order of States in respect of Col. 4.	MALES PER 1,000 FEMALES.	
	1881	1891.	TOTAL.	Males.	Females.		1881.	1891.
1	2	3	4	5	6	7	8	9
Makrai . . .	16,764	18,549	10·6	9·6	11·7	11	1,033	1,014
Bastar . . .	196,248	310,884	58·4	54·9	62·3	1	1,105	1,055
Kanker . . .	63,610	82,379	29·5	31·7	27·3	4	1,020	1,055
Nandgaon . . .	164,339	183,866	11·9	10·8	12·9	9	989	970
Khairagarh . .	166,138	181,184	9·1	7·7	10·4	14	990	967
Chhuikhadan . .	32,979	36,288	10·0	8·6	11·4	12	973	949
Kawardha . . .	86,362	91,813	6·3	7·9	4·7	15	978	1,006
Sakti . . .	22,819	25,374	11·2	10·8	11·6	10	989	983
Raigarh . . .	128,943	168,525	30·7	30·0	31·4	3	1,009	999
Sarangarh . . .	71,274	83,210	16·7	16·5	17·0	7	976	972
Bamra . . .	81,286	104,367	28·4	28·2	28·5	6	1,056	1,054
Rairakhol . . .	17,750	20,335	14·6	15·6	13·4	8	1,033	1,053
Sonpur . . .	178,701	195,245	9·2	8·4	10·2	13	1,014	998
Patna . . .	257,959	332,197	28·8	27·8	29·8	5	1,040	1,024
Kalahandi . . .	224,548	326,295	45·3	42·7	48·8	2	1,086	1,046
Total Feudatory States . .	**1,709,720**	**2,160,511**	**26·4**	**25·5**	**27·3**	...	**1,030**	**1,016**

As there are no registration returns available, comparison of the Census variation with the increase due to excess of births over deaths cannot be made, but I have noted on some of the circumstances that have apparently affected the growth of the population.

49. **Makrai.**—The small state of Makrai has increased by 10·6 per cent. since the last Census. It has no doubt benefited by the increased immigration to the Harda tehsil by which it is surrounded. On the other hand, the deposition of the Raja, which took place in 1890, has probably helped to reduce the number of foreign-born within the state. I have already noted the large falling off there has been amongst natives of Hoshangabad who are resident in Makrai, partly due it would seem to the state having ceased to be a refuge for vagabonds of all kinds.

50. **Bastar.**—The population of the Bastar state now amounts to 310,884 against 196,248 in 1881, an increase of no less than 58·4 per cent. The first cause to be assigned for this enormous variation is without doubt the greater accuracy of the present Census. Of the difficulties which were experienced in 1881, Mr. Drysdale gives an account at pages 12 and 13 of Appendix A of his Report. The state was then in a commotion owing to a feud in the family of the Chief. So late as the middle of January the latter was writing to the Assistant Commissioner at Sironcha asking that the Census might be put off for a year and a half owing to an insurrection against him headed by the Rani. An official from the Chanda district had meantime been deputed to the state to supervise

the preliminaries for the taking of the Census, but he and his men were for some time detained at Jagdalpur through fever which they had contracted in the dense forest country on the way there, and were only able to work in the intervals of sickness. The preparations for counting the inhabitants of this immense stretch of country were thus confined to some six weeks before the date fixed for the enumeration. Add to this the apathy of the state officials and the impossibility of finding persons who could read and write, and the omissions that must have occurred in the record can well be understood. On the present occasion the Census of the state was carried out under the direction of the Dewan, the late Rao Sahib Gopinath Guru. To the excellence of the arrangements which he made and to the zeal and energy which he displayed in carrying them through I have referred in the second part of the Report. The difficulty of finding enumerators was of course almost as great as ten years ago, but a staff numbering 484 persons was successfully got together as compared with 225 in 1881. In my opinion the record of the present Census of the Bastar State may be accepted as very fairly correct, and to this more particularly may be referred by far the greater part of the increase which it exhibits. Of the immigration which has taken place into Bastar, the most important items are these—the state contains 2,267 persons born in Chanda, 7,106 in Raipur, 5,712 in Madras, and 1,165 in the Nizam's Dominions; in 1881 the corresponding figures were—Chanda, 759, Raipur, 445, Madras, 2,859, and the Nizam's Dominions, 1,385. Allowing for inaccuracies, the fact remains that the state has gained considerably by immigration within the decade, the large influx of settlers from the district of Raipur being specially worthy of note.

51. **Chhatisgarh States.**—The birth-place statistics of nearly all of these are open to question except as regards persons born beyond Chhatisgarh. The population of Kanker has increased by 29·5 per cent., partly due to better enumeration, but chiefly on account of enhanced immigration from Raipur. The figures for the latter are unfortunately not reliable, on account of the state and district being given indiscriminately when returning place of birth, but a strong outward movement is known to have taken place from the Dhamtari tehsil of Raipur, of which also we have evidence in the comparatively slow rate of growth which the latter has been seen to exhibit. Nandgaon shows about the same percentage of increase as the neighbouring tehsil of Drug. The opening of the Nagpur-Chhatisgarh Railway in 1882 brought a considerable influx of traders and others into the state, but the general rise in prices which ensued has no doubt tended to act as a check upon the rapid natural growth of the population. The same remark applies to the state of Khairagarh, where the increase has been 9·1 per cent. on the population of 1881. The Kawardha state, which lies along the western border of Bilaspur, is remarkable as showing a comparatively low rate of increase, specially among females. To this I have already referred at paragraph 20. There are now only 1,171 persons born in Balaghat resident in the State against 2,135 in 1881, and 917 born in Mandla against 2,095, so that it would appear that Kawardha is not so popular with natives of these districts as it was ten years ago. If the supposition about incomplete record of males at the previous Census is correct, it would seem that part of even the small variation from the figures of 1881, which has resulted, should be referred to better enumeration. This leaves but a slight margin to be set down to natural increase, in which respect the state conforms to what has been already noticed in the case of the adjoining tehsil of Mungeli. The increase in the population of the small states of Chhuikhadan and Sakti, amounting, respectively, to 10·0 and 11·2 per cent. on the Census of 1881, calls for no remark.

52. **The Uria States.**—The growth in the enumerated population of these

states presents one striking feature in that it varies in size almost *directly* with the distance of the states from what was in 1881 their political head-quarters, Sambalpur. This is on the face of it an argument for holding that a substantial part of the increase should be set down to omissions in counting at the previous Census. Again in all the states there is a very large aboriginal population, and we have seen that generally among the forest and hill tribes a high proportion of children are born. The settled administration which the states now possess has also no doubt led to increased immigration, but the figures for the latter are not always sufficiently definite to fix on the share of the expansion which should be assigned to this cause. Again, the returns of 1881 having been evidently to a certain extent incomplete, we cannot by comparison be sure of the movements that have taken place since then. The same remark applies to emigration. To judge from the figures for the latter it would appear as if the states had lost largely within the last ten years by an outward movement towards Bengal. The Census Superintendent, Bengal, informs me that 3,792 persons in the British Districts of Chhota-Nagpur and Cuttack returned the Central Provinces as their place of birth, while the number so recorded from the Tributary States attached to these divisions amounted to no less than 62,402 persons. In 1881 the total number of emigrants to the whole Presidency of Bengal was only 40,486. The presumption is that the returns for the latter year were very wide of the mark, as it is impossible to conclude that fresh emigration to such an extent could have taken place alongside of the high rate of increase which has resulted in the Central Provinces Uria States, from which the great bulk of the emigrants must have been drawn. The same doubt attaches to the birth-place return of 1881 in the Agency Tracts of the northern Madras districts; there are now 8,832 natives of the Central Provinces resident in the Agency Tracts of the Ganjam, Vizagapatam and Godaveri districts against 1,530 ten years ago.

53. Admitting therefore that the migration figures give but an imperfect key to the variations that have taken place in the population of the Feudatories the following points may nevertheless be noted. Raigarh has gained by increased immigration from Bilaspur and from Bengal; the latter is recorded as the birth-place of 8,814 persons as compared with 7,322 in 1881. The opening of the Bengal-Nagpur Railway had also attracted workmen from Northern and Central India, but their numbers are comparatively insignificant. Altogether the immigration of the last ten years does not seem sufficient to account for the large increase in the population of the state. The variations in the population of Sarangarh, which is not so wild and was therefore less difficult to enumerate in 1881, has been much more normal. In Bamra construction work on the railway was actually in progress at the time of the Census, and the presence of a considerable body of railway employés, contractors and labourers from beyond the state helps to account for the large rise in its population. Sonpur, already highly cultivated and thickly peopled, has increased only 9·2 per cent. It has drawn a few additional settlers from Madras and the Cuttack states, but on the other hand, like the adjoining Bargarh tehsil of Sambalpur, it has contributed largely to the colonizing movement which has taken place into the Patna state. The inhabitants of the latter are now more than they were in 1881 by 74,238 persons, an increase of 28·8 per cent. The chief traces of increased immigration are from the places just noted, but this alone cannot account for such an immense rise in the population over and above what might be put down to natural growth; both in Patna and Kalahandi, where the increase has been 45·3 per cent., better enumeration has undoubtedly chiefly led to the results exhibited. In Kalahandi the only inward movements of importance have

been from Madras—there are 7,454 Madras-born against 2,144 in 1881 — and from Raipur, for which the figures have gone up by 1,752, so that a very large margin is left to be assigned to better counting.

For the varied nature of the increase in the sexes which is shown in the states of Bastar, where males have grown 7·4 per cent. less than females, in Kanker where the increase is 4·4 more, and in Kalahandi again less by 6·1, I can offer no further explanation than that put forward in paragraph 20.

CHAPTER III.

RELIGION AND SECT.

54. **General distribution of the People by Religion.**—Table VI shews the number of persons of each religion in the districts and states of the Central Provinces. In the Tables, in which are exhibited the statistics relating to age, civil condition and education, the distinction of religion has also been preserved, the reason being that in this country religion is not a mere system of faith, but is so indissolubly connected with the acts and customs of common life that it is impossible to overlook the influence which it must exercise over the subject-matter of these branches of enquiry. For the present we are, however, concerned only with the religion return as such, that is, with the general distribution of the people by religion and with the variations which are apparent when the return is compared with the results of the previous Census, while, lastly, it will be of use to consider the relative prevalence of the several religions in different localities in the Province.

The statement on the next page shews the number of persons returned as of each religion and the proportions which the followers of each bear to the total population. Variations in their numbers since 1881 will be separately noticed in a succeeding paragraph. The religions have been grouped for analysis according to what may, in some degree, be considered the order of development. The Animistic, or the religion of the forest and hill tribes, has been taken as the earliest; then follows the Brahminic or orthodox Hinduism, and below it the specially Indian offshoots of Sikhism, Jainism, Brahmoism and the new creed returned as Aryanism. Next has been taken Buddhism and Zoroastrianism, both sparsely represented in these Provinces; and lastly the three historic creeds, Judaism, Islam, and Christianity.

55. **Forest Tribes.**—To take first the forest and hill tribes, whose religion has been recorded as Animistic and who form nearly a sixth of the population of the Province. The rule for the guidance of the enumerators in making this return ran, that for a member of a forest tribe who did not call himself Hindu, Mussalman or any other religion, the name of his tribe should be entered, such as Gond or Bhil. So vague is the line that separates these classes from the lower grades of the Hindu community that the record we have got, though valuable when considered relatively in connection with distinctions of sex, age, and the like, can hardly be described as a full or accurate statement of the persons professing aboriginal forms of belief. The whole matter had necessarily to be left to the discretion of the Census agency, and the return is therefore what the enumerator, often not over-burdened with intelligence or free from prejudice, has made it, rather than a record of actually existing facts. One enumerator may describe the members of a forest tribe as of the tribal religion, while in the very next village the same class of people are being entered as Hindus. Attempts were, in some cases, made to preserve uniformity with the result that the return is as much open to doubt as ever, as real distinctions in form of belief were thus apt to be lost sight of through the rigid application of a general rule. The question is one which appears incapable of solution. All that we can say is that the persons who have been returned as animistic by religion are generally the wilder members of the hill tribes, but that there have been omissions and inclusions which the inherent difficulty of the subject renders

Statement showing the number of persons of each Religion in 1881 and 1891.

		Year.	Animistic.	Hindus.	Jains.	Mussalmans.	Christians.	Others.
		2	3	4	5	6	7	8
British Districts.	Total persons	1881	1,533,599	7,971,157	45,718	275,773	11,949	595
		1891	1,592,149	8,831,199	48,644	297,604	12,970	1,728
	Proportion per 10,000 of total population	*1881*	*1,559*	*8,102*	*46*	*280*	*12*	*1*
		1891	*1,477*	*8,189*	*45*	*276*	*12*	*1*
Feudatory States.	Total persons	1881	220,318	1,479,269	193	9,914	24	2
		1891	489,572	1,658,143	568	11,875	338	15
	Proportion per 10,000 of total population	*1881*	*1,289*	*8,652*	*1*	*58*	...	...
		1891	*2,266*	*7,675*	*3*	*55*	*1*	...
Central Provinces.	Total persons	1831	1,753,917	9,450,426	45,911	285,687	11,973	597
		1891	2,081,721	10,489,342	49,212	309,479	13,308	1,743
	Proportion per 10,000 of total population	*1881*	*1,519*	*8,183*	*40*	*247*	*10*	*1*
		1891	*1,608*	*8,103*	*38*	*239*	*11*	*1*
British Districts		Increase per cent.	3·8	10·8	6·4	7·9	8·5	...
Feudatory States			122·2	12·1	194·3	19·8	...	...
Central Provinces			18·7	11	7·2	8·3	11·2	...

Details of those shown as "Others."

		Arya.	Brahmo.	Sikh.	Buddhist.	Parsi.	Jew.	Agnostic.
		2	3	4	5	6	7	8
British Districts.	1881	...	7	97	17	399	63	...
	1891	265	3	172	322	781	176	9
	Net increase	*265*	*—4*	*75*	*305*	*382*	*113*	*9*
Feudatory States.	1881	...	...	2	...	...	...	...
	1891	10	...	1	3	...	...	1
	Net increase	*10*	...	*—1*	*3*	...	...	*1*
Central Provinces.	1881	...	7	99	17	399	63	...
	1891	275	3	173	325	781	176	10
	Net increase	*275*	*—4*	*74*	*308*	*382*	*113*	*10*

NOTE.—In 1881 twelve persons were shown as "Religion unspecified."

it impossible to prevent. Though their religious practices vary somewhat among the different tribes, the following description of the religion of the Gonds and Korkus from the pen of a most accurate observer, the late Captain Forsyth, may be taken as typical of most of the hill people of these Provinces.*

"*The Gonds.*—In religion the Gond tribes have passed through all the earlier stages of belief, and are now entering on that of idolatry, pure and simple—the last in which religion is still altogether dissevered from ideas of morality. As has been generally observed, however, the objects of worship of each new stage of development here form additions to those formerly reverenced, rather than supplant them.

"The foundaton of their creed appears to be a vague pantheism, in which all nature is ooked upon as pervaded by spiritual powers, the most prominent and powerful of which are personified and propitiated by simple offerings. Every prominent mountain top is the residence of the Spirit of the Hill, who must be satisfied by an offering before a *dhya* can be cut on its slopes. The forest is peopled by woodland sprites, for whom a grove of typical trees is commonly left standing as a refuge in clearing away the jungle. When the field is sown, the god of rice fields (Khodo Pen) has to be satisfied, and again when the crop is reaped. The malignant powers receive regular propitiation. The tiger god has a hut built for him in the wilderness that he may not come near their dwellings. The goddess of small-pox and of cholera receives offerings chiefly when her ravages are threatened. Among such elementary powers must be reckoned the ghosts of the deceased, which have to be laid by certain ceremonies. These consist in conjuring the ghost into something tangible, in one case into the body of a fish caught in the nearest water, in another, into a fowl chosen by omen. The object, whatever it is, is then brought to the house of the deceased and propitiated for a certain time, after which it is formally consigned to rest by burial. The spirits of persons killed by wild animals are believed to be specially malignant, and are "laid" with much care and ceremony.

"None of these powers of nature are represented by idols, nor have they any particular forms or ceremonies of worship. They are merely localised by some vague symbol; the mountain god by a daub of vermilion on some prominent rock; the tree god by a pile of stones thrown round the stem of a tree, and so on. At these the simple savage pays his devotion, almost fertively, as he passes in the gray of the morning to his day's labour, by a simple prostration, or perhaps by the offering of a handful of rice or an onion! More elaborate acts of worship are engaged in by the community at certain seasons, and then these primitive powers may be joined with the more personal deities derived from their neighbours in the general act of worship.

"In the next stage the tribes have added certain fetishes to the list of powers. The principal of these is an iron spear head called Phársá Pen, and he is supported by the Bell god, the Chain god, a god composed of some copper money hung up in a pot, shapeless stones, and many other objects, the power attributed to which is purely arbitrary, and unconnected with any natural agency. To this stage appears to belong the medicine man and dealer in witchcraft, who still possesses considerable power among the tribes. These medicine men can scarcely be called priests, and are not an hereditary caste. Their business is to exorcise evil spirits, to interpret the wishes of the fetish, to compel rain, and so on. Some of them seem to have acquired the power of throwing themselves into a sort of trance in which they are visited by the deity.

"In a still more advanced stage the Gonds have resorted to hero worship; but it is curious that all the deified heroes they reverence are of purely Hindu derivation. The chief are Bhimá, one of the five Pándú brethren, who is represented by his mythical club either in stone or wood; Hardyál, a Rájpút hero of much later date; Dulha Deo, the apotheosis of a bridegroom, and many others.

"Lastly come the recognised divinities of the Hindu pantheon. Amongst a race whose blessings are few and hardships many, it is not surprising that the malevolent members of the Hindu pantheon should have found more acceptance than the benevolent deities. Vishnú is scarcely recognised by them, except in his one terrible development of Narsingha or the Man-Tiger; while Siva, the Destroyer, with his formidable consort Káli and son Bhairava, are the favourite objects of reverence among the more advanced of the tribes. These are represented by rude idols, Siva himself in his usual phallic form; and a Brahmin in many cases officiates at their shrines. Here for the first time we find

* Highlands of Central India, pp. 148 and 154.

mythology—the science of priests—at work. In their earlier stages the tribes had no priests, no hierarchy of gods, and consequently no mythology. Now legends are invented to connect the tribes and their earlier gods with the great web of Hindu fiction, and bring them within the dominion of caste and priestdom."

"*The Korkus.*— "The religion of the Korkus is, I think, purer than that of the Gonds. The powers of nature are equally adored, such as the tiger god, the bison god, the hill god, the deities of small-pox and cholera. But these are all secondary to the Sun and the Moon, which, among this branch of the Kolarian stock as among the Kols in the far east, are the principal objects of adoration. I have seen nothing resembling Fetishism among them; and if, as some consider, that is the earliest form in which the religion of savages develops itself, the Korkus would seem in this respect to have advanced a stage beyond the Gonds. The sun and the figure of a horse (a Scythian emblem of the sun) are carved on wooden posts, and receive sacrifices. They also sacrifice to the manes of their dead, but only for a certain period to "lay" them. Belief in sorcery and witchcraft is not so prevalent among them as with the Gonds and Baigas. Their semi-Hindu chiefs have accepted Siva and his companions; but the common Korkus seem to care little about them, excepting in the immediate neighbourhood of his great shrine in the Mahadeo hills. A few glorified heroes receive attention, but not to nearly so great an extent as among the Gonds.

56. **Proportions of the different tribes who follow tribal Religions.**—Though it cannot be said that the Census furnishes us with an exact account of the number of persons professing aboriginal forms of belief, and though uniformity in the record has proved impossible of attainment, yet, as giving some indication of the tendencies which are at work, the following results which have been arrived at as regards the religions of particular tribes seem to be worth recording.

Statement shewing the number of the Forest Tribes *recorded as* Animistic *by Religion.*

Tribal Name.	1891.			Tribal Name.	1891.		
	Total.	No. recorded as Animistic.	Percentage of Col. 3 on Col. 2.		Total.	No. recorded as Animistic.	Percentage of Col. 7 on Col. 6.
1	2	3	4	5	6	7	8
Gond . . .	2,258,824	1,766,076	78·2	Khairwar . .	13,936	1,733	12·4
Khond . . .	196,400	153,946	78·4	Dhanwar . .	13,026	2,590	19·9
Sawara . . .	156,921	11,794	7·5	Kharia . .	9,953	3,894	39·1
Kawar . . .	127,093	4,175	3·3	Kamar . .	7,817	2,461	31·5
Baiga . . .	120,314	41,116	34·2	Bhunjia . .	6,329	1,063	16·8
Halba . . .	97,913	242	0·2	Holia . . .	4,566	537	11·8
Korku . . .	95,634	39,036	40·8	Arakh . .	2,106	1,166	55·4
Nahal . . .	8,766	2,028	23·1	Naksia . .	2,066	43	2·1
Kol . . .	87,516	11,260	12·9	Munda . .	5,185	2,282	44·0
Oraon . . .	23,264	15,380	66·1				
Bhil . . .	22,424	694	3·1	Birjia . . .	1,417	99	7·0
Bhumia . .	18,162	2,984	16·4	Bhuinhar . .	1,277	666	52·2
Bhaina . . .	17,151	1,907	11·1	Cherwa . .	982	53	5·4
Kuda . . .	16,296	4,923	30·2	Korwa . .	975	160	16·4
Bhuiya . . .	15,014	...	...				
Kisan . . .	13,982	8,249	59·0				

NOTE.—The above does not include 1,164 persons of aboriginal belief belonging to miscellaneous tribes.

The Khonds head the list with 78·4 per cent. of their number recorded as of aboriginal belief. Their isolated position in the remote state of Kalahandi quite accounts for this, but it is a surprise to find so many of the Gonds similarly returned, the more so as in British districts the proportion of the tribe shown as Animistic is as high as 82·7 per cent., while in the Feudatories it has fallen to 60·5. Throughout the Satpuras they have been almost universally denied any claim to Hinduism, and even in the Nerbada valley and in the districts of the Nagpur plain the number returned as Hindu is much smaller than might have been expected. As a matter of fact, Forsyth states that the Gonds have gone further in the adoption of Hindu sentiments than most of the aboriginal tribes; they are far more numerous, they occupy large tracts of country intermixed with the Hindus, their semi-Hindu chiefs possessed the ruling power of the country for many generations, and they have thus become more susceptible of modification than the others. This opinion must be accepted as a more accurate statement of the facts of the case than the Census figures. Taking the other tribes in their local order we may note first the Korkus, of whom 40·8 per cent. are returned as of the tribal religion; in the Betul District they have been mostly so recorded, but in Hoshangabad, Chhindwara, and Nimar the opposite has been the case. The Nahàls who resemble the Korkus occur almost solely in Hoshangabad and Nimar; they have very generally adopted Hinduism. The figures for Baigas include the Binjhwárs and allied tribes in Chhatisgarh. Among the Mandla Baigas 85·5 per cent. return their religion as aboriginal, in Balaghat the proportion is 44·4, while among the Binjhwárs of Chhatisgarh it falls to 3·4. The low percentage in Balaghat results almost wholly among the Binjhwár Baigas, the other Baigas are 70·0 per cent. animistic. The allied tribe of Bhumias is found chiefly in Jubbulpore, where nearly all its members have been shown as Hindus.

The remaining tribes, who are at all numerically strong, occur principally in the Chhatisgarh and Uria districts and states. First of all may be taken the Sawaras, who are numerous in Sambalpur, the Northern Uria States, and in the eastern part of the Chhatisgarh country; with them have also been classed the Saurs of Saugor and Damoh. They claim to be Hindus and have been almost universally regarded as such at the Census, the only places where the opposite is the case being the States of Patna and Sonpur; in Saugor and Damoh only 319 out of 23,201 persons have been shown of the tribal religion. The anxiety of the Kawars of Chhatisgarh to be considered Rajputs has been described by the writer of the Bilaspur Settlement Report, who mentions the recent assumption of the sacred thread by several of their *gots*. How universally this spirit pervades the tribe may be seen from the high proportion of their number, who describe themselves as Hindus. Next to the Kawars come the Halbas, all of whom practically claim to be Hindus by religion. In Bhandara the Halbas apparently refuse to admit their affinity to their namesakes of Bastar and Raipur, who are generally recognized as an off-shoot of the Gond tribe, but even the latter, it will be seen, have ceased to be treated as aborigines. The Kols are a scattered race; most of those enumerated in the Province are found as labourers in Jubbulpore and Mandla, though their affinities are mainly with the tribes of the Sambalpur country. In the latter part of the Province they are generally recorded as animistic by religion, the proportion so returned in Sambalpur and the Uria States being 55·5 per cent. of the numbers who have been enumerated there. Elsewhere they are for the most part looked upon as Hindus, only 5·7 per cent. being shown as animistic. The Oraons return 66·1 per cent. of their number as of aboriginal religion; 9,403 are found in the Bamra State, all of whom but 2 are so described, but as we come west to Raigarh and Bilaspur the tendency is to consider them Hindus. The Kisáns and Kudas are semi-Hinduized aborigines from Chhota-Nagpur. They have adopted tank-digging as a profession and therefore mix largely with Hindus, and are probably more Hindus in customs and belief than the Census figures show. The Bhainas,

Dhanwárs, and Khairwárs are chiefly found in Raigarh and the north of Bilaspur; in both places they have come to be very generally looked upon as Hindu. The only other tribe that need be mentioned is the Kharias; the Sambalpur district is the only part where they have been extensively described as animistic. Full details, by Districts and States, of the religions of the aboriginal races will be found in Table XVI, where the fourth group among castes has been allotted to the forest and hill tribes.

57. **Hindus.**—Next come the Hindus, who form the great mass of the inhabitants of the Central Provinces. Both in British districts and in the Feudatory States they number about four-fifths of the total population. At the Census of 1881 separate statistics were given for the two great dissenting sects, the Kabirpanthis and Satnámis, and also for a small sect, the Kumbhipáthias, found only in Sambalpur and the Uria States. On the present occasion all have been amalgamated with Hindus, but the numbers of the two former have been separately taken out and will be referred to later on. Under the term Hindu have been included the members of the depressed castes and, as has been mentioned above, all the semi-Hinduized aborigines who cared to return themselves as of that religion. The Enumerators' Instructions provided that low castes, such as Chamárs, Mahárs, etc., should be entered by the religion which they themselves returned, and that no dispute about it was to be raised. They were very generally recorded as Hindus—I find that the sample schedule for the guidance of enumerators contained an entry to that effect,— though now and again the caste name has been written in the column of religion, as an easy way out of the difficulty, which must have frequently beset the Hindu enumerator, as to whether these out-castes were to be admitted to be his co-religionists or not. The difficulty was, however, not wholly on the part of the enumerator. Among the depressed castes there are many who have very vague ideas of what their religious beliefs may be, and had the rule been strictly followed of entering only what they themselves expressed, the return could not, in many cases, have been made. Several of the district reports refer to the stumbling block which the columns for religion and sect proved to the less enlightened of the Census Agency, and to the frequent inability of the lower classes to afford any indication of their creed. The instance given from one of the Feudatory States where a Sawara persisted in saying that his *dharm* was cultivation, is an example of the species of reply which was often vouchsafed to the enquiries of the enumerator.

The difficulty experienced in recording the religion of the forest tribes has already been referred to. In the case, however, of some of the more civilized of the aboriginal races, the adoption of Hindu customs and beliefs has now been so far recognised that their claims to be admitted as Hindus can no longer be denied. Of the gradual fusion of the indigenous tribes of India with the Aryan settlers I cannot do better than again quote from Forsyth, who gives the following description of the process.*

"Still greater has been the effect on the Aryan religion of contact with these lower races. No religious system possesses such facility for proselytising as a polytheism; and history shows that when two such systems meet, there is nothing to stand in the way of their coalescing but the rivalry of their priests. Here there probably was no such rivalry. To judge from those which remain, the aboriginal tribes had no regular priesthood, and no systematic mythology. They had only inchoate gods, without a history and numerous as the natural object whose forces they represented. And when the tribes accepted the Hindu priest and his ceremonial, the priest found no difficulty in admitting to his accommodating pantheon a sufficient number of these to satisfy the conscience of the aboriginal Panthiest. Superficial inquiries have quoted Hinduism as a faith which cannot admit of a proselyte; but nothing could be more completely the reverse of the truth. Anything in

* Highlands of Central India, page 52.

the way of new gods may be brought by new worshippers within the pale of orthodoxy, provided only that they agree to accept the dominion of the Brahmin priest, together with the caste rules and ceremonial by means of which he exercises his power."

These remarks apply rather to the changes that have been wrought in the religious system of the Hindus throughout the ages they have been in contact with the indigenous races of India, but the process of absorption is still going on, and the tendency is for the latter to be more and more regarded as members of the Hindu community. That the admission of the aboriginal tribes within the pale of Hinduism has not been without its reaction on the Hindu settlers in their midst, is strikingly exemplified in the case of the people who first obtained a footing among the Gonds of the Central Provinces. "The older settlers, or Jharias, are much looser in their observances than later comers of the same caste, eating forbidden food and worshipping strange gods. For some generations after their arrival the northern importations generally keep up their home connection by marriage, fearing to ally themselves with degenerate brothers who may have carried their carelessness in social matters so far as to permit mesalliances and perhaps even to have contracted some taint of aboriginal blood. By degrees, however, the fear of distant public opinion wears off, and they find it convenient to follow the examples of their neighbours. Religious and social standards are thus very imperfectly maintained. Gods of most opposite tendencies find themselves associated in 'happy families' and indeed, some combination among them is probably needed to withstand the influence of the local deities, who muster very strong and recruit their influence from all quarters. Not only are there the elemental divinities of the hills and forests, but the spirits of the dead pass very rapidly from a state of canonization to one of deification. Thus in the Hoshangabad district the Ghori Kings of Malwa seem to have attained this dignity without distinction of persons, and a Hindu in difficulties would as soon invoke the 'Ghori Badshah' as any other supernatural power." *

58. **Sikhs.**—The Sikhs are a small community in the Central Provinces, the number of persons for whom the religion has been returned amounting to only 173. This does not include 234 persons who have been recorded as Sikh by caste and Hindu by religion, and probably all of whom are of the Sikh persuasion. The Nánakshâhis and Udásis, orders of Sikh devotees, have all been returned as Hindus at the Census; their numbers amount to 467.

59. **Jains.**—The Province contains only 49,212 followers of the Jain religion. The stronghold of the cult is the three northern districts of Saugor, Damoh and Jubbulpore, where no less than 62 per cent. of the total number of Jains are found. In the other parts of the Province the Jains are mostly immigrants from Marwar and Rajputana, while a few, found chiefly in the Maratha country, are from Guzerat. At one time—probably before the twelfth century—the Jain religion was paramount in Nimar and numerous remains of finely-carved temples are found at various places in Prânt Nimar, and at Khandwa and Mândháta in the modern district. The present representatives of the Jain religion in the Province are nearly all of the Bania caste, and are mostly engaged in money-lending and trade. The Jain Banias number 48,564 persons, other castes who return the religion are Rajput 84, Brahmin 15, Jati, an order of Jain devotees, 17, Darji 68, Rangári 38, and Kalár 388. Though every effort was made to get as correct statistics as possible for Jains, the caste tables which have only just been worked out long after those for religion were in print, disclose several instances of error which had remained undiscovered. These are chiefly cases

* Introduction to Central Provinces Gazetteer, p. cxxvii. See also, for an account of the superstitions prevailing in Chhatisgarh, the Bilaspur Settlement Report, p. 60.

where the words Jain or Digambri have been entered as sub-divisions of the Bania caste; such entries occur in respect of 679 persons, who, it would appear, should have, therefore, been classed among Jains, making the total number of the latter 49,891.

60. **Aryas and Brahmos.**—The number of persons representing themselves as professing the new creed returned as Aryanism is 275. Only three persons are shown as Brahmos; the record of the latter is, no doubt, incomplete, as it is to be presumed that several Brahmos have been entered as Hindus. Followers of the Aryan pervasion are found chiefly in the large towns, Saugor, Jubbulpore and Kampti furnishing considerably more than half of the persons of that denomination; others occur in the district of Bilaspur 38, Chhindwara 21, and Balaghat 19. The chief castes returning the sect are Rajput 33, Maratha 18, Brahmin 85, Káyasth 24, Sonár 11, Teli 22, Bania 9, while most of the other Aryas give no distinction of caste.

61. **Buddhists.**—Buddhists number 325; they are mostly Burmese prisoners in the Jails of Jubbulpore, Nagpur and Raipur; 11 persons are Chinese.

62. **Parsis.**—There are 781 Parsis in the Province, but if 12 persons are added, whose religion is given as Hindu and 3 who have been recorded as Mussalmans—all are properly followers of Zoroaster,—their numbers amount to 796. Almost half of them, 376, are found in Nagpur, while Nimar, Hoshangabad and Jubbulpore supply the greater part of the remainder. It is curious to note that the Parsi has not yet found his way into the country recently opened up by the Bengal-Nagpur Railway. There are only 8 Parsis in the districts to the east of Nagpur. None of them are found in the Feudatory States.

63. **Jews.**—The Jews number 176, but to these must be added 17, who have been wrongly entered by the enumerators as Mahomedans. Their total number, therefore, amounts to 193. Nagpur returns 98, Nimar 42, and Raipur 23.

64. **Christians.**—Christians, 13,308 persons, will be separately referred to, when the tables for sects are discussed; 10 Europeans and Eurasians returned themselves as Agnostics.

65. **Mussalmans.**—The Mahomedans of the Province number 309,479, of whom 297,604 are found in British districts where they form 2·8 per cent. of the population, and 11,875 in Feudatory States, where the proportion they bear to the total inhabitants is only 0·6. Regarding their local distribution, I shall have something to say further on. Of the Mussalmans of these parts the great mass are immigrants from Upper India. With the exception of Nimar and part of the Nerbada Valley, the rest of the country which is now the Central Provinces, may be said to have been out of the track of the Mahomedan invader; so the immigration that has taken place has generally been of a peaceful description, and has gone on side by side with the analogous Hindu colonization. In the Maratha country many of the Mahomedans have come from the Nizam's dominions and Berar. Only a few trace their ancestry as far back as the Gond Rajas; by far the greater portion came with and after the Marathas. From the Bombay side the Province has received Mahomedan traders in the shape of Bohras, Khojas and Memans; but the former alone muster in any strength, their most important settlement being found in Burhanpur. As has been seen to have been the case amongst Hindus, so with the Mussalmans of these parts, severance from their co-religionists and long residence among aliens have led them to adopt many of the customs and practices of the people amidst whom they dwell. Among the town population this process has not gone far, but in

the country of the Nagpur plain,* neglect of religious duties and assimilation to Hindu manners are common characteristics of the rustic Mahomedans. The isolated communities, who have for some two centuries dwelt among Hindus on the Satpura plateau, have gone still further in this respect. The Mussalman law of inheritance has for instance been so far influenced by Hindu practice that they habitually exclude daughters and widows from succession when there are sons or other male heirs.† The conversion to Islam of the Gond Rajas of Deogarh about the beginning of the last century was so much a matter of convenience, and the allegiance they owed to the Emperor at Delhi was so slight, that they appear to have made no attempt at active proselytism in the territories which they ruled. We may except the custom prevailing among the descendants of the house of Deogarh to the present day, according to which the members of the Raja's family can only marry with Gonds who have been previously taken and converted to Mahomedanism for the purpose. The only trace of proselytism which can be considered purely local is to be found in Nimar, where many of the Bhils were made to embrace Mahomedanism during the rule of that power in the district. The descendants of the converts now number 1,694 persons.

66. **Variations since 1881.**—The statement given at page 61 exhibits the variations which have taken place among the followers of the different religions since 1881. It is unnecessary to notice in detail the changes there have been among representatives of the minor or foreign creeds. With regard to the chief religions the following may be noted :—

Animistic.—In British Districts the number of persons returned as of aboriginal religion has increased only 4 per cent., while in the Feudatory States the variation is as high as 122 per cent. I have already referred to the difficulty which attaches to the making of this return owing to the vagueness of the line which separates the forest tribes from the lower classes of Hindus. A comparison of the figures for districts with those of 1881 shows that in many cases, and specially where the members of the forest tribes mix much with Hindus, the variation that has taken place is to be put down simply to different treatment of the matter by the Census agency. I give examples in the margin of instances of this kind. In Saugor the persons returned as of animistic belief are about half the number so returned in 1881, while in Damoh their numbers have more than doubled. Exactly the same thing has happened in Chhatisgarh. In the Raipur District there has been a considerable rise in the figures for aboriginal religions, while in the adjoining districts of Bilaspur and Sambalpur there has been a still more marked decline. It is impossible that these variations should represent actual changes in the religious beliefs of the people; they merely indicate that the Census staff in one district took a different view of the instructions on the subject from what their neighbours did in another. The examples, which I have given, are those which represent most divergence from the returns of 1881; elsewhere there has been no such marked variation, if we except Nimar, where 601 persons are recorded as of animistic religion against 5,282 at the last Census. The Bhils of Nimar have now been Hinduized to an extent that quite accounts for the small number.

District.	Number of Persons recorded as Animistic.		Variation + or —.
	1891.	1881.	
Saugor	9,960	19,144	—9,184
Damoh	14,375	5,421	+8,954
Jubbulpore	97,358	67,804	+29,554
Raipur	192,518	165,729	+26,789
Bilaspur	93,126	157,547	—64,421
Sambalpur	26,353	46,652	—20,299

* Bhandara Settlement Report, page 53.

† Digest of Civil Rulings of the Judicial Commissioner (1882), Hindu and Mahomedan Law, page 31.

of aborigines returned from the district under this head. As regards the large increase in the Feudatories, the Report on the Census of 1881 mentions that in the Uria States the aborigines were very generally returned as Hindus, "possibly through some loose local instruction, intended merely to make the Census agency recognize the frequent profession by aborigines of the Hindu religion being misconstrued into a general order to record them usually as of the Hindu religion." Something too may be put down to better counting at the present Census. The effect of any improvement in the enumeration will necessarily be most felt in remote and difficult tracts where the population consists almost entirely of aborigines, as yet wholly untouched by Hindu influences.

Hindus.—The remarks which have just been made as to the variation in the method of recording the religions of the aboriginal tribes, must also be considered as bearing upon the increase which results in the number of persons returned as professing the Hindu religion. Hindus and aborigines together have increased in British Districts by 9·66 per cent., or about the same rate, 9·61, as the total population, of which they form close upon 97 per cent. But while those who profess aboriginal forms of belief have advanced only 4 per cent., Hindus have increased by 11 per cent.; that is, the latter have increased at the expense of the former to the extent which these figures indicate. In the Feudatory States the opposite has been the case, as here the number of persons recorded as of Animistic religion has grown immensely at the expense of those returned as Hindu. The only method of comparison available is to combine the returns for Hindu and aboriginal religions, by which we get the following result:—

Combined figures for Hindu and Animistic Religions, 1881 and 1891.

	Number of persons of Hindu and Animistic religions.		Proportion of columns 2 and 3 per 10,000 of total population.		Increase per cent. calculated on actual numbers of Hindu and Animistic religions.	Increase per cent. in total population.
	1881.	1891.	1881.	1891.		
	2	3	4	5	6	7
British Districts	9,504,756	10,423,348	9,661	9,666	9·66	9·61
Feudatory States	1,699,587	2,147,715	9,941	9,941	26·37	26·37
Central Provinces	11,204,343	12,571,063	9,702	9,711	12·20	12·10

The variation conforms so much to the general rate observable among the total population that it seems unnecessary to discuss it in detail.

Jains.—The changes that have occurred among Jains in districts where they are numerous are noted in the margin. In Saugor and Damoh where they are exceptionally strong they have increased at a faster rate than the general population, the result probably of their more comfortable circumstances. The Nerbada valley districts and Betul possess apparent attractions for the Marwari to judge by the increased indication of his presence which the Census figures show. The Jains of Nagpur and Bhandara have evidently moved east

Statement showing variation amongst Jains.

District.	Jains.		Variation.	
	1881.	1891.	Number.	Per cent.
1	2	3	4	5
Saugor	16,432	17,413	981	5·97
Damoh	6,665	7,167	502	7·53
Jubbulpore	5,506	6,036	530	9·63
Narsinghpur	2,170	2,370	200	9·22
Hoshangabad	1,725	2,061	336	19·48
Nimar	1,247	1,455	208	16·68
Seoni	1,408	1,316	—92	—6·53
Betul	942	1,146	204	21·66
Chhindwara	1,451	1,491	40	2·76
Wardha	2,356	2,557	201	8·53
Nagpur	3,564	3,141	—423	—11·87
Bhandara	576	453	—123	—21·35

with the opening up of the Chhatisgarh country through recent railway enterprise; in the eastern districts and States there are now 1,123 Jains against 723 in 1881.

Mussalmans.—The only other religion the variation among whose followers need be noticed is the Mahomedan. These have increased by 7·92 per cent. in British Districts and by 19·78 in the Feudatory States. In most districts the rate of increase among the Mussalman community has been higher than among the general population. The following are, however, exceptions. In Chanda Mahomedans have increased only 1·9 per cent., in Raipur 2·2, in Betul 1·8, and in Balaghat 5·5. In Bhandara they number two persons less than at last Census, when there were no doubt many strangers in the district on account of the making of the narrow gauge railway. In proportion to their numbers, there can be hardly a doubt that there is more migration amongst Mussalmans, whether for purposes of service or of trade or on account of garrison changes, than amongst the great mass of Hindus. All three causes have probably brought some accession of Mahomedans to the Province, and especially to those districts where there are important trade or military centres, or where the number of their co-religionists is strong. The absence of some or all of these causes in the four districts mentioned may be taken to account for the small increase among Mahomedans which they exhibit. In Bilaspur, Sambalpur, and the States on the line of railway, the construction of the latter has materially added to the Mussalman population.

67. **Religious distribution of the population of each district.**—The following table exhibits the distribution of 10,000 of the population of each district according to the main religions:—

Distribution of 10,000 persons of each District by Religion.

District.	Animistic.	Hindu.	Jain.	Christian.	Mussalman.	Others.
1	2	3	4	5	6	7
Saugor	168	9,064	294	17	455	2
Damoh	441	9,024	220	1	314	...
Jubbulpore	1,301	8,073	81	30	512	3
Narsinghpur	1,204	8,359	65	3	369	...
Hoshangabad	1,365	8,119	39	17	458	2
Nimar	24	8,806	57	22	1,085	6
Mandla	5,520	4,328	10	4	138	...
Seoni	4,243	5,314	35	3	405	...
Chhindwara	3,722	5,931	37	2	307	1
Betul	3,685	6,119	35	2	159	...
Nagpur	554	8,748	41	73	572	12
Wardha	891	8,668	64	2	374	1
Chanda	2,366	7,459	11	3	161	...
Bhandara	1,201	8,615	6	2	176	...
Balaghat	2,450	7,361	8	1	180	...
Raipur	1,215	8,677	4	7	97	...
Bilaspur	800	9,101	...	3	96	...
Sambalpur	331	9,621	...	3	45	...

The figures speak for themselves. Jains, as has been already noted, are a strong body in the two northern districts and are also fairly represented in the Nerbada valley and in Wardha and Nagpur. Mussalmans are of course most numerous in proportion to the general population in Nimar, which was for long the seat of Mahomedan power. They are also found in greater numbers than might be expected from the isolated position of the districts in Seoni and Chhindwara. After the overthrow of the Deogarh Kingdom by the Marathas about the middle of the last century, the Government of the Seoni tract was entrusted to a Pathan family, the head of which bore the title of "Diwan." For the whole of the latter half of the century, the Pathans held sway above the Ghats, and it is probably owing to the footing which they had thus gained that the number of Mahomedans in this part of the country is so large. In the Native States the only places where Mussalmans muster strong are the western states of Khairagarh, Chhuikhadan and Kawardha; in these they form 105, 215 and 223 per 10,000 of the population respectively.

SECT.

68. **Sects of Hindus; Kabirpanthis and Satnamis.**—At the present Census the enumerator's schedule contained a column for sect, but no attempt was made to work out statistics for sects of Hindus except in the case of the two great dissenting bodies, the Kabirpanthis and Satnamis. The Census agency were instructed to return both as sects of the Hindu religion. It is needless to observe that sect was a subject which the ordinary enumerator did not

Kabirpanthi and Satnami Sects.

District or State.	Kabirpanthi.			Satnami.		
	Number.		Increase or Decrease.	Number.		Increase or Decrease.
	1881.	1891.		1881.	1891.	
1	2	3	4	5	6	7
Saugor	4,606	28,056	+23,450	245	14,611	+14,366
Damoh	2,423	17,621	+15,198	137	11,965	+11,828
Jubbulpore	11,701	90,130	+78,429	235	4,734	+4,499
Narsinghpur	411	7,561	+7,150	14	1,038	+1,024
Hoshangabad	3,372	37,514	+34,142	9	3,313	+3,304
Nimar	101	1,577	+1,476	54	135	+81
Mandla	5,686	19,956	+14,270	76	323	+247
Seoni	598	21,827	+21,229	9	333	+324
Chhindwara	5,528	10,118	+4,590	6	299	+293
Betul	132	2,106	+1,974	2	153	+151
Wardha	92	270	+178	2	...	—2
Nagpur	7,371	10,954	+3,583	416	116	—300
Chanda	1,064	2,092	+1,028	173	571	+398
Bhandara	2,169	11,430	+9,261	38	2	—36
Balaghat	8,574	40,706	+32,132	...	219	+219
Raipur	143,178	178,657	+35,479	223,447	252,674	+29,227
Bilaspur	87,318	112,018	+24,670	133,086	145,849	+12,763
Sambalpur	10,120	11,442	+1,322	212	116	—96
Total British Districts	*294,474*	*604,035*	+309,561	*358,161*	*436,451*	*+78,290*
Makrai	...	1,538	+1,538	...	27	+27
Bastar	3	1,666	+1,663	...	185	+185
Kanker	435	1,133	+698	44	335	+291
Nandgaon	14,676	25,616	+10,940	12,381	14,477	+2,096
Khairagarh	18,371	18,734	+363	16,332	15,199	—1,133
Chhuikhadan	3,286	4,703	+1,417	1,867	2,116	+249
Kawardha	5,618	5,200	—418	9,482	7,974	—1,508
Sakti	2,819	3,395	+576	...	43	+43
Raigarh	4,035	11,868	+7,833	129	92	—37
Sarangarh	4,253	4,973	+720	13	229	+216
Bamra	...	1,556	+1,556	...	...	...
Patna	14	878	+864	...	7	+7
Kalahandi	10	377	+367	...	225	+225
Total Feudatory States	*53,520*	*81,637*	*+28,117*	*40,248*	*40,909*	*+661*
Total Central Provinces	**347,994**	**685,672**	**+337,678**	**398,409**	**477,360**	**+78,951**

understand, and still less so the Hindu villager of these parts. As we are concerned, however, chiefly with the case of the Chhatisgarh districts and states, it may be well to state that there two great sect distinctions are observed; the orthodox Hindu is known as a Saktaha in contradistinction to the Kabirpanthi or follower of Kabir. The difference between the two was very generally recognized in the Census schedules; as the latter offered four columns—religion, sect of religion, caste and sub-division of caste—for the enumerator to fill up, he nearly always managed to get one or other of the sect names somewhere in one of these four places. The same was the case with Satnami which was in many cases promiscuously returned as religion or as caste. The only course to adopt in abstracting the figures for the sects was therefore to count the name, Kabirpanthi or Satnami, wherever it might occur, and in this way we have got as full a record as it is possible to have of the followers of the dissenting creeds. The results which have been obtained are set forth in the accompanying statement. As the intention with which the return of Kabirpanthis and Satnamis was worked out was to afford comparison with the figures of 1881, when the sects were deemed of sufficient importance to be treated as distinct religions, I have added the numbers which were then given. The first point that strikes us is the enormous variation which the figures for the Kabirpanthi sect exhibit; its members are almost double what they were shown to be ten years ago. Though it is certain that the simplicity and easy profession of the faith have made it popular among certain classes of the community, it can hardly be imagined that its followers have increased to the extent which these figures would tend to show. In 1881 there was only one column for religion in the schedule, which for Kabirpanthis and Satnamis was to be filled in with the names of these sects. There can be no doubt that in the case of Kabirpanthis many persons were recorded simply as Hindus owing to their being Kabirpanthis only in name or at most displaying a very loose observance of the precepts of the reformer. The following extract from the Report of 1881, Appendix A, para, 49, notes this:—

"One general difficulty was what should be shown as the religion of nominal members of the dissenting sects like Satnami and Kabirpanthi, who live as Hindus. The Seoni Report relates that 'a number of persons were shown in the books as of the Kabirpanthi religion. These simply acknowledge themselves as disciples of Kabir, while at the same time they observe caste and all the religious rites and ceremonies of the Hindus, and inter-marry amongst none but members of their own caste. As these men are Hindus in almost every particular and Kabirpanthis in nothing but name, the entries were accordingly corrected. These mistakes were common.' Indeed from the context it would seem that these are referred to among mistakes discovered and corrected at district head-quarters. This of course was never intended. The instructions in the enumerator's book recognized no distinction under religion between profession and practice."

I fear, therefore, that the comparison of the returns of the two enumerations will afford but a very imperfect idea of the progress which the sect is making. The Satnamis, however, belong so distinctively to Chhatisgarh, where on both occasions considerable pains was taken over their record, that in their case the same objection can hardly be said to arise.

69. *The Kabirpanthis.*—The two sects have been so fully described at pages 31—39 of the Census Report of 1881, that it is unnecessary to again enter upon a lengthened discussion of their rise, of the nature of their belief, or of the practice of the latter by the Kabirpanthis and Satnamis of these Provinces. Suffice it to say that the former sect was founded by Kabir, one of the followers of Rámánand who flourished about the end of the fourteenth century. In his teaching Kabir set himself against the whole body of Hindu superstitions. "He rejects and ridicules the Shástrás and the Puránás; he severely chastises the arrogance and hypocrisy of the Brahmins; he rejects every malevolent distinction of caste, religion and sect. All who love God and do good are brothers,

be they Hindus or Mussalmans. Idolatry and everything which approches it or may suggest it is severely condemned. The members of this sect, the Kabirpanthis, 'those who follow the path of Kabir,' form at present twelve principal branches, which have remained in communion with one another in spite of sundry differences in regard to both doctrine and practice. Their centre is at Benares, but we meet with them throughout the whole Presidency of Bengal, in Gujerat, in Central India, and as far as the Dekhan. Their number, difficult to estimate because of the pains they take to conform to the customs in the midst of which they live, appears to be pretty considerable."* The head of the faith in this part of the country resides at Kawardha, the chief town of the State of the same name. He appoints a certain number of deputies called Bhandáris or Mahants from the more advanced of his followers; these Mahants are spread all over the country, but besides them there are a number of hereditary lieutenants of the chief Guru with fixed seat or "Gádis" in various parts. There is also an itinerant order of ascetics of the sect, who travel about asking alms and reciting the precepts of their faith. With this organization a good many people belonging to the lower orders of Hindus are annually converted to Kabirism. As the creed, as at present practised, does not involve the loss of caste or any other sort of social degradation, as it does not impose any wearisome or costly ceremonial, as fasting and penance are no part of its teachings, and, above all, as its doctrines are more simple and better suited to the apprehension of the masses than those of Hinduism, and as they are embodied in a series of simple verses easily understood and remembered by all, Kabirism has gone on increasing in strength and prosperity in the midst of the decline of other sects, which have not the same elasticity to support them.† There is no prohibition against the admission of any caste, but, as a matter of fact, proselytism among the lower classes of the community has come to be discouraged. Several castes have almost wholly adopted the faith, at least in name. In Chhatisgarh the Pankas and Gándas are Kabirpanthis to a man, and there are numerous converts among the Telis, Koshtis, Kumhárs, and several others.

Regarding the numbers of Kabirpanthis returned at the Census, I have already said that comparison with the figures of 1881 will be for the most part meaningless. As far as the present enumeration is concerned, it may be noted that the districts in which Kabirpanthis form a considerable portion of the population, whose religion has been returned as Hindu, are Jubbulpore where they amount to 14·9 per cent., Balaghat 14·4, Mandla 13·6, Raipur 13·0, Seoni 11·1, Bilaspur 10·6, and Hoshangabad 8·7. In Nimar, Betul, Wardha, Nagpur, Chanda, Bhandara, and Sambalpur, they are less than 2 per cent. of the total number of Hindus.

70. *The Satnamis.*—The sect was founded some time in the fifteenth century by Rohidás who is said to have been, like Kabir, a desciple of Rámánand and to have lived in the country lying to the south of Oudh and in Rewa. The doctrines of the two sects closely resemble one another, that of Rohidás proclaiming the perfect equality of all men and the worship of the one true God under the title of "Satnám" or the true name. It does not appear that Satnamism ever attracted any number of proselytes from the better classes of the Hindus; only the lowest of the people availed themselves of the relief opened out by Rohidás, not so much by an intelligent appreciation of his doctrines as to avoid the degradation and contempt in which they, as outcastes, were held. The most notable feature in connection with the Satnami movement is the revival of the faith which began to be preached by Ghásidás, the Chamár reform-

* Barth's Religions of India (Trubner's Oriental Series), page 239.

† See the excellent account of the sect by Mr. Banerjee of Raipur, quoted by Mr. Drysdale.

er in Chhatisgarh between the years 1820 and 1830. The mission of Ghásidás has often been described; briefly, his object was to raise his fellows in the social scale and to free them from the tyranny of Brahminism. The movement which he began soon extended to nearly the whole Chamár community of Chhatisgarh, but the faith he preached—the belief in an immaterial omnipresent God to be worshipped without any visible sign or representation—has been too abstruse for a rude illiterate class like the Chamárs, and most of them have lapsed from strict observance of his doctrines. Practically all Chamárs call themselves Satnámis, but only a portion observe the precepts of the sect, abstaining from forbidden food, from the use of tobacco, which is also interdicted, and from the worship of strange gods.

The first thing that strikes one in the return of Satnámis at the Census is the large number of followers of the creed who are found in the northern districts of Saugor and Damoh and in the districts of the Nerbada valley. In 1881 the presence of Satnamis in these districts was hardly indicated, but they now form a considerable body, especially in Saugor and Damoh, where their numbers are 14,611 and 11,965, respectively. The examination of 100 books, in which Satnamis were found, in each district disclosed the information which I have noted in the margin, regarding the castes of the persons returned as Satnamis. The great majority, it will be seen, are Chamárs, and all the others belong to classes of low standing in the community. As the levelling of all caste distinctions is one of the first principles of true Satnamism, we may assume that the profession of the creed in these northern districts is merely nominal. The so-called Satnamis of the country outside Chhatisgarh do not acknowledge the spiritual leadership of the descendants of Ghásidás; they have probably taken the title of Satnámi simply as a distinction whereby to raise themselves in the social scale. Most would probably have adopted Kabirism, which would have better served their purpose, were it not for the tendency which is known to exist towards excluding members of the lower castes from admission to the latter faith. The Satnamis of Chhatisgarh have increased in the Raipur District by 13·1 per cent., in Bilaspur by 9·6, while in the Native States their numbers are about the same as at last Census. In Raipur the Chamár population amounts to 285,551, of whom no less than 88·5 per cent. have been shown as Satnamis; in Bilaspur there are 266,745 Chamárs, of whom only 54·7 have been so returned. These proportions hardly differ from the corresponding results in 1881, so that it would seem as if Satnamism, whether nominal or real, has found more of a footing in the former than in the latter district. Of the four States which form the western portion of Chhatisgarh, Nandgaon, Khairagarh, Chhuikhadan and Kawardha, the three former, which are contiguous to Raipur, return 43,705 Chamárs, of whom 72·7 per cent. are Satnamis; in Kawardha the proportion of the community recorded as Satnami is 57·7.

Castes of Satnamis in 100 books of Saugor and Damoh.

Caste.	Saugor.	Damoh.
Chamar	2,880	1,611
Mehra	...	303
Ahir	...	109
Dhobi	19	71
Teli	17	72
Kalar	...	87
Basor	34	28
Nai	...	62
Parka	...	60
Gadaria	...	53
Kumhar	...	39
Dhimar	13	21
Kori	23	...
Chandar	16	6
Saur	15	...
Bairagi	14	...
Other castes	20	...
Total	3,051	2,522

71. **Mahomedan Sects.**—The following table exhibits the distribution of Mussalmans by sects:—

Mahomedan Sects.

Districts.	Total.	Sunni.	Shiah.	Sect not given.
1	2	3	4	5
Saugor	26,898	24,509	1,111	1,278
Damoh	10,231	9,050	369	812
Jubbulpore	38,269	36,326	1,322	621
Mandla	4,699	3,996	313	390
Seoni	15,006	13,612	223	1,171
Narsinghpur	13,528	12,886	342	300
Hoshangabad	24,290	22,544	645	1,101
Nimar	27,501	24,843	1,911	747
Betul	5,122	4,201	192	729
Chhindwara	12,524	11,646	134	744
Wardha	15,003	13,230	327	1,446
Nagpur	43,356	39,031	2,379	1,946
Chanda	11,200	10,370	176	654
Bhandara	13,100	11,886	176	1,038
Balaghat	6,901	5,898	169	834
Raipur	15,324	12,416	661	2,247
Bilaspur	11,101	8,399	701	2,001
Sambalpur	3,551	3,325	180	46
	297,604	*268,168*	*11,331*	*18,105*

Feudatory States.	Total.	Sunni.	Shiah.	Sect not given.
6	7	8	9	10
Makrai	1,030	1,025	4	1
Bastar	1,064	840	52	172
Kanker	388	335	51	2
Nandgaon	1,592	1,319	114	159
Khairagarh	1,905	1,632	92	181
Chhuikhadan	779	748	1	30
Kawardha	2,051	1,869	33	149
Sakti	205	159	2	44
Raigarh	848	696	138	14
Sarangarh	308	240	1	67
Bamra	226	205	21	...
Rairakhol	62	59	3	...
Sonpur	549	488	8	53
Patna	541	400	92	49
Kalahandi	327	257	70	...
Total Feudatory States	*11,875*	*10,272*	*682*	*921*
Total British Districts	*297,604*	*268,168*	*11,331*	*18,105*
Total Central Provinces	309,479	278,440	12,013	19,026

Out of 309,479 Mahomedans in the Province 278,440, or 90 per cent., are Sunnis, 12,013, or 3·9 per cent., are Shiahs, while for the remainder, 6·1 per cent., the sect column was either not filled up or contained other information than that wanted. No persons returned themselves as Wahabis; probably owing to the political signification attaching to the sect, its name has fallen into disuse, followers of the Wahabi tenets calling themselves Ahlihadis, or more often simply describing themselves as Sunnis. The Sunnis of these parts belong mostly to the Hanifite persuasion, but the distinction is known only to the better educated of the community. The Shiahs are found in any strength only in Saugor, Jubbulpore, Nimar, and Nagpur, in each of which they exceed 1,000 persons. In most places the chief element among the Shiahs is the Bohra and Khoja traders from Bombay; other Shiahs are Moghals or recent Mahomedan immigrants from Upper India.

72. Christians—Variation since 1881.—Christians have increased in nine districts of the Province, and decreased in the remaining nine. Those in which the change in their numbers has been greatest within the past ten years are shown in the margin. The districts which have increased most are those affected by the new Bengal-Nagpur Railway; to this must also be ascribed the rise in the Christian population of the Feudatory States. In Nagpur there is a large Native Christian community, 2,360 persons, but despite the fact that within ten years there must have been considerable natural increase amongst its numbers—to say nothing of the advance due to missionary enterprise—the community is actually less than it was in 1881 by 9 persons, see the statement at para. 74. The falling off is to be ascribed to the withdrawal of the Madras troops from Nagpur and Kampti, to migration of Native Christians to places along the line of rail, as well as to possible variation in the record—to the latter point I shall refer hereafter. That the Christian population of Nagpur, as a whole, has increased is therefore mainly due to the large augmentation of the European and Eurasian communities which the establishment of the head-quarters of the new Railway at Nagpur has brought about. In Saugor and Jubbulpore the change of garrison has led to a considerable falling off amongst Native Christians; but in the former district the opening of the line between Saugor and Bina, which is now an important Railway centre, has to a great extent counteracted the decline. Nimar also shows a large decrease among Christians; Native Christians have gone down in numbers, and the fact of there being no longer a detachment of British troops in the fortress of Asirgarh has further contributed to the result which the Census figures show.

Increase and Decrease amongst Christians.

Increase.				Decrease.			
District.	Number.		Difference.	District.	Number.		Difference.
	1881.	1891.			1881.	1891.	
Hoshangabad.	783	914	+ 131	Saugor .	1,034	1,005	— 29
Nagpur .	4,850	5,521	+ 671	Jubbulpore.	2,476	2,230	— 246
Raipur .	821	1,094	+ 273	Nimar .	789	565	- 224
Bilaspur .	35	389	+ 354	Chanda .	289	227	— 62
Sambalpur	110	239	+ 129	Bhandara	157	121	— 36

	Total Christians, 1881.	Total Christians, 1891.	Increase.
Total British Districts . .	11,949	12,970	+ 1,021
Total Feudatory States . .	24	338	+ 314
Total Central Provinces . .	11,973	13,308	+ 1,335

73. Christian Sects.—The sects of Christians—for which figures are given in Supplementary Table A—were not always correctly recorded, as generally when Native Christians fell to be censused by a Hindu enumerator, the latter unless specially instructed made hardly an attempt to get at the correct sect name. To this must be ascribed the large return of persons entered as Protestants without any denomination being specified. The following table exhibits the results of the Census as regards the sects of the European, Eurasian and Native Christian communities, for which separate details have been taken out.

Christians *by* Sect *and* Race.

Sect.	Number of persons of each sect.	Percentage of sect on total Christians.	Sects by Race. Percentage of Persons of each Sect who are Europeans.	Eurasians.	Native Christians.	Races by Sect. Europeans. Total.	Percentage on total Europeans.	Eurasians. Total.	Percentage on total Eurasians.	Native Christians. Total.	Percentage on total Native Christians.
1	2	3	4	5	6	7	8	9	10	11	12
1. Church of England	4,478	33·6	68·9	19·9	11·2	3,084	63·9	894	40·6	500	7·9
2. Presbyterian	482	3·6	27·8	7·7	64·5	134	2·8	37	1·7	311	5·0
3. Roman Catholic	5,547	41·7	19·9	14·6	65·5	1,103	22·8	812	36·9	3,632	57·8
4. Methodist	298	2·3	29·9	47·3	22·8	89	1·8	141	6·4	68	1·1
5. Wesleyan	157	1·2	84·7	9·6	5·7	133	2·8	15	·7	9	·1
6. Congregationalist	4	...	75·0	25·0	...	3	·1	1	...	...	...
7. Baptist	121	·9	22·3	5·8	71·9	27	·6	7	·3	87	1·4
8. Plymouth Brethren	6	...	...	...	100·0	...	...	...	...	6	·1
9. Society of Friends	89	·7	11·2	...	88·8	10	·2	...	...	79	1·3
10. Lutheran	263	2·0	15·6	1·5	82·9	41	·8	4	·2	218	3·5
11. Greek Church	7	...	100·0	...	...	7	·1	...	...	...	...
12. Protestant	1,371	10·3	9·5	19·8	70·7	130	2·7	271	12·3	970	15·5
13. Unsectarian and sect not given.	485	3·7	13·8	4·1	82·1	67	1·4	20	·9	398	6·3
Total	13,308	100	36·3	16·5	47·2	4,828	100	2,202	100	6,278	100

The most numerous body in the Central Provinces are the Roman Catholics, who form 41·7 of all Christians. The majority of them are Native Christians; in Nagpur the converts to the Church of Rome number 1,867 persons, or one-third of the Catholic population of the Province. The sect includes the Indo-Portuguese community, 583 strong, all of whom have been classed among Native Christians. Next comes the Church of England, whose adherents are for the most part Europeans, the nationality of the greater portion of the European troops stationed in the Province being English. The Wesleyans, 157, are also nearly all British soldiers. Of the persons returned as Protestants 763, or more than half, are Native Christians in Raipur. There is an important missionary settlement of the American Reformed Church at Bisrampur, near the border of the Raipur and Bilaspur Districts, to which 728 of the converts would appear to belong. In Protestant have also been included the following denominations returned at the Census, Disciple of Christ 10, Sion Mission 1, American Mission and American Church 10. Presbyterians muster strong only in Nagpur 250, and in Bhandara, 58; in both districts there are missions established. The Methodists, 298, have a large following amongst the Eurasian community, especially in Jubbulpore. The Lutherans 263, who have been taken to include both the Swedish and the German Churches, are almost solely a missionary body; they have been most successful in Saugor, where they have 48 converts, and in Raipur and Bilaspur, where the latter number 153. In the Nerbada and Satpura Districts, according to the Census, their efforts have been almost in vain, there being about one person of European descent to every Native Christian; it is probable, however, that some of the latter have been entered as Protestants or have been shown under 'sect not given.' The Baptists have a strong connection in Sambalpur.

74. **Statistics of Native Christians.**—The following table exhibits the figures for Native Christians in ten districts where they number over 100 persons. Their distribution has already been generally referred to :—

Statement showing Districts in which Native Christians *number more than 100.*

DISTRICTS.	TOTAL NATIVE CHRISTIANS.			DISTRIBUTION BY SECTS, 1891 ONLY.								
	1881.	1891.	Increase or decrease.	Church of England.	Presbyterian.	Roman Catholic.	Methodist and Weslyan.	Lutheran.	Baptist.	Society of Friends.	Protestant.	Others and Unsectarian.
1	2	3	4	5	6	7	8	9	10	11	12	13
Nagpur . . .	2,369	2,360	*−9*	151	1-1	1,867	11	1	...	...	61	88
Raipur. . . .	734	1,011	*+277*	10	4	153	...	74	...	...	763	7
Jubbulpore . .	751	605	*−146*	146	7	398	30	...	...	...	22	2
Hoshangabad . .	370	506	*+136*	38	9	326	7	...	2	79	19	26
Bilaspur . . .	28	271	*+243*	5	...	77	...	79	...	...	14	96
Saugor . . .	410	251	*−159*	12	...	174	...	48	...	...	7	10
Nimar . . .	362	241	*−121*	6	...	188	13	...	...	...	15	19
Sambalpur . .	70	179	*+109*	8	1	72	...	...	83	...	7	8
Chanda . . .	195	156	*−39*	24	5	68	...	...	...	...	24	35
Mandla . . .	108	108	...	64	...	6	...	..	...	..	18	20
Other Districts and States . . .	367	590	*+223*	36	104	303	16	16	2	...	20	93
Total Central Provinces, 1891 .			6,278	500	311	3,632	77	218	87	79	970	404
Total Central Provinces, 1881 .			5,764	393	317	4,258	12	8	25	...	430	321
Variation			+514	+107	−6	−626	+65	+210	+62	+79	+540	+83

At the last Census 1,060 Christians were shown in the Sect Table as of race unspecified ; but in the Report at page 45 all have been classed with Non-British-born Europeans—for whom separate figures were taken out—and Eurasians, the term unspecified having been applied only to "persons of European name or mother tongue who omitted to record whether they were European or Eurasian." Following this classification, the number of Native Christians in 1881 amounted to 5,764 as against 6,278 at the present Census, while other Christians, that is Europeans and Eurasians, are now 7,030 as compared with 6,209 at the last enumeration. In other words, while Native Christians have increased only 8·9 per cent., other Christians have grown by 13·2. The result is certainly surprising, but too much reliance cannot be placed upon the figures we have got. In the first place, it is extremely difficult to obtain a correct record of Native Christians through the tendency, which we may take to be becoming more and more common, of using the term Eurasian as the race designation of persons whose claims to any trace of mixed descent are probably imaginary. In the same way the number of Europeans is, no doubt, unduly swelled by many Eurasians being incorrectly recorded as of foreign descent. There will thus always be a tendency for the figures for Europeans and Eurasians, real or so-called, to grow at the expense of those for Native Christians. If allowance is made for such possible grounds of inaccuracy, it is to be presumed that we should find that the numbers of native converts have really advanced at a faster rate than has been shown. Again, in accounting for the apparent anomaly in the growth of the different races of Christians, we must remember that the causes which since last Census have chiefly affected the Christian population of the Province—the opening of the Bengal-Nagpur Railway and the garrison changes—have both tended to bring about the result observed, namely, to largely augment the number of Europeans and Eurasians and to diminish the number of native converts. Though it cannot, perhaps, after all be said that Christianity is making much headway among the natives of these Provinces, the above considerations have an important bearing upon the low rate of increase which the Census results exhibit.

Rule 5 of the Instructions to Enumerators directed that in making the return, column 5, which for Hindus and others was to contain sub-divisions of caste, tribe or race as the case might be, should for Native Christians be filled in with any racial or caste sub-division that might be given, such as Goanese, Madrasi, etc. The results obtained are set forth in the general table of castes and races, but the following, as showing the chief sources from which the converts to Christianity are drawn, may be of interest:—2,471 Native Christians are shown as Tamils or Telugus, 583 are Goanese, 51 Gonds, 8 other aborigines, 32 Tantis and Koris, 28 Dheds, 26 Káyasths, 24 Ahirs, 23 Kunbis, 21 Mális, 20 Mahárs, 19 Rajputs, 18 Chamárs, and 17 Mussalmans, while others belong to various castes or have simply been recorded as Native Christians. The comparative absence of converts from among the better castes may be remarked. On this subject it is worth noting what Mr. Baines has said in the Bombay Census Report of 1881, namely, that "as long as the abandonment of caste is an essential on reception into Christianity, the success of Christian Missions will be for a long time more marked among the lower classes than among the rest, and that for two reasons; first, the consideration of social interests, which makes a Hindu of good position so much more tenacious of his religion than one of lower caste who has less to lose; and secondly, the greater receptivity of the latter with regard to emotional appeals which neither his intelligence nor his education dispose him to analyse."

CHAPTER IV.

SEX AND AGE.

SEX.

75. The distinctions of Sex and Age, especially the former, have been observed in several of the tables published in the second volume of this Report, but for the present we are concerned only with the figures that have been given regarding them in Table VII. The latter contains the actual statistics of sex and age for the several districts and states, but in order that the inferences to be drawn from them may be more clearly observed, it has been necessary to work out certain proportions which are given in tabular form in Appendix C. Before, however, attacking these formidable arrays of figures, it will be of use to note upon one or two matters connected with the distribution of the sexes apart from the complication of age. In other words, though a consideration of the age statistics may to some extent help us to see how the disproportions that exist have come about, we may first examine the broad results of the Census as regards the distribution of the sexes in different parts of the Province and among different races of the people.

76. **Relative proportions of the sexes in different districts.**—This has already been referred to in the chapter dealing with the increase in the population. The statement given below again exhibits the proportions between the

Number of Females per 1,000 Males by Districts.

	District, etc.	1891.	1881.	Serial order in respect of column 2.	Serial order in respect of column 3.
	1	2	3	4	5
Females more than males.	Raipur	1,042	*1,018*	1	*1*
	Bilaspur	1,031	*1,018*	2	*2*
	Bhandara	1,026	*1,006*	3	*5*
	Chhindwara	1,016	*1,003*	4	*6*
	Chhatisgarh States	1,015	*1,009*	5	*4*
	Balaghat	1,011	*1,017*	6	*3*
	Sambalpur	1,007	*1,001*	7	*7*
	Seoni	1,006	*993*	8	*8*
Females less than males.	Narsinghpur	994	*957*	9	*16*
	Jubbulpore	990	*968*	10	*13*
	Betul	987	*974*	11	*12*
	Mandla	982	*965*	12	*14*
	Chanda	980	*986*	13	*9*
	Nagpur	979	*982*	14	*10*
	Uria States	979	*963*	15	*15*
	Wardha	972	*980*	16	*11*
	Hoshangabad	958	*936*	17	*17*
	Damoh	946	*925*	18	*18*
	Saugor	936	*916*	19	*19*
	Nimar	932	*9 2*	20	*20*
	Total British Districts	998	*984*	...	...
	Total Feudatory States	984	*970*	...	...
	Total Central Provinces	996	*982*	...	...

sexes in the several districts, and numbers are added to show the order in which the latter stand as regards excess of females over males. Leaving consideration of the figures till afterwards, we may note that in the first seven districts given females exceeded males both in 1881 and 1891, and at the last Census Seoni has been added to their number. Narsinghpur and Jubbulpore, which stood low in the scale in 1881, have now risen high, while in the Maratha districts of Chanda, Nagpur, and Wardha females are now comparatively fewer than they were at the previous enumeration. In the districts of the Nerbada Valley, besides those which have been mentioned, and in Saugor and Damoh females have always been scarce, and the same is the case in the Feudatory States of the Uria country. The latter is a point specially deserving of notice, considering that in all the rest of the east of the Province females are generally in excess of males.

77. **Relative proportions between the sexes in different religions.**—The Census gives the following results with regard to the prevalence of the female sex among the followers of each religion, the latter being arranged in the order which they occupy in this respect :—

Number of Females per 1,000 Males by Religions.

Religion.	1891.	1881.	Serial order in respect of column 2.	Serial order in respect of column 3.
1	2	3	4	5
Animistic	1,015	*1,010*	1	*1*
All religions	**996**	**982**	**2**	**2**
Hindu	994	*978*	3	*3*
Jain	957	*936*	4	*5*
Mussalman	946	*960*	5	*4*
Parsi	747	*506*	6	*7*
Christian	659	*667*	7	*6*

Animistic.— The preponderance of the female sex among the jungle tribes is most marked, both at the present Census and that of 1881. If we examine the distribution of persons of aboriginal religion by districts, we find that in every district of the Province, except Saugor, Nimar, Nagpur, and Chanda, females are in excess of males; in Nagpur the sexes almost balance, but the disproportion is slightly to the disadvantage of females, of whom there are 992 per 1,000 males. In the two first of the excepted districts the aborigines are few in number, and in their ways of life are hardly distinguishable from the lower classes of Hindus among whom they live, and the same is the case to some extent in Nagpur. Whatever causes therefore have brought about the low average of females among the general population of these districts may be supposed to have had also an effect upon the semi-Hinduized aborigines which they contain. In Chanda, however, the circumstances are different ; here we have a large population of forest tribes, many of them the most primitive in the country. Whatever the reason may be, it is a singular fact that whereas among the aborigines of the Satpuras and the north of the Province generally females are in excess of males, in the great jungle tracts of the south the opposite is the case. The accompanying abstract illustrates what

Aborigines of the Southern Hills.

District.	Females per 1,000 males.	Some aboriginal tribes peculiar to the places mentioned in column 1.	Females per 1,000 males.
1	2	3	4
Chanda	987	Koi	996
Bastar	952	Mária	966
Kanker	973	Koitur	980
Patna	968	Muria	959
Kalahandi	927	Khond	945

In column 2 the proportions are calculated on the figures for Animistic religion. The numbers in column 4 are taken from the Caste Table, those for Khonds being for the Feudatory States only.

I say. The whole question of sex evolution is so difficult that the causes for many of the divergences we find are almost impossible to discover; but from the Age returns which will be afterwards discussed it would seem as if the dearth of females in the tracts in question were due to excessive mortality among the sex in the after years of life. I may note that in the Bamra State there are more males than females among persons of aboriginal religion, but owing to the construction of the Bengal-Nagpur Railway there was at the time of the Census a large influx of labourers from the Chhota-Nagpur direction, which may well account for the fact.

In 1881 it was suggested, as a possible reason for females being more numerous than males among people shown as of animistic belief, that women would have less desire to be inscribed as Hindus at the Census than men:—

"Not only would widows and other women supporting themselves be disposed to adhere more closely than males to their inherited superstitions, but even if they wished to be recorded as Hindus they would have less influence than men to induce such entry by the enumerators."

The reason given appears too slight to have any effect upon the return; and moreover the caste and tribal statistics of the present enumeration are distinctly against the theory, a preponderance of females being almost invariably observable amongst the members of the aboriginal tribes who have been returned as Hindus, as well as amongst those who are shown as of the tribal religion. Among Hindu Gonds there are, for instance, 1,026 females per 1,000 males, and the same will be noticed in the case of most of the other tribes. The Bajgas of Mandla and Balaghat show a preponderance of females amongst those of them who conform to Hindu usages, but of males amongst those who have made less advance in civilization. Apart, therefore, from any question of religion, we find that among the aboriginal tribes of the north and centre of the Province the female sex is more numerous than the male, while in the great forest tracts of the south the ratio suddenly changes, and males are uniformly in excess.

Jains.—The proportion of females among Jains has risen since the last Census, and the community has now changed places with the Mahomedans who were over the Jains in this respect in 1881. Except in the north of the Province the Jains are mostly immigrants from Rajputana, engaged in money-lending and trade; they are apparently taking more to settling down with their wives and families in the districts where they are found, the improved state of communications probably conducing to this result.

Mahomedans.—Among Mussalmans the proportion between the sexes has changed somewhat since last Census, females being now comparatively less numerous than they were in 1881. Looking at the figures for districts, it will appear that the causes which lead to a high proportion among females generally, equally affect the preponderance of the sex among Mahomedans. Thus, if we take the seven British districts which head the list in the latter respect, we find that in four of them—Seoni, Balaghat, Bhandara, and Raipur—Mahomedan females are more numerous than Mahomedan males; in all four there is a long-settled Mussalman community, and there is comparatively no immigration to upset the balance between the sexes, as is the case in many other parts of the Province.

Parsis.—It has been seen that there are now double the number of Parsis in the Central Provinces that there were in 1881; the rise in the proportion between the sexes shows that many more have come to stay than was the case ten years ago.

Christians.—The presence of a European army affects the sex return for followers of the Christian religion. Among Native Christians there are 919 females per 1,000 males.

78. **Migration as affecting the proportions between the sexes.**—This is a matter which more than any other tends to produce inequality between the figures for the sexes, but to estimate its incidence is not always an easy task. Calculations exhibiting the sexes amongst migrants for different districts will be found in Chapter IX, which deals with the birth-places of the population; they show that generally between two adjoining districts there is a greater interchange of females than of males, chiefly due to marriages across the border, but between places situated at a distance from one another, the greater part of the migrants are males. The interchange of population that takes place between districts which are close to one another may be practically left out of account; as, if one district, Chhindwara, gives to another, Nagpur, more females than males, the latter sends back to the former an almost equal proportion of females in return.* But immigration from a distance, say, from the North-West Provinces and Oudh, to the districts of the Central Provinces cannot be similarly left out of reckoning; we get 123,009 persons from the former province, of whom 66 per cent. are males, while we return 12,179 persons, amongst whom, it so happens, women are more numerous than men. Thus, to all the districts into which people from Northern India have flocked, there has been a large accession of males, two having come on an average for every female. As from this Province there is no extensive emigration to a distance to counteract the steady inflow of people which as an undeveloped country it attracts, it follows that in the districts to which settlers have principally been drawn we should find a higher proportion of the male than of the female sex. And this we see to be the case. I cannot here repeat the statements which are printed in Chapter IX, but reference may be made to them for detailed information on the points which I am now to notice.

The distant parts of India from which the Central Provinces have received the greatest accession of population are Bengal,—excluding the Tributary States of Chhota Nagpur and Cuttack,—Bombay, Madras, the North-West Provinces, Oudh, the Punjab, and Rajputana; and the districts to which immigrants from these places have uniformly been drawn are Saugor, Jubbulpore, Hoshangabad, Nimar, Nagpur, and to a less extent Wardha. The incomers have almost entirely avoided Narsinghpur, and it is to this that the high position occupied by the district in respect of the proportion of females to males, which has been remarked on at paragraph 76, may in great degree be attributed. Here then we have at once a reason for the excess of males, which we find in the districts whose names I have given. An additional cause for the low proportion of females in the northern districts will be found in the figures for emigration to the Central India States; while the birth-place returns show that among the immigrants we have received from Central India the sexes almost balance—there are 994 females per 1,000 males—they show that among the persons we have sent to Central India females are largely in excess of males, the proportion being 1,229 per 1,000. Much of the emigration I believe to have taken place from Saugor and Damoh, so that these are probably the two districts most affected in this respect. With the above exception, the proportions between the sexes are little disturbed by emigration beyond the Province; very few persons go to a distance, nearly all simply cross the border into Berar or into the adjoining country in other parts, and, as has been seen, interchanges of population with such border territory have little effect upon the matter under discussion. In the districts on the Satpuras and in the eastern districts and states the migrations of the people are generally of such a local nature that they can similarly be disregarded.

79. **Relative proportions of the sexes at different ages.**—At Ap-

* See Tabular Statement D, Chapter IX.

pendix C will be found tables showing the relative proportions of the sexes at each age-period in every district of the province; figures are given for the total population, and also for persons of aboriginal religion, as the sex statistics for the latter show some variance from the general rule. The subject of age is rather a complicated one, or at all events must look so, from the mass of figures which are necessarily involved in any calculations into which it enters. As to the value which these figures possess, I shall have something to say later on, but here it may be noted that mis-statements with regard to age will hardly affect the relative proportions between the sexes at different periods. More especially will this be the case in the early years of life; there can be no reason why a father should make a mistake about giving the age of an infant daughter, while that of a son is correctly returned. If mistakes are made, as there is no doubt they are, they will be made of both sexes equally. Later in life there is, however, a chance that the ages of the sexes will not be returned with an equal freedom from prejudice; there will probably be a tendency to make mis-statements about the ages of girls at the time of life that marriage ordinarily takes place, and when we come to the forties and fifties we shall find that, as a rule, the ages of men are stated in greater detail than those of women, for whom it is more the custom to return round numbers. But, dealing as we are with statistics for some thirteen millions of people, we shall see that when an average is struck on numbers so large, there are certain laws which these follow with an amount of regularity that precludes their being sensibly affected by mis-statement. The more we descend to detail the less certain do we become of our ground, but of the main facts which are brought out by the averages to be presently given we can speak with a very tolerable degree of conviction.

80. **General review of the sex averages at each age.**—We may first take the figures for the Central Provinces as a whole, and see how they compare with those of some other countries and with those of the previous Census:

Average number of Females to 1,000 Males at each age-period.

Age-period.	British Districts.		Central Provinces.				India, 1881.	England and Wales.	Italy.
	1881.	1891.	Animistic.	Mussalman.	Jain.	Total population.			
1	2	3	4	5	6	7	8	9	10
Under 1 year	1,013	1,014	1,022	1,005	907	*1,015*	1,004	998	**956**
1 "	1,056	1,082	1,095	1,028	1,215	*1,080*	1,036	1,004	962
2 years	1,090	1,100	1,134	1,044	1,066	*1,104*	1,072	1,003	965
3 "	1,096	1,131	1,144	1,079	1,100	*1,133*	1,070	1,006	962
4 "	1,007	1,050	1,085	1,068	1,047	*1,057*	992	1,004	978
Total under 5 years	1,054	1,077	1,101	1,047	1,045	*1,080*	1,034	1,003	964
5—9 years	923	978	981	1,001	980	*976*	926	1,006	966
10—14 "	**809**	**830**	850	797	**754**	*828*	**795**	**997**	959
15—19 "	960	948	1,036	858	827	*954*	922	1,008	1,025
20—24 "	1,183	1,176	1,250	1,009	905	*1,178*	1,088	1,093	1,017
25—29 "	1,058	1,083	1,145	952	1,003	*1,077*	991	1,087	1,027
30—34 "	923	977	1,007	910	996	*971*	955	1,077	1,027
35—39 "	895	945	951	789	906	*935*	861	1,069	1,005
40—44 "	893	891	**836**	929	1,008	*877*	964	1,079	1,010
45—49 "	875	843	845	**721**	782	*845*	885	1,103	996
50—54 "	984	958	909	997	1,124	*952*	1,021	1,104	1,020
55—59 "	1,028	1,049	1,156	804	933	*1,068*	936	1,111	986
60 and over	1,260	1,289	1,246	1,285	1,368	*1,294*	1,195	1,187	980
TOTAL	984	998	1,015	946	957	*996*	959	1,055	995

NOTE.—The figures in thick type show the period at which the ratio of females to males is lowest.

To save multiplication of tables, I have added columns to show statistics for persons who are Mahomedans, Jains, or Animistic by religion; Hindus form such an overwhelming majority of the inhabitants of the Province that the averages which result for them do not differ materially from those which are given for the whole population, and I have not therefore burdened the statement with an extra column on their account. In the whole Province we find the following variations to take place in the proportions between the sexes. There is a preponderance of—

(*a*) Females from . . . . . . 0 to 4 years of age.
(*b*) Males " . . . . . . 5 " 19 " " "
(*c*) Females " . . . . . . 20 " 29 " " "
(*d*) Males " . . . . . . 30 " 54 " " "
(*e*) Females " . . . . . . 55 upwards.

0—4 years.—The first matter to engage our attention is the fact that there are a greater number of female infants under one year of age than of males at the same period, the proportion being 1,015 to 1000. Now, it is a regular feature of the registration returns that there are more male births than female. The discrepancy is most marked, but two explanations are possible. First, as the birth of a son and heir is generally an occasion for greater jubilation than of a female child, there is some probability of more accurate registration of the former sex than of the latter; and second, the regular tendency of the figures given is to show that in the early years of life male mortality is much greater than female. Assuming the sexes to start off equal, at the end of six months there will be more females alive than males, and this will be still more the case among children who are just entering on the second year of their existence, and this is what the Census disproportion means. Instead of the Census figures being at variance with those which we get from the vital statistics returns, I think they rather bear them out. In the second year of life, as will be seen, females are able to gain on males 65 points in 1,000; in the first year, therefore, it is almost certain that they have gained more than the 15 points which the Census averages show. It may therefore be accepted that there are more male children born than female; the registration returns invariably show this result, and the Census, though at first sight apparently contradicting the fact, must be taken as pointing to the same conclusion.

To judge from the average given there seems to be somewhat of a tendency to the birth of female children among the aboriginal population and a strong tendency to the birth of male children among the Jains. One of the many theories put forward to account for a preponderance of male births is that in cases where the husband is the elder the child is male, and *vice versâ*. But as remarked by Mr. Baines in the Bombay Census Report of 1881, "as the number of cases in which the above theory would practically exclude altogether the birth of female children is overwhelming, it is clear that some supplementary influence is required." The theory can hardly be strictly applied in the case of the Jains of these Provinces; in Saugor, the only district in which they are at all numerous, the sexes at infancy are almost equal, and elsewhere the Jains occur in such small numbers as to be beyond the law of averages. But in the case of the aborigines it is possible that traces of the tendency referred to may be found; the ages of the sexes at marriage are much more evenly balanced among the hill tribes than amongst the other sections of the community, and to this may, in some measure, be attributed the large number of female children found in their midst. The whole subject, however, partakes too much of the theoretical to enable any particular deduction to be made from the figures which have been given.

The excessive mortality of males in the early years of life is as noticeable a fact in India as in European countries. Among natives a very decided opinion prevails that male babies are more difficult to rear than female, and this the Census figures bear out in a marked degree. To judge from the ratios given, the mortality amongst male infants is less severe among the Mahomedans and Jains than amongst the other classes of the population, as presumably their children are better cared for than are those of the aborigines and of the depressed castes, who form so large a portion of the Hindu community.

Five to Nineteen years.—Between the ages of 5 and 9 there is a decline in the value of female life, which is again still more marked in the next lustrum, 10 to 14 years. At this period there is, as has been remarked, a chance of the ages of females being understated, but it is also a time most fatal to female life both in this country and in Europe, though in the former the prevalence of early marriage greatly intensifies the mortality amongst girls of this age. Of Jain girls between 10 and 14 years two-thirds are married, and we see that amongst them fewer survive this period than is the case with the girls of other classes. Had we, however, separate statistics for the better castes of Hindus, we should probably find them to exhibit a like result; as it is, the overwhelming numbers of the aboriginal tribes and of the depressed classes who have been inscribed as Hindus, and amongst whom the practice of early marriage is little followed, raise the average for the Hindu community. Among the members of the hill tribes who are recorded as of aboriginal religion, only a fifth of the girls between 10 and 14 years are married, and we therefore find a high percentage of them living at this age. From 15 to 19 years there are everywhere signs of recovered vitality among females; among aborigines they again become more numerous than males.

Twenty to Twenty-nine years.—Between these years women are in these Provinces more numerous than men amongst all races except the Jains and Mahomedans; in every district, except Nimar, the same feature is observable. This is the more remarkable as it is at this period that we might expect to find the greatest inflow of immigration, bringing to the Province an accession of males. As a matter of fact, traces of this will be found in some of the district averages, those for places which have attracted many in-comers tending to fall more than is the case in parts unaffected by immigration. Amongst aborigines who receive no recruitment from this source the proportion of females is especially high.

Thirty years and over.—After the age of 30 years the ratios given are not very reliable for any particular period, but in general they show that up to old age male life is everywhere better than female. The averages for the latter in many cases tend to see-saw, being higher at periods which, like 40—44, include a round number than for intermediate periods, such as 45—49, which would very seldom be returned for women. After the age of 60 women are everywhere more numerous than men, but among aborigines there are fewer old women than among the other races, due probably to their being less able to stand the hard life they lead than men.

Comparing the returns for England with those of the Central Provinces, it would appear that the mortality amongst male children, which all the world over is more severe than among female, is much intensified in this country, where the conditions of life are harder. In England females suffer less in after-life than they do in India; they are married at a later age, when they are better able to tide over the perils of child-bearing; some portion of them, moreover, are never subjected to these perils, whereas in this country practically every woman is married. In England again we find that the ratio of females to males rises rapidly between the ages of 20 and 24, these being the years at which many young men leave the country for abroad. In Italy where the proportion between the sexes is the same as in these Provinces, we find that the result has come about in almost an exactly opposite way; in the European country females are fewer in infancy and old age, but more numerous in the middle stages of life.

81. **Sex averages at each age in certain districts.**—Here I shall remark upon a few of the most striking features which are presented by the district returns given at Appendix C.

The Vindhyan and Nerbada Valley districts.—A most noticeable circumstance about four of these districts—Saugor, Damoh, Jubbulpore and Narsinghpur—is the excess of male infants under one year over female. They are the only parts of the Province where this is seen to be the case. Some support is given by the marriage returns of these districts to the sex theory which would ascribe a preponderance of male children to unions where there is considerable disproportion between the ages of husband and wife; such disproportion is here caused by the late age at which men marry rather than by child-marriage among the female sex, for the latter is by no means a distinctive feature of the northern districts. It is impossible to give elaborate statements showing this, but in the abstract in the margin are noted certain proportions which bear upon the subject. In Saugor between the ages of 15 and 24 only 53·9 per cent. of the men are married, against 66·8 per cent. in Wardha and 70 per cent. in Raipur, but there is no such marked inequality in the numbers of married women at this time of life. In all the districts young wives are common, but in the northern districts young husbands are in a minority as compared with what is the case in other parts of the Province; in the former a preponderance of male children might therefore be expected, while in Raipur, where the balance between the ages of the sexes is most evenly preserved, the tendency to the production of male children is reduced. The restriction upon widow re-marriage which, as has been seen,* is carried further in the northern districts than elsewhere must also tend to produce the same effect, by diminishing the number of wives at the more advanced stages of life. So far as I am aware, there is no reason to suppose that the dearth of female infants in these districts is in any way due to infanticide. Another point to be remarked about all this part of the country is the very low proportion of females between the ages of 10 and 14. It is true that with a reduced average of the sex to start with, the proportion of females at this time of life should be correspondingly low, but the figures are even smaller than might thus be allowed for. Child marriage is not the sole reason for this, but it may be that there is more concealment of the age of girls at this period in these districts than in other places where females are kept in less seclusion.

Females per 1,000 Males up to 15 years of age.

Age.	Saugor.	Damoh.	Jubbulpore.	Narsinghpur.	Hoshangabad.	Provincial average (British Districts).
1	2	3	4	5	7	8
0	955	960	991	967	1,019	1,014
1	1,037	1,041	1,086	1,079	1,085	1,082
2	1,112	1,076	1,072	1,078	1,087	1,100
3	1,101	1,086	1,149	1,072	1,093	1,131
4	1,026	1,024	1,068	1,026	1,003	1,050
0—4	1,049	1,038	1,077	1,043	1,055	1,077
5—9	948	938	968	970	963	978
10—14	765	779	810	777	788	830

District.	Percentage of Married on Total of each Sex between Ages 15 and 24.	
	Males.	Females.
Saugor	53·9	90·1
Narsinghpur	58·8	92·3
Wardha	66·8	95·2
Raipur	70·0	92·7

Chhatisgarh and the Eastern States.—The only other part of the Province to which I would draw attention is the eastern districts and states, and here it is to the proportions of the sexes in old age that I shall specially refer.

* See Chapter II, paragraph 28. Chapter V may also be referred to.

Females per 1,000 Males in old age.

District, etc.	Total Population.		Animistic Religion.	
	50—59 years.	60 years and over.	50—59 years.	60 years and over.
Raipur	1,101	1,577	1,160	1,710
Bilaspur	1,065	1,481	1,020	1,652
Sambalpur	1,031	1,418	1,032	1,348
Provincial average	**972**	**1,294**	**943**	**1,246**
Bastar	805	1,040	788	879
Patna	896	1,245	871	1,150
Kalahandi	881	1,174	762	942

The phenomenal number of old women found in Chhatisgarh is most striking. I cannot do better than quote what Mr. Ismay, who has an intimate knowledge of Chhatisgarh, said upon the subject in 1881. Speaking of the Raipur district, he wrote:—

"As in 1872, so in the late (1881) Census females are found to be in excess of males. The same result is found in Bilaspur and is admitted to be correct by all with whom I have ever spoken on the subject. The only reasons I have ever heard advanced are—(1) that in other districts, owing to prejudice, a percentage of females is kept off the returns of the Census officer; (2) that in Chhatisgarh the great mass of the women are employed in agricultural and other out-door pursuits, and the strength and physique thus acquired secure them a longer span of life than is enjoyed by their wealthier, but more effeminate, sisters in other districts. This argument is, I think, not without weight, for the number of old women which even a small village can turn out is something surprising."

The longevity of the women of the aboriginal tribes in Chhatisgarh proper is also marked; in most other parts of the Province they do not live so long as the women of the other classes.

Turning next to the figures for the three southern States, I think we have here a clue to the remarkable dearth of women which distinguishes them. We cannot for one moment imagine that any of the ladies, who among the aborigines of these southern wilds are in the sere and yellow of life, have any idea of what their ages are, but neither have their lords and masters, nor for that matter their sisters in other parts. The age return is probably, therefore, based chiefly on the estimate of the enumerator, but it is in all likelihood a near enough approach to the actual circumstances of the case. The Census in the States was carefully taken, and the result has been to show that females instead of being in excess of males, as they are amongst the hill tribes elsewhere, are here largely in a minority. To bring this about it is necessary that they should die off more readily, and this we found to be the fact, as in the semi-savage existence of the aborigines of the southern hills, but few females survive the middle years of life.

82. **Summary of the above conclusions as to the relative proportions between the sexes.**—I think from what we have seen that it is superfluous to assume that concealment of females has had any effect upon the sex returns at the present Census; in almost every case we can otherwise account for the low proportion of females in the districts where this result is found. As I have remarked in Chapter II, the inclination to distrust the Census is becoming less at every enumeration, and as this is the fourth Census the Province has seen within the last twenty-five years, it can hardly be supposed that any concealment worth the name is now attempted, whatever may have been the case in former days. The conclusions at which we have arrived above as to the varying proportions between the sexes may be summarized as under:—

(a) Among the aboriginal tribes females generally exceed males, except in the southern parts of the Province; the excess is most marked in the earlier periods of life, fewer women surviving to old age than amongst other classes of the community. In Bastar and Kalahandi the excess of males appears to be due to the greater mortality among females in after-life, which is specially noticeable among the aborigines of the southern hills.

(*b*) The Vindhyan and Nerbada valley districts—with the exception of Narsinghpur—and the districts of Wardha and Nagpur, have attracted a great deal of immigration from distant parts of India. Among the immigrants the male sex largely predominates, so that the balance of the sexes in all these districts has been sensibly affected by the influx of settlers to their midst. In Narsinghpur, where there has been comparatively no immigration, the sexes are much more nearly equal.

(*c*) It is probable that almost everywhere more males are born than females; this is specially the case in Saugor, Damoh, Jubbulpore, and Narsinghpur. The first five years of life are more fatal to male children than to female, but between the ages of 10 and 14 there is excessive mortality among the female sex.

(*d*) The districts and states of Chhatisgarh are remarkable for the longevity of the female sex, due probably to late marriages and to the active life which females in those parts lead.

It seems unnecessary to go over the conditions of each district and see how these laws apply; enough has already been said on the subject to explain the variations that arise.

83. **Comparison with other Provinces.**—Before leaving this subject it may be of interest to see how the Province compares with other parts of India as regards the proportion between the sexes. This will appear from the statement appended :—

Relative proportions of the sexes in different parts of India—Census of 1891.

Province or State.	Females per 1,000 males.	Province or State.	Females per 1,000 males.
Madras	1,020	Berar	942
Bengal	1,005	Bombay	939
Central Provinces	996	North-West Provinces and Oudh	931
Hyderabad	966	Central India	914
Burma	964	Rajputana	896
Assam	943	Punjab	850

Note.—Except in the case of Madras, Berar, and Bombay, the proportions are calculated on the preliminary returns for the Provinces given.

AGE.

84. **The record of age.**—In the previous portion of this chapter, when discussing in connection with age the relative proportions of the sexes among the population, it has been seen that inaccuracy in the record of age could be to a great extent disregarded, as hardly affecting the ratios in question. But the case is different when we come to consider the average number of persons living at each age, and attempt to compare the figures for one period with another, Here we find the most marked discrepancies in the statistics we have got. Nothing else was perhaps to be expected when it is considered that in this country and especially in the Central Provinces with its large aboriginal population, very few persons who are at all advanced in life have any idea what their ages are. The strange thing is the amount of method we find in the irregularities that exist; even the most pronounced among them will be seen to run through every district and to affect the returns for almost every religion alike.

Perhaps the most extraordinary feature in the returns is that which is presented by the age statistics for young children. One would naturally expect the ages in the first few years of life to be accurately returned, for there can hardly be the same chance of mistake about the age of a young child as about the age of a person more advanced in years. But this is far from being borne out by the Census results. Supposing the birth-rate to remain constant, the number of children in the second year of life will be less than those in the first year, as there must have been more deaths amongst those who have been two years in existence than amongst those who have been only one. So in the third year there should be fewer children than in the second, and int he fourth year than in the third. But what we find from the Census figures is this: in the second year of life the number of children is very much lower than in the first, but in the third the number suddenly rises until we get more children in existence even than there are infants under one year of age; in the fourth year there is a still further rise; in the fifth year the number slightly declines, but still is greater than at the age period, 0—1. Similarly in the lustrum 5—9, there are far more children than there are in the first five years of life. Something of the same kind was observable in several of the Indian Provinces at the last census, so that the circumstance of the irregular record of children's ages is not altogether fortuitous. Again it will be seen from the detailed statements printed at Appendix C (Nos. III and IV) that there is in every case a tendency towards returning round numbers like 30 or 40 in preference to odd numbers between the decennial periods. It may also be taken that there is very general under-statement of age in the case of the old and middle aged. In the case of the latter, it will evidently be misleading to go by the five-year periods which are given in Table VII; over 30 the ages are therefore grouped according to ten-year intervals in most of the tabular statements which follow.

85. **General distribution of the population by age.**—The appended table shows the age distribution of 10,000 persons of each sex, and compares the results of the Census in this respect with the statistics for 1881 and with those of two European countries:—

Age-distribution of 10,000 persons of each sex.

Age Period.	British Districts. 1881.		British Districts. 1891.		Central Provinces. 1891.		England and Wales.		France.	
	Males.	Females	Males.	Females.	Males.	Females.	Males.	Females.	Males.	Females.
1	2	3	4	5	6	7	8	9	10	11
0	281	289	286	290	284	289	298	282	188	181
1	284	305	194	210	198	215	270	257	177	171
2	305	338	310	342	311	345	278	265	191	187
3	354	394	337	382	347	395	273	260	190	188
4	333	341	322	339	325	345	272	258	184	183
Total under 5	*1,557*	*1,667*	*1,449*	*1,563*	*1,465*	*1,589*	*1,391*	*1,322*	*930*	*910*
5—9	1,483	1,424	1,578	1,546	1,605	1,572	1,241	1,184	901	891
10—14	1,102	906	1,203	1,001	1,209	1,006	1,109	1,048	890	871
15—19	703	686	691	656	699	669	1,003	959	848	841
Total under 20	*4,845*	*4,683*	*4,921*	*4,766*	*4,978*	*4,836*	*4,744*	*4,513*	*3,569*	*3,513*
20—24	759	913	707	833	707	836	880	912	922	968
25—29	898	966	840	911	839	908	776	800	732	696
30—39	1,476	1,370	1,449	1,402	1,447	1,392	1,254	1,276	1,365	1,341
40—49	981	886	1,034	910	1,018	888	966	998	1,222	1,206
50—59	554	558	560	546	539	526	687	721	1,005	1,020
60 and over	487	624	489	632	472	614	693	780	1,185	1,256

Leaving detailed explanation till afterwards, we may note the following as matters of interest :—

(*a*) The falling off in children 0—4 years of age as compared with 1881, and the rise in the number of children aged 5—9.

(*b*) The large number of young children under 5 and under 10 years in this country as compared with Europe, and more especially with France, where the number of children is particularly low.

(*c*) In old age the European countries gain on India, the number of persons who in Europe attain the age of 50 and over forming a larger portion of the total population than in the East.

(*d*) Both in this country and in Europe the number of old women is considerably larger than the number of old men.

86. The early years of life.—*Comparison with 1881.*—First we may examine the averages which result for the earlier years of life. On the peculiarity of the returns for the years 0—9, I have already remarked, but the apparent divergences are so striking and run with such strange regularity throughout the figures, both for districts and races, that they can hardly be dismissed as meaningless. To take, for instance, the quinquennial periods, it must be remembered that the children returned in 1891 at the ages 0—4 have been born within the years 1886—90, those at 5—9 within the years 1881—85, while those at 10—14 are the same as the children who were shown at ages 0—4 at the census of 1881, and similarly with the others. Now, in Chapter II we have seen that the years 1886—90 were bad years throughout the Province; food was scarce, and the general health was low; in the first half of the decade, on the other hand, there were prosperous seasons. Of both these periods we have the clearest trace in the averages which have been given; during the five years 1881—85 more children were born, and with plenty in the land more of these would survive than during the five lean years which followed; and to this is to be ascribed the high proportion of children between the ages of 5 and 9. Previous to the last census the seasons had been generally favourable; the birth-rate rose, infant mortality was low, and at the present day we find the children born during this period, and now aged 10 to 14 years, to be in a large majority when compared with those of similar age at the enumeration of 1881.

Distribution of 10,000 persons in British districts for quinquennial periods 0 to 20.

Age-period.	1881.		1891.	
	Males.	Females.	Males.	Females.
0—4	1,557	1,667	1,449	1,563
5—9	1,483	1,424	1,578	1,546
10—14	1,102	906	1,203	1,001
15—19	703	686	691	656

Infant life.—Dealing thus with groups of years we see that the Census results are not so unreliable as they at first sight seem to be; but, descending to the annual periods which have been retained in Table VII for the first five years of life, we come to more uncertain ground. The immense falling off in the number of children, between the ages of under one year and over one year, may very reasonably be taken as in some measure an indication of the terrible mortality of the year 1889. The number of deaths was then 81,000 more than in any one year during the

Distribution of 10,000 persons in British districts for ages 0—4.

Age-period.	1881.		1891.	
	Males.	Females.	Males.	Females.
0—1	281	289	286	290
1	284	305	194	210
2	305	338	310	342
3	354	394	337	382
4	333	341	322	339
Total 0—4	1,557	1,667	1,449	1,563

decade, and the birth-rate also fell lower than it had been during the previous years of the same period. The small number of children under one year of age is less explicable. It must be borne in mind that the returns for infants under one year or age have been artificially increased from two causes: first, the tendency to write all young children down as "infant," the word used in the schedule; and second, the fact that we have got in this age-period all the children who were one year old when the preliminary enumeration commenced, *plus* the number born in the five or six weeks the enumeration was in progress. The instructions were to return the age that each person would have attained onthe 26th February, the day of the Census, but it is hardly likely that the rule was much attended to. If deductions are made for both these causes, the average of infants of one year and under will be sensibly reduced; and, as it is proved that a year of distress checks the natural fecundity of the population, we might infer that the number of children in the first year of life, *i.e.* begotten during or immediately following the hard season of 1889, has been brought down in consequence. The birth-rate in 1890 was certainly low, 38·41 per mille, but we find the very same phenomenon of a low average of children returned as under one year of age in 1881, when in the year preceding the Census the birth-rate was abnormally high, 44·87 per mille. It would therefore appear as if there was an inherent failing to make a correct return of the age of very young children, or the average of the last census has been unduly lowered by some cause of which we are not now aware. Altogether, the returns for the individual ages of children in the first five years of life appear to be devoid of meaning; all we can say is that for the small number of children under 2 years of age returned at the present Census we can in part account by the depressed vitality of the time immediately preceding the enumeration, but that for anything less than the five yearly period the age statistics cannot be looked upon as reliable.

Variation in the age distribution of the sexes.—This can be far more clearly understood from the ratios which were worked out in the previous section of this chapter, and which showed that in infancy female life is better than male, but that between the ages of 10 and 14 there is a marked falling off in the value of the former. The matter can be also treated thus: the number of persons living in the Central Provinces who are between 5 and 9 years of age amounts to 1,605 per 10,000 of the population in the case of males, and 1,572 on a like average in the case of females. At the age of 10 to 14 years the number of males has fallen to 1,209, or a decrease of 25 per cent. in the five years; females, on the other hand, have declined to 1,006, a loss of 36 per cent. in their number in the same period. The figures are approximate only, but they probably represent nearly enough the ratio which female bears to male mortality at this time of life, and which may thus be roughly taken to be as 7 is to 5.

87. **Middle and old age.**—If the age statistics for the earlier years of life are frequently open to doubt, those for middle and old age must be regarded as infinitely more so. The figures we have got are in nine cases out of ten the merest fancy; a villager whose age is 50 years will, if asked, return himself as 30, not from any desire to appear younger than he is, but simply from ignorance of what he is saying. If, however, we assume that the same mistakes have been made in every part of the Province, the age statistics, though specifically unreliable, may yet be looked upon as of value from a comparative point of view, as from them we may gather some idea of the relative proportions of the young and old in different parts of the country. The matter may be best considered in connection with what has been called the economical age distribution of the population; or, as Mr. Baines has put it in the Bombay Census Report of 1881, we may "divide the period of life into the productive and the onerous, and measure the

condition of the people by the ratio found to exist between the sums of these two classes. A population has to be judged, according to this standard, by the ratio of the total of those who reach maturity, not by that of those who come into the world only to leave it before the day of work has been reached." The appended abstract shows how the Province compares in this respect with some other parts of India, and with the two European countries for which detailed age statistics have already been given :—

Age-distribution of 10,000 persons of each sex according to the productive and dependent periods of life.

Province or Country.	Males.					Females.				
	0—9	0—19	60 and over.	Total of columns 3 and 4.	20—59	0—9	0—14	45 and over.	Total of columns 8 and 9.	15—44
1	2	3	4	5	6	7	8	9	10	11
Central Provinces	3,070	4,978	472	*5,450*	4,550	3,161	4,167	1,370	*5,537*	4,463
Berar	2,629	4,360	578	*4,938*	5,062	2,923	3,885	1,524	*5,409*	4,591
Bombay	2,853	4,718	427	*5,145*	4,855	2,983	3,869	1,453	*5,322*	4,678
North-West Provinces	2,635	4,639	501	*5,140*	4,860	2,724	3,665	1,632	*5,297*	4,703
Madras	2,821	4,737	507	*5,244*	4,756	2,830	3,761	1,522	*5,283*	4,717
England and Wales	2,632	4,744	693	*5,437*	4,563	2,506	3,554	1,954	*5,508*	4,492
France	1,831	3,569	1,185	*4,754*	5,246	1,801	2,672	2,864	*5,536*	4,464

Note.—Columns 6 and 11 represent the productive, and columns 5 and 10 the dependent part of the population.

In males the working age has been taken as 20 to 59; the lower limit might better be put at 18 years, but as this period does not appear in the Age Tables and as in the case of the other provinces and countries, I have no proper means of deducing it, the limit of 20 may be allowed to remain. For females 15 to 44 has been taken as the working age. The Central Provinces, it will be seen, are distinguished from the other parts of India by the high proportion of young children which they return, and by the comparative smallness of the productive population which is brought about in consequence. In Berar, where there is much immigration, the figures for the working male population are very high as compared with those for the other provinces given. The peculiar distribution of the people in France, where there is a dearth of children, and a resulting excess in the proportion of workers, is a noticeable feature of these returns.

88. **Mean Age.**—The mean age of the population as deducible from the Census figures is 24 years, being 23·83 in the case of males and 24·18 in the case of females. According to the Census of 1881 the average age of the total population was 24·07 years, of males 23·89 years, and of females 24·25 years. The mean age of the female sex is thus slightly in excess of that of males, but in both cases it is no doubt pitched too low owing to understatement in the later years of life.

89. **Age statistics for the principal religions.**—The age distribution

of the followers of each religion will appear from the statement which is subjoined :—

Age-distribution of 10,000 persons of each Religion.

Age.	Males.					Females.				
	Hindus.	Jains.	Mussalmans.	Christians.	Animistic.	Hindus.	Jains.	Mussalmans.	Christians.	Animistic.
1	2	3	4	5	6	7	8	9	10	11
0—4 . .	1,466	1,086	1,222	976	1,511	1,588	1,187	1,353	1,442	1,639
5—9 . .	1,600	1,233	1,339	994	1,685	1,567	1,263	1,417	1,584	1,629
Total under 10 . .	*3,066*	*2,319*	*2,561*	*1,970*	*3,196*	*3,155*	*2,450*	*2,770*	*3,026*	*3,268*
10—14 . .	1,212	1,208	1,138	812	1,211	1,006	952	959	1,087	1,014
15—19 . .	707	860	726	657	654	669	743	659	1,022	667
Total under 20 . .	*4,985*	*4,387*	*4,425*	*3,439*	*5,061*	*4,830*	*4,145*	*4,388*	*5,135*	*4,949*
20—29 . .	1,550	1,797	1,764	3,699	1,473	1,745	1,789	1,827	1,960	1,731
30—39 . .	1,447	1,559	1,587	1,447	1,419	1,391	1,564	1,453	1,317	1,380
40—49 . .	1,011	1,179	1,098	780	1,035	890	1,146	1,011	813	855
50—59 . .	538	608	609	386	528	529	684	619	425	491
60 and over .	469	470	517	249	484	615	672	702	350	594

The Hindus form such a large portion of the total inhabitants of the Province that their distribution hardly differs from that which we have seen to result for the general population. Among Jains the number of young people is small and the number of workers is large, due in part to the inherited thrift of the race which no doubt operates as a prudential check upon the unlimited production of children, and in part to the presence of a considerable body of immigrants who swell the ranks of those who are of a working age. The Mahomedan community also displays a far lower proportion of children than the average of the general population ; both amongst males and females the ratio of persons who are over 60 years of age is higher among Mussalmans than amongst any of the other races. The statistics for Christians are of course abnormal on account of the age distribution of the European population ; 37 per cent. of the males are between 20 and 30 years of age, this period including the greater part of the British garrison of the Province. The figures for the aboriginal population are most noteworthy. A very large number of children are brought into the world only to die off, most of them during the early years of life. Among a community so improvident as are most of the hill tribes, the propagation of the race will naturally go on untrammelled by any consideration as to the future well-being of the offspring they produce. Some allowance should be made, however, for the greater mortality which must necessarily exist among people who lead so hard a life, and which will thus reduce the number of the old among the aboriginal races, at the same time heightening the proportion which the young must bear to a population so reduced. But, everything considered, the number of children among these tribes must appear exceedingly great.

90. Age statistics for districts.—These are given in detail at Appendix C, Tables III and IV. In the accompanying abstract I have summarized the result

Age-distribution of 10,000 males by districts.

District, etc.	0—4	0—9	0—19	20—59	60 and over.
Saugor	1,256	2,791	4,838	4,796	366
Damoh	1,268	2,835	4,988	4,653	359
Jubbulpore	1,321	2,908	4,957	4,684	359
Narsinghpur	1,396	2,857	4,819	4,798	383
Hoshangabad	1,341	2,686	4,625	4,955	420
Nimár	1,335	2,644	4,527	5,009	464
Mandla	1,587	3,355	5.332	4,344	324
Seoni	1,458	2,991	4,927	4,615	458
Chhindwara	1,491	3,034	4,991	4,499	510
Betul	1,431	2,971	4,930	4,532	538
Wardha	1,276	2,559	4,293	5,023	684
Nagpur	1,250	2,571	4,391	4.819	790
Chanda	1,434	2,982	4,763	4,675	562
Bhandara	1,566	3,140	4,857	4,506	637
Balaghat	1,486	3,052	4,827	4,597	576
Raipur	1,644	3,427	5,151	4,337	512
Bilaspur	1,585	3,361	5.214	4,381	405
Chhatisgarh States	1,637	3,394	5,094	4,438	468
Bastar	1,488	3,128	4,972	4,556	472
Sambalpur	1,451	3,081	5,289	4,344	367
Uria States	1,511	3,270	5,423	4,249	328

for males, as from this the conditions of the several districts can be sufficiently understood without burdening the statement with sex details. The chief points noticeable are the excess of children in the districts on the Satpura plateau and in the south and east of the Province, the dearth of the very old in the northern districts of Saugor, Damoh, and in the districts of the Nerbada valley, and the large number of old people in the districts of the Nagpur country.

91. Excess of Children.—This is one of the most prominent points in the statistics which have been given, and, as has been seen, distinguishes the Province from most of the other parts of India for which returns have as yet been received. As has been noted at the close of the last paragraph, the proportion of children to the total population can be raised by reducing the number of adults by early death. Thus, if in any community few persons attain maturity, the proportion of children among such, as calculated upon the total strength of the community, will necessarily be greater than when many persons live to middle and old age. That, death comes at an early age in many of the districts where children are most numerous can be judged from some of the ratios which have been given; in Raipur there are, on an average, 600 more people alive in 10,000 at the age of 9 years than in Damoh, but at 19 the excess amounts to little over 150. Allowing, therefore, that the high proportion of children in the districts where this is found, is to some extent exaggerated by the greater mortality among the population which takes place later in life, the fact remains that in the districts mentioned a very large number of children are born. The matter has already been noticed when discussing the increase in the population, and it has been seen* that, despite the unhealthy climate and high mortality of several of these districts,

* See page 34, Chapter II.

the population has risen some 10 per cent. or over compared with a slight increase in many other parts of the Province. To the reasons for this excess of children which have been given in Chapter II, I hardly know that I have much to add. Briefly the causes which bring about this result may be stated to be (1) abundance of food, (2) a low standard of comfort among the people, and (3) the greater prevalence of the married state in all the districts where the number of young children is large.

The abundance of food is due to the more abundant return which the land makes of rice, which is the great staple of the districts of the south and east of the Province, and both in these districts and in those on the Satpuras to the absence of an export market and to the surplus produce of the soil being thus made available for home consumption. The population of all the districts, where there is a noted excess of children, is very largely composed of the lower classes of Hindus and of the aboriginal tribes. In Chhatisgarh we find the Kurmi and Teli castes to be stongly represented, but in both there is a numerous section which has been settled in the country from time immemorial, and whose members differ little in their mode of life from their neighbours who are not usually reckoned so high in the social scale. Amongst all classes the standard of comfort is exceedingly low, and with plenty of food to eat there is no check upon the unlimited production of children which is so marked a feature of the eastern districts. The picture which Mr. Bannerjee of Raipur has drawn in the last Census Report of the Chamár of Chhatisgarh living in a hovel, "with an army of children of all ages squatting round him on the floor," can very well be taken to apply to most of the other inhabitants of that part of the country. Again, among the aboriginal tribes who, specially in the Satpura districts, form so a large portion of the population, and among the Hindu castes of Chhatisgarh, widow remarriage is universal, and if it be the case, as remarked by Mr. Ibbetson in the Punjab Census Report of 1881, that "early marriage by forcing the girl into premature puberty, or at least into child-bearing before she is fully developed, not only reduces the number of wives who survive to become mothers, but lessens their reproductive powers," we get another reason for the increased production of children which most of these districts display, as compared with others where the conditions are adverse to this end. In other words, we find more married women and among them a greater expectation of offspring, and this cannot but have an appreciable effect upon the number of children that are born.

92. The above is a very inadequate review of the age figures, but I have thought it best to avoid all actuarial calculations, partly because of the imperfect nature of the figures on which they must be based, and partly because the subject is a difficult one, demanding more time than I can now spare for its treatment, and I have no desire to publish a mass of undigested statistics from which to deduce imaginary rates of mortality or impossible standards of duration of life.

CHAPTER V.

CIVIL CONDITION.

93. Statistics showing the Civil Condition of the population are given in Table VIII. The subject has already been referred to in the chapter dealing with the variations that have taken place in the number of the people since last census, as marriage, being one of the first factors in the reproduction of the race, must have an important bearing on all questions regarding the growth of the population. Before coming to a review of the figures, it may be as well to premise that those relating to age are necessarily open to question on account of the incorrectness with which, as has been seen, ages have been returned at the Census; in the present chapter the statistics for civil condition will be considered from more than one point of view in connection with age, but in at least two of the modes in which they will be examined it can be seen that inaccurate statement of age will hardly affect the comparisons that are made. On this I shall note when the age statistics come to be discussed.

94. **The record of civil condition.**—At the enumeration the instructions issued for making the return directed that every person should be asked whether he or she was married or not, and that the answer should be put down without further enquiry. In most cases this was supplemented by local instructions, to the effect that the forms of marriage compact, known as *pát* and *churi pahinána*, should be recognized, and persons united by such ties should be recorded as married. The necessity for this arose from the very free manner in which such unions can be contracted and dissolved. This is especially the case in the Chhatisgarh country where, amongst almost all classes, "there is a singular absence of restraint on their women, and a marvellous facility afforded the latter for forming new alliances when those originally contracted have been found distasteful or have been severed by death. These convenient alliances are effected without much ceremony. The parties having agreed, they collect their friends and give a feast, in the course of which the woman is divested of her former ornaments and adorned anew with a great array, perhaps 20 or 30 on each arm, of coloured glass bangles. Having assumed these, she swears fealty before the assembled guests to her new lord, and then takes up a wife's recognized position in her new home. The peculiarity of this arrangement is that the compact is as easily dissolved as contracted, for, if after an interval the woman leaves the house and breaks up the glass bangles on her arm, she is supposed to sever the connection, leaving both parties free to make a fresh selection.*" No special instructions were issued regarding the entry of civil condition for the divorced or for persons between whom a compact of the nature just described has been dissolved, but all such were ordinarily recorded as unmarried.

95. **Scope of the present Chapter.**—As the treatment of the subject of civil condition involves rather elaborate calculations, resulting in perplexing arrays of figures, I shall here set forth the general arrangement which I intend to follow in the review of the subject which will be made in the present Chapter

* Bilaspur Settlement Report, page 63. See also the account of the Chamárs given by Mr. Banerjee in the Census Report for 1881. After describing the remarriage ceremonies of *churi* and *paithu*, Mr. Banerjee remarks that "if the Penal Code were strictly administered in Chhatisgarh, almost every tenth Chamár might be made amenable to one or other of the sections relating to marriage, and a good many women would go to jail for bigamy. But laws which are above the working level of society can scarcely be effectively administered and the law is almost a dead letter in the face of facts which are held to be quite consistent with good sense and Chhatisgarh morality."

First, the civil condition of the total population, irrespective of age, will be noted, and the Province compared in this respect with other parts of India and with one or two European countries. Similarly the statistics of civil condition for each religion may be broadly compared. The age returns will next be taken up and discussed in accordance with the scheme proposed by the Census Commissioner; it will be seen how the persons in each civil condition stand in relation to age, and how those at each age stand in relation to civil condition, while again the number of persons at each age will be compared together by sexes, that is, the proportion of wives to husbands and of widowers to widowed. Any special features regarding the civil condition of the people in any particular part of the Province will last fall to be remarked upon.

96. **Civil condition of the general population.**—The appended statement contrasts the civil condition of the people in the Central Provinces with the results of the census of 1881 and with those of some other provinces returns for which have reached me:

Distribution of 10,000 persons of the population of each Province or Country by Civil Condition.

Province or Country.	Males.			Females.		
	Single.	Married.	Widowed.	Single.	Married.	Widowed.
Central Provinces British Districts, 1881	4,631	4,939	430	3,439	5,080	1,481
Central Provinces British Districts, 1891	4,668	4,890	442	3,560	4,960	1,480
Central Provinces Total	**4,748**	**4,833**	**419**	**3,685**	**4,891**	**1,424**
Berar	3,838	5,588	574	2,635	5,769	1,596
Bombay	4,712	4,812	476	3,238	5,152	1,610
Madras	5,378	4,279	343	3,785	4,363	1,852
N.-W.-P. and Oudh	4,503	4,864	633	3,071	5,253	1,676
England and Wales	6,193	3,463	344	5,928	3,314	758
France	5,513	3,954	533	5,041	3,934	1,025

Comparison with last Census.—One of the most noticeable features in the proportions which have been given is the fall that is apparent in the number of married persons since the last enumeration. Comparison can be made only for the British districts of the Province, as marriage statistics were not collected for the Feudatory States in 1881; in the former there are now only 4,960 women married in every 10,000 of the sex against 5,080 ten years ago, a decline of 120; among males there is a similar falling off amounting to 49. In both cases, as the married have decreased, the number of unmarried has gone up. The explanation is to be found in the fact that there are now a much large number of persons alive in the early years of life than was the case in 1881, as the abstract in the margin shows. As the unmarried state predominates among persons under 15 years of age, the increased proportion of the latter must necessarily be followed by a corresponding rise in the number of unmarried, and this we find to be the case.

	Year.	Males.	Females.
Number of persons aged 0-14 per 10,000 of the total population	1891	4,230	4,110
	1881	*4,142*	*3,997*
Number of unmarried per 10,000 of population	1891	4,668	3,560
	1881	*4,631*	*3,439*

Comparison with other parts of India.—Contrasting the Province with other parts of India, we may note as a most conspicuous point in these returns the low number of widows which we have got, being 1,424 per 10,000 of the whole female population against an average of between 1,600 and 1,800 elsewhere. This is mainly the result of the less restriction which exists in this part of the country upon the remarriage of widows, but some allowance is also to be made for the fact that there are here fewer women alive in the latter years of life than in the other provinces, for which statistics have been compiled. From the abstract accompanying it will be seen that in the Central Provinces there are only 1,370 females in 10,000 living after the age of 45, so that the number of widows must be proportionately less than in places where the average longevity of the female sex is greater. The same is the case also with the widowed among males, but in respect of the latter Madras ranks lowest amongst the provinces given. Similarly, with a surplus of young children such as this Province possesses, the number of unmarried is larger than in places like Berar and the North-West Provinces where, as has been shown at paragraph 87, young children are comparatively in a minority. Madras is conspicuous by the high average of unmarried it returns, more than half its male population being shown as single, so that in the southern Presidency marriages take place in general at an even later age than is the case in this part of India. The proportion between husbands and wives cannot be exactly judged from the statement given, but it will be noticed that the sexes are more equally balanced as regards the married state in the Central Provinces than in the other places shown.

Province.	Number of widows per 10,000 of female population.	Number of females aged 45 and over per 10,000 of female population.
Central Provinces	1,424	1,370
Berar	1,596	1,524
Bombay	1,610	1,453
North-West Provinces and Oudh	1,676	1,632
Madras	1,852	1,522

Comparison with Europe.—Comparing the marriage statistics for an Indian province with those for a European country, the first point that strikes us is the high proportion of married and widowed which is exhibited by the former. In the Central Provinces about half the population is married against only a third in England and Wales. Among widowed the greatest difference is found in the returns for the female sex, there being on an average two widows in India, or at least in this part of it, to one in the mother country. In Europe the number of spinsters is largely in excess of the number of married women, whereas in the East the opposite is the case. The country which most nearly approaches the Indian standard is France, where far more people are married and where there is a larger proportion of widowed than in England.

97. **Civil condition in the several religions.**—The statement appended shows the average number of persons among 10,000 of the followers of each religion who are single, married, or widowed. Amongst Hindus the married state is more common than amongst the general population, the average for which is reduced by the low proportion of married among the aboriginal tribes. With the latter the marriage ceremony does not take place until both bride and bridegroom have reached maturity, though with the spread of Hindu ideas there is in some quarters a tendency for parents to marry their daughters at an early age. That the Hindu practice has not been carried far must, however, be apparent from the high proportion of unmarried among the forest tribes; to the latter the excess of children which we have seen to be characteristic of the aboriginal races must also be taken as contributing. The number of widows is naturally small amongst the aborigines owing to the prevalence of widow marriage.

Distribution of 10,000 persons of each religion by civil condition.

Religion.	Males.			Females.		
	Single.	Married.	Widowed.	Single.	Married.	Widowed.
All religions	4,748	4,833	419	3,685	4,891	1,424
Hindu	4,643	4,935	422	3,562	4,992	1,446
Jain	4,751	4,615	634	2,675	4,642	2,683
Animistic	5,254	4,360	386	4,334	4,440	1,226
Mussalman	4,847	4,662	491	3,529	4,620	1,851
Christian	6,955	2,789	256	5,116	3,841	1,043

"With the Gonds," writes Colonel Ward, "widows are expected to remarry; it may be said to be the general rule, and the Gond customs provide for it in two ways. The first consists simply in the woman proceeding to the house of the man she has agreed to live with after her husband's death. The other is where the younger brother marries the elder brother's widow. This he is expected to do by the custom of the tribe, unless the widow should insist upon making some other arrangement for herself." Among Jains the number of unmarried females is exceedingly low, and the number of widows is very great; it will be noticed that in point of single men the community hardly differs from the general population. Thus, it would seem that Jain girls are married at an early age to men who are considerably their seniors, and to this and to the strict prohibition of remarriage of widows may be assigned the high proportion of the latter which we find among the Jains. Though the remarriage of widows is not forbidden by Mahomedan law, the number of widows among Mussalmans is very much greater than the average of all other communities except the Jain. With regard to this we may note, first, that among Mahomedans the number of women who live to old age is greater than amongst the other races, and second, that whereas among the aborigines and the common Hindu castes who allow widows to remarry such remarriage is so general as almost to be the rule; with Mahomedans there is no such universal custom demanding that women should not be left single after the death of a husband. The statistics for Christians are necessarily distorted in the case of the male sex by the presence of a European army composed of unmarried soldiers; single females are, it will be seen, much in excess of married, due to late marriages; in this respect the returns approach more nearly the European standard.

98. **Civil condition in connection with age.**—Two statements are given on the following page, in which are shown—

(A) the number of persons in each civil condition distributed according to age, and

(B) the number of persons at each age distributed according to civil condition.

It is of course out of the question to note upon half the matters which these tables disclose. After attempting a lengthened review of one of sets of figures I find what I have written to be such a mass of repetition that I think it better to leave the tables to speak for themselves, merely noting on some of the more striking features they present.

I take first the table marked A, which shows the proportion which the single, married, or widowed at any age bear to the total number of persons in each condition. It may be remarked that, like the proportional statements referred to in the last part of the previous chapter, the present table is open to the objection of wrong statement of age, but by adopting, as has been done, large periods of years, we sensibly reduce the amount of error to which these age returns are liable.

A.—Distribution of 10,000 persons of each Civil Condition *by* Age.

Religion.	Civil Condition.	0—14		15—24		25—39		40—49		50 and over.	
		Males.	Females.	Males.	Females.	Males.	Females.	Males.	Females.	Males.	Females.
1	2	3	4	5	6	7	8	9	10	11	12
All Religions	Single	8,408	9,572	1,160	330	343	66	54	16	35	16
	Married	580	1,277	1,721	2,739	4,175	4,144	1,868	1,170	1,656	670
	Widowed	162	109	565	312	2,528	1,747	2,130	2,177	4,615	5,655
Hindu	Single	8,514	9,654	1,081	258	316	58	54	15	35	15
	Married	645	1,412	1,797	2,740	4,127	4,055	1,816	1,141	1,615	652
	Widowed	174	118	578	317	2,534	1,763	2,137	2,178	4,577	5,624
Animistic	Single	8,154	9,257	1,385	617	387	89	46	19	28	18
	Married	273	591	1,328	2,692	4,403	4,613	2,135	1,317	1,861	787
	Widowed	110	63	505	270	2,489	1,599	2,080	2,131	4,816	5,937
Jain	Single	7,092	9,908	1,679	48	885	26	218	2	126	16
	Married	335	1,549	2,064	3,104	4,091	3,867	2,005	1,061	1,505	419
	Widowed	44	118	451	592	2,031	2,540	2,370	2,434	5,104	4,316
Mussalman	Single	7,395	9,467	1,807	360	627	105	103	33	68	35
	Married	234	813	1,436	2,979	4,448	4,354	2,022	1,243	1,860	611
	Widowed	110	65	531	311	2,606	1,780	2,146	2,292	4,607	5,552

Note.—If the numbers in each horizontal line are added separately for each sex, the result is 10,000.

B.—Distribution of 10,000 persons of each age-period *by* Civil Condition.

Religion.	Civil Condition.	All Ages.		0—14		15—24		25—39		40—49		50 and over.	
		Males.	Females.	Males.	Females.	Males.	Females.	Males.	Females.	Males.	Females.	Males.	Females.
1	2	3	4	5	6	7	8	9	10	11	12	13	14
All Religions.	Single	4,748	3,685	9,329	8,464	3,916	807	712	105	254	67	166	51
	Married	4,833	4,891	655	1,499	5,915	8,898	8,825	8,813	8,869	6,442	7,920	2,877
	Widowed	419	1,424	16	37	169	295	463	1,082	877	3,491	1,914	7,072
Hindu.	Single	4,643	3,562	9,239	8,266	3,551	610	641	91	247	59	163	46
	Married	4,935	4,992	744	1,693	6,276	9,085	8,892	8,800	8,861	6,402	7,917	2,844
	Widowed	422	1,446	17	41	173	305	467	1,109	892	3,539	1,920	7,110
Animistic.	Single	5,254	4,334	9,721	9,369	5,489	1,787	917	169	232	97	146	73
	Married	4,360	4,440	269	613	4,364	7,992	8,650	8,972	8,992	6,845	8,017	3,219
	Widowed	386	1,226	10	18	147	221	433	859	776	3,058	1,837	6,708
Jain.	Single	4,751	2,675	9,553	7,793	4,485	80	1,726	28	880	4	553	31
	Married	4,615	4,642	439	2,114	5,354	8,936	7,745	7,228	7,846	4,298	6,444	1,434
	Widowed	634	2,683	8	93	161	984	529	2,744	1,274	5,698	3,003	8,535
Mussalman.	Single	4,847	3,529	9,690	8,961	5,572	815	1,213	156	454	114	295	92
	Married	4,662	4,620	295	1,007	4,261	8,817	8,277	8,459	8,587	5,687	7,698	2,137
	Widowed	491	1,851	15	32	167	368	510	1,385	959	4,199	2,007	7,771

Note.—If the numbers in each vertical line are added separately for each religion the result is 10,000.

Distribution of the unmarried by age.—By far the larger portion of the unmarried are naturally under the age of 15 years. At the other periods we may note the considerable number of men amongst the Jains who remain unmarried at a late stage of life; 12 per cent. of Jain bachelors are aged 25 and over, as compared with 8 per cent. of Mahomedans and 4 per cent. of Hindus. The tendency among Jains to defer marriage until a somewhat advanced age is probably augmented by the fact that many persons belonging to the community in these Provinces are fortune-seekers, who put off marrying until they return to their country with some accumulation of worldly goods. The universal prevalence of the married state among the female sex in this country is very clearly illustrated by the figures which have been given; of unmarried females less than one per cent. are over the age of 25. The low proportion may be, in some measure, due to concealment of age, as there is a wide-spread and deep-rooted feeling of shame attaching to the presence in the family of an unmarried woman after this time of life. But, as this is also the very reason which induces parents to see that their daughters are married early in life, it may be taken that the low average of unmarried elderly females is a fair enough approximation to the actual facts. Many of them are probably women of immoral life, whilst others may have been unable to find a husband through deformity or for other reasons; but old maids in the home sense of the term are few and far between in India.

Distribution of the married by age.—At the first age-period, 0—14 years, the Jains return the highest proportion of married females on the total of the sex in that condition, over 15 per cent. of their married women being under 15 years of age against 14 per cent. among Hindus, 8 per cent. among Mahomedans, and 6 per cent. among aborigines. Though the Jains marry their daughters at a tender age, it will be observed that they marry their sons much later in life than Hindus; of married Hindu males over 6 per cent. are under 15 years of age, while among Jains only 3 per cent. of the married are boys under that age. Between the ages of 15 and 24 the Jains still occupy a leading position as regards the number of married females; at this time also the proportion of married among the male sex is higher in the case of the Jains than of the other races. Among the followers of every religion the married state is most prevalent between the ages of 25 and 39; at this period and in the more advanced years of life, it is further to be noted that amongst aborigines, and to a certain extent also amongst Mahomedans, the proportion of married of both sexes is considerably in excess of what obtains among the Hindus and Jains, with whom early marriage is more common.

Distribution of the widowed by age.—The most marked results are to be seen, as usual, in the Jain community. Had we separate statistics for the higher castes of Hindus, we should find almost the identically same features of early marriage and enforced widowhood among them as are apparent in the case of the Jains, but as no distinction has been preserved between the higher castes and those lower in the social scale, and as, moreover, amongst Hindus have been included a host of semi-Hinduised aborigines, the significance of the returns is to a great extent destroyed. Nearly one-third, 32·5 per cent., of Jain widows are under 40 years of age, against 21·6 per cent. among Mahomedans, and 19·3 per cent. among aborigines.

99. **Civil condition of the people at each age-period.**—I next come to the distribution of persons at each age-period according to civil condition, details for which have been set forth in statement B above. The proportions given in this table are of more than ordinary significance, as it can be seen that they are little affected by mis-statement of age or by fluctuations in the number of children among the different races. We are not comparing one age-period with another, but have only to look how the people of any given age, be they few or many, are situated as to civil condition, and as any inaccuracy in the return of age will

naturally affect both sexes alike, we can also see how the sexes stand when compared together in this respect. I have had worked out statistics for every district of the Province in the form which is subjoined, but as little could be made out of such a wilderness of figures as results, I give on the next page the returns for only six districts which may be looked upon as more or less representative.

Comparison by religions.—It is hardly necessary to go over this ground again. The same features can be observed as have been noted on in the last paragraph of early marriage and consequent early widowhood among Jain females, of late marriage among the Mahomedans and the aboriginal races, and of the very small number of females amongst all classes of the community who remain unmarried after middle age. As the figures are now presented, prominence is given to the fact that between the ages of 15 and 24 so many as 18 per cent. of the female sex among the aboriginal tribes remain unwed; among Mahomedans only 8, and among Hindus 6 per cent. of the women of this age are single, while among Jains the proportion falls below 1 per cent. The explanation is to be found in the fact that 16 or 17 years is a common age for the marriage of girls among the forest tribes, so that at the commencement of the age-period entered in the table many are still unmarried.

Comparison by districts.—One of the first things to note in the district returns is the extent to which early marriage takes place in different parts of the Province. To begin with, the high average of the married under 15 years of age in Raipur may be remarked. In Chhatisgarh there are few representatives of the better Hindu castes, amongst whom child marriage is more of an established institution, but despite this fact we can see that early marriage prevails to a considerable degree. In Raipur and Bilaspur in every 10,000 boys under 15 years of age, 877 and 924 respectively are married; in Saugor the proportion is as low as 413. Among girls the preponderance of married is not so great in comparison with other parts of the country, but the proportion is still very considerable, being 1,597 per 10,000 in Raipur, and 1,667 in Bilaspur. In Saugor, Damoh and Hoshangabad child marriage is not nearly so prevalent as it is usually taken to be, the proportion of married females under 15 years of age being 1,471 in Saugor, 1,380 in Damoh, and 1,403 in Hoshangabad. The districts where the custom most prevails are Jubbulpore with an average of 1,789 girl wives Nimar 1,844, Wardha 2,741, Nagpur 2,466, and Chanda 2,023. The matter will be further referred to below in connection with the subject of infant marriage.

Next we may note the high average of the male sex who in the northern districts remain unmarried until late in life. In Saugor nearly half the men between 15 and 24 years of age are bachelors; in Raipur the proportion falls below one-third. Between 25 and 39 there are still a large number of men unmarried in Saugor, one man in every ten being single. Though the male sex marries late in these northern districts, there is no such delay in the case of females; the subject has already been referred to in the previous chapter in connection with the tendency which is taken to exist towards male children being born of unions in which the ages of the husband and wife are so disproportionate as they are here found to be. In the districts where the aboriginal population is large, we discover a high proportion of females unmarried between the ages of 15 and 24. Mandla is to some extent exceptional, but in Chhindwara 1,235 females in 10,000 are unmarried at this time of life; in Betul 1,559, and in Balaghat 1,319; the reason is that given in the previous paragraph, *viz.* that girls are not generally married among the aborigines until 16 or 17 years of age, so a considerable portion of their number at the beginning of the age-period in question are still single.

Distribution of 10,000 persons of each age-period by civil condition in certain districts.

(a)—Males.

Civil condition.	District.	All ages.	0—14	15—24.	25—39.	40—49.	50 and over.
1	2	3	4	5	6	7	8
Single.	Saugor	4,925	9,575	4,415	1,196	574	376
	Mandla	5,061	9,315	3,754	739	260	194
	Narsinghpur	4,599	9,261	3,863	775	318	208
	Wardha	3,972	9,217	3,173	536	238	160
	Raipur	4,591	9,107	2,812	391	132	82
	Sambalpur	4,878	9,437	3,550	427	132	108
Married.	Saugor	4,482	413	5,389	8,117	8,088	6,907
	Mandla	4,598	669	6,044	8,803	8,948	8,115
	Narsinghpur	4,812	714	5,877	8,507	8,494	7,262
	Wardha	5,473	765	6,679	9,024	8,808	7,673
	Raipur	5,059	877	6,997	9,179	9,150	8,377
	Sambalpur	4,815	556	6,340	9,201	9,123	8,264
Widowed.	Saugor	593	12	196	687	1,338	2,717
	Mandla	341	16	202	458	792	1,691
	Narsinghpur	589	25	260	718	1,188	2,530
	Wardha	555	18	148	440	954	2,167
	Raipur	350	16	191	430	718	1,541
	Sambalpur	307	7	110	372	745	1,628

(b)—Females.

Civil condition.	District.	All ages.	0—14	15—24.	25—39.	40—49.	50 and over.
Single.	Saugor	3,435	8,484	302	66	48	33
	Mandla	4,062	8,616	735	108	58	56
	Narsinghpur	3,253	8,222	376	46	27	29
	Wardha	2,753	7,197	231	67	41	32
	Raipur	3,647	8,377	526	81	52	25
	Sambalpur	4,031	8,768	1,056	158	104	74
Married.	Saugor	4,698	1,471	9,087	7,970	5,047	1,959
	Mandla	4,751	1,354	9,014	8,897	6,382	2,805
	Narsinghpur	4,992	1,724	9,228	8,486	5,518	2,148
	Wardha	5,637	2,741	9,520	8,913	6,660	2,797
	Raipur	5,032	1,597	9,269	9,139	7,076	3,261
	Sambalpur	4,728	1,207	8,691	8,801	6,393	3,096
Widowed.	Saugor	1,867	45	611	1,964	4,905	8,008
	Mandla	1,187	30	251	995	3,560	7,139
	Narsinghpur	1,755	54	396	1,468	4,455	7,823
	Wardha	1,610	62	249	1,020	3,299	7,171
	Raipur	1,321	26	205	780	2,872	6,704
	Sambalpur	1,241	25	253	1,041	3,503	6,830

Explanation.—The Table should be read thus. Of every 10,000 males between 0 and 14 years of age in the Saugor district, 9,575 are single, 413 are married, and 12 are widowed; between the ages of 15 and 24, 4,415 in every 10,000 are single, 5,389 are married, and 196 are widowed.

The prevalence of the married state among adults in those districts where remarriage of widows is chiefly practised is also worthy of note. The matter is of some importance as bearing upon the increase in the population, and has in this connection been referred to at paragraph 28 of Chapter II. Conversely, we find in the districts mentioned comparatively few persons living in widowhood, specially in the middle periods of life; in Saugor of every 10,000 females between the ages of 25 and 39, 1,964 are widowed, and in Narsinghpur, 1,468, while in Mandla the proportion is 995, and in Raipur it falls as low as 780. The late age at which men marry in the northern districts must also conduce to an excess of widows, as the old husbands must die off more rapidly than their youthful wives.

100. **Child marriage.**—A very important question in connection with these returns is whether they furnish us with any sign that child marriage is on the decrease. In 1881 no detail of age was kept under the age of 10 years, but in the accompanying abstract I give the figures for two intermediate periods which have been shown in our tables at the present Census, as well as compare the results of the two enumerations with regard to children under 10. It is of course chiefly in respect of female children that the question of early marriage may be properly said to arise, and it is therefore to them that the proportions given have reference. The districts of the Nagpur plain are the part of the Province where the practice of girl marriage most obtains,—in Wardha, of girls under the age of 10, 12 per cent. are married, in Nagpur 10·1, and in Chanda 9·4,—and it is to its prevalence among the Hindu castes of this part of the country that the provincial average for Hindus is brought so high. Jains marry 4·7 per cent. of their daughters at this age, and Mahomedans 2·6, while among the aboriginal tribes the proportion falls to 1·9 per cent. Among the followers of every religion, except Mahomedans, there is a slight decrease in the extent of child marriage within the last ten years, and the same is observable in the returns of every district given, except Mandla. It is probable that the decline may have been, to some degree, affected by the agitation which there was, just previous to the Census, in connection with the Criminal Law Amendment Act, which has raised the age of consent to 12 years, but how far the statistics may have been influenced in this respect it is impossible to say.

Percentage of females between the ages of 0—9 who are married.

(*a*) Districts.

Districts.	1891. 0—4	1891. 5—9	1891. 0—9	1881. 0—9
Saugor	0·5	5·2	2·9	3·6
Jubbulpore	1·1	12·1	6·8	7·0
Mandla	1·4	8·5	4·9	4·0
Narsinghpur	0·7	10·2	5·4	6·4
Wardha	1·6	22·7	12·0	15·1
Nagpur	1·3	18·9	10·1	10·7
Chanda	2·4	16·8	9·4	11·3
Bhandara	1·2	12·7	6·8	8·4
Raipur	1·4	12·1	6·6	8·0
Sambalpur	0·4	4·7	2·6	3·0
British Districts	1·2	11·2	6·2	6·9

(*b*) Religions.

Religions	1891. 0—4	1891. 5—9	1891. 0—9	1881. 0—9
Hindus	1·3	13·0	7·1	8·1
Mussalmans	0·5	4·6	2·6	2·6
Jains	0·5	8·7	4·7	6·4
Animistic	0·6	3·2	1·9	2 1

Marriage under the age of 5 years takes place amongst several of the castes in the Maratha districts, but is not very common elsewhere, except in the districts of Jubbulpore and Mandla. In the latter district the proportion of married girls even among the forest tribes is high, amounting to 3·5 per cent. under the age of 10 years, or nearly double the provincial average for the aboriginal races. To the ultra-Hinduism of the Raj Gonds of Mandla, reference will be found in the chapter on Caste, where an extract on the subject from Colonel Ward's Settlement Report of the district, page 130, has been given.

101. **The proportion between the sexes in each civil condition.**—A statement showing the number of females per 1,000 males in each civil condition at the different age-periods is given on the next page. Similar proportions are shown for the followers of each religion, but omitting detail of age. With regard to the latter, the ratios which I had had worked out simply point to the same general conclusions as have already been noticed, so it would hardly be worth while to publish them. It would also have to be considered that these ratios must be affected by the variation in the proportions between the sexes at different periods of life; if for instance among the forest tribes there are 1,144 females per 1,000 males between the ages of 15 and 24, the ratios shown for each civil condition can hardly be compared with similar averages among the Jains, where the female sex is in a pronounced minority at this age.

The comparison by age calls for little comment. Between the ages of 15 and 40 the number of spinsters is very small compared with the number of bachelors; to every 10 of the latter there are on an average, about 2 of the former. Married women are in excess of men up till middle age, after which husbands are more numerous than wives, the balance being turned by the excess of widows. That there is not more disproportion among the widowed when compared by sexes, is a matter for surprise, but the explanation lies in the universality with which the practice of widow remarriage obtains among the aboriginals and all the common Hindu castes. Among Jains, on the other hand, we find 11 widows to every widower under 15 years of age, and 5 widows to every widower between the ages of 15 and 40; the same would, no doubt, be observable among the better classes of Hindus, but the returns are obscured by the overwhelming preponderance of the lower castes.

Number of females per 1,000 males of the same age and civil condition.

Age-period.	Single.	Married.	Widowed.	Total population.
0—14	880	2,218	2,274	970
15—24	220	1,604	1,869	1,066
25—39	149	1,000	2,339	1,002
40—49	229	631	3,459	869
50 and over	347	408	4,188	1,122
All ages	773	1,008	3,385	996

Comparison by religions.—Omitting the detail of age, we find that there are, in general, more wives than husbands among Hindus and aborigines, and more husbands than wives among Jains and Mahomedans. Polygamy is most common among the forest tribes, where between 3 and 4 men in every hundred have a second wife. The disproportion between the married in the Mahomedan and Jain communities is to be set down to migration. In the districts where there have been little or no immigration from a distance, such as Seoni, Chhindwara, Balaghat, Bhandara and Raipur, wives nearly equal, and sometimes out-number, husbands among Mahomedans. On the other hand in places like Saugor, Jubbulpore, Nimar, and Nagpur the number of married men who are temporarily residents in these parts as soldiers or in service of one kind or another, leads to an excess of married men over women. The same is the case with the Jains, many of whom leave their wives and families in their country and come here only as temporary sojourners.

Number of females per 1,000 males of same civil condition.

Religion.	Single.	Married.	Widowed.	Total of religion.
All religions	773	1,008	3,385	996
Hindu	763	1,006	3,405	994
Jain	539	962	4,047	957
Animistic	837	1,034	3,223	1,015
Mussalman	889	937	3,566	946

Comparison by Districts.—The statement accompanying shows the number of wives per 1,000 husbands for each district of the Province. As the aboriginal races return a superabundance of married women, I have added a column exhibiting the ratios which obtain in all districts where they are numerous. There are fewer wives than husbands in the four districts which form the northern border of the Province, Saugor, Damoh, Hoshangabad, and Nimar, due, presumably, to immigration from other parts of India of married men unaccompanied by their wives. The same cause has no doubt also conduced to this result in Sambalpur, where there were many persons temporarily resident in the district in connection with the railway construction which was taking place at the time of the Census. So far as I am aware, there can be no other cause than immigration of married males, for husbands being in excess of wives; but it is worthy of note that in all the southern parts of the Province, in Chanda, Bastar, Kanker, and generally in the Uria states, this result is observable. Among the aboriginal races of the southern states, the custom which ordains that the younger brother should take his elder brother's widow to wife is very exceptionally practised, and again the strangers who have penetrated these wilds would naturally leave their wives behind them, so that for both reasons a dearth of married women might be expected. The districts where we find polygamy to be most common are those on the Satpuras; here the practice just referred to is usual among the aboriginal races.

Number of wives per 1,000 husbands, British districts.

Districts.	Total population.	Animistic religion.
Saugor	981	...
Damoh	993	...
Jubbulpore	1,005	1,040
Narsinghpur	1,031	1,059
Hoshangabad	987	1,055
Nimar	973	...
Mandla	1,014	1,050
Seoni	1,021	1,068
Chhindwara	1,036	1,060
Betul	1,016	1,035
Wardha	1,001	1,043
Nagpur	1,006	1,015
Bhandara	1,035	1,069
Balaghat	1,035	1,073
Chanda	979	992
Raipur	1,037	1,054
Bilaspur	1,031	1,044
Sambalpur	989	992
British Territory	**1,012**	**1,045**
Feudatory States	**982**	**997**
Total Central Provinces	**1,008**	**1,034**

102. **Marriage statistics for Christians.**—In the preceding paragraphs no note has been made of the marriage statistics for Christians or for followers of the other religions, which are hardly represented in these Provinces. In the case of Christians the returns are affected to such an extent in respect of the male sex by the presence of the European troops that hardly any remark regarding them seems necessary. As in 1881, so at the present Census a certain number of children under 10 and still more between 10 and 15 years of age, are shown as married; it is probable that these results in the case of the earlier age are in some degree due to mistakes in record or abstraction; 12 children, 7 boys and 5 girls

are recorded as married under the age of 10, and 43 between the ages of 10 and 15. Between the ages of 15 and 24, 42 per cent. of the women are single, but at the next period, 25 to 39 years, only 8 per cent. remain unmarried. There are, on an average, 91 wives to every 100 husbands among Christians; in the European community the wives of many of the married men are resident in Europe. Similarly among the Parsis we find only 64 wives to every 100 husbands, the latter very commonly leave their wives behind them in their settled place of abode.

CHAPTER VI.

INFIRMITIES.

103. **The record of Infirmities.**—The infirm regarding whom information has been obtained at the Census are (1) the Insane, (2) Deaf-mutes, (3) the Blind, and (4) Lepers. In the case of deaf-mutes only those persons were to be entered in the schedules who were both deaf and dumb from birth; for the blind only blindness of both eyes was to be recorded; and for the leprous only true or corrosive leprosy. Instructions to these effects were issued to the enumerators, but there can hardly be a doubt that they have not been in all cases very literally carried out; wrong entries were not infrequently discovered when the results were being worked out. As regards insanity no attempt was made to distinguish between the imbecile and the insane—the matter would be beyond the understanding of the ordinary enumerator—,so the return we have got must to some extent include both. The record of deaf-muteness gave some trouble in abstraction, entries of "deaf" alone or of "dumb" alone being now and again met with. The former had perforce to be left out of account, but the latter was taken as an infirmity, the word employed generally signifying deaf-muteness. About the blind there was hardly any chance of mistake, but in the case of leprosy there is scarcely a doubt that the record is far from correct; in the first place, we cannot always be certain that white leprosy has not now and again been returned instead of black; while, on the other hand, we may take it that there has been some amount of concealment of the infirmity, especially in the case of females.

The infirmity statistics are divided into two parts in the Final Tables contained in the second volume; the afflicted are first shown according to certain specified age-periods—Tables XII to XV,—and again according to castes, tribes and races—Tables XII A to XV A. In the remarks which follow I shall begin by noting on the prevalence of each infirmity in different localities, comparing at the same time the provincial results with those of other parts of India, for which I am in possession of figures. The number of infirm at different ages will next be examined, while lastly note may be made of the proportions who are afflicted in the several castes or tribes.*

PERSONS OF UNSOUND MIND.

104. **Comparison with last Census and with other Provinces.**—There are in the Central Provinces 2,034 persons of unsound mind, of whom 1,758 are in British districts, and 276 in the Feudatory States. In other words one person in every 6,364 is insane; in British districts one in 6,129, and in the Feudatory States one in 7,827. The decrease at the present Census is most marked, but it may be observed Berar and the North-West Provinces and Oudh show exactly similar results. In Berar in 1881 one person was insane in every 3,212 as against one in 6,062 at the present enumeration, and in the North-West Provinces and Oudh one in 6,949 ten years ago

Insanes—British Districts.

Year.	Number of insanes.	Number of persons among whom one is insane.
1872	1,612	5,743
1881	2,528	4,568
1891	1,758	6,129

* To save multiplication of tables the caste, etc., statistics will be considered for all the infirmities together Reference to this matter will not therefore be found in the separate sections of the chapter which deal with individual infirmities.

against 8,404 in 1891. Such violent changes can hardly be accounted for in any other way than by variation in the system of enumeration. At the present Census we have tended to go back to the standard of 1872, as will be seen from the abstract which I have given.

The relative prevalence of insanity in some of the other Indian Provinces for which results have reached me are noted in the margin. I have added also the proportions for one or two European countries, the returns given being those of the preceding Census. The striking difference exhibited between the average of insane in this country and among most European nations, has been the subject of frequent remark. The fact is usually attributed to the intemperate habits of the labouring classes in the west and to the greater mental strain and anxieties of modern civilized life.

Province or Country.	In 10,000 persons of each sex the average number who are insane.	
	Males.	Females.
North-West Provinces and Oudh	1·6	·8
Berar	1·9	1·4
Central Provinces	2·0	1·1
Madras	2·5	1·8
Burma	9·8	8·3
Italy	8	6
England and Wales	31	33
United States of America	35	32
Scotland	38	39

105. **District distribution of persons of unsound mind.**—In the accompanying table I have arranged the districts of the Province in the order in which they stand as regards the proportion of insane among their population. The figures given for Jubbulpore and Nagpur are abnormal on account of their including the inmates of the lunatic asylums, which these districts contain. During the year 1890 the number of patients in the Jubbulpore asylum was 156 and in Nagpur 152. Putting aside these two districts, we are left with the districts of Narsinghpur and Nimar in the Nerbada valley and the districts on the Satpuras at the head of the list, as regards the prevalence of insanity. It is, perhaps, rather bordering on theory to attempt to assign reasons for their position in this respect; but if it be taken that the chief predisposing causes to insanity in this country are the intemperate use of noxious drugs and indulgence in strong liquor, we have here in part a reason for insanity being specially a feature of the Nerbada valley and of the Satpura hill country. In the former we find a considerable population of semi-Hinduized aborigines, who have copied only too readily the vices of the northern races by whom they were overrun; the besotted condition of many of the Bhils, Gonds and of the other village drudges of the Nerbada districts has long been a matter of common note, and in this respect they are closely run by some of the immigrant races themselves. On the Satpuras the craving for drink is a failing not only of the aboriginal tribes but of several of the cultivating and industrial castes as well. Turning to the east of the Province, the spread of the Kabirpanthi and Satnami doctrines has certainly induced habits of sobriety among the inhabitants of the Chhatisgarh plain, and to this may in

District Distribution of Insanes.

District.	Number of Insanes.	Number of persons among whom one is insane.
Jubbulpore	244	3,066
Nagpur	220	3,353
Narsinghpur	89	4,124
Chhindwara	87	4,684
Betul	68	4,753
Nimar	50	5,070
Seoni	70	5,297
Mandla	60	5,656
Wardha	68	5,895
Hoshangabad	89	5,954
Saugor	94	6,295
Balaghat	55	6,970
Damoh	41	7,942
Sambalpur	98	8,127
Bilaspur	124	9,388
Bhandara	78	9,524
Chanda	73	9,556
Raipur	144	11,003
British Districts	1,758	6,129
Feudatory States	276	7,827
Central Provinces	2,034	6,364

some degree be assigned the low average of insanity which we find throughout this part of the country.

106. **Comparison by Age and Sex.**—In the accompanying abstract is shown, (1) the distribution of 1,000 persons of unsound mind by age, and (2) the proportion of afflicted to the total number of persons at each age-period. It will be seen that it is in the prime of life that insanity is most prevalent, and that it attacks females at a much earlier age than males. More than a fourth of the insane of the female sex are girls or young women between the ages of 10 and 20 years. From the proportions given in columns 4 and 5 we gather that the value of the life of the insane decreases with advancing years at a faster rate than that of the general population. At all ages there are more persons of unsound mind among males than among females; the average of the latter tends, however, to rise in old age.

Age and Sex Distribution of the Insane.

Age-period.	Proportion at each age of 1,000 afflicted.		Proportion of afflicted to 10,000 persons at each age.		Afflicted Females per 100 Males.
	Males.	Females.	Males.	Females.	
1	2	3	4	5	6
0—9	67	*80*	·4	*·3*	68
10—19	174	*265*	1·8	*1·8*	87
20—29	221	*196*	2·8	*1·3*	51
30—39	251	*208*	3·4	*1·7*	48
40—49	161	*129*	3·2	*1·7*	46
50—59	77	*69*	2·8	*1·5*	52
60 and over	49	*53*	2·1	*·9*	61
All Ages	1,000	*1,000*	2 0	*1·1*	57

DEAF-MUTES.

107. **Comparison with last Census and with other Provinces.**—The number of deaf-mutes returned at the Census was 6,440, being 5,463 in the British districts of the Province and 977 in the Feudatory States. Comparison with the returns of the two previous enumerations is made in the marginal statement. As was the case with insanes, so also in respect of the deaf and dumb, the figures more nearly approach the results of 1872 than those of 1881. On the latter they show a decided falling off, there being now one insane in every 2,010 persons against one in 1,720 at the previous Census.

Deaf-mutes—British Districts.

Year.	Number of deaf-mutes.	Number of persons among whom one is deaf-mute.
1872	4,185	*2,212*
1881	6,712	*1,720*
1891	5,463	*2,010*

In the accompanying abstract the prevalence of the infirmity in some of the other provinces of India and in one or two European countries, is compared with the results which we have got. In respect of deaf-muteness it will be observed that in general the statistics for most of the Indian provinces differ but slightly from the European standard, though in both the east and west there are some noticeable divergences from the usual average.

Province or Country.	In 10,000 persons of each sex the average number who are deaf and dumb.	
	Males.	Females.
Berar	2·1	1·5
Burma	5·5	4·7
Central Provinces	5·7	4·2
Madras	8·3	6·2
N.-W. Provinces and Oudh	8·7	5·1
Scotland	3	2
England and Wales	6	5
United States of America	7	6
Austria	15	11

108. **District Distribution of Deaf-mutes.**—The districts are here arranged serially in the order in which they stand as regards the relative proportion of afflicted. Assuming the return to be, as it purports, a record of congenital deaf-mutism only, the district distribution hardly helps us to an explanation of the probable tendencies which conduce to the infirmity. Amongst these, the most commonly accepted is consanguineous marriages, but there could hardly be differences in this respect so great as to place Hoshangabad and Narsinghpur at the head of the list, while the districts of Nimar and Jubbulpore, which adjoin these, come at the other end. The Satpura districts again stand high as regards the number of afflicted they contain. In 1881 Sambalpur, where now the number of deaf-mutes is abnormally low, far exceeded all the other districts in point of prevalence of the infirmity. In the Uria states one person is deaf and dumb in every 2,249, also a low average, so that it is impossible to account for the high figures of the previous Census That such variations should occur shows how uncertain is the record obtained regarding the infirmity. Omission to note that only persons deaf and dumb *from birth* should be entered in the schedules, and the temptation to record persons whose sole ailment is dullness of hearing, have necessarily perturbed the returns.

District Distribution of Deaf-mutes.

District.	Number of deaf-mutes.	Number of persons among whom one is deaf-mute.
Hoshangabad	385	1,376
Chanda	473	1,475
Narsinghpur	238	1,542
Seoni	234	1,584
Betul	187	1,734
Bhandara	417	1,781
Mandla	187	1,815
Nagpur	410	1,848
Balaghat	205	1,870
Chhindwara	210	1,940
Bilaspur	581	2,004
Wardha	196	2,045
Damoh	154	2,114
Saugor	252	2,348
Jubbulpore	318	2,353
Raipur	647	2,449
Nimar	91	2,786
Sambalpur	278	2,865
British Districts	5,463	1,974
Feudatory States	977	2,211
Total Central Provinces	6,440	2,010

109. **Comparision by Age and Sex.**—This will appear from the table which I append. As we are dealing with congenital deaf-mutism it must follow that the greatest number of afflicted should be found in the earlier years of life before their ranks have been thinned by death. This we see to be the case, although the figures for the first decade are to some extent abnormal, as there would naturally be some hesitation in showing as deaf-mutes young children who might be late in developing the power of speech. Could we be certain that the returns do not include persons who have contracted deafness with failing years, the proportions given in columns 4 and 5 would point to there being greater longevity among the deaf and dumb than among the population at large. Passing their lives in comparative freedom from toil, many of them no doubt live to a good old age, but the large rise in their strength, when measured by the ratio they bear to their equals in years, is to be attributed as much perhaps to mis-

taken record as to actual long-livedness among the infirm. This would seem to

Age and Sex Distribution of Deaf-mutes.

Age-period.	Proportion at each age of 1,000 afflicted.		Proportion of afflicted to 10,000 persons at each age.		Afflicted Females per 100 Males.
	Males.	Females.	Males.	Females.	
1	2	3	4	5	6
0—9	191	*198*	3·6	*2·6*	75
10—19	227	*206*	6·8	*5·2*	66
20—29	175	*173*	6·5	*4·2*	72
30—39	154	*135*	6·1	*4·1*	64
40—49	112	*98*	6·3	*4·6*	64
50—59	68	*72*	7·3	*5·8*	77
60 and over	73	*118*	8·8	*8·0*	118
All Ages	1,000	1,000	5·7	4·2	73

be specially the case in the return of females, the number of old women shown as deaf and dumb being to all appearance unduly large.

THE BLIND.

110. Comparison with last Census and with other Provinces.—

The Blind—British Districts.

Year.	Number of Blind.	Number of persons among whom one is blind.
1872	12,003	*771*
1881	25,260	*457*
1891	18,567	*581*

There are 20,470 blind persons in the Province, of whom 18,567 are in British districts and 1,903 in the Feudatory States. In other words, there is one person blind in every 632 of the population, being one in 581 in British territory and one in 1,135 in the Feudatories. As in the case of the infirmities before noticed, the returns of the present Census show a remarkable falling off, as compared with those of ten years ago. There are now three blind persons for every four there were in 1881; in 1872 there were only two on a like proportion. There can ordinarily be little mistake about the enumeration of the blind, so the decrease in their number at the present Census as compared with that preceding—a decrease which is common to other provinces as well as this—must be looked upon as a satisfactory result of the spread of vaccination, and of the greater readiness of the people to avail themselves of medical treatment for the infirmity.

Compared with other provinces this part of the country returns a comparatively low average of blindness. An examination of the district figures in the next paragraph will show, however, that in the tracts which border on Berar and in those which more resemble Northern India, the numbers of the blind are even greater than they are in those parts of India. In Berar one person in every 428 is blind, and in the North-West Provinces and Oudh, one in 427; this average is surpassed by the proportion of the infirm in Saugor, Jubbulpore,

Province or Country.	In 10,000 persons of each sex the average number who are blind.	
	Males.	Females.
Madras	9·7	*9·9*
Central Provinces	14·4	*17·0*
Burma	17·2	*22·9*
Berar	22·7	*24·1*
N.-W. P. and Oudh	22·8	*24·1*
Italy	8	*7*
England and Wales	9	*8*
Ireland	11	*12*
United States of America	10	*9*

Narsinghpur and Hoshangabad and is closely approached by that in Wardha and Damoh.

111. District Distribution of the Blind.—The arrangement of the districts of the Province as regards the prevalence of blindness closely follows that which resulted at the last Census. The comparative immunity of the Uria country from the infirmity is as marked now as it was then shown to be. Taking the Uria Feudatory States by themselves, we find the proportion of the afflicted to be as low as one person in 1,406; in Sambalppr there is only one person blind in 1,522. Another noticeable feature about the Uria country is the fact that there are more blind men than women, there being 714 of the former to 684 of the latter. Everywhere else the prevalence of the infirmity is shown to be greater among females than among males. It seems impossible to account for the remarkable variations that are apparent between the districts in the north and west of the Province and those in the centre, south and east, in any other way than by the different character of the country. Something may, perhaps, be said for the fact that in the former there are more old people than in the latter, and as blindness to a great extent comes with age, the number of blind will naturally be greater in places where there are many old. On the other hand, in the nine districts which stand at the head of the list, the people are probably better housed and are more cleanly in their habits than in the remaining nine, so that they should be less liable to blindness on this account than otherwise. Neither can the greater prevalence of the infirmity be assigned to small-pox, a common source of blindness in this country, as the ravages of the disease are by no means more severe in the northern districts than in the other parts of the Province.

District Distribution of the Blind.

DISTRICT.	Number of blind.	Number of persons among whom one is blind.
Narsinghpur	1,134	*323*
Hoshangabad	1,489	*355*
Saugor	1,583	*373*
Jubbulpore	1,987	*376*
Wardha	917	*437*
Damoh	742	*438*
Seoni	735	*504*
Nimar	488	*519*
Nagpur	1,226	*618*
Bilaspur	1,808	*643*
Raipur	2,275	*696*
Betul	459	*704*
Balaghat	535	*716*
Chhindwara	568	*717*
Mandla	447	*759*
Chanda	855	*815*
Bhandara	796	*933*
Sambalpur	523	*1,522*
British Districts	**18,567**	**581**
Feudatory States	**1,903**	**1,135**
Central Provinces	**20,470**	**632**

112.—Comparison by Age and Sex.—From the table here given it

Age and Sex Distribution of the Blind.

AGE-PERIOD.	PROPORTION AT EACH AGE OF 1,000 AFFLICTED.		PROPORTION OF AFFLICTED TO 10,000 PERSONS AT EACH AGE.		AFFLICTED FEMALES PER 100 MALES.
	Males.	Females.	Males.	Females.	
1	2	3	4	5	6
0—9	118	*70*	5·5	*3·8*	70
10—19	132	*83*	10·0	*8·4*	73
20—29	128	*101*	12·0	*10·0*	93
30—39	136	*123*	13·5	*15·2*	108
40—49	140	*131*	19·9	*25·4*	111
50—59	112	*127*	29·9	*39·1*	127
60 and over	234	*365*	71·7	*102·2*	184
All Ages	1,000	*1,000*	14·4	*170*	118

will appear that blindness is specially an infirmity of the old. A third of the blind among males and a half among females are over the age of 50 years. Its increasing prevalence in the later years of life can be seen from the high proportion which the number of blind bears to the total of persons alive in old age. Amongst old women the percentage of the afflcted amounts to over one per cent.; in Narsinghpur the proportion rises to one blind in 57, in Saugor one in 54, in Hoshangabad one in 55, and in Wardha one in 61.

LEPERS.

113. Comparison with last Census and with other Provinces.—The number of persons returned as lepers is 6,614; in British districts 5,355, and in the Feudatory States 1,259. There is thus one person afflicted with leprosy in over 1,957 of the population, the proportion being one in 2,014 in British territory and one in 1,716 in the Feudatories. Again we find the figures of the present Census to show a decline on the high average of 1881. In Berar and in the North-West Provinces and Oudh there has similarly been a decrease in the numbers of persons returned as smitten with the disease.

Lepers—British Districts.

YEAR.	Number of lepers.	Number of persons among whom one is a leper.
1872 . . .	2,807	3,298
1881 . . .	6,443	1,804
1891 . . .	5,355	2,014

In the Province as a whole leprosy is more common than in Madras and Northern India, but it does not prevail to anything like the extent which we find in the Berars. As will be seen from the next paragraph, however, the Wardha district is even more affected than Berar; in the latter there is one leper in every 783 persons, while in Wardha the proportion is one in 772.

PROVINCE.	IN 10,000 PERSONS THE AVERAGE NUMBER WHO ARE LEPERS.	
	Males.	Females.
Madras . . .	5·4	1·8
North-West Provinces and Oudh.	5·7	1·3
Central Provinces . .	6·7	3·5
Burma . . .	11·7	5·1
Berar . . .	19·3	5·8

114. District Distribution of Lepers.—The table here given presents the most remarkable variations in the prevalence of the disease. Throughout the Nagpur country and Chhatisgarh it is much more rife than in the districts of the north and centre of the Province. The number of lepers in the districts of Wardha and Nagpur is especially great, but even there it is hardly likely that we have a complete return of all the persons who are afflicted. Dr. Harris, the Civil Surgeon of Nagpur, has informed me that in the Nagpur district the number of lepers is certainly greater than the Census returns bring out. The record, as has already been remarked, is by no means easy to make; incipient cases are overlooked, and there is no doubt some concealment of the disease. The inferences to be drawn from the d strict figures are, of course, a matter for professional opinion, but it seems clear that the disease has got a firmer hold

District Distribution of Lepers.

DISTRICT.	Number of lepers.	Number of persons among whom one is a leper.
Wardha	519	772
Nagpur	773	980
Raipur	1,073	1,476
Bhandara	471	1,577
Chanda	423	1,649
Bilaspur	635	2,305
Sambalpur	312	2,552
Nimar	99	2,560
Hoshangabad	205	2,585
Chhindwara	153	2,663
Balaghat	126	3,042
Saugor	154	3,842
Betul	81	3,990
Narsinghpur	91	4,033
Mandla	54	6,099
Seoni	60	6,179
Jubbulpore	102	7,334
Damoh	24	13,567
British Districts . . .	**5,355**	**2,014**
Feudatory States . . .	**1,259**	**1,716**
Central Provinces . . .	**6,614**	**1,957**

in the part of the Province that lies to the south of the central hill range, than in the tracts on the Satpuras and beyond. In the present unchecked state of the disease, there is little probability that the hold will in any way be relinquished, though unfortunately the return is hardly exact enough to enable us to compare with certainty the results of different enumerations.

115. **Comparison by Age and Sex.**—About three-fourths of the lepers in these Provinces are over the age of 30 years, the proportions as taken from columns 2 and 3 being 77 per cent. in the case of males and 70 per cent. in the case of females. It is evident therefore, as will also appear from the figures

Sex and Age Distribution of Lepers.

Age-period.	Proportion at each age of 1,000 afflicted.		Proportion of afflicted to 10,000 persons at each age.		Afflicted Females per 100 Males.
	Males.	Females.	Males.	Females.	
1	2	3	4	5	6
0—9	22	*42*	·5	*·5*	101
10—19	61	*108*	2·2	*2·2*	90
20—29	147	*146*	6·4	*2·9*	51
30—39	220	*223*	10·2	*5·5*	52
40—49	261	*210*	17·3	*8·2*	41
50—59	158	*123*	19·7	*8·2*	40
60 and over	131	*148*	18·7	*8·4*	58
All Ages .	1,000	*1,000*	6·7	*3·5*	51

given in columns 4 and 5, that it is after the middle stage of life has been passed that the disease chiefly manifests itself. The great disproportion between the sexes of the afflicted in the case of adults is to be remarked; on an average two men are lepers to every woman. It may be taken that this result is in some degree to be attributed to the reluctance which would naturally be felt about disclosing the existence of the disease among the women of the family.

INFIRMITIES BY CASTE, ETC.

116. The castes of the infirm are set forth in four long tables, and it is by no means an easy matter to deal with the large amount of detail which has there been collected. Provincial figures showing the proportion of the afflicted in the more important castes have been worked out and are printed in this chapter, but in the case of infirmities which are perhaps more local than racial, such as blindness and leprosy, it is evident that unless the proportions for different districts are taken into account, the results will have but little meaning. This must, however, be left for more specialized inquiry, as the space at my disposal will hardly permit of such detailed treatment of the subject.

Infirmities by Castes, etc.

Class and Group.	Caste.	Total Population.	IN 10,000 PERSONS THE AVERAGE NUMBER WHO ARE									
			Insane.		Deaf-mutes.		Blind.		Lepers.		Total afflicted.	
			Males.	Females.	Males.	Females.	Males.	Females.	Males.	Females.	Males.	Females.
1	2	3	4	5	6	7	8	9	10	11	12	13
A.—AGRICULTURAL.												
I.—Military and Dominant.	Gujar . . .	48,501	2	...	6	3	22	30	7	3	37	36
	Rajput . . .	379,731	2	1	8	5	16	16	6	2	32	24
	Group I .	468,540	2	1	8	5	17	18	6	3	33	27
II(*a*).—Cultivators	Bhoyar . . .	45,340	2	2	12	7	11	16	3	...	28	25
	Káchhi . . .	122,646	3	1	6	4	24	34	3	2	36	41
	Kawar, Kaonra .	142,814	2	1	7	5	12	14	4	3	25	23
	Kirár . . .	43,316	4	1	8	4	13	19	5	3	30	27
	Kolta . . .	110,200	2	1	6	4	8	5	3	2	19	12
	Kunbi . . .	801,766	1	1	7	5	17	22	10	4	35	32
	Lodhi . . .	287,241	2	1	7	4	21	21	4	3	34	29
	Máli, Marár . .	357,988	2	1	6	5	13	17	9	4	30	27
	Mána . . .	42,774	...	...	4	5	11	13	15	3	30	21
	Group II (*a*) .	2,186,165	2	1	6	4	15	19	7	3	30	27
II(*b*).—Graziers, etc. .	......	1,011,225	1	1	5	4	11	14	6	3	23	22
II(*c*).—Labourers .	......	71,665	1	...	6	7	15	20	7	3	29	30
IV.—Forest and Hill Tribes.	Baiga . . .	120,314	1	1	4	4	7	12	7	6	19	23
	Bhil . . .	22,424	4	2	3	...	30	40	6	2	43	44
	Gond . . .	2,247,459	2	1	5	4	14	18	6	3	27	26
	Khond . . .	196,400	1	1	5	3	7	8	14	6	27	18
	Kol . . .	87,516	3	1	5	1	22	15	2	1	32	18
	Korku . . .	95,634	2	1	6	5	11	15	9	4	28	25
	Sawara . . .	156,921	1	2	4	2	8	8	6	3	19	15
	Group IV .	3,173,194	2	1	5	4	13	16	6	3	26	24
B.—PROFESSIONAL.												
V.—Priests . .	...	383,013	4	1	6	3	19	20	4	2	33	26
VI.—Devotees . .	...	98,277	3	1	5	3	17	17	6	4	31	25
VII.—Temple Servants.	...	12,274	3	...	5	5	12	11	12	10	32	26
VIII.—Genealogists .	...	23,710	2	3	3	5	25	33	4	1	34	42
IX.—Writers . .	...	47,126	4	1	5	5	17	17	7	5	33	28

Infirmities by Castes, etc.—contd.

Class and Group.	Caste.	Total Population.	In 10,000 persons the average number who are: Insane. Males.	Insane. Females.	Deaf-mutes. Males.	Deaf-mutes. Females.	Blind. Males.	Blind. Females.	Lepers. Males.	Lepers. Females.	Total afflicted. Males.	Total afflicted. Females.
1	2	3	4	5	6	7	8	9	10	11	12	13
C.—COMMERCIAL.												
XIV.—Traders	Bania	129,270	4	3	8	5	18	22	5	3	35	33
	Group XIV	144,813	4	3	8	5	17	21	6	3	35	32
XVI.—Carriers	...	56,092	4	1	3	4	8	10	1	...	16	15
D.—ARTISANS AND VILLAGE MENIALS.												
XVII.—Goldsmiths	...	99,315	4	3	6	6	17	19	5	2	32	30
XVIII.—Barbers	...	140,882	3	...	8	4	19	25	6	3	36	32
XIX.—Blacksmiths	...	150,546	2	1	6	5	14	17	7	4	29	27
XX.—Carpenters, Masons and Turners.	...	77,646	3	1	9	7	16	22	10	4	38	34
XXI.—Brass and Copper Smiths.	...	20,921	2	1	10	9	8	12	5	2	25	24
XXII.—Tailors	...	35,968	5	1	9	4	22	28	6	2	42	35
XXII(*a*).—Perfumers, Drug Sellers and Betel-leaf Sellers.	...	29,135	1	3	9	5	16	25	9	3	35	36
XXIII.—Weavers, Callenderers and Dyers.	Ganda	291,768	1	1	4	3	7	5	3	2	15	11
	Katia	43,940	4	...	6	4	14	13	3	2	27	19
	Kori	44,700	4	2	4	3	28	32	5	1	41	38
	Koshti	137,891	2	1	9	5	11	12	11	3	33	21
	Panka	162,631	2	1	6	4	16	16	6	3	30	24
	Group XXIII	750,981	2	1	6	4	12	12	6	3	26	20
XXIV.—Washermen	...	136,541	2	1	4	5	16	16	8	5	30	27
XXV.—Cotton-cleaners.	...	36,669	1	2	2	4	11	13	5	2	19	21
XXVI.—Shepherds and Wool-weavers.	...	62,283	2	2	4	6	15	18	4	2	25	28
XXVII.—Oil-pressers	...	734,935	2	1	7	5	14	17	12	7	35	30
XXVIII.—Potters	...	102,682	3	1	7	5	13	20	5	5	28	31
XXXV.—Fishermen, Boatmen, Palki-bearers, Water-carriers, Cooks, etc.	Dhimar	218,007	2	2	8	7	17	21	7	4	34	34
	Kewat	192,700	1	1	4	3	10	13	10	6	25	23
	Group XXXV	473,175	2	1	6	5	13	17	9	5	30	28

Infirmities by Castes, etc.—concluded.

Class and Group.	Caste.	Total Population.	In 10,000 persons the average number who are: Insane. Males.	Insane. Females.	Deaf-mutes. Males.	Deaf-mutes. Females.	Blind. Males.	Blind. Females.	Lepers. Males.	Lepers. Females.	Total afflicted. Males.	Total afflicted. Females.
1	2	3	4	5	6	7	8	9	10	11	12	13
D.—Artisans and Village Menials—*continued.*												
XXXVI.—Distillers and Toddy-drawers.	...	181,101	2	1	6	6	13	14	7	3	28	24
XXXVIII.—Leather-workers.	...	886,800	1	1	4	3	18	21	5	3	28	28
XXXVIII(*a*).—Village-watchmen.	Baláhi . . .	41,000	5	1	7	5	26	38	5	4	43	48
	Mahár, Mahra .	670,932	2	1	6	5	13	15	9	4	30	25
	Group XXXVIII(*a*)	786,359	2	1	6	5	16	18	8	4	32	28
XXXIX.—Scavengers .	...	83,079	3	2	6	4	12	14	7	6	28	26
E.—Vagrant, Minor Artisans and Performers, etc.												
XLI.—Earthworkers and Stone-dressers.	...	18,723	4	...	2	2	7	16	3	...	16	18
XLIII.—Matmakers, Cane-splitters, Grass-cutters, etc.	Basor . . .	47,294	1	...	8	3	22	24	3	...	34	27
	Group XLIII .	123,410	2	1	7	3	14	15	5	3	28	22
F.—Races and Nationalities.												
XLVIII.—Asiatic races of reputed non-Indian descent.		254,984	3	1	6	4	16	18	5	3	30	26
Total Central Provinces.			**2**	**1**	**6**	**4**	**14**	**17**	**7**	**3**	**29**	**25**

Note.—Groups of castes, in which there are less than 10,000 persons, are not entered in this table though they are included in the Provincial Total.

Insanes.—A feature in the returns is the prevalence of insanity among the better castes, such as Brahmins, the writing castes, Banias and Sonárs. They are perhaps the classes of the population whose avocations correspond more closely to the busy life of the West, and the greater mental strain thus involved has apparently an effect similar to what we find in European countries. The Bhils, Baláhis and Koris are specimens of the debased drudges of the Nerbada valley districts to whom reference has been made in paragraph 105; among all a large proportion are of unsound mind.

Deaf-mutes.—The figures given for this infirmity are hardly capable of explanation, without a much more detailed inquiry than is possible at a census.

Why it is that the Bhoyars of Betul and Chhindwara should be specially afflicted—two persons are deaf and dumb for every one in the Province generally—is a point which can hardly be cleared up without expert local investigation. Amongst some of the artizan castes a high proportion of deaf-mutism exists; such are the carpenters, brass and copper smiths, tailors, and Koshtis amongst weavers.

Blind.—Blindness, as has been seen, would appear to be more of a local than of a racial infirmity. Hence we find a high average of afflicted among northern castes, such as Gujars, Káchhis, Lodhis, Kols—the great bulk of whom are from Jubbulpore,— Koris and the like, and a low average among the castes and aboriginal tribes of the centre and east of the Province. The Bhils and Baláhis of Nimar are, it will be seen, largely afflicted with blindness.

Lepers.—This disease we have also seen to be to a great extent local, being much more prevalent in the tracts south of the Satpuras than elsewhere. The proportions exhibited in the above table exhibit the same fact in a different light. It may, however, be of interest to know the relative prevalence of the infirmity among some of the principal castes of the districts of Wardha and Nagpur where leprosy is most firmly estabished. This has been done in the statement which is given in the margin. The highest average is found among the aboriginal tribes, who in these districts are among the lowest of the population. Next comes the comparatively well-to-do caste of oil-pressers. The predominating castes in both districts are the Kunbis among whom one person in every 949 is a leper and the Mahárs where the proportion is one in 1,136.

Prevalence of Leprosy among certain castes in Wardha and Nagpur.

Caste, etc.	Total of caste, etc.	Number of persons amongst whom one is a leper.
Forest tribes	93,079	633
Oil-pressers—*Teli*	101,043	660
Kalár	12,768	672
Carpenters, etc.	20,185	673
Fishermen	25,770	716
Bania	16,945	737
Graziers, *Gaoli, Gowari, etc.*	33,296	757
Máli-Marár	49,028	766
Kunbi	235,437	949
Barbers	16,591	1,106
Mahár	181,835	1,136
Mussalmans	51,335	1,222
Koshti	52,477	1,381
Brahmin	33,778	1,608

CHAPTER VII.

EDUCATION.

117. The statistics regarding instruction are contained in two Tables IX and C. In the former are given details of religion and age in connection with education: the latter is a list of castes and races with the numbers recorded against each, of those who are literate and of those who know English. In Table IX the population has been distributed under three educational heads, *learning*, *literate* and *illiterate*. As the entries under the first of these three heads are open to considerable doubt, I shall first note the rules issued for the guidance of the enumerating staff in making the return, and shall remark upon the defect which would appear to exist in the manner in which they have been carried out. The rules ran thus:—

Column 12. (Instruction).—Enter as literate persons who can read and write, and are not still under instruction. Enter as learning persons who are learning to read and write at home or at school, or who have learned to read and write, but are still at school or college or learning at home. Enter as illiterate those who are not under instruction and who do not know how to both read and write or who can read but not write, or can sign their own name but not read.

Column 13. (Language known by literate).—Enter here the language which those shown as literate in column 12 can both read and write. Enter one language only that best known. But if a person knows how to read and write English as well as a vernacular, enter "English" also. This column is to be left blank for those shown in column 12 as learning or illiterate.

Both these rules were, I am convinced, frequently broken; there was a great temptation to enter boys who were well able to read and write as literate in cases where they were still under instruction, and I am inclined to think that the addition of the extra column in the schedule for language known, first introduced at the present Census, has to some extent conduced to this result. The rules require to be carefully read and considered before their full meaning is understood, and unless they were thoroughly drilled into the enumerator, the latter would naturally miss their point. The simple question of learning or not learning could present no difficulty, but when it was confounded with the other question of knowing or not knowing a language, the former was apt to be lost sight of, and only the latter taken into account. The use of the word *jánta*, or knowing, for "literate" in the Hindi schedule may have in some degree contributed to this; in Hindi districts the proportion of literates to learners among persons under 14 years of age is 26 per cent., as compared with 16 in Marathi districts where the schedule word was more definite. Be this as it may, the presence in the schedule of a column for language known would undoubtedly appear to have led the more ignorant of the enumerating staff into returning persons as knowing or literate, who should have really been described as learners. To record a school boy, who could probably read and write better than the enumerator himself, as not knowing any language, must have appeared to be little less than a fabrication. And even where the entry of 'learning' had been properly made, there seems to have been a general temptation to overlook the provisions of rule 14 and add the language learnt. In the abstracting office such mistakes were frequently discovered; others may have escaped notice, as in the hurry of the work the abstractor readily fell into the trap of listing all with a language entry to their names among literates. But the very prevalence of the error made this one of the points which the checking staff were specially directed to examine, and I think that as regards abstraction there has been no mistake to speak of in this respect. The entry in the schedules of literate instead of learning was, however, a defect which could not be cured. It is of wide enough extent to impair the value of the figures for persons under instruction, but the return is, it is now admitted, of little importance, and for any future Census its abandonment has been practically decided on. At the Census Conference held at Simla in October last, it was recommended that the enquiry should henceforth be confined to those who can read and write and those who can not (Vol. II, Census Proceedings, page 78). As regards the two heads, literate and illiterate, as thus defined, the present Census may be taken to give trustworthy returns. By combining the figures for learning with those for literate, as the word was used at the Census, we get the number of persons who are literate in the new sense of the term; for convenience sake, I shall adopt the expression educated, *viz.*, of those who are able to read and write. In the combined total the mistake disappears; it is only in the component parts, one of which has gained at the expense of the other, that confusion exists.

118. **Census figures compared with Education returns.**—At this point it will be well to note how the results of the present Census contrast with those for the Census of 1881 and with the returns of the Educational Department. At the Census of 1872 the figures for instruction were admitted to be unreliable and so may be left out of account.

*Education statistics—British districts.**

Years.	Education Department: number of persons under instruction.	Census.		
		Number of persons under instruction.	Number of literates.	Total Educated.
1872 . .	85,956	...	...	...
1881 . .	79,551	80,020	161,210	241,230
1891 . .	105,009	80,207	237,574	317,781

The most striking features in the above abstract are, first, the remarkable variation during the two last decades in the number of persons under instruction, as shown by the returns of the Education Department; second, the great difference between the latter and the Census results; and third, the enormous increase in educated persons since last Census. With regard to the fall in the number of pupils noticeable in 1881, the Inspector General of Education wrote at the time that though there had been a great and undoubted advance in primary education during the ten years, 1871 to 1881, the advance had been obscured by two events, the collapse of private aided schools in Bhandara during 1873-75 and of the same class of schools in Sambalpur in 1877. In the five years from 1881-82 to 1885-86 there was a recovery, and the number of pupils went up by bounds; in the latter year they numbered over 100,000. The increase is attributed by the Inspector General in his Annual Report for 1884-85 to the opening of a large number of aided and unaided schools. During the last five years the number of scholars has gone on growing though more slowly than during the first half of the decade. The average daily attendance, however, has not quite kept pace with the increase in the number of enrolled pupils; in 1890-91 it was only 200 more than in 1886-87, when the number of scholars was less by over 4,000. But in general the attendance may be set down at 66 per cent. or about two-thirds of the pupils on the rolls.

Coming next to the Census results it will at once be seen that we have far too few persons under instruction. At the Census should have been brought under record all persons learning at home or in any of the indigenous schools

* In 188 the Education return was not made for the Feudatory States. Information regarding them has, therefore, been excluded from the abstract given.

which do not appear in the Education returns; the latter should therefore show fewer persons under instruction than the Census Tables, but the opposite is the case. Even if a liberal allowance is made for part of the one-third of the children not attending school, being either too young to be recognized as learners or so casual in their visits as hardly to come under that category, the fact still remains that the Census figures are far lower than they should be. The explanation is to be found as has been already pointed out in the phenomenal increase that has taken place in the number of literates, the latter including many persons, specially in the earlier age-periods, who should properly have been recorded as learners.

119. **State of Education in the Province.**—Statements are appended which show the comparative state of education in different parts of the Province, and the progress that has taken place since last Census; for the Feudatories, however, the education return was not made in 1881. In the Table given on the next page the Districts and States are arranged in the order in which they stand as regards the relative strength of the educated male population.

Comparison of combined figures of Literate and Learning for 1891 with those of former Census.

Districts.	Educated males per 10,000 of male population.			Educated females per 10,000 of female population.		
	1881.	1891.	Advance during last decade.	1881.	1891.	Advance during last decade.
Saugor	673	795	122	37	41	4
Damoh	580	722	142	14	19	5
Jubbulpore	776	875	99	33	41	8
Mandla	164	279	115	4	8	4
Seoni	306	457	151	21	25	4
Narsinghpur	661	862	201	22	27	5
Hoshangabad	740	904	164	18	24	6
Nimar	1,093	1,128	35	22	25	3
Betul	306	418	112	5	6	1
Chhindwara	278	357	79	4	5	1
Wardha	635	786	151	7	14	7
Nagpur	826	941	115	42	64	22
Chanda	353	306	43	7	6	—1
Bhandara	354	455	101	6	8	2
Balaghat	297	364	67	3	7	4
Raipur	287	365	78	8	14	6
Bilaspur	240	291	51	7	8	1
Sambalpur	391	521	130	14	18	4
British Districts	472	568	96	15	20	5

British Districts.—It will be seen that the districts which head the list are those in which there is either a large town population, or in which there are large numbers of the better cultivating castes. The most backward are naturally the districts in which the towns are few or unimportant, or where there is a high proportion of the aboriginal element. Nimar takes the first place with one man or boy in every nine able to read and write; for many years it has occupied a similar leading position in the returns of the Education Department. But this place it seems hardly likely to keep, for since 1881, when it led the other districts even more prominently than it does now, its progress has been slow. Next to Nimar come Nagpur, Hoshangabad and Jubbulpore, where one male out of every eleven has been or is being taught to read and write. The advanced state of education in the towns of Nagpur, Kampti, and Jubbulpore raises the average for the first and third of these districts. Hoshangabad one would scarcely expect to find so high in the scale of education; but it is evident that instruction is well diffused among the peasantry of the Nerbada valley, as the position occupied by both Hoshangabad and Narsinghpur goes to show. Both have made substantial progress since 1881. The next districts in order are Saugor, Wardha, and Damoh, all three well settled and advancing in education. A long way behind comes Sambalpur, where judging from the disproportion existing between the returns for learning and literate, the teaching of the old indigenous schools has left its mark upon the population, many more of whom are educated than the figures for those attending school would lead one to expect. Then follow Seoni, Bhandara, and other districts containing large numbers of aborigines or depressed castes. Chhindwara, Bilaspur, and Mandla occupy the foot of the list; in all there are immense tracts of jungle where schools are unknown.

Feudatory States.—Turning to the Feudatories one would hardly have thought to find the small State of Makrai with so high an average of educated men as one in thirteen. Sarangarh comes next with one male in every nineteen able to read and write; here as in Makrai the proportion of children at school is high. In Bamra the number of literates has been abnormally increased by the large numbers of railway employés, contractors, and skilled workmen, who happened to be in the State at the time of the Census. Rairakhol also shows an inordinate number of literates; its proximity to the former political head-quarters, Sambalpur, may possibly afford a reason for this, as presumably something of the old indigenous school system of that district was at one time in force in the State. The proportion of school-going children in Sakti and Kawardha is noticeable; both States have been for some time under the management of the Deputy Commissioner of Bilaspur. In many of the remaining States education is exceedingly backward; in Kanker only one man in 72 and in Bastar one in 98 is able to read and write.

Statement showing Education in Districts and States.

District or State.	Males.					Females.					Educated females per 10,000 educated males.
	Total Educated.	Proportion per 10,000 of male population.			Number amongst whom one is able to read and write.	Total Educated.	Proportion per 10,000 of female population.			Number amongst whom one is able to read and write.	
		Learning.	Literate.	Illiterate.			Learning.	Literate.	Illiterate.		
1	2	3	4	5	6	7	8	9	10	11	12
Nimar	14,800	191	937	8,872	9	308	3	22	9,975	400	208
Nagpur	36,021	248	693	9,059	11	2,404	20	44	9,936	156	667
Hoshangabad	24,458	184	720	9,096	11	614	5	19	9,976	417	251
Jubbulpore	32,893	227	648	9,125	11	1,538	14	27	9,959	244	468
Narsinghpur	15,864	202	660	9,138	12	494	10	17	9,973	370	311
Saugor	24,313	174	621	9,205	13	1,157	17	24	9,959	244	476
Wardha	15,987	211	575	9,214	13	267	5	9	9,986	714	167
Damoh	12,075	174	548	9,278	14	300	5	14	9,981	526	248
Sambalpur	20,687	86	435	9,479	19	742	7	11	9,982	556	359
Seoni	8,455	125	332	9,543	22	457	11	14	9,975	400	541
Bhandara	16,685	156	299	9,545	22	293	4	4	9,992	1,250	176
Betul	6,799	122	296	9,582	24	102	2	4	9,994	1,667	150
Chanda	13,956	117	279	9,604	25	195	2	4	9,994	1,667	140
Raipur	28,315	112	253	9,635	27	1,161	7	7	9,986	714	410
Balaghat	6,938	101	263	9,636	27	134	3	4	9,993	1,429	193
Chhindwara	7,213	78	279	9,643	28	102	1	4	9,995	2,000	141
Bilaspur	16,664	64	227	9,709	34	484	2	6	9,992	1,250	290
Mandla	4,775	72	207	9,721	36	131	4	4	9,992	1,250	274
Total British Districts	306,898	141	427	9,432	18	10,883	7	13	9,980	495	355

Statement showing Education in Districts and States—contd.

District or State.	Males.					Females.					Educated females per 10,000 educated males.
	Total Educated.	Proportion per 10,000 of male population.			Number amongst whom one is able to read and write.	Total Educated.	Proportion per 10,000 of female population.			Number amongst whom one is able to read and write.	
		Learning.	Literate.	Illiterate.			Learning.	Literate.	Illiterate.		
1	2	3	4	5	6	7	8	9	10	11	12
Total British Districts, brought forward	*306,898*	141	427	9,432	18	*10,883*	7	13	9,980	495	355
Makrai	*712*	143	619	9,238	13	*5*	1	4	9,995	2,000	70
Sarangarh	*2,172*	141	388	9,471	19	*153*	20	16	9,964	278	704
Bamra	*2,405*	63	386	9,551	22	*90*	2	16	9,982	556	374
Rairakhol	*393*	56	321	9,623	27	*58*	...	58	9,942	169	1,476
Sakti	*428*	98	242	9,660	29	*15*	...	12	9,988	833	350
Kawardha	*1,222*	101	164	9,735	38	*41*	3	6	9,991	1,111	336
Raigarh	*2,044*	45	198	9,757	41	*39*	1	4	9,995	2,000	191
Chhuikhadan	*404*	52	177	9,771	44	*42*	1	22	9,977	435	1,040
Sonpur	*2,227*	36	192	9,772	44	*32*	...	3	9,997	3,333	144
Nandgaon	*1,993*	37	183	9,780	45	*69*	1	6	9,993	1,429	346
Khairagarh	*1,833*	44	162	9,794	49	*67*	2	5	9,993	1,429	366
Patna	*3,118*	41	145	9,814	54	*49*	1	2	9,997	3,333	157
Kalahandi	*2,536*	38	114	9,848	66	*97*	1	5	9,994	1,667	382
Kanker	*590*	43	96	9,861	72	*13*	...	3	9,997	3,333	220
Bastar	*1,624*	16	86	9,898	98	*28*	...	2	9,998	5,000	172
Total Feudatory States	*23,701*	46	172	9,782	46	*798*	2	6	9,992	1,343	336
Total Central Provinces	*330,599*	125	385	9,490	20	*11,681*	6	12	9,982	553	353

Note.—Columns 2, 6, 7 and 12 combine the statistics for learning and literate, as returned at the present Census.

120. **Female Education.**—Of the backwardness of female education in the Province the figures which are given in column 11 give an exaggerated idea. It is well known that there exists in India a prejudice against describing grown-up females as literate, and of this the Census results bear the fullest impress. To take, for instance, Saugor, about which the Inspector General of Education wrote in 1882, that it was the only district in which girls' schools really flourished; Saugor has returned 478 girls under instruction, a very fair proportion, but after all the years of flourishing girls' schools, it only shows 679 females as literate. Seoni, where female education has always been well cared for, is another notable example, with 196 females recorded as learning, and only 261 as literate. The figures are manifestly wrong. A better index of the state of female education will be got by examining the figures for girls returned as learning, as here,

there is generally no concealment. From these the most advanced district is shown to be Nagpur, with Saugor and Jubbulpore next. In all three it must be remembered there are large European and Eurasian communities, so that the figures for native females are still lower than what I have given. The only other districts in which female education would appear to have made any headway are Narsinghpur, Nimar, Seoni, and Hoshangabad. The Chhatisgarh districts also show a considerable proportion of females able to read and write, as compared with the number of educated males. For the comparatively high position occupied by some of the Native States, it is not easy to account. Rairakhol, for instance, shows no learners, but 58 women have been taught to read and write; this is probably another surviving trace of the defunct indigenous school system to which reference has been already made. In Sarangarh 86 girls were under instruction at the time of the Census; it is the only State where there appears to be any sign of activity in the matter of the education of females.

COMPARATIVE TABLE OF INSTRUCTION BY AGE AND RELIGION: BRITISH DISTRICTS.

(a) Percentage of Males and Females of each age-period who are learning or literate.

Age-period.	Education.	Total Population.		Hindus.		Mahomedans.		Christians.		Jains.		Parsis.		Animistic.	
		Males.	Females.	Males.	Females.	Males.	Females.	Males.	Females.	Males.	Females.	Males.	Females.	Males.	Females.
5—14	Learning	4·41	·26	4·58	·19	10·33	·78	62·27	54·23	32·85	3·02	62·33	33·65	·49	·02
	Literate	1·01	·09	1·07	·07	1·94	·38	12·38	12·18	9·61	1·19	16·88	22·11	·11	·00
	TOTAL EDUCATED	5·42	·35	5·65	·26	12·27	1·16	74·65	66·41	42·46	4·21	79·21	55·76	·60	·02
15—24	Learning	1·20	·02	1·22	·01	4·09	·09	7·40	8·79	3·56	·13	26·66	5·55	·19	·00
	Literate	8·69	·28	8·81	·18	23·68	1·62	81·23	55·26	59·53	2·65	72·00	75·92	·63	·00
	TOTAL EDUCATED	9·89	·30	10·03	·19	27·77	1·71	88·63	64·05	63·09	2·78	98·66	81·47	·82	·00
25 and over.	TOTAL EDUCATED	6·38	·14	6·54	·08	18·12	·80	82·17	52·70	54·27	·50	94·88	70·24	·40	·00
All Ages.	TOTAL EDUCATED	5·68	·19	5·83	·13	17·45	1·07	74·52	50·49	47·03	1·62	80·08	55·98	·45	·00

(b) Number of Persons in each Religion among whom one person is able to read and write.

	Total Population Males	Total Population Females	Hindus Males	Hindus Females	Mahomedans Males	Mahomedans Females	Christians Males	Christians Females	Jains Males	Jains Females	Parsis Males	Parsis Females	Animistic Males	Animistic Females
	18	495	17	732	6	92	1	2	2	61	1	2	216	8,677

121. **Education by Religion.**—I next come to examine the education returns in connection with religion. In the statement accompanying the proportions for the learning and literate of different religions are exhibited in conjunction with age. Three age-periods have been kept with the intention of distinguishing in persons returned as learning, those who are receiving primary instruction from those who are pupils of higher institutions. In the first age-period, 5—14 years, all learners, it is presumed, are under instruction in elementary subjects, while those from 15—24 may be taken to be receiving

higher education of one kind or another. Over 25 includes all others. Unfortunately it has been seen that the Census returns cannot be trusted for the number of learners, so that the purpose for which the statistics were taken out by ages is to some extent frustrated. For Hindus and Mahomedans, I have also given a table in which the relative strength of the educated in each district among the followers of these religions is set forth.

Percentage of Educated on Total Population: Hindu and Mussalman Religions.—British Districts.

Districts.	Hindus.		Mussalmans.	
	Males.	Females.	Males.	Females.
Saugor	6·46	·26	14·06	·58
Damoh	6·54	·13	12·86	1·00
Jubbulpore	8·73	·21	16·79	1·16
Mandla	5·20	·11	23·10	·82
Seoni	6·59	·35	15·14	·79
Narsinghpur	9·12	·26	14·82	·75
Hoshangabad	9·56	·13	16·96	·82
Nimar	10·52	·07	12·95	·45
Betul	5·88	·05	22·23	1·04
Chhindwara	4·85	·05	12·97	·19
Wardha	7·99	·11	14·46	·60
Nagpur	8·31	·21	19·20	2·23
Chanda	4·56	·04	23·09	·95
Bhandara	4·62	·06	24·09	·90
Balaghat	4·03	·06	23·90	·72
Raipur	3·72	·12	24·34	1·45
Bilaspur	2·91	·06	19·94	1·09
Sambalpur	5·24	·16	26·82	4·89
British Districts	**5·83**	**·13**	**17·46**	**1·08**

Parsis.—From the last line in the first statement it will be seen that the best educated community are the Parsis, amongst whom 80 per cent. of the men and 56 per cent. of the women are able to read and write. The education of their boys is carefully attended to; about 80 per cent. of those between 5 and 14 are shown as either learning or literate; the remaining 20 per cent., it is to be presumed, have been thought too young to send to school, but that all at one time or another are taught to read and write will appear from the fact that between the ages of 15 and 24 years, 99 Parsis out of every 100 are educated. The proportion of the young men between these ages, who are still under instruction in the higher branches of study, is about 27 per cent., an average which is nearly four times higher than that for Christians which comes next in order. In the education of females the Parsi community also occupies the first place; of the younger generation, 15 to 24 years, over four-fifths of the women have received instruction.

Christians.—Turning next to Christians it is a matter for surprise to find such a considerable proportion of children not at school and unable to read and write; of the female children no less than one-third would appear to be growing up illiterate. Of youths between 15 and 24 the number under instruction must appear exceedingly small, but for this there is a reason. The explanation is found in the fact that the total number of persons in this age-period is abnormally raised by the large number of British soldiers who are under 25 years of age. Calculated on this total, the proportion of those among the resident Christian community, who between the years of 15 and 24 are under instruction, is necessarily much reduced.

Jains.—The Jains who are next in order are, as might be expected from their main avocation being trade, a well educated class. There are two noticeable features in the figures given with regard to them. The first is the very small number of boys over 14 who are recorded as learning; it is evidently thought fitting that a youth who has reached this age should join his father in his shop rather than pursue the more advanced branches of study. The Jains are a practical money-making community to whom the advantages of the higher education appeal in vain. The other point, which calls for remark, is the great want of instruction among their women. In this respect they are scarcely any better than the Mahomedans and Hindus; like the latter they would seem to be averse to admitting that their grown-up females can read and write. In Saugor, where are found more than one-third of the total number of Jains in the Province, 123 females are recorded as learning against 110 returned as literate.

Mussalmans.—Coming next to Mahomedans it may strike one as rather surprising that considering all that is said about the backward state of education in the community, the average number of learning and literate should be so high as compared with the figures given for Hindus. The reason is that Mahomedans are usually found in towns, where the standard of education is fairly high. Amongst Hindus, on the other hand, it must be remembered, are included all the low and depressed castes, who form such a large proportion of the population of every district and amongst whom education has made but little headway. If the return showing the average number of educated among the two communities in detail of districts is examined, further light is thrown upon the statistics for Mahomedans. In all the districts with a scanty Mahomedan population principally engaged in service or in trade, the proportion of literates is at once seen to rise. Such are Mandla, Betul, Chanda, Bhandara, Balaghat, and the districts of the Chhatisgarh division. In the Vindhyan and Nerbada districts and in Seoni and Chhindwara there is a large Mussalman community engaged in cultivation; amongst them the standard of instruction is comparatively low.

Hindus and Aborigines.—The education returns for Hindus and aborigines give such small averages as almost to preclude remark: the subject can better be examined in connection with the statistics of caste to which reference will be found further on.

122. **Town and Country.**—The abstract in the margin contrasts the difference between education in town and country for Hindu and Mahomedan males. The figures for females, as has been seen, are of little statistical value, and therefore hardly call for comparison. The Cantonment of Kampti, in which is stationed a full battalion of European troops, possesses the highest standard of education. The percentage of literacy among its Mahomedans is also specially noticeable; the latter result is in part attributable to the high rate of instruction among the Mussalman troopers of the Madras Cavalry regiment. Saugor occupies second place with one-fourth of its male population able to read and write. The town of Burhanpur has the best educated Hindu community, while illiteracy is, on the other hand, greatest among its Mahomedan population. The latter result was unlooked for, as the town is a stronghold of the Bohra traders, who are known to be a well instructed class. But in Burhanpur there is a large Mussalman community of another kind; many of them subsist by weaving, and they are described as poor and ignorant to a degree; it is to the presence of the latter that the low position occupied by the Mahomedans may be ascribed. In point of education among its rural population, Nimar, it will be noticed, takes chief place among the districts given.

Percentage of Educated among Hindu and Mahomedan Males in Town and Country.

Town.	Town.			Surrounding Country.		
	All religions.	Hindus.	Mussalmans.	All religions.	Hindus.	Mussalmans.
Nagpur	21·64	19·69	18·05	} 5·50	5·50	15·35
Kampti	28·22	22·50	25·81			
Saugor	25·18	22·36	22·30	6·50	5·39	9·80
Jubbulpore	23·73	21·48	20·74	6·71	7·21	12·70
Burhanpur	20·79	24·62	12·03	8·49	7·97	7·86

123. **Castes of literates.**—In supplementary Table C will be found the number of persons of every caste and race who are literate and amongst these the number who know English. In the appended statements I have set forth the numbers and percentages which result for certain of the chief castes among whom education has made considerable progress, and also for some of the larger castes who are conspicuously illiterate. I think it will give a better idea of the subject if only the figures for males are considered, and if we confine our enquiries to the British districts of the Province; the returns for the Feudatory States are available in Table C for any one who may wish to refer to them.

Castes in which literacy has made considerable progress—British Districts.

Caste.	Total males.	Total males literate.	Total males knowing English.	Percentage of column 3 on column 2.	Percentage of column 4 on column 3.	Number of males among whom one is literate.
1	2	3	4	5	6	7
Káyasth	14,346	6,823	545	47·56	7·99	2
Bania	63,524	24,692	226	38·87	·92	3
Bidur	5,405	1,909	58	35·32	3·04	3
Brahmin	184,339	59,487	3,159	32·27	5·31	3
Saiad (M)	11,600	2,502	182	21·57	7·27	5
Bairági	15,536	2,848	8	18·33	...	5
Maratha	15,968	2,701	160	16·92	5·92	6
Sonár	43,822	6,964	84	15·89	1·21	6
Shaikh (M)	65,968	9,698	592	14·7	6·10	7
Pathan (M)	42,604	5,311	237	12·47	4·46	8
Bhát	10,938	1,294	8	11·83	...	8
Gosain	12,927	1,419	15	10·98	1·06	9
Bhulia	6,014	590	2	9·81	...	10
Darji	17,787	1,729	30	9·72	1·74	10
Barai, Tamboli, etc.	13,654	1,327	28	9·72	2·11	10
Kalár	66,630	5,378	50	8·07	·93	12
Rajput	182,676	13,689	360	7·49	2·63	13
Ját	3,937	288	2	7·32	...	14
Kolta	38,906	2,664	3	6·85	...	15
Dángi	12,979	865	1	6·66	...	15
Kohli	9,851	638	2	6·48	...	15
Koshti	65,208	4,038	24	6·19	·59	16
Agharia	5,941	348	1	5·86	...	17
Khangár	7,525	357	3	4·74	...	21
Kápewár	5,473	246	47	4·49	19·11	22
Barhai	35,207	1,271	14	3·61	1·10	28
Kirár	22,168	713	...	3·22	...	31
Gujar	24,395	783	1	3·21	...	31
Kunbi	395,019	12,582	213	3·19	1·69	31
Kahár	9,225	291	22	3·15	7·56	32
Nai, Mháli	65,417	1,896	31	2·90	1·64	34
Dahait	6,273	176	...	2·81	...	36
Máli	57,663	1,532	30	2·66	1·96	38
Káonra	7,972	208	1	2·61	...	38
Lodhi	131,519	3,366	14	2·56	·42	39
Dom	5,702	146	2	2·56	...	39
Teli	313,117	7,736	38	2·47	·49	40
Lohár	64,677	1,429	13	2·21	·91	45
Bhoi	7,491	150	19	2·0	12·67	50

NOTE.—Percentages are not given in column 6 when the number of English-knowing is under 10.

In the first place it must be remembered that we are comparing the number of persons who are literate according to the census definition, which excludes such as are only learning, with the total number of people in each caste. The figures would have more meaning if we could effect comparison only with adults, but in the absence of age details for individual castes this cannot be done; roughly speaking, however, the proportion of persons in the better castes who are over the age of 15 years may be taken as 60 per cent. Were education universal we might therefore expect 60 persons in every 100 to be literate, and it is on this basis that we should found the comparisons we make. Thus in the case of the Káyasths who are the best instructed caste, we find 48 per cent. who can read and write; in other words, 48 out of every 60 adults, or four-fifths of the total who are of an age to have finished their education, are shown as literate. In the same way 39 Banias in every 60 or about two-thirds of the caste are educated, and so with the others.

But to take the proportions as they stand, we may note that both in point of general literacy and knowledge of English, the Káyasths take a pre-eminent lead. I have not given details for the numerically unimportant castes, but may here note that like the Káyasths, the other writing castes are also well instructed; among Parbhus 50 per cent. are literate, and amongst the Uria Mahantis, 46 per cent.; or if we judge of the latter by the total of their number in Feudatory States as well as British districts, the proportion becomes 41. Next to the writing castes come the Banias, of whom 39 per cent. are educated; as their avocation does not, however, demand a knowledge of English, the number of the caste who return the language is exceedingly small. Of the Brahmins 32 per cent. are literate, and 5 per cent. of these have a knowledge of English. In the latter respect they are surpassed by the Saiyads and Shaikhs among Mahomedans and by the persons returned as Marathas. It is unnecessary to pass each caste in review, but attention may be called to the large number of persons among the Kápewárs, a Hindu caste of Chanda and Nagpur, who have learned English, the proportion so recorded being as high as 19 per cent. of the total literate. In the statement given no mention is made of the Telugu and Tamil castes of Nagpur and Kampti, among whom English has become a second tongue; among the persons who gave their caste as simply Tamil, half are English-knowing, and among Telugus about one-fifth, whilst of the Balija and Vellálar castes 60 and 71 per cent., respectively, are similarly returned.

If we leave out of account Europeans and Eurasians we find the following general results in respect of literacy and instruction in English for the whole Province:—

Statement of literacy amongst the male population, excluding Europeans and Eurasians.

	Total population.	Number literate.	Number knowing English.	Percentage of	
				Column 3 on column 2.	Column 4 on column 3.
	2	3	4	5	6
British Districts	5,392,635	226,929	7,891	4·2	3·5
Feudatory States	1,088,926	18,646	321	1·7	1·7
Central Provinces	**6,481,561**	**245,575**	**8,212**	**3·8**	**3·3**

124. Castes which are largely illiterate.— This hardly amounts to more than giving the names of the chief aboriginal tribes and of the depressed castes among Hindus. The high position occupied by the Khonds is due to only those who are resident in Sambalpur being taken into account; in the Feudatory states where they are chiefly found, they are as illiterate as the rest of the forest tribes. Among the low castes, it is extremely difficult for education to make any headway; their out-case condition has rendered them apathetic as to the instruction of their children, and even where attempts have been made to introduce schools for their benefit, they have often ended in failure. The Inspector General of Education wrote in 1882:—

Castes which are largely illiterate—British Districts.

Caste.	Total males.	Total males literate.	Total males knowing English.	Percentage of column 3 on column 2.
1	2	3	4	5
Mahár, Mehra	311,132	3,110	67	1·00
Khond . .	9,846	97	1	·99
Katia . .	21,214	202	1	·95
Gaoli . .	28,932	256	9	·88
Dhangar .	10,210	87	3	·85
Chandár .	15,170	128	2	·84
Marár . .	94,768	729	..	·77
Halba . .	36,627	274	1	·75
Mána . .	21,176	151	...	·71
Kawar . .	36,986	217	1	·59
Gahra . .	27,826	150	...	·54
Ráwat (Chhatisgarhi) .	93,657	503	...	·54
Banjára .	23,335	111	...	·48
Gánda .	80,783	381	...	·47
Gond . .	880,935	3,331	13	·38
Baiga . .	46,856	139	...	·30
Chamár .	400,097	1,173	8	·29
Gowári .	59,628	150	2	·25
Kol . .	41,554	65	...	·16
Bhil . .	11,103	16	...	·14
Korku . .	46,100	58	...	·13

For Mahárs special schools have sometimes been opened, but they rarely last long. The teacher is generally a Mahomedan, as Brahmins and others of the better castes among the Hindus object to be appointed to teach Mahár boys. After a time the low caste boys disappear and their place is taken by Mahomedans. Dhers and other low castes also attend village schools; they often read in the school house verandah. Masters receive nothing from their hands; slates, for instance, which have to be examined for the working of arithmetical questions or for composition or dictation, are pushed along the ground to and from the master. If the master accidentally touches a boy, the master has to bathe before he is pure. Of course the low caste boys cannot be punished with a cane, perhaps this is an advantage. Chamárs, too, are seldom seen in schools except in Chhatisgarh, there they are Satnámis and attend Hindu schools. To Government schools boys of all castes are admitted, no questions are asked, but social prejudices do undoubtedly tend to keep the lower castes from school, and their own poverty and dislike to instruction also keep them away from school. Most of the Dhers are weavers; their children are employed from the earliest years, that is, from six years and upwards, in their fathers' calling.

125. Literacy among females.—The number of females who have been educated are so few that it is useless attempting to reduce the results which we have obtained to proportionate figures. The chief castes all show a certain number of their women as knowing how to read and write; Rajputs return 460 literate females, Brahmins, 1,205, of whom there are 11 knowing English; Banias, 482, and Káyasths, 226, of whom 10 have been taught English. The figures are for the whole province. Literacy among Parsi and Mahomedan females has been already referred to under the head of religion.

CHAPTER VIII.

LANGUAGES.

126. **Classification of languages adopted in Table X.**—The resolution of the Government of India, dated 1st July 1890, prescribed for the table showing the parent tongue of the population, a geographical classification, as being the most convenient form for the Provincial Returns. In Table X this classification has not been strictly carried out. The languages recorded at the Census have been grouped according to provinces and countries, an arrangement based on political rather than on purely geographical limits. The first place has been assigned to vernaculars of the Central Provinces. It is not easy in every case to say what the latter are, so much is the Province beholden to other parts of India for its people and its languages. The term has, however, been taken to apply to languages which are spoken by homogeneous masses of the population inhabiting definite portions of the Province. In this category I have not ventured to include Telugu; it is, no doubt, the vernacular of a small part of the southern border of Chanda and the Bastar State, but the numbers returning it are such a fraction of the Telugu-speaking race, that I have preferred to treat it as an extra-Provincial language. On the other hand, the language of the Kols and Mundas and several of the dialects included in "other Dravidian" and "other Kolarian" have been taken amongst the Provincial vernaculars, as they are spoken by aborigines widely scattered over the eastern part of the Province, though, as is the case generally with aboriginal dialects, they do not form the sole vernacular of any well defined area. The accompanying abstract shows the population distributed over the different groups. From the fact that the first part of Group A is chiefly composed of the three great languages, Hindi, Marathi, and Uria, all of which are main vernaculars of other Provinces, the language return gives no clue to the number of persons who are foreigners from other parts of India. Groups B, C, and D give the number of persons who by speech are of descent foreign to India. These form but an infinitesimal portion of the population, a fact that is sufficiently accounted for by the isolated position and backward development of the Province.

Group.	Number.
A (*a*)—Vernaculars of the Province .	12,764,105
(*b*) Ditto of other Provinces .	173,298
Indian languages	12,937,403
B—Other Asiatic languages . .	138
C—European languages . . .	7,261
D—African dialects	3
Total .	12,944,805

127. **Linguistic classification of languages.**—The abstract here given is an attempt at a linguistic classification of the languages returned at the Census, based on the scheme contained in the Census Commissioner's Note W, dated 24th September 1891. The scheme follows in general that laid down by Mr. Cust in his book on the "Modern Languages of the East Indies." The following, which appears at page 49 of that work must, however, be taken to be in several particulars erroneous:—

Still more numerous are the Semi-Kolarian dialects. The language of the Bhils in the Bombay Province, Rajputana, and Central India is understood to be a dialect of Hindi. The race has lost its peculiar language, but kept a great many words and no doubt phonetic variations. Many persons assert that the Bhil language still exists, but the only vocabulary which I have seen is composed entirely of Hindi words. In the Central Provinces the Laria or Chhatisgarhi dialect is conspicuous, and the Halba, Parja or Tagara,

Linguistic Classification of the Languages appearing in Table X.

INDIAN LANGUAGES.

Family.	Group.	Language.	Dialect.	Number returning.
I.—ARYAN.	(a.) Eranic.	Pashtu	...	652
		Baluchi	...	3
			Total Group (a.)	655
	(b.) Indic.	Panjabi	...	1,154
		Sindhi	...	9
		Hindi	...	7,277,344
			Urdu	158,332
			Halbi	103,385
			Márwári	22,566
			Nipáli	124
			Total Hindi	7,561,751
		Hindi-Kolarian	Bhili	21,715
			Baigáni	7,974
			Total Hindi-Kolarian.	29,689
		Hindi-Dravidian or Gypsy dialects.	...	29,750
		Gujerati	...	17,389
		Marathi	...	2,127,908
			Goanese or Gomantaki.	532
			Total Marathi.	2,128,440
		Bengali	...	1,648
		Uria	...	1,602,732
			Total Group (b.)	11,372,562
		Total Family I		11,373,217

Family.	Group.	Language.	Dialect.	Number returning.
II.—DRAVIDIAN.	(a.) Southern.	Tamil	...	5,953
		Telugu	...	117,132
		Canarese	...	5,761
		Malayalam	...	19
			Total Group (a.)	128,865
	(b.) Northern.	Khondi	...	66,149
		Gondi	...	1,228,076
		Other Dravidian dialects.	...	8,944
			Total Group (b.)	1,303,169
		Total Family II		1,432,034
III.—KOLARIAN.	...	Kol	...	14,388
		Munda	...	34,486
		Korku	...	74,846
		Other Kolarian dialects.	...	8,076
		Total Family III		131,796
IV.—TIBETO-BURMAN.	...	Burmese	...	346
		Chin	...	4
		Karen	...	1
		Total Family IV		351
V.—TAI OR SHAN.	...	Shan	...	5
		Total Indian Languages		12,937,408

LANGUAGES FOREIGN TO INDIA.

Family.	Group.	Language.	Number returning.
I.—ARYAN.	(a.) Eranic.	Persian	112
		Armenian	3
		Total Group (a.)	115
	(b.) Greek.	Greek	7
	(c.) Italic.	Italian	2
		French	55
		Spanish	1
		Total Group (c.)	58
	(d.) Teutonic. Germanic.	German	23
		English	7,109
		Flemish	1
	Scandinavian.	Norwegian	2
		Swedish	26
		Total Group (d.)	7,161

Family.	Group.	Language.	Number returning.
I.—ARYAN—*contd.*	(e) Celtic.	Welsh	1
		Gaelic	2
		Irish	32
		Total Group (e)	35
		Total Family I	7,376
II.—SEMITIC.	...	Arabic	7
		Hebrew	11
		Total Family II	18
III.—MONGOLIAN.	...	Chinese	5
IV.—HAMITIC.	...	East African Dialects.	3
		Total Non-Indian Languages	7,402

and Bhuttia (Bhatri) of Bastar. To these must be added the dialect of the Bhogtas, near Palamow in Chutia-Nagpur of the Bengal Province, and the Kharwar, Byga, Binjhwar, Panka, Mehra, and Katya. Vocabularies are supplied.

To class the Hindi spoken in Chhatisgarh among semi-Kolarian dialects does not appear correct, and the same remark must apply to Panka, Mehra, and Katia. Pankai has been returned as a dialect only from the Seoni district; Katiai is recorded in the books of Seoni, Hoshangabad, Betul and Chhindwara. References to these districts have elicited replies to the effect that the patois of the Pankas and Katias is only a low form of Hindi, containing nothing of the aboriginal element. It may be that in some places from members of the two castes residing amongst Gonds, they occasionally know a few Gondi words, but in that case the admixture would be Dravidian and not Kolarian. As, however, in the classification scheme the term Hindi-Dravidian has been specially applied to the dialects of the vagrant tribes, it seems best to exclude from this heading the local dialects, which, though now and again they may have given currency to an aboriginal expression, are strictly Hindi in basis. The Bastar dialects mentioned by Cust, I shall refer to later on; they are, if anything, allied to Gond and are not Kolarian.

128. I now come to the consideration of the individual languages returned at the Census. Though the great number of names appearing in the language column of the schedules must not be taken to represent proportionate diversity of speech, it is nevertheless probable that many of them represent real differences. It is unfortunately next to impossible to conduct satisfactory enquiries as to what these differences are through the medium of correspondence. The present returns, however, even where we know little or nothing about their significance, may be of use as suggesting the lines of further research; to this end I have given in detail the dialects, real or so-called, which have been included in each main language. The latter may best be noted on in the order in which they come in Table X.

Distribution by Language of 10,000 of the People of each District or State.

District or State.	Hindi including Halbi.	Urdu.	Marathi.	Uria.	Vagrant dialects.	Aboriginal dialects.	Marwari	Telugu.	All Indian languages.
(a) Districts.									
Saugor	9,845	58	24	...	...	39	8	2	9,987
Damoh	9,914	18	14	...	...	37	2	...	10,000
Jubbulpore	9,291	286	30	2	2	322	6	14	9,978
Mandla	5,714	43	22	...	32	4,174	8	..	9,999
Seoni	5,267	212	519	2	29	3,934	12	1	9,999
Narsinghpur	9,915	19	24	...	...	25	5	1	9,997
Hoshangabad	8,408	151	102	...	18	1,152	131	6	9,990
Nimar	5,989	445	1,654	...	206	1,160	47	16	9,986
Betul	3,664	108	2,325	...	9	3,880	6	1	9,999
Chhindwara	4,332	117	1,869	1	31	3,621	19	4	9,999
Wardha	540	370	7,884	...	22	1,050	58	53	9,999
Nagpur	1,397	549	7,126	1	5	585	48	152	9,957
Chanda	567	157	6,130	1	53	1,901	10	1,161	9,998
Bhandara	1,988	157	6,616	...	2	1,176	8	19	9,999
Balaghat	5,241	107	2,574	...	15	2,014	4	4	9,999
Raipur	9,048	31	85	563	29	223	9	6	9,999
Bilaspur	9,844	16	30	5	14	78	3	5	9,999
Sambalpur	1,995	21	14	7,478	22	435	4	16	9,999

Distribution by Language of 10,000 of the People of each District or State—contd.

District or State.	Hindi including Halbi.	Urdu.	Marathi.	Uria.	Vagrant dialects.	Abori-ginal dialects.	Marwari	Telugu.	All Indian languages.
(*b*) *States.*									
Makrai	6,569	80	44	...	68	3,159	78	...	10,000
Bastar	3,830	26	95	69	120	5,479	11	363	10,000
Kanker	5,138	3	84	6	...	4,731	37	...	10,000
Nandgaon	9,593	21	217	1	4	104	43	5	9,999
Khairagarh	9,599	46	157	3	2	153	17	12	9,994
Chhuikhadan	9,803	24	131	...	...	37	...	...	10,000
Kawardha	9,826	18	62	3	3	81	2	3	10,000
Sakti	9,723	41	29	3	20	169	...	14	10 000
Raigarh	7,547	15	18	1,725	53	631	...	3	9,999
Sarangarh	6,865	5	29	2,797	73	228	2	...	10,000
Bamra	568	16	2	7,643	9	1,746	1	2	9,999
Rairakhol	49	1	...	9,508	...	442	...	...	10,000
Sonpur	106	18	...	9,738	3	113	2	15	10,000
Patna	178	6	...	9,745	2	56	...	11	10,000
Kalahandi	241	5	...	7,636	3	2,010	...	104	10,000
Total Central Provinces	5,702	122	1,644	124	23	1,131	17	90	9,994

VERNACULARS OF THE PROVINCE.

129. **Hindi** is the language of about three-fifths of the population of the Province. As will appear from the general abstract given above, it is the leading vernacular of 13 out of the 18 districts, and in one form or another of 9 of the 15 Feudatory States. It is spoken throughout the Jubbulpore and Nerbada Divisions, except on the southern border, where in the tehsils of Burhanpur, Multai, and Sausar it finds a rival in Marathi, the language of the Nagpur country and Berar. The dividing line may be taken to be the southern crest of the Satpura range. In the Balaghat District the same line of division is continued, the part of the Burha tehsil below the hills being chiefly Marathi-speaking, while the remainder of the district is Hindi. Here the line turns off to the south, the boundary following the range of hills which divides the Nagpur country from Chhatisgarh. The language of the latter tract is the form of Hindi, to which it gives its name; while in the large dependency of Bastar to the south, the prevailing speech is also a kind of Hindi known as Halbi. The hilly barrier separating the Sambalpur country from Chhatisgarh is the eastern boundary of the Hindi tongue. In Sambalpur it is extensively spoken under the name of Laria in the zemindaries of Phuljhar, Chandarpur, etc., which lie to the west of the district. The dividing line runs through the States of Raigarh and Sarangarh, Laria being the language of 109,254 of the inhabitants of the former State and of 54,531 of the latter. Outside the limits just described, in the Nagpur plain, there are large colonies of Powars, Lodhis, and other northern races who still retain their Hindi mother-tongue, but the predominating language of this part of the country is Marathi.

Tehsil, etc.	Percentage on total Population of persons speaking	
	Hindi.	Marathi.
Burhanpur	20	45
Multai	45	31
Sausar	19	50
Burha	51	31
	Hindi.	Uria.
Raigarh	75	17
Sarangarh	69	28
Sambalpur: Phuljhar	49	49
Sambalpur: Borasambhar	10	88
Sambalpur: Chandarpur	93	4
Sambalpur: Padampur	20	75
Sambalpur: Malkhorda	95	3

130. The dialects which have been included in Hindi are given in the margin. Many of the terms are simply the names of castes, who use amongst themselves a particular form of speech for which the caste name appeared to the enumerator the most natural expression, such are Bhoyari, Gowari, Katiai, Powari, etc. Others are well known local dialects, as Chhatisgarhi, Bundeli, Bagheli, whilst some are mere fancy terms derived chiefly from names of places, *e.g.*, Raipuri, Nagpuri, Sirgujia. In no case has the return for any of the well known dialects of Hindi been at all complete. The enumerator's instructions contained no express directions on the subject, and the entry of the general term for mother-tongue was, therefore, followed. The figures given have consequently no meaning in most cases. I append the following notes as to some of the dialects returned.

Hindi Dialects.

Dialect.	Number of persons returning.
Aheráni	136
Bagheli	842
Bhojpuri	57
Bhoyari	1,153
Bundeli	211
Brij	3
Chhatisgarhi	562,426
Laria	324,090
Sadri	138
Satnámi	23
Kánkeri	9
Raipuri	6
Makaria	30
Raut	14
Others	8
Total Chhatisgarhi	886,744
Dhandhári	121
Gaheri	84
Gowári	361
Katiái	4,249
Maghia	128
Málwi	11
Mandláha	188
Maithili	10
Nágpuri	56
Nágri	793
Nimári	977
Pachhái	9
Pahári	1
Pardeshi	4
Pankái	5
Powári	3,490
Purbi	152
Rajhari	80
Ránchi	8
Rángdi	2
Sirgujia	36
Others	8

Aherani is recorded as the mother-tongue of some Sonars in Burhanpur; at the last Census the dialect was returned by 37 persons as against 136 in 1891. Bhojpuri, Brij, Dhandhari, Malwi, Maghia or Magadhi, Maithili, Pachhai, Pahari, Perdeshi, Purbi are names for the Hindi of Behar, the North-West Provinces, and Central India. Bagheli and Bundeli are well known dialects of Hindi, extensively spoken in the northern districts of the Province. "In Jubbulpore the language of the district is the dialect of Hindi known as the Bagheli. One of its peculiarities that particularly attracts the attention of a stranger from Northern India is the elision of nearly all the short vowels."—*Central Provinces Gazetteer*, page 225.

Bhoyari, Gowari, Katiai, Powari, etc., represent the patois spoken by the castes whose names they bear. An interesting point in connection with these so-called dialects is the question how far they may be diluted with aboriginal terms picked up from among the tribes with whom the first settlers of the castes came in contact. The Deputy Commissioners, from whom I have made enquires, have generally reported that the aboriginal element does not enter into the speech of any of the castes, for whom a separate caste language has been returned. Almost the sole exception is Powari, which is reported from Bhandara to be much diluted with aboriginal terms. At page 51 of the Report of the Central Provinces Ethnological Committee (1866-67), the language of the Powars is said "to savour most of Urdu, but they have adopted or corrupted words from the Gondi and Marathi dialects." In Berar at the Census of 1881, Rajhari or Lajhari was put by Mr. Kitts as a variety of Gondi, containing a slight sprinkling of Marathi words. At the present Census Rajhari has been returned only from the Betul district, where it is reported to be a kind of Hindi and to be in no way allied to or mixed with Gondi. The general tenor of the replies received as to the other language terms is to the same effect. On the whole, it seems best to conclude that there is nothing distinctively aboriginal in any of these caste dialects. They are recorded mainly from the southern districts of the Satpuras, Betul, Chhindwara, Seoni, and Balaghat, Powari and Gowari being returned also from Bhandara. Occurring as they do on the meeting ground of the Hindi and Marathi-speaking races, their composition might naturally be expected to partake of both; Hindi predominates in all, but the intermixed foreign element to which the dialects owe their individuality is Marathi rather than any of the aboriginal tongues.

Nimari has been returned for only about 1,000 persons. It is the language of the district from which its name is derived. Captain Forsyth writes of it in the Nimar Settlement Report:—

The Nimari dialect is a mixture of the common Hindi of Malwa and the Upper Nerbada valley with Marathi, considerably dashed with high flown Persian words and idioms bequeathed to it by its numerous Mahomedan population of former times, and often strangely mangled in their modern uses. The Hindi element preponderates north of the Central hill range and the Marathi to the south of it.

The Chhatisgarhi dialect has not been fully returned; it is the almost universal speech of the people of Chhatisgarh. To the east of the Chhatisgarh plain in the States of Raigarh, Sarangarh, and the Sambalpur zemindaries, the dialect is known as Laria. As to the application of the terms Colonel Bowie writes to me:—

To the people of these parts the Chhatisgarh country proper, *i.e.*, Raipur and Bilaspur, is the Laria country, and Sambalpur, the Uria country. Laria is simply the Chhatisgarhi dialect of Hindi: it is, I believe, quite pure Hindi, introduced by immigrants from the North-West Provinces.

The Bilaspur Settlement Report notes that a few aboriginal words have found currency in the dialect, but "it rests on a strictly Hindi basis, and there are comparatively few Urdu words in use." Raipuri, Satnami, Kankeri are fancy names invented by the enumerator; they have been put under Chhatisgarhi. Sadri is reported to be an equivalent of Laria.

About the other dialect terms it seems hardly necessary to make any remark. Mandlaha is evidently a coined expression, it has been returned in Bilaspur by Mahto Teli immigrants from Mandla. Nagpuri recorded in the books of the Sambalpur District refers to the Hindi of Chhota-Nagpur, as do also the terms Ranchi and Sirgujia.

131. **Urdu.**—In this has been included Hindustani spoken by 292 persons and Mussalmani by 107 persons. The distinction between Hindi and Urdu has been thus referred to by Mr. Baines in his circular on the classification of languages:—

The vernacular is Hindi and the term Urdu is correctly applied only to the dialect in use in the chief towns of Northern India, where it was introduced by the Mussalman invaders. It is distinguished by the number of Persian and Arabic words it contains, and with much local variation is used as a *lingua franca*, especially amongst Mussalmans, over the greater part of India. At the present Census nearly the whole of the vernaculars of the North-West Provinces and Oudh will be found to be returned as Hindustani. On the other hand, across the political frontier in Behar and the Central Provinces, the return will be that of Hindi or one of its larger sub-divisions. The best solution of the question seems to be to enter the language as Hindi wherever it is the vernacular of the tract, as a whole, and to restrict the use of the title Urdu to tracts where the language in question is either foreign or the dialect of a class, such as that section of the local Mussalmans who do not return as their mother-tongue the vernacular of their place of residence.

In the Central Provinces the entries under the term Urdu are in accordance with the distinction above drawn. In the northern districts, with the exception of Jubbulpore, the number of persons returned as speaking Urdu is comparatively small, the current vernacular Hindi being most probably recorded of nearly all Mussalmans. In Nimar and the four principal districts of the Nagpur Division, it is likely that almost all the better class of Mahomedans have returned Urdu as their mother-tongue. The figures in places like Jubbulpore and Nagpur are, no doubt, considerably increased by the number of persons foreign to the Province, whose language has been given as Urdu.

132. **Marathi** is the language of the districts of Wardha, Nagpur, Bhandara, and Chanda in the Nagpur Division. It has been already seen that it is also strongly represented in the parts of the Nimar, Betul, Chhindwara, and Balaghat Districts, which form the southern outskirts of the Satpura range. The dialects included in Marathi are for the most part unimportant. Koshti, which is a mixture of Hindi and Marathi spoken by the weaving class, has been put amongst Marathi rather than Hindi, as the name implies a Southern origin. Of the 5,929 persons returned as speaking the Koshti dialect, 4,271 are from the Chanda District, and of the remainder all but 12 persons belong to the Nagpur Division. Kewati is returned from the Mul Tehsil of Chanda, and is reported to be mixed Hindi and Marathi. It should probably be put amongst the latter, though in 1881 it was included in Hindi. The Chanda Settlement Report, page 38, speaks of the Kewats as being Marathas.

Marathi Dialects.

Dialect.	Number of persons returning.	Dialect.	Number of persons returning.
Berári	26	Konkani	3
Bonái	20	Koshti	5,929
Burdi	143	Kumbhári	108
Dekhani	7	Mahári	141
Dhangari	11	Netkáni	87
Ghetli	28	Others	11
Kewati	5,074		

133. **Uria** is the language of Sambalpur and of the States of Bamra, Rairakhol, Patna, Kalahandi, and Sonpur, and, in part, of Raigarh and Sarangarh. There are also a few Uria speakers on the eastern border of the Bastar State, where it borders on Jeypore. Comparative figures are given in the general abstract. The dialects returned are unimportant, being, if anything at all, mere varieties spoken by different castes.

Uria Dialects.

Dialect.	Number of persons returning.
Betra	22
Bhulia	9,106
Dami	288
Jharia	33
Kuli	14
Ludha	38
Turi	637
Utkali	15
Others	12

134. **Halbi and Bastar Dialects.**—The Halbi dialect is peculiar to the Bastar State, as are also several forms of Gondi, which will be noted on under that language. A few persons speaking these dialects are found across the border in Chanda, Bhandara, etc., but all are probably Bastar people. Almost the only available information regarding the languages of Bastar is contained in Colonel Glasfurd's note, printed at page 46 of his Bastar Report :—

Halbi Dialects.

Dialect.	Number of persons returning.
Adkuri	511
Bastari	1,322
Chandári	328
Gachikolo	38
Mehari	241
Mirgáni	1,429
Muria	497
Sundi	15
Others	10

The languages in Bastar are numerous; nearly every caste has its dialect, and they are most of them so similar that they cannot be considered as different languages. They may, however, be classed as under :—

1 Halba. | 2 Maria. | 3 Telugu.

The first closely resembles the Chhatisgarhi dialect. There is a great admixture of Marathi in it, or rather there are many Marathi affixes, and it often happens that a pure Hindustani word is taken and a Marathi termination added. The whole language in this part of the country is a jargon of Marathi and Hindi words; grammar and idioms all jumbled up into undescribable confusion. It is spoken by the Halbas and Murias, and may be said to be sub-divided into the Parja or Tagara and Bhatra dialects. It is spoken by all in Jagdalpur from the Rajah to the lowest of his subjects.

Then comes a statement of the limits of the three languages, which may be summarised as follows. The Halbi dialect extends for the most part over the northern and eastern portion of the State. A line running roughly from north-west to south-east divides it from Maria, which is spoken in the Central hills, and from Telugu, which is the language, of the country towards the Godaveri. Colonel Glasfurd, however, notes that Halbi is pretty extensively spoken throughout the dependency. On the south, where the Marias border on Sironcha, and where they come more into contact with the Telingas, they are generally able to understand Telugu, talking their own language only among themselves. Wherever the Maria or Halbi borders on the Telugu, many words of the latter are introduced into the former; and the same is the case with the dialects of Halbi, where they border on Uria, as in the disputed country lying between Bastar and Jeypore.

In Halbi has been included a number of terms, all of which signify the dialects of particular castes. About a third of the people in the State are returned as speaking Halbi; a half speak Gondi, while the remaining one-sixth use Hindi, Telugu, Uria, etc.

135. Dialects of Vagrants.

—The dialects listed under this head are given in the accompanying abstract. Of these by far the most important is Labhani, the language of the Banjaras, for which a separate statement is given, showing the number of persons in each district who have returned it as their mother-tongue. On the classification of these dialects, the Census Commissioner's directions were:—

Dialects of Vagrants.

Dialect.	Number of persons returning.
Badak	19
Bhámti	14
Burgándi	10
Gárodi	25
Kanjar	7
Kaikári	140
Kolháti	7
Labháni	25,519
Banjári	2,228
Bepári	540
Berári	115
Gowári	53
Naiki	768
Ratan	28
Others	20
Total Labhani	29,271
Nati	5
Nunyás	3
Párdhi	110
Sánsi	27
Sikligari	13
Shikári	14
Waddari	85
Total Hindi-Gypsy	29,750

> Lastly, come the different dialects used by certain tribes of vagrants from Cape Comorin to the Punjab. It seems that most of these have combined vulgar Hindi with some one of the Dravidian languages, usually Tamil or Telugu, so that they have a kind of thieves' Latin available for their purposes wherever they may wander. These dialects will be put in a separate group under the title of Hindi-Gypsy.

The persons whose speech has been returned as Badak, Kanjar and Sansi are all found within the precincts of the Thugi Lines or Central Jail at Jubbulpore. In Mr. Hislop's papers relating to the aboriginal tribes of the Central Provinces is given a vocabulary of the speech used by the Kaikaris; it is part Tamil, part Telugu with a mixture of other words. Kaikari has been returned as the mother-tongue of 58 persons in Jubbulpore, 45 in Nimar, and 37 in the districts of the Nagpur Division. Burgandi is another term for Kaikari; it is recorded of ten persons from the Nimar District. The language of the Bhamtas is said by Colonel Gunthorpe to be mainly Telugu; it has been given as the mother-tongue of 14 per-

Distribution of Persons speaking Labháni.

District.	Persons returning.
Saugor	7
Damoh	15
Jubbulpore	54
Mandla	1,097
Seoni	1,089
Narsinghpur	10
Hoshangabad	962
Nimar	5,156
Betul	279
Chhindwara	1,274
Wardha	702
Nagpur	368
Chanda	3,681
Bhandara	180
Balaghat	592
Raipur	4,664
Bilaspur	1,593
Sambalpur	1,738
Feudatory States	5,810
Total Labhani	29,271

sons in Nagpur. The Pardhis speak a version of the Gujerati language amongst themselves; Wardha returns 85 and Chanda 25 persons using the Pardhi dialect. Waddari is reported by the Deputy Commissioner of Wardha to be a corrupt form of Tamil; of the 85 persons of whom it is recorded 76 are from Wardha and 9 from Raipur. There remain the dialects appearing as Garoḍi, Kolhati, Nati, Nunyas, Shikari and Sikligari. Mr. Kitts, in the Berar Census Report of 1881, calls the two first a mixture of base Gujerati and Marathi. Nati is reported by the Deputy Commissioner, Chhindwara, to be a low form of Hindi, with a good deal of thieves' slang. The other three are probably somewhat similar. The language of the Banjaras is akin to Marwari; of the dialects included in it some are named after well known epithets of the Labhana tribe, others derived from names of places are evidently fanciful.

136. **Gondi.**—The number of persons speaking Gondi is 1,228,076. At the last Census, when the language return was not available for the Feudatory States, the number of Gondi speakers in the British districts was 967,500. In this were included persons whose mother-tongue was given as some of the dialects which at the present Census have been classified under Khondi, "other Dravidian" and even "other Kolarian." An adjustment of the figures gives the following comparative results:—

Number of persons speaking Gondi (British districts), { 1881— 961,098 ; 1891—1,005,313 }

There has thus been an increase of about 44,215 persons, or 4·4 per cent. on the number for 1881. The increase may be put down partly to natural increment and partly to more careful enumeration of some of the wilder tracts at the present Census. In the margin I have noted the divergence from the figures of 1881 for all districts in which Gondi is returned in any strength. The increase is most marked in Jubbulpore, whilst the districts of Narsinghpur and Hoshangabad, lower down the Nerbada valley, show a considerable falling off in the number of persons who speak Gondi. For the increase in Jubbulpore it is not easy to find a reason, unless it be assigned to the large influx of harvesters into the district which is reported to have taken place about the time of the Census. Of these labourers a great number were from Mandla and the Rewah State, and it is safe to assume that a large proportion of them were Gonds. In the settled part of the Nerbada valley where the Gonds have now been long the drudges of Hindi-speaking cultivators, it is natural to find them abandoning their aboriginal tongue. That the numbers who speak it in the Nagpur country have not declined is a matter for surprise. In Saugor and Damoh and in Chhatisgarh the process would appear to have gone much further, the Gonds

Distribution of Persons speaking Gondi.

District.	Number speaking Gondi.		Difference.	Total Gonds.	Proportion speaking Gondi.
	1881.	1891.			
Saugor	3,747	2,338	—1,400	30,327	7·7
Damoh	3	1,191	+1,188	31,404	3·8
Jubbulpore	8,509	24,126	+15,617	112,463	21·5
Mandla	129,627	140,058	+10,431	170,591	78·0
Seoni	134,276	145,872	+11,596	159,449	91·5
Narsinghpur	5,592	936	—4,656	48,021	1·9
Hoshangabad	53,282	39,784	—13,498	65,907	60·4
Nimar	3,217	2,166	—1,051	1,590	136·2
Betul	87,968	93,999	+6,031	96,101	97·8
Chhindwara	131,755	135,194	+3,439	152,096	88·9
Wardha	41,412	42,079	+667	44,790	93·9
Nagpur	43,060	44,310	+1,259	47,526	93·3
Chanda	132,348	132,598	+250	168,623	78·6
Bhandara	84,126	87,347	+3,221	93,638	93·3
Balaghat	74,156	76,262	+2,106	93,453	81·6
Raipur	...	27,822	...	250,595	11·1
Bilaspur	...	8,459	...	159,502	5·3
Sambalpur	...	763	...	64,455	1·2
Feudatory States	...	222,763	...	459,293	48·5
Total Central Provinces	...	1,228,076	...	2,258,824	54·4

NOTE.—Owing to inclusion of other aboriginal dialects, the figures of 1881 for the Chhatisgarh districts cannot be ascertained. In Nimar Gondi has been returned as the mother-tongue of tribes other than Gonds. In Bastar many of the tribes who have been reckoned as allied to Gonds use the Halbi language; this has conduced in great part to the low proportion of Gondi-speakers in the Feudatory States.

who have retained their distinctive form of speech being small in comparison with the strength of the tribe.

Of the dialects included in Gondi, Bharia is found only in the Chhindwara district, Ojhi in Seoni, Betul, Chhindwara, Chanda and Balaghat, Kolami in Wardha, and Deogarhi in Bilaspur. The remainder belong almost exclusively to Chanda and the Bastar State; figures for these have, therefore, been separately given in the appended abstract. Maria or Mari, Koi and Gotte are the dialects of the well known tribes of the same name. I have classed them under Gondi, but Maria, at least, is quite a distinct language, although doubtless having a common root (*Chanda Settlement Report*, page 43). All three dialects are said to be allied (*Ethnological Committee's Report*, page 39). Hislop gives vocabularies in his work. Naiki is the dialect of the Darwe Gonds of Chanda. Whether I am right in including in Gondi the Parji, Tagari, and Bhatri dialects of the Bastar State is somewhat open to doubt. As has been seen in the extract quoted under Halbi, Colonel Glasfurd considered Parji or Tagari and Bhatri to be dialects of Halbi. In the appendix to his Bastar Report he uses Parji and Bhatri as synonyms. This would hardly seem to be the case as Hislop assigns them separate places in his vocabulary of aboriginal terms, and the words he gives appear quite different in each. Nor can the two dialects be considered as simply offshoots of Halbi, which, it is agreed, is a mere low form of Chhatisgarhi. Hislop and following him the Ethnological Committee class Bhatri and Parji among the aboriginal tongues, and I have adopted this classification. I have been unfortunately unable to obtain any local information as to the exact significance of the various Bastar dialects; the field is one that has still to be explored.

Dialects of Gondi.

DIALECT.	Chanda.	Bastar.	POVINCIAL TOTAL.
Bharia	...	...	1,989
Bhatri	...	29,396	29,414
Deogarhi	...	...	2
Gotte	7,856	4,711	12,567
Parji	...	10,144	10,144
Koi	5,405	7,283	12,688
Tagari	...	116	116
Kolámi	...	...	1,612
Mári	5,970	27,032	33,004
Abuj-Mard	...	352	352
Jhoria	...	54	54
TOTAL MARI	5,970	27,438	33,410
Naki	195	...	195
Ojhi	13	...	171

137. **Khondi** is the language of the Khonds of Kalahandi. A few Khondi speakers are found in the other Uria States and in Sambalpur. Kutia, 832 persons, and Tekria, 24, are included both being spoken by Khonds. Kutia is the term which in Kalahandi is specially applied to the hill Khonds.

138. **Other Dravidian dialects.**—Next comes a class of aboriginal dialects, which, for convenience sake, has been styled other Dravidian. Of these the Oraon is found mainly in Raigarh and the Sambalpur District. Of the terms listed under Oraon, Dhangari and Kurukh are synonyms, derived from names for the tribe. Of the Dhanwari dialect the Deputy Commissioner of Bilaspur writes:—"The Dhanwari is a dialect more allied to the Gondi and is spoken by the Dhanwars, a class of professional Shikaris, from whom it derives its name." Kamari is returned from the Raipur District, 3,743 persons, and

Other Dravidian Dialects.

DIALECT.	Number of persons.
Oráon	1,761
Bára	88
Báràgucha	125
Dhángari	2,229
Kurukh	98
TOTAL ORAON	4,301
Bhaina	3
Dhanwári	228
Kamári	4,009
Sawara	401
Sadana	2
TOTAL OTHER DRAVIDIAN	8,944

from Bastar, 146; at the Census of 1881 the tribe was classed as Dravidian. In the Raipur Settlement Report the Kamars are described as for the most part living in the wildest jungles, so that it is probable that the speech of the less civilized among them is to some extent aboriginal. According to the Settlement Report, the tribal dialect is akin to Uria as is also that of the Sawaras, who, following the Census Report of 1881, have been wrongly classed as Dravidian. Sawara has been recorded as a dialect only in Sambalpur, but Colonel Bowie informs me that the Sawaras of the Sambalpur District have no language except Uria. Dalton in his Ethnology of Bengal mentions that the Sawaras living between the Khond country and the Godaveri still retain a primitive form of speech, but elsewhere Uria is their mother-tongue. It may be doubted whether the 401 persons in Sambalpur, who are returned as speaking Sawara, have any connection with the Sawaras of the Ganjam hills, but the entry has been retained among the aboriginal dialects; it should have been classed as Kolarian. About Bhaina recorded of the tribe of that name and Sadana recorded of Bhuiyas nothing is known; the entries are probably fanciful.

139. **Kolarian dialects.**—The **Korku** language is confined to the western parts of the Satpuras. Like Gondi it appears to be holding its ground, the number of Korku speakers in British districts being 70,754 as against 65,271 at the last Census. In Korku has been included Nahali. Of the Nahals Captain Forsyth writes in the Nimar Settlement Report that they have no separate language, but talk that of the Korkus in the wilder parts of the district.

Dialect.	No.	Districts.	No.
Korku	65,808	Hoshangabad	21,265
Mowási	8,762	Nimar	5,726
Naháli	62	Betul	31,404
Pahári	214	Chhindwara	12,359
		Feudatory States	4,092
Total	74,846	Total	74,846

Bhili, including Kotli spoken by 33 persons, is practically confined to the Nimar district, the sole exception of any note being its return as the mother-tongue of 186 persons of the tribe resident in the Kanker State. "The Bhils have no aboriginal tongue, but speak a dialect composed of Hindi, Marathi, and some other elements difficult to analyse, but probably aboriginal." (Forsyth). In 1881 only 4,897 persons returned the dialect as against 21,715 at the present Census.

Baigani has been recorded as the mother-tongue of Baigas, and of the allied races of Binjhwars, Bhumias, and Bhunjias. Colonel Ward in the Settlement Report of the Mandla district says that the only language the Baigas know is Hindi. On enquiry being made, as a test case, whether the entry of Baigani returned at the present Census, had any significance, the following note has been received from Mr. Balmukund Purohit, the Tehsildar of Ramgarh, who has had much experience of the Baigas :—

Dialect.	Number of persons.	District.	Number of persons.
Baigáni	2,616	Mandla	1,590
Binjhwári	4,447	Hoshangabad	6
Bhumiái	44	Balaghat	944
Bhunjia	867	Raipur	3,782
		Bilaspur	310
		Sambalpur	1,027
		Feudatory States	315
Total	7,974	Total	7,974

I have often been through the villages mentioned and have conversed with the Baigas. I have found that the language they speak is not a separate language but a corruption of Hindi. The speech they use among themselves can always be understood, save where Gondi words occur, which they have learned by mixing among the Gonds.

It would appear that the Binjhwars and Bhunjias of Raipur have also no distinctive dialect, but talk ordinary Chhatisgarhi (*Ethnological Committee's Report*, pages 94—97).

Dialect.	Number returning.
Kol	14,388
Munda	1,765
Beldár	34
Disli	35
Kuda	9,499
Kisán	22,816
Lanjar	25
Mirdha	272
Others	40
Total Munda	34,486
Kharia	6,804
Mátia	77
Total Kharia	6,881
Bhogta	13
Gadba	375
Kawar	570
Khaira	30
Korwa	71
Mánjhi	20
Mahto	60
Sáota	56

140. Kol, Munda, and the dialects classed as "other Kolarian" are recorded almost solely from Sambalpur and the Uria States. The entries under Munda, with the exception of Kisan, have all been returned of Kudas, and may, therefore, be looked upon as Mundari. The language of the Kisans is reported by the Deputy Commissioner of Sambalpur to be akin to Kol, the latter term, I may add, being used in a general way so as to include almost all the aboriginal dialects returned from the district. The Urias in the Census Office assert that the Kisans and the Kudas are identical and speak the same dialect, which is described as a jungly form of speech. Kisan has therefore been listed with Munda.

Of the Kharia dialect Cust writes :—

The Kharias are found in the district of Singbhum in a very wild state, living in backwoods and on the tops of hills. They are more civilized in Chhota-Nagpur and are agriculturists. Of their language we have vocabularies supplied by Dalton, but nothing beyond. There are affinities to Mundari and Juang. There is no character, and this language will probably die away.

Bhogta is mentioned by Cust as a semi-Kolarian dialect. It has been returned as the mother-tongue of Kols in Sambalpur. I quote from the Ethnological Committee's Report, page 6, as to the Gadba, Mahto and Manjhi dialects :—

The Gadbas are said to inhabit the eastern portion of Bastar and Jeypore where they are numerous: they become scarce as you go west in Bastar. Captain Glasfurd says that they seem allied to the Marias, we presume, by manners and customs, but a glance at the few words given in Captain Glasfurd's table, shows that their language differs from that of the surrounding tribes, while comparison with the Kol and Korku lists will show that some of the most important words in the Gadba tongue are identical with those used by the Korkus in the west, and by the Kols and Santhals in the east. It is interesting to find a Kolarian specimen imbedded among the Dravidians down in the south-east. The dialects of the Manjhi and Mahto would appear from Mr. Chisholm's vocabulary to belong to the Kolarian family, and the location of these tribes helps this inference.

At the present Census the Gadba dialect has been returned from Bastar, 286 persons, and Kalahandi, 89. Mahto is found in the Bilaspur zemindaris and Manjhi in Raigarh. Saota spoken by 56 persons in Bilaspur has been put amongst Kolarian dialects, but of its existence as a separate language there must be considerable doubt. According to Dalton the Saotas of Sirgujia have no language but a rude Hindi; the tribe is allied to the Korwas, of whose dialect Dalton gives a vocabulary. The Korwa speakers returned at the Census are all found in the Raigarh State. Whether there are any such dialects as Khaira and Kawar, I am unable to say. Khaira is recorded from the Sambalpur district, and Kawar from Sambalpur, 88 persons, and from Raigarh, 482. The terms have been put under Kolarian dialects in default of any other classification. In Chhatisgarh proper the Kawars speak only Hindi, and though the district note published at page 99 of the Ethnological Committee's Report suggests the probability of the tribe having a separate dialect, the present returns would seem to be against the theory, seeing that out of the great mass of Kawars only some 500 have been shown as having a distinctive form of speech.

OTHER INDIAN LANGUAGES.

141. Of these **Marwari** and **Gujerati** are represented in every district of the Provinces. Marwari is returned in greatest strength in the districts of the Lower Nerbada valley, Hoshangabad and Nimar, and in Wardha, Nagpur and Raipur where there are many members of the community engaged in money-lending and trade. Gujerati is spoken by 11,565 persons in the Nimar district, of whom 8,220 are found in the town of Burhanpur. The connection of Burhanpur in the old days with Surat and the establishment of a strong Gujerati colony in its midst, have brought the language into extensive use, especially among the mercantile classes of the town.

DIALECTS.	Number of persons returning.
Gujerati	17,009
Pársi	35
Kachhi	339
Others	6
TOTAL GUJERATI	17,389

142. The accompanying abstract shows the districts from which **Canarese** has been principally returned. The Golars or Golkars are a pastoral tribe of nomadic proclivities whose dialect is allied to Canarese. This is the language also of the Holias, a low caste of leather workers and musicians, found chiefly in the Nagpur and Bhandara districts. Kuramwar, which in Table X had been included in Telugu on the analogy of the classification adopted in 1881, is apparently Canarese. "The Kuramwars are a wild-looking race of shepherds, speaking a dialect of Canarese."—*Chanda Settlement Report*, page 56.

DISTRICTS.	Canarese.	Golari.	Holia.	Kuramwár.
Seoni	325	139	125	...
Nagpur	74	171	301	...
Chanda	812	27	3	2,316
Bhandara	614	1,013	466	...
Balaghat	404	910	109	...

143. **Telugu.**—There are considerable numbers of Telugus in almost every district of the Province, but the most important colonies are found in the towns of Kampti and Nagpur. In the southern parts of Chanda and Bastar which lie along the north bank of the Godaveri, Telugu is the current vernacular. Its local distribution is noted in the margin; the language as spoken is described to be barbarous and harsh. In Telugu had been included Kuramwar, but this I have now taken as Canarese. Kapewar recorded of 2,914 persons has been put with Telugu, as has also Yerukala, 16 persons, a dialect spoken by a primitive tribe of the same name.

TEHSIL ETC.	SPEAKING TELUGU.	
	Number of persons.	Percentage on Population.
Mul Tehsil, excluding Ahiri	30,021	15
Ahiri	6,547	25
Sironcha	32,091	76
Bastar	11,287	4

144. Tamil with its synonyms Arvi, Madrasi, and Dravidi is recorded as the mother-tongue of about 6,000 persons, of whom two-thirds are found in Kampti and Nagpur. Of the Bengali speakers, 1,648 in number, over one-fourth are found in Jubbulpore and one-fourth in Sambalpur, the remainder being scattered over the rest of the Province, where they are employed chiefly as clerks, etc. Panjabi is recorded of 1,154 persons, who are for the most part soldiers, skilled workmen or vagrants. The 652 people who speak Pashtu belong mainly to the latter class. With one or two exceptions, the persons whose mother-tongue is Burman or Shan are prisoners in the central jails.

NON-INDIAN LANGUAGES.

145. As has been already noticed the number of persons who speak languages foreign to India is so small as hardly to call for remark. The table in the margin compares the figures for the language and birth-place of foreigners so far as comparison is possible. The number of Persian speakers returned is out of all proportion to the number of people born in Persia. Some of the persons who have recorded their place of birth as Afghanistan, have no doubt given Persian as their mother-tongue, but the discrepancy is rather due to the classic language being affectedly returned instead of a vernacular. To the same cause has probably to be assigned the occurrence of Hebrew as a parent tongue. The numbers of China and Arabia-born are largely in excess of the figures for the languages corresponding. The persons in question are mostly Mahomedans, who have been returned as speaking Urdu Of the English-speaking only 41 per cent. give their birth-place as the United Kingdom, the Colonies or America, the remainder being Eurasians and Indian-born Europeans. The French returned at the Census are for the most part connected with the service of the church; their numbers are recruited from France and the language and birth-place details therefore closely agree. On the other hand, there is a considerable difference in the case of the Swedes between persons speaking Swedish and persons born in Sweden; some of the missionaries have families born in India, and the latter represent the divergence in question. There are no language entries to correspond with Switzerland, Russia, or Turkey in Europe; the persons returning these countries have been recorded as speaking French, German, Greek, and in some cases English.

Persons foreign to India by language and birth-place.

Language.	Number returning	Country.	Number born.
Persian	112	Persia	5
Arabic	7	Arabia	37
Armenian	3	Turkey in Asia	5
Hebrew	11		
Chinese	5	China	17
English, Welsh, Gaelic, Irish	7,144	United Kingdom, Gibraltar, etc., African and Australian colonies, and America	2,949
French	55	France	54
German	23	Germany	16
Flemish	1	Belgium	2
Swedish	26	Sweden	15
Norwegian	2	Norway	2
Spanish	1	Spain	2
Italian	2	Italy	2
Greek	7	Greece and Ionian Islands	5

CHAPTER IX.

BIRTH-PLACE.

146. **Scope of the Return**—*British Districts.*—Before noting on the birth-place returns for the population of the Province, it will be well to remark upon one or two matters, which are worthy of observation in connection with the scope of the Table (No. XI) in which they are contained. First of all the table shows for each District and Feudatory State the place of birth of every person found within its limits at the time of the Census. To get this information for a particular district shown at the top of the table, the latter should be read *vertically*: the entries appearing against each name in column 1 represent the number of persons resident in the district, who have been born in that place. Excluding the figures which appear against the name of the district itself, the remainder of the entries in each vertical column represent the number of immigrants into the district from other parts of the Province and beyond. Read *horizontally* the figures against each name in column 1, show the distribution of persons of that place of birth over the several districts. If we take the first four pages of the table, in which the districts of the Province appear in column 1, we get for each district so appearing the present place of residence of every person born within it who is still living in the Central Provinces. By excluding the persons resident in the district itself, the remaining entries in each horizontal line show the emigrants from each district into other parts of the Province. For emigrants from any district, say Nagpur, to another part of India, it would of course be necessary to go to the Census returns of the Province or State where persons born in Nagpur may now happen to be residing. At the Census such persons may have returned Nagpur as their birth-place, but in the compilation of the returns of the Province or State, no separate record was required to be kept of outside districts. The entries for all persons born in the Central Provinces have been lumped into one, and this total is alone available. There is thus no record of the number of persons born in any one district of the Central Provinces who have been enumerated in other parts of India. In other words, we have detailed information regarding local emigration from one of our own districts to another, but regarding foreign emigration we have none.

147. *Feudatory States.*—In Part II of the Tables are given the birth-place returns of the Feudatory States. The instructions for filling up the enumerator's schedule were to the ordinary effect that the district in which each person was born should be stated, and if the person were not born in the Central Provinces, the name of the Province or State should be added. Throughout the Hindi Feudatory States of Chhatisgarh, the name of the district, Raipur or Bilaspur, within which the State used to be included, has been almost universally entered as the place of birth instead of the State itself. The error would have been to a great extent prevented, had the instructions been more precisely worded by making it clear that for persons born in one of the Feudatories, the name of the Feudatory should be recorded. Unhappily at the time the rules for filling the schedule were drawn up, I was unaware of the prevailing custom of regarding the States as an integral portion of the district with which they had formerly been in political connection. In the Uria States the mistake has been avoided by the insertion in the specimen schedule of the names of Feudatories in the birth-place column. But in all the Hindi States, except Nandgaon and Bastar, the returns are vitiated. In Raigarh and Sarangarh the results are not so bad, as part of the Census was taken in Hindi and

part in Uria. The strange thing is that the same mistake appears to have been made without being discovered in the British districts of Raipur and Bilaspur which return only 487 and 463 persons respectively as being born in the States, when by the actual facts there should have been as many thousands in all probability as there are hundreds. For the Chhatisgarh Districts and States it will not, therefore, be always possible to supply proportional details to correspond with those given for other districts. With the above exception the record of birth-place has been generally complete. It was sometimes difficult to make out the names of places in other parts of India, but the number that have remained unclassed is exceedingly small. The greater part of the entries in the table under "Central Provinces unspecified" were recorded of Europeans and Eurasians who frequently failed to give their district of birth.

Birth-place.	Number.	Proportion per 10,000 of total population.
A.—India.		
I.—Within the Province	12,412,439	9,589
II.—Elsewhere in India	528,407	408
Total A.—India	12,940,846	9,997
B.—Other Asiatic Countries	888	1
C.—Europe.		
I.—United Kingdom	2,861	2
II.—Other Countries	119	...
Total C	2,980	2
D.—Elsewhere	91	...
Total	12,944,805	10,000

148. General Distribution of the Population by Birth-place.—The accompanying statement shows the general distribution by birth-place of the persons enumerated in the Central Provinces. Thus 95·9 per cent. of the population have been born within the limits of the Province, and 4·1 per cent. are immigrants from beyond. In 1881 the percentage of the indigenous to the total population was 95·2, immigration supplying the remaining 4·8. An examination of the returns shows that it is in immigrants from other parts of India that the decrease has taken place.

	Immigrants from other parts of India.	Immigrants from beyond India.
1881	546,644	3,272
1891	528,407	3,959

The figures for immigration from other Provinces and States are noticed in detail in the next paragraph. Those for immigration from beyond India have been already referred to in the chapter on languages.

149. Immigration from other Provinces.—*Central India.*—The part of India from which the Province draws most of its immigrants is the Central India States, by which it is surrounded on the north-west and north-east. The number of immigrants from these States has fallen considerably since 1881. Previous to the last Census the famine of 1877-78 had driven a large number of persons from Central India across the border into the northern districts of the Province; many of them settled down and remained as field labourers and cultivators. Though, after the lapse of 13 years, the traces of this movement as evidenced by the birth-place return have necessarily in part disappeared, a glance at the Immigration table, Statement A, printed in the present chapter, will show how largely the districts, more especially of Saugor, Damoh, Jubbulpore, and Hoshangabad, are peopled by natives of the Central India States. In Jubbulpore and Damoh they form about a fourteenth of the population.

North-West Provinces and Oudh.—Next to Central India comes the North-West Provinces and Oudh. In the Census Report of 1881 the immigration figures then returned for the former were reported to have been abnormally increased by the number of refugees who after the famine had settled down in the Central Provinces. The decrease at the present Census may be partly due to this reason. From Oudh, on the other hand, the number of immigrants has nearly doubled; the increase may be attributed to the congested state of the population in that part of Northern India. Of this some idea may be gathered from the fact that the population of Oudh has increased over 11 per cent. during the last ten years, the density being now 522 persons per square

Immigration *from* other Provinces *compared with 1881.*

Province or State.	1881. British Districts.	1881. Feudatory States.	1881. Central Provinces.	1891. British Districts.	1891. Feudatory States.	1891. Central Provinces.	Proportion of col. 7 to total immigrants.	Female immigrants per 1,000 males.
1	2	3	4	5	6	7	8	9
Bengal	20,278	8,549	28,827	11,284	10,053	21,337	4·0	656
Bengal Feudatory States	845	22,037	22,882	9,692	24,712	34,404	6·5	1,054
Berar	52,089	222	52,311	51,703	407	52,110	9·9	1,433
Bombay and Feudatory States	26,106	404	26,510	24,002	552	24,554	4·7	826
Madras and Feudatory States	21,083	7,336	28,419	9,748	17,047	26,795	5·1	829
North-West Provinces and Feudatory States	102,509	3,081	105 590	87,518	2,525	90,043	17·0	575
Oudh	16,375	673	17,048	32,056	910	32,966	6·2	379
Punjab and Feudatory States	2,725	109	2,834	6,006	445	6,541	1·2	291
Hyderabad	26,553	1,480	23,033	20,489	1,396	21,885	4·1	1,023
Rajputana	18,098	1,202	19,300	19,381	2,661	22,042	4·2	553
Central India States	212,405	1,716	214,211	190,830	1,753	192,583	36·5	994
Other parts of India	674	5	679	2,992	155	3,147	·6	498
Total	459,830	46,814	546,644	465,791	62,616	528,407	100	829

Distribution by British Districts *of 10,000 persons born in each Province and State.*

District.	Bengal.	Bengal Feudatory States.	Berar.	Bombay and Feudatories.	Madras and Feudatories.	North-West Provinces and Feudatories.	Oudh.	Punjab and Feudatories.	Hyderabad.	Rajputana.	Central India States.
Saugor	237	...	3	127	106	2,604	782	2,278	22	631	1,778
Damoh	50	...	1	15	12	269	154	133	4	123	1,217
Jubbulpore	1,172	1	17	393	512	2,490	1,494	1,765	173	588	2,974
Mandla	86	13	2	48	15	250	332	190	3	115	424
Seoni	89	...	11	34	51	237	334	266	29	138	118
Narsinghpur	85	...	6	122	34	296	255	161	13	225	536
Hoshangabad	307	...	144	857	283	796	1,433	676	213	2,431	1,334
Nimar	101	...	345	4,484	146	436	1,024	558	218	921	419
Betul	43	...	865	38	31	107	411	198	96	176	29
Chhindwara	46	...	286	44	33	149	167	162	37	319	93
Wardha	63	...	5,232	742	103	207	496	156	267	888	63
Nagpur	355	3	1,384	1,651	4,445	920	1,388	1,726	1,187	1,282	65
Chanda	53	3	1,201	238	557	143	384	171	7,422	226	54
Bhandara	41	...	314	155	67	98	132	228	82	324	18
Balaghat	32	...	40	29	45	79	103	190	17	125	36
Raipur	282	...	21	446	722	280	349	343	104	834	42
Bilaspur	2,872	6,196	79	249	165	455	596	402	60	530	764
Sambalpur	4,086	3,784	49	328	2,673	184	166	397	53	124	36
Total	10,000	10,000	10,000	10,000	10,000	10,000	10,000	10,000	10,000	10,000	10,000

mile. In the North-West Provinces the corresponding figures are an increase of 4·76 in population and a mean density of 419. Of the immigrants from Oudh a very large proportion are persons engaged in service of various kinds, while others are petty traders.

Berar.—From Berar there has been no alteration in the figures for immigration into the Central Provinces.

Madras.—The withdrawal of the Madras garrison from some of the military stations accounts in great part for the falling off which has taken place in British districts in the immigration from the Madras Presidency. Comparative figures are given in the margin for the most important districts. At the time of the Census there were Madras troops in two districts only, Nagpur and Sambalpur. The Madras force in the former had been reduced since 1881, as the figures sufficiently show; in Sambalpur there has been but little change. The large increase in the Native States of persons born in Madras is noteworthy; there are no published returns to show in what States immigrants from Madras were found in 1881, so individual comparison is impossible, but at the present Census they are recorded from Bastar 5,712 persons, Sonpur 1,656, Patna 1,670, and Kalahandi 7,454. There can be little doubt that new comers have been largely attracted to take up cultivation in the Feudatory States by the settled administration which these now possess.

Immigration from Madras.

District.	1881.	1891.
Saugor	1,750	103
Jubbulpore	2,742	498
Nagpur	6,398	4,306
Chanda	2,480	543
Hoshangabad	1,183	276
Raipur	2,717	698
Sambalpur	2,547	2,449

Bombay.—From the Bombay Presidency immigration has somewhat declined. Bombay troops are now stationed at Kampti and Raipur, and the number of persons in the latter district and Nagpur have therefore increased. The increase does not, however, in any way balance the falling off that was apparent by the departure of the Madras troops; the latter move about with a host of female relations and hangers on, which are not found with a Bombay or Bengal regiment. The presence of the latter merely represents an increase of foreign-born little over the number of the rank and file. Many of these, too, in the case of Bombay troops are persons from Rajputana and Northern India, so that the change of garrison has brought into the Province comparatively few persons born in Bombay. By far the greatest number of immigrants from the Western Presidency are found in Nimar. Since the last Census their numbers have gone down from 13,415 to 10,763 at the present time, and it is to this decline that the variation in the Provincial total during the last decade is due; in other districts there has been hardly any change. Except in Nimar, where many are cultivators, the persons born in Bombay are for the most part traders or their agents. The 545 persons returning their birth-place as the Bombay Feudatory States are also traders; at the last Census their number was only 7, but the number of Cutchis and others from that part of the western coast is probably greater than even the present figures go to show; the native country of several has no doubt been entered under the general heading of Bombay.

Bengal.—From Bengal proper immigration has fallen off considerably, but if the figures for the Presidency are combined with those for the Tributary States of Chhota Nagpur and Cuttack, the decline becomes an increase. At the last Census, as at the present, an attempt was made to keep the British part of the Presidency distinct from the Feudatory, but with misleading results as a comparison of the figures for 1881 and 1891 for immigration into Bilaspur and Sambalpur will sufficiently show.

Year.	Born in Bengal (British).		Born in Feudatories of Chhota Nagpur and Cuttack.		Bengal Presidency.	
	Bilaspur.	Sambalpur.	Bilaspur.	Sambalpur.	Bilaspur.	Sambalpur.
1881	7,551	8,832	68	777	7,619	9,609
1891	3,241	4,611	6,005	3,667	9,246	8,278

They are the two districts which attract most settlers from the Bengal Presidency, and of these the greater portion are from Chhota Nagpur and Cuttack, both British and Feudatory. The number of immigrants from these parts into the Native States of the Central Provinces has increased by over 4,000; many of them are labourers employed on the Railway works which were in progress at the time of the Census.

Rajputana, &c.—Of persons born in the Nizam's Dominions, there has been a falling off in almost every district, the difference being most marked in Chanda, where there is a decrease of 3,598 persons. Rajputana, on the other hand, has sent the Province 2,742 more persons than was the case in 1881. The immigrants from this part are generally connected with money-lending and trade, more particularly the former. The districts which show the largest return of people born in Rajputana are Hoshangabad, Nimar, Wardha, Nagpur, and Raipur: in the two former it is probable that some proportion of these are agriculturists. The increase is most noticeable in the eastern districts of the Province, which were just beginning to be opened up to trade, by the building of the Bengal-Nagpur Railway. Raipur shows, for instance 1,617 persons of birth-place Rajputana, as compared with 846 in 1881: Bilaspur and Sambalpur give 1,028 and 241, as compared with 698 and 162. In the Feudatories, the numbers have gone up from 1,202 at the last Census, to 2,661 at the present time: of these 575 are found in Nandgaon and are chiefly traders, while 1,430 in Bamra are contractors, traders or workmen connected with the Railway construction. Immigrants from the Punjab have become more numerous in nearly every district. The chief increase, due to garrison changes, is in Saugor and Jubbulpore; in Saugor there are now 1,389 persons hailing from the Punjab, against 193 in 1881, and in Jubbulpore the present number is 1,069, instead of 612. In the eastern districts and States, also, the Railway works attracted considerable numbers of Panjabis. The persons returned as born in other parts of India are so few as hardly to call for mention. Mysore sends 832 persons to the Province, of whom 520 are resident in Nagpur; Ajmir-Merwara is returned as the birth-place of 732 people chiefly from Hoshangabad, Nimar, and Nagpur.

The proportion between the male and female immigrants from different parts, which is shown in the last column of the statement, exhibits a principle which runs through these returns, *viz.*, that for places close to one another the number of female immigrants is as a rule in excess of male, and the further apart places are the more do the male immigrants exceed the female. In the case of the Punjab and Oudh the proportion of females is abnormally low. From the former the Province gets soldiers and workmen, most of whom are without their families. The large number of persons who leave their homes in Oudh in quest of service are also for the most part single men.

150. **Emigration beyond the Province.**—Of the number of persons who have emigrated from the Province to other parts of India, full details have not yet been communicated to me. The accompanying statement contrasts the figures so far as they have been ascertained with the same returns for 1881, as well as with the number of immigrants from the corresponding places.

In Assam there were at the time of the Census 3,844 persons who were

Gain or loss resulting from migrations beyond the Province.

Province or State.	Emigrants.			Immigrants.		Gain or loss to Province.	
	1881.	1891.		1891.			
	Total.	Total.	Proportion of females per 1,000 males.	Total.	Proportion of females per 1,000 males.	1891.	1881.
Assam	825	3,844	735	16	...	—3,828	—825
Berar	185,142	216,488	977	52,110	1,433	—164,378	—132,831
Bombay and States	10,537	10,494	586	24,554	826	+14,060	+15,973
Burma	310	527	109	374	...	—153	—266
Madras and States	4 936	16,253	840	26,795	829	+10,542	+23,483
Mysore	1,063	2,016	856	832	...	—1,184	—742
North-West Provinces, Oudh and States	29,361	12,179	1,160	123,009	517	+110,830	+93,277
Punjab and States	1,441	1,095	674	6,541	291	+5,446	+1,393
Bengal and States	40,486	85,742	805	55,741	881	—30,001	+11,223
Central India States	78,258	117,878	1,229	192,583	994	+74,705	+135,953
Hyderabad	13,287	6,782	781	21,885	1,022	+15,103	+14,746
Total	365,646	473,298	...	504,440	...	+31,142	+161,384

natives of the Central Provinces. Nearly all are probably coolies imported chiefly from the Uria country; their numbers have more than quadrupled during the last ten years. In Berar emigration from the Central Provinces has increased about 17 per cent. Noting on the large influx of immigrants into Berar from this Province at the Census of 1881, Mr. Kitts wrote:—

"Of the immigrants from the Central Provinces nearly one-half are found in the Amraoti District, and more than one-third in Wun. The Morsi and Chandur taluks adjoin the Central Provinces, and the number of immigrants in each of these is very high being respectively 16 and 26·7 per cent. of their total population; so too in the Yeotmal and Wun taluks of the Wun District, which also border on the Central Provinces, where the proportions are 32 and 17 per cent. respectively. The sexes are equally represented in these four taluks, a fact which shows that the immigrants are settlers, and not mere temporary residents, or men come in advance of their families to prospect the land."

The movement to judge by the figures above given still continues, but it is probable that the increase at the present Census is largely of a temporary sort. Mr. Drysdale writes from Wardha, that a large number of persons annually leave the district, temporarily to work as shearers of the rabi harvest in Berar. The shearing was still going on when the Census was taken, and as the cold weather harvest in the Wardha District was a poor one, it is probable that the number of persons who went into Berar was largely increased on this account. A comparison of the figures for the sexes of the emigrants may also be taken to point to the same conclusion. Berar sends to this Province, presumably in marriage, a large number of females, they are in the proportion of about three to every two males. Were there no field for labour in the Berars, it is probable that the returns would show a like strong female migration from the Central Provinces to Berar; the settlers would naturally send to the old country for wives, and the proportion of females might thus be expected to be specially high. But as it is, the number of males who go to Berar in quest of work at the harvest season, tends to preserve the balance between the sexes. Of the male migration, therefore, a considerable proportion is probably only temporary.

In Burma, the number of persons born in the Central Provinces is 527, as against 310 in 1881; I presume that most of the persons so returned are connected with Madras regiments formerly stationed here. The difference in the figures for emigration to Madras would appear to be due to the incomplete return of birth-place in the Agency Tracts of the three Northern Districts at the last Census. In 1891, 8,832 people living in the Agency Tracts have recorded the Central Provinces as their place of birth. The withdrawal of the Madras

A.—Immigration.—*Read* vertically *this table shows the distribution of* 10,000 *of the population of each District according to birth-place. Read* diagonally *from the upper left-hand corner it shows the relative strength of the* indigenous *population in each District.*

Birth-place.	Saugor.	Damoh.	Jubbulpore.	Mandla.	Seoni.	Narsinghpur.	Hoshangabad.	Nimar.	Betul.	Chhindwara.	Wardha.	Nagpur.	Chanda.	Bhandara.	Balaghat.
Saugor	8,705	372	41	21	27	143	29	6	5	12	3	9	1	1	15
Damoh	127	8,623	157	5	4	40	4	1	1	1	...	1	...	...	1
Jubbulpore	17	158	8,425	284	108	134	24	6	3	13	5	12	1	2	13
Mandla	2	12	56	8,896	126	2	1	...	...	3	...	1	...	1	127
Seoni	6	1	23	220	8,493	44	2	1	3	190	3	18	1	22	326
Narsinghpur	56	13	60	8	123	9,080	114	2	4	162	1	2	...	...	2
Hoshangabad	6	2	7	11	5	116	8,765	177	160	88	1	4	5	1	1
Nimar	...	...	2	...	...	2	40	8,568	13	1	1	4	1	...	...
Betul	1	..	1	...	3	2	103	3	9,445	162	11	9	...	1	...
Chhindwara	3	...	2	5	199	30	12	1	83	8,923	21	98	1	4	11
Wardha	...	...	...	...	1	...	...	...	3	10	7,824	133	66	12	3
Nagpur	4	2	12	6	56	4	9	15	27	251	814	8,785	83	150	41
Chanda	...	...	1	...	6	...	1	..	...	2	267	121	8,997	95	4
Bhandara	...	...	1	1	130	..	5	2	1	16	131	264	145	9,282	810
Balaghat	...	...	1	96	546	1	...	1	...	9	9	18	2	288	8,488
Raipur	1	2	6	11	4	1	1	1	1	2	6	10	293	78	110
Bilaspur	...	...	2	81	1	...	...	...	...	1	...	2	1	1	39
Sambalpur	3	...	...	...	...	...	...	1	...	...	...	1	...	...	...
Feudatory States	...	...	...	1	...	...	8	1	...	3	...	...	20	...	...
Immigrants from other parts of the Province.	226	562	372	750	1,339	519	353	218	304	926	1,278	707	620	656	1,508
Bengal	5	2	18	3	3	3	7	4	2	1	2	5	1	1	1
Berar	...	...	1	...	2	1	14	70	138	36	675	94	89	22	5
Bombay and Feudatory States	5	1	13	3	2	8	39	425	3	3	44	52	8	5	2
Madras and Feudatory States	2	...	7	...	1	1	5	6	1	1	2	57	8	1	1
N.-W. P., Oudh and Feudatory States	428	87	355	96	85	93	218	280	69	45	85	165	36	16	27
Punjab and Feudatory States	23	2	14	3	4	3	8	13	4	2	2	14	1	2	3
Hyderabad	1	...	5	...	2	1	8	18	6	2	14	32	218	2	1
Rajputana	21	7	15	7	7	12	89	70	11	15	43	33	6	8	6
Central India	573	713	759	238	61	279	481	315	17	44	30	16	15	5	18
United Kingdom	9	...	9	...	...	...	2	3	...	...	...	17	...	...	...
Elsewhere in India and beyond	2	3	7	4	1	...	11	15	...	2	6	23	1	...	...
Total Immigrants	1,295	1,377	1,575	1,104	1,507	920	1,235	1,487	555	1,077	2,176	1,215	1,008	718	1,567

B.—Emigration.—*Read* horizontally *this table shows the distribution of 10,000 persons born in each district, mentioned in the first column.*

Birth-place.	Saugor.	Damoh.	Jubbulpore.	Mandla.	Seoni.	Narsinghpur.	Hoshangabad.	Nimar.	Betul.	Chhindwara.	Wardha.	Nagpur.	Chanda.	Bhandara.	Balaghat.	Raipur.	Bilaspur.	Sambalpur.	Feudatory States.	Total Emigrants from districts mentioned in column.
Saugor	9,505	224	57	13	19	96	28	3	2	9	2	13	1	2	10	4	6	1	5	495
Damoh	249	9,281	389	6	5	49	7	1	1	2	...	2	...	...	1	1	3	...	3	719
Jubbulpore	15	78	9,588	146	60	74	19	3	2	8	3	13	1	2	7	8	11	4	8	462
Mandla	4	12	132	9,461	147	2	2	...	...	3	...	3	1	3	152	5	40	1	32	589
Seoni	10	1	49	213	8,994	46	4	...	2	221	3	39	2	46	357	5	2	1	5	1,006
Narsinghpur	91	12	124	7	126	9,269	168	2	4	183	1	4	1	...	2	2	2	...	2	781
Hoshangabad	8	1	10	8	4	87	9,522	92	106	73	1	6	7	1	1	2	10	1	60	478
Nimar	1	...	7	...	1	3	96	9,889	19	3	3	15	2	1	...	3	1	...	6	161
Betul	2	...	2	...	3	2	170	3	9,550	207	14	21	1	2	1	1	...	...	21	450
Chhindwara	4	...	4	4	191	28	19	1	70	9,428	22	192	2	8	11	4	2	...	15	577
Wardha	...	...	1	...	1	...	...	...	3	13	9,502	305	139	26	4	2	1	...	3	498
Nagpur	3	1	12	3	28	2	7	5	12	137	440	8,966	77	150	21	43	18	21	54	1,084
Chanda	...	...	1	...	3	...	1	...	...	1	162	139	9,492	106	3	22	9	1	60	508
Bhandara	...	...	1	1	63	...	3	1	...	9	69	261	132	8,991	405	13	5	2	44	1,009
Balaghat	1	...	2	87	541	1	...	...	...	10	10	36	4	571	8,639	28	6	2	62	1,361

C.—Gain *or* Loss *to each district by* Migrations within *the* Province.

	Saugor.	Damoh.	Jubbulpore.	Mandla.	Seoni.	Narsinghpur.	Hoshangabad.	Nimar.	Betul.	Chhindwara.	Wardha.	Nagpur.	Chanda.	Bhandara.	Balaghat.
Immigrants from other Districts	13,417	18,318	27,828	25,496	49,667	19,059	18,911	5,571	9,797	37,767	51,055	53,646	43,169	48,654	57,638
Emigrants to other Districts	26,836	21,759	30,537	17,206	35,233	26,269	23,296	3,541	14,368	22,269	16,443	76,747	33,591	77,369	50,949
Gain (+) Loss (−)	−13,419	−3,441	−2,709	+8,290	+14,434	−7,210	−4,385	+2,030	−4,571	+15,498	+34,612	−23,101	+9 578	−28,715	+6,689

D.—Proportion of Female per 1,000 of all Migrants.

(1) *Read* vertically *gives the figures for* Immigrants *from places mentioned in column I.*

(2) *Read* horizontally *gives the figures for* Emigrants *from places mentioned in column I.*

Birth-place.	Saugor.	Damoh.	Jubbulpore.	Mandla.	Seoni.	Narsingh-pur.	Hoshan-gabad.	Nimar.	Betul.	Chhind-wara.	Wardha.	Nagpur.	Chanda.	Bhandara.	Balaghat.	Raipur.	Bilaspur.	Sambal-pur.
1	2	3	4	5	6	7	8	9	10	11	12	13	14	15	16	17	18	19
Saugor	...	683	479	415	494	576	464	413	333	419	358	374	...	...	392	448	403	...
Damoh	641	...	542	417	387	509	469	...	...	...	...	...	...	...	...	...	...	...
Jubbulpore	528	576	...	448	493	574	464	394	...	491	380	481	...	410	391	454	393	333
Mandla	118	412	501	...	535		...	...	...	...	...	...	...	...	518	488	485	...
Seoni	428	...	551	507	...	542	598	...	...	565	426	528	...	528	514	436	...	...
Narsinghpur	561	590	629	383	450	...	603	...	453	485	...	455	...	...	...	...	...	...
Hoshangabad	544	...	434	452	419	652	...	472	470	462	...	452	496	...	...	...	462	...
Nimar	...	...	262	...	...		483	...	427	...	...	399	...	...	...	...	...	...
Betul	...	...	...	...	527	...	495	...	...	522	530	572	...	...	...	...	...	...
Chhindwara	298	...	488	343	554	519	533	...	576	...	562	619	...	487	428	540	...	...
Wardha	...	...	...	...	...	...	...	...	...	486	...	592	559	500	564	...	...	...
Nagpur	301	...	562	449	509	466	469	485	543	615	542	...	525	572	491	468	484	412
Chanda	...	...	...	...	538	...	...	...	...	...	567	609	...	608	549	467	491	...
Bhandara	...	...	...	...	497	...	484	...	...	542	469	547	528	...	555	393	337	219
Balaghat	...	...	...	475	519	...	...	...	...	490	436	476	494	583	...	447	428	...
Raipur	...	...	484	474	497	...	...	...	...	...	514	488	430	452	493	...	516	452
Bilaspur	...	...	221	491	...	...	...	...	...	...	...	404	...	...	504	519	...	518
Sambalpur	...	...	...	...	...	...	...	...	...	...	...	...	...	...	...	454	528	...
Feudatory States	...	...	...	..	...	...	575	...	...	538	...	...	488	...	...	483	479	554
Bengal	292	...	421	...	320	...	384	289	...	...	..	406	...	...	...	220	425	352
Berar	...	...	...	...	...	...	508	510	547	618	612	615	577	487	498	444	483	391
Bengal States	...	...	...	...	...	...	...	...	...	...	...	...	...	...	...	...	491	519
Bombay and States	325	...	368	202	...	339	355	574	...	292	386	416	372	315	...	321	244	309
Madras and States	456	...	521	...	...	...	413	415	...	...	360	402	383	...	...	514	391	388
North-West Provinces, Oudh and States	469	343	366	272	277	318	310	271	261	302	215	330	206	278	262	288	301	212
Punjab and States	179	...	221	181	235	...	235	212	281	...	...	297	173	259	371	172	220	190
Hyderabad	...	...	420	...	...	...	498	455	472	...	432	492	526	375	...	432	398	385
Rajputana	406	423	393	428	362	405	360	336	356	331	334	366	258	303	284	323	401	303
Central India	525	496	506	456	347	526	548	578	414	405	161	330	512	351	341	299	457	198

troops has also tended to increase the number of persons born in the Central Provinces, who are now living in the Madras Presidency. For the large falling off in emigration to the North-West Provinces and Oudh, I am unable to give any proper explanation. It is possible that the greater part of the emigration in 1881 may have been local, *i.e.*, confined mainly to the border districts of the Province, but as the last North-West Provinces Census Report did not give extra-Provincial details by districts, the exact scope of the movement cannot be ascertained. The large proportion of females may be possibly accounted for by the desire, prevalent among the better class of Hindus who have migrated to the Central Provinces, to keep up their connection with the north country by sending back their daughters there in marriage.

151. **Migrations within the Province. Explanation of Comparative Statements**—I next come to the movements that have taken place between different districts in the Province. These can be much better understood from the three proportional statements A, B, and D which have been prepared and which I have tried to make as explicit as possible, than from any written description that can be given. To take first statement A: of every 10,000 persons residing in each district appearing in the heading, the number born in each recorded place of birth is given in the vertical line under the name of the district. For example in Chhindwara of every 10,000 persons resident in the district at the time of the Census 12 were immigrants from Saugor, 13 from Jubbulpore, 190 from Seoni, and 8,923 were born in Chhindwara itself. Going down the column we can see that 926 of the people of Chhindwara or about a tenth of the population came from other districts in the Province. The number of immigrants from beyond the Central Provinces is, as might be expected in such an out of the way place, comparatively small; they are only in the proportion of 151 in 10,000. Next looking to statement B, the horizontal line opposite each district in column 1, tells us where every 10,000 persons born in the district are now living. As has been already observed, this information is available only regarding persons who are residing within the Province; of people who have gone to other parts of India there is no trace. From Chhindwara the number of persons who have emigrated beyond the borders of the Province will probably be small; Berar is the only place where many such might be found. Reading along the line opposite Chhindwara it will be seen that of 10,000 persons born in the district, four have emigrated to Saugor, 191 to Seoni, 192 to Nagpur, and so for the other districts. 9,423 people still live in Chhindwara, and the remaining 577 have gone to other parts of the Province. The *comparative* value of this statement is of course vitiated by the fact that of the 15 districts given in the table all but five are adjacent to foreign territory for which complete detailed information regarding emigration is not available. Thus whereas 577 per 10,000 nearly represents the total emigration from the Chhindwara district, 495 is no index of the total emigration from Saugor. All that the statement purports to show is the proportions in which persons born in a particular district tend to move to other districts within the Province. The net gain or loss resulting from inter-district migrations is shown in statement C.

152. **Relative proportion of the Sexes amongst Migrants.**—Statement D is of importance as explaining the nature of the migrations under discussion. Read vertically for any district in the heading, it shows the proportion of females per 1,000 of all immigrants from any of the places mentioned in the birth-place column. Thus of immigrants from Saugor to Chhindwara 419 per 1,000 are females, from Seoni the proportion is 565, and from Nagpur 615. If the horizontal line opposite Chhindwara in column 1 is taken, the figures give similar proportions for persons born in Chhindwara who have gone to other districts, *e.g.*, of emigrants to Saugor, 298 per 1,000 are females, to Seoni 554, and to Nagpur 619. In the statement details have been filled in only for districts

between which the migration figures exceed 100; for anything below this amount comparison is unnecessary. Taking each district and noticing the proportions between the sexes that are exhibited, the following general rule is deduced, *viz.*, that women are in excess of men amongst migrants between adjacent districts, whilst the opposite is the case amongst migrants between places at a distance from one another. As it is between adjoining districts that the figures for migration are naturally largest, it will be seen that it is the movements of the female population rather than the male that more especially affect the birth-place returns. The high proportion of female migrants for districts adjoining one another, is to be set down to marriages across their borders. Where the number of female migrants is proportionately less than the number of male migrants between two neighbouring districts, it is in most cases possible to account for the divergence from the rule. The case of Berar has already been noticed; there it was the field for labour that had apparently led to the exception. Nimar may also be taken as an example of where the rule is departed from. The next districts to Nimar are Hoshangabad and Betul, yet it sends to both, as well as receives from them, more men than women. The explanation is that the affinities of its people lie rather towards Bombay, Berar, and Central India than towards the Nerbada valley or the Satpuras; that this is the case is at once apparent from the fact that the former send to the district a considerably larger number of females than of males. The further deductions to be made from the figures which exhibit the proportions between the sexes are that in cases where the number of men among the migrants exceed the women, the movement is temporary rather than lasting. More especially is this the case if such disproportion is apparent between districts which adjoin one another, and are peopled by a common race, and where we should therefore expect to find more females than males among the migrants. Where the sexes tend to balance, it may be assumed that the migration is more of a permanent nature; particularly will this hold good when the migration is between places at a distance, the inference being that the men have not left their homes to look for employment but have gone to settle down taking with them their wives and families.

153. **Immigration statistics for districts.**—I have here arranged the districts in the order in which they stand, as regards the proportion of immigrants to their total population. It would be useless, as I have said, to compare them as regards emigration, since the border districts, whose people migrate to the surrounding States, would stand low in the list as compared with central districts, emigrants from which rarely go outside the Province. In point of immigration, Wardha takes the lead, with more than one-fifth of its inhabitants born outside its limits, chiefly in Nagpur, Berar, and Chanda. From Berar, the proportion of female immigrants is high, less so from Nagpur and Chanda, while from most other places the in-comers are principally men. The district, as a centre of the cotton industry, presents great attractions for labour and trade, to which the large extent of its immigration may be attributed. On the other hand, it sends large numbers of its people to Nagpur and the Berars as agriculturists and workmen. Jubbulpore, from its importance as a commercial and military centre, has also a large foreign element amongst its population. It is somewhat sur-

Serial No.	District.	Proportion of immigrants per 10,000 of total population.
1	Wardha	2,176
2	Jubbulpore	1,575
3	Balaghat	1,567
4	Seoni	1,507
5	Nimar	1,437
6	Damoh	1,377
7	Saugor	1,295
8	Hoshangabad	1,235
9	Nagpur	1,215
10	Mandla	1,104
11	Chhindwara	1,077
12	Chanda	1,003
13	Narsinghpur	920
14	Bhandara	718
15	Betul	555

prising to find the two inland districts of Balaghat and Seoni next in order as regards immigration. Both, also, it will be seen, send forth a large number of emigrants. These movements take place to a great extent between the districts themselves, and there is further a large interchange of population between Balaghat and Bhandara. The Deputy Commissioner of Seoni writing about these figures remarks:—

"I would also note that in former days the Seoni District included all that are now the Katangi, Lalbarra, and Wara-Seoni Purganas of the Balaghat District, and it may well be that illiterate people, in giving their places of birth, said indiscriminately, Seoni or Balaghat zilla, without being very sure what zilla it was: and this may account for the apparent interchange between the two districts."

The same doubt attaches to the returns for Bhandara, out of which a large patch was taken to form the district of Balaghat. It is probable that in Seoni and Balaghat some allowance should be made for possible error on this account, but both would appear to have attracted settlers in considerable numbers. Nimar draws the most part of its immigrant population from the Bombay Presidency and Central India. The large influx of people from the latter into Damoh, Saugor, and Hoshangabad has already been noticed. One would scarcely expect to find Nagpur so low in the scale of immigration, but compared with its three quarters of a million of inhabitants, the proportion of in-comers it attracts is not so high as in districts like Wardha or Nimar, with only half or one-third its population. The districts to which settlers are least drawn are Narsinghpur, Bhandara, and Betul. The first of these is already one of the most densely-populated parts of the Province; there is not much of a field for labour or trade, so that the proportion of male immigrants is comparatively low. There is, on the other hand, a very considerable interchange of females between Narsinghpur and most of the neighbouring districts. Bhandara is also a well-settled district, with no special industries to draw new comers to its midst. In Betul the isolated position of the district must in a great measure account for the high rate of its indigenous population.

154. **The Chhatisgarh Districts and States.**—I shall now add a few words about the Chhatisgarh Districts and States, which I have had to exclude from the proportional statements, on account of incorrectness in their birth-place returns. The abstract in the margin shows the change that has taken place in immigration from outside Chhatisgarh into the British districts since 1881. The first thing that strikes one is the falling off in the figures for the Raipur district. With the exception of the town of Raipur, there is no place of commercial importance in the district, and even Raipur itself must have suffered in this respect from Raj-Nandgaon being till recently the terminus of the railway. For agricultural settlers there is no field, the land is to a great extent already fully cultivated, and the people of Chhatisgarh have few or no affinities with the outside world. The overwhelming numbers of the Chamár population, act no doubt as a further deterrent to immigration. In the Census Report of 1881, Mr. Drysdale was of opinion that it was the want of a sufficient market for the produce of the country, which kept agriculturists from coming to Chhatisgarh. "As it is isolation which has kept down prices in these districts, we may expect that the extension of railway communication will result in attracting more colonists into Chhatisgarh." This result has up to the present time certainly not been realized, and for the reasons I have given above, I think there is little likelihood of increased immigration taking place to any marked extent, at least into the

DISTRICT.	Immigration from the Western districts of the Province.		Immigration from beyond the Province.	
	1891.	1881.	1891.	1881.
Raipur . .	8,219	10,762	8,796	11,150
Bilaspur .	5,705	7,465	32,498	29,691
Sambalpur .	2,384	1,054	15,511	13,888

plain country. At the time of the Census the construction of the Bengal-Nagpur Railway had practically been completed in Raipur; in Bilaspur work was also nearly finished, but in the eastern part of Sambalpur it was still in progress. In Raipur, therefore, we find few railway workmen of outside birth-place, whereas in Bilaspur and Sambalpur, the numbers of these have had an appreciable effect upon the returns. Like Raipur, the greater portion of Bilaspur is a country shunned by the cultivating classes of other parts. Only along the northern parts of the district, is there extensive immigration from the neighbouring States in Chhota Nagpur and Baghelkhand. In 1881, the number of persons born in the Central India States, was 15,088, and at the present Census, 14,589; but from Bengal, the numbers have risen from 7,619 to 9,246, the extra field for labour having no doubt contributed to the increase. In Sambalpur, 1,574 persons are shown as having been born in Nagpur; these figures, it has been discovered, are misleading, as in many of the Uria books by Nagpur is evidently meant Chhota-Nagpur; the number of persons returning Bengal or its Feudatories, will therefore be somewhat increased. As has been already said, almost the whole of the growth of immigration into Sambalpur seems to be explained by the presence of large numbers of contractors and their workmen, chiefly from the west and north of India.

155. **Immigration statistics for Feudatory States.**—In all the Feudatory States, the birth-place return may be accepted as correct for all places outside the districts and States of Chhatisgarh. In Khairagarh, Chhuikhadan, Kanker, Kawardha and Sakti, the place of birth of persons born in the States has been almost invariably recorded as Raipur or Bilaspur. In Sarangarh the return of Sambalpur as the birth-place of 28,270 persons, or 34 per cent. of the population, is also incorrect, and some suspicion attaches to Raigarh where 14,777, or 8·8 per cent. of the inhabitants are likewise so recorded. In Nandgaon there is a little doubt about the entry of Raipur, but most of the other figures would appear to be correct. In the other States the return may be taken as reliable as regards the migrations between the several States, and between the States and the districts in which they were formerly included. The accompanying abstract exhibits the main features of the immigration into the States whose figures it is possible to accept. There is no means of comparison with the returns of 1881, as detailed statements were not published at the last Census. The Uria States, it will be seen, are attracting settlers in large numbers, a result which was to be looked for with the improved administration they now possess. From the figures in column 3 it appears that Sambalpur contributes largely to the immigration into these States, some of which have received strong drafts of colonists from the British district; in Patna alone they number over twenty-one thousand, or about a sixteenth of the population,

Immigration into the Feudatory States.

State.	Total Population.	Immigrants from							
		District to which formerly attached.		Other Districts.		Other Feudatories.		Beyond the Province.	
		Number.	Percentage on column 2.	Number.	Percentage on column 2.	Number.	Percentage on column 2.	Number.	Percentage on column 2.
1	2	3	4	5	6	7	8	9	10
Makrai	18,549	2,847	15·3	612	3·3	1	...	766	4·1
Bastar	310,884	2,267	·7	7,373	2·4	1,037	·3	7,342	2·4
Nandgaon	183,866	23,537	12·8	4,214	2·3	7,142	3·9	1,949	1·1
Raigarh	168,525	14,777	8·8	7,188	4·3	4,178	2·5	9,960	5·9
Bamra	104,367	9,784	9·4	1,204	1·2	1,588	1·5	13,141	12·6
Rairakhol	20,335	997	4·9	52	·3	2,248	11·1	2,460	12·1
Sonpur	195,245	9,187	4·7	368	·2	4,463	2·3	9,094	4·7
Patna	332,197	21,057	6·3	9,740	2·9	27,854	8·4	5,425	1·6
Kalahandi	326,295	1,143	·4	3,930	1·2	6,868	2·1	8,899	2·7

There is at the same time a very considerable counteracting movement from the States into Sambalpur, but the net result of the migration that takes place is greatly to the advantage of the former. From outside the Province, immigration takes place mainly from the Chhota Nagpur and Cuttack Tributaries into the neighbouring States of Raigarh, Bamra, Rairakhol, and Sonpur; from the Agency Tracts of the northern Madras districts into Kalahandi and Bastar, and to a less degree from the Nizam's Dominions into the latter State. Nandgaon and Khairagarh are the only places that have attracted immigrants from distant parts of India. Bamra we may exclude, as the people from Northern and Western India, enumerated in the State, were mere temporary residents brought there by the construction of the railway.

156. The birth-place returns are further discussed in Chapter II, which deals with the movements of the population. There I have noted also on some of the statistics for emigration beyond the Province, figures for which were not available when the present chapter was written.

CHAPTER X.

CASTES, TRIBES, AND RACES.

157. The present chapter deals with the division of the people into Castes, Tribes, and Races, particulars regarding which will be found in Table XVI of the second volume of the Report. The subject of caste has also been taken up in connection with censused infirmities, Tables XII-A to XV-A, and in connection with education, Supplementary Table C; in both cases it has been dealt with in the chapters which relate to these matters respectively.

158. **The Record of Caste.**—In the enumerator's schedule two columns were kept, one for the record of main caste and the other for that of caste sub-divisions. The rules for the guidance of the census agency ran as follows:—

Column 4 (Caste, etc.).—Enter the caste of Hindus and Jains, as Brahmin, Bania, Chamar, Rajput, etc., and tribe or race for others, as Pathan, Moghal, Bhil, Gond, etc. Enter Christians as European, Eurasian, or Native Christian; or the caste of the latter may be entered if recognized. Vague terms, like Pardesi, Marwari, Hindustani, Madrasi, etc., must not be used.

Column 5 (Sub-division of Caste, etc.).—If the caste has been entered in column 4, enter here its sub-division, as Kanaujia, Deshasth, for Brahmins; Agarwal, Oswal, for Banias. If tribe has been entered, enter its sub-division, as Pardhan, Raj Gond, for Gonds. If European has been entered in column 4, enter nationality, as English, German, Irish, etc., and, if Native Christian, any racial or caste sub-division that may be given, as Goanese, Madrasi, etc. If no sub-division of caste or tribe be given, repeat the entry in column 4, but do not leave the column blank.

As was to be expected, the question, more especially of caste sub-division, proved a source of frequent bewilderment to the enumerating staff. It was of course impossible to issue set rules on the matter with the object of procuring what might be considered uniformity. Uniformity of some kind we should no doubt have attained by such a method, but it would have been at the expense of accuracy in the record as representing actually existing facts. The staff had, therefore, to be left pretty much to its own devices, though care was generally taken to inculcate that it was only main sub-divisions, and not *gots* or petty and local sections, that were required to be entered in the census books. Despite such precautions, however, the record was in too many instances crowded with a multifarious assortment of family patronymics and of titles derived from names of places, occupations, and the like, while *gots* and religious sects were also strongly in evidence in column 5 of the schedule. Frequently the enumerator or the person enumerated could not rise to giving even names such as these for caste sub-divisions, and the name of the main caste was then repeated in the sub-division column according to the closing portion of the second of the rules which have been given.

159. **The Compilation of the Caste Statistics.**—According to the directons of the Census Commissioner, contained in his note P, dated 30th April 1891, every caste and every sub-division of caste was to be abstracted from the Census books and separately tabulated in the village registers.* It soon became

*"The abstraction should include every caste, etc., and every sub-division found in the schedule. From the abstraction sheets an index is to be prepared, in which each caste, etc., with its sub-divisions, should appear in alphabetical order. In a Province, such as the Punjab, where the question of caste distribution was fully dealt with in connection with the last census, it has been found unnecessary to tabulate more than certain locally important sub-divisions. Elsewhere it will be advisable for a complete table, showing the strength of each item, to be recorded for further enquiry."

apparent that the time and labour that would be thus involved would be very great, and Mr. Baines suggested notice being taken only of those which might be deemed to be locally of importance. With this end in view nominal lists of castes and sub-divisions which had been prepared from the abstraction sheets were circulated to certain districts, and the opinions of the district officers invited on the names thus submitted to them. The replies received were generally unsatisfactory ; no time could be allowed for conducting the research that was necessary over so wide a range of enquiry ; the work in the Census office had to be pushed on, and any delay would have thrown a large portion of the tabulating establishment out of employment. Again, such varying accounts were furnished from different districts of the caste sub-divisions which were locally important, that I was almost in as much doubt as ever as to the sub-divisions which I should take up and those which might be altogether disregarded. I may here remark that there was practically no previous record to go by, nor, with the exception of Mr. Hislop's Papers and the report of the Ethnological Committee—both of which deal only with the aboriginal tribes,—are there any books of reference available regarding the castes of the Central Provinces. Some of the old Settlement Reports, all of which were published close upon a quarter of a century ago, contain excellent notes on some of the main cultivating castes in several districts, but the local caste sub-divisions have hardly in any case been touched upon. Being thus left in the dark as to how to proceed, the only solution that presented itself was to go on with the tabulation of the caste sub-divisions, as in this way alone could be ascertained what sub-divisions were numerically important, and what were mere petty or family names returned by only a few persons. In the case of the lower castes it was considered hardly worth while to pursue the investigation, but in the case of the important cultivating, priestly, and mercantile castes, as well as of the aboriginal tribes, it was thought best to work out the full details with which the census books had furnished us. In this way it was hoped that the work would be curtailed without at the same time any information at our disposal being lost as regards the chief castes and tribes of the Province. This decision taken, the work of tabulation was actively pushed on. It involved, even for the limited number of castes for which full details of sub-divisions were worked out, a very considerable amount of labour, but the task was a light one when compared with the magnitude of the work, which was afterwards necessary in collecting and arranging the innumerable different items which were scattered throughout the village registers. The districts of Saugor, Damoh, and Jubbulpore in the north, and of Nagpur in the south, of the Province were those which gave most trouble. In each of the former, castes like the Kurmis, Káchhis, Lodhis, etc., returned sub-divisions which in every case could be counted by hundreds, and the same was the case with many of the cultivating classes in Nagpur. The aboriginal tribes were also a source of very considerable difficulty, mainly on account of the multitude of *gots* or sectional names which had everywhere been recorded regarding them.

160. After a great deal of time and labour the compilation of castes, and of sub-divisions in the case of the prescribed castes, was completed, when another difficulty presented itself in connection with the wonderful transformation which the names of both had undergone in being transcribed from the census books to the working sheets, from the latter to the village registers, and from these again to the compilation papers. In many instances there was no resource but to refer to the original schedules, though this was of course unnecessary in the case of minor sub-divisions, which the compilation had shown to be represented by only a few persons. As the adjustments of the errors made in transcribing names occupied a considerable time, I may here remark that what more than

anything else conduced to such mistakes was the Central Office system for compiling the census returns, which was adopted for the Province. Excluding Sambalpur and the Uria States, more than two-thirds of the entries in the enumeration books were in the Hindi character. In the Census Office, partly owing to difficulty in obtaining workers from the Hindi districts, and partly owing to the abundance of Maratha candidates for employment in Nagpur, the majoriy of the persons employed were Marathas. Of these a very large proportion had to be put to abstracting the entries in the Hindi books. As a rule they could read Hindi well enough for all practical purposes, but when it came to transcribing uncommon names, such as those entered for sub-division of caste, they made numerous mistakes, and these were carried on, frequentlyi n an intensified form, in the subsequent processes through which the work passed. It would be of course too much to hope that had Hindi speakers alone been employed in abstracting the Hindi books, we should have been spared any mistakes of this sort; errors in transcribing will always arise, but not to the extent which working with a mixed staff, such as was employed in the Census Office on the present occasion, has produced. At a future census the advantage of having local names read by local men, to whom they are more or less familiar, would to me appear a strong argument in favour of having the results prepared at separate centres and not at a single head-quarters, as has been the case in 1891.

161. **The final results—Explanation of the Table.**— Such were the main difficulties with which we had to contend in dealing with the compilation of the caste statistics. Now that the Table showing the distribution of the people by caste has been made up, the result must, I fear, be considered somewhat inadequate, when the time that has been spent on the work is taken into account. A great mass of detail has been collected, much of which must perforce be left out of consideration, as, before it can be properly treated, much local inquiry will be necessary, and a fuller acquaintance with the people than can be derived from a two years' residence at Nagpur brought to bear upon the subject. As it is, for all the principal cultivating castes and for others which are of fair social standing, the chief sub-divisions are shown in detail of districts in Table XVI. In the case of the Feudatory States, sub-divisions have not been inserted in the published Table, but in the notes on individual castes, which are given in the present chapter, the figures for caste sub-divisions in the Feudatory States are taken into account as well as those for British districts. It must be remembered that the numbers shown against any particular subdivision do not necessarily represent the actual number of persons belonging to that sub-division. To take, for instance, the Kurmi caste, one of the most important of its sub-divisions is the Chandnáhu, the members of which in British districts and the Feudatory States are shown as 45,895. We cannot, however, say that there are only this number of Chandnáhu Kurmis in the Central Provinces; other members of the sub-division may have given a *got* or family name as sub-caste, while others again may have omitted to record the subdivision altogether. Thus the return can never be said with certainty to be complete, although every care was taken to see that all terms which were synonymous were combined with the sub-division to which they might correspond. Though therefore we may not be sure of the exact number of Chandnáhus, the figures which have been worked out give us a fair indication of the relative strength of the sub-division, and they enable us to ascertain in what part of the Province its members are found; in the case of the Chandnáhus this will be seen to be the districts and states of Chhatisgarh.

162. **Scheme of Caste Classification.**—The scheme drawn up by the Census Commissioner according to which all castes, tribes, etc., have been

arranged in the census tables will be found at page 137 of the second volume of the report. All are classified in 53 groups, which again are shown under six main heads or classes, as given in the margin. The arrangement of the different castes and tribes according to this method is not in every case such a simple matter as it seems. For instance, in the case of some of the tribes of aboriginal descent, all the members of which have now practically taken to agriculture and have come to be regarded as belonging to the Hindu community, it has been thought best to include them amongst cultivators, in Group II (*a*), rather than among forest and hill tribes Group IV, to which they might otherwise belong. There are several castes or tribes which might thus be classified under different groups, and I am not certain that the classification which I have adopted is in every case the right one. As, however, the tables for infirmities by caste, XII-A to XV-A, had been drawn up previously to the whole question of caste classification being fully gone into in connection with the caste table proper, it was thought best to allow the classification at first adopted to remain Otherwise difficulties would have arisen in calculating the proportion of the infirm for any particular group were the latter to contain different items in the several tables.

Classes of Castes, etc.
A.—Agricultural.
B.—Professional.
C.—Commercial.
D.—Artisan and village menial.
E.—Vagrant, minor artisans, and performers, etc.
F.—Races and nationalities.

163. **Scope of the present chapter.**—At the present Census no attempt has been made to work out information with regard to occupations or civil condition in conjunction with caste. The only matters which are therefore possible of discussion may be said to be, first, the relative strength of the different items, that is, individual castes, and the same by groups and classes, in proportion to the total population ; second, the proportions of the sexes among castes, and, third the variation since the last census in the numbers returning a particular caste. In addition to the above I have ventured on giving a short review of the more important castes, showing their strength in the chief districts where they are found, and the principal of their sub-divisions. So far as I am aware, there is nothing of the sort at present on record for the Central Provinces. At the census of 1881 the subject was practically not touched upon, and anything that has been written about the different castes and tribes will be found only in the two books to which I have referred at paragraph 159 , or scattered over the several district reports of the old Settlement. The account which I can give will necessarily be of the briefest, both the time and space at my disposal being limited, and as I am almost wholly dependent on the works above-mentioned for the information which I can supply, I have left detailed reference for those who require it to be made to the originals. With regard to the castes of the Maratha country the Berar Census Report of 1881 contains much useful information, and I have also received considerable help from Mr. Crooke's Ethnographical Hand-book for the North-West Provinces and Oudh (1890), and from the official edition of Mr. Risley's "Tribes and Castes of Bengal," published in 1891. The latter in many cases sheds quite a new light on the *terra incognita*—at least to most people in these Provinces—of the tribes of the lower Mahanadi basin and the parts which border on Chhota-Nagpur. Of the caste sub-divisions whose names are mentioned in the following pages, I scarcely know sufficient to venture upon very detailed accounts. The matter is one which requires much more extended investigation than is possible at a census, and in general little can be ascertained regarding them through the ordinary channels of correspondence, the replies received from districts about those on which reference was made, being frequently of such an inauthoritative nature that their publication would be of little use.

164. Though the general matters—the proportions of the several castes on the total population, and of the sexes in different castes—should more

properly be taken up to begin with, I defer noticing them until after the general eview of individual castes and tribes, as the latter is in part written and ready for the press. On the colonization of the Province by Hindu settlers from Upper and Western India I have already remarked at paragraph 3 of the first chapter of the Report. In Chapter III, which deals with the religions of the people, it has been seen how many of the original colonists have in course of time abandoned the strict observance of the social rules which are binding on their fellow-castemen in other parts. On the other hand, some of the immigrant classes who are lower in the social scale, and many of the aboriginal tribes, have benefited by the general laxity of the caste system which obtains nearly all over the Province to rise to heights in the way of caste ceremonials and observances, to which they could probably never have aspired under the more rigid caste *régime* of the long settled parts of India.

CLASS A.—AGRICULTURAL CASTES AND TRIBES.

165. This class is divided into three groups, showing (1) the military and dominant agricultural castes, (2) other agricultural castes, arranged according as they are, (*a*) cultivators, (*b*) cattle-breeders and graziers, and (*c*) field labourers, and (3) the forest and hill tribes. The relative strength of the different groups is shown at paragraph 261.

166. **I. Military and Dominant Castes.—Gujars.**—This important northern caste is found principally in the Nerbada valley. The Lilorha Gujars are said to have come from the Gwalior direction about the beginning of the seventeenth century, and are thus amongst the oldest cultivators in the valley. They occur chiefly in the Narsinghpur district and in the Sohagpur tehsil of Hoshangabad. They are a fine manly set, with none of the character for turbulence for which the Gujar race has long been known in the north of India, and are reckoned very good cultivators. The Mundal Gujars, who are found in the southern part of the Nerbada valley, in the Nimar district and in the Harda tehsil of Hoshangabad, are immigrants from Marwar. They are called Mundal, because when they eat they take off their turbans and expose their shaven heads, while the Lilorhas eat with the turban on.* The Nimar Gujars, of whom the Mundals form considerably more than half, are distinguished for their love of ostentation which leads them to spend their money on fine clothes and houses rather than in increasing their agricultural stock.† They are noted for their breed of fine trotting bullocks. The Jádam, Bargujar, and Reve are other sub-divisions occurring chiefly in Nimar. Eight Gujars are shown as Mussalman by religion; they are probably natives of Upper India, where many of the Gujars profess Mahomedanism.

Gujars, 48,501—37 per 10,000 of the population.

Chief sub-divisions.	Number.	Chief districts.	Number.	Percentage of district population.
Bargujar .	1,775	Saugor .	435	·1
Jádam .	2,222	Narsinghpur .	5,065	1·4
Lilorha .	19,917	Hoshangabad	23,969	4·5
Mundal .	14,769	Nimar . .	16,436	6·5
Reve .	1,802	Chhindwara .	743	·2
Kanwa .	747			
Gadwáe . .	800			

The *Játs* number 7,453, of whom 1,122 occur in the Narsinghpur district and 4,654 in Hoshangabad; in the latter they occur along the Nerbada in the Hoshangabad and Seoni tehsils. The Játs in this part of the country came originally from Bhartpur, but halted in Marwar on their way; at the census 1,182 of the Játs in Hoshangabad returned Marwari as a sub-division of their caste. They are excellent cultivators. Elsewhere Játs are met with in any

* Hoshangabad Settlement Report, page 62. † Nimar Settlement Report, page 261.

number, only in Saugor and Jubbulpore, where many of them are persumably soldiers in Native regiments; 19 are Sikhs and 17 Mussalmans by religion.

167. **Marathas,** 32,571, occur throughout the Province, but are most numerous in the three districts of Nimar, Betul, and Chhindwara, which form the northern border of Berar, in Wardha, where they number 7,607, in Nagpur 11,375 and in Chanda 1,792, while in Raipur the presence of 3,190 Marathas bespeaks the former dominance of the race in Chhatisgarh. Members of other castes have no doubt in some cases been shown simply as Marathas, so that the name probably includes several persons who do not belong to the military tribe to whom the term more properly applies; but as all persons who styled themselves Maratha and gave sub-divisions, such as Kunbi, have been put amongst their proper castes, the return may be taken as generally correct. The Marathas are the people from whom the great military leaders of the race have sprung; they have numerous sub-divisions, but all eat together and intermarry, though the widespread distribution of the caste and the high position to which some of the Maratha families have attained, have tended to raise up barriers in this latter respect.

168. **Rajputs.**—Under this name have been shown all the tribes of pure or impure descent who are generally looked upon as Rajputs. Without distinguishing between the varying elements that compose the caste, we find it to be most strongly represented in the lower parts of the Nerbada valley, Hoshangabad, and Nimar, in the Seoni district on the Satpura plateau, and in Bhandara and Balaghat in the Maratha country. In the three latter districts the preponderance of the caste is due to the presence of the Powárs, by far the largest section of the Rajputs in these parts.

The *Powárs* trace their origin to the Pramaras of Malwa, whence the members of the caste have spread over Northern India and in later times formed the

Rajput, 379,731.—293 per 10,000 of the population.

Sub-divisions.	Number.	Sub-divisions.	Number.	Districts.	Number.	Percentage of district population.
Baghel	3,381	Gautam	1,166	Saugor	18,347	3·1
Bágri	7,363	Gujar	76	Damoh	9,191	2·8
Bais	14,905	Jádam	20,152			
Baksaria	2,129	Kachhwáha	2,863	Jubbulpore	22,430	3·0
				Narsinghpur	17,082	4·7
Banáphar	277	Nágbansi	1,033	Hoshangabad	59,956	11·3
Bhadauria	949	Pál	527	Nimar	21,603	8·5
Bhanj	49	Parihár	5,087			
Bháradwáj	271	Powár	128,158	Mandla	2,189	·6
Bisen	547	Purbia	1,285	Seoni	25,888	7·0
				Chhindwara	8,677	2·1
Bundela	1,930	Ráchewár	87	Betul	6,501	2·0
Chandel	3,376	Raghubansi	16,590			
Chauhán	12,638	Raghwa	5,053	Wardha	3,087	·8
Daharia	1,310	Ráthor	5,670	Nagpur	12,169	1·6
Daraiha	1,807	Senghar	113	Chanda	2,127	·3
				Bhandara	70,040	9·4
Dhákar	186	Solanki	2,337	Balaghat	43 564	11·4
Dikhit	951	Sombansi	1,212			
Gaharwár	777	Surajbansi	6,419	Raipur	13,502	·9
Gahlot	887	Tawar	3,936	Bilaspur	14,909	1·3
Gaur	17,196	Tilokchandi	446	Sambalpur	6,596	·8
				Feudatory States	21,873	1·0

extensive colonies which we find in the Wainganga valley at the present day. In the northern districts of the Province it is probable that the Powárs are offshoots from the settlements in Upper India, but in the Nagpur country and on the Satpuras the Powárs are immigrants of a later period from Dhar in Central India, which is the traditional home of the tribe. Their first appearance in these parts was at Nandardhan near Ramtek, in the Nagpur district, where they built a fort and settled several villages, and whence as time went on they spread themselves to the east of the Wainganas. Some of the more influential members of the caste accompanied Chimnaji Bhonsla in the Cuttack expedition, and on their return were given lands in the lowlands of the present districts of Bhandara and Balaghat. From here about the commencement of the present century they first set out to people the waste lands above the ghats, where they have all along been among the most successful of the settlers who have helped to reclaim these wilds. Regarding them the writer of the Seoni Settlement Report has noted :—

"As agriculturists this class ranks high, and their cultivation may almost be termed scientific. From long practice they have acquired great skill in the arrangement of irrigation works and an extraordinary eye for the levels of the country over which water for irrigation is led for miles by them. They have also unusual aptitude for the management of the aboriginal classes, through whose agency they get the whole of their rough work of cultivating and clearing jungles and making the commencement of ir igation works effected. Their capabilities are proved by what they have effected within a century in Katangi —now part of Balaghat—and in the eastern portions of the Seoni tehsil. In respect of their energy and enterprise they are interesting, but from their litigious tricky habits and servile manners, and their close illiberal dispositions, they are not pleasant to deal with. They are almost all well-to-do, and mostly carry on money dealings chiefly with their tenants and servants."

The distribution of the Powárs in the three districts of the upper Wainganga valley is worth noting; they occur, it will be seen, all over Balaghat, but in Seoni they are confined to the southern portion of the district, and in Bhandara to the northern tehsil.

District and Tehsil.	Number of Powárs.
Seoni—	
Lakhnadon	46
Seoni	16,665
Balaghat—	
Burha	34,415
Behir	6,836
Bhandara—	
Tirora	52,343
Bhandara	8,730
Sakoli	2,480

Next to the Powárs come the *Jádums*, 20,152, a tribe found chiefly in Hoshangabad, where they number 18,940, of whom 14,636 are returned from the Hoshangabad tehsil. They claim descent from the Jadonbansis, one of the thirty-six royal tribes of Rajputs enumerated by Tod, but in Hoshangabad they are said to be all of impure blood.

The *Raghubansis*, 16,590, are an important cultivating class in Jubbulpore 2,283, in Narsinghpur 1,553, in Hoshangabad 7,362, and in Chhindwara 3,114. In Hoshangabad they are found chiefly in the Sohagpur and Seoni tehsils, where they number 3,445 and 3,300, respectively. "They are a queer class, all professing to be Rajputs from Ajodhia, although on cross-examination they are obliged to confess that they did not come here straight from Ajodhia, but stopped in Bundelkhand and the Gwalior territory by the way. They are obviously of impure blood, as they marry only among themselves; but whenever they get wealthy and influential, they assume the sacred-thread, stop all familiarity with the Gujars and Kirárs, and profess to be very high caste Rajputs indeed.—" (*Hoshangabad Settlement Report*, page 60). The Raghwas of the Nagpur country, said to be impure Rajputs, are probably the same as the Raghubansis of the Nerbada valley. Besides being agriculturists, they engage in trade, ghee being one of the commodities in which they specially deal.

The *Bais* Rajputs, 14,905, who are found in every district, trace their origin to the tract known as Baiswara in Oudh. Tod gives them as one of the thirty-six royal tribes, but there seems considerable doubt as to whether they are really pure Rajputs In the Central Provinces they muster strong in Chhatisgarh, where their numbers amount to 4,616. Chauháns, with their sub-divisions Bhadauria, 949, and Purbia, 1,275, number 14,862, of whom nearly a third,

4,846, are returned from Hoshangabad. Gaurs, with whom have been included the persons recorded as Gorae Rajputs, are found principally in Narsinghpur, from which 6,194 have been returned. The Chamar Gaurs, 4,432, are the highest of the three branches of the Gaur tribe; they are said to be so called because one of their women, far advanced in pregnancy, took refuge in a Chamár's hut, and was there delivered under his protection.* The Bágris are an important tribe in the Seoni district, where 4,985 are found, nearly all in the Seoni tehsil. In Saugor the Bágris belong to the Central Indian stock, who have long had a name for professional robbery. 6,419 persons returned themselves as of the solar race, Surajbansi, and 1,212 as of the lunar race, Sombansi or Chandrabansi; of the Surajbansis about half are found in Betul. Of the other sub-divisions, most of which are well-known Rajput clans, it is hardly necessary to speak; nearly all are represented by a few persons in every part of the Province. Among less known or local sub-divisions we may however note the Baksarias, Daharias, and Daraihas, returned chiefly from Chhatisgarh; the two latter are described as having so far deteriorated that they would not be acknowledged by the up-country race at all. The Pál is an impure Rajput tribe returned from Hoshangabad. In Kalahandi and others of the Uria States many persons have recorded themselves as Rajputs, giving their sub-divisions as Nágbansi, Paik, Bhanj, etc.; many are probably of very doubtful Kshatriya descent.

169. **II(a) Cultivators.**—*Agharias*, 26,219, are found in Sambalpur and the surrounding States of Raigarh, Sarangarh, Bamra and Patna; they occur chiefly in the borderland between Chhatisgarh and the Uria country. According to their tradition they derive their name from having originally come from Agra (Dalton). They are tall and well-built and are orthodox Hindus in most customs, but they allow their widows to remarry and bury their dead.

Alias, or cultivators of the ál plant, number 136, of whom all but 19 are found in Nimar.

The *Arewárs*, 2,344, *Ayawárs*, 359, and *Barewárs*, 762, are Telugu agricultural castes returned principally from the Chanda district. Of the Arewárs more than half have given Khaire, a title of the Kunbis, as a sub-division of their caste.

Bankas, 7,884, are recorded mainly from Kalahandi, 7,657; they are the same as Páiks- the latter term has been returned as a sub-division by 212 of their number—and serve as rural police and village watchmen. *Páiks* number 15,250, and are found in Raipur 2,494, in Patna 3,034, and in Kalahandi 9,691. From the number of names of other castes returned as Páik sub-divisions, the class appears to be recruited from various quarters. 2,570 Páiks and Bankas styled themselves Rajputs.

Bargáhs, 1,436, a tribe of people in Northern India who take service with the better classes of Hindus, have found their way through Rewa into Chhatisgarh, where the members of the caste are now engaged in agriculture. Bilaspur returns 1,130 and Raipur 162.

Bishnois, 677, occur only in Hoshangabad; they are immigrants from Upper India and resemble the Játs in appearance. They follow the precepts of Jámbhaji, a Rajput of Bikanir, who lived in the fifteenth century; the settlers in the Nerbada valley, like their fellow-castemen in the north, have abandoned the Mahomedan customs and religious rites which they formerly practised.† Crooke classes them amongst Banias. At the Census 273 of the Bishnois returned Marwari as a sub-division of their caste, but this only signifies that they, like the Játs, are immigrants from Marwar.

* Crooke's Ethnography, North-Western Provinces and Oudh, páge 154.
† Hoshangabad Settlement Report, page 62; Crooke's Ethnography, North-Western Provinces and Oudh, page 17.

170. *Bhoyars.*—These are an important cultivating class in the Betul and Chhindwara districts. In the former they are found chiefly in the Multai tehsil, 16,347; in Chhindwara they occur both above and below the ghats, in the Chhindwara tehsil their numbers amounting to 7,849. They are believed to have come originally from northern India, and are described as hardworking and industrious cultivators, ever ready to avail themselves of any means of irrigation. Hard drinking is said to be one of their failings.

Bhoyar 45,340—35 per 10,000 of the population.

Chief Sub-divisions.	Number.	Chief districts.	Number.	Percentage of district population
Powár	27,534	Betul	19,626	6·1
Jagdepowár	2,293	Chhindwara	14,378	3·5
Dholewár	2,519	Wardha	8,908	2·2
Chaurasia	261	Nagpur	2,333	·3

The *Burmese and Shans*, 314, enumerated in the Province, are nearly all prisoners in the three Central Jails. The entry includes 4 Chins, 2 Shans, 7 Talaings, and 1 Karen.

Chasas number 20,528, of whom 11,269 are found in Bamra, 5,772 in Rairakhol, and 2,290 in Sonpur. They are the chief cultivating caste of Orissa, and are said by Mr. Risley to be for the most part of non-Aryan descent, the loose organization of the caste system among the Urias making it possible for outsiders to be admitted into the caste. The name Chasa, it may be remarked, simply means cultivator of the soil.

The *Cherwas*, 982, are returned chiefly from the north of Bilaspur, 536, and from Raigarh, 372. They are evidently the same as the Cheros, a formerly dominant tribe of Chhota-Nagpur, who are described by Dalton at page 125 of his "Ethnology of Bengal."

171. **Dángis.**—Of the 25,070 Dángis enumerated at the Census, 23,111 are found in the Saugor district and 1,019 in Damoh. The following description of the caste has been furnished by the Deputy Commissioner of Saugor:—

Dángis, 25,070—19 per 10,000 of the population.

Chief Sub-divisions.	Number.
Bhadonia	2,223
Nadiya	3,799
Nahonia	3,.83
Nakoria	1,016
Mahobia	645
Basia	452
Atwaria	422

"The Dángis appear to be an offshoot of the Rajput tribe. The name is, according to some, derived from *dáng* (fraud), the Dángis being the issue of wives detained fraudulently by a certain chief; according to others, it is a corruption of the word *dági* (stained). The common story runs thus. The Chief of Garhpahra, or old Saugor, 7 miles from its present situation, detained twenty-two palanquins of married women by force and kept them as his wives. The issue of the illicit intercourse were named Dángis, and there are thus twenty-two sub-divisions of these people. Besides these there are three other sections who are considered the most respectable in their community. They are Nahonias, Bhadonias, and Nadiyas. These are pure Rajputs who migrated from Central India (Narwar and Bhadawar), and being cut off from their own domicile, mixed with the Dángis of the Saugor district. The Nahonias are Kachhwáha Rajputs, Bhadonias are Bhadauria Chauháns, and Nadiyas are said to be the descendants of Nadwania Rajputs. The pure Rajputs accept daughters of these three clans in marriage, but do not give theirs to Dángis. Similarly, the three superior clans named above accept daughters from the twenty-two inferior sections specified, but will not give theirs to them. The Dángis were always a troublesome and disreputable set of people They are an ignorant race, and education seems to have had little effect on them, and to this day they preserve their rude and uncouth manners."

They predominate in the Saugor and Khurai tehsils, where they number 10,975 and 6,915 respectively; the town of Khurai was in former times given by Aurangzeb in jagir to a Dángi chief.

Deswális.—Among these have been included 819 persons who returned their caste as Mina; the total of the two castes thus amounts to 8,186. In

Hoshangabad the Deswális number 6,694, or 1·3 per cent. of the population of the district; there are 815 in Nimar and 495 in Makrai. The 124 persons recorded from Saugor are all up-country Minas. The Deswális first came to the Nerbada valley from Khandesh, whither they had emigrated from Malwa; others were attracted from Jaipur at a later period. According to the Hoshangabad Settlement Report they are the same race as the Minas of Ajmir, who with the Bhils have borne the credit of all the robberies committed in Rájasthán and Malwa for many generations. 3,010 persons gave Mina as a sub-division of their caste, while 341 returned the sub-division Dekhani, a name that would point to their having been at one time settled in Khandesh.

172. **Káchhis.**—This important cultivating caste is found in nearly every part of the Province, but from the abstract in the margin it will be seen that it is returned in strength only from the northern districts. In Saugor the Káchhis are between a twelfth and a thirteenth part of the population of the district. The Káchhis are noted for the excellence of the garden crops they raise. Their chief sub-division in this part of the country is the Kachhwáha. Mr. Crooke inclines to the belief that the Káchhis have at least a totemistic connection with the Kachhwáha tribe of Rajputs, who take their name from *kachhwa*, the tortoise, which was probably the tribal symbol.*

Káchhi, 122,646—95 per 10,000 of the population.

Chief Sub-divisions.	Number.	Chief districts.	Number.	Percentage of district population.
Kachhwáha	73,799	Saugor .	45,896	7·8
Hardia .	15,051	Damoh .	15,722	4·8
Siloria .	11,477	Jubbulpore .	27,294	3·6
Alaha .	5,537	Narsinghpur .	13,733	3·7
Saksena .	1,092	Hoshangabad	9,331	1·8
Kanaujia .	766	Nimar . .	2,447	1·0
Jiri . .	410	Mandla .	3,164	·9
		Seoni . .	1,792	·5
		Chhindwara .	1,191	·3

The *Kápewárs*, 12,705, are a cultivating caste in the Chanda district, where 9,634 of them are found; Nagpur returns 1,146 and the Bastar State 1,348. According to the Chanda Settlement Report "the Kápewárs hold the same position among Telugus that Kunbis do among Marathas, their speciality being rice and sugarcane; but they are also the best stone-masons in the country, and it seems probable that they were originally brought to Chanda to build the many miles of cut-stone rampart which guards the city, and that when the work was finished their descendants took to agriculture in default of other employment." The name of Kápewár would appear to be interchangeable with the term Munurwár, which in the tables has been shown as a sub-division, but is, according to all accounts, a synonym for the main caste.

173. The **Kawars** are an important aboriginal tribe in Chhatisgarh and in the Uria country, in the former of which they are principally found. They number 44,302 in Bilaspur, or 3·8 per cent. of the population, and 27,435 in Raigarh, or 16·3 per cent. of the inhabitants of the State; 3,860 Kawars are returned from Chanda, where they occur solely in the Brahmapuri tehsil which adjoins Chhatisgarh. Of the Kawars a full account is given in the Bilaspur Settlement Report (1868), page 54, where they are described as fired with an ambition to pass as Rajputs. To this desire is to be ascribed the adoption of such high-sounding terms as Kawarbansi, Tawar, etc., among their sub-divisions. The similarity of the tribal name to the well-known Rajput title has proved a convenient means of transition to the higher rank to

Kawar, 127,093—98 per 10,000 of the population.

Chief Sub-Divisions.	Number.
Dudhkawar	4,069
Paikara	64,380
Rathia	27,447
Tawar	1,139
Kawarbansi	7,109
Telási	864
Mánjhi	404

* Crooke's Ethnographical Hand-Book, North-West Provinces and Oudh, page 111.

which the more influential members of the tribe aspire; and if report be true, the claim of those who call themselves Tawar to be of Rajput lineage has, by dint of judicious importuning coupled with arguments of a more substantial nature, been in recent times recognized by one of the leading of the Central India Chiefs. The writer of the Raipur Settlement Report, page 35, is inclined to consider that the Kawars really are imperfect Rajputs, who settled in early times among the hills of the Vindhyan range, and so failed in becoming Hinduized like other warlike immigrants.

The *Kaonras*, 15,721, were in 1881 classed along with Kawars, but on the present occasion they have been kept distinct. They nearly all occur in the Narsinghpur district, the Deputy Commissioner of which reports regarding them as follows:—

"The Kaonras trace their descent from the Kauravas, one of the two legendary families of the Lunar race. They wear the sacred-thread, burn their dead and generally observe the Hindu religion, being guided in all matters of ceremonial by Brahmins. But they differ from strict Hindus in two important points: they eat flesh and allow their widows to remarry. They imitate Rajput manners and customs. It is only in this last respect and in their practice of eating flesh that they appear to resemble the Kawars; and it is to be observed that like the Kawars they do not drink liquor. The two castes would appear to be perfectly distinct."

According to Mr. Risley the Kawars of Chhota-Nagpur set up the same claim to descent from the Kauravas of the Mahábhárata, and the Dudh Kawars among them follow the Hindu doctrine and have Brahmin priests. Further research will probably disclose the identity of the Narsinghpur Kaonras with the Kawars of the eastern districts.

174. *Kirs*, 6,941, are found in Hoshangabad 5,978, and in Narsinghpur 849; they are found along the riverside, where they grow melons in the sand and castor-oil plant and vegetables in the alluvial soil. They are immigrants from the Marwar direction; 244 have recorded Marwari as a sub-division, while 449 returned themselves as Rajputs.

Kirárs.—These are an important caste in the Nerbada valley and on the Satpura plateau, but as cultivators they are considered inferior to most of the other agricultural classes of these districts. More than half of the Kirárs, 28,041, have returned themselves as Dhákars, a sub-division of the Rajput caste. According to a report furnished by the Deputy Commissioner of Betul,* the Kirárs say that they are Dhákar Rajputs, and that they formerly belonged to Dháránagri, whence they were driven by Mahomedan invasion. To conceal their identity they styled themselves Kirárs, from Kirargaon, a place where they had settled. The Kirárs of Betul hold intercourse with their castemen in the other Satpura districts and in Nagpur, with whom they eat and intermarry, but have apparently been cut adrift from those in the Nerbada valley and Berar.

Kirár 43,316—34 per 10,000 of the population.

Chief districts.	Number.	Percentage of district population.
Narsinghpur . . .	12,496	3·4
Hoshangabad . . .	10,448	2·0
Betul	7,829	2·4
Chhindwara . . .	4,750	1·2
Seoni	2,894	·8
Nagpur	4,105	·5

175. The **Kisáns** and **Kudas** are returned solely from Sambalpur and the Uria States; they number 13,982 and 16,296 respectively. Like Chasa the term Kisán simply means cultivator of the soil. Colonel Dalton has a note upon the tribe at page 131 of his "Ethnography of Bengal." Both in appearance and in customs they resemble the Kols, but they repudiate all connection with that race and would scorn to eat with them. Their affinities are altogether towards Chhota-Nagpur, as they are found almost entirely in the Bamra State, 5,876, and in Sambalpur, north of the Mahanadi—all the 7,988 Kisáns enumerated in the district are recorded from the Uttartir,—whilst hardly any occur in the

* For another account of the Kirárs, see Hoshangabad Settlement Report, page 60.

Southern Uria States, or in those which border on Orissa. The Kudas are said to be analogous to the Kisáns, and though tank-digging and earthwork generally is their characteristic profession,—the name Kuda is derived from the Uria word for digging,—in late years they have largely taken to cultivation. Mr. Risley considers the Kudas or Koras to be probably an offshoot from the Munda tribe; with them he classes the Khairas, of whom 955 have been returned at the Census, but have been shown in the Caste Table in Group IV among aboriginal races. Combining the figures for Kudas and Khairas, the strength of the tribe becomes 17,251; they are much more widely distributed than the Kisáns, 9,846 in Sambalpur being found in both tehsils of the district, while in Sarangarh there are 1,041, in Bamra 899, in Rairakhol 875, in Sonpur 1,778, in Patna 1,898, and in Kalahandi 349. Among Kisáns 59·0 per cent have returned their religion as animistic and amongst Kudas and Khairas 28·5; both are semi-Hinduized, the Kudas especially affecting to be orthodox Hindus, worshipping the regular gods and calling themselves Saktas or Vaishnavas according to the cult to which they incline. The sub-divisions of the tribes which have been recorded are for the most part unimportant. Kudas also call themselves Mirdhas, 1,754 being so returned; other titles are Munda, 158, Nágbansi, 158, Mánjhi, 37, Raotia, 20, while Kisán has been shown as a sub-division of 255 persons whose main caste was given as Kuda. Similarly, Kuda has been returned as a sub-division of the Kisans, so that in Sambalpur, as has been reported by the Deputy Commissioner, the two tribes can hardly be considered as very distinct.

176. The **Kohlis** or **Kohris**, 19,739, are found almost solely in the districts of Bhandara, 12,097, and Chanda, 7,602. In the former they occur chiefly in the south—8,130 are returned from the Sakoli tehsil, where the numerous tanks offer facilities for raising their favourite crops of sugarcane and rice. In Chanda 6,578 of their number are found in the Brahmapuri tehsil. Regarding their origin the writer of the Chanda Settlement Report notes:—

"In the Bhandara Settlement Report it is surmised that they were originally brought to Chanda from the Benares Province by a prince of the Bhonsla* line and that from Chanda they spread to Bhandara, but no story of this sort is found among the Chanda Kohlis, who not only have held tanks long before the Maratha invasion, but have neither, in appearance, dress, customs, religion, language, nor traditions, the faintest tinge of anything connected with Upper India. They believe themselves to have been always in Chanda, and though now, like the Mánas, copying the Maratha Kunbis, retain many Gond customs and have the same Bháts as the Mánas."

The sub-divisions of the caste returned at the Census do not help us to a solution of the question; the only sub-division containing even a moderate number of persons is the Jháre, 230, recorded in the Bhandara books, which would point to the caste having been long settled in the Province. The theory of the writer of the Bhandara Report that the Kohlis first came from Northern India in the suite of a Bhonsla prince of the Chanda branch who had performed a pilgrimage to Benares is evidently untenable, but it is possible that they may have been introduced by one of the Gond princes of Chanda, who may have sojourned in Upper India. At all events the similarity of their name and style of cultivation would point to their affinity to the Koiris of the North-Western Provinces who resemble the Kurmis, the only distinction being that the Koiris are generally market-gardeners as well as agriculturists. Benares is, moreover, the traditional home of the Koiris, who say they were produced by Mahadeva and Párvati to look after the gardens of the sacred city.†

177. The **Koltas**, 110,200, are the chief Uria cultivating caste. In Sambalpur, where they hold most of the best villages in the district, the Koltas number 77,499, or about a tenth part of the population; they are widely scattered over

* Query. May not 'Gond' be meant?

† Crooke's Ethnographical Hand-book, North-West Provinces and Oudh, page 111.

the Uria States, Raigarh containing 8,346, Sarangarh 3,798, Sonpur 6,510, Patna 10,373, and Kalahandi 2,556. It was owing to the footing the Koltas obtained in the latter State, where their thrift and industry enabled them to supplant the aboriginal holders of the soil, that the Khond rising took place in 1882.

178. **Kunbis, Kurmis.**—At the Census the two names have often been used indiscriminately, so that it would be of little use to give separate district

Kunbi, Kurmi — 801,766 — 619 per 10,000 of the population.

Kunbis.		Kurmis.		Chief Districts.	Number.	Percentage of district population.
Chief Sub-divisions.	Number.	Chief Sub-divisions.	Number.			
1	2	3	4	5	6	7
Báone . .	60,525	Atharia . .	3,703	Saugor . .	26,511	4·5
Dekhani . .	2,031	Baiswár . .	2,038	Damoh . .	24,193	7·4
Dália . .	135	Bargaiya . .	3,459			
Deshkar . .	6,805	Bundele . .	1,898	Jubbulpore . .	35,578	4·8
				Narsinghpur .	7,256	2·0
Dhanojé . .	54,800	Chandnáhu . .	45,895	Hoshangabad .	22,975	4·3
Ghátul . .	1,133	Chauria . .	10,383	Nimar . .	22,999	9·1
Jádo . . .	2,080	Delwár . .	6,461			
Jháre . . .	36,135	Desaha . .	5,299	Mandla . .	5,737	1·7
		Dholewár . .	5,504	Seoni . .	7,980	2·2
Kadwa .	278			Chhindwara .	26,130	6·4
Khaire . .	86,879	Gahoi . .	19,499	Betul . .	49,879	15·4
Khedula . .	40,092	Gawel . .	2,089			
Lewa . . .	1,665	Gore . .	4,077	Wardha . .	81,455	20·3
		Kanaujia . .	12,952	Nagpur . .	153,982	20·3
Lonhare . .	42,122	Manwa . .	35,306	Chanda . .	102,535	14·7
Mána . .	7,266			Bhandara . .	86,618	11·7
Tirale . .	170,873	Patharia . .	1,134	Balaghat . .	19,303	2·7
Wándhekár . .	6,215	Sanaurhia . .	15,625			
		Santora . .	6,494	Raipur . .	67,731	4·3
		Singrore . .	11,883	Bilaspur . .	51,015	4·4
		Usrete . .	36,181	Sambalpur . .	3,177	·4
				Feudatory States .	15,712	·7

details for the northern and southern branches of the great cultivating caste. The sub-divisions of one or the other can, however, be sufficiently distinguished, and all that are of any importance have been classed in the appended table according as they are Kunbi or Kurmi tribes. The Maratha *Kunbis* are found in greatest strength in the districts of the Nagpur plain; both in Wardha and Nagpur they form more than a fifth part of the population. Outside the Maratha country proper the Kunbis occur principally in Nimar, where nearly all are of southern or western origin, in Betul where more than four-fifths of the combined strength of the caste are Marathas, and in Chhindwara where also the caste is almost wholly of this stock. In Seoni and towards Chhatisgarh the *Kurmi* element predominates; in the Kawardha State, it is true, a large number of Kunbis have been returned, but an examination of the sub-divisions given shows that most of the members of the caste are of northern origin. In the northern districts and generally throughout the Nerbada valley the Kurmi takes the place of the Maratha Kunbi who is here seldom met with, being practically confined to the Harda tehsil of Hoshangabad, where 5,192 persons returned themselves as Kunbis.

The caste is so well known that I need not here do more than refer to some of the most noteworthy of its sub-divisions, which, so far as the Central Provinces are concerned, have now for the first time been brought out at the Census. To take first the Kunbis; by far the strongest body among them are the Tirales, to whom belong the great bulk of the caste in Nimar, Chhindwara, Wardha, and Nagpur; in 1881 they formed over 60 per cent. of the whole Kunbi population of Berar. There is a tradition that they were once Rajputs, said to have come from a place named Therol in Hindustan.* Next to the Tirales in number come the Khaires, whose stronghold is the Chanda district, though many are found also in Wardha and Nagpur. The Dhanoje Kunbis are the other great division of the caste in Chanda; they are proverbial for the excellence of their cattle, and occupying the lands along the bank of the Wardha river are chiefly employed in growing jowari and cotton, while the Khaire Kunbis of the centre and south cultivate principally jowari and rice. The Báone and Jháre Kunbis occur mostly towards Bhandara, where in the valley of the Wainganga the Khedulas are also found; the latter sub-division extends down the valley into the Chanda district, in the Brahmapuri tehsil of which it is strongly represented. In Betul the Kunbis belong mainly to the Lonhåre sub-division. Among Gujerati Kunbis, nearly all of whom are found in Nimar, the chief sub-divisions returned are the Lewa, Kadwa, and Dália. The Kurmis of the northern part of the province belong principally to the Usrete, Gahoi, Santora, and Sanaurhia sub-divisions, while those of the Chhatisgarh country are Chandnáhus, who greatly predominate, Manwas—found largely in the Simga tehsil of Raipur—Singrores and Delwárs. The Chaurias are an important sub-division in Hoshangabad. Throughout the Province the caste is known as a thrifty and hard-working class of cultivators. They rarely follow any other profession, and the real secret of their unfailing success in agricultural pursuits generally does not appear to lie so much in their reputed superior skill, as in the fact that the women are engaged equally with the men in carrying on the work of their fields, while the women of several other agricultural classes are precluded from prejudice or custom from assisting the male population in their labours.

The *Lodhas*, 5,353, are found only in Hoshangabad, where they are said to be distinct from the Lodhis, none of whose sub-divisions they return.

179. **The Lodhis** are most strongly represented in the four northern districts of Saugor, Damoh, Jubbulpore, and Narsinghpur, while south of the

Lodhi, 287,241—222 per 10,000 of the population.

Chief sub-divisions.	Number.	Chief districts and states.	Number.	Percentage of district population.
Basyán	4,017	Saugor	47,197	8·0
Bhadauria	2,610	Damoh	39,211	12·0
Chandpuria	1,683			
Chhaparha	15,875	Jubbulpore	47,560	6·4
		Narsinghpur	32,947	9·0
		Hoshangabad	7 704	1·5
Dondasia	3,707			
Gudleya	1,894			
Hardia	2,342	Mandla	5,008	1·5
Jángra	65,945	Seoni	5,067	1·4
		Chhindwara	9,451	2·3
Janghele	11,894	Nagpur	8,509	1·1
Jaria	36,123	Bhandara	20,903	2·8
Kirbanaya	4,113	Balaghat	18,607	4·9
Lohbansi	1,728			
		Raipur	8,259	·5
Mahálodhi	54,691	Bilaspur	8,869	·8
Mahdele	17,149	Nandgaon	3,948	2·1
Narwaria	3,718	Khairagarh	16,612	9·2
Ráwat	1,621	Chhuikhadan	3,952	10·9
Singrore	20,897	Kawardha	1,677	1·8

* Berar Census Report, 1881, page 113.

Satpuras there are large colonies of the tribe in Bhandara and Balaghat and in the States of Nandgaon, Khairagarh, and Chhuikhadan. Of their numerous sub-divisions, only those have been shown which contain more than 1,000 persons. In the north of the Province the Lodhis were among the earliest of the settlers from northern India and they have attained to considerable position as cultivators and landholders. In Damoh "the principal talukdars and landholders are of the Lodhi caste, the Mahdele sect predominating over all others, and they consider themselves superior to the Lodhis of the Nerbada valley, who are mostly Mahálodhis. As agriculturists they are scarcely inferior to the Kurmis; they are somewhat better looking, both men and women, the former with a martial swagger, noticeable even among the purely agricultural members. They are, however, the opposite of the Kurmi in natural temperament, being short-tempered, hot-blooded, revengeful, and ever ready to join in any disturbance." The description holds fairly true of the caste as found throughout the northern districts and in the Nerbada valley. Towards this side their chief tribes are the Mahálodhis in Narsinghpur and Saugor, the Chhaparhas and Singrores in Jubbulpore, the Jarias in Saugor and the Mahdeles in Damoh. These are very sparsely represented in the southern colony of the Nagpur country and the Chhatisgarh border, where the greater portion of the Lodhis met with belong to the Jángra sub-division of the caste. Four-fifths of the Lodhis in the native states are of this tribe, which also predominates in the Chhindwara district above the ghats. The Lodhis of Bhandara are described as well set up, fine, powerful men, living always in the open air and following no profession but that of the plough; they are a quiet and peaceful people with none of the character for turbulence which attaches to their brethren on the other side of the Satpuras.

180. **Mális and Marárs.**—These are an important cultivating class in several districts of the Province, their special pursuit being the raising of garden produce which is the traditional occupation of the castes. If we leave out Sambalpur and the Uria States, Marár may be said to be the name generally returned for the gardener class throughout the eastern half of the Province, in which may be included the districts of Mandla, Seoni, Bhandara, and Chanda. In the two latter districts Mális are also largely met with; in Nagpur and Wardha and in the western Satpura districts and Nimar they are almost universally returned, while in the Nerbada valley and the two northern districts the place of both Máli and Marár is taken by the Káchhi of Upper India. Among Marárs the chief sub-divisions are the Bhoriya, 52,353, returned of four-fifths of the caste in the Balaghat and Seoni districts, and the Bhoyara, 44,859, which is recorded of a large number of persons in Bhandara, Balaghat, and Chhatisgarh; I am unable to tell whether the names are synonymous. The Bhoyaras are immigrants from Northern India; the Phulmarárs, on the other hand, have come from the Berars and occur principally in the Bhandara district. The Kosria Marárs, 53,182, are numerous in Raipur and Chanda. In the latter district they are the only agricultural caste, who are allowed to plant turmeric with their own hands; they are debarred from the use of liquor whichis not forbidden to the Phulmarárs.—(*Chanda Settlement Report*, page 54). Hardia Marárs, who take their name from the native word for tur-

Máli, 141,086—109 per 10,000 of the population.
Marár, 216,902—168 per 10,000 of the population.

Chief districts.	Number.		Percentage of total on district population.
	Mális.	Marárs.	
Hoshangabad	5,314	5	1·0
Nimar	6,778	167	2·7
Betul	4,837	...	1·5
Chhindwara . . .	7,011	1,174	2·0
Wardha . . .	17,808	4	4·4
Nagpur	30,288	928	4·1
Mandla	84	3,730	1·1
Seoni	959	10,627	3·1
Balaghat . . .	1,088	52,743	14·0
Bhandara . . .	7,660	24,890	4·4
Chanda	13,741	22,634	5·2
Raipur	3,972	88,547	2·7
Bilaspur . . .	522	33,125	2·9
Sambalpur . . .	11,843	2 408	1·8
Feudatory States . .	26,055	25,892	2·4

meric, are returned almost solely from Bilaspur. Other sub-divisions are Pabiya, 1,926, and Kanaujia, 543, found in Bilaspur, the latter presumably denoting the northern origin of the Marárs of Chhatisgarh. Among the Mális the sub-divisions resemble those of the Marárs; the chief ones are the Gáse 21,011, Kosre 33,271, Lonháre 16,561, Phulmáli, 37,138, Pandra, 9,836, Jiri, 1,658, Baone, 2,104, Hardia 2,689, and Bhoriya 899. With the exception of the Pandra sub-division, all are very generally distributed over the western districts where Mális occur; in the Uria country the sub-divisions chiefly found are the Kosria, Phulmáli, and Pandra, the latter being also extensively returned from Raipur. Except in Sambalpur where the Gandhmális,* a section of the caste, are employed in temple service, the Malis of these Provinces are purely gardeners and agriculturists.

181. Of the **Mánas**, 42,774, nearly three-fourths, or 30,063, are found in the Chanda district; there are 4,454 in Balaghat and 4,134 in Nagpur, while others occur in Wardha and Bhandara.

"Tradition asserts that previous to the Gond conquest the Mánas reigned over the country, having their strongholds at Surjagarh in Ahiri and at Manikgarh in Hyderabad territory, and that after a troubled rule of two hundred years, they fell before the Gonds. In appearance they are of the Gond type, and are strongly and stoutly made, while in character they are hardy, industrious, and truthful. They are among the best rice cultivators in the district—" (*Chanda Settlement Report*, page 50).

In Chanda the Mánas are found chiefly west of the Wainganga, 19,145 in the Warora tehsil, and 9,187 in Brahmapuri. The only sub-division of the tribe which is returned in any strength is the Badwaik, 3,151, which is recorded from all the districts.

The *Sudhs*, 7,908, are a small caste of Orissa who believe their original occupation to have been personal service, but are now for the most part engaged in cultivation. At the Census they have been recorded chiefly from Sambalpur 1,572, Sonpur 3,224 and Rairakhol 1,939. Of the four sub-divisions of the caste given by Mr. Risley three are returned, Bara Sudh 3,239, Sáno or Kabatkonia Sudh 224, and Butka Sudh 1,308.

"The most primitive of the sub-divisions about which tolerably full data are available appears to be the Butka Sudh. They wander about reclaiming waste lands and tapping date or palm trees for their juice. Bara Sudhs believe military or personal service to have been their original occupation. Some of them hold service tenures under the chiefs of the Orissa Tributary Mahals, and the fact that they bear the title Paik seems to show that they must once have formed part of the rude militia which once existed in that part of the country. The Sáno Sudhs believe that their original profession was the cultivation of date and palm trees. The social status of both groups is considerably higher than that of the Butka Sudhs, who can hardly be reckoned as coming within the pale of Hinduism at all"—(*Risley*).

182. **Minor agricultural castes.**—The Doras, 2,968, are Telugu cultivators, found principally in Kalahandi, where they number 2,512. Kalangas, 5,106, are agriculturists in Raigarh 1,216, Sambalpur 2,086 and Patna 1,739. The Khandaits, or swordsmen of Orissa, are found to the number of 1,394 in Sambalpur and the Uria States; they are now generally engaged in cultivation. Máropis, 305, are recorded from Bhandara; the name is said to be a corruption of Marwari, the persons so styled being immigrants of long standing from the Jodhpur country. They are reported to be of Rajput lineage, but in the table have been classed as ordinary cultivators. Mowárs, 1,490, are found in Bilaspur, and the adjoining States of Raigarh and Sarangarh; they are cultivators akin to Kurmis. The Panáras, 3,436, are pán cultivators and gardeners; in Bastar, where they number 3,022, they grow only vegetables. Sunkars, 7,329, are found chiefly in Chhatisgarh, where they are market gardeners, whilst in Nimar they are said to be stone-dressers; they are evidently the same as the Sunkár caste

* See Group VII in Caste Table.

of the North-Western Provinces, who are described as earth-workers. Their sub-divisions, Kosria and Kachhela, point to their being here vegetable growers by profession, while Deswári, recorded of 258 persons, indicates the northern origin of the caste.

183. **II (b) Graziers.**—The distribution of the pastoral class has been dealt with at paragraph 261; it is hardly necessary to give district details for each caste, as the latter are so much alike, their names being frequently interchangeable, that it would serve but little purpose to do so.

Ahirs.—First in point of numbers as well as of importance comes the Ahir caste, the great pastoral tribe of Northern India. They are found all over the northern districts, in the Nerbada valley, and in the Satpura districts with the exception of Betul, while in Chhatisgarh they are generally known as Gahras and Ráwats, names which will be separately referred to. In Northern India their three main branches are the Nandbans, Jadbans, and Goalbans, which acknowledge no connection except being all Ahirs; with the exception of the last they have numerous sub-divisions, by which they have usually been returned at the Census. The largest of these, the Kaora, is a section of the Nandbans tribe; they are found specially in the districts of Jubbulpore, Mandla, Seoni, Chhindwara, and Narsinghpur. The Kamarias, who are identical with the Kaoras, occur principally in Jubbulpore; the Bharotia and Jijhotia are northern sections of the caste returned mostly from Saugor and Damoh.

Ahir, 202,683—157 per 10,000 of the population.

Chief subdivisions.	Number.
Bharotia	8,965
Dauwa	37
Dhanror	383
Gondi Ahir	518
Gundera	1,101
Goalbans	17,232
Jadbans	1,997
Jharia	5,351
Jijhotia	16,462
Kamaria	5,610
Kanaujia	8,812
Kaora	71,756
Kopa	1,554
Kosaria	4,186
Narwaria	3,288
Nandbans	9,350

Though these tribal names all point to the Ahirs of the Central Provinces having come from the north of India, the period of their immigration would in many cases seem to have been very remote. In Damoh they are considered to be almost aboriginal; "possibly some of them may have come from the Brij, or the country round Mathura and Bhartpur, as in other parts of India, but they appear to have quite lost their nationality and even their peculiar patois which many castes in the Nerbada valley have retained almost unaltered to the present day"—(*Damoh Settlement Report*, page 43). The Ahirs are said to be distinct from the Gaolis who, before the rise of the Gonds to power, held sway in a great part of the country which now forms the Central Provinces, but like the Gaolis—who also point to Mathura as their original home—many of them would appear to have settled in these parts before the regular tide of immigration from Northern India had set in.

Though the tending of cattle is the traditional occupation of the caste, a great portion of its members have now taken to cultivation. In Mandla the Narwaria Ahirs are described by Colonel Ward as among the best malguzars of the district; they are as a rule pushing and enterprising men who have devoted themselves entirely to agriculture. The Jharia, Kosaria, and Kanaujia Ahirs occur chiefly in Chhatisgarh; in common with several other castes the two former have been settled from time immemorial in the Upper Mahanadi valley, while the Kanaujias are comparatively recent immigrants from the north-west. The Kopa Ahirs are found principally in Jubbulpore, where they number 1,432; the term appears to be derived from Kopa, one of the tutelary deities—presumably connected with Gopa—of the Ahirs in the northern districts. The Dauwas derive their title from their providing wet nurses for the Bundelas of Central

India. The Gond Ahirs, with whom it would appear the Gunderas are identical, are allied to the Gonds with whom they eat but do not intermarry.

184. The **Gaolis** are found in Saugor, in the lower Nerbada valley, on the southern Satpuras and in the western part of the Maratha country. In Betul and Chhindwara they are especially numerous, forming about 4 per cent. of the population in both districts. The chief interest attaching to the name lies in the fact of a Gaoli tribe having once been paramount in the Satpura country, until some time in the sixteenth century they fell before the rising power of the Gonds. "Of their former dominance traces still remain in the names of Gawálgarh, the fort of the cowherd, and Asirgarh, which is said by Ferishta to be the fort of Asá, the Ahir, or herdsman. From Deogarh on the plateau, which, according to popular tradition, was the last seat of the Gaoli power on the Satpuras, the very names of the Gaoli chiefs are handed down. In Saugor there are traditions of Gaoli supremacy of even a later date. The tracts of Etawa and Khurai, both north-west of Saugor, are said not to have passed out of the power of the Gaolis until the close of the seventeenth century." The distribution of the Gaolis at the present day corresponds almost exactly with the account given of the ancient dominance of the caste in the western and southern parts of the Province; but beyond this there is extremely little to establish their identity with the former ruling race. Mr. Grant in his introduction to the Central Provinces Gazetteer, from which the above facts about the Gaolis have been taken, writes that notwithstanding the most persevering investigation nothing of any interest has been elicited as to the origin of the present members of the tribe. "All their traditions and legends seem to point to Mathura, the classic land of the cowherds, and they make no claim to local sovereignty for their ancestors. They are said in some districts to differ from other Hindus in appearance, but they worship the same gods and speak the same language as their neighbours." The writer of the Chhindwara Settlement Report would seem to indicate the connection of the Gaolis, who in Chhindwara claim a high origin and pride themselves on the purity of their descent, with the former dominant race, while in Hoshangabad the tribe is merely said to have come in with the general immigration from Bundelkhand and Upper India. The probability is that amongst the present Gaolis there are representatives both of the old settlers and of comparatively recent in-comers, although it may be noted that we do not find among them the surname of Jharia, which in the case of many other castes is always taken to signify long residence in the country.

Gaoli 56,653—44 per 10,000 of the population.

Subdivisions.	Number.	Districts.	Number.	Percetage of district population.
Bhokar . . .	1,122	Saugor . .	934	·2
Dholia . . .	728	Seoni . . .	5,020	1·4
Dudhgaoli . .	10,164	Hoshangabad .	4,565	·9
Goalbans . .	969	Nimar . .	3,622	1·4
Khetária . .	416	Betul . .	13,433	4·2
Málwi . . .	2,522	Chhindwara .	16,093	3·9
Nandbans . .	26,326	Wardha . .	4,508	1·1
Raghubans . .	512	Nagpur . .	2,336	·3
Ránya . . .	2,168	Chanda . .	3,101	·4
Ráthor . . .	1,126	Bhandara . .	1,726	·2

Of their sub-divisions the chief is the Nandbans, which we have seen to be one of the three chief branches of the cowherd class in the north of India; it occurs in greatest strength in the three hill districts which were more particularly the seat of former Gaoli power. In Chhindwara the Nandbans Gaolis are agriculturists as well as keepers of cattle and many of them are proprietors of villages. The Dholia, Khetária, and Málwi Gaolis are found in Betul, the latter also occurring in Hoshangabad. From the Raghubans Gaolis being found both in Saugor and in Seoni we may infer that in both districts the Gaolis are of the same stock. The Rányas are returned from Nimar, Hoshangabad, and the Satpura districts. As a general rule the Gaolis have hardly taken to cultivation; with the exception of the Nandbans division, and the Khetárias who take their name from being agriculturists, nearly all are engaged in the care of their herds of cattle.

185. The **Gowáris**, 120,247, are the cowherds of the Maratha country, 5,598 being also found in the southern and eastern parts of Seoni, and 2,079 in the Sausar tehsil of Chhindwara. Among the Gowáris we find no trace of a northern origin, none of the sub-divisions which have been given for the Ahirs and Gaolis being recorded of the caste. Nearly all of them are returned as Dudh-Gowáris, the number of persons so shown amounting to 109,260, while other sub-divisions given are Injhwár 1,106, Máládhári 910, and Gond-Gowári 717. In Bhandara they are described as among the most valuable of the menial classes; they have in their hands the care of all the cattle of the country, and are but seldom employed in actual field work.

Gaoláns, 1,764, found in Betul and in the Harda tehsil of Hoshangabad, are inferior in rank to the Gaolis. The *Bhárurs*, 2,144, are cattle herds in the Khandwa tehsil of the Nimar district. *Ghosis*, 10,698, are returned mainly from the northern districts, more than half their number being found in Saugor. In the North-West Provinces the Ghosis are Mahomedan Ahirs; here all have been recorded as Hindus. *Golars*, 1,127, occur principally in Seoni, Chanda, Balaghat, and Bhandara, while *Golkars*, 3,015, are almost all returned from Chanda, where they are described as wild-looking people, who are scattered about the least cultivated parts of the district and live by tending cattle. The Telugu *Gollas* are also a Chanda caste; 621 of them are shown as belonging to the Era Golla sub-division.

186. The cattle herds of Chhatisgarh and the Uria country remain to be referred to. In the former the cattle-tending castes are, besides the Ahirs already noticed, the *Ráwats*, *Gahras*, and *Thethwárs*. The chief sub-divisions are given in the margin. The Desaha and Kanaujia Ráwats are more recent immigrants and are generally of better standing than the old settled Jharias and Kosarias. The *Gaurs* are the herdsmen of the Uria country; their great sub-division is the Magadha, to which three-fourths of their number belong.

RÁWATS.		GAURS.	
Sub-divisions.	Number.	Sub-divisions.	Number.
Ráwat (*Total*)	228,169	*Gaur* (*Total*)	245,234
Desaha	18,838	Dudhkaura	1,372
Jharia	99,998	Dumál	417
Kanaujia	24,604	Gopapuria	543
Kaora	7,818	Jharia	26,903
Kosaria	33,878		
Magadha	18,958	Kalanjia	330
		Kanaujia	1,225
Gahra (*Total*)	96,083	Khandwál	200
		Kosaria	2,151
Thethwár (*Total*)	3,187	Magadha	181,309
Kanaujia	2,407		

187. **II (c) Labourers.**—In this group have been entered some semi-aboriginal tribes who have now been Hinduized or have so far ceased to belong to the jungles that inclusion under the present heading seemed the most appropriate classification to apply to them. Other caste names have also been included about which I had no definite information at the time the table was prepared; in one or two cases they should more properly have been shown elsewhere.

The *Arakhs*, 2,106, found mostly in Chanda, are an offshoot of the Pási tribe and their regular occupation is bird-catching and shikar.* In Chanda they are generally employed as house and field servants. At the Census 1,166 persons, or more than half their number, recorded their religion as Arakh or Gond; these semi-Hinduized Arakhs occur all over the Province, 357 being returned from Jubbulpore. *Audhálias*, 855, are a pig-rearing caste in Bilaspur. The *Bhilálas*, 14,243, are found almost solely in Nimar, 9,623, and Hoshangabad 4,431.

"The Bhilálas are usually held to be descended from one of those commixtures of Rajput and aboriginal (in this case Bhil) blood, which appear to have been not uncommon when the Rajput clans were acquiring for themselves the lordship of Central India. The only Bhilálas who show a marked infusion of the Rajput blood are the families of the chiefs, who do not intermarry with the common Bhilálas. The latter, though believed to be really undiluted aborigines, yet differ considerably from the other tribes of Bhils. They

* Berar Census Report, 1881, page 157.

have for a much longer time been in contact with 'civilization' and are in consequence much greater scoundrels, just as the tame Gond is much worse than the wild one"—(*Nimar Settlement Report*, page 247).

The *Dhákars*, 8,036, are recorded principally from Bastar, 7,207, where they are said to be the illegitimate offspring of Brahmins.* In some cases the name may signify Dhákar Rajput; the Dhákars returned in Hoshangabad have been classed as such.

188. *Dhánuks*, 6,745, are found in the Nerbada valley, chiefly in Narsinghpur, where 5,610 of their number are returned. In the North-Western Provinces they are described a "low tribe who act as watchmen and village drudges." Here they are employed as field servants or general labourers. The *Dhuris*, 2,797, are a Chhatisgarh labouring class, largely engaged in parching rice. *Khadáts*, 1,443, are immigrants into the Uria country from Ganjam; 1,018 are recorded from Sonpur. They are employed as domestic servants, cartmen, doolie-bearers or as general labourers. *Mannepus*, 1,510, and *Naiks*, 3,021, are Telugu labouring castes in Chanda. *Pábs* or *Pabias*, 15,760, are said by Mr. Risley to be the same as the Páns, a weaving and servile caste of Orissa and southern Chhota-Nagpur, who have been classed among weavers in Group XXIII; in Sambalpur they are described as field and general labourers, and had been entered accordingly in Table XVI before I was aware of their identity. In these Provinces they occur principally in the north of Bilaspur, 2,527, in Raigarh, 2,332, and in Sambalpur, 9,897, mostly in the northern part of the district. On the analogy of last Census the *Parkas* of the three northern districts have been kept separate from the Panka caste, but they are in all probability the same; they number 2,486, chiefly returned from Jubbulpore. The *Rajbhars*, 3,025, are akin to the Bhars, an aboriginal race of Central and Northern India. "According to Sir H. M. Elliot the Bhars consider themselves superior to the Rajbhars, but this claim to superiority is not admitted by the latter. They do not eat or drink together. †" In the North-Western Provinces the Bhars are swineherds and outcastes, while the Rajbhars are counted among Hindus. In these parts the Rajbhars alone are found; they are thoroughly Hinduized and are generally employed as day labourers. The *Rajjhars*, 5,296, occur chiefly in the hilly parts of Hoshangabad and the three southern Satpura districts; they are apparently akin to the Gonds, over whom, however, they claim social superiority. The *Ráwats* of the northern districts are labourers, resembling the Saurs, and are distinct from the herdsmen of Chhatisgarh; they number 3,683, of whom 1,064 are returned from Saugor and 1,684 from Jubbulpore.

189. **IV. Forest and Hill Tribes.**—In this group come the aboriginal tribes who are found in greater or less strength in every part of the Province. According to the classified table their numbers amount to 3,173,194, or 24·5 per cent. of the total population. As has already been seen there are some races of aboriginal descent, such as the Kudas, Rajjhars, etc., who at least in this part of the country have come to be looked upon as sections of the Hindu community and have been entered accordingly under non-aboriginal heads. The present group, therefore, as its name implies, contains only those aborigines who more distinctively belong to the forests and hills.

The Baigas.—Properly speaking the term Baiga is applied to a race of aborigines, found chiefly in the most inaccessible parts of the uplands of Mandla and Balaghat, and to a less extent amidst the hill ranges of Chhatisgarh bordering on those districts. Allied to or identical with the Baigas are other tribes found recorded at the Census under different names, chiefly in the jungle tracts of the Chhatisgarh country, such as the Binjhwárs, Binjhias, and Náhars. All have been entered as sub-divisions of the Baiga tribe in the caste table for

* Glasfurd's Bastar, page 36.

† Crooke's Ethnography, North-Western Provinces and Oudh, page. 41.

British districts, but in the feudatories table where sub-divisions have not been distinguished, the subordinate tribes are shown in separate entries. There is another name, Bhumia, which is in most cases synonymous with Baiga, but as it is a term of rather indefinite application and may possibly include the members of other tribes, it has been thought best to keep it distinct. The nomenclature of the tribes tends to be rather confusing, but the following statement will help to show under what names and where they have been recorded at the enumeration.

Distribution of Baigas and allied tribes over the chief districts where found.

	Tribal Name.	Damoh.	Jubbulpore.	Mandla.	Seoni.	Balaghat.	Raipur.	Bilaspur.	Sambalpur.	Chhatisgarh Feudatories.	Uria Feudatories.	Provincial, Total.
	1	2	3	4	5	6	7	8	9	10	11	12
Baigas Proper.	*Baiga* . Bharotia . .	9	...	5,354	...	1,713	...	581	...	670	...	8,327
	Baiga . Binjhwár . .	...	196	3,280	659	3,449	2	108	...	74	...	7,768
	Baiga . Mundia . .	...	660	2,680	7	...	...	...	...	...	...	3,347
	Baiga . Narotia or Náhar	...	...	16	...	1,886	...	...	...	135	...	2,037
	Baiga . Tribe not given .	...	1,669	5,885	206	264	18	125	...	276	...	8,447
	Bhumia of Mandla, Balaghat and the hills north of Chhatisgarh.	...	...	10	...	1	721	4,395	...	958	...	6,085
	Total Baigas .	9	2,525	17,225	872	7,313	741	5,209	...	2,113	...	36,011*
Tribes allied to Baigas.	*Binjhwár* *Binjhál.* Of eastern Chhatisgarh and the Uria country.	...	...	...	...	...	8,820	10,220	45,258	12	24,870	89,180
	Binjhia . Ditto . .	...	...	...	...	...	...	214	...	...	...	214
	Birjia . Ditto . .	...	...	...	...	...	...	...	833	...	584	1,417
	Náhar . Ditto . .	...	...	...	...	...	171	88	37	442	256	994
	Bhumia . Of Damoh, Jubbulpore, etc.	743	11,289	...	...	...	...	...	5	40	...	12,077†

* Includes 4 Baigas from other districts. † Inclndes 11 Bhumias from other districts.

The Baigas so called have been returned from Jubbulpore, from Mandla, Seoni, and Balaghat on the Satpuras, and from Kawardha and the hill country north of Chhatisgarh. Regarding their origin, customs, and religious beliefs a most complete account has been furnished in Colonel Bloomfield's "Notes on the Baigas of the Central Provinces," published at Nagpur in 1885. Forsyth has also given an excellent description of the Baigas of the Maikal range in the east of Mandla in his book "The Highlands of Central India," from which I take the following passage :—

"The real Baiga of the hill ranges is still almost in a state of nature. They are very black, with an upright, slim, though exceedingly wiry frame, and show less of the negretto type of feature than any other of these wild races. Destitute of all clothing but a small strip of cloth, or, at most, when in full dress, with the addition of a coarse cotton-sheet worn cross-wise over the chest, with long, tangled, coal-black hair, and furnished with bow and arrow and a keen little axe hitched over the shoulder, the Baiga is the very model of a hill aborigine. He scorns all tillage but the *dhya* clearing on the mountain-side, pitching his neat habitation of bamboo wicker-work, like an eagle's eyrie, on some hill-top or ledge of rock far above the valleys, penetrated by pathways ; and ekes out the fruits of the earth by an unwearying pursuit of game. Full of courage, and accustomed to depend on each other, they hesitate not to attack every animal of the forest, including the tiger himself. Though thus secluded in the wilderness, the Mandla Baiga is by no means extremely shy, and will placidly go on cutting his *dhya* while a train of strangers is passing him, when a wild Gond or Korku would have abandoned all and fled to the forest. They are truthful and honest almost to a fault, being terribly cheated in consequence in their dealings with the traders ; and they possess the patriarchal form of self-government still so perfectly that nearly all their disputes are settled by the elders without appeal, though these, of course, under our alien system possess no legal authority. Serious crime among them is almost unheard of."

The Baigas in Mandla have three main divisions, which again are subdivided into several *gots*. They are the Binjhwár, the Mundia, and the Bharotia. In Balaghat the first and the last of these are found, but Colonel Bloomfield is unable to identify the Mundias of Mandla with any of the tribes found in Balaghat. In the latter the place of the Mundias is taken by the Narotias or Náhars. The Binjhwárs are the highest sub-division, from them the priests of the tribe and of the Gonds are chiefly derived ; they live apart from every other tribe, and though nominally often in the same village as Gonds, the Baiga settlement is usually at some distance, often on the very top of a high hill overlooking the Gond village.* In Balaghat, however, the Binjhwárs are among the most civilized of the tribes, in the villages of the Mau valley many having long been regularly settled as plough cultivators. At the Census 84 per cent. of the Balaghat Binjhwárs gave their religion as Hindu, while the other tribes show but a small proportion so returned ; on the other hand, the Mandla Binjhwárs are nearly all—93 per cent.—shown as animistic by religion. The Binjhwárs are particular as to their food and drink, refusing to eat with the other tribes of Baigas and with outsiders. The Mundias are known by the head being shaven all but one lock ; the Binjhwárs, on the other hand, wear their hair long. In Balaghat both the Bharotias and Narotias cut their hair whenever they think proper ; neither are very particular about their food and will eat almost anything except beef, which is forbidden. The Bharotias are the wildest of all the tribes in the Balaghat district.

190. The **Bhumias** are returned principally from Damoh and Jubbulpore and from the northern zemindaris of Bilaspur. I have been unable to ascertain who the Bhumias of the two northern districts are, but they are probably Gond medicine-men or priests chosen from among the Gonds themselves. They have given a great number of sub-divisions of their tribe, but all, except in the case of one or two persons, are quite distinct from those recorded of the Baigas of Mandla. Their principal section is the Ráthor, returned for 4,693 persons. In Mandla, according to Colonel Ward, the two words "Bhumia" and "Baiga" are certainly synonymous, as the people apply both names equally, and such is also the case in Bilaspur. Of the Bhumias of Lapha in the north of the latter district, Forsyth writes :—

"Here the tribe is known only by the name of Bhumia, the term Baiga, which is their commoner tribal name in Mandla, being restricted to their priests and medicine-men in these more eastern regions. They spoke capital Hindi and were not at all shy in conversation, though wilder in appearance even than those who live in the Mandla district."

At the Census the Bhumias of Bilaspur in several cases returned the Baiga sub-division, Bharotia, as one of their clans. They are found chiefly in the Mungeli tehsil, 2,516, and in Bilaspur, 1,854 ; in Seorinarayan there are only 25. In Raipur of 721 Bhumias recorded at the Census, 641 are from the north of the Drug tehsil ; these are also Baigas.

191. The **Binjhwárs, Binjhias, and Binjháls** of Eastern Chhatisgarh and of the Uria country are believed to be identical with the Baigas, but they do not call themselves by the latter name. In Raipur nearly all are found in the eastern part of the Raipur tehsil, on the further side of the Mahanadi. In Bilaspur they occur also in the eastern or north-eastern parts of the district ; 7,849 are found in the Bilaspur tehsil and 2,581 in Seorinarayan, while in Mungeli they are hardly, if at all, represented, the four persons returned being probably Binjhwár Baigas. All over the Uria country the tribe occurs usually under the name of Binjhál, their numbers in the Sambalpur district alone amounting to no less than 45,258. It will thus be seen that the whole of the Chhatisgarh plain separates the Baigas of the Maikal hills from the Binjhwárs of further Chhatisgarh. The

* Colonel Ward's Mandla Settlement Report, page 154.

tribe is also found in the south of Chhota-Nagpur, chiefly in the States of Sarguja and Gangpur. Regarding them Mr. Risley states that their traditions associate them with the Vindhya hills and that their original habitat is said to have been Ratanpur in Chhatisgarh, whence they moved eastward in the direction of Borasambhar in Sambalpur. At the Census they have been generally recorded as of the Hindu religion. The *Birjias* are presumably identical with the Binjhias or Binjhwárs, but as I am not certain of who they are, I have shown them separate in Table XVI.

The *Náhars* of the eastern districts and states are probably the same as the Náhar Baigas. From Raipur their occupation is reported to be basket-making. In Kawardha the 135 persons shown as Náhars in Table XVI were recorded as Bhumia Náhar; elsewhere Náhar alone has been returned as the tribal name.

192. The **Bhils,** 22,424, are almost solely confined to the Nimar district, where 21,460 of their number occur, the chief exceptions being 412 who are found as far afield as Sambalpur, and 302 returned from the Kanker State. 1,694 Bhils gave their religion as Mussalman; of these 1,546 belong to the Burhanpur tehsil, which was formerly the seat of Mahomedan power in the district. "They now retain no observance of any save the most elementary rites of that faith, and, particularly the women, have returned to the worship of the semi-Hindu, semi-elemental deities reverenced by most of the wild tribes. These converted Bhils are, with few exceptions, a miserable lot, idle and thriftless, and steeped in the deadly vice of opium eating—" (*Nimar Settlement Report*, page 246).

193. **The Gonds** with their allied tribes number 2,258,824; in the British districts they amount to 1,799,531, or 16·7 per cent. of the total population, and in the Feudatory States to 495,293, or 21·3 per cent. These figures are not very precise, as the Gonds, in common with the lower classes of Hindus, frequently adopt occupational titles, such as Nagárchi, Dholi, and the like, and when these are recorded by themselves it is impossible to say whether the persons they represent are Gonds or not. As a rule, unless accompanied by a Gondi sub-divisional name, such terms have been treated as ordinary Hindu castes. The chief divisions of the Gonds and the numbers recorded against each at the Census will appear from the appended statement. No note has been taken of the petty

Gond Tribes.

Chief sub-divisions.	Number.	Chief sub-divisions.	Number.
Ahir (Gondi)	6,012	Lohár (Gondi)	8,171
Andh	18	Magadha	1,187
Bharia	31,762	Manjhi	634
Bhima	274		
Bhoi	5,694	Manne	507
Burar (Gondi)	3,265	Nagárchi (Gondi)	1,650
		Ojha	5,459
Darwe or Naik	6,203	Pardhán	72,278
Desai	3,795		
Dholi	4,199	Ráj Pardhán	17,251
Dhur	501,009	Parganiya	870
Dhurwa	7,501	Pathári	16,295
Gaiki	2,798	Raj Gond	614,276
Gaite	5,521	Ráwanbansi	220,166
Gowári	7,403	Thotia	4,496
Khatulha	11,875	Sonjhara (Gondi)	68
Kolábhut	920	Others and unspecified	473,348
Kolám	1,914		
Kondar (Gondi)	532	TOTAL	2,037,351

TRIBES ALLIED TO GONDS.

Locality where found.	Tribes.	Number.
Throughout the Province	Agaria	5,832
Bastar State	Bhatra	33,087
	Jhoria	936
	Parja	13,491
	Tagara	396
	Muria	54,071
Bastar and south of Chanda	Gotte	8,159
	Koi	24,304
Bastar and north-east of Chanda	Koitur	22,530
	Mária	58,667
Grand Total of Gonds		2,258,824

or local sub-divisions and *gots* which have been returned in the utmost profusion by the Gonds of every part of the Province. All have, however, been worked out at the cost of much time and labour and are on record for the purpose of any future enquiry that may be made regarding them.

194. The *Agarias* are iron smelters; they will be noted on hereafter as the main strength of the tribe has been shown under a separate group—No. XXXIV. The Gondi *Ahirs* are pure Gonds eating and drinking with other Gonds, the only difference being that they do not intermarry. They are most numerous in the district of Chhindwara. The *Bharias* are found principally in Jubbulpore and Chhindwara. In the latter they are described as among the wildest of the hill tribes, but though living amongst Gonds and inhabiting some of the remotest parts in the north of the district, they talk no language but Hindi. Nearly all are shown as of aboriginal religion, while in Jubbulpore the Bharias are equally universally returned as Hindus. The *Darwe* or *Naik* Gonds of Chanda are found in the south of the district, chiefly in the Mul tehsil where they number 3,163. "They appear in the time of the Gond kings to have been employed as soldiers and to the present day prefer sepoy service with a zemindar to agricultural work."* The *Manne* Gonds of Chanda are said to be identical with the Darwes, Manne being the name in use among the Telugus. The *Dholis* or *Dholias* are so styled from their playing on the dhol, a kind of kettle-drum; the *Nagárchis* are performers on the nagára, also a kind of drum. The wives of both act as midwives in Hindu as well as in Gond families. The *Dhur* Gonds are the common Gonds of the Nerbada valley, of the open country of the Satpura plateau and of the Chhatisgarh plain. Dhurwa is properly speaking a *got* name, but is presumably used as equivalent to Dhur. The *Gaikis* are village herdsmen in Betul as are the *Gowáris* in the Maratha districts. The *Gaitis* are described at page 21 of Hislop's Papers. They are found mainly in the Sakoli tehsil of Bhandara, 665, in the Brahmapuri tehsil of Chanda, 215 and in the north of the Bastar State, 4,535. According to Hislop their chief peculiarity, not found among common Gonds, though it may exist even among them, is to have in each village a separate tenement set apart for the occupancy of the unmarried men during the night. This is called the *gotalghar* (empty bed-house), and in some villages there is a like provision made for the unmarried Gaiti women. In this connection I may remark that a report received from the Dewan of Kanker states the custom to be prevalent among the Gonds of that State, who mostly belong to the common or Dhur Gond tribe. *Khatulha* Gonds are found in most districts of the Province, but have been most numerously returned from Saugor 6,478, and Narsinghpur, 3,176. Hislop mentions that the name is applied to those of the Gonds who have more especially begun to conform to the Hindu religion and to ape Hindu manners.† The *Kolábhuts* and *Bhimás* are vagrants

Gond, 2,258,824—1,745 per 10,000 of the population.

District.	Number.	Percentage on total population of the districts.
Saugor	30,327	5·1
Damoh	31,404	9·6
Jubbulpore	112,463	15·0
Narsinghpur	48,021	13·1
Hoshangabad	65,907	12·4
Nimar	1,590	·6
Mandla	179,591	52·6
Seoni	159,449	43·0
Chhindwara	152,096	37·3
Betul	96,101	29·7
Wardha	44,790	11·2
Nagpur	47,526	6·3
Chanda	168,623	24·2
Bhandara	93,638	12·6
Balaghat	93,453	24·4
Raipur	250,595	15·8
Bilaspur	159,502	13·7
Sambalpur	64,455	8·1
Feudatory States	459,293	21·3

* Chanda Settlement Report, page 49.

† Hislop's Papers, page 5.

"whose women are dancing girls in both senses of the word. They follow their profession chiefly among the Hindus, it being reckoned disreputable by the people of their own race."* The *Kolám* Gonds are confined to the Wardha district, where they occur chiefly in the Arvi tehsil. Gondi *Kondars* and *Lohárs* are iron smelters and workers, like the Agarias.

195. The *Ojhas, Pardháns, Patháris, Desais*, and *Thothias* are all bards or minstrels of the Gonds. The Ojhas are very generally distributed, being found in greater or less numbers in almost every district of the Province; among them there are two classes, the first acts as musicians, dancers, and beggars, the other as fowlers and snarers. Both classes eat together and intermarry. Among the Ojhas it is only the men who dance, and when thus engaged they put on special attire and wear anklets with bells.† In someparts of the Western Satpuras the Ojhas are also the minstrels of the Korkus; but they have no connection with the latter, being called in, it would appear, simply because there are no others available in the depths of the forest. They beg equally from Hindus, Gonds, and Korkus. Pardhán, Patħári and Desai are given by Hislop as synonymous terms for the name of the great Bhát class of the Gonds, whose genealogies they repeat, describing the exploits of their ancestors and reciting the myths of their religion in rhyme. The Pardháns are found in greatest strength in the lower Nerbada valley, on the Satpuras and in the districts of the Nagpur country; in Chhatisgarh their place is taken by the Patháris, who are also most numerous in Jubbulpore and Mandla. The Desai Gonds belong principally to Chhatisgarh. In some parts the Pardháns and Patháris have a bad reputation for thieving, the Patháris of Bilaspur being well known in this respect. The Thothias are returned principally from Betul and Chanda, where they are described as a low class of Gonds, chiefly subsisting by making bamboo mats. According to Hislop the name Thothia signifies maimed or inferior; they are also frequently called Mátias, from the goddess of small-pox being the chief subject of their songs.

196. The *Ráj Gonds* are the highest class among the Gonds. According to Forsyth the Ráj Gonds are in many cases the result of the alliance between the Rajput adventurer and the Gond, many of the descendants of the petty chiefs of the days of the Gond rule showing the clearest signs of possessing a mixture of Hindu and aboriginal blood. "The Hindu element in such cases has not been the debased article current among the masses of the labouring population, but the purer strain derived from the aristocratic families of Rajputana. In other cases, among the lower races of aborigines, crosses also appear to have taken place; but in such cases it appears to have been the already debased Hindu of the lower orders that has furnished the foreign element."‡ From the great number of Ráj Gonds who are found in every part of the Province, it must also appear that the tribe has been largely recruited by aspirants to higher rank from amongst the more influential members of the other tribes; more than a fourth of the Gonds enumerated at the Census have returned themselves as belonging to the premier clan. The return of religion is evidently misleading in the case of the Ráj Gonds, only 16·6 per cent. of whom have been shown as Hindus. According to Colonel Ward they are Hindus in most of their ceremonies, "outdoing the highest caste Hindu in the matter of purifying themselves and aping them in all their religious ceremonies. The true Ráj Gond wears the sacred thread and considers himself deeply insulted if compared in status with a Gond. Mr. Hislop says that he carries his passion for purification so far that he has the faggots with which his food is cooked, sprinkled with water before

* Hislop's Papers, page 7. | † Census Report, 1881, page 198. | ‡ "Highlands of Central India," page 142.

use." The *Ráwanbansi* is the Gond of the northern Satpuras, being met with in great numbers in the districts of Mandla and Balaghat, and to a less extent in the adjoining parts of Seoni and Jubbulpore.

197. **The Gonds of Bastar** and the south of Chanda are so far distinct from the tribesmen of the Satpura country that they may be separately referred to. The *Bhatras* are found almost solely in the north-east of Bastar, between Jagdalpur and the Raipur zemindaris, in the latter of which 96 of their number are recorded. Nearly all are shown as Hindus by religion. According to Colonel Glasfurd they are cultivators, and a good many of them have the hereditary privilege of wearing the sacred thread. The *Gottes* are confined to the south of the Chanda district and of the Bastar state; they resemble the *Kois*, amongst whom they are found, but keep more aloof from civilization and are more restless in their habits than the latter tribe. The Kois are distinct from the *Koiturs*. In the Chanda district the Kois occur only in the Sironcha tehsil, 10,305, and in the south of Mul 6,718. The Koiturs, on the other hand, are returned solely from the north-eastern part of the district, being confined to the Brahmapuri tehsil; they are also found in Bhandara, in the Nandgaon state and in Raipur. According to the Chanda Settlement Report * the Koiturs are identical with the *Márias* and this is borne out by the distribution of the tribe, as all occur along the border of that part of the Bastar state which is the stronghold of the Mária race. Combining the figures for the two tribal names we find the Márias distributed as is here shown.

Distribution of Márias.

District, etc.	Number.
Chanda—	
Brahmapuri	42,288
Mul	7,070
Other Tehsils	58
Bhandara—	
Sákoli	4,551
Raipur—	
Drug, Dhamtari	1,117
Nandgaon	229
Bastar	25,855
Elsewhere	29
Total Márias	81,197

198. Interesting accounts of the tribe will be found in the Settlement Report of the Chanda district and in Colonel Glasfurd's report on Bastar. From the latter I extract the following description of the Márias:—

"They inhabit the densest jungles and are a shy race, avoiding all contact with strangers and flying to the hills on the least alarm. In appearance they are more uncivilized than the Murias and Bhatras; about the same height, but far surpassing them in strength and agility. Their dress depends a good deal on their distance from civilization and upon the accessibility of the localities they inhabit. Near Bhopalpatnam and Vijapur they are better clad, but in the wilder and more unfrequented parts, such as among the Baila Dilas, their clothing is of the very scantiest description. They shave the head all but the topknot, and as they use an iron knife for this purpose, it is not surprising that they dread the disagreeable operation, and have recourse to it as seldom as possible; consequently their hair which gets excessively matted is all gathered up into one knot behind or on the crown. Necklaces of beads, red and white, frequently worked into collars of an inch or two in width, are suspended round the necks of the younger men; the elder seldom wear them. On the wrists the men wear brass bracelets and round the waist is often a girdle of cowries. A small knife without any sheath, made of iron slightly tempered is invariably stuck in the girdle behind; they sometimes wear sandals made of the skin of the bison, or wild buffalo, and of the rudest description and shape, being secured round the instep and great toe by cords made of grass; a hatchet hanging from the shoulder, or a bow and arrows, completes the costume of the Mária, as seen in his native wilds. The Márias are a timid, quiet race, docile, and although addicted to drinking, they are not quarrelsome. They are a most cheerful, light-hearted people, always

*"The Gonds are seen in their purest type in the Márias, or, as they are called towards the north, the Koiturs, who inhabit the wild wastes of hill and forest which lie beyond the Wainganga. Whether the Márias are the root from which the other Gonds have sprung remains at present an open question; but it is worthy of remark that in villages bordering upon the more cultivated tracts the change of name from Mária to Koitur, then to jungly Gond, and then to plain Gond, can be seen in progress; and it is not difficult to imagine that a well-to-do Mária family settled in the plains and calling itself Gond may in two or three generations adopt the more fashionable designation of Ráj-Gond—" (*Chanda Settlement Report*, page 40).

laughing and joking amongst themselves. Seldom does a Mária village resound with quarrels or wrangling among either sex; and in this respect they present a marked contrast to those in more civilized tracts. They in common with many other wild races bear a singular character for truthfulness and honesty, and when once they get over the feeling of shyness, which is natural to them, they are exceedingly frank and communicative."

199. With the Márias have been amalgamated the Máris—the similarity of the names rendered it impossible to keep them separate— who are akin to the former tribe. They inhabit the wild and difficult country called Abujmard in the west of Bastar, and from living in a wilder tract are poorer and more uncivilized than the Márias who live in the more level country. The connection between the two is kept up by intermarriage. The *Jhorias* are found in the north-western parts of Bastar towards the Kanker border. They are said by Colonel Glasfurd to be a numerous class, but only 936 are returned at the Census. The similarity of the name, which was frequently written Jhuria, to that of the next tribe, the *Murias*, made it difficult to keep the terms separate in abstraction, but an examination of the books of some of the tracts where the Jhorias are found, showed that the great preponderance of the entries were of Murias. The Jhorias are, however, more akin to the Márias than to the Murias; they resemble the former in dress and like them prefer a life in the woods to the attractions of a civilization even so mild as that of the Bastar country.

The Murias, on the other hand, who are found in the more open parts around Jagdalpur and in the north-east of the state, are good cultivators; they are active, hardy and well-behaved and their villages are generally clean and comfortable. The *Parjas* and *Tagaras* are found south from Jagdalpur; they are a poor race, subsisting partly by cultivation and partly by hunting, and are not so well-clothed as the Murias and Bhatras.

200. As the races which have been described, together with the Halbas who will presently be noticed, form such a large proportion of the inhabitants of the Bastar state, the figures given in the margin are of interest as showing the extent to which the population of the dependency is composed of the different tribes.

Aboriginal tribes of Bastar.

Tribe.	Number.	Percentage of population.
Gond	70,069	22·5
Bhatra	21,459	6·9
Gotte	5,070	1·6
Jhoria	936	·3
Koi	7,281	2·4
Mária	25,855	8·3
Muria	53,960	17·4
Parja	13,467	4·3
Tagara	396	·1
Halba	13,865	4·5
Others	1,679	·5
TOTAL	214,037	68·8

201. The **Halbas**, 97,913, are returned chiefly from Bhandara 18,425, Chanda 7,199, Raipur 47,273, and from Nandgaon 2,324, Kanker 5,879, and the Bastar state 13,865. In Raipur they are said to have come from Bastar and this is borne out by their being found almost solely in the Dhamtari tehsil, 29,099, and in Drug 17,671. In Bhandara they occur mainly in the Tirora tehsil, 10,559, and in Sakoli, 7,829. The Halbas of Bhandara, according to a report received from that district, disclaim any connection with the Gonds, to whom the remnant of the original stock in the Bastar state are said to be related.* In Raipur Colonel Bowie informs me, they are looked upon and consider themselves as of Gond descent, but they have now universally adopted the religious beliefs of the Hindus.† In Bastar "they are scattered over the more level and cultivated tracts, but are seldom found south of the Indrávati. They dress and live better and have a better appearance than most of the other castes; they do not eat the flesh of cows nor of swine and wear the sacred-

* In the Bhandara Settlement Report, page 48, the Halbas are described as an offshoot of the Kunbis, apparently because their calling is agriculture.

† See also Hislop's Papers, page 21.

thread as a caste." In Bhandara the Halbas eat swine's flesh and do not put on the sacred-thread, so that, as far as outward appearances are concerned, they have no cause to be nervous, as they seem to be, about acknowledging their kinship to the Bastar Halbas. In their ceremonies the Bhandara Halbas resemble those of Raipur, of whom a description is given at page 36 of the Settlement Report of that district.

202. **The Khonds,** 196,400, are found all over the Uria country, but largely predominate to the south-east, where in the states of Patna and Kalahandi they number 52,798 and 104,709, or 15·9 and 32·1 per cent. of the population respectively. At the Census they, like the Gonds, have returned a very large number of sub-divisions, the chief of which are here given. The Kutias, the largest section recorded of the tribe, are the hill Khonds of the Kalahandi state, from which also have been returned the Jharias, Kachharias, and Paikarias. In the southern states the Khonds are very generally shown as animistic by religion, very few of them having as yet taken to Hindu customs, but in Sambalpur where they mix more with the Urias, 87·4 per cent. of the tribe are recorded as Hindus. The Khonds admit into their community members of other stocks with the exception of some of the debased castes, and to this practice Mr. Risley thinks may in some degree be due the fine physique of the race.

Khond, 196,400—152 per 10,000 of the population.

Chief sub-divisions.	Number.
Dal	2,149
Jharia	4,596
Kachharia	24,760
Kutia	31,087
Paikaria	13,666
Ráj	7,697

203. **The Korkus** are distributed as shown in the statement subjoined. The tribe has been so frequently described—the excellent account given by Sir Charles Elliott at pages 250-264 of the Hoshangabad Settlement Report may be specially referred to—that it is needless for me to remark upon it here. The Mowási Korkus are found in Chhindwara, 11,081, in Hoshangabad, 8,508, and in Betul, 2,175; the Rumas are confined to Betul, 5,629, and to Hoshangabad, 3,965. The persons recorded from the Wardha district as Bopchis are Korkus.

Korku 96,218—74 per 10,000 of the population.

Chief sub-divisions.	Number	Chief districts.	Number.	Percentage of district population.
Mowási . .	21,768	Hoshangabad .	36,772	6·9
Ruma . .	9,699	Betul .	31,880	9·9
Ráj Korku .	2,677	Nimár . .	10,118	4·0
Bauria . .	1,727	Chhindwara .	12,559	3·1
Bondai . .	1,321			
Moghia . .	123			
Bopchi . .	584			

The *Nahâls*, 8,766, are returned principally from Hoshangabad, 3,383, and Nimar, 3,502. They are now for the most part village drudges and have almost ceased to exist as a separate tribe. They mix much with the Korkus, talking their language in the more hilly parts, but are considered inferior to the latter in the social scale.

204. **The Kols** in these Provinces are found in greatest numbers in the districts of Jubbulpore and Mandla. In the former they amount to 61,705 persons, or about a twelfth part of the population; in Mandla they number 8,313, while a few have spread into the surrounding districts of Narsinghpur, Seoni and Chhindwara. In all these places they are employed mainly as day labourers, and are generally looked upon as members of the Hindu community. In the eastern parts of the Province which border on Chhota-Nagpur, we find the tribal Kol. According to Mr. Risley the term Kol is a generic name applied by Hindus to the Munda and Oraon tribes and sometimes also to the Bhumij and Kharias. At the Census Kol was recorded as main tribe for these and several other races; in each case the Kol-Mundas, Kol-Kharias, etc., have been classed under their proper

tribe, but a considerable number of people still remain who were either returned simply as Kols or for whom tribal sub-divisions were recorded which could not be identified with any of the known races of the Chhota-Nagpur country. Kols thus undefined occur principally in Bamra, 1,818, in Sonpur, 875, and in Patna, 736.

The whole system of nomenclature of these eastern tribes is very confusing to one unacquainted with their composition; thus Munda-Kharias, Kharia-Oráons, and many other such combinations were continually cropping up, and presenting problems as to what they should be taken to be. Mr. Risley, I see, takes the last name of the combination as main tribe, putting Munda-Kharias among Kharias and Kharia-Oráons among Oráons; but at the time the results for the eastern districts and states were compiled, I was not aware of this, and generally adopted the opposite method, making the first name the main tribe and the second the sub-division in the ordinary way.

205. The **Sawaras, Sabars or Saurs** are found in two localities, the first is the Vindhyan hills north of the Nerbada in the districts of Saugor or Damoh, the second is the east of Chhatisgarh and the Uria country. They have almost everywhere adopted the religious customs of the Hindus. In Saugor and Damoh the Brahmin officiates at their ceremonies and they burn their dead, but in the Uria country, according to Mr. Risley, the original faith of the tribe has been less modified by the influence of Hindu usage. How a branch of the tribe came to be settled in the districts of Saugor and Damoh is unknown, unless it be that as a wandering race they spread over the Bundelkhand highlands, where a portion of their number remained and have thus got separated from the eastern stock. In Saugor the Saurs call themselves Dángiwálas or those attached to the Dángis, while the Saurs of Bundelkhand are known as Bhadaurias, or those coming from the Bhadáwar state. They have no tradition of how or when they came to live in the part of the country where they are now found.

Sawara 156,921—121 per 10,000 of the population.

Chief districts.	Number.	Percentage on district population.
Saugor	18,448	3·1
Damoh	4,753	1·5
Hoshangabad	553	·1
Raipur	5,916	·4
Bilaspur	1,898	·2
Sambalpur	76,155	9·6
Feudatory States	48,998	2·3

206. **Aboriginal Tribes of the Chhota-Nagpur border and of the Uria country.**—The numbers of these tribes and the principal localities where they are found are exhibited in the appended statement. First come

Aboriginal Tribes of Chhota-Nagpur and the Uria Country.

Name of tribe.	Number.	Localities where chiefly found.
Bhaina	17,151	Along the southern border of Chhota-Nagpur: Mandla, Bilaspur—8,695 in Bilaspur tehsil,—Raigarh and Sambalpur.
Bhuinhár Bhuiya	16,291	Raigarh 2,415, Sambalpur 8,359, Bamra 4,901.
Bhunjia	6,329	South-east of Raipur—6,020 in Raipur tehsil.
Bhumij	36	Bamra.
Debgunia	507	Sambalpur and the Uria States.

Aboriginal Tribes of Chhota-Nagpur and the Uria Country—continued.

Name of Tribe.	Number.	Localities where chiefly found.
Dhanwár	8,842	North-east of Bilaspur—7,090 in Bilaspur tehsil,—Raigarh 2,449, Bamra 516.
Lodha	3,119	
Sonwáni	1,065	
Total Dhanwár .	*13,026*	
Kamár	7,817	South-east of Raipur—4,720 in Raipur tehsil.—Bamra 1,302, and the Uria country.
Khairwár	3,224	Bilaspur—4,842 in tehsil Bilaspur and 2,461 in Seorinarain,—Raigarh 4,684.
Mánjhi	10,289	
Máhto	423	
Total Khairwár .	*13,936*	
Kharia	8,930	Raigarh and Sambalpur.
Oraon	293	
Dhelki	537	
Dudh-kharia . . .	193	
Total Kharia .	*9,953*	
Korwa	975	North of Bilaspur and Raigarh.
Munda	5,185	Sambalpur 1,831, Raigarh 1,035, Bamra 1,733.
Naksia	2,066	Sambalpur, 1,078, Raigarh, 741, Bamra 235.
Oraon	21,567	Distributed all along southern border of Chhota-Nagpur: Bilaspur 1,122, Sambalpur 8,068, Raigarh 3,886, Bamra 9,403.
Dhángar . . .	1,697	
Total Oraon .	*23,264*	
Rautia	477	Raigarh; a few in north of Bilaspur and Sambalpur.
Saota	283	North of Bilaspur.

the *Bhainas*, a tribe whose idenity I am unable to trace, but believe the name to be simply a variation of the widespread designation, which as Bhuiya or Bhumia is frequently applied to the aboriginal tenants of the soil all over these central hills. At the last Census the term was reported to be identical with Bhuinhár, which, on the other hand, following Dalton's Ethnology, was taken to be distinct from Bhuiya. Mr. Risley, however, gives Bhuiya and Bhuinhár as synonymous. Who and what the *Bhuiyas* are is a matter involved in considerable doubt. The name Bhuiya, originally signifying some sort of connection with the soil, is at present adopted as a title by many tribes and castes, from Assam to Rajputana and from Behar to Madras, but here we see it employed as the sole designation of a distinct tribe. This Mr. Risley considers to have come about in something like the following manner :—

"The advanced guard of the Aryan immigrants pressing forward in quest of land, and seeking a name for the alien races whom they found in possession of scanty clearings in the forest-clad tract of Central India, whither they had themselves been driven, would naturally ignore the tribal names of the groups with which they came in contact, and would call the strangers Bhuiyas, or children of the soil. In course of time, as the Aryan domination grew, the name conferred by the conquering race would abide, and the older savage designations would pass away and be forgotten. But wherever the title of Bhuiya, conferred in this rough general fashion by the new settlers on all the non-Aryans whom they came across, chanced to be adopted by a compact tribe, it would become the tribal name of that aggregate, and would be used by them for the purpose of describing themselves collectively. Thus, it would seem, may have arisen the distinction, well known in most parts of Chhota-Nagpur, between a "Bhuiya by tribe" and a "Bhuiya by title." The Bhuiyas of Bonai and Keunjhar described by Colonel Dalton belong to the former category; the Bhumij, Mundas, and Oraons to the latter. The distinction will be made somewhat clearer if it is explained that every "tribal Bhuiya" will as a matter of course describe himself as Bhuiya, while a member of the other tribes mentioned in the last sentence will only call himself Bhuiya if he is speaking with reference to a question of land, or desires for some special reason to lay stress on his status as a landholder or agriculturist. It is a plausible conjecture that the tribal Bhuiyas, properly so called, as distinguished from the titular Bhuiyas of other tribes or castes, may have had their original settlements in the Tributary States to the south of the Chhota-Nagpur plateau. In Gangpur, Bonai, Keunjhar and Bamra the organization of the tribe is more complete than elsewhere, and the name Bhuiya is unequivocally recognized as the tribal designation."

The titular use of the word Bhuiya, it may here be noted, is exemplified among the Gonds of these Provinces. In Saugor we find a class of the latter known as Bhoi, regarding whom Colonel Hogg informs me that they have a separate dialect which they call Pársi, and their form of worship and marriage and funeral ceremonies are of a distinctively aboriginal nature. The name, as applied to them, may therefore be taken to signify that they are the primitive occupants of the soil; the word Bhumia is similarly used, as we have seen, both among the Gonds and the Baigas.

The *Bhunjias* of the southern zemindaris of Raipur are the same as the Bhuiyas of the country further east. At page 116 of the Ethnological Committee's Report, Mr. Hewitt identifies the Bhunjias with the eastern "Bhumias," and states that all their traditions point to their having come from the eastern Garhjat states of Sambalpur. At page 5 of the same compilation the opinion is put forth that the Bhunjias correspond to the Bhumij, another of the Chhota-Nagpur tribes, who are akin to the Mundas. The former of these two views may be taken as the correct one; from the similarity of the name to that of the Bhuiyas who are extensively distributed over the country adjoining the tract where the Bhunjias occur—whereas the Bhumij are scarcely represented in these parts,—and from the fact of the eastern origin of the Bhunjias, it must appear that the name of the latter is nothing other than the Chhatisgarh equivalent for the Bhuiya tribe.

207. Regarding the *Debgunias*, Mr. Priest informs me that they were originally the priests of the Bhainas, their calling being, as the name imports, to prophesy the advent of the gods. Their main occupation is at present to recite the genealogies of the Bhaina chiefs; they are the bháts of the Bhainas. The *Dhanwárs* are a race of professional shikaris in Sambalpur, but from the northern hills of Bilaspur they are reported to subsist by rude cultivation and by gathering forest produce. One of their sub-divisions is the Lodha, and by this name alone they have sometimes been recorded at the Census. The *Kamárs* of the southern zemindaris of Raipur, who form the largest part of the tribe in these Provinces, are described as living in the most remote jungles, supporting themselves on jungle fruits and small game. In Bengal and in Chhota-Nagpur the term Kamár is merely an occupational one, implying a worker in metals; it includes persons of aboriginal as well as non-aboriginal stock. The application of the name in these Provinces has no doubt arisen in the same way—in some cases Kamárs were shown in the Census books as workers in iron,—though it would

appear that the bulk of the tribe, as it at present exists, have now taken to jungle pursuits.

208. With *Khairwárs* have been amalgamated the Mánjhis and Mahtos of the hills north of Raigarh and Bilaspur. According to Mr. Risley both Mánjhi and Mahto are in Bengal the titles of several castes or tribes, amongst them being Khairwárs. Colonel Dalton at page 129 of his Ethnology of Bengal gives Mánjhi and Mahto as sub-divisions of the Khairwár tribe in those parts of Chhota Nagpur which adjoin the place where they are found in the Central Provinces. Both have therefore been put with Khairwárs, though it may be remarked that Mánjhi—village headman—has frequently been recorded, specially in the Uria country, as a title of several of the aboriginal tribes. The Khairwárs have generally been shown as of the Hindu religion at the Census.

209. The *Kharias, Korwas, Mundas, Rautias, Oraons, and Saotas* are well-known tribes of Chhota-Nagpur. The Saota or Saont is the southern name for the Santál. Nágbansi, a term of somewhat indefinite application, is sometimes found recorded from the eastern districts and states; it would appear to be generally used of the Mundas, 602 of whom gave Nágbansi as a sub-division in the Census schedules; Nágbansi recorded alone has therefore been shown under Munda in Table XVI. The *Naksias,* who have been classed among forest and hill tribes, their occupation being given as dhya cultivation and hunting, are reported by the Deputy Commissioner of Sambalpur to be low-caste Hindus equal in status to the Pábs and Domárs.

CLASS B.—PROFESSIONAL.

210. The most important castes included in this class are Priests, Group V, Devotees, Group VI, and Writers, Group IX.

V. Priests.—The distribution of *Brahmins* in the several districts of the Province is given in the accompanying abstract. As will be seen the priestly caste is strongest in the northern district of the Province and in the Nerbada valley; in the Nagpur country Brahmins occur chiefly in the Wardha and Nagpur districts, in Chanda they are only 1 per cent. of the population, in Bhandara ·8, and in Balaghat ·6. These are the three districts in which the caste is proportionately weakest. In the Satpura districts and in Chhatisgarh the average tends to rise, and in the better parts of the Uria country the number of Brahmins is very considerable, in Sambalpur amounting to over 3 per cent. of the inhabitants of the district.

Brahmin 382,938—296 per 10,000 of the population.

District.	Total.	Percentage on district population.
Saugor	45,803	7·7
Damoh	24,737	7·6
Jubbulpore	61,468	8·2
Narsinghpur	26,162	7·1
Hoshangabad	33,604	6·3
Nimar	12,671	5·0
Mandla	6,840	2·0
Seoni	6,547	1·8
Chhindwara	7,124	1·7
Betul	3,427	1·1
Wardha	11,124	2·8
Nagpur	22,654	3·0
Chanda	6,834	1·0
Bhandara	6,104	·8
Balaghat	2,362	·6
Raipur	21,678	1·4
Bilaspur	25,371	2·2
Chhatisgarh States	6,219	1·0
Bastar	1,693	·5
Sambalpur	25,154	3·2
Uria States	24,205	2·0

Subjoined is a statement which has been prepared showing the principal sub-divisions of the caste which have been returned at the Census; the arrangement of the table follows the scheme laid down by Mr. Sherring in his work on Hindu castes. The percentages cannot be taken very strictly, as allowance must be made for the fact that about a twelfth of the Brahmins returned sub-divisions which could not be readily classed, without a greater amount of research than could be given to the subject. Allowing for these it may be roughly stated that about four-fifths of the Brahmins of these Provinces belong to the Panch-Gaur or northern race, while of the remaining one-fifth the greater number, more than two-thirds, belong to the Panch-Dravid or southern race, the balance being local Brahmins, who do not properly fall within either of these orders. In other words, out of every hundred Brahmins 80, 14, and 6 belong approximately to the three classes that have been given.

Sub-divisions of Brahmins.

Group	Division.	Sub-division.	TOTAL.	Percentage of sub-division on division and of division on total Brahmins.
PANCH-GAUR.	Kanaujia .	Jijhotia . .	31,154	13·3
		Kanaujia . .	78,554	33·5
		Pardesi (Agni-hotri 986) . .	19,020	8·1
		Sanádhya . .	3,226	1·4
		Sanaurhia . .	36,979	15·8
		Sarwaria (Mahápátra 410) .	65,268	27·9
		Total Kanaujia .	234,201	61·2
	Sáraswat .	......	550	·1
	Gaur . .	Adgaur . .	3,307	22·0
		Bhárgao . .	1,612	10·7
		Deswáli Chhannát (Chnannáti 105, Daima 260, Gujargaur 1,248, Parikh 137) .	1,750	21·7
		Palliwár . .	1,337	8·9
		Pushkarna . .	288	1·9
		Shrigaur . .	997	6·6
		Gaur (Bengali Brahmins 93, Márwári 245, Nandwáná 234, Sewak 77) .	5,709	38·2
		Total Gaur .	15,000	3·9
	Maithila .	Ojha . . .	732	·2
	Utkali .	Jháre . . .	6,791	21·7
		Raghunáthia .	3,194	10·2
		Utkali (Susári 140, Balrámgotri 261, Sáhu 177) .	21,300	68·1
		Total Utkali .	31,285	8·2
	PANCH-GAUR UNSPECIFIED .		77	...
	Total Panch-Gaur .		281,845	73·6
PANCH-DRAVID.	Maháráshtra	Deshasth . .	22,433	51·4
		Kánnav . .	2,837	6·5
		Karháde . .	1,237	2·8
		Kokanasth . .	3,229	7·4
		Mádhyanjan .	1,738	4·0
		Málwi . .	1,955	4·5
		Maháráshtra (Charak 408. Abir 140, Devrukhe 3, Hiranya 877, Kalanki 1) . .	10,189	23·4
		Total Maháráshtra . . .	43,618	11·4
	Tailanga .	......	1,249	·3
	Dravid .	......	145	...
	Karnáta .	......	47	...
	Gurjar . .	Audich . .	363	10·2
		Khedáwál . .	1,526	43·0
		Nágar . .	646	18·2
		Gujeráti Audambar 75, Jambu 120) . . .	1,014	28·6
		Total Gurjar .	3,549	1·0
	PANCH-DRAVID UNSPECIFIED .		57	...
	Total Panch-Dravid .		48,665	12·7
SUPPLEMENTARY TRIBES.	Supplementary Tribes.	Ahiwási . .	1,686	8·9
		Báwisá . .	1,071	5·6
		Bhagore . .	3,089	16·2
		Golápurab . .	1,360	7·2
		Náramdeo . .	9,928	52·3
		Rikhishwar . .	1,332	7·0
		Others (Káshmiri 11, Sákaldwipi 187, Shenvi 14, Shringrishi 148, Jháre 191) .	551	2·8
		Total Supplementary Tribes .	19,017	5·0
	BRAHMIN UNSPECIFIED .		33,411	8·7
	GRAND TOTAL .		382,938	100

211. *Panch-Gaur Brahmins.*—Among the Panch-Gaurs by far the strongest division are the Kanaujias, hailing from the country round Cawnpore and Benares; their number is, according to the classified list, 234,201. A third of these have returned themselves simply as Kanaujias; they are more generally distributed than most of the other sections of the northern Brahmins, and they form the chief element of the caste as found in Chhatisgarh. Jijhotias are more especially the Brahmins of Saugor and Damoh. Mr. Crooke remarks that, according to their own account, they connect their name with the Yajurveda, but it is more probably a geographical designation from Jajhoti, the ancient name of Bundelkhand. The Sarwaria Brahmins occur in greatest numbers in Jubbulpore, where 36,159, or about three-fifths of the caste in the district, belong to this section. The Sanádhyas or Sanaurhias are returned principally from Saugor 10,968, Damoh 3,315, Jubbulpore 4,055, Narsinghpur 11,495, and Hoshangabad 5,641. The two names are undistinguishable, though the Sanádhyas are more properly Brahmins from the Ganges-Jamna Doab, while the Sanaurhias are the well-known criminal class of Bundelkhand. The latter claim to be Brahmins and akin to the Sanádhyas. According to Mr. Crooke, the Sanaurhia "is a strict Brahmin, renews his thread annually at the Rakshábandan, is a total abstainer from flesh and wine, never destroys life in any form, observes the same ceremonies connected with births, marriages, and deaths that other Brahmins do, worships the cow and the serpent, and when he is sick employs none but Brahmin sorcerers to expel the evil spirit from his body." Though it would be impossible to expect the two names to be properly distinguished at the Census I may state for what it is worth, that the results as finally worked out show the Sanaurhias to out number Sanádhyas in the proportion of about 12 to 1.

The Gaur Brahmins come mostly from further north than the Kanaujias, whilst other representatives of the division in these Provinces are from Malwa and Rajputana, and some are from Bengal. More than a third of the Gaurs are returned from the Hoshangabad district, 5,425, whither most of them have come from Marwar and Jaipur or from the country beyond; they are all more or less infected with the Marwari taint of money-lending and mercantile pursuits.* The Deswáli Chhannát is the Gaur of Malwa.

The Utkalis are the Brahmins of the Uria country. The numbers of the sub-division are properly much larger than shown in the table, as in it should be included almost all the Brahmins who have been shown from Sambalpur and the Uria states among "others and unspecified," about a fourth of the caste in those parts.

212. *Panch Dravid Brahmins.*—Chief amongst these come the Maratha Brahmins of Nimar and the districts of the Nagpur plain. About a fourth of the caste have not returned distinct sub-divisions, but amongst those who have, it will be seen that the section which most largely prevails is the Deshasth, the dwellers on the tableland above the Western Ghats. Allowing for the indefinite record of part of the Maratha Brahmins, it may be taken that the Deshasths number something like 70 per cent. of the caste in these Provinces. Next in importance are the Kokanasths or Chitpáwans, who number 3,229; the Maratha Peshwas belonged to this community. There is a fairly strong Maratha colony in Saugor, 1,282, where throughout the latter half of the last century the caste was dominant; nearly half of its number belongs to the Karháde sub-division.

The Gurjar Brahmins of Gujerat are found principally in Hoshangabad 1,108, and Nimar 820; their chief sub-divisions are the Khedáwál—here generally employed as bankers and traders—and the Nágar Brahmins of Nimar, regarding whose establishment in that part of the country an account is given in Captain Forsyth's Settlement Report of the district, page 61.

* Hoshangabad Settlement Report, page 67.

213. Among the supplementary Brahmin tribes the principal is the Náramdeo, the local Brahmin of the Nerbada valley, where are also found the Golápurabs, mostly returned from Narsinghpur, and the Báwisas, who are peculiar to Nimar. The former are said to have come originally from Bundelkhand. The Ahiwásis are recorded from the upper part of the valley, more than half of their number occurring in Jubbulpore. In the north of India "they claim to be Brahmins, but local jealousy denies them the honour. Their favourite occupation is the carrying trade—trading in their own carts they carry salt from Rajputana all over northern India, bringing back sugar and other commodities in return."* The Bhagore and Rikhishwar are two local sections of Brahmins; the latter found almost solely in Chhindwara, and the former in that district and along the Nerbada, like most of the other local tribes.

The *Dhámis* of Saugor and Damoh, 75 in number, are worshippers of Pránnáth in the Panna state. All are recorded as Hindus at the Census, but the class observes Hindu and Mahomedan rites without distinction.

214. **VI. Devotees.**—The accompanying statement exhibits the districts in which the number of religious mendicants is high or low in proportion to the total population. Hoshangabad, along the whole of whose border flows the sacred river Nerbada, heads the list in the first of these respects, and Narsinghpur which lies next to it takes third place. In Chhatisgarh the ascetic class is found chiefly in the northern part of the plain. The chiefs of Chhuikhadan and Khairagarh belong to the Bairági caste, and the class is also of some standing in Bilaspur, where they hold the proprietary right of a considerable number of villages. It is needless to state that here almost all the devotee castes have largely abandoned asceticism.† In Nagpur and Wardha the high average of devotees returned at the Census is to some extent accounted for by the inclusion of the Gárpagáris, the local hail-averting caste.

Religious Mendicants.

Average High.			Average Low.		
District, etc.	No.	Percentage on population.	District.	No.	Percentage on population.
Hoshangabad .	8,298	1·56	Chanda .	2,161	·31
Bilaspur .	14,605	1·25	Bhandara	3,537	·48
Narsinghpur .	3,836	1·04	Damoh .	1,701	·52
Nagpur .	6,928	·91	Betul .	1,881	·58
Wardha .	3,634	·91	Saugor .	3,494	·59
			Seoni .	2,257	·61
			Balaghat .	2,369	·62
Chhuikhadan .	591	1·63			
Sakti .	376	1·48			
Kawardhas	1,288	1·40			

Most of the castes which have been entered in the present group are so well known as hardly to call for detailed mention. 36 *Aghoris* were found at the Census. They are a class of mendicants who extort alms by eating human ordure, bones, or other filth; they are now rapidly disappearing; in 1881 ninety-three persons returned themselves as Aghoris. Of the 38,180 *Bairágis*, 18,593 or 48·7 per cent. are recorded from the two Chhatisgarh districts and from the states of Kawardha, Chhuikhadan, Khairagarh, Nandgaon and Sakti, which form the more open part of the plain. Here, as has been remarked, the caste has generally taken to worldly pursuits.

215. The *Basdewas*, 2,494, are "a sect of 'merry beggars,' known by their wearing a cap of peacock feathers. The stems are bound together and surmounted by a sham snake, while the feathers shade the face. They beg only in the morning; each man has his beat which another Basdewa dare not infringe, unless bareheaded."‡ The *Gárpagáris* occur only in the Maratha districts; the Gárpagári is, or rather used to be, one of the regular village servants, but now the potency of the spells by which he averts the hail from the standing crops would appear to be but little believed in. The *Gosáins* number 25,834; their chief recorded sub-divisions are the Giri 9,643, Puri 6,236, Bhárthi 1,463, Ban

* Crooke's Ethnography, North-West Provinces and Oudh, page 5.
† *Cf.* Bilaspur Settlement Report, page 53.
‡ Berar Census Report, 1881, page 68.

386, Aran 68, and Jati 48. The *Sanyási* is properly a person who has renounced the world; the order is open to Brahmins alone, and its members profess to live in a state of celibacy, but the term is ordinarily used loosely as an equivalent of Bairági or Gosáin. To this may be ascribed the fact that, according to the census returns, the sexes are found in about equal proportions in the caste; it is recorded almost solely from Chhatisgarh, where the slack observance of religious vows by people of this class has already been remarked upon. The other devotee castes who are most strongly represented in these Provinces are the *Jogis* 6,994, *Náths* 5,714, *Jangams* 1,640, *Gondhalis* 510, *Mánbhaus* 630, and *Nánakshdhis* 467. In many cases the names were so intermixed that the figures given can be looked upon as indicating only comparatively the numbers belonging to each order. Amongst all, except the Mánbhaus and Nánakshâhis, the average of females is high. The Nánakshdhis are Sikh devotees; among them have been included 314 *Udásis* and 25 *Suthráshâhis*.

216. **VII. Temple Servants.**—The class is practically found only in the Maratha country and in Sambalpur. In the former the temple servants are *Guraos* 7,240, and *Viramushtis* 73, the latter being Telugus from Chanda; in the Uria country they are represented by the *Thanápatis* 2,423, and *Gandhmálıs* 2,538, terms which, from one being frequently entered in the census books as a sub-division of the other, would appear to be synonymous. These castes are attendants in the temples and sellers of flowers and *bel* leaves for offerings to the idol.

217. **VIII. Genealogists.**—These are the *Bháts* and *Raos*, who together number 23,710 persons. Only 169 Mahomedan Bháts have been returned at the Census. The Bháts are attached to many castes, whose names they take, but no account has been kept of these in the returns.

218. **IX. Writers.**—These are the *Káyasths*, 29,414, of the northern districts, the *Bidurs* 11,852, and *Parbhus* 438, of the Maratha country, and the *Karans* or *Mahantis* 5,378, of Sambalpur and the Uria states. The sub-divisons recorded of the Káyasths are given in the margin: more than three-fourths of the caste belong to the Shriwástab sub-division. The three districts in which the Káyasths are proportionally strongest are Saugor 5,748, Jubbulpore 5,795, and Narsinghpur 4,544. Akin to the Káyasths are the Parbhus, nearly half of whom are found in Nagpur; 138 of them return the sub-division Chandraseni, so called from the name of their progenitor. Bidurs, with whom have been included *Krishnapakshis*,* are conventionally included among the writing castes, but many are cultivators, traders, or shop-keepers. The caste is most largely represented in Nagpur 4,169, Chanda 1,954, and Wardha 1,567. The Mahantis or Karans are the Káyasths of the Uria country; they return the ordinary Uria sub-divisions, Utkali, Jhádwa, etc.

Sub-divisions of Káyasths.

Chief Sub-divisions.	Number.
Shriwástab	23,334
Saksena	1,506
Unáya	565
Gaur	407
Bhatnágar	150
Máthur	119
Nigam	85
Amisht	53
Karan	19
Kulashresth	18
Ayatháne	9
Válmiki	2
Surajdhwaj	2

219. **X. Astrologers, etc.**—The principal caste is the *Joshi*, numbering 2,562, recorded mainly from Saugor, Damoh, and the Nerbada valley districts. In the Maratha country the astrologers are the *Sarodis* 832, a mendicant class found chiefly in the Wardha district, where 516 of their number are returned.

* "A distinction is sometimes raised by maintaining that the father of a Bidur may be a Kunbi or a man of even a lower caste, while the male parent of a Krishnapakshi is always a Brahmin or another Krishnapakshi."—Berar Census Report, 1881, page 123.

220. **XI—XIII. Musicians, Dancers, etc.**—The only caste whose numbers are at all considerable is the *Nagárchi*, 4,796, a low caste of musicians in the south-eastern parts of the Satpuras. The members of the caste "claim to be Hindus, are generally recognized as such, and do not kill cows or eat beef; but they worship Gond deities, and will take food from a Gond, by whom they are considered an inferior race." * Though the name is adopted as an occupational title—literally, player on the *nagára* or drum—by some of the Gonds, it is probable that the generality of the tribe are out-caste Hindus, who, from living among the Gonds, have adopted many of their religious ceremonies and beliefs.

CLASS C.—COMMERCIAL.

221. **XIV. Traders.**—The chief trading caste is the **Bania**, particulars regarding which are shown in the appended abstract. At the Census 37·6 per cent. of the Bania caste recorded their religion as Jain; the chief sub-divisions returning the creed are set forth below, but it must be remarked that members of these sub-divisions sometimes returned themselves as Hindus, while again Jains were occasionally found among the more distinctively Hindu sections of the caste. As the caste predominates so largely in the northern districts, the greater part of the Banias in these Provinces may be taken to be of northern origin. Marwari Banias are common in the lower part of the Nerbada valley, in the Maratha country, and throughout the eastern districts,† and more especially in the two former tracts many Gujerati Banias are met with. The sub-divisional returns, however, are not complete enough, nor are the names always sufficiently distinct, to enable us to note the distribution of the caste, according to its locality of origin, with anything like precision.

Bania 129,270—100 per 10,000 of the population.

Hindus.				Jains.		Chief districts.	No.	Per cent.
Chief sub-divisions.	No.	Chief sub-divisions.	No.	Chief sub-divisions.	No.			
Agarwál	15,880	Khandelwal	830	Charnágar	2,683	Saugor	22,920	3·9
Agrahari	975	Lád	2,818	Golápurab	6,672	Damoh	10,874	3·3
Ajudhiabási	1,717	Lingáyat	4,166	Oswál	3,881	Jubbulpur	17,664	2·4
Asáti	3,071	Lohána	41	Parwár	29,034	Narsinghpur	10,224	2·8
Dasá	1,294	Mahesri	5,021	Saitwál	2,857	Hoshangabad	8,278	1·6
Dhákar	221	Márwári	1,156	Vinaikwár	873	Nimar	8,510	3·4
Dhusar	1,064	Mor	298			Wardha	6,710	1·7
Gahoi	7,103	Nema	4,024			Nagpur	10,235	1·4
Gangráda	1,104	Palliwár	878					
Kasarwáni	5,308	Shrimáli	543					
Kasaundhi	4,108	Umre	2,066					
Kharáta	230							

The chief class of Banias in the Central Provinces are the Parwárs; they are found in every district, but are most numerous in Saugor 12,519, Damoh

* Report of Deputy Commissioner, Balaghat.

† Compare the language return in Table IX. There are very few Marwari speakers in the northern districts, while they abound in Hoshangabad 6,926, in Nimar 1,204 — though many of these are no doubt persons other than Banias — in Chhindwara 782, in Wardha 2,326, in Nagpur 3,652, in Chanda 699, in Bhandara 613, and in Raipur 1,434.

3,704, Jubbulpore 4,885, and Nasinghpur 1,973. They are generally Jains by religion, but over a tenth of them are returned as Hindus. In Saugor and Damoh, where they form the bulk of the Bania community, they are all of Bundelkhandi or local origin, and speak nothing but pure Bundeli. In the southern districts of the Province the Parwárs are mostly from Rajputana, from which also have generally come the Agarwáls, Oswáls, Mahesris, Saitwáls, Khandelwáls and others. The Gahois and Golápurabs are from Bundelkhand; the latter, according to a report received from Saugor, appear to belong to the same stock as the Parwárs, being a reformed minority, specially in details of marriage. The Lád, Lingáyat, and Shrimáli Banias are the principal sections of the caste from Western India; the Láds are met with chiefly in Nimar 1,215, and the Lingáyats in Wardha and Nagpur.

222. The *Komtis* are a class of Telugu traders found chiefly in the Nagpur country, 76·0 per cent. of their number being from Chanda. *Wanjáris* 2,712, occur principally in the Wardha and Chanda districts; they are distinct from Banjáras. In 1881 Mr. Kitts has in Berar classed Wanjáris as a cultivating caste, and states that in every respect they resemble Kunbis; at the present enumeration Wanjári was returned a Kunbi sub-division by 28 persons, but in general about Nagpur the Wanjáris are petty traders.* Their chief sub-divisions are Bhusárjin 557, and Rautjin 489. *Khatris*, 3,354, the great trading and writing caste of northern India, are found in every district, but are numerous only in Hoshangabad 560, and in Nimar 815; in the latter district the caste occurs mainly in Burhanpur, where they are weavers from Gujerat. The *Bohras* number only 2,673, but many more must have been shown simply as Mussalmans; Nimar returns 1,750.

223. **XVI. Carriers**—The **Banjáras** are a numerous class in these Provinces, amounting to 56,092 persons. They are widely distributed, but occur in greatest strength in the districts of Hoshangabad, 4,306, Nimar, 5,892—here they number 2·3 per cent. of the inhabitants—Chhindwara, 2,822, Raipur, 7,238, Bilaspur, 3,832, and Sambalpur, 4,701. In the native states there are many in Bastar, 4,685, Raigarh, 1,638, and Kalahandi, 2,167. The traditional occupation of the class has now largely disappeared. It is unfortunately almost impossible to effect comparison between the figures for the caste and those for the occupation of carrying by pack-bullocks. In the first place, the latter is extensively followed by persons other than Banjáras—in all the northern districts a large number of people have been returned as engaged in the work of *lád*, whereas very few Banjáras are recorded from that part of the Province. Again, in cases where carriers, say, of grain, have been shown as also sellers or dealers, they have been entered in the Occupation table among the latter. But generally in all places where the country has been opened up by the railway, we find the Banjáras to have mostly abandoned their original pursuit; this will be found to be specially the case in the lower Nerbada valley and in the Maratha districts. In Nimar there are only 13 carriers by pack-bullocks returned from the district, though the Banjáras, as we have seen, exceed five thousand persons.

The Banjáras have a dialect of their own, known as Labháni; it has been recorded as the mother-tongue of 29,271 persons, or 52·2 per cent. of the caste. Of the Nimar Banjáras, 5,156—nearly the whole strength of the tribe in the district—are shown as speaking Labháni. In Chanda 3,681 persons speak the dialect, whereas the number of Banjáras appearing in Table XVI is only 2,165; the mistake is due to confusion arising from the use of the term Naik, which is applied alike to the Banjáras† and to a class of Telugus. Elsewhere the title

* *Cf.* Also Chanda Settlement Report, page 58.

† "Each *tánda*, as their camps are called, is commanded by a chief called the *naik*, whom all obey, and who, in council with the elders, disposes of inter-tribal offenders, even to the extent of capital punishment, it is believed." Forsyth's Highlands of Central India, page 108.

was taken as synonymous with Banjára, but in Chanda the distinction has not been observed; the tribe in the latter district may therefore be taken to number at least 4,000 persons instead of the figures which have been given.

The chief sub-divisions of the Banjáras are those which are shown in the margin. The tribe is recorded under several names; they are very commonly styled Labhánas, which, though more properly a sub-divisional term, is often used as a general name for the whole caste. Such is also the case with the title Naik; frequently also the Banjáras call themselves simply Bepáris. The highest class among the Banjáras is the Mathuria, who say they are Brahmins and wear the sacred thread. The Cháran Banjáras, with the Chauháns, Powárs, Ráthors, Taurs, and Rajput Banjáras all claim to be of Rajput origin; the Bartia Banjáras who are found principally in the eastern districts and states are given by Mr. Kitts as a sub-tribe of the Chárans.* The Mukeris or Multánis are Mussalman Banjaras; those in the Central Provinces are nearly all settled in the Saugor district where they deal in cattle.

Sub-divisions of Banjáras.

NAME.	No.
Bartia	1,884
Cháran	1,356
Chauhán	1,074
Powár	1,629
Rajput	8,269
Ráthor	3,021
Taur	125
Goár	2,508
Gugeria	773
Jharbala	462
Láhoria	1,142
Mathuria	1,338
Mukeri	1,023
Thuria	988

CLASS D.—ARTISANS AND VILLAGE MENIALS.

224. This class contains 25 groups, which will be noticed individually below. For details of district distribution it will be necessary to refer to the table in the second volume, as most of the castes are hardly of sufficient importance to call for separate note in this respect.

225. **XVII. Goldsmiths.**—The *Sonár* caste, including the Telugu *Sarábus* and *Kamsalas*, numbers 91,935 or 71 per 10,000 of the inhabitants of the Province. They are found in greatest strength in the richer and more settled districts; in Jubbulpore, Narsinghpur, Nimar, and in the districts of the Nagpur division—if we take the Pancháls into account in Chanda—they number more than 1 per cent. of the population. On the other hand, in the Chhatisgarh districts and states the proportion falls to between ·2 and ·3 per cent. The chief sub-divisions of the Sonár caste are those which have been given in Table XVI. Others are the Aherán and Dhália Sonárs of Burhanpur, numbering 358 and 310 respectively; the Dewángan 240, Pándhre 422, and Purània 1,126, the two former found principally in the Maratha country, and the latter in the northern districts. Marwari goldsmiths number 1,040. Six hundred and fifty-five Sonars returned themselves as Pancháls, and the latter term by itself has been recorded of 7,380 persons, nearly all belonging to the Nagpur division, Chanda alone returning 4,505. Panchál is properly a collective name applied to all the five chief artisan castes, but it is more particularly used of the Sonárs and Kasárs; from the sub-divisions returned for Pancháls at the Census, Dewángan, Vaishya, etc., it would appear that the term in general represents only the former caste, and all Pancháls have therefore been classed among goldsmiths in the final table. A distinctive feature about the Panchál Sonars is that they take their religious teachers from among their own caste.

226. **XVIII. Barbers.**—The Barber caste is recorded under various names in different parts of the Province; in the Hindi districts the caste is known as *Nai*, *Khawás* and *Mardánia*, in the Maratha country as *Mháli*, among the Telu

* Berar Census Report, page 151.

gus as *Mangala*, and among the Urias as *Bhandári*. The barbers number 140,197 at the Census, or 1·1 per cent. of the population; they muster in force in the three northern districts of Saugor, Damoh, and Narsinghpur, where they exceed 2 per cent. of the inhabitants. The functions of the caste are so well known as hardly to call for description; the barber is generally one of the village servants, receiving an allowance in grain for every grown up male in the family, the same fee including also his wife's attendance on the womankind. The *Maháwats*, 54, who have been classed under the heading of barbers, are a branch of the caste "who do ear-cleaning and cupping, which is performed with a cow's horn, which has a hole at the pointed end, through which they exhaust the air. They are chiefly found in large towns where they practise as a low order of quack doctors."* *Báris*, 685, are a northern caste of leaf-plate makers and torch-bearers, here engaged mainly in personal service.

227. **XIX. Blacksmiths.**—*Lohárs, Khátis or Kammaris* are pretty evenly distributed over all the districts and states of the Province. They number 149,496 or 1·2 per cent. of the population, the districts with the highest proportion of blacksmiths being Bhandara, where they form 1·8 per cent. of the inhabitants of the district, and Saugor 1·7, while in Wardha the proportion sinks to ·8 and in Nimar to ·5 per cent. The sub-divisions recorded of the caste include Agarias 2,852, and Gondi Lohárs 4,679, the former returned chiefly from Jubbulpore, and the latter from the Satpura districts; both are in all probability mostly employed in collecting and smelting iron ore. Jharia or Jháde Lohárs are returned, the former from Chhatisgarh, the latter from the Maratha country, where also chiefly occur the Panchál and Baone Lohárs, numbering 2,309 and 1,467 respectively. The Panchâls are described "as a wandering caste of smiths living in grass-mat huts, and using as fuel the roots of thorn bushes, which they batter out on the ground with the back of a short-handled axe peculiar to themselves. They move from place to place with buffaloes, donkeys, and occasionally ponies to carry their kit." From the large number of Panchâls returned at the Census it is however probable that the name is used more often as denoting that Lohár is one of the Pánch-Panchál castes, than that the persons of whom it is recorded belong to the vagrant tribe. Barhai Lohárs, who unite carpentry with blacksmiths' work, number 4,608; they occur mainly in the Maratha districts. Kamár—see para. 207—has been returned as a sub-division by 193 persons in Sambalpur. The *Ghantras*, 1,007, are inferior blacksmiths in the Uria country.

228. **XX. Carpenters, Masons and Turners.**—So unevenly distributed are the workers in wood in different parts of the Province that it is worth while comparing the figures which result for some of the districts where the average of carpenters is high, and for others where the Barhai caste can hardly be said to exist. It will be seen that in the Satpura districts and throughout Chhatisgarh and the Uria country the carpenter's profession is practically unknown. The same feature is observable in the Occupation table, the reason being that the implements of agriculture in these parts are of so rough a kind that the cultivator prepares his own. In addition to the sub-divisions given in the caste table only two need be recorded, the Kokás 660, and the Chamár

Barhai 69,833 — 54 per 10,000 of the population.

Average High.			Average Low.		
District.	Number.	Percentage of district population.	District.	Number.	Percentage of district population.
Saugor	6,438	1·1	Seoni	1,116	·3
Damoh	4,256	1·3	Mandla	323	...
Narsinghpur	5,837	1·6	Balaghat	301	...
Hoshangabad	7,446	1·4	Raipur	157	...
Wardha	6,791	1·7	Bilaspur	244	...
Nagpur	13,061	1·7	Sambalpur	328	...
			Feudatory States	625	...

* Crooke's Ethnography of the N.-W. P. and Oudh, page 122.

Barhai 22. The *Kharádis* and *Kunderas* are turners; *Lakheras*, 2,736, are workers in lac, bangles being their chief article of manufacture; they are found principally in the northern parts of the Province. *Chitrakárs* or *Mahâranas* are painters of wooden idols returned from Sambalpur and the Uria states. Masons, *Larhia, Ráj, Gaundi*, number 3,547, of whom nearly four-fifths occur in the two districts of Saugor and Jubbulpore; in the Maratha districts and in Chhatisgarh, members of the Gaundi caste, as the masons are there called, are found only to the number of a score or two.

229. **XXI. Brass and Copper-smiths.**—Amongst these the principal castes are the *Kaseras* or *Kasárs*, 10,489, who take their name from the bell-metal in which they work, the *Tameras*, or workers in copper, 3,677, *Otáris* or *Watkaris*, 1,535, *Khadras*, 2,012, *Bharewas*, 1,713, and *Audhias*, 1,002. It is of interest to note that in the three northern districts of Saugor, Damoh, and Jubbulpore, almost the sole representatives of the craft are the Tameras or copper workers, and the same is also the case, though to a less extent, in Narsinghpur. On the other hand, throughout the Maratha districts the workers in bell-metal, of which both the Kasár and Otári are founders and casters, hold almost undisputed sway. The distinction is probably more nominal than real, as both classes of workmen use copper and bell-metal in the manufacture of their wares. In Mandla the Bharewas are the makers of the bell-metal vessels, for which the place has a reputation. Of the Audhias, Seoni returns considerably more than half, 597, while the Khadras are found almost solely in Sambalpur and the Uria states. Sambalpur, it may be observed, returns a much larger proportion of workers in the baser metals than any other district in the Province, and a similar high average of these artificers is noticeable in some of the Uria States, particularly Raigarh and Sonpur.

230. **XXII. Tailors.**—*Darsis*, in the Maratha country commonly known as *Simpis*, and among the Telugus as *Merewárs*, number 35,968, or ·28 per cent. of the population. Sixty-eight of their number are recorded as Jain by religion, but all belong probably only to the Jain sub-division of the caste, and are not followers of the creed of that name. The caste is sparsely represented in the hill districts and in the eastern districts and states.

231. **XXII (*a*) Grain-parchers and Confectioners** number 5,282. *Bharbhunjas* are the only caste recorded who are parchers of grain, but the industry is extensively followed by other classes, notably the Dhuris, Kewats, Dhimars, etc. The *Gurias* are the confectioners of the Uria country, and the *Halwais* of the other parts of the Province.

232. **XXII (*b*) Perfumers and Betel-leaf sellers.**—The former occupational class is represented by only 48 persons. Betel-leaf growers and sellers are the *Barais*, in the Maratha districts generally known as *Báris*, 24,614, the *Pansáris* 908, and the *Tambolis* 2,294. The Barais are more specially the growers of the betel and the Tambolis the sellers, but the distinction is imperfectly preserved. Nagpur and Wardha in the south of the Province, and Saugor and Damoh in the north, are the districts from which the castes are returned in greatest strength. The chief sub-divisions recorded are the same for all the three castes; Chaurasia Barais are found throughout the northern districts, and Golait and Kumhárdang Báris in the districts of the Nagpur plain. Purània is returned as a sub-division by 1,026 Barais and Báris, and Surajbans by 1,355; Kumráwat is given as the sub-caste of 341 Tambolis in Hoshangabad and Nimar.

233. **XXIII. Weavers, etc.**—The castes included in this group number 750,981 persons or 5·8 per cent. of the population, but along with them should properly be reckoned the persons shown under the heading of village watchmen, as nearly all of the latter are primarily weavers by profession. Combining the figures for the two groups, we find that the weaving classes amount to about 12 per cent. of the inhibitants of the Province. The castes which are numerically

strongest in the present group are the *Gándas* and *Pankas* of Chhatisgarh and the Uria country; their distribution is noted in the margin. The two names are generally considered as synonymous, but the writer of the Bilaspur Settlement Report gives the proper name of the caste as Panka, and limits the application of the term Gánda to those who have taken to village service, and to the inferior musician class known as Bajgariya Gándas. In Sambalpur and the Uria states, however, it will be seen that the almost universal name for the caste is Gánda. The most notable feature about the Pankas is the fact that in Chhatisgarh almost the whole caste has adopted the Kabirpanthi creed, and they thus abstain from meat and do not drink liquor. On the other hand, the Gándas of the Uria country are ordinary low-caste Hindus; in Sambalpur there are 91,006 Gándas, while all the Kabirpanthis in the district number only 11,442; in Sonpur, where there are 26,650 Gándas, no Kabirpanthis are returned, and in Patna, where the caste numbers 57,452, there are only 878 followers of the dissenting sect. Though weaving was the original occupation of the Panka or Gánda caste, a large proportion of its members are now engaged in agriculture, but their style of cultivation is not of a very high order. They also furnish nearly all the village watchmen of the part of the Province where they are found.

Gánda 291,768 — 225 per 10,000 of the population; Panka 162,631—126.

Chief districts, etc.	Number.		Percentage on Population.		
	Gándas.	Pankas.	Gándas.	Pankas.	Both castes.
Mandla .	12	14,528	...	4·3	4·3
Raipur .	39,733	34,494	2·5	2·2	4·7
Bilaspur .	31,162	72,272	2·7	6·2	8·9
Chhatisgarh States.	12,593	14,268	2·1	2·4	4·5
Sambalpur .	91,006	7,929	11·4	1·0	12·4
Uria States .	111,475	12,073	9·1	1·0	10·1

234. Though the Gándas, and like them the Mehras, are the largest castes by whom weaving is generally carried on as a profession, the most important industrial class in this respect is the Koshti caste of the Maratha country, the Koshta of the Hindi districts. In the latter, with the exception of Raipur, the caste is not so common, but in the districts of the Nagpur plain it is strongly represented, as the appended figures show:—

Koshti 137,891—106 per 10,000 of population.

Chief sub-division.	No.	Chief district.	No.	Percentage on district population.
Dewángan	7,001	Jubbulpore	3,690	·5
Gadhewál	12,428	Chhindwara	3,242	·8
Halbi	25,262	Wardha	7,652	1·9
Lád	897	Nagpur	44,825	5·9
Sálewár	4,896	Chanda	10,647	1·5
		Bhandara	18,006	2·4
		Raipur	19,983	1·3
		Bilaspur	10,934	·9

By far the largest sub-division among the Koshtis is the Halbi, to which more than five-sixths of the caste in the Nagpur district belongs; they are the people who make the fine white cotton cloths with silk borders, for which more especially the towns of Nagpur and Umrer are famous. The Halbis have an admixture of Gujerati in their speech. The Sálewárs are Telugu Koshtis, chiefly found in Chanda; the cloths they weave are generally of coloured patterns.

The *Sális* are silk weavers, nearly all returned from the Nimar district, where they occur solely in the town of Burhanpur and its precincts. The *Patwas* string necklaces and make waistbands of silk and cotton thread; they are found specially in the northern districts of the Province. The *Chhipias* of Bilaspur are also necklace-makers. The *Netkánis*, 2,333, and *Koskátis*, 1,553, are

Telugu castes returned from the Chanda district; the former are weavers, the latter deal in tassar cocoons, and are spinners and weavers of the silk.

235. The *Koris* are the Hindu weaving caste of Northern India in contradistinction to the *Juláha* or *Momin*, who are Mahomedans. At the Census the Koris number 44,700, of whom three-fourths are found in the districts of Saugor, Damoh, Jubbulpore and Narsinghpur. The *Kolis* of Nimar and of the tracts which border on the Berars have been entered along with Koris in the final Table. In Nimar they are hardly distinguishable from the Bhils, with whom they occupy the western hill parts of the district; their numbers at the Census, including also the Koris, were 1,936; they are mostly in the position of the village watch. In Berar the Kolis "have acted aforetime as guardians of the hill passes. Along the north of the province up to the eastern boundary of the Akola district ran a chain of out-posts or watch-towers, some of which were held by Kolis, and others by Bhils."* Many of them live by hunting, but the caste has now taken largely to agriculture. The Juláhas and Momins occur principally in Nagpur. The *Katias*, 43,940, are an important weaving and village watchman caste, found mainly on the Satpuras and in Hoshangabad; in the latter district and in Seoni and Chhindwara they number over 2 per cent. of the population. They are said to be an industrious race, but are addicted to drinking. The *Bhulias*, 24,758, are the weavers of the Uria country, whence also are returned the *Páns*, 12,233, and *Taalas*, 1,813. With the Páns Mr. Risley identifies the Pábs, classed in group II (*c*), and *Tantis*, all of them low castes of Dravidian origin; the Gánda is also said to belong to the same stock.

236. The chief printing and dyeing castes are the *Chhipa*, 5,023, *Rangrez*, 1,546, and *Rangári*, 7,196. The Chhipas are generally printers, but some are also dyers; they are found throughout the northern districts and in Bhandara and Balaghat; 1,348 are returned from the Narsinghpur district, where stamped cotton fabrics are largely produced, chiefly in the Gádarwára tehsil. The Rangrez are the Mahomedan dyers of the northern parts of the Province; in the Maratha country their place is taken by the Hindu dyeing caste of Rangáris, more than half of whom belong to the Bhaosar sub-division. 870 Rangáris returned Chhipa as their sub-caste. The caste is said to have come originally from Gujerat, which may possibly account for 38 of them being recorded of the Jain religion.

237. **XXIV. Washermen,** known in different parts of the Province as *Dhobi*, *Warthi*, *Bareth*, and *Chákli*, number 136,541 or 1·06 per cent. of the population. The caste largely preponderates in Chhatisgarh, a part of the country where, at least to the superficial observer, it would scarcely seem as if its services were much availed of; both in Raipur and Bilaspur the Dhobis number over 20,000 persons. In both districts the washerman is one of the recognized village servants; but, as a rule, he gets no fixed payment, and the great body of cultivators dispense with his services altogether. According to the Raipur Settlement Report he is employed by the ryots only to wash the clothes of the dead, and he is never found among a population of Satnámis. We may therefore take it that in Chhatisgarh the Bareth caste has largely taken to cultivation. In all the hill districts the Dhobis are very sparsely distributed; in Betul and Balaghat they form only ·4 and ·3 per cent. of the population respectively. In the more settled districts of the west and north of the Province, and in Wardha and Nagpur, the proportion rises to 1 per cent. and over.

238. **XXV. Cotton-cleaners.**—These, when Mahomedans, are known as *Pinjáras* or *Bahnas*, when Hindus, as *Kanderas*. The two first are by far the most numerous. The Bahnas, 15,719, are the cotton carders of the north of the Province, being found almost solely in the districts of Saugor, Damoh, Jubbulpore and Narsinghpur. In Hoshangabad and throughout the southern Satpuras

* Berar Census Report, 1881, page 132.

and the Maratha country the caste is known as Pinjára, which name has been returned for 17,356 persons at the Census, of whom all but 758 are Mussalmans. The Kanderas, 3,594, like the Bahnas, belong chiefly to the north of the Province. The Pinjáras of the hill districts, though professing the Mussalman religion, at the same time follow many of the customs and ceremonies of the Hindus; their marriages are celebrated both according to the Hindu and Mahomedan rites, and in their rules of inheritance our courts have held that they are subject to Hindu and not Mahomedan law. Their surnames also are similar to those common among the Hindus, showing that they are converts from the latter race.*

239. **XXVI. Shepherds and Wool-weavers.**—Of these there are three castes in these Provinces, the northern *Gadaria*, numbering 38,497, the *Dhangar* of Nimar and the Maratha country, 20,870, and the *Kuramwár*, 2,916, the last a class of shepherds of Canarese origin found principally in the Chanda district. All three are hereditary tenders of sheep and goats; together they amount to 62,283 persons or ·5 per cent. of the population, the districts where they are most strongly represented being Jubbulpore, 7,023, Nagpur, 6,838, Chanda, 6,358, and Wardha, 6,587. In the latter district they form 1·6 per cent. of the inhabitants; with this we may compare Berar, where, at the Census of 1881, the Dhangars were no less than 2·8 per cent. of the entire population. To the tending of sheep and goats they add the calling of weaving coarse blankets of the wool they get from their flocks. Few of the shepherd class are, as a rule, engaged in cultivation. Besides the sub-divisions which have been given in Table XVI, the following have been returned at the Census; of Dhangars, Ládse 515, Hatkar, said to be akin to Bangi, 310, Kánare 786, Ahir 143, Nikhar 34, and Dhengre 12; and of Gadarias, Málwi 599, Kosaria 179, and Pardesi 2,141.

240. **XXVII. Oil-pressers.**—The distribution of the Teli caste is shown in the appended statement:—

Teli 734,935—568 per 10,000 of the population.

Chief Sub-divisions.	No.	Districts.	No.	Percentage on total population of the district.
Báthri	37,995	Saugor	15,207	2·6
Dobaile	85,511	Damoh	7,601	2·3
Endele	13,263			
Ekbaile	9,686	Jubbulpore	18,637	2·5
Gándli	3,779	Narsinghpur	7,864	2·1
		Hoshangabad	9,530	1·8
Gulháni	7,147			
Haldia	17,814	Nimar	5,711	2·3
Halia	10,824			
Jharia	335,902	Mandla	8,856	2·6
Matha	5,474	Seoni	6,944	1·9
		Chhindwara	13,126	3·2
Ráthor	23,871	Betul	8,261	2·6
Sáo	19,379			
Shriwás	6,126	Wardha	39,862	9·9
Taráne	48,980	Nagpur	61,181	8·1
		Chanda	37,490	5·4
Umre	1,296	Bhandara	40,613	5·5
Kosaria	3,072	Balaghat	6,889	1·8
Kanaujia	10,606			
Gadhoria	3,563	Raipur	235,679	14·9
		Bilaspur	82,144	7·1
		Sambalpur	27,230	3·4
		Chhatisgarh States	71,450	11·9
		Uria States	29,081	2·4

* *Cf.* Chanda Settlement Report, page 58.

Though the manufacture and sale of oil is the traditional occupation of the caste, the oil-pressers returned in the Occupation Table number only about a seventh part of the persons for whom caste name has been recorded. In every part of the Province the Telis are an important agricultural class, but this is more especially the case in Chhatisgarh, where the Telis have long been settled as cultivators of the soil. The caste is also largely engaged in shop-keeping, and the Telis, specially of the central hill districts, drive an extensive trade in exporting grain, oil-seeds, mhowa, and other jungle products, in return for which they import salt, cocoanut, and sundries.*

At the Census the caste has returned a large number of sub-divisions, the chief of which are shown in the statement which has been given. Among the Telis of the northern districts the principal sub-castes are the Báthri, Gulháni, and Ráthor. Of the latter there is an interesting account in Colonel Ward's Settlement Report of the Mandla district, where they form the best cultivating class in the Ramgarh tehsil. The Ráthors of Mandla number 3,256 persons; they have entirely given up oil-pressing as a profession, and have dropped the designation of Teli, calling themselves simply Ráthors, to which they frequently add the title Mahto, which they have adopted. The Ráthors have also found their way into the north of the Bilaspur district, where 4,106 of them are found, but here, as a rule, they preserve their original caste designation. The Telis of the Maratha country generally return the sub-divisions of Dobaile, Ekbaile, Endele or Erandal, Sao and Taráne; the Gándlis are the Telugu Telis of Chanda. The names of the two first classes are derived from their respectively yoking two bullocks and one in their mills, while the Erandal Telis are found principally in Chanda, where they abound in the parts which lie east of the Wainganga; their sole occupation is agriculture, the chief crops they grow being sugarcane and rice. The Mathas are the trading Telis of Betul and Chhindwara. In Chhatisgarh the Telis are represented by the Jharia, Kosaria, Kanaujia, and Halia sub-divisions. Of these the two first are among the oldest settlers in the country, and the Jharias, who form the great bulk of the caste, are reckoned excellent cultivators. The Kanaujia and Halia Telis are more recent immigrants; the former from Northern India, and the latter from the Nagpur direction.

241. **XXVIII. Potters** are represented by the well known *Kumhár* caste, 102,682 in number, or ·8 per cent. of the population. The Kumhár is most in evidence in the northern districts of Saugor and Damoh, and in the districts of the Nerbada valley, where the caste forms over 1 per cent. of the inhabitants; in Saugor and Damoh the proportion is as high as 1·5 and 1·6 per cent. respectively. In the other districts the average strength of the caste is only about a third of this rate, or ·5 per cent., with the exception, however, of Sambalpur, where the proportion again rises to about 1 per cent. The same excess is noticeable throughout the Uria states; in Patna over 2 per cent. of the inhabitants belong to the potter caste. In the Central Provinces the Kumhár does not generally rank as one of the village servants like the Barhai or Lohár. His social standing is low, "far below that of the Lohár, and not very much above that of the Chamár, for his hereditary association with that impure beast, the donkey, the animal sacred to Sitala, the small-pox goddess, pollutes him, as also his readiness to carry manure and sweepings."†

242. **XXIX. Glass workers, etc.,** comprise three small castes—the *Kacheras* 1,898, *Turkáris* 574, and *Sisgars* 865; the main occupation of all of these is the manufacture of glass bangles. Both the latter castes and a third part of the first are Mahomedans by religion.

* Betul Settlement Report, page 41.
† Ibbetson's Punjab Ethnography, section 632.

243. **XXXIII. Gold washers** are represented by the *Sonjharas*, 2,783; this includes also the *Jhiras* or diamond-washers of the Mahanadi. The caste is found chiefly in Seoni, Bhandara, and Chanda, and in Bilaspur, Sambalpur, and some of the Uria states; in Bamra there are 1,238 and in Sonpur 537. From the Occupation Table it would appear as if the industry had almost died out, only some 230 persons in the Province returning gold-washing as a means of livelihood; the presence of the caste in various places denotes, however, the parts where gold was formerly found. In Seoni and Bhandara the Sonjharas worked chiefly in the Wainganga, but the gold obtained was impure and not very valuable. "One trait of theirs, illustrative of their low state, may be mentioned, and that is that they avoid any spot where luck attended former efforts. They flee from it as from an accursed thing."* In Chanda gold exists in minute particles in some of the eastern streams, and is also found in the Godaveri opposite the lower portion of the Sironcha tehsil. The Sonjharas returned at the Census are mostly from Brahmapuri in the Wainganga valley; "they have a superstition that he who finds gold will be childless, and hence the search is dreaded by many."† In the eastern districts and states gold washing was formerly carried on in the Mahanadi and its affluents, but the process is said to have scarcely been remunerative. Before we took the country, some fifteen or twenty villages in Sambalpur were granted rent-free to the Jhiras, in consideration of their undertaking the search for diamonds in the bed of the Mahanadi, but the industry has now practically died out, though the people who followed it still retain their distinctive name. Gold-washing is to a small extent followed by members of the jungle tribes; among Gonds, Sonjhara as a sub-division has been recorded of 68 persons.

244. **XXXIV. Iron-smelters.**—The tribes who follow the profession of smelting iron-ore have been returned in such various ways at the Census that it is difficult to ascertain what their real numbers may be. The occupation is chiefly engaged in by a class of people known as *Agarias*, who, in these Provinces at least, are looked upon as Gonds, and have frequently described themselves as such at the enumeration. Again, there is an Agaria class among blacksmiths, and to these we may add the Gondi Lohárs, many of whom make it their chief business to collect and smelt iron-ore, while numbers of the Kamárs and Lohárs in the wilder parts of the southern and eastern states are also similarly employed. All the latter must be, however, left out of account, and we need only notice the iron-smelting castes who have returned themselves by names distinctive of their profession. Agarias, including those found among Gonds and Lohárs, number 5,832, of whom 1,850 are found in Jubbulpore, 564 in Mandla, 306 in Raipur, and 2,013 in Bilaspur; 656 are recorded from the Feudatory states, principally Raigarh. Of the process as carried out in the hills north of Bilaspur, to which the manufacture of iron in that part of Chhatisgarh is practically confined, the following description is of interest.

"The profession is scarcely an inviting one, for, although the native process of manufacture is extremely rude, the labour involved is very considerable. There is the charcoal to be made and the ore to be collected. The ore is then taken and mixed with charcoal and is placed in a clay furnace about three feet high. A regular current of air is kept playing on the furnace from a primitive pair of bellows worked by the feet. When the ore is smelted, the manufactured article comes rushing out in a lava-like stream from a crevice at the bottom of the furnace. It is then hammered and made into broad bars fit for sale. The iron which is made is of fair quality, but has no special reputation in the market."

* Bhandara Settlement Report, page 49.
† Chanda Settlement Report, page 105.

The *Dángris* are returned from the Maratha country, but few of them are now engaged in the preparation of the ore; in fact the introduction of European iron is rapidly driving the native-made material from the market, so that smelting is confined to supplying the needs of only the more inaccessible tracts. In Saugor, Damoh and Jubbulpore we meet with the *Kondars*, who number in all 1,274 persons. In Saugor nearly all the Kondars returned from the district, 479, have been described as Gonds. Many of them are said to be leaving the district on account of the stringency of the forest laws making it difficult for them to obtain the supplies of charcoal they require.

245. **XXXV. Fishermen, boatmen, etc.**—The most important fishing castes in the Central Provinces are the *Dhimars*, who number 218,007, or 1·7 per cent. of the population, and the *Kewats* 192,700, or 1·5 per cent. The total number of persons in the group amounts to 473,180, or 3·7 per cent. of the population. The Dhimars are most strongly represented in the four northern districts of Saugor, Damoh, Jubbulpore, and Narsinghpur—in the two latter they number 4 per cent. of the inhabitants,—and in Chanda and Bhandara, where the proportion rises to 4·7 and 4·5. The Kewats are the great fishing caste of Chhatisgarh and the Uria country; in Raipur and Bilaspur they form 3·7 per cent. of the population, and in Sambalpur 4 per cent. In the Uria states the Kewats are naturally found principally in the tracts which border on the Mahanadi or its larger affluents; thus they are numerous in Sarangarah, 2,935, in Sonpur, 13,757, and to a less extent in Patna, 7,654, while in the great dependency of Kalahandi the whole of the fishing castes are represented by only 491 persons. *Kahárs*, 19,000, occur chiefly along the Nerbada—in Hoshangabad they form over 1 per cent. of the inhabitants of the district—and in Bilaspur, where 3,778 of them are found. The *Bhois*, 15,616, are specially the fishermen of the Wardha valley, 6,150 occurring in the Wardha district, and 2,354 in Nagpur. The isolated colony of 638 returned from the Saugor district are probably nearly all identical with the Gond Bhois, to whom reference has already been made. On the Wainganga we find a fishing caste of the name of *Injhwár*, 11,322, recorded from the districts of Bhandara and Balaghat; the name occurs also as a subdivision of the Gowáris, and it was further often entered in the census books as Vinjhwár, and was thus hardly distinguishable from Binjhwár, the chief Baiga tribe of Balaghat. *Malláhs*, 4,852, belong mainly to the upper Nerbada, in the districts of Narsinghpur and Jubbulpore. The *Wadewárs* or *Odewárs*, 4,597, are the Telugu fishermen of the Godaveri.

The traditional occupation of all the castes is fishing, but to show how largely the castes have taken to other pursuits, it is worth while noting that in Table XVII only 124,742 persons have been recorded as subsisting by catching and selling fish; this number amounts to little more than a fourth part of the fisher castes returned at the Census. In the north of the Province the Dhimars and Kahárs are very generally water-carriers; in the chapter on Occupations it has been remarked that in the four northern districts of Saugor, Damoh, Jubbulpore and Narsinghpur there are 23,596 persons employed as water-bearers, or more than 66 per cent. of the total number recorded for all the British districts. All the northern castes of Hindus, including Brahmins, take water from the Kahárs; but this is not the case in the southern districts, where even the common Hindu castes refuse to drink from their hands. A very large number of Dhimars and Kewats are parchers of grain, the operation being one which specially engages the female members of the castes. Others again are water-nut growers, while in districts where tassar silk is produced, almost the whole of the cocoon-rearing industry is in their hands. Few find employment as palki-bearers in these parts, but as boatmen and carriers by water they are extensively engaged on all the larger rivers. From the preponderating number of the castes it is also evident that many of their members have taken to the cultivation of the soil.

246. XXXVI. Distillers, etc.—The appended abstract shows the districts in which the spirit-distilling caste is most strongly represented. It is found very

Kalár (including Sundi) 177,207—136 per 10,000 of the population.

Chief Sub-divisions.	No.	Chief Sub-divisions.	No.	Chief Districts.	No.	Percentage of population.
Chaukse . .	3,699	Máhore . .	501	Seoni . . .	4,277	1·2
Daharia . .	6,438	Málwi . .	2,675	Chhindwara .	6,194	1·5
Dandsena . .	29,398	Maratha . .	4,146	Nagpur . .	9,661	1·3
Indge . . .	488	Rai . . .	11,170	Chanda . .	11,247	1·6
Jain . . .	16,085			Bhandara . .	29,072	3·9
		Sao . . .	574	Balaghat . .	7,622	2·0
Jaiswár . .	5,689	Surajbans . .	2,143			
Kanaujia . .	4,506	Sihore . .	2,862	Raipur . .	21,833	1·4
Kosre . . .	15,341	Tili . . .	2,283	Chhatisgarh States	16,674	2·7
Lád . . .	550	Umre . .	407	Bastar . .	8,806	2·8

generally in every part of the Province, but is proportionately most numerous in the Maratha country, specially in the districts of Bhandara and Balaghat. In the adjoining states to the east the Kalárs are also a very large body; in Khairagarh, Nandgaon, and Bastar they form between 2 and 3 per cent. of the population, while in Kanker they number, according to the Census, no fewer them 5,092 or 6 per cent. of the inhabitants of the state. Although the legitimate business of the caste is the distilling and selling of *mhowa* liquor, many of its members are well-to-do cultivators, whilst others are shop-keepers and grain-sellers; in the hill districts a large part of the trade in salt and the miscellaneous commodities known as *kirána*, which is partly carried on through pack bullocks, is in their hands. Of the Bhandara Kalárs there is the following notice in the Settlement Report of that district:—

"They are divided into three classes. The Jain Kalárs are renegades from the Bania caste, who, on their first advent a century ago, took up the excise and drug trade, and hence came to be called Kalárs. While they were from the western coast, the Sihore Kalárо descended on the Nagpur country from Bundelkhand, and for a very long time were then known as Umre Banias; apparently, only that section of them who came to the towns of the Bhandara district—for they are not found in the agricultural villages—have taken to the wine trade, while their more orthodox brethren still remain as grain sellers. The original Kalárs seem to be Pardesis, who came from Hindustan, but they are not numerous, and most of the wine trade is in the hands of the Jain Kalárs."

The Jain Kalárs are Hindus by religion; close upon 400 of them have been shown as of the Jain creed, but this is probably a mistake on the part of the enumerators, who have been misled by the similarity of the sub-divisional name. They are peculiar to the districts of the Nagpur plain. The Dandsenas are the Kalárs of the Chhatisgarh country; in Bastar and in Sambalpur and the Uria states we find the *Sundi* liquor-distilling caste of Bengal, of whom 15,420 have been returned at the Census. The *Pásis*, 3,170, are described by Mr. Crooke as "a tribe of agriculturists, toddy-drawers, watchmen, and thieves." They are found in all parts of the Province, many of them presumably in the last of these capacities; a third of them occur in Jubbulpore. Among the recorded sub-divisions of the tribe are the Báwaria 1,467, Bahelia 72, Baurási 86, and Kaithwása 364.

247. XXXVII. Butchers.—The castes included under this head, *Chikwa*, *Kasai*, and *Khatik*, number 7,176 persons, of whom 9·3 per cent. are Mahomedans by religion.

248. XXXVIII. Leather-workers.—The *Chamár* caste is found in great force in the northern districts of the Province and throughout the Chhatisgarh plain, as the appended abstract shows:—

Chamár 876,060—677 per 10,000 of the population.

Northern districts.	No.	Percentage on population.	Chhatisgarh.	No.	Percentage on population.
Saugor	74,467	12·6	Raipur	285,551	18·0
Damoh	40,416	12·4	Nandgaon	20,061	10·9
Jubbulpore	37,765	5·0	Khairagarh	20,734	11·4
Narsinghpur	19,108	5·2	Chhuikhadan	2,910	8·0
Hoshangabad	20,395	3·8	Bilaspur	266,745	22·9
			Kawardha	13,823	15·1
			Sarangarh	6,491	7·8

Compared with the proportions here given the smallness of its numbers in the hill districts and in those of the Maratha country is most marked; in several of them the Chamárs do not amount to even 1 per cent. of the population. In the chapter on Occupation it is remarked that in the northern districts the persons who work in leather are much more numerous than in the rest of the Province, but in all of them a very large proportion of the Chamár community is also employed in labour of various sorts. In the margin I have compared the caste-figures with those for occupation, from which it will be seen that what Mr. Crooke says of the Chamárs of Upper India holds good of their caste-fellows in Saugor, Damoh, and the Nerbada valley. "The Chamár is properly the caste of curriers and tanners; but all through the province he is a field labourer and cooly. He does all the rough work of the village, and is generally obliged to give a certain amount of forced labour (*begár*)."* In the chapter on Religion I have noted that many of the Chamárs in the northern districts have taken to calling themselves Satnámis. I see that Mr. Crooke also mentions that there has recently been a revival among the Chamárs of Upper India, of which the return of Satnámi at the Census for a large number of the caste, specially from Saugor and Damoh, is probably a trace.

DISTRICTS.	Chamárs by caste.	Leather-workers by profession.	Percentage of col. 3 on col. 2.
Saugor	74,467	23,018	30·9
Damoh	40,416	17,514	43·3
Jubbulpore	37,765	19,474	51·6
Narsinghpur	19,108	10,363	54·2
Hoshangabad	20,395	15,762	77·3

249. Of the Chamárs of Chhatisgarh a full account has been given at pages 34—39 of Mr. Drysdale's (1881) Report, so I pass over all notice of their religious beliefs and social customs; on the former I have already remarked in chapter III. They are found in greatest numbers in the north and west of the Chhatisgarh plain, a fact from which Mr. Hewitt argues, in the Settlement Report of the Raipur district, that they are immigrants of comparatively recent date. The Chamárs themselves lay claim to a very high antiquity among the inhabitants of Chhatisgarh; at the Census they nearly all return the sub-division Jhádwa or Jharia, which implies long residence on the soil. The Chamár of Chhatisgarh is almost invariably a cultivator, but as such, though generally industrious, he is careless and not very successful. "The Chamárs are slovenly and untidy in

Chhatisgarh Chamárs.

Tehsilwar Distribution.			Sub-divisions returned at the Census.	
	Tehsil.	Percentage on population.	Chief Sub-divisions.	No.
Raipur.	Simga	28·8	Jhádwa	372,911
	Raipur	19·3	Kanaujia	14,002
	Drug	16·9	Kosariya	2,809
	Dhamtari	7·5	Aharwár	1,710
Bilaspur.	Mungeli	36·4		
	Bilaspur	15·9		
	Seori Narain	19·9		

* Crooke's Ethnography of the N.-W. P. and Oudh, page 62.

their habits, and the houses of even the wealthiest of them are generally miserable hovels. Though frugal in the extreme, indulging in no extravagance in dress or jewellery, they rarely make money and seem to want the talent of getting on in the world. As a class, however, they do not present the same degraded appearance as their brethren in other parts of India, and, as a rule, they are lighter in colour than the other cultivating castes, while some of the men and many of the women are remarkable for good looks."*

Of the other leather-working castes the principal are the *Holias*, 4,560, a tribe reputed to be of Canarese origin, found chiefly in the districts of Seoni, Nagpur, Bhandara, and Balaghat. The articles which they generally make are leather buckets (*mots*) and ropes, but they are also employed as drum-beaters on festive occasions. The *Mádgis*, 2,467, are Telugu leather-workers from Chanda.

250. **XXXVIII(*a*). Village watchmen.**—The group as it appears in the final table does not properly represent all of the classes who perform village service; the exercise of the *Kotwár's* profession is so generally combined with the weaving of coarse cloth, that the castes who follow it may be looked upon as weavers or watchmen indiscriminately. The Gándas and Pankas of Chhatisgarh have been shown under the former head, so that in the eastern part of the Province the number of the village-watchman class, as it stands in the table, must appear unduly small. The principal of the castes on whom the duties of the village Kotwár devolve is the *Mahár* of the Maratha country, the *Mehra* of the Hindi districts. In Wardha the Mahárs amount to 14·5 per cent. of the population, in Chanda to 12·0, in Nagpur to 16·3, and in Bhandara to 17·3 per cent.; in the two last districts they number as many as 123,877 and 128,540 persons respectively. The Mehras are numerous in Mandla, where they are 3·5 per cent. of the inhabitants, in Narsinghpur 5·1, in Betul 9·3, in Chhindwara 6·8, in Seoni 5·9, and in Balaghat 8·9. In Hoshangabad they are the village servants of the northern tehsils of Sohagpur and Hoshangabad; in Seoni and Harda their place is taken by the Baláhis, who are also the Kotwárs of the Nimar district, where they number 21,205 or 8·4 per cent. of the population. In Saugor and Damoh the village watchmen belong generally to the *Chandár* and *Khangár* castes, principally the former. In Jubbulpore both these castes occur, as do also the *Dahait* and Mehra, the two latter predominating. In Chhatisgarh, as has been already noted, the chief village servants are the Gándas and Pankas; besides these there is a caste known as *Chauhán*, which also performs the Kotwárs' duties.

Just as we have seen the Chamár to be largely the day labourer of the northern part of the Province, so is the Mahár the principal labourer of the districts of the Nagpur plain. Many members of the caste, more especially the female portion of the community, are employed in spinning or in weaving coarse cloth—in the villages almost every other Mahár or Mehra household has its spinning-wheel or loom,—but the great majority are the common day labourers of the districts where they are found. In Mandla and Seoni, it may be noted, many of the Mehras have adopted Kabirpanthism, which is essentially the weavers' creed. As village watchman, besides his more distinctively official duties, the Mahár is general referee in all matters concerning the village boundaries or customs. He receives certain grain dues from the cultivators of the village, and is entitled to the carcases of cattle that die within its bounds. The only other of the Kotwár caste that calls for remark is the Chauhán of Chhatisgarh. The caste has no connection with the Rajput tribe of the same name; in general they are village servants or petty cultivators, but are never weavers like the Gándas or Pankas. At the Census Chauháns have been recorded principally from the Bilaspur district, but they also occur in Raipur, though in compilation the members of the caste appear to have got mixed up with Rajputs, as only 10

* Raipur Sett. Report, page 34.

are returned for the district. The Chauháns say they came originally from Manipuri in the North-West Provinces; in Chhatisgarh many of them have rather a reputation for thieving.

251. **XXXIX. Scavengers.**—The *Doms* are the chief caste in this group, but, according to Mr. Risley, they believe their original occupation to be the making of baskets and mats. This is still the calling which is followed by a great portion of the caste, but the degraded position forced upon all Doms by reason of the functions which some of them perform is in the whole acquiesced in by the entire community. Their distribution as shown in the printed table is open to doubt. In the British districts they are found principally in the north of the Province and in Raipur; in the Feudatory states, of 56,979 who have been returned at the enumeration, all except 461 are shown as occurring in the Kalahandi state. Exactly the same thing happened, I notice, in 1881—see the abstract given at page 179 of Mr. Drysdale's Report, volume II,—so that the figures of the present Census may possibly be correct. Generally the name by which the caste is known in the Uria country is Dom, but occasionally it is written Dumár, and as such is hardly distinguishable in abstraction from Dumál, a sub-tribe of the Gaurs or herdsmen of Sambalpur and the eastern states. The latter is extensively returned from the adjoining feudatories of Patna and Sonpur, while none occur in Kalahandi; it is therefore almost certain that there has been confusion in working out the figures for the two caste names. The *Mehtar* or *Bhangi* caste forms the sweeper class throughout the Province; as a rule they engage in no other occupation. 1,305 members of the caste have given their religion as Mahomedan.

CLASS E.—VAGRANT MINOR ARTIZANS AND PERFORMERS, etc.

252. *Criminal Tribes.*—In this class are shown certain menial and vagrant castes, many of the latter being more or less professional criminals. The distribution of the criminal tribes is a matter of some importance from an administrative point of view, but it is not very easy to give a detailed account of the various thieving tribes without a greater knowledge of the subject than I possess. In the case of several castes it is for instance necessary to discriminate between those persons amongst them who in certain localities are known to be criminally inclined, and those who in other places are generally well behaved members of the community. Such are, to give well known examples, the Bágris, Minas, Patháris, and others. The Bágris are largely criminal along the Bundelkhand border, a reputation which they do not possess in Seoni; the Minas of the Nerbada valley are for the most part settled cultivators, while the few found in the other districts are probably of the northern stock, which in most parts of Upper India is almost invariably criminal. Certain of the tribes also which appear in the present section of the Caste Table are probably wrong-doers in certain localities, but lead a settled life in others. The preparation of a reliable statement of criminal tribes, which would show the places where they are found, I must therefore leave to some one better acquainted with all the corners of the Province than I can be.

253. **XL. Grindstone-makers and stone-quarriers.**—The *Sánsias* are a small caste of stone-quarriers in Sambalpur; so far as is known they are permanent residents of the place. The *Takáras* 43, and *Waddars* 313, affect almost solely the districts of Nimar and Wardha; both are vagrants, and at least the Takáras are criminal.

254. **XLI. Earth-workers and stone-dressers.**—Most of the castes under this heading are more or less vagrants, but as a rule they are well behaved. The chief is the *Beldár*, which is found distributed over every part of the Province; many of them are Telugus and Urias, specially in the Maratha districts

and in Chhatisgarh. The *Murhas*, 3,522, and *Nunias*, 4,781, belong more particularly to the northern districts. *Pindháris*, 397, are recorded chiefly from Hoshangabad 233, from Bhandara 38, and from Balaghat 110. In the first of these districts all but one are Mahomedans by religion. Regarding them the Settlement Report states that they were not originally Mahomedans; "their forefathers were the children of Gonds and Korkus, carried off by the Pindháris in their raids, circumcised and made to follow their profession. When the Pindháris were put down, the men mostly returned to their native villages; they are utterly without religion, not practising the rites of their faith, nor yet those of their families."

255. **XLIII. Mat and Cane-workers, etc.**—The principal castes in this group are the *Burars*, otherwise known as *Basors* or *Kandras*, who number 47,294, of whom considerably more than half are found in the three northern districts of Saugor, Damoh, and Jubbulpore, the *Ghasias* of Chhatisgarh and the Uria country, numbering 39,544, and the *Mángs* of the Maratha districts, 18,975. The ordinary occupation of the three castes is the weaving of mats and baskets, but all also act as musicians on festive occasions. Of 449 *Kaikáris* recorded at the Census, 85 are from Jubbulpore, 209 from Nimar, and nearly all the remainder from the districts of Wardha, Nagpur and Chanda; they are a well known criminal tribe, and under various names occur all over the Indian Peninsula.

256. **XLIV. Hunters and Fowlers, etc.**—Of these the chief are the *Bahelias* of the northern districts and Chhatisgarh, 2,648, the *Párdhis*, 1,996, who are found throughout the Province, but are most common in Nimar, 328, Wardha, 347, and Nagpur, 316, and the *Moghias*, 690, of the northern districts and of the Nerbada valley. All three have criminal tendencies. The Moghias of Hoshangabad and Betul are presumably Korkus, as the latter return both Moghia and Bauria as sub-divisions, the term being evidently assumed by members of the tribe who engage in the chase.

257. **XLV. Miscellaneous castes.**—The only caste of importance included under this head is the *Bhámta*, 2,533 persons, which is returned mainly from the three districts of Wardha, Chanda and Nagpur. The Bhámtas are noted thieves; many members of the caste are engaged in the cultivation of hemp, from which they make ropes and mats.

258. **XLVI. Tumblers and Acrobats.**—These are represented by several castes found in every quarter of the Province. The chief are the *Berias*, 906, *Kanjars*, 300—among whom have been included 36 *Sánsis*,—*Kuchbandhias*, 638, and *Nats*, 580, of the northern districts, the *Gopáls*, 681, of Nimar and the Nagpur country, where also and in Chhatisgarh are found the *Kolhátis*, 243. *Pahalwáns*, 591, are found chiefly in Chhatisgarh,—there are 318 in Bilaspur— where they are described, according to the Census Report of 1881, to be a class of singing beggars and to have no connection with wrestling.

CLASS F.—RACES AND NATIONALITIES.

259. **XLVIII. Asiatic Races of non-Indian descent.**—To these it is hardly necessary to refer, except as regards the tribes of Mahomedans, and these are so ill-defined in this part of the country that but little significance can attach to the figures which have been given. The predominant tribe is the Shaikh, to which 132,333 or more than half of the Mussalmans belong, while Pathans, 88,025, form over a third of the community; 23,614 persons returned themselves as Saiads and 4,831 as Moghals.

260. **L—LII. Non-Asiatic Races, Eurasians and Native Christians.**—Excluding seven Africans, there are now in the Province 4,825 persons of non-Asiatic descent, of whom 3,541 are males and 1,284 are females. Comparison with the results of 1881 is impossible, as then only 3,919 persons were recorded as of

European or American descent, while over 1,000 persons were recorded as of "race unspecified," a term applied to persons of European name and mother-tongue, neither Portuguese or British born, who omitted to record whether they were Europeans or Eurasians. In the same way comparison cannot be made in the case of Eurasians, who now number 2,207. There are 583 Indian Portuguese against 206 in 1881, and 6,278 Native Christians of all kinds against 5,764. To the variation in the number of the latter, reference will be found in the chapter which deals with the religions of the population.

GENERAL.

261. Distribution of the different classes of castes by Districts.—The following table exhibits the proportion which each of the classes shown in the Caste Table bears to the total population of each district; in the first class the groups of dominant and ordinary agricultural castes, of pastoral castes, and of the forest and hill tribes are distinguished :—

Percentage of Classes of Castes on total Population by Districts.

District.	A.—Agricultural.					B.—Professional.	C.—Commercial.	D.—Artisans and village menials.	E.—Vagrant minor artisans and performers, etc.	F.—Races and Nationalities.
	1. Military and Dominant.	2(a). Cultivators.	2. (b) Graziers.	4. Forest and Hill Tribes.	Total.					
1	2	3	4	5	6	7	8	9	10	11
Saugor	3·3	24·5	6·0	8·3	42·3	9·8	4·2	38·2	2·2	3·3
Damoh	2·9	24·8	5·1	11·4	44·4	9·5	3·4	37·7	2·7	2·3
Jubbulpore	3·1	15·1	4·7	24·9	48·5	10·2	2·5	32·6	1·8	4·4
Narsinghpur	6·4	22·7	3·2	13·2	47·4	10·0	3·0	35·5	1·6	2·5
Hoshangabad	16·8	14·1	2·8	20·1	55·1	8·7	2·5	28·7	1·2	3·7
Nimar	15·8	13·5	3·3	14·5	51·0	6·5	6·7	25·2	1·1	9·4
Mandla	·7	5·3	7·4	60·3	73·9	3·0	1·2	19·6	1·1	1·2
Seoni	7·2	7·9	9·3	43·4	68·2	3·4	1·7	22·8	·9	3·0
Chhindwara	2·6	15·8	8·0	40·3	67·0	3·4	1·6	25·3	·7	2·0
Betul	2·4	25·5	5·1	39·5	73·0	2·1	·9	21·7	·8	1·5
Wardha	2·7	27·7	3·8	11·3	45·6	4·9	2·6	41·1	2·2	3·6
Nagpur	3·1	27·4	2·4	6·3	30·2	5·1	1·7	46·6	1·5	5·7
Bhandara	9·6	20·9	7·0	15·1	52·6	1·9	·7	42·8	·5	1·5
Balaghat	11·4	22·8	9·1	26·7	70·0	2·1	·9	25·0	·4	1·0
Chanda	·6	27·8	3·2	25·2	57·5	2·0	1·4	36·6	·8	1·5
Raipur	1·1	9·5	10·3	20·7	41·6	2·4	·8	53·4	·8	1·0
Bilaspur	1·4	12·3	8·5	17·8	40·5	3·8	·8	52·6	1·4	·9
Sambalpur	·8	17·2	12·5	30·3	62·1	4·7	·8	30·0	1·8	·5
British Territory	4·1	17·7	6·8	22·1	51·8	4·8	1·7	88·5	1·8	2·4
Feudatory States	1·1	12·8	12·8	36·6	68·9	2·7	·8	80·7	1·1	·6
Total Central Provinces	3·6	16·9	7·8	24·5	58·4	4·5	1·5	87·2	1·2	2·1

The table hardly calls for remark, as it is merely intended as a synopsis of the caste review which has been made. We may note, however, the prevalence of the dominant agricultural castes in Hoshangabad and Nimar, where about a sixth of the population is composed of Rajputs, pure and impure, and of Játs, Gujars, and the like. In Bhandara and Balaghat the presence of the Powárs raises the average for the dominant groups in these two districts. Ordinary cultivating castes are scarce in the Satpura districts, where their place is taken by the aboriginal races, and in Chhatisgarh, where a great part of the cultivators are Telis, Chamárs, Pankas, etc. In the latter part of the Province and in the Uria country the pastoral group is strongly represented, but, as can be seen from the analogous table given in the chapter on Occupation, agriculture rather than pasture is here the pursuit of the main body of the grazing castes. The professional class, comprising Brahmins and Káyasths, is most numerous in the northern districts of Saugor and Damoh and in the Nerbada valley. Nimar comes to the front in respect of the importance of its commercial community, 6·7 per cent. of its population returning trading castes; there is a large number of Banias in the district, and, as has been noticed, a strong settlement of Banjaras, amounting to close upon 6,000 persons. Vagrant minor artisans, class E, are most numerous in Saugor, Damoh, Jubbulpore, Wardha, and Sambalpur, chiefly on account of the numbers of the mat and cane working castes they return; the first four districts are also a favourite resort of many castes of less reputable modes of life. In class F the preponderating element is the Mahomedan; to the distribution of persons of this religion reference will be found in Chapter III.

262. **Principal castes; variation since the last Census.**—The following table has been prepared to show the numbers returning some of the principal castes, and compares the latter in this respect with the previous census. In all cases it is not easy to say that we are dealing with exactly the same people, as difference of classification at the two enumerations has occasionally led to variance in the caste return.

Statement showing the principal castes and tribes in the Central Provinces, and the variation in their numbers since last Census.

(*a*) Principal Hindu Castes.

Castes.	Number returning.		Net increase.	Increase per cent.	Proportion of females per 1,000 males.	Percentage of total population.
	1891.	1881.				
Kolta	110,200	92,827	17,373	18·7	997	·8
Kawar, Kaonra	142,814	121,436	21,378	17·6	1,022	1·1
Kewat	192,700	165,591	27,109	16·4	1,044	1·5
Gánda, Panka	454,399	391,859	62,540	16·0	1,020	3·5
Mahár, Mehra, Dher	671,882	580,315	91,567	15·8	1,009	5·2
Teli	734,935	636,244	98,691	15·7	1,015	5·7
Ahir, Ráwat, Gahra, Gaoli, etc.	588,919	509,526	79,393	15·6	995	4·6
Chamár	876,060	760,101	115,959	15·3	1,003	6·8
Kumhár	102,682	89,201	13,481	15·1	981	·8
Gaur	245,034	214,936	30,098	14·0	997	1·9
Dhobi	136,541	119,936	16,605	13·8	1,032	1·1
Máli, Marár	357,988	316,721	41,267	13·0	1,006	2·8
Dhimar	218,007	194,453	23,554	12·1	1,007	1·7
Lohár, Kháti	149,169	133,476	15,693	11·8	1,006	1·2
Rajput	379,731	347,133	32,598	9·4	961	2·9
Gowári	120,247	110,363	9,884	9·0	1,012	·9
Kunbi, Kurmi	801,766	740,528	61,238	8·3	989	6·2
Lodhi	287,241	265,147	22,094	8·3	988	2·2
Nai, Mháli	140,143	131,614	8,529	6·5	992	1·1
Brahmin	382,938	359,886	23,052	6·4	898	3·0
Koshti	137,891	129,559	8,332	6·4	982	1·1
Bania	129,270	122,358	6,912	5·6	937	1·0
Káchhi	122,646	116,677	5,969	5·1	965	·9
Kalár, Gaundla	162,027	156,308	5,719	3·7	1,001	1·3

(*b*) Principal aboriginal Tribes.

Tribes	1891.	1881.	Net increase.	Increase per cent.	Proportion of females per 1,000 males.	Percentage of total population.
Khond	196,400	149,758	46,642	31·1	951	1·5
Bhil	22,424	17,583	4,841	27·5	989	·2
Sawara	156,921	130,719	26,202	20·0	1,014	1·2
Baiga, Binjhwár	120,314	102,942	17,372	16.9	996	·9
Gond, Halba	2,345,372	2,040,153	305,219	15·0	1,022	18·1
Kol	87,516	76,148	11.368	14·0	1,002	·7
Korku	95,634	84,909	10,725	12·6	989	·7

The statement is given chiefly as a summary of the main results of the caste enumeration, so I need hardly expatiate upon the figures it contains. In Chapter II the general increase in different parts of the Province has been dealt with at length, and the variations in the numbers returned for each caste are simply the same matter put in a new light. The castes which are common in the east and south of the province have grown most since 1881; such are the Khond Sawaras, Telis, Koltas, etc. The Mahárs or Mehras and the Gond tribes also show considerable increase; the latter are now 15 per cent. more numerous than they were at the last census.

263. Taking the classification adopted in the Caste Table at the present Census, the following is the broad result of the variation in the aboriginal population of each district since the last enumeration :—

Variation in the Aboriginal Population of each district since 1881.

District.	Aboriginal Tribes.		Net variations.	Increase or decrease per cent.	Increase per cent. in general population.
	1881.	1891.			
Saugor	45,606	*48,781*	3,175	7·0	4·7
Damoh	37,483	*37,097*	—386	—1·0	4·0
Jubbulpore	153,392	*186,135*	32,743	21·3	8·8
Mandla	184,247	*204,571*	20,324	11·0	12·9
Seoni	145,945	*160,968*	15,023	10·3	10·4
Narsinghpur	47,665	*48,431*	766	1·6	0·5
Hoshangabad	93,233	*106,641*	13,408	14·4	8·4
Nimar	30,379	*36,708*	6,329	20·8	9·5
Betul	122,771	*127,667*	4,896	4·0	5·9
Chhindwara	152,505	*164,410*	11,905	7·8	9·2
Wardha	43,615	*45,495*	1,880	4·3	3·5
Nagpur	43,932	*47,584*	3,652	8·3	8·6
Chanda	154,975	*175,877*	20,902	13·5	7·5
Bhandara	100,531	*111,849*	11,318	11·3	8·6
Balaghat	96,473	*102,143*	5,670	5·9	12·5
Raipur	296,775	*328,257*	31,482	10·6	12·7
Bilaspur	184,476	*207,717*	23,241	12·6	14·4
Sambalpur	209,485	*241,332*	31,847	15·2	14·8
British Districts	**2,143,488**	**2,881,668**	**238,175**	**11·1**	**9·6**
Feudatory States	**589,874**	**791,581**	**201,657**	**34·2**	**26·1**
Total Central Provinces	**2,733,362**	**3,173,194**	**439,832**	**16·1**	**12·0**

Both in British districts and in the Feudatory states the aboriginal tribes have increased at a faster rate than the general population. Taking the population of the Province as whole it may be said that but little of this increase is due to immigration; there has been some accession to the numbers of the aborigines by immigration from Rewa across the border into the Jubbulpore district and a certain number of the tribesmen of Chhota Nagpur have also been attracted to the east of the Province by the construction of the Bengal-Nagpur Railway. But beyond these there has probably been hardly any movement from outside, of aboriginal races into the Central Provinces. The increase is therefore to be attributed to the rapid natural growth of the hill tribes and to better enumeration. In Chapter IV it has been seen that ordinarily among the forest tribes the production of children is greater than amongst the general population, and any improvement in the enumeration will naturally affect the remoter tracts which are almost wholly peopled by aborigines.

Coming to details of districts we can be less sure of the comparisons we make, as difference in the record and the more complete classification which was possible at the present Census, when all the tribal sub-divisions were taken out, may to some extent affect the statistics which are given, when compared with those of 1881. In the above table care has been taken to make the figures of the two enumerations as homogeneous as possible, and thus eliminate any chance of error as far as this can be done. In Saugor the aboriginal tribes have increased by 7 per cent.; the only two tribes in the district are the Gonds and Saurs, among the former of whom the rate of increase has been 2·4 per cent. and among the latter 14·5. The forest tribes in Damoh have actually decreased, due, it would appear, to the drain made on the southern or hilly part of the district for labourers to reap the harvest in Jubbulpore. In the latter district the aborigines have increased 21·3 per cent.; the Kols, who number 61,705, have grown by 15,322 or 33 per cent., and the Gonds 110,578 by 12,194 or 12·4. Immigration from the surrounding districts has largely conduced to the increase which is apparent. In Narsinghpur the aboriginal tribes show almost the same stationary condition as the general population of the district. In Hoshangabad there is a marked increase among both the Gonds and Korkus of the district, in the former amounting to 7·3 per cent. and among the latter to 29·2. In Nimar there has been a rise of 21 per cent. chiefly in the number of the Bhils who are now 21,460 against 16,935 in 1881. What the cause may be I know not, but it would appear as if part of the difference were due to the Mussalman Bhils having been kept out of the table at the last census. In Betul we find the Gonds of the district to have increased by 6·2 per cent., while among the Korkus there has been a decline amounting to 2·3 per cent. The immense rise in the number of the Korkus in Hoshangabad may mean that the Betul Korkus are moving into the latter district, though of this the birth-place returns give us no indication. With the ill-defined territorial limits of a tract so wild as Kalibhit which intervenes between the two districts, it is, however, hardly likely that movements about the border would be very exactly recorded, so the increase in the Hoshangabad Korkus may reasonably be taken to explain the falling off apparent in their number in Betul. In Chhindwara the Korkus are now 13·3 per cent. more numerous than they were in 1881, while the Gonds of the district have increased by 7 per cent. The only other district which calls for remark is Balaghat; here the total population has grown 12·5 per cent., but the aboriginal tribes show an increase of only 5·9. This is mainly due to difference in the record; Baigas have decreased by 5·5, but at both enumerations the return is defective on account of its being difficult, in abstracting the entries in the enumerators' books, to distinguish between Binjhwárs, who are Baigas, and Injhwárs, who are fishermen.* Both have certainly got mixed to some extent. In Mandla there are now 17,215 Baigas against 11,493 in 1881, an increase of nearly 50 per cent., and though here again there has been difference in the record,† it may be taken that the Baigas are certainly not decreasing. Again, in the case of the Gonds of Balaghat, if we include amongst the latter the Nagárchis, as was apparently done at the last census, we find the race to have grown by 9 per cent. The difference between the variation in the general population and that in the aboriginal tribes of Balaghat is therefore apparent rather than real; the latter have probably increased quite as much as have the former. In Chanda and in the Feudatory states a good deal of the growth in the numbers of the forest tribes is to be put down to better counting; the matter has been fully treated of in Chapter II of the Report.

264. **Proportion between the sexes.**—In this respect also there is little to add to what has already been written in Chapter IV. The castes and tribes of

* See paragraph 245. In 1881 there were only 806 Injhwars; in Balaghat there are now 4,256; it is impossible to say which is correct, though at the present Census the sub-divisional terms returned enabled us to distinguish between the names more readily than could be done in 1881.

† From Baigas being mixed up with Gonds, and *vice versâ*, in the enumeration entries.

the hill districts and of the east of the Province generally contain more females than males, while those of the northern districts and of the Nerbada valley, and to some degree those of the Nagpur country, show an excess of males. The castes or tribes, with the lowest proportions of females, are the Brahmins, among whom there are 898 females per 1,000 males, Banias 937, Khonds 951, Rajputs 961, and Káchhis 965. All these castes, except the Khonds, occur principally in the northern and western districts of the Province, and their numbers have been much effected by immigration, resulting, as has been seen, in a preponderance of the male sex. The marriage system of these districts, according to which men marry later in life than in the centre and east of the Province, and the restriction on widow re-marriage which obtains, have been taken as possible explanations of the marked tendency to the production of male children which these districts exhibit, the theory being that when the ages of husband and wife are thus disproportionate the progeny is more likely to be male than when the parents are more of one age. Among the Khonds the reason for the dearth of females appears to be the excessive mortality of the latter sex, which is apparent in after life among the aborigines of the southern hill tracts of the Province. As we have no age statistics for individual castes, it is impossible to treat separately of the proportions between the sexes which each exhibits; the subject can only be dealt with territorially, and thence we can argue as to the probable inferences to be drawn regarding the sex statistics for castes which are strongly represented in any particular part of the country.

CHAPTER XI.

OCCUPATION.

265. Statistics regarding the occupations of the population are set forth in three Tables, XVII-A, B and C. In Table XVII-A details are given for the occupations of—(*a*) the total population, (*b*) the town and (*c*) the country. XVII-B contains the distribution of occupation by districts, and XVII-C shows the number of persons who combine agriculture with other occupations. In Part A of the Tables, with the object of giving some indication of the distribution between workers and dependents, three age-periods have been kept, namely 0—4, 5—14 and 15 and over, while in Part C the distinction of sex, which has been preserved in the first two parts, has been dispensed with. The compilation of the returns, which appear in these Tables, has taken up an almost inconceivable amount of time and labour, to which in great measure has been due the extended nature of the Census operations. Some allowance must be made for a certain amount of defectiveness in the materials with which we have had to deal, as well as for the difficulties of classification inherent in so complex a subject; but no pains have been spared to make the results obtained as clear and correct a representation of the facts recorded at the Census as it was possible to get, and the efforts that have been made in this direction may be regarded as having met with a very fair measure of success. Before proceeding to discuss the statistical facts observable in the mass of details which take up nearly a hundred and fifty pages of closely printed figures, it is necessary to explain shortly how these have been arrived at; that is, I shall note upon, first, the record of occupations in the enumeration books, and, second, the manner in which these have been abstracted and finally arranged in the form in which they appear in the printed tables.

266. **Record of Occupations at the Census**—*Definition.*—The rule for the guidance of the enumerators ran:—

"Column 11 (*Occupation or means of subsistence*).—Enter here the exact occupation or means of livelihood of all males and females who do work or live on private property, such as *house-rent, pension, etc.* In the case of children and women who do not work, enter the occupation of the head of their family, or of the person who supports them, adding the word 'dependent,' but do not leave this column unfilled for any one, even an infant. If a person have two or more occupations, enter only the chief one, except when a person owns or cultivates land in addition to another occupation, when both should be entered."

"No vague terms should be used, such as "*service*," "*Government service*" "*shop-keeping*," "*writing*," or "*labour*," etc., but the *exact service*, the *goods sold*, the *class of writing or labour*, must be stated. When a person's occupation is connected with agriculture, it should be stated whether the land is cultivated in person or all let to tenants; if he be an agricultural labourer, it should be stated whether he be engaged by the month or year, or is a daily field labourer. Women who earn money by occupations independent of their husbands, such as *selling firewood, cowdung-cakes, grass* or by *rice-pounding, weaving or doing house-work* for wages, should be shown under those occupations. If a person makes the articles he sells, he should be entered as "maker and seller" of them. If a person lives on alms, it should be stated whether he is a religious mendicant or an ordinary beggar. When a person is in Government, Railway or Municipal service, the special service should be entered first, and the word Government or Municipal, etc., after, as a clerk, *Government*; sweeper, *Municipal*; labourer, *Railway*."

In amplification of this, instructions were issued as under:—

"The following distinctions should be observed in entering the occupations of persons who own or cultivate land:—"

(1) A person owns land, of which he cultivates, himself or through labourers, a part or the whole: enter in column 11 the ordinary term for his ownership, as Malguzar, Mafidar, Pattidar, etc.

(2) A person owns land, all of which he lets out for cultivation to tenants, he cultivating no part himself or through labourers: in column 11, to the ordinary terms as above, add "land all let to tenants."

(3) A person has no land of his own but rents land from others for cultivation: in column 11 enter the word "cultivator."

267. In connection with the record of occupations, we may observe the following points.

(1) *The Census shows the number of people living by, not exercising, an occupation.*—In the first place it will be seen that for every person, whether man, woman, or child, some means of livelihood was to be entered, the word "dependent" being added for those who did not work. Here I may remark that in the subsequent compilation of the returns, the distinction between workers and dependents was not retained, so that what we have got is a record of all persons *living by* an occupation, which, as was suggested at the Conference of Census officers held at Agra in the end of 1889, is both more accurate and useful in this country than that of the number of persons *exercising* an occupation. In this latter respect the voluminous returns of 1881 were so defective that no attempt was made to follow up the clue which might have been given by the word "dependent" at the present Census.

(2) *When a person has two occupations, only the chief one is given, except when one is connected with the land.*—It not unfrequently happens that a person follows more than one occupation, in which case the obvious course is to enter only the one on which he principally depends. An exception is, however, made in the case of agriculture, which is often followed by persons who at the same time work at other occupations. It is most desirable that we should know the exact number of persons who have a direct interest in the land, and this could not be ascertained unless we took into account all persons, who, whatever their trade, are in addition either owners or tenants of land. To show the number of persons who thus combine agriculture with some other occupation, a separate statement has been prepared which forms Part C of the Occupation Tables. All such persons are entered in Parts A and B under their respective special headings, so as not to affect the completeness of the return of the non-agricultural occupations, which take up an equal or probably greater part of their time. Thus a money-lender, who is an owner of land, will appear in Parts A and B among the money-lending class. In Part C he and all others like him, who have other means of subsistence besides income from land, are separately shown; to their total is added the number of land-owners who have no other occupation returned against them, and in this way the full number of people who own land is ascertained. Here I may note that in Part C a column has been added to show the number of persons who are farm servants or field labourers besides being otherwise employed. As the instructions required that only those "who own or cultivate land in addition to another occupation" should be so entered in the schedule, the return of people who similarly do field as well as other work is necessarily incomplete. As a matter of fact, a great part of the lower classes of the village population occasionally work as field-labourers, but the number we have got shows only 9,943 persons thus recorded, a result which is obviously misleading. If the information is called for at a future Census, specific instructions for its record will require to be added.

(3) *Traditional combined occupations.*—There is in this country another important class of combined occupations, of which, however, no trace has been kept at the present Census, through the rules first framed for the guidance of the enumerators not having contained explicit directions on the subject. In the primitive state of society, which we find in the Indian village, the industries which are necessary to supply the simple needs of the villagers are for the most part prosecuted within the village itself. Within such narrow limits there exists no field for the minute division of labour which is so distinctive an industrial feature of countries more advanced in civilization; on the other hand, we sometimes see combined in one and the same person separate occupations which would otherwise be kept distinct. Thus, the blacksmith is frequently also a carpenter, the barber employs himself in making leaf plates, mat and broom, makers do duty as musicians, while the fisherman devotes part of his time to the trade of parching grain. These are not exceptional cases of two occupations being followed by a single person, but are well established instances of hereditary pursuits which are nearly always combined in the same caste. Of such complex industries the Census has given us no record, the instruction that only the main occupation should be entered in the schedule having directly prevented their return. A few examples, which appeared in the enumeration books, are given under order XXII in the classified list; elsewhere, they are distributed under the headings of the specific occupations, which the Census agency may have taken to be the principal source of income to the persons by whom they are followed.

(4) *Mistakes found in the enumeration.*—Chief amongst these must be put the record, despite very explicit instructions to the contrary, of indefinite terms for occupations, such as service, shop-keeping, etc. The careful classification of the entries which was carried out in the Census Office served to correct many of the errors that were found; in a population of nearly 13 millions, only some 8,659 persons, or 7 in 10,000, have been shown as of occupation undefined. But the process was a long and tedious one, and more time than I fear should have been spared, has been given to eliciting the meaning of doubtful and erroneous returns of occupation. The use of the word "dependent" was also an occasional source of stumbling to the Census agency. On the whole, the purport of the instructions was well understood, but sometimes entries were found in which means of livelihood was entered only for the head of the house, all the members of the family being shown simply as "dependent," without repetition of the occupation entry. Some latitude had necessarily to be left to the abstracting staff in dealing with such entries, but generally no mistake could be made about their meaning. In discussing individual occupations I shall hereafter notice other instances in which the Census staff sometimes failed to understand what was required of them; but, considering the detailed, and, in some points, difficult nature of the record which they were asked to make, I think it is astonishing how well they acquitted themselves.

268. **Compilation of the Returns.**—Though this matter properly belongs to the second part of the Report, I refer to it here, as it may be more advantageously discussed when the general scheme of the occupation statistics is under review than otherwise. As the occupations stood recorded in the books, one and the same means of livelihood was ordinarily written in half a dozen different ways. It was obviously impossible that, throughout the whole process of tabulation of the statistics, each separate designation should be kept distinct; allowing that some amount of combination had to be made, the difficulty existed of laying down rules as to what names should be combined and what discretion was to be given to the tabulating staff in this respect. After trying one or two plans which were cumbrous as well as of doubtful advantage, recourse was had to the method suggested by Mr. Drew, the Census Superintendent of the Bombay Presidency. On the basis of the scheme for the classification of means of livelihood contained in the

Census Commissioner's note O, dated 29th April 1891, an index of occupations was drawn up in which a serial number was assigned to each main occupation, and the names of others which might be considered synonymous entered alongside under the appropriate number. The latter were taken from nominal lists which had previously been prepared for certain districts, showing the occupation terms entered in the schedules. With this index to go by, a set of clerks were put to work to mark against each occupation appearing in the sheets on which the entries from the books had been abstracted, the serial number under which it stood recorded in the index. The numbering of occupations in this manner was very carefully carried out, and though the method might at first appear laborious, its adoption proved successful on various grounds. First, the combination of synonymous names for occupations was effected on a fixed and well arranged plan by a selected body of men, who very soon became such adepts at the process that the unceasing check which was exercised over their work very seldom revealed a wrong combination. Had the combination been left to the general body of tabulators, it is probable that many mistakes would have cropped up, which in the tabulated registers it would have been very difficult to correct. On the other hand, by the plan adopted the combination was effected and checked before the process of tabulation was taken in hand, so that the latter was very much simplified. Again, the entries in the abstraction sheets were very often vague or unintelligible, but as each numbering clerk had beside him the original books of the Census charge on which he was engaged, he could in case of necessity refer to the original entries, and in this way many difficulties were cleared up. Any entries of uncommon occupations, which did not appear in the index list, were at the same time brought up for orders as to the head under which they should be included. Lastly, in tabulation and throughout the whole process of compilation, there was considerable saving in time effected by having to write only numbers instead of lengthy terms for occupations. The method was, I think, entirely satisfactory and might well be adopted at a future Census. I would add, however, that on the present occasion the system was rather unnecessarily expanded by keeping distinct subordinate occupations which might very well have been combined from the commencement. This left us with a great deal of detail which caused great delay in compilation; for instance, under Government servants, officers of the various departments were separately numbered and tabulated, only to be put all together in the end under the general head. It would have saved much time had the inclusion been made to begin with.

269. **Classification of Occupations.**—This was, as has already been remarked, carried out in accordance with the general scheme laid down by the Census Commissioner, which has been printed at pages 168—69 of Volume II of the Report, and which is thus described in Mr. Baines' Circular.

"The object in view is to group the entries in the Census schedules as far as possible in accordance with the distribution of occupations in India in general, and at the same time to allow room for the designation of special features found only in certain Provinces. It is superfluous, therefore, to discuss the classification in use at the Census of communities further advanced in economic differentiation, or one based simply on the abstract laws of sociological science. The classification now published is not altogether scientifically correct, but it will serve its purpose if it collects under one head occupations known to be akin to each other, and keeps apart others which are but nominally related."

"In the first place the aggregate of the various means of livelihood are divided into the following main classes:—

A.—Government.

B.—Pasture and agriculture.

C.—Personal services.

D.—The preparation and supply of material substances.

E.—Commerce and transport of persons, goods and messages, and the storage of goods.

F.—Prefessions, learned, artistic and minor.

G.—Indefinite occupations, and means of subsistence independent of occupation.

"Subordinate to the seven classes come 24 orders, as shown below, bracketed according to their respective main heads :—

Class.	Orders.
A.	I.—Administration. II.—Defence. III.—Foreign and Feudatory State Service.
B.	IV.—Cattle-breeding, etc. V.—Agriculture.
C.	VI.—Personal services.
D.	VII.—Food and drink. VIII.—Light, firing and forage. IX.—Buildings. X.—Vehicles and vessels. XI.—Supplementary requirements. XII.—Textile fabrics and dress. XIII.—Metals and precious stones. XIV.—Glass, pottery and stone ware. XV.—Wood, cane and leaves. XVI.—Drugs, gums, etc. XVII.—Leather.
E.	XVIII.—Commerce. XIX.—Transport and storage.
F.	XX.—Learned and artistic professions. XXI.—Sports and amusements.
G.	XXII.—Complex occupations. XXIII.—Indefinite occupations. XXIV.—Independent of work.

" The first few explain themselves. As regards the seventh, eighth, ninth, tenth and eleventh, the object the article or service is intended for is placed more prominently than the material dealt with. On the other hand, from the twelfth to the seventeenth, the latter is regarded as more characteristic of the occupation than the object for which the prepared article is intended. The distinction is, of course, conventional and not economic, as in both orders the makers and the sellers of an article are combined, and it is only in the eighteenth order that special mention is made of those who return themselves as exclusively engaged in distribution."

The classification next passes into sub-orders and, where still further definition is thought necessary, into groups below the sub-orders. Of the latter, there are 77, which are shown, with their groups, in the general scheme.

270. Two points in connection with the above method of classification are worthy of special note :—

(1) *The classification of the special functions undertaken by the State which are distinct from the main end of administration—Protection and Defence.*—These are to be classed, not under the general head of Government service, but under their special designation. Thus, Public Instruction comes under Education, and Engineering, Agricultural training, Medical practice and administration under these heads, respectively; and so also with the service of local and municipal bodies, where only persons actually engaged in administration are entered under those titles.

(2). *The classification of Village Industries.*—These are an important class in this country where, in the absence of a high development of manufactures and commerce, production and distribution are frequently in the hands of one and the same person. The great bulk of the village artisans,—the blacksmith, the carpenter, the potter, the weaver and the like,—sell as well as make the articles in which they work. In the larger towns the division of industry is, however, much more complete; here the employment of capital has called into existence manufactures which are followed as a distinct pursuit, entailing separate distribution of the goods produced. But in the classification scheme it has not been thought advisable to make any difference between the two kinds of industry. Thus, no distinction has been kept between those who make and those who sell special goods, though in the sub-divisional groups separate places have been assigned to the general dealer, the commercial agent and other middlemen.

271. Other cases in which the classification of special occupations appears worthy of remark will be noticed in reviewing the body of statistics which have been worked out. To these I shall now turn my attention. The subject is a wide one and is not easy to approach, but the following may be taken as an outline of the course which I intend to pursue. First of all, I shall deal with the general distribution of the people by occupation. In doing so, it will be occasionally necessary to refer to one or all of the special branches into which the enquiry divides itself, *viz.* the occupations of males and females, and those in which juveniles bear a part, the occupations of the town and country and those which are followed in combination with agriculture, while lastly comes the local distribution of means of livelihood throughout the Province. Of some of these matters, separate note will be afterwards made as well. The native states are generally so backward in development that the subject of the occupation of their population had better be treated of apart from that of the more advanced British districts.

GENERAL DISTRIBUTION OF THE POPULATION BY OCCUPATION.

BRITISH DISTRICTS.

272. The following table gives statistics for the distribution of the population of British districts by the different classes of occupations :—

Occupation Distribution for British Districts.

Class.	Name.	Total population.	Proportion per 10,000 of total population.	Males.		Females.	
				Total number of persons.	Proportion per 10,000.	Total number of persons.	Proportion per 10,000.
A	Government	208,920	194	121,317	225	87,603	163
B	Pasture and Agriculture	7,173,480	6,651	3,623,092	6,713	3,550,388	6,591
C	Personal Service	262,639	243	137,006	254	125,633	233
D	Preparation and supply of material substances	2,017,982	1,870	978,930	1,814	1,039,052	1,929
E	Commerce, Transport and Storage	197,694	184	112,505	208	85,189	158
F	Professions	132,149	122	74,985	139	57,164	106
G	Indefinite and Independent	791,430	736	349,469	647	441,961	820
	Total	10,784,294	10,000	5,397,304	10,000	5,386,990	10,000

Distinction of sex.—Separate details are given for the sexes, but the differentiation is not of very much importance, as the whole system of enumeration of means of livelihood is based on a principle that obliterates sex distinction. I refer to the Census being, as has already been explained, a record of persons who live by, and not who exercise, an occupation. No doubt, from there being a preponderance of females depending on one means of livelihood as compared with males, we can infer that the occupation is one in which females more especially bear a part, but from the intermixture of workers and dependents that has taken place, we can have only a general indication of the extent to which the particular pursuit is really engaged in by the female sex.

Distinction of age.—Similarly the detail of age, which has been worked out in connection with occupation, can only be employed in an indefinite manner to show how far the persons subsisting by any occupation are actual workers or dependents. All children under five years of age are, of course, dependents, juveniles, from 5 to 14 years, may or may not be so, while of adults the greater part, amongst males, may be looked upon as workers. The age return can, perhaps, be turned to account in a general way, in comparing the results of one part of the country with another, but its principal object, so far as our present purpose is concerned, may be taken to be the index which it gives to the occupations in which (1) juveniles and (2) adult females compete with the adult males employed.

Use to which the details of sex and age may be turned.—I shall explain my meaning better by giving two examples. To take first juveniles: ordinarily all children are shown as depending on the occupations followed by their fathers, but in some cases they are recorded under separate means of livelihood. For instance, the son of, say, an agricultural labourer is frequently returned as herding cattle. If we distribute 10,000 males of the total population over the whole list of occupations, we find that 300 persons result as depending on the care of cattle for their living; 10,000 male juveniles, that is from 5 to 14, similarly distributed, show 461 persons so returned. Thus we can infer that the herding of cattle is one in which young boys are largely engaged. It is the same thing with females, but in their case it will be of no use to enquire as to the preponderance or otherwise of juvenile workers. The scheme of the return, according to which nearly all young girls are entered as of the father's occupation, while grown up women may have been shown as following different pursuits, is against our obtaining correct information on the subject. Thus, take the case of fishermen; of 10,000 females of all ages, 69 are shown as depending on fishing for their means of livelihood, of 10,000 from ages 5—14 the proportion amounts to 82. From this it would at first sight appear as if young girls were engaged in fishing more than grown up women, but the inference would be wrong, as the high proportion is due to the large number of children recorded as of their father's profession, while their mothers are otherwise employed. But the age returns can be made use of to show us more distinctly than we could otherwise know whether any particular occupation is one in which females extensively compete with males. This can best be ascertained by comparing the number of adult females with the number of adult males recorded against any particular means of livelihood. To take the instance of firewood and grass-gatherers; the total number of females is to the total number of males as 217 to 100; but if we consider only those who are grown up, the proportion becomes 275 to 100. The latter is the strongest indication we can get that the occupation is one in which women largely bear a part.

The distinctions of sex and age as above described will be shown in the detailed tabular statements which follow.

273. *Comparison with the returns of 1881 impossible.*—Of the population of the British districts of the Province 1·94 per cent. belong to the class who are engaged in Administration and Defence, 66·51 are employed in Pasture and Agriculture, 2·43 in Personal services, 18·70 in Industrial occupations, 1·84 in Transport and Commerce, 1·22 come under the head of Professions, while the remainder, 7·36, live by indefinite labour, or are supported independently of occupation. These proportions are reviewed in detail below. Up to the present none of the tables for other Provinces have reached me, so that I am unable to compare the results which they display with the figures I have given. To show how impossible is comparison with the returns of 1881, when a record was made only of *actual workers*, I may note that 44·5 per cent. of the

male population and 31·7 of the female—these percentages include Feudatory States—were then returned as belonging to the cultivating class. The result appears misleading on account of the large number of persons shown as of no occupation, and it certainly does not represent the actual conditions of a Province where agriculture is notoriously the means of subsistence of the great body of the population. It is true that by dividing off the number of people shown in 1881 as of no occupation, according to the proportions which each class of workers bears to the total of employed, we might get an estimate of what the number of persons living by any class of occupation may then have been, but the result would be so problematical and the time at my disposal is so short that I think it best to leave consideration of the 1881 return altogether out of account. The following remarks have therefore reference solely to the present distribution of the means of livelihood of the people.

CLASS A.—GOVERNMENT.

274. Class A is divided into 3 orders, (1)—persons engaged in administration, (2) persons engaged in defence, and (3) persons in the service of Foreign or Feudatory States.

Occupation Statistics—Class A.

Order.	Sub-order.	Name.	Total Population. No.	Total Population. Distribution of 10,000 persons.	Males. No.	Males. Distribution of 10,000. Total	Males. Distribution of 10,000. 5—14	Females. No.	Females. Distribution of 10,000.	Adult females per 100 adult males.	Distribution of 10,000 persons living in towns.	Percentage of employed who live in towns.
1	2	3	4	5	6	7	8	9	10	11	12	13
I.—Administration.	1	Government Service.	49,652	46	28,109	52	36	21,543	40	70	380	56·6
	2	Service of Local Bodies.	5,729	5	3,242	6	5	2,487	5	72	63	81·4
	3	Village Service .	140,697	131	80,627	149	137	60,070	111	65	52	2·7
	Total Order I.	Administration .	196,078	182	111,978	207	178	84,100	156	66	495	18·7
II.—Defence.	4	Army . .	12,327	12	9,014	17	5	3,313	6	26	163	97·6
	5	Navy and Marine .	6	...	3	...	...	3	...	...	...	...
	Total Order II.	Defence . .	12,333	12	9,017	17	5	3,316	6	26	163	97·6
III.—Feudatory States Service.	6	Administrative Service.	467	...	301	1	...	166	1	46	2	37·5
	7	Army . .	42	...	21	...	...	21	...	...	...	...
	Total Order III.	Foreign, etc., Service.	509	...	322	1	...	187	1	48	2	40·5
Total Class A.—Government .			208,920	194	121,31	226	183	87,603	163	62	660	23·4

I.—Administration*. (1) *Government.*—In the first sub-order, Government service, three divisions have been recognized, which may be described as superior, intermediate and menial, and which stand to one another in the proportion of 2·7, 17·8 and 79·5 per cent. of the total of the sub-order. Amongst menials, 39,480, we find a high average of males—there are only 66 women per 100 men—due chiefly to the inclusion of the rank and file of the police force. All persons for whom the indefinite term "Government Service" was entered in the schedules have come under the third head,

* In the heading of this and the following paragraphs the figures in Roman character refer to the serial numbers of Orders of occupations, and those within brackets to Sub-orders.

as most of them probably belong to the inferior class. It has already been observed that the employés of Government in such special branches, as Engineering, Education, Survey, etc., have been classed under these professions respectively and not amongst Government servants.

(3). *Village Service.*—This comprises headmen who are not agriculturists, 90, accountants or patwaris, 14,887 and watchmen, 125,720. In the Central Provinces the village headman, or *mukadam*, is almost invariably a cultivator, and the instructions being that in such case he should be shown under the heading. "Agriculture", he is scarcely represented in these returns. The village watchman class shows a low proportion of female dependents, 63 adults per 100 males, the explanation being that the women of the kotwar's family are usually engaged in weaving, which is the traditional pursuit of the class. The Bhumak, or hereditary village watchman and priest, has been put under the heading of Religion, as more properly belonging to the latter category; the Bhumaks, returned at the Census, number 2,385. The kotwar is essentially the village drudge, he is made use of on all occasions, such as bringing the tenants together at rent times, serving as the village messenger and in general doing the headman's biddings; but he is also supposed to be a general referee on all points connected with village boundaries, tenure of land, ancient customs, etc. In remuneration for his services, he generally holds a plot of rent-free land, receiving besides certain fees usually in kind, and is entitled to the carcases of cattle dying within the village. As the name of the sub-order implies, the persons whom it includes are found mainly in the country; only 2·7 per cent. of the total have been recorded in towns.

275. **II.—Defence.**—This comprises persons serving in the army and their families, and six persons who belong to the navy and marine. Of the latter, one, a railway passenger, was returned as a "Sailor, Government," and the other five were recorded from Kampti as dependents of a person in the Bombay Marine Battalion. Of the persons shown under the heading Army, 2,126 are entered as followers. There was at first some uncertainty as to the occupations to be included under this head, but a reference to the Census Commissioner resulted in its being directed that all persons exercising well defined professions, which were not exclusively military, should come in the classes to which these belonged. Thus, regimental cooks, mochis, syces and barrack watchmen are shown under these heads, the follower class being therefore mainly limited to transport drivers, dooly bearers and the like. The army population is of course almost solely confined to the towns; males are nearly three times as numerous as females, and of the former over 86 per cent. are adults.

276. **III.—Service of Feudatory States.**—This contains 509 persons in the service of native states, who happened to be enumerated in the Central Provinces; these are classed under two sub-orders, administrative and military. The places where most persons connected with Feudatory States were found are Saugor, Jubbulpore, Hoshangabad, Raipur and Bilaspur; in Hoshangabad the presence of the deposed Raja of Makrai accounts for the large number of people of this class recorded from the district.

CLASS B.—PASTURE AND AGRICULTURE.

277. This class is divided into two orders: (1) persons engaged in keeping and grazing cattle and other stock, and (2) persons who have an interest in land, as owners and tenants, persons who are agricultural labourers, and persons who are growers of special products or who are engaged in agricultural training or supervision. The former contains 2·48 per cent. of the total population of the Province, and the latter 64·03, amongst whom persons having an interest in land largely predominate.

Occupation Statistics—Class B.

Order.	Sub-order or group.	Name.	Total Population. No.	Total Population. Distribution of 10,000 persons	Males. No.	Males. Distribution of 10,000. Total.	Males. Distribution of 10,000. 5–14.	Females. No.	Females. Distribution of 10,000.	Adult females per 100 adult males.	Distribution of 10,000 persons living in towns.	Percentage of employed who live in towns.
1	2	3	4	5	6	7	8	9	10	11	12	13
IV.—LIVE-STOCK.	8 A.	Horses and Horned Cattle	248,704	231	166,274	308	468	82,430	153	53	61	1·8
	8 B.	Other Draught Animals	177	...	148	...	...	29	...	21	...	18·2
	8 C.	Small Stock	17,035	16	11,035	21	28	6,000	11	55	14	6·3
	Total 8	Stock-Breeding and Dealing	265,916	247	177,457	329	496	88,459	164	53	75	2·1
	9	Subsidiary Services to stock	909	1	533	1	1	376	1	69	7	59·4
	Total Order IV.	Live-Stock	266,825	248	177,990	330	497	88,835	165	53	82	2·3
V.—AGRICULTURE.	10	Interest in Land	4,909,195	4,552	2,500,310	4,633	4,742	2,408,885	4,472	97	800	1·2
	11	Agricultural Labourers	1,936,200	1,795	909,630	1,685	1,643	1,026,570	1,906	119	354	1·4
	12	Growers of Special Products and Trees	45,787	42	25,632	47	40	20,155	37	72	108	17·5
	13	Agricultural Training and Supervision	15,473	14	9,530	18	11	5,943	11	53	21	9·9
	Total Order V	Agriculture	6,906,655	6,403	3,445,102	6,383	6,436	3,461,553	6,426	102	1,283	1·4
Total Class B.—Pasture and Agriculture			7,173,480	6,651	3,623,092	6,718	6,933	3,550,388	6,591	100	1,365	1·4
PARTICULAR OCCUPATIONS.	21.	Herdsmen	241,498	224	161,843	300	461	79,655	148	53	52	1·6
	34, 35, 36.	Farm Servants	820,564	761	556,904	1,032	930	263,660	490	36	130	1·2
	37, 38.	Field Labourers	1,115,636	1,034	352,726	653	713	762,910	1,416	266	224	1·5

IV.—Live-Stock.—This order is sub-divided, so as to show separately (1) persons who are connected with (*a*) horses and horned cattle, (*b*) with other draught animals, and (*c*) with small stock, and (2) persons who perform subsidiary services to stock.

(*8a*) *Horses and horned cattle.*—Of the 266,825 persons employed about live-stock, by far the greater portion have to do with the care of cattle, their numbers amounting to 248,507. In the occupation tables a further distinction is kept between persons who are simply herdsmen, 241,498, and persons who are breeders or dealers of cattle and buffaloes, 7,009, while all those recorded in the enumeration books as tending the household cattle have been transferred to the heading Agriculture, this being generally the duty of a juvenile member of the cultivator's family. It is hardly to be expected that the figures for these divisions are very precise, as both dealing, and tending the household kine may have sometimes been entered under the general term *dhor rakhnā*. As a matter of fact, there are very few breeders worthy of the name in these Provinces, so that nearly all the persons shown as breeders or dealers of cattle belong simply to the latter category; those who breed cattle do so for purposes other than dealing. In Saugor a large number of dealers, 1,286, have been returned, due partly to the district being a head-quarters place of a class of people known as Mukeris, who trade in cattle, and partly to the great cattle fair at Garhakota having occurred at the time of the enumeration. Herdsmen are an important class in all districts. Regarding them we may note, first, the low number of females dependent on the occupation, 53 per 100 males, and second, that the tending of cattle is one of the occupations in which youths from 5 to 14 are largely employed, the proportion of males who are between those ages being 42·7 per cent. of the whole; in the general population only 27·8 per cent. of the males are between the ages of 5 and 14.

(*8b*) *Other draught animals.*—Under this head are entered 177 people, returned as breeders or keepers of donkeys; all are probably Kumhars, amongst whom there is a section called *Gadhera*, who keep asses for the purpose of their trade; none of them in all likelihood breed to sell. Camel-keepers have all been classed under the head "Carriers by pack animals," to which in this Province they properly belong.

(*8c*) *Small stock.*—16,617 persons are shown as having the care of sheep and goats; they include breeders, dealers and hired shepherds, and as amongst herdsmen, a large proportion of them are juveniles aged from 5—14, 38·1 per cent. of the males being so returned. Along with the keeping of sheep is usually combined the occupation of blanket-weaving (No. 179), which is returned of 17,581 persons, most of whom are also shepherds. In Chanda, which returns the highest number of shepherds, 2,617, of any district in the Province, there is a strong body of Kuramwárs, a nomadic race of Canarese origin, employed in the tending of sheep; 418 persons are returned at the Census as pigbreeders and swineherds; pigs are kept by many of the lower classes, such as Dhimars, Basors, Pankas, etc., and by most of the aboriginal tribes.

(*9*) *Subsidiary services to stock.*—This group, 909 in number, includes veterinary surgeons, farriers, horse-breakers and trainers.

The chief pastoral districts according to the return given at paragraph 323, are those on the Satpuras, and Chanda, Balaghat, Raipur and Bilaspur. The Sambalpur district is notable as returning very few persons employed about stock; the breed of cattle in the district is probably the worst in the Province, no attention being paid to their keep. Among the Urias milk is not ordinarily an article of diet. The Uria States, I may add, return a similarly low proportion of cattle herds.

278. **V.—Agriculture.** (*10*) *Interest in land.*—From the table which has been given above it will be observed that no less than 4,909,195 persons, or 45·5 per cent. of the population, are directly interested in the land as owners or occupants or as tenants or sharers. If to these we add the persons exhibited in the special return, Table XVIIC., as combining agriculture with other occupations, the number amounts to 5,121,549, or 47·5 per cent. of the population. The relative proportions of these who are (1) owners or occupants; and (2) tenants, in the combined total of agriculturists, will appear from the statement which is here given.

Interest in Land.

Agricultural Occupation.	Number of persons for whom occupation in column 1 is recorded by itself.	Number of persons combining the same with non-agricultural occupations.	Total of columns 2 and 3.	Proportion of column 4 on total population.
1	2	3	4	5
Owners or occupants	275,616	13,276	288,892	2·7
Tenants	4,633,579	199,078	4,832,657	44·8
Total Interest in Land	4,909,195	212,354	5,121,549	47·5

For the present we may leave out of account all notice of the particular occupations which the persons shown in column 3 follow in combination with agriculture; the matter can better be treated of in a separate note.

Land-owners and occupants.—Taking up, then, only the subject of agriculture by itself, we may first turn our attention to the land-owning class. In the Imperial Table three distinctions have been observed in connection therewith, the class being divided into (1) land-owners who do not cultivate, but let all their land to tenants, (2) land-owners cultivating, and (3) lessees of villages. Before proceeding further it will be well to note what the figures for land-owners mean, and here, I may say, that at the Census it is exceedingly difficult, with the half-educated enumerators we had to employ, to be certain of the result we have obtained in this respect. To make the matter as clear as possible, the rule for making the return ran—that in each case the status of the land-owner should be specified, such as zemindár, talukdár, málguzár, pattidár, málik-makbuza, máfidár, or whatever the term for the ownership might be. In this way it was hoped that we should be able to get a distinct return of persons owning land, and that the latter would not be merged in the general term of cultivator, which would almost certainly have otherwise been the case. The plan worked on the whole satisfactorily, but it would be unsafe to assume that we have attained real accuracy; for the latter the records of the settlement department are the proper guide,—the census figures can be looked upon only as an approximation. This being the case, no attempt has been made to publish details of the different kinds of proprietorship, though these, it may be remarked, were separately worked out; the figures for owners of land include therefore every person so returned, from zemindars in possession of estates which cover hundreds of square miles, down to the plot proprietor or rent-free holder, who has only an acre of land, or perhaps less, which he can call his own. Of this rather heterogeneous class, 1,406 persons, or ·5 per cent., are returned as land-owners not cultivating, 267,052, or 96·9, are shown as cultivating proprietors, and 7,158, or 2·6, are lessees of villages. The extreme fewness of non-cultivating landlords is worthy of note, but the figures are probably a very fair indication of the actual state of affairs; almost everybody who is an owner of land, however much of it he may let out to tenants, has at least an acre or two in which cultivation is carried on on his own account, even if it be only to grow vegetables or other produce for home consumption. Lessees of villages are numerous in Seoni, 1,033, in Raipur, 2,948, and in Bilaspur, 1,506.

Tenants and Sharers.—Under this head have been included all the multifarious terms by which the actual cultivation of land, otherwise than as an owner, was returned in the Census schedules. No attempt was made to obtain a record of the different kinds of tenancy; all were to be entered under the general designation *Kástkári.* Such being the instructions issued to enumerators, no account has been kept of different kinds of occupancy when shown in the enumeration books, nor of different styles of cultivation, such as the *dhya* or wood-ash system, as the return would in every case be fragmentary. From the almost even balance which is preserved between the sexes—there are 97 adult females for 100 males—we may take it that the figures we have got are very fairly correct. There is always somewhat of a tendency to return the wife of a cultivator as simply doing field work, but very generally some word is added to show that it is in her husband's land that she works; in all such cases she has been classed as a cultivator, and not as an agricultural labourer. In cases where it was not shown that she was employed in home cultivation, she had of course to be included in the latter category, but such were the exception, rather than the rule. Amongst tenants have been included sharers of all kinds, and there is a further class, entered in the table as "cultivators subsidiary," who may also be looked upon as tenants. They are the persons who tend the household cattle, a duty which in the greater number of cases falls upon some member usually a juvenile, of the cultivator's family; of the 5,851 persons, male and female, thus returned, more than half, 3,021, are boys from 5 to 14 years of age. All are properly dependent on the family holding for their living, and have been shown accordingly in the occupation statistics.

279. (*II*) *Agricultural Labourers.*—First come farm servants in fixed employ; these number 820,564, or 7·61 of the population. An attempt has been made to distinguish between those who are paid by the year and those who are paid by the month, but the return can hardly be looked upon as very reliable The ordinary method of payment is by the year, and from the largeness of the number of persons who are shown as paid by the month—they amount to 155,177—I suspect that a considerable proportion of labourers who are engaged only for the harvest, and who can hardly therefore be looked upon as farm servants proper, have come in the return. Farm servants on yearly wages—amongst whom have been included persons for whom have been given such terms as *harwáha,* etc., whether coupled with the word "yearly" or not,—number 601,239, whilst others for whom no further specification than farm service was returned, amount to 64,148. The chief point to be noticed in connection with the figures for this occupation is the very low proportion of females who are shown as belonging to it, there are only 36 women to every hundred men. The wives of the farm servant class have generally been returned as ordinary field labourers and are therefore included in the occupation which follows, in which, as will be seen, the proportion of females to males is as high as 266 per 100. Agricultural labourers and crop-watchers together number 1,115,636, or over a tenth part of the population. It must be borne in mind that a large proportion of the persons who are returned as general labourers in Order XXIII must also to a great extent take part in the work of the fields; usually in the villages there is little other labour of a general kind to be done.

280. **Strength of the agricultural population in different districts.**—The appended statement shows the proportions which the different

classes of agriculturists bear to the total population in the several districts of the Province :—

Proportion of different classes of Agriculturists per 10,000 of the population of each district.

Districts.	Interest in Land.			Labourers.			Total Agriculturists.
	Owners.	Tenants.	Total.	Farm servants.	Field labourers.	Total.	
Saugor	355	3,253	3,608	294	806	1,100	4,708
Damoh	443	3,681	4,124	446	810	1,256	5,380
Jubbulpore	277	3,565	3,842	386	1,172	1,558	5,400
Narsinghpur	217	3,340	3,557	315	680	995	4,552
Hoshangabad	150	3,392	3,542	705	617	1,322	4,864
Nimar	1,738	2,356	4,094	357	1,471	1,828	5,922
Mandla	124	5,564	5,688	680	973	1,653	7,341
Seoni	214	4,402	4,616	1,138	707	1,845	6,461
Chhindwara	291	4,437	4,728	793	1,591	2,384	7,112
Betul	163	4,776	4,939	638	1,214	1,852	6,791
Wardha	271	2,485	2,756	976	2,959	3,935	6,691
Nagpur	210	2,443	2,653	676	1,729	2,405	5,058
Chanda	157	3,375	3,532	630	1,779	2,409	5,941
Bhandara	269	3,710	3,979	960	1,490	2,450	6,429
Balaghat	209	4,328	4,537	1,363	1,266	2,629	7,166
Raipur	180	5,390	5,570	1,109	618	1,727	7,297
Bilaspur	212	6,555	6,767	415	522	937	7,704
Sambalpur	141	5,365	5,506	1,277	48	1,325	6,831
Total British Districts	255	4,297	4,552	761	1,034	1,795	6,347

The deductions to be drawn from the figures I must leave to persons better acquainted with the agricultural conditions of the Province than myself. I would only note the following as explanatory of some of the more marked variations which are exhibited. In the first place, the above refers only to persons whose calling is solely agriculture; people combining the latter with other occupations have not been included, as I have not district details concerning them by me as I write. It may, therefore, be that in some districts the low proportion of land-owners is in part due to the exclusion of the landholding saucar, from the figures I have given. In Nimar the high average of owners exhibits the peculiar tenure of the district, where many of the cultivators are proprietors of their holdings. In the hill districts and in Chhatisgarh and Sambalpur, the number of cultivating tenants appears high in proportion to the population, when compared with the more advanced districts of the Nerbada valley and the Nagpur plain. In the latter, a larger portion of the people are engaged in industrial pursuits, and it will also be seen that whereas the class that has an interest in the land is weak, the agricultural labouring community is correspondingly strong. The reason for the disproportion which these districts exhibit in this respect is hardly to be sought for in the grasping of a landlord class dispossessing the ryot of his land, though in some cases this force may have been, or may still be, in operation. It should rather be set down to the fact that in the old settled parts of the Province land is scarce, and the expenses of cultivation high, in comparison with what is the case in the hill districts, where land is to be had almost for the asking, and where the cultivation is of the rudest and can be carried on by any hill-man with none of the resources which are necessary to the cultivator of the plains.

The figures for field labourers present the most remarkable variations of any in the statement which has been given. As has been already remarked, the return depends a good deal on the treatment of the subject by the enumerating staff. Practically, nearly all labourers in the country are more agricultural labourers than anything else and should properly have been reckoned so at the Census. The high proportion, amounting to nearly 30 per cent., of the population so recorded in the Wardha district, is in all likelihood due to the Deputy Commissioner, Mr. Drysdale, with the experience of the Census of 1881 to go by, having recognized this fact and forbidden the use of the indefinite term "general labour", which found such favour in other places. In Sambalpur, where less than ½ per cent. of the population is recorded as belonging to the agricultural labouring class, nearly 10 per cent. of the inhabitants of the district have been shown as common labourers.

281. (*12*) *Growers of Special Products and Trees.*—The sub-order includes several occupations, which, with one or two exceptions, are of an agricultural nature. The number of persons of whom *quasi*-agricultural pursuits have been returned is 30,022, whilst others, whose occupations are not so distinctively agricultural, amount to 15,765. Among the former we may first notice betel-vine growers, 4,199, found principally in the four northern districts of Saugor, Damoh, Jubbulpore, and Narsinghpur, and in the south of the Province, in Wardha and Chanda, the latter of which especially is noted for its pán gardens. Many growers of betel are at the same time sellers of the leaf, and must have been shown as such in sub-order 19. Madder or ál growers number only 311; they are principally returned from Damoh, Chhindwara, Nagpur, Bhandara, and Balaghat. Though it is no doubt the case that ál is being steadily supplanted by dyes of European manufacture, yet the number of growers of the plant must appear unduly small; some may probably have been entered as ordinary cultivators. Fruit-growers, 399, market gardeners, 20,110, and gardeners 5,002, were frequently hardly distinguishable in the enumeration schedules; the districts in which, according to the Census, the growers of garden crops predominate, are Saugor, Damoh, and Jubbulpore in the north, and Raipur in the east of the Province, but the return is hardly reliable, as the raisers of such produce have in many cases been shown as engaged in agriculture without further distinction.

Of the non-agricultural occupations comprised in the present sub-order the principal is the forest service, in which 41 persons are shown as officers and their dependents, and 8,320 as employed in clerical and subordinate establishments. Water-nut growers number 7,317, of whom 3,134 are returned from the Jubbulpore district. Water-nut cultivation is also largely carried on in Nagpur, Bhandara, and Balaghat; it appears to be unknown in Sambalpur. The calling is usually followed by the Dhimar caste, and has been returned in conjunction with the occupation of fishing by 871 persons shown in Order XXII—Complex Occupations.

282. (*13*). *Agricultural Training and Supervision.*—Under this head come zemindárs' and málguzárs' agents and clerks, 4,565, and the persons returned as málguzárs' havaldars, 10,896. The latter is almost a village servant, but he may be more properly considered as the málguzár's bailiff, who looks after the village affairs and collects rents in his absence.

CLASS C.—PERSONAL AND HOUSEHOLD SERVICES.

283. The class contains three sub-orders: (1) persons engaged in personal and domestic services, (2) persons employed as hotel or rest-house keepers, and (3) persons connected with the work of sanitation.

Occupation Statistics—Class C.

Order.	Sub-order or group.	Name.	Total Population. No.	Total Population. Distribu-tion of 10,000 persons.	Males. No.	Males. Distribution of 10,000. Total.	Males. Distribution of 10,000. 5—14.	Females. No.	Females. Distribution of 10,000.	Adult Females per 100 adult males.	Distribution of 10,000 persons living in towns.	Percentage of employed who live in towns.
1	2	3	4	5	6	7	8	9	10	11	12	13
VI.—PERSONAL AND HOUSEHOLD SERVICES.	14	Personal and domestic services.	244,610	227	127,989	237	213	116,621	217	90	725	21·9
	15	Non-domestic establishment	359	...	195	1	...	164	...	77	3	65·2
	16	Sanitation	17,670	16	8,822	16	16	8,848	16	102	115	48·0
	Total Order VI.	Perso Household Services.	262,639	243	137,006	254	29	125,633	333	90	843	23·7

VI.—Personal and Household Services. (*14*) *Personal and Domestic Services.*—The persons following this branch of employment number 244,610 or 2·27 of the total population. The barbers, 86,815, are the largest body among them; their women do oil-anointing, and plait and dress the hair of females; all thus returned have been classed under the present heading, so that it was scarcely to be expected that the women dependent on the trade would be so few in number as compared with the men, to whom they stand in the proportion of 66 to 100. Many are no doubt engaged in the making of leaf plates, an occupation which is generally carried on in the barber's family in the northern and eastern districts of the Province; amongst leaf plate makers there are 3,604 women to 565 men. Others are probably engaged as indoor servants or, in the country where members of the profession are not so well off, are employed in field work. 290 persons are shown as tattooers. Tattooing is carried to its greatest extent among the Gonds, of whom Forsyth writes:—

"The Gond women have the legs, as far as they are suffered to be seen, tattooed in a variety of fantastic patterns, done in indigo or gunpowder blue. The Pardháns are

the great artists in this line, and the figures they design are almost the only ornamental art attempted by these tribes. It is done when the girl becomes marriageable, and the traveller will sometimes hear dreadful screeches issuing from their villages, which will be attributed to some young Gondin being operated upon with a tattooing needle."

Persons engaged in washing clothes number 58,447, of whom rather more than half are females. Among water carriers, 35,577, there is also a preponderance of females who number 148 per 100 males. The distribution of the occupation is worthy of remark, the four northern districts of Saugor, Damoh, Jubbulpore and Narsinghpur containing no less than 23,596 persons employed as water bearers, or 66·3 per cent. of the total for the Province. Elsewhere the employment of special servants for the purpose, if we exclude places with a European or Eurasian population, would appear to be the exception rather than the rule. Cooks number 5,870, of whom 3,231, or considerably more than half, are found in the districts of Nagpur and Jubbulpore; 4,819 of the total number occur in towns. Among natives the cooking is usually done by the wives of all classes, rich as well as poor, caste prejudices and the unvarying custom of the country preventing the employment of hired cooks. The indoor work is in like manner almost universally done by the women of the family, and this accounts for the very small number of the class, 36,912, returned at the Census. Grooms, mahouts, etc., number 12,569, and the last sub-division of domestics, door-keepers, or private sepoys, 8,087 ; these include, probably, many persons who should more properly have been classed among messengers, the indefiniteness of the terms returned frequently making classification a matter of difficulty.

The relative strength of the domestic class in proportion to the population of each district is shown at paragraph 323. Above also particular instances have been noted, which indicate that in the northern districts of Saugor, Damoh, Jubbulpore, Narsinghpur and Hoshangabad, where there is a preponderance of well-to-do people, living in the more pretentious style of the better class of natives of Northern India, the number of domestics is far greater than in the other parts of the Province. We may except Nagpur, where, in the large towns of Nagpur and Kampti with a large European and Eurasian population, there is also a high proportion of people engaged in personal services. Elsewhere the people are generally so poor or conform to such a low standard of living that domestics are but rarely employed.

(16) *Sanitation.*—Under this head 17,670 persons are returned. As the work of scavenging is wholly confined to one class which is practically debarred from following any other avocation, the proportions of the sexes, it will be noticed, are nearly equal.

CLASS D.—PREPARATION AND SUPPLY OF MATERIAL SUBSTANCES.

284. The industrial class in which, as has been explained, the makers and sellers of an article are combined, has been divided into several orders, particulars of which have already been given. From their nature the occupations which it includes are specially distinctive of the town population, of whom no less than 45·46 per cent. are returned as belonging to the class.

Occupation Statistics—Class D.

Order.	Sub-order or group.	Name.	Total Population. No.	Total Population. Distribution of 10,000 persons.	Males. No.	Males. Distribution of 10,000. Total.	Males. Distribution of 10,000. 5–14	Females. No.	Females. Distribution of 10,000.	Adult females per 100 adult males.	Distribution of 10,000 persons living in towns.	Percentage of employed who live in towns.
1	2	3	4	5	6	7	8	9	10	11	12	13
VII.—FOOD AND DRINK.	17	Animal food	160,802	149	83,891	155	157	76,911	143	90	252	11·6
	18	Vegetable food	162,346	151	61,143	113	107	101,203	188	191	576	26·2
	19	Drink, condiments, and narcotics	119,115	110	59,717	111	96	59,398	110	101	288	17·9
		Total Order VII.—Food and drink	**442,263**	**410**	**204,751**	**379**	**360**	**237,512**	**441**	**124**	**1,116**	**18·7**
VIII.—LIGHT, FIRING AND FORAGE.	20	Lighting	90,361	84	41,230	76	77	49,131	91	128	157	12·9
	21	Fuel and forage	125,487	116	40,768	76	82	84,719	158	256	271	16·0
		Total Order VIII.—Light, firing, and forage.	**215,848**	**200**	**81,998**	**152**	**159**	**133,850**	**249**	**190**	**428**	**14·7**
IX.—BUILDING.	22	Building materials	15,711	15	8,816	16	13	6,895	13	71	64	30·3
	23	Artificers in building	27,781	26	16,132	30	23	11,649	21	65	191	50·8
		Total Order IX.—Buildings	**43,492**	**41**	**24,948**	**46**	**36**	**18,544**	**34**	**67**	**255**	**43·4**
X.—VEHICLES AND VESSELS.	24	Railway plant	4,573	4	2,838	5	3	1,735	3	50	37	60·4
	25	Carts and carriages, etc.	707	1	438	1	1	269	1	56	5	52·6
	26	Ships and boats	1	...	1	...	...	...	...	...	...	...
		Total Order X.—Vehicles and vessels	**5,281**	**5**	**3,277**	**6**	**4**	**2,004**	**4**	**51**	**42**	**59·3**

Occupation Statistics—Class D—continued.

Order.	Sub-order or group.	Name.	Total Population. No.	Total Population. Distribution of 10,000 persons.	Males. No.	Males. Distribution of 10,000. Total.	Males. Distribution of 10,000. 5–14	Females. No.	Females. Distribution of 10,000.	Adult females per 100 adult males.	Distribution of 10,000 persons living in towns.	Percentage of employed who live in towns.
1	2	3	4	5	6	7	8	9	10	11	12	13
XI.—Supplementary Requirements.	27	Paper, etc.	321	...	165	...	...	156	...	85	1	30·8
	28	Books and prints	1,615	1	884	2	1	731	2	78	19	86·9
	29	Watches, clocks, and scientific instruments.	168	...	96	...	...	72	...	67	2	97·0
	30	Carving, engraving, etc.	244	...	146	...	...	98	...	59	3	89·8
	31	Toys, curiosities	1,033	1	462	1	1	571	1	131	10	71·6
	32	Music and musical instruments	1,610	1	907	2	2	703	2	71	1	6·6
	33	Necklace, bracelets, beads, sacred threads, etc.	40,428	37	19,802	37	34	20,626	38	109	129	23·6
	34	Furniture	242	...	133	...	...	109	...	91	2	63·2
	35	Harness	828	1	502	1	1	326	1	61	7	61·5
	36	Tools and machinery	2,471	2	1,360	3	2	1,111	2	76	18	53·4
	37	Arms and ammunition	1,420	1	737	1	1	683	1	91	6	33·6
		Total Order XI.—Supplementary requirements	**50,380**	**44**	**25,194**	**47**	**42**	**25,186**	**47**	**103**	**198**	**29·2**
XII.—Textile Fabrics and Dress.	38	Wool and fur	20,432	19	10,353	19	18	10,079	19	96	11	3·8
	39	Silk	9,278	9	3,660	7	6	5,618	10	181	59	47·4
	40	Cotton	617,168	572	298,495	553	528	318,673	592	111	1,294	15·6
	41	Jute, flax, coir, etc.	10,081	9	5,323	10	9	4,758	9	85	14	10·4
	42	Dress	69,685	65	35,069	65	56	34,616	64	98	280	29·7
		Total Order XII.—Textile Fabrics and Dress.	**726,644**	**674**	**352,900**	**654**	**617**	**373,744**	**694**	**109**	**1,658**	**16·9**

Occupation Statistics—Class D—continued.

Order.	Sub-order or group.	Name.	Total Population. No.	Total Population. Distribution of 10,000 persons.	Males. No.	Males. Distribution of 10,000. Total.	Males. Distribution of 10,000. 5—14	Females. No.	Females. Distribution of 10,000.	Adult females per 100 adult males.	Distribution of 10,000 persons living in towns.	Percentage of employed who live in towns.
1	2	3	4	5	6	7	8	9	10	11	12	13
XIII.—METALS AND PRECIOUS STONES.	43	Gold, silver, and precious stones	60,523	56	32,421	60	52	28,102	52	84	217	26·6
	44	Brass, copper and bell-metal	17,961	17	9,660	18	17	8,301	16	85	73	30·2
	45	Tin, zinc, mercury, and lead	1,337	1	721	2	1	616	1	83	13	70·3
	46	Iron and steel	89,271	83	48,738	90	87	40,533	75	78	67	5·6
		Total Order XIII.—Metals and Precious Stones	**169,092**	**157**	**91,540**	**170**	**157**	**77,552**	**144**	**81**	**370**	**16·2**
XIV.—GLASS POTTERY, AND STONEWARE.	47	Glass and chinaware	141	...	89	...	...	52	...	52	1	63·1
	48	Earthen and stoneware	59,889	56	30,081	56	54	29,808	55	98	64	7·9
		Total Order XIV.—Glass Pottery and Stoneware	**60,030**	**56**	**30,170**	**56**	**54**	**29,860**	**55**	**98**	**65**	**8·0**
XV.—WOOD, CANE, AND LEAVES.	49	Timber and wood	66,068	61	38,829	72	61	27,239	51	61	137	15·3
	50	Cane-work, matting, and leaves, etc.	79,283	74	37,195	69	72	42,088	78	121	91	8·5
		Total Order XV.—Wood, Cane, and Leaves, etc.	**145,351**	**135**	**76,024**	**141**	**133**	**69,327**	**129**	**89**	**228**	**11·6**
XVI.—DRUGS, GUMS, DYES, ETC.	51	Gums, wax, and similar forest produce	7,554	7	3,694	7	7	3,860	7	109	9	8·5
	52	Drugs, dyes, pigments, etc.	4,620	4	2,405	4	4	2,215	4	98	22	35·5
		Total Order XVI.—Drugs, Gums, Dyes, etc.	**12,174**	**11**	**6,099**	**11**	**11**	**6,075**	**11**	**104**	**31**	**18·8**

Occupation Statistics—Class D—concluded.

Order.	Sub-order or group.	Name.	Total Population. No.	Total Population. Distribution of 10,000 persons.	Males. No.	Males. Distribution of 10,000. Total.	Males. Distribution of 10,000. 5—14	Females. No.	Females. Distribution of 10,000.	Adult females per 100 adult males.	Distribution of 10,000 persons living in towns.	Percentage of employed who live in towns.
1	2	3	4	5	6	7	8	9	10	11	12	13
XVII.—LEATHER, HORNS, BONES, ETC.	53	Leather, etc.	147,427	*137*	82,029	*152*	160	65,398	*121*	74	155	7·8
		Total Order XVII.—Leather, horns, bones, etc.	**147,427**	**137**	**82,029**	**152**	**160**	**65,398**	**121**	**74**	**155**	**7·8**
Total Class D.—Preparation and supply of material substances			**2,017,982**	**1,870**	**978,980**	**1,814**	**1,783**	**1,039,052**	**1,929**	**110**	**4,546**	**16·7**
PARTICULAR OCCUPATIONS.		72. Fishermen	99,250	*92*	61,881	*115*	115	37,369	*69*	51	81	6·0
		73. Fish-dealers	15,385	*14*	4,445	*8*	8	10,940	*20*	257	24	11·3
		74. Grain-dealers	45,996	*43*	24,458	*45*	39	21,538	*40*	88	160	25·6
		75. Grain-parchers	35,749	*33*	8,878	*16*	19	26,871	*50*	400	40	8·2
		76. Pulse-preparers	38,616	*36*	9,620	*18*	19	28,996	*54*	421	183	35·1
		103. Oil-pressers	89,705	*83*	40,867	*76*	76	48,838	*91*	120	153	12·6
		109. Firewood gatherers	105,686	*98*	33,304	*62*	70	72,382	*134*	275	169	11·8
		186. Cotton-ginners	4,438	*4*	1,086	*2*	2	3,352	*6*	404	31	51·6
		187. Cotton-cleaners	21,144	*20*	11,190	*21*	19	9,954	*18*	87	34	12·0
		190. Cotton-spinners	144,615	*134*	32,400	*60*	76	112,215	*208*	516	111	5·7
		191. Cotton-weavers	419,724	*389*	239,563	*444*	407	180,161	*334*	68	978	17·2
		214. Goldsmiths	54,777	*51*	29,350	*54*	47	25,427	*47*	84	168	22·7
		228. Blacksmiths	84,112	*78*	45,978	*85*	82	38,134	*71*	78	60	5·3
		236. Potters	58,026	*54*	29,117	*54*	53	28,909	*54*	98	62	7·9
		242. Carpenters	59,115	*55*	34,383	*64*	55	24,732	*46*	64	106	13·3
		265-268. Leather-workers	145,344	*135*	80,866	*150*	158	64,478	*120*	74	148	7·6

VII.—Food and Drink.—442,263, or 4·1 per cent. of the population, are shown as employed in the preparation and supply of food and drink. They are arranged according as they deal in animal or vegetable food, or in drinks, condiments and narcotics.

(17) *Animal Food.*—The purveyors of animal food number 160,802, of whom 24 per cent. are connected with the supply of milk, butter, and ghee, 71·3 per cent. with the supply of fish, while the remainder, 4·7 per cent., are butchers or fowl-dealers. In the first class of occupation a very high proportion of females is employed; there are 215 to every 100 males. Of the persons engaged in the supply of fish, 99,250 are returned as catching and curing fish, while 15,385 are shown as dealers; in the former men take most part, in the latter women are generally employed, the proportion of females to 100 males being 51 in the one, and 257 in the other. Among the fishing castes there are many persons who work also as boatmen, as water-carriers, as grain-parchers and as water-nut growers. Grain parching is specially the occupation of the female members of the fisherman's family; it is returned of only 8,878 males, but the number of females of whom it is recorded, amounts to 25,871, the greater portion of whom belong to the Kewat, Dhimar, and other fishing castes. The purveying of flesh is necessarily an occupation which is not much followed in this country; of the persons engaged in it 66·9 per cent. live in towns.

(18) *Vegetable Food.*—This sub-order numbers 162,346 persons, or 1·51 of the total population; 74·6 per cent. of these are connected with trade in grain and pulses, 21·2 deal in vegetables and fruits, and 4·2 are confectioners or public cooks. Grain-dealers number 45,996, and include all from grain-lenders who are in a large way of business down to the petty shop-keeper. The latter has, however, more commonly come under the heading "flour and pulse preparers and sellers," who number 38,616. The grinding of flour is in this country generally a household duty of the women of the family, and it is improbable that the high proportion of females shown under the occupation at the Census perform this work for wages; they outnumber the males by 421 to 100.

285. (19) *Drinks, Condiments, and Narcotics.*—The three heads which this sub-order includes are distributed as follows: 21,890 persons, or 18·4 per cent. of the total, prepare or deal in drink, 85,342, or 71·6 in condiments, sugar, salt, etc., 11,883, or 10·0 in narcotics, tobacco, opium, etc. Country spirits distillers and sellers, 20,152, are in a very distinct minority in the northern districts of Saugor, Damoh, and in the Nerbada valley; in Saugor there are only 204 persons dependent on the occupation, in Damoh 138, and in Narsinghpur 188. In the Satpura districts, where there is a large aboriginal population, their numbers at once rise; in Seoni there are 755, in Chhindwara 758, and in Betul 1,054, Balaghat returns 1,551, and in the Maratha country proper they are also in force, especially in Chanda, where they number 4,080. In Chhatisgarh the people are, it would seem, more temperate, as in the eastern districts liquor-vendors fall off in number; this may be perhaps attributed to the presence of the Kabirpanthis and Satnamis, who include such a large proportion of the lower castes of these districts and who are generally believed to be abstainers. Of the 1,615 toddy-drawers and sellers returned at the Census, 1,503 are found in Wardha, Nagpur, and Chanda, the former district returning the greater portion of them, 954.

The sugarcane cultivators invariably carry on the process of molasses-making in these Provinces, so that of the 3,097 persons returned as makers and sellers of the commodity, probably nearly all are dealers. Betul, from which *gúr* is an important article of export, returns 711 persons under this occupation, the highest of any district in the Province. Salt sellers number 6,680, of whom 3,798 are found in the three eastern districts of Raipur, Bilaspur, and Sambalpur. This side of the Province used formerly to be supplied with salt brought from

Cuttack by Banjara carriers, but with the opening of the railway the trade has of late tended to fall into the hands of the Kachhi merchants from Bombay, who have a monopoly of the import in most other parts. Next come grocers, or sellers of *kiráña*, 26,649; they are for the most part petty dealers in sugar, spices, and other condiments. Besides these, there are a large number of persons who were returned at the Census as dealing in two or more miscellaneous commodities, one or other of which should properly have come under different headings in the scheme of classification adopted. Such are dealers in *gûr* and tobacco, dealers in *gûr* and cloth, dealers in grain and salt; all have been, for the sake of convenience, classed together and are shown in the present sub-order. They amount to 35,540, of whom somewhat more than half are females, indicating that a considerable proportion of their number are merely petty vendors. Betel leaf and areca nut sellers number 11,591; they are very sparsely represented in Chhatisgarh. Of tobacco and snuff preparers and dealers, 10,803, considerably more than half, 6,387, are found in the districts of the Nagpur division.

286. VIII. **Light, firing, and forage.** (20) *Lighting.*—Oil-pressers and sellers, 89,705, form almost the entire bulk of the persons included in this sub-order. Women are employed more than men, presumably in retailing oil.

(21). *Fuel and forage.*—Of 125,487 persons listed under this head, the greater number, 105,686, are shown as firewood and grass gatherers and sellers. They are ordinary labourers who collect head-loads of grass and sticks for sale; the occupation is largely followed by the women of the poorer classes—females out-numbering males by 275 to 100. Grass-cutters engaged on wages are also included. Separate places have been assigned to persons who are contractors and dealers in firewood, 3,622, and in hay, 5,427, but from the indefiniteness of the entries in the schedules, the distinction was difficult to observe; in both females largely outnumber males, so that it is probable that most of the persons entered under these occupations are only head-load retailers. Charcoal-burning, returned as the occupation of 2,505 persons, is followed chiefly in the Jubbulpore and Saugor districts. 3,659 persons are returned as dependent on the coal-mining industry, of whom 3,080 are connected with the mines at Warora, and 546 with those belonging to the Nerbada Coal and Iron Company at Mohpani in the Narsinghpur district. A few other persons were shown in other districts as coal-miners; they are presumably persons temporarily absent from their work, or by mistake include persons employed on the railway lines as coal-labourers. The entry of coal-miners does not include enginemen and mechanics employed about mines, all of whom have been classed under the head of mechanics (171).

287. IX. **Buildings.** (22) *Building materials.*—Brick and tile burning is followed by 12,796 persons, and is frequently carried on in conjunction with potter's work, under which the greater part of the Kumhárs have been returned.

(23) *Artificers in building* are chiefly masons, 12,300, and mud-wall builders, 10,112; the latter a very doubtful entry, as it was almost impossible to say what the expression "*matti-ka-kám*" signified whether it stood for mud-wall building or simply for doing earth-work. It has been taken as the former. The mason builds with bricks, burnt or unburnt, and is according to the district distribution table more common in the northern than in the southern districts, where his place is taken by the mud-wall builder, almost half of whom are found in the districts of Wardha and Nagpur. 62·6 per cent. of the persons entered as masons are recorded as living in towns.

288. X. **Vehicles and vessels.** (25) *Carts and carriages.*—Palkis, of which eleven makers are returned, are out of fashion in these Provinces. They are recorded only from Mandla and Sambalpur, where difficulties of communication make it necessary to use doolies, especially in the rainy season.

289. XI. **Supplementary requirements.**—Under this head are included rather a miscellaneous assortment of arts, the chief of which is the manufacture of trinkets, necklaces, beads, etc.

(27) *Paper.*—Damoh is the only district where paper is made to any appeciable extent in the Central Provinces. The Settlement report of the district (1867) states that large quantities of superior native paper are manufactured at Panchamnagar on the Bias river and exported to the valley of the Nerbada, where no paper is manufuctured, the consumption being principally of inferior paper of European manufacture imported from Bombay; at the present time the persons employed in the industry number 184. There are also a few people, 28, in Nimar, who make paper; elsewhere the persons who are shown as paper makers and sellers belong to the latter category, and should have properly come under stationers, the next occupation entered in the Table.

(28). *Books and Prints.*—Under this heading 1,615 persons are returned, nearly all of whom live in towns, the chief exception being 94 persons recorded from Raipur, who are employed at the Bisrampur Mission Press in that district. The greatest number of printers is found in Nagpur, which returns 822 persons so employed.

(32) *Music and Musical Instruments.*—Drum and horn-makers, 1,573, are returned almost solely from the three Eastern districts, Sambalpur alone showing 1,037. These people are generally Ghasias. Elsewhere drums are fashioned by Basors, who do bamboo work as well.

290. (33). *Necklaces, Bracelets, Beads, etc.*—The distinction was kept between the makers of bangles, etc., in lac, in wood and bone, and in glass, but the record has not been always sufficiently definite to give precise returns under these heads; hence a preponderance of persons shown under makers of such ornaments without specification of material. The bangles ordinarily worn are made of lac or glass, there being 3,347 makers of bangles in the former material and 2,928 in the latter. Bangles in bone and wood are not much in use in these Provinces, but a few makers of them are shown in the Maratha country and in Chhatisgarh; among them have been listed bangle painters, of whom there were some returned at the Census, as the bangles painted are bone ones. 13,967 persons are shown as makers of ornaments, which include bangles, armlets, toe-rings, etc., without the substance in which they work being indicated. Imitation and pewter jewellery is made by 7,036 people; the lower classes generally adorn their persons with these ornaments. The figures shown under this and the preceding occupation, representing workers for such a large class of the population, seem disproportionate when compared with those for goldsmiths, 54,777, who work for a smaller class, the explanation being that workers in brass, copper and bell-metal, sub-order 44, also make pewter jewellery. As the rather indefinite entry "*zewar banáná*" has been classed under the occupation goldsmith, it is also probable that the latter class contains a certain number of the people who work in materials other than silver and gold. Next come dealers in beads, 6,407, who include the persons whose occupation has been shown as *manihári*; these generally sell glass beads, but they also deal in miscellaneous articles of hardware.

(35).—*Harness.*—The making and repairing of country saddles is returned of 751 persons; it is chiefly the occupation of the Jingar caste. Only 8 people have been recorded as making saddle cloths, others having probably been included amongst saddlers. Narsinghpur is noted for its saddle cloths.

(36). *Tools and Machinery.*—Under this head are entered 194 persons who make knives, axes, etc., 369 knife and tool grinders—*sikalgars*,—1,070 loom and loom-comb makers, and 838 mechanics who are not connected with the railway.

Half the loom and loom-comb makers are found in the districts of Nagpur and Bhandara, the former, which is a centre of the country weaving industry, returning 415. 295 mechanics in the Chanda district are nearly all blacksmiths, enginemen, etc., connected with the Warora Colliery. In other places the people for whom the occupation is returned are generally mill-wrights employed in cotton factories and ginning presses.

(37) *Arms and Ammunition.*—97 persons are shown as making and mending guns, of whom 22 occur in Saugor and 30 in Narsinghpur. Jubbulpore, in which is situated the village of Katangi, which in former times used to be famed for the manufacture of gun barrels, returns only 8 persons thus employed. Gunpowder and fireworks makers and sellers have been shown separate, but as a rule both commodities are sold by one and the same person; the persons dealing in them number 1,203.

291. **XII.—Textile Fabrics and Dress.**—This is a very numerous order, including 726,644 persons, or 6·74 of the total population of the Province. It is sub-divided into (1) persons working in wool, (2) persons working in silk, (3) persons working in cotton, (4) persons working in flax, etc., and (5) persons engaged in making and selling clothes and piece-goods. Workers in cotton greatly predominate; they number 617,168, or 5·72 per cent. of the inhabitants of the Province.

(38) *Wool and Fur.*—The blanket weavers and sellers, 17,581, are, as has already been noticed, generally shepherds, who make coarse black blankets from the wool they get from their flocks. The spinning of the yarn is chiefly the occupation of their women, of whom 2,432 are thus employed against 166 men. The pursuit is one which appertains almost wholly to the country. 49 carpet-weavers are found in the towns of Nagpur and Jubbulpore, and 2 are returned from Seoni. The 18 shawl sellers are Kabulis who go about hawking dried fruits and shawls. It is worthy of note that no occupations under the heading wool are returned from the Balaghat and Sambalpur districts; in both also the number of shepherds is small. The chief wool-producing tracts in the Province are the districts of Chanda and Raipur.

292. (39) *Silk.*—9,278 persons are entered in this sub-order, but as in these Provinces few people work exclusively in silk, there can hardly be a doubt that the return is not precise. The gathering and rearing of tassar cocoons, which is an important industry, specially in the eastern districts of Bilaspur and Sambalpur, is represented by only 96 persons, of whom 30 are from Bilaspur and 12 from Sambalpur. The explanation may be that at the time of the Census the collecting and rearing season being past, the persons who follow this occupation were then employed on other work.*

Silk carders and spinners number 3,641 and weavers and dealers 5,387. The industry is practically limited, according to the Census returns, to Nimar, Nagpur, Bhandara, and Chanda; while in Raipur, Bilaspur, and Sambalpur silk-weavers are found, but not to the extent which the prevalence of the trade, especially in the two latter districts, would demand. The reason given is that the weavers of tassar silk do not confine themselves to the weaving of tassar alone, but also work in cotton, the latter giving them employment for the chief part of the year. In the Maratha districts the preparation of silk thread is carried on principally in Bhandara, where tassar culture is followed by the Dhimar and other castes. Silk-weaving in all the three districts is for the most part confined to the manufacture of the fine borders, which are a distinctive feature of the cloths for which Umrer and Nagpur more particularly are famous. The silk used is imported. The weavers number 3,323 in Nagpur, 639 in Chanda, and 294 in Bhandara; but from the body of the cloths they make being cotton, it is probable that the

* Cf. Bilaspur Settlement Report, page 78.

return is in many cases confused with persons who work only in the latter material. Silk spinners and weavers number 184 in Burhanpur and its neighbourhood: here silk is employed in conjunction with gold wire to make up the fine embroideries which are still, though to a limited extent, manufactured in the city. Of the persons returned, the greater portion, 113, are shown as spinners of silk, but this is misleading, as the silk is nearly always imported spun; 22 sellers of the imported article have come under this head, while most of the others are persons employed in plaiting the thread with wire (*batna*). The weaving entry is evidently incomplete. Silk dyeing is followed by 154 people, nearly all of whom are found in the principal silk-weaving districts. It remains to add that among silk-weavers a very high proportion of women has been returned; they number 238 to 100 men: the latter do the weaving, so that the excess of females is difficult to understand, unless, as from the schedule entries would appear to be the case, the women are specially engaged in unwinding (*kholna*) and preparing the thread, while the men have come amongst general weavers from working in both silk and cotton.

293. (40) *Cotton.*—In this sub-order have come, without distinction, all cotton spinners and weavers of country cloth, as well as the mill hands engaged in both of these branches. So also ginners and pressers, 4,438, include persons employed in cotton presses and ginning factories. Cotton ginning is usually done by females, who are to males engaged in the occupation as 404 to 100. When ginned the cotton is ready for the press, if intended for export, or for carding, if intended for home consumption. The carding removes any stains or dirt which would otherwise interfere with the spinning or appear in the material when made up. Cotton carders or cleaners are as a rule Bahnas and Pinjáras, who also fill quilts, cushions and clothes, in the districts where cotton-stuffed garments are used. Carding demands more strength than ginning, and is usually more of a man's occupation; according to the Census, for every 100 grown-up men employed in cleaning cotton there are only 87 women. Dealing in cotton, whether as gathered, *kapás*, or ginned, *rui*, is returned of 5,518 persons; dealers in cotton-seeds, which are used for fodder or oil, have come under order VIII, to which they properly belong. During the year 1890-91, 276,703 maunds of cotton, valued at R41,50,545, were exported from the Province, of which more than half was consigned to Bombay. The remainder was shared by places in the Bombay Presidency, in the North-West Provinces, and in the Berars in the proportion of 8, 2, and 1.

Next comes spinning, which is, like ginning, essentially a feminine occupation, the proportion of adults engaged in it being 516 females to 100 males. The number of cotton spinners is 144,615. In weaving both sexes are employed, the preliminary part, unwinding the yarn and getting it ready for the loom, being chiefly the duty of the women; 8,031 women were returned under the term *sut ukalná*, or preparing the warp, against 1,668 men, the proportional figures for adults being 721 females to 100 males. In actual weaving there are 237,895 males employed as compared with 172,130 females; here the latter are in a minority in the proportion of 64 to 100. Combining the figures for the two processes, we find that 419,724 people are connected with the cotton-weaving industry. The occupations of cotton weaving and spinning are ones in which very many castes are engaged; the chief are the exclusively weaving classes, the Koshtis, Sális, Koris, etc.; but the making of coarse cloth is also very extensively carried on by members of the depressed castes, such as the Mahárs, Dheds, Gándas, and Pankas.

294. At the time of the Census there were three cotton mills at work in the Province, particulars of which, as taken from the Administration Report for 1890-91, are given in the margin. At the enumeration 321 persons have been returned as being employed on the managing or clerical establishments of mills, and 2,117 are shown as factory hands unspecified. In every case, when the process in which the mill hand was employed was definitely stated, he was classed accordingly as mechanic, spinner, weaver, etc. At the last Census there was only one mill working in the Province, *viz.*, that at Nagpur; there are now factories at work at Hinganghat in the Wardha district (established 1881) and at Jubbulpore (1885). Three more mills are under construction, or have been opened since the Census took place—one at Nagpur, another at Pulgaon in the Wardha district, and a third at Raj Nandgaon in Chhatisgarh.

Statistics of spinning and weaving factories.

PLACE, ETC.	Number of looms.	Number of spindles.	Amount of cotton worked up during year.	Description of goods.	Average number of persons employed.
			Cwt.		
Nagpur—The Empress Mills.	700	42,232	74,626	Twist and piece-goods.	2,872
Hinganghat .	...	18,248	23,719	Yarn .	835
Jubbulpore—The Gokaldas Balabhdas Mills.	105	11,600	11,025	Yarn of low counts and coarse cloth.	495

Cotton printers number 2,572 and dyers 15,444; in both the sexes are equally employed. Makers of cotton tape and of rope number 885 and 172. Tents and carpets are made by 40 and 178 persons respectively; the former are manufactured only in Jubbulpore, where the occupation has been entered for inmates of the School of Industry. Cotton durries are made in several places, but their manufacture has been returned in greatest strength from Nagpur, where 148 persons are thus employed, some of them in the Empress Mills.

The distribution of persons engaged in the cotton industry scarcely calls for remark, beyond the fact that they are necessarily most numerous in the cotton producing districts, and least so in places like Mandla and Chhatisgarh, where no cotton is grown.

295. (41) *Flax, Coir, etc.*—2,131 persons are returned as flax spinners, weavers, and sellers; all are spinners or sellers of the raw material, the only weaving done in these Provinces being sacking and gunny making, which is separately entered against 3,790 persons. 3,744 hemp rope makers are returned and 416 makers of nets. In the latter are included net bags, which are used for the transport of raw cotton, and are made principally in Wardha, 318 persons, and in Nagpur, 82. The chief flax and hemp working castes are the Bhámtas, Kumráwats, Lorhas, Banjáras, etc., and the industry seems to be most largely followed in the districts of the Nerbada valley and in Chanda and Nagpur.

296. (42) *Dress.*—This sub-order comprises 69,685 persons, of whom the most important are tailors, 42,921, and piece-goods dealers, 25,384. Hosiers and haberdashers seem rather a strange find in the Central Provinces; under these terms have been included sellers of ribbons, scarves, etc., when separately returned.

Eight hundred fifty-eight people have given their occupation as making embroideries, lace, and muslin; of 610 adults thus engaged, 483 are females. Gold lace embroidery is made in Burhanpur, where 196 people have been shown as employed in its manufacture; of these the greater number are makers of borders in which the gold-plated silver thread made in the town is worked up along with silk. Many of the weavers of the finer fabrics of Burhanpur are classed among silk-workers or ordinary weavers, as the entries in the Census schedules were not usually explicit enough to provide for their separate classification. *Kashida*, embroidered needle-work, is the principal item in the present occupation; it is done by women, and is returned more specially from Narsinghpur 42 persons,

Wardha 76, Nagpur 287, and Bhandara 80. 97 persons are returned from Chanda as engaged in the shoe embroidery, for which the town is noted; others are presumably listed under the general heading of shoe-making.

The entry of piece-goods dealers, 25,384, is probably fairly correct, as males number considerably more than females, being in the proportion of 100 to 76 for adults; it is therefore unlikely that the occupation includes the women of the weaver's household who occasionally sell the products of the family loom, and who should, according to the scheme of classification adopted, properly come under the heading weavers and sellers.

297. **XIII.—Metals and Precious Stones.**—(43) *Gold, Silver, and Precious Stones.*—Gold and silver dealers are shown as 951; the entry is not very explicit, and can hardly be distinguished from gold and silver workers, who number 54,777, the latter including all persons who work in the precious metals, as well as those for whom indefinite term, such as *sewar dágina banána* were recorded. The districts with the highest proportion of gold and silver workers are those of the Nerbada valley and of the Nagpur plain. Goldsmith's dust-washers, 1,210, probably include several persons who wash for gold in the sand of rivers. The latter, styled Sonjharas, number 139, of whom 36 are returned from Chanda, 57 from Bilaspur, and 36 from Sambalpur. Gold is found in the Ib and Mahanadi in the last of these districts and in the Jonk river in Bilaspur. In Bhandara gold-washing used to be carried on in the Wainganga and its tributaries, but the pursuit has not been specially recorded at the present Census. The family of a manager of a gold mine, enumerated in Kampti, represent the seven persons shown under this head in Nagpur. Two gold prospectors—the Census was taken before the Chhota Nagpur gold bubble had burst—had found their way into the Sambalpur district, where also were recorded the two persons entered as prospectors for diamonds. 76 people have returned themselves as employed in buying up and burning old silver lace for the purpose of obtaining the precious metal.

298. Gold and silver wire-drawing is recorded as the occupation of 2,646 persons, of whom all but 6 are found in Burhanpur or its neighbourhood. The following is a summary of the description given in the Central Provinces Gazetteer of the gold and silver thread work done in Burhanpur.

"The silver after testing is cast into the shape of a square ingot, *pásá*, weighing from 32 to 60 tolas and measuring about 2 feet long and 1¼ inches square. These silver bars are covered with a thin gold leaf, the amount allotted to each *pásá* being from ½ to 6 per cent. on the amount of the silver. The adhesion appears to be effected purely by mechanical skill on the part of the workmen called *pásá-tániás*. It is then passed by the same workmen through a series of holes in steel plates of diminishing size by manual power, applied by means of a spoked wheel of the rudest construction. After passing through forty of these holes it is reduced to about the size of an ordinary soda-water wire. Thence it goes into the hands of another set of operatives called *tániás*, who still further reduce it through a gradation of 40 more holes, the last of which is as fine as a human hair. Their apparatus is of somewhat more delicate construction, but the work requires neither the same skill nor hard work as the first operation. The wire is drawn by them down to various degrees of fineness, according to the work for which it is destined. The round wire is given to the *chaprias*, who flatten it into an almost impalpable film by hammering between two polished steel surfaces—an operation requiring, it is said, superior skill. In this state it is termed *bádlá*, and is used for some few sorts of work. The greater part of it has, however, to be spun into a thread along with silk before being woven up. This is done by persons called *bitais*, who use no sort of apparatus for this purpose, except a couple of wooden spindles twirled by the hand. The beauty of the result obtained by such primitive implements must strike every one with amazement; the layer of gold on the finest wire must be of almost inconceivable thinness. The mixed thread is called *kalábatun*, which is woven into *kinkhábs* and other brilliant fabrics. The wire-workers were originally Pathans introduced from Upper India by the Emperor Akbar, but now all castes work at the trade.

"The cloth-weaving business of the city is quite distinct from the operation of drawing the wire and spinning the *kalábatun* thread above described. The chief fabrics still made in the city are *sari*, a very rich light stuff in which the flattened wire is interwoven with silk in the warp, with a thread woof, chiefly made up into scarves and sáris worn by females on wedding and other high occasions. *Selári* is half silk and half thread with brilliant edging and borders of silk and gold thread, mostly in the form of sáris and dopattas. *Pitámbar*, all silk with the same edging, is a better sort of the same. The gold thread is also much woven up with silks into rich borders and edgings, exported to be attached to the cloth manufactures of other places."

At the Census 19 persons were returned in Burhanpur as engaged in *chaprai* and 16 in making *kalábatun*; both have been rather incorrectly entered among embroiderers (No. 209). *Bitai* is returned of 15 people and *tanai* of 18. Of 2,356 persons who have been recorded in the town as engaged in wire-drawing, all, except these 33, are shown as doing *tárkashi* work; the term properly applies only to drawing, but is in general use as including all the processes connected with the manufacture of the thread. Outside the limits of the town itself the operation gives employment to 284 persons; they are said to be all *bitais*, that is spinners of the thread with silk, the more difficult processes of drawing and flattening being confined to the town. It has been seen that only 196 embroiderers and 188 workers in silk have been returned from the Nimar district; the figures are out of all proportion to the number of persons engaged in the gold wire-drawing industry. For this two reasons may be assigned,—first, that the *kalábatun* thread is very largely exported to other parts of India without being woven up; and, second, that makers of the fabrics in which the thread is employed are very generally shown under terms which can be classed only under the general head of cloth-weaving.

Dealers in pearls and precious stones number 298, while 334 persons have been recorded as selling coral and coral beads, the latter being the form in which coral is mainly dealt in in these parts.

299. (44). *Brass, Copper, and Bell-metal.*—An attempt was at first made to keep separate the workers in these substances, but with such unsatisfactory results that in the general table all have been listed together. Most of the 17,691 persons returned in the sub-order are makers and sellers of pots of these metals; a few were also returned as image-casters and brass measure-makers. Persons who gave their occupation as the manufacturers of pewter ornament shave come in a different sub-order, No. 33.

300. (46) *Iron and Steel.*—Iron smelting is given as the occupation of 3,070 people, the principal districts from which it is returned being Mandla, 323, Narsinghpur, 359, Chanda, 586, Bhandara, 332, Bilaspur, 270, and Sambalpur, 296. Iron ores exist in nearly every part of the Province, but now that the imported article can be so readily obtained, smelting is carried on to a very limited extent. The castes usually employed in the operation are the Kondars in Saugor and Damoh, and the Agarias and sometimes the Gonds elsewhere.

Blacksmiths number 84,112; they include makers of agricultural implements that are made of iron. In the smaller villages it frequently happens that the same person is both blacksmith and carpenter; 734 people thus returned have been shown under Complex occupations, Order XXII. From the caste table we learn that 4,747 persons were returned as Lohár-barhai under the main caste Barhai, while 4,608 were similarly shown as Barhai-Kháti under the caste Lohár, but the combination of the occupations is probably more common than even these figures indicate. In the blacksmiths' profession adult males outnumber females in the proportion of 100 to 78; the latter have sometimes been recorded as bellows-blowers and classed under the general occupation. Dealers in articles of hardware number 2,072, of whom only one-fourth are found in towns; the entry in all likelihood includes several persons who are really blacksmiths.

301. **XIV.—Glass, Pottery, and Stoneware.** (47) *Glass, etc.*—Only 141 persons are returned as working or dealing in glass, the main use to which the latter is put being the manufacture of glass bangles which has been shewn in sub-order 33; probably every one of the people recorded under the present heading as glass-blowers, etc., are bangle makers or sellers. We may except Nimar, where in the town of Burhanpur the manufacture is carried on of large glass globes locally known as *sischur*, which are silvered inside with lead and then broken up for purposes of ornamentation. 7 persons are shown in Table XVII-B as thus employed, but 7 others have been wrongly tabulated in sub-order 33, the similarity of the name to the common term for glass bangles having given rise to the error. 5 persons returned their occupation as dealing in *dheba*, a silicate imported chiefly from Mirzapur for glass manufacture.

(48) *Earthen and Stone Ware.*—Potters number 58,026, amongst whom the sexes are about equally divided. 1,678 persons make and mend grindstones. Soapstone is found and worked in more than one place in the Province—Chanda, Jubbulpore, etc.—but no return has been made at the Census of persons specially employed in working it, though it is likely that some of the people, 149, shewn as making pestles, etc., also fashion cups out of soapstone.

302. **XV.—Wood, Cane, Leaves, etc.** (49) *Timber and Wood.*—Chief among this class come carpenters, 59,115. Their women follow other occupations to a considerable extent, there being only 64 adult females per 100 males. The most noticeable feature about the return of carpenters is their comparative absence from the districts of Mandla, where only 220 persons follow the occupation, Balaghat, 802, Raipur, 890, Bilaspur, 471, and Sambalpur, 272. In the Settlement Report (1868) of Bilaspur, page 161, is given a list of the village servants as found in Chhatisgarh; the list, while including the blacksmith, makes no mention of the carpenter. Regarding this the writer remarks that in the matter of carpentering, the implements used are of so rough a kind that the cultivators generally prepare their own, or if pushed make for the nearest town. The same observation is made at page 50 of the Raipur Settlement Report. There is, on the other hand, no want of blacksmiths in these districts; in Raipur alone there are 12,782 persons dependent on the trade, so that the general repair of agricultural implements, when not done by the cultivators themselves, would appear to devolve upon the blacksmith. Turning to the Caste Table we find the Barhai or carpenter caste similarly unrepresented in the districts indicated; the caste numbers in Mandla 323, in Balaghat 301, in Raipur 157, in Bilaspur 244, and in Sambalpur 328. Timber and bamboo agents number 2,464; as a rule only persons shown as dealing in building timber or bamboos have been brought under this head, other wood sellers being shown in sub-order 21. 4,417 people gave their occupation as wood or bamboo cutting.

(50) *Cane Matting, and Leaves.*—This includes workers in bamboos 11,550, basket-weavers 52,320, mat (tatti) makers 6,453, leaf-plate makers 4,169, broom-makers 2,281, brush and comb makers 2,055, and a few others. Leaf-plates and brooms are largely made by females, the proportion of women to 100 men being 855 in the one and 301 in the other. The former occupation is frequently carried on in the barber's family.

303. **XVI.—Drugs, Gums, and Dyes.** (51) *Gums and Forest Produce.*—Collectors and sellers of forest produce number 7,554, but these figures hardly indicate the extent to which the gathering of jungle products is at certain seasons engaged in by members of the forest tribes, who have been returned under the other occupations which they generally follow. Gum collecting and selling is returned of 512 persons, of whom no less than 503 are found in the Saugor district. Catechu, made from the pith of the khair tree, is prepared by 1,098

persons, chiefly found in Saugor 169, Damoh 224, Jubbulpore 129, and Chhindwara 340. Lac-gatherers number 3,675 persons; from the Raipur district 2,194 are returned, of whom about three-fourths occur in the Raipur tehsil and one-fourth in Dhamtari. Large quantities of lac are found in all the districts of the Province, but more particularly in the eastern parts; a considerable amount is consumed locally for the manufacture of bracelets and other articles, but most districts also export to a greater or less extent. In 1890-91, 38,954 maunds of stick lac, value R7,01,172, was exported from the Province; the quantity is almost half what it was two years before, since when the export has declined. The incrustation is collected about the commencement of the cold season by the jungle tribes, who make it over to Lakheras if for home consumption, or to the export agencies which are established at various parts. Wax, honey, and minor forest products are gathered and sold by 2,227 persons. The entry includes a few people who collect or deal in myrabolams (*harra*), the export of which amounted in 1890-91 to 244,938 maunds, value R7,04,197, nearly 100,000 maunds less than it had been in the previous year. The collecting season is the hot weather, so that the occupation scarcely existed at the time of the enumeration.

(52) *Drugs, Dyes, etc.*—1,438 persons are shown as druggists and chemists; almost all are merely sellers of medicinal herbs and roots. Indigo workers and sellers number 241, of whom 190 occur in the cloth-weaving districts of Nagpur and Bhandara. Madder (*ál* or *ánchi*) and safflower workers are returned as 281, of whom 70 are found in Damoh, 66 in Nagpur, and 89 in Bhandara; the growers of the *ál* plant have been separately shown under sub-order 12. The introduction of European dyes has made madder of less value than it formerly was, and it is now used to a much more limited extent.

304. **XVII.—Leather, Horns, etc.**—The first four entries, tanners and curriers, shoemakers, general workers in leather, and leather bucket makers, can hardly be distinguished, the tanning and currying being usually done by persons who also make shoes or other articles. The combined strength of the three occupations is 145,344, amongst whom males predominate, there being 74 females to 100 males. The northern districts of Saugor, Damoh, Jubbulpore, Narsinghpur, and Hoshangabad show the greatest expenditure of leather; in the three former the number of shoemakers, etc., approaches 20,000, in Saugor 23,000, and in the two latter considerably exceeds 10,000. Elsewhere leather-workers fall below this number. 85 preparers of catgut are returned; they were frequently shown as combining the occupation with the making of brooms, but all have been shown in the present sub-order.

CLASS E.—COMMERCE, TRANSPORT, AND STORAGE.

305. The class has been sub-divided to show (1) persons who are engaged in commercial pursuits, and (2) persons who are connected with the transport of passengers, goods and messages, and with the storage of goods. It has already been seen that, according to the system of classification adopted, all persons engaged in the distribution of special goods have been shown along with persons employed in their manufacture. The commercial class, according to the Census Tables, is therefore limited to persons engaged in money-lending or general merchandise and to middlemen; it excludes dealers in grain, cloth, cotton, and other commodities, whose affinities lie rather with the commercial than the industrial class. As thus restricted the commercial community numbers 112,006, or 1·05 per cent. of the total population, while persons engaged in transport and storage amount to 85,688, or 0·79 per cent. of the population.

Occupation Statistics.—Class E.

Order.	Sub-order or group.	Name.	Total Population. No.	Total Population. Distribution of 10,000 persons.	Males. No.	Males. Distribution of 10,000. Total.	Males. Distribution of 10,000. 5—14.	Females. No.	Females. Distribution of 10,000.	Adult females per 100 adult males.	Distribution of 10,000 persons living in towns.	Percentage of employed who live in towns.
1	2	3	4	5	6	7	8	9	10	11	12	13
XVIII.—COMMERCE.	54	Dealers in money and securities . . .	46,392	*43*	23,791	*44*	39	22,601	*42*	97	209	33·3
	55	General merchandise .	972	*1*	597	*1*	1	375	...	58	3	20·1
	56	Dealing unspecified .	41,661	*39*	25,124	*47*	32	16,537	*31*	58	222	39·3
	57 (a)	Brokers, etc. . . .	11,179	*11*	6,168	*11*	8	5,011	*9*	76	94	61·8
	57 (b)	Contractors and farmers .	11,802	*11*	6,591	*12*	10	5,211	*10*	72	40	25·2
		Total Sub-order 57.—Middlemen, etc. .	**22,981**	**22**	**12,759**	**23**	**18**	**10,222**	**19**	**74**	**134**	**43·0**
		Total Order XVIII.—Commerce . .	**112,006**	**105**	**62,271**	**115**	**90**	**49,785**	**92**	**75**	**568**	**87·4**
XIX.—TRANSPORT AND STORAGE.	58 (a)	Administration, Railway	2,574	*2*	1,446	3	2	1,128	*2*	77	30	86·2
	58 (b)	Working staff, Railway .	14,236	*13*	8,548	*16*	10	5,688	*11*	55	99	51·4
		Total Sub-order 58.—Railway . . .	**16,810**	**15**	**9,994**	**19**	**12**	**6,816**	**13**	**58**	**129**	**56·7**
	59 (a)	Cart, carriage, and tramway owners and drivers	18,496	*17*	11,867	*22*	15	6,629	*12*	45	131	52·5
	59 (b)	Carriers by pack-animals	21,483	*20*	12,274	*23*	19	9,209	*17*	70	13	4·5
		Total Sub-order 59.—Road . . .	**39,979**	**37**	**24,141**	**45**	**34**	**15,838**	**29**	**58**	**144**	**26·7**
	60	Water	1,944	*2*	1,114	*2*	2	830	*2*	74	3	9·9
	61 (a)	Post, etc. . . .	9,784	*9*	5,686	*10*	8	4,098	*7*	64	51	38·4
	61 (b)	Telegraph and telephone	823	*1*	441	*1*	...	382	*1*	68	9	82·5
		Total Sub-order 61.—Messages . . .	**10,607**	**10**	**6,127**	**11**	**8**	**4,480**	**8**	**64**	**60**	**41·8**
	62	Storage and weighing .	16,348	*15*	8,858	*16*	12	7,490	*14*	77	148	66·8
		Total Order XIX.—Transport and Storage	**85,688**	**79**	**50,234**	**93**	**68**	**35,454**	**66**	**62**	**484**	**41·8**
Total Class E.—Commerce, Transport, and Storage . . .			**197,694**	**184**	**112,505**	**208**	**158**	**85,189**	**158**	**69**	**1,052**	**39·8**

306. **XVIII.—Commerce.** (54) *Dealers in Money and Securities.*—32,685 persons have returned their occupation as money-lending; amongst them have been included all native bankers or saucars. Grain-lending is perhaps the most common form of usury in the country; when separately shewn—it was thus recorded of 1,472 persons—the entry has been put among grain merchants in sub-order 18, many of whom are probably lenders as well. Among money-lenders the sexes are about equally distributed. The districts in which they muster in most strength in proportion to the population are Saugor, where there are 66 per 10,000 of the population, Damoh 53, Narsinghpur 66, Nimar 86, Wardha 70, and Nagpur 65. In Mandla, Seoni, Chhindwara, Balaghat, Raipur, and Bilaspur they number under 20 on the same proportion, the district where they are least in evidence being Mandla, where the average falls to 6. 11,630 persons are shown as saucars' munims, gumáshtas, clerks, etc., and 2,037 as money-changers (shroffs). It may be noted that while only 21·6 per cent. of money-lenders are found in towns, the proportion of the other two occupations recorded as urban rises to 59·1 and 71·5 per cent. respectively. In the country the money-lender generally dispenses with the services of a clerk, and any money-changing that is done devolves upon the ordinary shop-keeper.

(55) *General Merchandise.*—This, returned of 972 persons, was an entry of very indefinite application in the census books. As far as possible only those occupations have been brought in the sub-order which represent wholesale general dealing, but the large item of 422 persons in Chanda recorded as *bepáris* is a remnant which we failed to classify. From the scanty return of pack-bullock carriers from the district, it is probable these are really Banjaras.

(56) *Dealing unspecified.*—In the sub-order comes a very large class returned as shop-keepers' and money-lenders' servants. It contains 33,809 persons, for most of whom some vague term implying service in a shop or with a saucar was recorded; dunners, etc., are also included. The people employed on these duties are often up-country men, who are in many cases single; hence we may in part account for the small number of females dependent on the occupation, there being only 52 women to every 100 men. Shop-keeping unspecified has been returned of 5,052 persons, while 1,934 are shown as pedlars and hawkers. Of the latter by far the largest number is recorded from Sambalpur, 1,229, where there is a considerable class of traders who hawk cloth and brass and copper pots about the district.

(57) *Middlemen.*—The 6,711 persons entered in the table as agents include gumáshtas, ám-mukhtiars, and other general agents; while among brokers, 4,468, are shown brokers of grain, cattle, timber, etc., all except brokers of cotton, who have been classed with raw cotton exporters and dealers. Among contractors and farmers, 11,802, several distinctions have been kept, the most important being farmers of liquor, opium, etc. 4,268, farmers of tolls, ferries, etc. 562, and emigration agents 61. The latter are recorded from Jubbulpore, 7, and Sambalpur, 54.

307. **XIX.—Transport and Storage.** (58) *Railway.*—Railway servants and their dependents number 16,810, of whom 2,574 are connected with the administration of the different lines and 14,236 compose the working staff.

(59) *Road.*—Among the 15,096 persons recorded as carters and cart-drivers a very low proportion of females is noticeable, 43 adults per 100 males. Considering its population, Sambalpur returns a very scarce allowance of cartmen, only 173 being given for the whole district; in Bilaspur and some of the hill districts the use of carts would also appear to be rare. Of the 2,269 palki and dooly bearers returned at the Census, Raipur furnishes 1,269 and Bilaspur 697. From Sambalpur the occupation has not been given; the people who carry palkis in the Uria country are chiefly Betras, who are at the same time workers in bamboos, and have evidently been recorded as such. Regimental dooly-bearers have been entered amongst army followers.

Nineteen thousand seven hundred twenty-eight carriers by pack bullocks are recorded. Their distribution is worthy of note; in the four northern districts of Saugor, Damoh, Jubbulpore, and Mandla 11,877 are returned; in the Nerbada valley and Nimar there are only 905; in the three Satpura districts of Betul, Chhindwara, and Seoni they number 2,034; in the Maratha country 639, of whom 489 are from Balaghat; and in the two Chhatisgarh districts and Sambalpur their numbers amount to 4,273. Thus the chief parts of the Province where the trade can still be said to exist are, first, the northern districts between which and the Central India States there is a large traffic carried on by pack animals; and, second, Chhatisgarh and the Uria country, whence there are important Banjara routes, principally in the direction of Rewa and Chhota Nagpur and towards Cuttack and the East Coast. The recent opening of the Bengal-Nagpur Railway, of which a branch runs from Bilaspur through the Rewa State to Katni, will do much to reduce the carrying trade by pack bullocks in this part of the country. I may add that when carriers of salt, grain, etc., were represented as also selling these articles, they have been classed among dealers. The 1,290 carriers by pack horses and donkeys are nearly all from the northern districts of the Province. 465 camel drivers are mainly the persons who in the cold weather are employed to carry the tent equipage of Government officers on tour.

(61) *Messages.*—4,745 persons belong to the Postal and 823 to the Telegraph service. In the sub-order have also been included a miscellaneous list of messengers, peons, etc., who could not be classified otherwise; these number 5,039.

CLASS F.—PROFESSIONS.

308. In this class are shown (1) persons connected with the learned and artistic professions, Religion, Law, Science, etc., and (2) persons who are de-

Occupation Statistics.—Class F.

Order.	Sub-order or group.	Name.	Total population. No.	Distribution of 10,000 persons.	Males. No.	Distribution of 10,000. Total.	Distribution of 10,000. 5—14	Females. No.	Distribution of 10,000.	Adult females per 100 adult males.	Distribution of 10,000 persons living in towns.	Percentage of employed who live in towns.
1	2	3	4	5	6	7	8	9	10	11	12	13
XX.—Learned and Artistic Professions.	63 (a)	Priests, Ministers, etc.	19,942	19	11,322	21	17	8,620	16	70	60	22·1
	63 (b)	Subsidiary Religious services	49,141	46	27,080	50	42	22,061	41	80	136	20·5
		Total sub-order 63.—Religion	69,083	65	38,402	71	59	30,681	57	77	196	21·0
	64	Education	10,620	10	6,199	12	8	4,421	8	66	63	43·5
	65	Literature	3,417	3	1,878	3	2	1,539	3	77	27	58·8
	66	Law	4,422	4	2,322	4	4	2,100	4	93	50	83·6
	67 (a)	Practitioners	7,821	7	2,673	5	4	5,148	10	225	39	37·2
	67 (b)	Subsidiary Medical services	1,618	2	913	2	2	705	1	70	17	75·7
		Total sub-order 67.—Medicine	9,439	9	3,586	7	6	5,853	11	186	56	43·7
	68 (a)	Engineers, Architects, and Surveyors	165	...	99	...	...	66	...	63	2	86·7
	68 (b)	Subsidiary staff	5,274	5	3,961	8	3	1,313	3	24	26	36·0
		Total sub-order 68.—Engineering and Surveying	5,439	5	4,060	8	3	1 379	3	25	28	37·5
	69 (a)	Astronomy, etc.	6	...	4	...	...	2	...	...	...	...
	69 (b)	Minor Sciences	1,020	1	555	1	1	465	1	83	4	27·4
		Total sub-order 69.—Other Sciences	1,026	1	559	1	1	467	1	83	4	27·7
	70	Pictorial Art and Sculpture	307	...	158	...	...	149	...	77	3	78·5
	71	Music, Acting, Dancing	22,971	21	14,695	27	24	8,276	15	46	64	20·7
		Total Order XX.—Learned and Artistic Professions	126,724	118	71,859	133	107	54,865	102	73	491	28·6
XXI.—Sport and Amusements.	72	Sport	3,607	3	2,057	4	4	1,550	3	64	4	7·6
	73 (a)	Catching, training, and exhibiting animals	237	...	145	...	...	92	...	65	...	1·3
	73 (b)	Conjuring, fortune-telling and other exhibitions	1,259	1	738	2	2	521	1	65	2	9·2
	73 (c)	Acrobatics and athletics	186	...	107	...	...	79	...	71	...	8·6
	73 (d)	Service of places of entertainment	136	...	79	...	...	57	...	70	1	44·9
		Total sub-order 73.—Exhibitions and Games	1,818	1	1,069	2	2	749	1	66	3	10·8
		Total Order XXI.—Sport and Amusement	5,425	4	3,126	6	6	2,299	4	65	7	8·6
Total Class F—Professions			132,149	122	74,985	139	113	57,164	106	72	498	28·7

pendent on exhibitions, sports, and amusement. It has been already noted that persons employed under Government in any of the special functions, such as education and engineering, which in this country are undertaken by Government, are grouped according to the professions to which they belong, and have therefore come under the present heading. The general distribution of the professional classes will be seen from the statement subjoined.

309. **XX.—Learned and Artistic Professions.** (63) *Religion.*—Of 69,083 people returned at the Census as performing services connected with religion, 48,182, or 69·7 per cent., are shown as religious mendicants, ascetics, etc., without distinction of caste or creed, while 14,983 persons, or 21·7 per cent., have recorded themselves as priests, mullahs, or ministers of religion other than Christian. It is perhaps impossible to draw much of a distinction between the two classes; of the six duties of a priest enjoined by the Shástras, all except the last, receiving of alms, are often more honoured in the breach than the observance, so that the offices of mendicant and priest thus tend to overlap. The only places in which priests outnumber mendicants are Chanda and Sambalpur, the preponderance in the latter district being as high as seven to one, and the same feature is observable in the occupation statistics of the Uria States. From the neighbourhood of this part of the country to Puri, I should have looked for almost an opposite result. In Chanda the return of persons, 2,068, recorded as priests, has been unduly swelled by the inclusion of 1,638 Bhumaks, a class of aboriginal priests and village watchmen, of whom 2,385 have been returned at the enumeration. Of the Bhumaks a full account was given in the Census Report of 1881, at pages 122 and 194-5. They are the priests and exorcists of the Korkus of Hoshangabad and Betul, and of the Gonds of the Southern Satpuras; in the Maratha country the Bhumak is perhaps more of a village watchman. From the five districts of the Nagpur division 2,251 Bhumaks are recorded, so that, if we exclude these, only a few of distinctly priestly profession have been enumerated at the Census.

The Baigas, of whom 55 have been included in the entry for Bhumaks given above, are the aboriginal priests of Mandla and of the northern parts of Chhatisgarh. Of the Mandla Baigas, Forsyth writes that "they consider themselves and are allowed to be superior to the Gonds, who take their priests of the mysteries or medicinemen from among them. Theirs it is to hold converse with the world of spirits who are everywhere present to aboriginal superstition; theirs it is to cast omens, to compel the rain, to charm away the tiger or disease. The Baiga medicineman fully looks his character. He is tall, thin and cadaverous, abstraction and mystery residing in his hollow eyes. When wanted he has to be sent for to some distant haunt of gnomes and spirits, and comes with charms and simples hung in the hollow of a bottle gourd. A great necklace, fashioned with much carving, from the kernels of forest fruits marks his holy calling.*" In Chhatisgarh, even among the non-aboriginal population, the Baiga is a man of considerable influence; without his being called in to invoke the blessing of Thakurdeo, the tutelary deity of the fields, no agricultural operations can be performed. The Baiga is usually well-to-do as compared with his neighbours, and it is in this mundane light that he has been almost universally regarded at the Census. Thus very few of the Baigas appear among the priestly class; in nearly every case they have been described simply as cultivators or as followers of other worldly pursuits.

Readers, or *purániks*, 3,697, are a class of religious instructors who read and

* Highlands of Central India, page 37.

explain the Hindu sacred books; with them have been included reciters and chanters (*haridás*). Exorcists, hail averters, and amuletiers number 718. As has been noted above with regard to Bhumaks and Baigas, the ordinary occupations of the persons who exercise the powers and spells which superstition attributes to them have almost invariably been recorded in preference to the supernatural ones. The return of the latter is therefore very fragmentary. The Gárpagáris, whose duty it is to preserve the crops from hail, are numerous all over the Maratha country, but the exercise of their profession is scantily returned. The same is in some degree the case with the *guniyas* who practise exorcism, and with the class of people who deal in charms, generally in the form of some mantra written on a leaf, which is enclosed in a locket or amulet to be worn on the arm or round the neck.

310. (64-71) *Other Learned and Artistic Professions.*—The followers of these are so few in number as hardly to call for any remark. The entry of literature is unduly increased by the inclusion of 3,189 clerks, for whom no special branch of employment was specified; most of them are in all probability mercantile. The large number, 3,115, of survey menials returned is due to the measurement operations which were in progress in several districts of the Province; in Hoshangabad and Betul a party of the Trigonometrical Survey of India was at work. Astrologers and horoscope-casters number 1,020; they are found principally in the Maratha districts, where they are represented by the *joshis*, whose functions are too well known to need description. The 19,387 musicians are mainly the performers on drums and horns, who supply music at weddings and funerals; 16,073 of their number are found in the country. As the musicians are generally of low castes, Mángs, Ghasias, Nagárchis, etc., their women are largely engaged in other work; there are only 38 adult females dependent on the profession for every 100 men. Musicians who accompany dancing girls come in the next occupation, under which have been entered actors, singers, and dancers and their accompanists; these amount to 3,552, among whom a low proportion of young children is noticeable. 39·5 per cent. of their number, chiefly singers and dancers, are found in towns; in the country the occupation is mainly confined to the *rásdháris*, an itinerant class of actors and mimes.

311. **XXI.—Sport and Amusements.**—5,435 persons return themselves as employed in connection with sport and amusements. Of these 3,601 are professional shikaris. The remainder are principally exhibitors of bears, monkeys, etc. 234, buffoons or *bhánds* 121, ballad-reciters or *bháts* 200, exhibitors of puppets—*bádsháhi*—98, conjurers or *gárodis* and other showmen 840, and tumblers and acrobats—*kabutris, nat-bedias, etc.*—186. These occupations are nearly all returned from the country.

CLASS G.—INDEFINITE AND INDEPENDENT.

312. In this class have been shown (1) persons for whom complex village occupations—see paragraph 313—have been returned, (2) persons who perform unskilled labour or subsist by disreputable means, and (3) persons who do not work, but live by charity or endowments, or who are supported at the public charge. As will be seen from the statement which is appended, the composition of the class is of rather a miscellaneous nature. Its strongest element is the labouring community, who form 5·96 per cent. of the total population of the Province; the preponderance of females in the class is due to the large number of women returned as doing coolie or labouring work.

Occupation Statistics.—Class G.

Order.	Sub-order or group.	Name.	Total Population. No.	Total Population. Distribution of 10,000 persons.	Males. No.	Males. Distribution of 10,000. Total.	Males. Distribution of 10,000. 5—14	Females. No.	Females. Distribution of 10,000.	Adult females per 100 adult males.	Distribution of 10,000 persons living in towns.	Percentage of employed who live in towns.
1	2	3	4	5	6	7	8	9	10	11	12	13
XXII.—COMPLEX OCCUPATIONS.		**Total Order XXII—Complex Occupations**	6,327	6	2,924	5	5	3,403	6	111	7	8·2
XXIII.—INDEFINITE.	74 (a)	Special branches	58,486	54	29,222	54	45	29,264	54	98	138	17·4
	74 (b)	General labour	584,068	542	240,184	445	487	343,884	639	164	510	6.5
		Total Sub-order 74—Unskilled labour	642,554	596	269,406	499	532	373,148	693	155	648	7·5
	75	Undefined, etc.	9,188	9	4,144	8	6	5,044	9	125	27	21·6
		Total Order XXIII—Indefinite	651,742	605	273,550	507	538	378,192	702	155	675	7·7
XXIV.—INDEPENDENT OF WORK.	76 (a)	Property and allowances	1,610	2	649	1	1	961	2	186	17	78·3
	76 (b)	Charity and endowments	118,393	110	63,473	118	99	54,920	102	86	186	11·6
		Total Sub-order 76—Property and Alms	120,003	112	64,122	119	100	55,881	104	87	203	12·5
	77 (a)	Pensions	8,546	8	4,445	8	8	4,101	7	93	88	75·8
	77 (b)	Prisoners	4,812	5	4,428	8	...	384	1	8	63	96·8
		Total Sub-order 77—Supported at the public charge	13,358	13	8,873	16	8	4,485	8	42	151	83·3
		Total Order XXIV—Independent of Work	133,861	125	72,995	135	108	60,366	112	80	354	19·6
Total Class G.—Indefinite and Independent			791,430	736	349,469	647	651	441,961	820	136	1,036	9·7

313. **XXII.—Complex Occupations.**—To these reference has already been made at different places. The return is obviously fragmentary, the rule that only the chief of two non-agricultural occupations should be entered in the schedules operating to this effect. The principal item among the complex occupations returned is the entry of fishermen and grain-parchers numbering 2,403, amongst whom there are 252 adult females per 100 males.

314. **XXIII.—Indefinite.**— (74) *Unskilled Labour.*—Earth-workers and tank-diggers have been kept separate in the table, though the distinction can hardly be considered very precise. Raipur and Bilaspur furnish 1,330 of the 1,621 tank-diggers returned at the Census. Railway permanent-way gangmen and labourers are a strong body in Bilaspur, 1,265, and Sambalpur, 2,232, where they were employed in large numbers in connection with the new

Railway works. In all these branches of labour males outnumber females, the preponderance being greatest in the case of Railway labourers, amongst whom there are only 50 grown-up women for every 100 men. Quarrymen and stone-splitters number 6,453; stone-breaking is an operation demanding strength, and is therefore more of a man's employment. In rice-husking, on the other hand, women are almost solely engaged; they are in the proportion of 1,271 per 100 men. Of 9,056 rice-huskers returned at the Census, 5,243, or 57·9 per cent., are recorded from the two Chhatisgarh districts and Sambalpur.

General labour—the usual term employed was *ám majuri*—has been given as the occupation of 584,068 persons, amongst whom adult females predominate over males in the proportion of 164 to 100. The districts from which the indefinite term has been most numerously recorded are Saugor, 83,172, Sambalpur, 71,660, and Hoshangabad, 65,059. Narsinghpur, in proportion to its population, also returns a very large number of general labourers, 54,602. It is probable that many of the people who have come in this class are in reality principally engaged in field labour of one sort or another, but the presence of such a large proletariat, especially in the northern districts and the Nerbada valley, is significant, as showing a difficulty in finding regular employment, which in some measure bears out the low rate of increase in that part of the country, as well as the tendency towards emigration to the surrounding States, which in most of these districts has been seen to exist.

(75) *Means of Livelihood Undefined.*—The sub-order includes 2,570 persons, who have returned disreputable means of livelihood, prostitutes, etc. 527 of the latter are recorded from Bilaspur, which at the time of the Census was the last stage of civilization on the new Railway line, and was therefore a resort of disreputable characters.

315. **XXIV.—Independent of Work.** (76) *Property and Alms.*—118,221 persons returned their means of subsistence as begging. Religious mendicants were separately recorded and classed, their numbers being 48,182. Combining the figures for the two classes, we find that the district which contains the strongest element of mendicancy in proportion to its population is Hoshangabad. The sacred river Nerbada runs along the entire length of Hoshangabad, and to this may in great part be ascribed the large number of beggars returned from the district. Among non-religious mendicants it will be seen that the Province returns more males than females; probably the instruction as to recording whether mendicancy was associated with religion or not has been imperfectly carried out at the Census, and many Bairagis and fakirs shown in the present sub-order who might perhaps have more properly been described as religious mendicants.

Statistics of Beggars.

DISTRICT.	Number of mendicants religious and ordinary.	Percentage of column 2 on total population.
1	2	3
High average of mendicancy.		
Hoshangabad	17,880	3·4
Damoh	8,464	2·6
Narsinghpur	9,230	2·5
Saugor	14,016	2·4
Nimar	6,165	2·4
Low average of mendicancy.		
Seoni	4,421	1·2
Bilaspur	13,712	1·2
Raipur	17,075	1·1
Mandla	3,578	1·1
Balaghat	3,996	1·0
Sambalpur	7,211	0·9
Bhandara	6,948	0·9
Provincial average	166,403	1·5

(77) *Supported at the Public Charge.*—Inmates of asylums number 128; in Jubbulpore the lunatics in the asylum were returned as of the occupations which they had followed before their confinement. Among prisoners are found a few young children who by the prison rules are allowed to accompany their mothers to jail.

OCCUPATIONS IN THE FEUDATORY STATES.

316. The accompanying table exhibits the distribution of the population of the Feudatory States by occupation. The only information which I need note upon is that contained in column 8, wherein are set forth the proportions which the number of persons engaged in each order or class of occupations bears to the total population. In column 9 are shown the corresponding figures for British districts.

Occupation Statistics—Feudatory States.

Class and order.	Name.	Males.		Females.		Total.		Corresponding proportion per 10,000 in British Districts.	Percentage of employed who live in towns.
		Total number of persons.	Proportion per 10,000.	Total number of persons.	Proportion per 10,000.	Total number of persons.	Proportion per 10,000.		
1	2	3	4	5	6	7	8	9	10
CLASS A .	GOVERNMENT.								
Order I	Administration	21,877	201	18,053	169	39,930	185	182	6·9
„ II	Defence	25	...	14	...	39	...	12	...
„ III	Foreign and Feudatory State service	2	...	...	...	2	...	...	...
	Total Class A.—Government	21,904	201	18,067	169	39,971	185	194	6·9
CLASS B .	PASTURE AND AGRICULTURE.								
Order IV	Provision and care of cattle	34,011	312	24,774	231	58,785	272	248	·6
„ V	Agriculture—								
	Sub-order 10—								
	29-31 Land-owners	27,891	256	26,522	248	54,413	252	255	·9
	32, 33 Tenants	610,411	5,605	577,972	5,394	1,188,383	5,501	4,297	·4
	TOTAL SUB-ORDER 10.—INTEREST IN LAND	638,302	5,861	604,494	5,642	1,242,796	5,753	4 552	·4
	Sub-order 11—								
	34 Farm servants	96,469	886	67,424	620	163,893	759	761	·7
	37, 38 Field labourers	42,857	393	67,044	625	109,901	508	1,034	·1
	TOTAL SUB-ORDER 11.—AGRICULTURAL LABOURERS	139,326	1,279	134,468	1,254	273,794	1,267	1,795	·5
	Others	4,913	46	4,348	41	9,261	43	56	2·8
	TOTAL ORDER V.—AGRICULTURE	782,541	7,186	743,310	6,937	1,525,851	7,063	6,403	·4
	Total Class B.—Pasture and Agriculture	816,552	7,498	768,084	7,168	1,584,636	7,336	6,651	·4
CLASS C .	PERSONAL SERVICES	15,586	143	16,160	151	31,746	147	243	10·5
CLASS D .	PREPARATION AND SUPPLY OF MATERIAL SUBSTANCES.								
Order VII	Food and drink	33,440	307	42,161	393	75,601	350	410	7·2
	89 Country spirit distillers and sellers	7,583	70	7,845	73	15,428	71	19	·9
„ VIII	Light, firing, and forage	7,625	70	9,873	92	17,498	81	200	9·0
„ IX	Buildings	937	9	657	6	1,594	7	41	19·8
„ X	Vehicles and vessels	167	2	139	1	306	1	5	37·3
„ XI	Supplementary requirements	3,930	36	4,033	38	7,963	37	44	12·8
„ XII	Textile fabrics and dress	80,248	737	85,682	800	165,930	768	674	2·8
	Sub-order 40, Cotton	76,212	700	82,099	766	158,311	733	572	2·3
„ XIII	Metals and precious stones	13,797	127	13,167	123	26,964	125	157	4·9
„ XIV	Glass, pottery, and stoneware	7,629	70	7,607	71	15,236	71	56	2·6
„ XV	Wood, cane, and leaves, etc.	6,331	58	6,300	59	12,631	58	135	5·2
„ XVI	Drugs, dyes, gums, etc.	1,141	10	1,502	14	2,643	12	11	·7
„ XVII	Leather	3,533	32	3,311	31	6,844	32	137	7·3
	Total Class D.—Preparation and supply of material substances	158,778	1,458	174,432	1,628	333,210	1,542	1,870	4·8

Occupation Statistics—Feudatory States—continued.

Class and order.	NAME.	MALES.		FEMALES.		TOTAL.		Corresponding proportion per 10,000 in British Districts.	Percentage of employed who live in towns.
		Total number of persons.	Proportion per 10,000.	Total number of persons.	Proportion per 10,000.	Total number of persons.	Proportion per 10,000.		
1	2	3	4	5	6	7	8	9	10
CLASS E .	COMMERCE, TRANSPORT, AND STORAGE.								
Order XVIII	Commerce . . .	6 436	50	4 701	44	11,137	51	105	13·5
" XIX	Transport and storage .	7.350	68	5,109	48	12,459	58	79	17·4
	Total Class E.—Commerce, Transport, and Storage	13,786	127	9,810	92	23,596	109	184	12·6
CLASS F .	PROFESSIONS.								
Order XX	Learned and Artistic professions	6,157	56	5,151	48	11,308	52	128	12·6
	Sub-order 63.—Religion .	3,974	37	3.436	32	7,410	34	65	12·0
" XXI	Sport and Amusements .	611	6	553	5	1,164	6	4	·4
	Total Class F.—Professions	6,768	62	5,704	53	12,472	58	122	11·5
CLASS G .	INDEFINITE AND INDEPENDENT.								
Order XXII	Complex occupations . .	424	4	294	3	718	3	6	16·2
" XXIII	Indefinite	47.503	436	71,849	670	119,352	552	605	3·1
" XXIV	Independent of work . .	7,710	71	7,100	66	14,810	69	125	6·9
	Total Class G.—Indefinite and Independent . .	55,637	511	79,243	739	134,880	624	736	3·6

317. *Class A.—Government.*—1·85 per cent. of the inhabitants of the States are shown as employed in the work of administration; of the 39,930 thus described, no less than 37,862 are engaged in menial service or in the village watch. A great part of these consist of the rude militia, who more particularly in the Uria States are the constituted guardians of law and order. They can hardly be considered to come under the head of Defence, their duties being more akin to those of the police in British territory. Order II, Defence, therefore comprises only a few persons, miscellaneously described as *topdars* or by some other term of a more or less warlike nature.

318. *Class B.—Pasture and Agriculture.*—Under this head are comprised no less than 73·4 per cent. of the population of the Feudatories, as compared with 66·5 per cent. similarly employed in British districts. The provision and care of cattle is the occupation of 2·7 per cent. of the people; in the Uria States, as has already been seen to be the case in Sambalpur, comparatively few persons are employed in pastoral pursuits, whereas in the Chhatisgarh country and in Bastar the herdsmen class musters strong, the percentage which it bears to the total population being 4·0 in the former and 3·2 in the latter, compared with only 2·0 per cent. in the Uria Feudatories.

Agriculture in one form or another is followed by 70·6 per cent. of the inhabitants of the States, made up as follows: 2·5 per cent. are land-owners, 55 per cent. are tenants or ordinary cultivators, 7·6 per cent. are farm servants in regular employ and 5·1 per cent. are field labourers, while the remainder, ·4 per cent., are engaged in semi-agricultural pursuits, such as the growth of garden crops and other special products. It is difficult to say whether the distinction between land-owners and ordinary tenant cultivators has been everywhere sufficiently preserved, but it is singular that the former class is scarcely represented in the States of Kanker and Bastar. Throughout the Feudatory States the ratio of persons who have a direct interest in land is much higher than in the British districts of the Province, being 57·5 per cent. of the whole population against 45·5; the agricultural labouring community is on the other hand proportionally less strong, the percentage being 12·7 in the Feudatory States against 18·0 in British territory.

The figures are indicative of the pristine conditions of life which obtain in the undeveloped country which stretches along the south and east of the Province; industries are few, the great bulk of the people are engaged in the cultivation of the soil, and of these a far larger proportion are directly connected with the land than in the more advanced British districts.

Combining with the above the figures, which we get in Table XVII—C., for persons following other occupations in addition to agriculture, the following result is obtained:—

Interest in Land.

Agricultural occupation.	Number of persons for whom the occupation in column I is recorded by itself.	Number of persons combining the same with non-agricultural occupations.	Total of columns 2 and 3.	Proportion of column 4 on total population.
1	2	3	4	5
Owners or occupants	54,413	842	55,255	2·6
Tenants	1,188,383	68,869	1,257,252	58·2
TOTAL INTEREST IN LAND	1,242,796	69,711	1,312,507	60·8

319. *Class D.—Preparation and Supply of Material Substances.*—On this there is little to remark, except that in most of the occupations which come under this head, comparatively few persons are engaged, when the number of the population to whose wants they minister is taken into account. The liquor-seller is a notable exception however; in every 10,000 persons, 71 are employed in the manufacture and sale of country spirit, as compared with 19 on a like proportion in British districts. In the Bastar State the ratio rises as high as 162, there being no less than 5,040 liquor-sellers in the dependency. Another point worth noticing is the large number of people who are engaged in spinning and weaving cotton, being 7·3 per cent. of the population as against 5·7 per cent. in British territory. It is evident that manufactured cloth has not yet found its way into the Feudatories to any large extent, judging by the large number of persons who are employed on the country loom.

320. *Class E.—Commerce, etc.*—Fifty-one persons in every 10,000 are engaged in commercial pursuits. The money-lender is not such a conspicuous figure in the community in most of the Feudatories as he is in British districts. In the whole of Bastar, for instance, there are only 64 persons dependent on usury in a population of over 300,000. Taking all the Native States, there are 14 money-lenders amongst every 10,000 persons; in British territory the proportion is 43. Of the 12,459 people who are shown as occupied in transport and storage, nearly half are carriers by pack animals, there being 5,602 so returned.

321. *Class G.—Indefinite and Independent.*—The professional class hardly calls for remark, about two-thirds of its members being connected with religion. There are 3,409 religious mendicants. Combining these with the 13,633 persons who live by ordinary begging, we get 17,042 persons dependent on alms, or

about ·8 per cent. of the population as compared with 1·5 per cent. in British territory. In Bastar the percentage of mendicancy is as low as ·5, in the Chhatisgarh States it rises to 9, and in the Uria Feudatories to ·8 per cent.

GENERAL.

322. **Occupations combined with Agriculture.**—The statement subjoined shows the occupations which are more commonly followed in conjunction with agriculture. In Table XVII—C. columns have been kept distinguishing land-owners, tenants and field labourers, but it is only for the two first of these that full information is available.

Occupations which are commonly combined with agriculture.

Order and sub-order.	Name.	BRITISH DISTRICTS. Total returning the occupation, including those combining it with agriculture.	BRITISH DISTRICTS. CONNECTED WITH THE LAND. Number of persons in column 3 who are owners or tenants of land.	BRITISH DISTRICTS. CONNECTED WITH THE LAND. Percentage of col. 4 on col. 3.	FEUDATORY STATES. Total returning the occupation, including those combining it with agriculture.	FEUDATORY STATES. CONNECTED WITH THE LAND. Number of persons in column 6 who are owners or tenants of land.	FEUDATORY STATES. CONNECTED WITH THE LAND. Percentage of col. 7 on col. 6.
1	2	3	4	5	6	7	8
I. 3	Village service	140,697	23,697	16·8	26,741	12,522	46·8
IV.	Provision and care of cattle.	266,825	8,130	3·0	58,785	2,261	3·8
VI.	Personal and household services.	262,639	22,081	8·4	31,746	4,218	13·3
VII.	Purveyors of food and drink.	442,263	25,233	5·7	75,601	9,131	12·1
VIII. 20	Oil-pressers, etc.	90,361	15,509	17·2	11,686	4,586	39·2
XII. 38	Workers in wool and fur	20,432	1,501	7·3	1,430	82	5·7
40	" " cotton	617,168	20,713	4	158,311	17,509	11·1
42	" " dress	726,644	25,930	3·6	4,466	318	7·1
XIII. 43	" " gold, silver, etc.	60,523	6,824	11·3	3,307	361	10·9
46	" " iron and steel	89,271	9,833	11·0	21,023	1,743	8·3
XIV. 48	" " earthen and stoneware.	59,889	4,211	7·0	15,228	4,822	31·7
XV. 49	" " timber and wood.	66,068	6,946	10·5	1,920	71	3·7
XVII. 53	" " leather	147,427	8,989	6·1	6,844	886	12·9
XVIII. 54	Dealers in money and securities.	46,392	17,045	36·7	2,989	906	30·3
XIX. 59	Carriers by road	39,979	3,218	8·0	6,421	392	6.1
XX. 63	Religious services	69,083	7,215	10·4	7,410	1,256	17·0
	All others	793,238	5,279	·7	210,013	8,647	4·1
Total non-agricultural Population.		**3,938,899**	**212,354**	**5·4**	**643,921**	**69,711**	**10·9**

NOTE.—For total agricultural population, including the persons shown in columns 4 and 7 above, see paragraphs 278 and 318.

The sixteen items here given include 95 per cent. of the entries recorded of agriculture being followed along with another occupation. In the Feudatory States close upon half of the persons who form the village watch or the rude police of the south-eastern part of the Province are cultivators. Both in the case of village servants and of such personal servants as barbers and washermen, the grant of a field is occasionally made in return for their services to the village community; thus throughout the Province we find a considerable number of these engaged in agriculture. Amongst purveyors of food and drink, Order VIII, there is a comparatively large number of persons connected with the land, especially amongst vendors of vegetables and betel-leaf, these articles being in many cases grown by those who sell them. Liquor-sellers, too, come out strongly as owners and tenants of land, 11 per cent. of their number in British districts and 21 per cent. in the Feudatory States being so returned. The oil-pressing class is, it will be observed, largely engaged in cultivation, the proportions so employed being 17·2 and 36·7 per cent. in British and Feudatory territory respectively. The only other occupational group, to which I need refer, is that which comprises dealers in money and securities. In the British districts of the Province there are—exclusive of money-changers and of money-lenders' clerks, etc.—32,685 persons whose occupation is money-lending. Of these, 16,349, or exactly half, have an interest in land, 6,589 as owners and 9,760 as tenants. The former of these figures deserves to be noted from another point of view. From Table XVII—C. it will be seen that there are 13,276 persons who are owners of land in addition to following another occupation, so that we find that for nearly half of these that other occupation is money-lending. The figures refer to British territory only; in the Feudatories the money-lender is not so much in evidence, but there, too, he has got a firm grasp of the land.

323. **Local distribution of Occupations.**—The extent to which the several classes of occupations are followed in each district will appear from the statement which is subjoined :—

Local distribution of Occupations.

	PERCENTAGE OF THE POPULATION OF EACH DISTRICT WHO ARE ENGAGED IN							
	Government service. Class A.	Pasture. Class B.	Agriculture. Class B.	Personal services. Class C.	Industrial occupations. Class D.	Commerce. Class E.	Professions. Class F.	Indefinite occupations. Class G.
1	2	3	4	5	6	7	8	9
Saugor	2·25	1·52	47·77	4·79	23·45	2·44	1·66	16·12
Damoh	1·83	1·89	55·26	4·68	24·37	1·97	1·75	8·25
Jubbulpore	2·16	1·77	55·41	4·34	21·41	3·43	1·52	9·96
Narsinghpur	2·01	1 53	46·08	5·09	24·16	2·35	1·75	17·03
Hoshangabad	2·74	2·19	49·57	3·84	21·66	2·68	2·26	15·06
Nimar	3·22	1·59	59·46	2·34	23·12	4·25	1·98	4·04
Mandla	1·73	3·65	73·78	·91	10·84	1·44	·71	6·94
Seoni	1·83	3·05	65·00	2·21	15·16	·98	·90	10·87
Chhindwara	1·99	2·61	71·37	2·08	17·15	1·12	·96	2·72
Betul	2·50	2·80	67·93	1·44	17·18	1·00	1·00	6·15
Wardha	1·76	1·69	67·31	1·98	17·22	2·70	1·75	5·59
Nagpur	3·18	1·58	51·24	3·46	29·04	4·27	2·56	4·67
Chanda	1·46	2·66	59·92	1·70	27·63	1·86	1·05	3·72
Bhandara	1·69	1·62	64·68	1·53	26·06	1·38	·89	2·15
Balaghat	1·74	2·34	71·96	1·58	17·74	·76	1·28	2·60
Raipur	1·47	4·40	73·69	1·85	12·22	·87	·76	4·74
Bilaspur	1·18	3·27	77·31	1·36	8·88	·88	·63	6·49
Sambalpur	2·14	·98	68·48	1·09	14·90	·99	·51	10·91
Total British Districts	1·94	2·48	64·04	2·44	18·71	1·83	1·22	7·34
Chhatisgarh States	1·54	3·96	74·12	2·13	12·70	1·02	·81	3·72
Bastar	·68	3·20	77·35	·58	11·27	1·06	·28	5·58
Uria States	2·27	1·99	67·39	1·36	17·74	1·13	·54	7·58
Total Feudatory States	1·85	2·73	70·62	1·47	15·42	1·09	·58	6·24
Grand Total, Central Provinces	1·92	2·52		2·27	18·16	1·71	1·12	7·16

The subject has already been referred to under the various occupation headings in the first part of this chapter; the present table is given as a synopsis of the general distribution of means of livelihood throughout the Province. In the more advanced districts of the north and west of the Province, and in the districts of the Nagpur plain, the industrial, commercial, and professional classes are strongly represented, compared with what is the case in the less developed tracts of the centre, south, and east. In the latter, pasture and agriculture is still the calling of close upon three-fourths of the population.

CENSUS OF 1891.

PART II.

THE OPERATIONS OF THE CENSUS.

PART II.

THE OPERATIONS OF THE CENSUS.

CHAPTER I.

PRELIMINARY MEASURES.

1. The Census operations were commenced in the Central Provinces by the issue of a letter, Book Circular XVI, dated 15th April, from the Secretary to the Chief Commissioner, to all Deputy Commissioners, giving some general directions as to the procedure that was to be followed. About this date the Superintendent of the Operations was appointed, and the further conduct of the work took place in accordance with instructions issued by him from time to time.

2. **Territorial Sub-division into Census Areas.**—The lowest Census sub-division was the *Block*, being the area, the census of which was to be taken by a single *Enumerator*. Above the block came the Census *Circle*, under a *Supervisor*, and next the *Charge*, over which was a *Superintendent*, and which was the highest sub-division. The procedure adopted for dividing off the census areas, which were to be formed in each district, was the same as that followed in 1881, and it was therefore hoped that some assistance might be got from the records and maps of the last Census; but on enquiry it was found that in most districts these were in a very incomplete state. Census Circular A, dated the 30th April, set forth the general lines on which the division should take place. A large scale map was to be taken, and on this census circles were to be marked off, the average size of the circle being fixed at ten blocks, each of 60 houses or 300 persons. The boundaries of police station-house and out-post areas were to be adhered to, and no circle was to fall partly in one such area and partly in another. Circles were next grouped into charges. In almost every district, the grouping was so arranged as to have the charge area also in accordance with police sub-division boundaries. As a general rule, the police sub-divisions were themselves taken as charges, but in cases where they were too large or populous to be thus treated, two or more charges, as might be necessary, were framed of the circles in the police area. In this connection a difficulty was at the outset experienced owing to the manner in which throughout the Province police sub-divisions have been drawn up without regard to tehsil boundaries. It was obviously inexpedient that a Superintendent of a Census charge should be under the orders of two separate Tehsildars, so the arrangement of charges according to police areas had in such cases to be departed from. The framing of Census charges and circles was generally completed during June. The formation of blocks was left to a later stage of the operations, and will be noticed further on.

3. **Appointment of Supervising Staff.**—Throughout the operations the matter of establishment has been one of the main difficulties with which District

Officers have had to deal. Though this remark applies more particularly with regard to enumerators, the practical withdrawal of the Patwari establishment from Census work resulted in a supervising staff having to be entertained, which was in many cases inefficient. The following extract from the Secretary to the Chief Commissioner's letter, above referred to, first announced the extent to which the Patwari staff would be at the disposal of Deputy Commissioners for employment on Census :—

"Although Patwaris cannot be employed in every district for the work of the Census without interrupting settlement operations, they can be utilized almost everywhere in the preliminary work of checking the correctness of maps of circles with regard to villages included therein. They will also be able to help (during the rains) in the selection and instruction of Enumerators and in checking the building lists prepared by the latter. When the work is well started and the more helpful non-officials come to be known, selections to relieve Patwaris of the work of supervision can be made."

Appended to this letter is a memorandum by the Commissioner of Settlements and Agriculture, from which I quote :—

"Briefly, then, for the Census work to be done during the rains, Patwaris can everywhere be made available, except in Mandla and parts of Raipur and Bilaspur, provided they are allowed to do Census work in their spare time, and are permitted to begin early so as to be free by 15th October. Our monsoon establishment of Inspectors is wholly engaged in office work. Not a man can be spared. At last Census there was not a Revenue Inspector in the Provinces, or a Patwari for the matter of that in five districts, and I do not see why their services should be indispensable now.

"I now come to the enumeration work of January and February. In all circles to which Patwaris have been posted and the settlement work of which has been completed, the Patwaris can be made available for census work in these months. This is the case with all circles in the Sambalpur District, with the circles of one tehsil in the Bilaspur District, and with about 150 circles in the Raipur District. Details are given in the margin of the number of circles in which settlement work will probably be completed in each of the other three divisions. The figures are approximate only, as the full extent of completed work will not be accounted for another two months. The number of Patwaris in column 3 would be available for census work in January and February, provided that they were allowed to return for a short time to settlement work if their services were required."

District.	Total number of circles.	Number in which settlement work will probably be completed by January 1891.
Saugor	420	250
Damoh	174	174
Jubbulpore	398	360
Mandla	Patwaris on general staff.	
Seoni	128	10
Narsinghpur	277	277
Hoshangabad	435	300
Nimar	220	50
Betul	174	...
Chhindwara	146	30
Wardha	209	100
Nagpur	259	100
Chanda	144	10
Bhandara	185	10
Balaghat	98	...

As the Patwaris were, of all others, the persons wanted for the duties of Circle Supervisor, the fact that their services could only be partially availed of was a serious difficulty. In most districts it was preferred to employ the permanent staff from the beginning, so as to avoid the inconvenience that would arise from the change of establishment that must take place on Patwaris being withdrawn for settlement work. The division of the district into census areas in conformity with police circle limits more or less suggested the employment of the police as a supervising staff, and nearly everywhere, at least to begin with, the conduct of the operations was carried out through them. Many non-officials also were forthcoming as Supervisors, service, as a rule, being accepted without demur, it being considered rather a distinction to have been singled out for a superior post. A detailed list of the establishment employed will be found at paragraph 14.

4. **Preparation and Test of Circle Lists of Villages.**—Simultaneously with the division of the district into Census circles and charges, lists were prepared of the villages and hamlets in each circle, with the number of houses in each

according to the Census of 1881. The information was written up in columns 2 and 3 of the form of Circle List appended to Circular B.* Sketch maps of circle and charge areas, showing the villages and hamlets they contained, were also made for the use of Supervisors and Superintendents. Each Supervisor was then required to go over his circle and check the correctness of the villages in the circle list supplied him. New villages that had sprung up were to be entered in the list; old ones that had disappeared were to be struck out, and any marked change in the number of houses in an existing village was to be noted. The necessity for this preliminary check was most marked in districts in which there are large forest and jungle areas, as the two extracts given below will show:—

"**Hoshangabad.**—In the thinly-populated portions south of the Railway and on the Betul border, villages which existed at the last Census had in many cases been abandoned, or had been replaced by others with new names and on new sites. The lists of villages and hamlets were prepared from information collected from Police out-posts and from the Forest Department, the information on record at head-quaters being quite insufficient. The lists thus obtained had to be very carefully checked, as errors, omissions, or duplicate entries were only too common. New villages were constantly being brought to notice and had to be located on the map."

And again—

"The police, whatever may have been expected, have shown that they are far from having a complete knowledge of the villages in their circles. In one or two instances they discovered villages at the last moment which had not been included in any circle, and whose names and location no one seems to have remembered."

"**Bilaspur.**—The lists and maps of the malguzari portions of the tehsils were found fairly correct. A new hamlet had sprung up here and there, and the number of houses in the villages had to be generally revised. But in the zemindari and Government forest eserves the changes were very great. Whole vilages has disappeared and new ones had been established in many places. The names in the trace maps, the names in the district record-room lists, and the names in the papers of the previous census, were all at variance with each other and with the facts as ascertained on the spot."

It was therefore a matter of the first impotance to have the record of existing villages and hamlets fully and carefully made. As this part of the work fell to be done during the rains, the difficulties experienced in the more remote parts, specially of Chanda and Bilaspur, were very great. It would be well if in future the step were carried out during the hot weather before the Census, as it is hardly likely that at least the next decade will find in these wild tracts many persons of sufficient education to undertake the task, and it is next to impossible to get imported men to work in them during the rainy season.

5. **Outline of other Preliminaries.**—Along with the check of the record of villages, each Supervisor at the same time devised the most convenient division of his circle into blocks according to instructions given him. He was also required to make proposals for the selection of suitable Enumerators on the spot, and, this done, to return the circle list with the above details filled in for examination and correction where necessary,—see the example appended to Circular B. On receiving it back, his next duty was to arrange for the writing up, by the Enumerators appointed, of all the houses in each block in a form of block list, a rough copy of which was first to be prepared and sent for approval. The actual numbering of the houses was not to take place until this list was passed. I shall in another place note what I think the best plan of procedure to be for a future Census. The one just detailed was, I think, rather too elaborate, and required too much sending for sanction. It must, of course, be remembered that at the present Census we had to deal with a very backward staff, and it was necessary, above all, to make sure of every step that was

* See Appendix A.

taken. Though the method adopted then was slow, there is no doubt that, under the circumstances, it was the one best suited to ensure that every part of the operations was duly carried out, and without it there would not have been the same certainty as to the results obtained. The following remark from the Bilaspur report is to the point :—

"Where the preparation of building lists can be checked by a Superintendent, Tehsildar or other intelligent official, it will save time if the preparation of the building lists and the printing of the numbers are done together ; but where the work has to be entrusted to a subordinate agency, it is better that the lists should first be completed and subjected to scrutiny before the numbers are painted, or much of the work may have to be done over again."

An obvious plan of simplifying the procedure was that adopted in one or two districts, *viz.*, to get the Supervisor to prepare rough block lists at the same time as he submitted his rough circle list. When the original instructions on the subject were issued, it was thought that on the Enumerator would devolve all the details of the work as far as the block was concerned ; the listing of houses and the painting of numbers were therefore left to him. As a matter of fact, the work to a great extent fell on the Supervisor, and it would have been as well to have had the rough block list prepared by him at once. Another difficulty that arose from the lengthy procedure adopted at the present Census was that the indents for Enumerators' books were based on the number of houses entered in the block lists, and the length of time that it took to have the latter prapared seriously delayed the submission of indents to the Press.

6. **Formation of Blocks.**—The plan of having this done by Supervisors appears to have on the whole worked well. The instructions given were acted on in all well-settled districts. "As a rule, an Enumerator's block should not contain more than about 60 houses or 300 persons. Two or more small villages near to one another may be made into one block, or a block may contain parts of different villages, or the whole of one and part of another. Any village, though containing less than 60 houses, may be made into a separate block if there are sufficient competent Enumerators available." Here it would be well to state what is meant by the word "village." At the present Census, as will be noted hereafter, the population of hamlets was, in many cases, enumerated apart from that of the main village, thus giving considerable trouble to the Census agency, and occasionally creating confusion in the compilation of the returns owing to its being difficult to tell whether a name was that of a main village or a hamlet, or whether a hamlet belonged to one main village or to another.

For Census purposes the village should be taken to mean the *mauza, i.e.*, the parent village with its subordinate hamlets. As we want to ascertain separately the population of each village, as here defined, this object can best be obtained by keeping every village as distinct as possible from its neighbours. The rule that allows two or more villages to be put together in one block is therefore hardly a good one, and for a future Census I would suggest that if a village is so small that it need not have a separate Enumerator, it should still remain a block by itself. Two or three such blocks might of course be given to one Enumerator. The matter is a slight one ; but anything that tends to simplify Census procedure should not be overlooked. Further remarks on the size of blocks will be found in the paragraph dealing with the final division into Census areas.

7. **Definition of a House.**—The next question to which reference may be made is that of the definition of a house,—a matter which more than any other has puzzled the heads of the Census staff. The general definition adopted was the standard one, a rider being appended dealing with the subject of enclosures.

"By house is meant the dwelling place of one or more families, with their dependents and servants, having a separate principal entrance from the public way."

NOTE.—A bungalow with servants' out-houses should be reckoned as single house.

"In Chhatisgarh and elsewhere, where there are enclosures containing separate huts or houses, the enclosure will be marked with a serial number, and the separate huts and houses with separate sub-numbers, *e..g*, where 16 is the serial number of an enclosure containing three huts, the numbering of the latter will be $\frac{16}{1}$, $\frac{16}{2}$, $\frac{16}{3}$."

In connection with this definition the Census Commissioner wrote :—

"As regards the note to the house definition, I should recommend the addition of a fractional number, if not a separate number, to servants' quarters, as they will be enumerated apart from the bungalow. Moreover, they are just as independent of the main building as the houses round an enclosure in Chhatisgarh."

The note was therefore amended as follows :—

"Servants' out-houses attached to a bungalow will bear the number of the latter with sub-numbers added, *e.g.*, where 20 is the number of a bungalow, its out-houses will be numbered $\frac{20}{1}$, $\frac{20}{2}$, $\frac{20}{3}$, etc.

The above was the definition of a house as it finally stood. The rule about enclosures had been introduced in accordance with the Census Commissioner's proposals for the Census of the Province, embodied in his Note C, dated 22nd February 1890 :—

"The standard definition of a house seems to be inapplicable only in the Chhatisgarh Division, where, in order to retain the means of comparison with last census as well as to bring the numbers into something like uniformity with those in adjacent districts of Bengal, Mr. Drysdale proposes a system of sub-numbers for enclosures, which in the latter tracts would be treated as single houses. The question is no easy one to settle, and the above proposition will meet the special difficulty under consideration."

The application of the standard definition was sometimes in itself a by no means easy matter, but any dificulty it may have caused was very slight in comparison with the trouble that was given by the rule about sub-numbering in enclosures. In many districts sub-numbering was entirely dispensed with after various attempts at carrying it out proved it to be unsatisfactory. In others it was partially carried out ; but uniformity was not always maintained, as some of the district reports go to show.

8. **The enclosure.**—It will have been seen that what led to separate notice being taken of enclosures was the existence of what has been called the Chhatisgarh enclosure. Although this form of homestead prevails in Chhatisgarh it is not unknown in other districts also. It has been well described in the Bilaspur District Report, from which I again quote :—

"Every Chhatisgarh family, however poor, has at least two separate huts, one of which serves as a cooking and sleeping place, and the other as a store-house for grain or fuel, a place for pounding rice and a guest chamber. These huts are surrounded by some kind of a wall or hedge. If the family is well-to-do, it has a larger number of huts ; and as the married members of the family increase, it becomes necessary to increase the number of sleeping places. Thus, when the eldest son marries, it is the custom for the parents to give up their own house to the newly-married couple and retire into a smaller hut ; the number of huts in an enclosure thus tends to multiply. It is not uncommon to permit a field servant to construct his dwelling hut within the family enclosure ; and sometimes even a neighbour's farm servant may be allowed this privilege. It follows that an enclosure may contain only one family or several distinct families either cognate or unrelated."

It soon came to my notice that the rule as to giving one number to an enclosure and sub-numbering the houses it contained was difficult of application, and I began to find it being used in a manner that was scarcely intended. The Superintendent of Kalahandi wrote in October that in that State there were "many enclosures made of split bamboos, within which live several independent families," and asked how such enclosures should be numbered. I also came across large closed courtyards in towns, containing frequently a considerable number of separate houses, which had been treated according to the enclosure rule, though the latter was evidently inapplicable. Instructions were therefore issued that in all, except enclosures of a private nature (*khâs bâri*), *i.e.*, inhabited by inter-dependent families, the inside of the enclosure should be treated as the common way and the buildings it contained listed as separate houses according as they fell within the standard definition or not. As it was found that the use of sub-numbers had led to the greatest confusion, it was recommended that only the serial number should be used for enclosures treated as a single house, and that sub-numbers should, as far as possible, be omitted. In most districts the numbering was carried out in accordance with these instructions, but in some the wrong use of sub-numbers was still retained. As a consequence, it was ordered that when preparing the abstract in the Enumeration Book, all such sub-numbered houses should be counted as main houses. In this way greater uniformity than would otherwise have been the case was attained, though the result can still be hardly described as satisfactory.

9. **Suggestions for house definition at future Census.**—The first consideration that has to be taken into account is whether any definition of a house can be got which will possess a value for statistical purposes. It has been pretty generally conceded that any attempt at a definition that would assure this end would be beyond the understanding of the persons who would have to put it into practice, while houses differ in different localities to such an extent that a general rule would be most difficult of application. What is wanted is therefore a definition that will be of service for purposes of enumeration, that will serve the Enumerator as a guide to the work he has to do at the Census. I had asked District Officers to favour me with their suggestions as to a possible definition towards this end, giving it as my opinion that for enclosures a *chulhâwâr* definition was necessary. Most Deputy Commissioners have agreed with this, but I give below remarks on the subject from one or two of the district reports showing that this does not altogether meet the case:—

Jubbulpore.—Colonel Plowden writes:—"The principle laid down by you that where the enclosure consists of houses occupied by the members of one family or of dependent families, *i.e.*, eating from the same *chulha*, it should bear one serial number, if occupied by independent families, the inside of the enclosure should be considered as the common way, and the house of each family separately numbered, is the one which has been generally followed and may be adopted with advantage at the next Census. But it does not cover all cases. In villages houses are of such varying descriptions that no hard-and-fast rules can be laid down on the subject."

Mr. Crump writes:—"My experience in **Hoshangabad** has convinced me that any definition of a house is impossible, and frame what rules you will, it must ultimately be left to the discretion of the Supervisor and Enumerator. We do not want to estimate the number of families, and therefore any system based on separation in food will be liable to give erroneous figures. What we want to count is the number of houses, and I should be disposed to treat everything as a house which had a separate main entrance from the public way. I should not rely at all on separation in food, unless it was followed by separation in property also. My experience is that separation in food and generally in dwelling is only a slight matter, and does not cause any great change in the condition of the family who remain living in houses in the same enclosure. I would therefore treat the small enclosures as a single house, and should certainly abolish all sub-numbering."

Mr. K. K. Thakur, Extra Assistant Commissioner, in an interesting note appended to the Bilaspur Report, has also put forward objections to the adoption of a *chulhâwâr* definition for enclosures, on the ground that the result obtained will be useless as confusing families with houses. But at present I am unable to see any way out of the difficulty, and for a future Census would suggest that, while keeping the standard definition for ordinary houses, a rule should be added that enclosures containing houses occupied by inter-dependent families should be treated as a single house, while the interior of enclosures containing houses occupied by independent families should be taken as the public way, and the houses of the separate families separately listed according to the general rule. The addition of a column in the Block List for *Head of Family* would obviate the chance of any of the inter-dependent families grouped under one house-number being omitte dr om the enumeration.

10. **House-numbering.**—It has been seen that this was not allowed to be commenced until first done in the rough on paper. The writing up of the block list was the first part of the work that fell to be done by the enumerator. Being strange to it he made frequent mistakes, but those were to a great extent discovered by the scrutiny to which the list was subjected previous to the house numbering being taken in hand. The latter was not begun until after the rains had ceased, which was in most places about September or the commencement of October. To every house was to be affixed the serial number noted against it in the block list. For the purpose of keeping blocks and circles distinct, it was recommended that along with the house-number should be painted the distinguishing letter of the block and the number of the circle—the latter were numbered serially throughout each charge. Ordinarily then the house number stood thus (2) $\frac{A}{16}$, 2 being the circle number, A the block letter, and 16 the serial number of the house. The plan is rather an elaborate one and does not yield advantages commensurate with the extra trouble it gives to the Census agency, and I allowed it to be partly discontinued as the work went on.

The material used for painting the numbers was generally a mixture of *geru* and oil. Where possible a sheltered position under the eaves in front of the building was chosen and a square or round space whitewashed, on which the number was afterwards painted in red. In the case of the wattle and grass huts which form the dwellings of many of the people of the Province, a common plan was to plaster a patch with mud, on which the house number could then be affixed in the usual way. Numerous other devices were resorted to: numbers were painted on earthen pots, winnowing fans, pieces of wood and other articles which were left with the house-holder and which he was told to produce when the Census officer made his rounds. As in 1881 some difficulty was experienced with the wild tribes in the Raipur District, many of whom have an aversion to their huts being touched by an outsider. The Superintendent of Sarangarh reports a similar aversion on the part of the Kumbhipáthias in that State. The objection was got over by the house-numbers being written on pegs driven in the ground in front of the huts of the objecting parties.

11. **Separate record of hamlets.**—If a block were made up of several villages, or parts of villages, a separate block list and a separate series of numbers beginning with 1 was assigned to each. In the ordinary mauza which is the village unit adopted in the Census tables, besides the main village, there are generally several scattered hamlets; sometimes mere offshoots of the parent village containing only a few houses, sometimes distinct and considerable settlements. In different parts of the Province they are known by different names, *tola, dhána, páli, etc.* At the present Census the preliminary instructions contained no precise definition of the word village, and as a consequence in nearly every district hamlets were treated as villages, *i.e.*, the houses they contained were numbered apart from those of the main village under the rule above quoted, and separate block lists were prepared for them. So far there was no great difficulty; but when it came to having a separate enumeration book for every hamlet so listed, troubles at once arose. In the first place, the submission of indents for enumerators' books was seriously delayed by the time it took to work out calculations as to the number and size of the separate hamlets appearing in the lists. The number of books of the

smaller size was indefinitely multiplied, an enumerator frequently requiring four or five for his block when one large book might have sufficed. But the greatest inconvenience of any was caused when a large mass of very small books come to be dealt with in the Central Office. At a future Census it should be clearly laid down that by village is meant the mauza, and that all hamlets should be considered as part of the parent village. House-numbering should then be consecutive throughout the mauza, the houses in the first block being numbered, say, 1 to 60, and the second block beginning with 61. In the case of a large village or town in which there were more Circles than one, the numbers should run consecutively by circles. There might in some places be exceptional cases, where, from the hamlet having a distinctive share in the village lands, a separate record of its population might be desirable. For such, special provision could be made by permitting the hamlet in this instance to be listed and treated as a village, but ordinarily the experience of the present Census shows that the more closely the mauza is adhered to as the village unit the better it will be.

12. **Buildings not used as dwelling places.**—Circular B laid down that every building should be counted a house which was intended for or used as a human dwelling, whether actually occupied at the time or not. The instructions to enumerators went further, and directed that buildings like shops, schools, temples, etc., should be included in the block list and should each receive a serial number. It was afterwards pointed out by the Deputy Commissioner of Wardha that the inclusion of shops, cattle-sheds, etc., brought a mass of useless detail upon the block list, and that were a blank page to be kept in the enumeration book for all such buildings found empty at the time of the Census, considerable inconvenience might be experienced from schedules running short. It was also noticed that it would be unnecessary to separately number places like these merely because some one slept there for the night, as such persons would be enumerated at their houses, in accordance with paragraph 11 of the Instructions to Enumerators. The Final Instructions for Supervisors therefore allowed for buildings of the above description being scored out in the block list and for their being thus no longer treated as houses. Most Deputy Commissioners are of opinion that these buildings should be brought on to the block list and should receive a serial number, so as to guard against the possibility of any one being overlooked on the Census night. This is perhaps the best plan to adopt, and for a future Census the rule might run that all buildings in which any one is likely to be found at night should receive a place in the block list. I would then omit the part of the Enumerators' Instructions which directs that a blank page in the enumeration book should be kept for all buildings found empty at the time of the Census; the block list is quite a sufficient guide to such houses. Encamping grounds, halting places frequented by travellers and the like, were entered in the block list, but were not numbered as houses.

13. **Progress of the work.**—The subdivision of Districts into Charges and Circles had been set down for May, the remaining portion of the preliminaries being due for completion by the middle of October. Monthly reports were called for showing the progress made. The District Census reports give the approximate dates on which the various preparatory steps were completed; but considering the dificulties which had to be encountered in some districts as compared with others, a comparison of these is hardly a fair test of the work done. Almost everywhere the arrangement of districts into Census Charges and Circles was completed by the month of June, and the selection of Superintendents and Supervisors took place at the same time. The formation of blocks and the appointment of enumerators went on very slowly in some districts, but was generally completed, except in very remote tracts, in October. House-numbering was not finished until December. In most cases the bulk of the work had been executed long before these dates, and only the special difficulty of some forest tract or other unforeseen circumstance kept the work behind. In Jubbulpore the delay in starting the operations was great, and it was not until the appointment in October of Mr. H. C. Bose, Extra Assistant Commissioner, as Special Census Officer, that real progress began to be made. In Burhanpur a misunderstanding between the Hindus and Mahomedans hindered the work; the house-numbering had not been finished in the beginning of January, when the Census Commissioner and myself visited the town. In Bhandara and

Chanda the preliminary measures were late in being completed, the delay in the latter District being chiefly due to the apathy of the Brahmapuri tehsil staff In the Panabaras zemindari of Chanda the success of the Census was for a time endangered by a feud in the zemindar's family: there was a small civil war raging, each party accusing the other amongst other things of having burnt the Census papers. The matter was promptly dealt with, but accidents like these show that in tracts so backward in communication as many of the Central Provinces Districts are, a very early start should be made with the preliminary work of such an extensive operation as the Census.

14. **Statistics of (a) Census Divisions, (b) Census Agency.**—Statements are appended, showing—

(1) the number of Charges, Circles and Blocks in each District, and the number of Census Officers of each kind entertained, and

(2) the sources from which the latter were drawn.

Statement showing the distribution of Census Divisions in Districts.

District.	Population of District.	No. of Superintendents.	Charges.		No. of Supervisors.	Circles.		No. of Enumerators.	No. of Blocks.	Number per Enumerator.	
			No. of Charges.	Circles per Charge.		No. of Circles.	Blocks per Circle.			Inhabited houses.	Inhabitants.
Saugor	591,743	61	58	4·7	357	272	10·0	3,237	2,468	37	183
Damoh	325,613	26	26	5·4	141	141	10·8	1,509	1,520	47	216
Jubbulpore	748,146	45	45	6·9	313	310	11·8	3,622	3,671	44	207
Mandla	339,373	33	33	3·6	120	120	9·9	1,191	1,191	52	285
Seoni	370,767	36	36	3·8	138	138	10·1	1,397	1,397	53	265
Narsinghpur	367,026	23	23	4·9	112	112	14·3	1,625	1,599	50	226
Hoshangabad	529,945	53	58	3·9	225	225	10·3	2,320	2,320	46	228
Nimar	253,486	22	22	8·2	181	181	5·9	1,065	1,065	48	238
Betul	323,196	30	30	3·8	113	113	10·3	1,166	1,166	53	277
Chhindwara	407,494	35	35	3·4	120	120	11·4	1,370	1,370	58	297
Wardha	400,854	35	32	4·9	175	158	11·4	2,209	1,795	39	181
Nagpur	757,862	65	65	5·7	374	372	8·6	3,233	3,218	47	234
Chanda	697,610	49	49	5·1	249	249	10·5	2,620	2,620	50	266
Bhandara	742 850	43	43	5·3	229	229	12·5	2,848	2,874	49	261
Balaghat	383,331	20	20	8·7	175	175	8·0	1,398	1,398	51	274
Raipur	1,584,427	51	48	10·2	495	488	11·0	5,269	5,355	57	301
Bilaspur	1,164,158	37	37	12·5	461	461	9·9	4,534	4,550	57	257
Sambalpur	796,413	53	53	5·9	314	314	9·5	2,980	2,980	51	267
TOTAL BRITISH DISTRICTS.	10,784,294	717	713	5·9	4,292	4,178	10·2	43,593	42,557	49	247
Feudatory States	2,160,511	126	123	5·3	652	648	8·1	5,301	5,277	77	408
TOTAL CENTRAL PROVINCES.	12,944,805	843	836	5·8	4,944	4,826	9·9	48,894	47,834	53	265

NOTE.—The difference between the number of Census Officers and of Census Divisions is explained by the fact that sometimes an officer had charge of two divisions, if small; and sometimes one or more officers were appointed to a large division, see paragraph 9 of Circular B.

It will be seen that in only one District, Raipur, does the average number of inhabitants per enumerator exceed the standard of 300. In most Districts there were individual cases in which the number was no doubt frequently in excess, but the average has been reduced mainly owing to the operation of two causes—*first*, when there were men available, separate small villages had each a separate enumerator, and *second*, in forest tracts where villages are far apart and are composed of only a few huts, the blocks, though frequently very large in area, are necessarily small as regards number of inhabitants. It is this latter cause which, in all the more jungly Districts, has pulled down the size of the block. The Sambalpur Report instances blocks being formed, containing only 2 or 3 houses, the latter being so inaccessible as to necessitate separate enumeration. It has also to be considered that blocks were originally framed on the basis of houses, 60 being the number assigned to each, and as several of these turned out to be uninhabited, see paragraph 12, the size of the block as shown by persons enumerated has naturally declined. The District Reports do not furnish complete details as to special areas, such as municipalities, forest tracts, etc., so it is impossible to give separate statements for these. Sixty as the standard number of houses per block is generally looked upon as suitable, and I would retain it at a future Census. The number of blocks to a Circle, and of Circles to a Charge, varies considerably in different Districts. The necessity of having a good and sufficient staff of Supervisors is insisted upon in nearly all of the District Reports : on them has fallen the burden of the work at the present Census. The proportion of Superintendents is not of so much importance, and the number to be entertained might well be left to the discretion of the Deputy Commissioner according to the material at his disposal.

Statement showing the sources from which the Census Agency was drawn.

District	Superintendents.			Supervisors.				Enumeratosr.							
	Total.	Official.	Non-official.	Total.	Official.	Patwaris and their relatives.	Non-official.	Total.	Official.	Patwaris and their relatives.	Land-holders and cultivators.	Bankers and Traders.	School-boys.	Others.	Number paid.
Saugor	61	41	20	357	140	...	217	3,237	216	...	1,535	591	12	883	...
Damoh	26	24	2	141	92	4	45	1,509	54	97	810	55	2	491	...
Jubbulpore	45	41	4	313	68	2	243	3,622	151	117	2,576	251	38	489	...
Mandla	33	32	1	120	86	2	32	1,191	111	16	365	9	41	649	9
Seoni	36	22	14	138	66	1	71	1,397	109	2	1,039	74	19	154	2
Narsinghpur	23	23	...	112	5	...	107	1,625	34	48	1,060	126	107	250	...
Hoshangabad	53	50	3	225	21	1	203	2,320	149	213	1,004	194	6	754	...
Nimar	22	14	8	181	36	38	107	1,065	109	95	275	214	...	372	...
Betul	30	30	...	113	43	...	70	1,166	109	6	535	105	...	411	...
Chhindwara	35	22	13	120	30	...	90	1,370	128	112	374	230	...	526	...
Wardha	35	27	8	175	63	2	110	2,209	74	17	1,317	93	25	683	...
Nagpur	65	52	13	374	106	1	267	3,233	351	22	445	84	80	2,251	100
Chanda	49	43	6	249	26	9	214	2,620	190	27	729	177	64	1,433	53
Bhandara	43	40	3	229	56	7	166	2,848	111	22	1,489	185	53	988	4
Balaghat	20	20	...	175	93	...	82	1,398	5	...	...	...	...	1,393	34
Raipur	51	42	9	495	230	108	157	5,269	255	41	2,918	530	570	955	...
Bilaspur	37	26	11	461	120	19	322	4,534	123	61	2,851	353	263	883	12
Sambalpur	53	43	10	314	143	90	81	2,980	148	79	2,259	44	138	312	...
Total	717	592	125	4,292	1,424	284	2,584	43,593	2,427	975	21,581	3,315	1,418	13,877	214

The second statement given shows the classes from which the Census staff was drawn. The summary in the margin exhibits the extent to which the several Government Departments assisted in the work.

Department.	Superintendents.	Supervisors.	Enumerators.	Total employed.	Proportion of column 5 per 100 of all officials.
1	2	3	4	5	6
Revenue and Judicial	99	179	260	538	12
Police	351	271	353	975	22
Educational	45	617	983	1,645	37
Forest	57	207	354	618	14
Military	1	17	83	101	2
Others	39	133	394	566	13
Total	592	1,424	2,427	4,443	100

Revenue and Judicial.—Tehsildars were not employed as Charge Superintendents, but were held responsible for the general conduct of the operations in their tehsils.

Police.—As has been already noticed the police were very largely employed on Census duty, and many of the District Reports testify to the good work they have done. Several Deputy Commissioners are of the opinion that if Police Circle areas are made the basis of Census subdivisions, it is a good plan to let the management of the Census remain with the Police. It seems to me that in the upland Districts, where crime is comparatively rare, and where the Police have therefore more time on their hands, this arrangement could very well be adopted. But there is scarcely a doubt that the Police cannot attend to Census in addition to their own work in the more populous Districts : one of the two has to suffer, and naturally it is Census that must go to the wall. This has been the experience of the present Census in more than one District. Deputy Commissioners had, of course, no alternative but to utilize the services of the Police, but, in future, it would be well if, specially in the plains Districts, other agency were found.

Educational.—By a notification issued in April 1890, it was ordered that both Civil Courts and Schools should be closed from 20th January to the end of February in lieu of the ordinary vacation in May and June. The whole of the School staff were thus placed at the disposal of the District Officers for employment during the final enumeration. The assistance they rendered was invaluable. In several instances the Deputy Commissioner was able to draft off school-masters to manage the Census of difficult tracts. With school-boy enumerators the employment of the school-master as supervisor was found to be a good plan, and, generally speaking, the agency is one which should always be untilized to the full at an operation of this kind.

Forest.—The forest officials were necessarily employed, almost to a man, in taking the Census of the extensive forest reserves that exist in many Districts.

In one or two cases objections were raised about the Census interfering with the ordinary duties of subordinate officials, so the orders issued in 1881 as to the co-operation of all Departments in the work were repeated. As a general rule, however, there was little difficulty experienced in this respect, and the District Reports are full of reference to the willing manner in which all Departments worked side by side to make the Census a success.

——	Superintendents.	Supervisors.	Enumerators.	Total employed.	Proportion of column 5 per 100 of all non-officials.
Patwaris and their relatives.	1	284	975	1,260	3
Land-holders and cultivators.	91	1,581	21,581	23,253	53
Bankers and traders	12	218	3,315	3,545	8
School-boys . .	...	12	1,418	1,430	3
Others . .	21	773	13,877	14,671	33
TOTAL .	125	2,868	41,166	44,159	100

The proportion of the different classes of non-officials is given in in the margin. Unfortunately the Circle List form did not contain a column showing the occupations of Enumerators, and the information on this head is not so full as it might have been.

Patwaris.—It has already been seen that, on account of the pressing nature of settlement work, the services of the patwaris could not be made available for Census duty, except to a very limited extent. Their loss was keenly felt. It is not so much that the work could not be done without them, but their non-employment has been a severe strain on the District Officer and his staff. It is perhaps impossible that the general administration of the District should not suffer to some degree by the carrying out of an operation of such magnitude as the Census; by the employment, however, of a highly trained staff like the patwaris, the interference with the ordinary work of the District is reduced to a minimum. The performance of the whole of the Census preliminaries for his Circle would give the patwari very little trouble, and the work would be done quickly and well as compared with what has been the case at the present Census, when non-official agency had to be hunted for and kept at the task for several months, before even a fair amount of accuracy could be attained. With the patwaris at his service the District Officer should not suffer the woes of Census for more than three or four months, although before then, no doubt, some general arrangements would require to have been made. The experience of the present Census certainly shows that on a future occasion the utmost use should be made of the patwari staff, which will then be probably available for the duty. It may be noted that of the number shown under the heading "Patwaris and their relatives," a considerable proportion belongs to the latter category.

School-boys.—The return of these is by no means complete; they were a useful agency in rural tracts.

Of the 44,159 non-officials employed at the Census, only 214, or about ·5 per cent., were paid. The figures speak for themselves as to the goodwill with which the work was done. It must be remembered that this work was no light matter especially for the supervising staff, who for many months had to make frequent journeyings to and fro, were always at the beck and call of the Government officers, and had to put up with having their work freely criticized and often found fault with. Every District Report bears witness to the general good spirit that prevailed. There were no doubt occasional objections and complaints, more particularly at the beginning of the work, but, as a rule, these were easily met. It was mainly to enumerators sent from a distance to take the census of remote and difficult tracts that payment was made. In Kampti a number of paid enumerators were entertained, the expense falling on the Cantonment Fund.

15. I append extracts from the District Reports which discuss some of the more interesting points connected with the matter of the Census agency:—

Saugor.—Patwaris were not employed on Census duty. In several instances difficulty was found before the passing of the Act in getting the persons selected as Enumerators to work, but generally there was little cause for complaint.

Damoh.—There was but little reluctance to undertake the work, and almost every one employed worked well and zealously.

Jubbulpore.—The majority of the Superintendents were Police officials, either Chief or Head Constables. The Deputy Commissioner thinks it was a mistake to utilize the services of this class of officials so largely for Census work. If they neglected their ordinary duties, they incurred the displeasure of their superiors, so they could not devote to Census work the attention it required. "From another point of view the appointment of Police officials as Superintendents is undesirable, as it has an unsatisfactory influence on the subordinate Census staff. It is scarcely a desirable arrangement to place men in the grade of Head Constable, many of whom are not of very high intelligence or of very high social status, over a staff of Supervisors, the majority of whom are bankers and landlords. All said, however, it would have been difficult, if not impossible, to have got through the work without the assistance of the Police." The District Report in another place speaks of the appointment of Superintendents as being not of much use. "They simply do the work of forwarding papers, and that in a very perfunctory and dilatory manner. The real burden of the work rests on the supervisors and enumerators."

Mandla.—"No difficulty was experienced in making the appointments of Superintendents and Supervisors, as a sufficient number of Government officials and intelligent landholders was ready at hand and furnished the necessary materials. The main difficulty to be contended with was that of finding enumerators owing to the very backward condition of the District, and as was anticipated it was found impossible to secure a sufficient number of men able to read and write. This was specially the case in the Ramgarh tehsil, where the inhabitants are mostly Gonds and Baigas, and it was found necessary to arrange for the appointment of thirty paid men. In response to a notice inviting applicants to come forward, the services of only nine men could be secured. The consequence was that the work of filling in the enumerator's schedules and the preliminary arrangements in connection with the preparation of building lists, etc., devolved chiefly on Supervisors. Enumerators and Supervisors had to be sent from long distances and were required to be absent from their houses on several occasions for days at a time. Another difficulty was that enumerators were frequently not present in their respective blocks, when visited by the Superintendent or Supervisor, and work was retarded in consequence. The want of the patwaris was keenly felt."

In **Seoni** little difficulty was experienced in finding enumerators. Very little help was got from patwaris, concerning whom the Deputy Commissioner writes that, though they would be of service in carrying out the preliminary measures, they should not be employed in the actual enumeration, as trusting to their local knowledge, they would be inclined to record conjectural figures, without making village to village and house to house visits. Seoni is happily the only district from which such fears are expressed.

Hoshangabad.—Very substantial aid was had from the patwaris, survey work having been, to some extent, completed in the district. Mr. L. K. Laurie speaks highly of the work they did. "The number of patwaris appointed as enumerators does not accurately represent the extent of the services rendered by this body of men. Many malguzars would not have been able to perform their duties as enumerators without the assistance of the patwaris. At a future Census it would be advisable to make patwaris' circles and Revenue Inspectors' charges the basis of Census arrangements."

Betul.—"In this District, where the great majority of even the mukadams are illiterate, it can be easily imagined how difficult it was to get enumerators in the wilder tracts. Petition-writers and others had, in some instances, to be sent from Badnur and others of the larger villages. The work was, as a rule, willingly and well done, there was no grumbling or holding back, though in some cases a good deal of personal inconvenience had to be borne." As giving the other side of the question, which has been raised in the Jubbulpore Report, as to whether the Police make a good supervising staff, I give Colonel Vertue's remarks on the excellent work they did in the Betul District: "Much, in a matter of this kind, must always depend upon the controlling agency employed. From the outset I put the work in the hands of the District Superintendent of Police and his Chief Constables, and the result was so successful that if there was to be another Census in 1892, I would do the same thing again. The Police have enormous advantages in dealing with a work like this. They are scattered over a District in disciplined order, in a way in which no other Department is; they are feared by the people; can always be found when wanted; and, owing to their training, can always be trusted to carry out orders with exactitude. Moreover, as they are not regarded with any great favour by other Government Departments, their work is always open to unfavourable scrutiny should there be anything amiss with it. The advantages then of employing the Police were many, and not the least was the opportunity the plan gave for fearless criticism of their work by others. That an operation of such magnitude was carried out with perfect ease was mainly due to their exertions and those of the malguzars."

In **Narsinghpur, Chhindwara,** and **Nimar** enumerators were generally obtained without much difficulty, except in forest tracts, where special arrangements were necessary.

Balaghat.—The patwaris were engaged on settlement. Their services were much missed, as the agency employed was frequently not very competent. Paid enumerators were entertained for some of the wilder tracts.

Chanda.—The Deputy Commissioner writes: "The difficulty in finding enumerators was very great. The fact that they were not paid does not appear to have been the chief cause of the difficulty, but rather the absolute deficiency of competent men. This was specially the case in the zemindaris, many of which are very difficult of access. Panabaras, Jharapapra, Koracha, Ambagarh and other zemindaris lie 100 miles or so by road from the nearest Teshil, Police Station, or Government school: that road lies through forest in which the villages have been largely depopulated by man-eaters. In each there were perhaps one kámdar and one thanedar who could read and write, perhaps one or two lessees of forest produce and a policeman. The entire indigenous stock of literates in a zemindari like Muramgaon, covering 200 square miles, consisted of two persons when I reached it. The only plan was to import enumerators, but this was no easy matter, as at first hardly a man could be found to go." Later a better spirit prevailed, as the Report continues: "That we managed to get enumerators at all for the zemindaris was simply due to the willingness of the people to assist. This was beyond all praise." The Census of the large Ahiri zemindari was excellently managed by the zemindar, who spared neither pains nor expense to make the operations a success. The Deputy Commissioner was able to procure the services of only a few of the patwaris, and there can be little doubt, as he says, that in no other District was the loss of the patwaris so much felt as in Chanda.

The **Nagpur, Wardha,** and **Bhandara** District Reports note that there was some reluctance at first on the part of non-officials to undertake Census duty. Mr. Drysdale writes that it was easily overcome, and that generally a great deal of interest was taken in the work; those who were unwilling at first vying with their neighbours to see who would do best.

Raipur.—It was difficult to obtain the services of the patwaris, owing to the pressure of settlement work which was approaching a conclusion. Those employed were used chiefly as supervisors, and did good work. The zemindaris with the exception of Thakurtola gave no trouble. Several of them are under management, and the work was well looked after. There was certainly no such difficulty anywhere, as appears to have been the case in 1881.

Bilaspur.—The Census of the zemindaris presented great difficulties. People were not to be found who could read and write, and men of local influence had to be appointed as supervisors, though frequently illiterate. The District Report speaks highly of the services they rendered, getting the work done by their agents or by men they specially employed for the purpose. The patwaris were still busy with settlement, though it had been hoped that the services of those in the Bilaspur Tehsil would be available throughout: see the Settlement Commissioner's note at paragraph 3. On the representation of the Deputy Commissioner 140 men were, however, placed by the Settlement Commissioner at his disposal. The account of the work they did is of interest: "When the patwaris reported themselves, they were divided into parties and placed under the orders of the various Superintendents. None of them during the preliminary Census work were appointed supervisors or enumerators, but they were sent from circle to circle under the directions of the Superintendents helping supervisors in difficulties, writing up lists in arrears, and doing the work of supervisors unable to act themselves. The service they rendered in this manner was invaluable. The patwaris were also sent to the zemindaris where the supervisors were generally illiterate. In the northern zemindaris on the Maikal Range they suffered terribly from fever during the rainy season. Hardly one of the patwaris sent to this part of the district escaped, and in two months' time almost half of them had returned to head-quarters quite incapacitated for work, many of them being carried on charpoys. Two of them died from the fever they thus contracted. The accompanying statement shows the number of patwaris engaged in Census work from the end of August to the end of December, and the percentage of those that were invalided from sickness. The Settlement Commissioner withdrew 50 of the deputed patwaris on the 1st January and 40 on the 15th, leaving 50 for Census duty. These remained until the completion of the operations." The work done by the patwaris under such difficult circumstances fully deserves the praise it receives in the District Report.

MONTH.	Total No. of Patwaris on Census duty.	No. sent on duty to the zemindaris.	No. of sick and incapacitated patwaris at head-quarters.	Percentage of sick on the No. sent to the zemindaris.
August .	50	33	...	...
September .	87	53	7	13·2
October .	112	78	33	42·3
November .	140	98	49	50·
December .	140	91	57	62·6

Sambalpur.—"Enumerators taken from amongst school-masters and advanced schoolboys did their work well. This class should always be employed as enumerators when possible, as the work interferes less with their private affairs, and they are therefore much more willing to devote to it the time required. Many of the persons originally chosen as enumerators proved unfit for the work, a large number having to be rejected on account of their being able only to inscribe on palm leaves. As far as possible they were replaced, but a good deal of the preliminary work fell to be done by supervisors."

16. Preliminary Census Forms.—(1) *Letters of appointment.*—At the present Census the letter of appointment and the preliminary Instructions for enumerators were printed on the same sheet of paper. In order that the appointments might come under the Census Act, the form of letter could not be filled in and signed until the latter became law, and as this did not take place till October, a difficulty was experienced in issuing the Instructions to the enumerators selected. As it was, the sheets were sent out blank and afterwards returned for signature on the passing of the Act, or fresh slips containing the letter of appointment were issued. In future the Instructions should be issued by themselves, appointment slips being separately printed. (2) *Circle list.*—In this there should in future be two additional columns, 3 and 8. In column 3 subordinate hamlets will be shown separately from main villages in the list. At the present Census both have been written in the same column, and it is frequently impossible to tell which is main village and which hamlet. Even though the census of hamlets is not taken separately, it will still be necessary to show them in the Circle list, to ensure against any being omitted. (3) *Block list.*—To this I should add a column for heads of families: it will be useful in cases where more than one family reside in a building to which only one serial number has been given. At the present Census the enumerators' books did not contain a copy of the block list form. These were printed locally and issued in duplicate, one copy being used for drawing up the rough list of houses, the other for fair copying the list when passed. This last was pasted into the enumerator's book when received. In future each enumerator's book should contain the block list form, which will be filled in from a rough building list prepared beforehand.

All the preliminary forms in Hindi and Marathi were printed in Nagpur, where also the few Telugu forms required were lithographed. Uria forms were partly printed at the Raja of Bamra's Press and partly lithographed at Sambalpur. Of the Circle List Form, which was printed on foolscap paper, four copies for each Circle were issued to allow for fair copies for the Charge Superintendent and for the Census Office. For each block two copies—one for fair, and the other for rough—were ordinarily issued of the block list form, which was printed on paper of the same size as the enumerator's schedule ; but as in many cases all the houses of a large block would not come on one copy of the form, an extra supply was allowed for. For small blocks the half of the form was usually found sufficient. At a future Census it would be well to give at least five copies of the Circle List for each Circle to allow for the spoilage that invariably takes place when strange forms come to be filled. Only one copy of the block list for each block will be issued if the enumerators' books are to contain a copy of the form.

CHAPTER II.

THE ENUMERATION.

17. **The Schedule and Instructions.**—These will be found in Appendix A. The suitability of both has been discussed at a Conference held at Simla in October last, and to the recommendations then made I have little to add. I shall, however, note on a few of the points which have more specially come within my own experience at the present Census.

The Schedule.—The want of an entry at the top of each schedule, showing the name of tehsil and village was felt in the Abstraction Office, when, as occasionally happened, a leaf got misplaced. The size and form of the schedule were appropriate. By deepening the page so as to make it contain more lines I think the book would be rather unwieldy, and consequently more liable to get torn. As it was, the paper in numbers of the books used on the present occasion, particularly those supplied from Bombay, was found to tear very readily. At the Conference it was considered that the rule requiring a new page to be taken for every house was wasteful. This must be taken to include that a blank page should not be left for every unoccupied house. I think there can be little harm in dropping the rule in future: more important than the saving in paper would be the boon of having increased space to meet extraordinary entries on the Census night, a contingency for which it is not always easy to make provision. No difficulty was experienced in entering the occupants of several sub-numbered houses consecutively on the same page in this way. A matter which might, however, be noted in this connection is that no line should be drawn across the page separating the people of one house from those of the house following. This had been directed in the case of sub-numbered houses, with the consequence that in the hurry of abstraction it was sometimes difficult to tell whether the line, if drawn close to an entry in the schedule, was a dividing line or a line cancelling an entry. The proposal to have the column for serial number at the end instead of at the beginning of the schedule is a good one: by the present arrangement it is frequently wrongly filled in. The space given for the entry of occupation was not as a rule sufficient at the present Census. According to the instructions occupations have to be described in considerable detail, and when a long entry has to be repeated in full for all the numbers of a family, the utmost available space should be assigned to it.

18. **The Enumerator's Instructions.—Parts A and B** laid down the procedure to be followed on the first and second rounds. The rules were generally found to be suitable. As regards paragraph 2, in Maratha Districts directions might be given restricting the use of the Modi character as far as possible. It is not easily read by the Nagpur school-boy in abstracting. The Nimari character gave no trouble at the present Census. Amendments of paragraphs 3 and 5 have already been suggested. There was apparently no difficulty in working the provisions of paragraphs 6 and 11. So far as can be judged from the the district reports, there could have been little chance of applying the latter rule, as almost everywhere there appears to have been a dread amounting almost to a superstition of being found away from one's house on the night of the Census. Paragraph 10.—Instead of reading over the whole of the entries in the schedule, it was found sufficient if only the names of the members of the family were read out.

Part C contained the rules for filling up the schedule :—

Rule 1.—The serial number might, I think, be retained. It is occasionally of use as showing whether an entry which has been imperfectly scored out should be taken or not.

Rules 2 and 3.—In the Central Provinces the prevalence of the two great bodies of Hindu dissenters, the Kabirpanthis and Satnamis, makes the question of the retention of the column for sect worthy of some consideration. At present I am unable to discuss the results disclosed by the abstraction of the figures for these two sects; this will be done in the chapter on the religions of the people. But from the entries appearing in the enumerators' books I should say that it is not worth while to retain the sect column, more specially if the latter is to be omitted for the rest of India. Generally speaking, the enumerator has little idea of what the term implies, and the person enumerated still less. As a consequence sectarian terms are found scattered broadcast over all the four columns 2 to 5. Though abstractors had orders to write a person down as a Satnami, in whatever column the name might occur, I question whether the information thus obtained is very trustworthy. If the column were to be retained, it would be only on account of these two sects. For all other creeds, except Christian, no sect return is required. At the present Census, it is true we have worked out details for sects of Mahomedans, but it is generally conceded that the result is fragmentary, and it was on this ground that the Census Conference, which met at Agra in December 1889, decided that t was not worth while to obtain a return of the more emphatically theological schools or sects of the Mahomedan religion. Merely on account of the Satnamis and Kabirpanthis to burden the schedule with an extra column and to inflict upon the enumerators an extra crux in the instructions, seems to me to be uncalled for. On the present occasion the returns for religion and caste have been appreciably perturbed by the impossibility of getting the enumerators to grasp the meaning of the columns for sect and caste sub-division. Caste has been written for religion and sect for caste in a mnnner which, I would venture to believe, has been largely induced by the fact of there being four columns which had to be filled up somehow, and about the precise signification of which no clear idea seemed possible of being imparted. If it must be known what are the numbers of those who follow the two dissenting sects, a better plan would be to have the latter recorded as religions in the appropriate column. At the present Census the method of simply disposing of them as sects of the Hindu religion has been objected to on the ground that they are not offshoots of Hinduism, but entirely distinct creeds. Clear instructions for the record of both as separate religions would, therefore, probably be carried out without any difficulty, and would afford the information that is wanted. On any account I should not keep a sect column for their separate record alone.

Rules 4 and 5.—Caste and sub-division of caste. It was the general opinion of the members of the Simla Conference "that the statement of castes recorded at the Census of 1891 is as full and accurate as any that is likely to be obtained through the medium of a census, and therefore another record of the members of each caste will not be required at so short an interval as ten years." On this matter I shall remark when discussing the tables for caste in the first part of the report, but here I would note that if it be again decided to obtain a record of castes, the column for sub-division should be omitted. With clear instructions the main caste will very generally be intelligibly recorded. At the present Census the working out of details of sub-divisions of caste has necessitated an expenditure of time and money which must be considered out of proportion to the value of the results obtained. The information is not therefore likely to be again required, and if this is the case, I harcly think it is worth while, as has been suggested, to retain the column for sub-caste in the schedule, merely for the purpose of elucidating any doubtful entry of main caste that may be recorded. Like sect, the caste sub-division is frequently imperfectly understood, and to trouble the enumerator with entering in the schedule a mass of detail of which no notice will be taken except for reference in doubtful cases, appears to me to be unnecessary.

Rule 8.—No special instructions were issued about the entry of civil condition for the divorced, but they were ordinarily recorded as unmarried.

Rule 9.—The return of parent-tongue is, it is believed, of hardly any practical use; its omission was therefore generally agreed to at the Conference. If the return is, however, kept, a common mistake in the Uria books should be guarded against. Infants were frequently returned as *kundi*, a word said to signify speechless, instead of the tongue of the parents being recorded. As *kundi* might mean Uria, Laria or any of the aboriginal languages, the mistake does not permit of direct adjustment; it is also sometimes confounded with Khondi.

Rule 10.—The rule was loosely worded in the Central Provinces Instructions, and as a consequence the birth-place returns for some of the Native States in Chhatisgarh have been vitiated. The political control of these Feudatories until recently was in the hands of the Deputy Commissioners of Raipur, Bilaspur, and Sambalpur. Kawardha and Sakti still remain so. It had thus been the custom to look upon the States as forming an integral portion of these districts, much as is the case with the zemindaries attached to them. As the enumerators' instructions did not clearly lay down that persons born in one of the States should return the name of the State as place of birth, the mistake has frequently been made of entering the old district name instead. Thus for nearly all the people of Khairagarh, Raipur is returned as place of birth, Khairagarh being in the popular mind taken as a part of that district. More specific instructions should issue at a future Census

Rule 11.—Occupation.—This rule was no doubt the one which the enumerator found it most difficult to master. It will be better to defer my remarks on its working until the occupation tables are discussed in the results portion of the report.

Rule 12.—In future it has been recommended that the return of persons *under education* should be dispensed with. The instructions will be much simplified by the change.

Rule 14.—The experience of the present Census shows that this is one of the rules which enumerators make least effort to understand. Probably the fact that entries under it are of comparatively rare occurrence led to its being to some extent overlooked. The column contained all manner of mistakes: persons were returned as *deaf* only or *dumb* only and not as *deaf-mutes*, and lameness or some deformity was continually recorded. On a future occasion the instructions to supervisors should be amplified so as to guard against such wrong entries, and care should be taken to see that the rule is more thoroughly understood and acted on than has hitherto been the case.

19. **The Specimen Schedule.**—It is important to have a few good examples to which the Census staff may refer, and it was this consideration that led the Simla Conference to propose that as soon as the instructions and schedules are fixed upon, copies should be sent to district officers in order that sample entries may be prepared in accordance with them. The sample entries thus obtained will be of the greatest help to the Census Superintendent in drawing up a set of examples to suit every part of the Province. On the present occasion different specimen schedules were provided for Hindi, Marathi, Uria and Telugu speaking tracts. The change adopted in the manner of expressing occupations of agriculturists—see para. 9 (g) of the final Instructions to Supervisors, which were issued after the schedules had been printed—caused the entries of agricultural occupations in the specimen schedule to be somewhat misleading. An example might with advantage have been given in the Hindi schedule to illustrate rule 10—Birth-place, as applied to Native States. The schedule was printed so as to show the application of paras. 14, 15, and rule I, *i.e.*, a red ink entry was introduced at the foot of the schedule, one of the black ink entries was scored out in red, and the serial numbering of the entries was given in red ink.

20. **Translation of the Schedule, Instructions, etc.**—To this too much importance cannot be attached. On the present occasion an imperfect knowledge of the language and a total lack of acquaintance with the Province led me into error in this respect which might have been otherwise avoided. In such a matter as translation opinions will naturally differ, and most varying versions were given by different officers consulted of some of the terms for which it was sought to obtain the most suitable vernacular equivalent. The word "mazhab" for "religion" in the Hindi schedule is perhaps the instance, which has been most objected to, of a term being used which is not generally understood by the common people. No guidance was obtained from the record of the last Census, as all the vernacular schedules then in use had been destroyed.

21. **Training of the Census Agency.**—The District Reports detail various methods for the training of the Census Agency. In one case the whole of the superior staff was got together and put through a written examination in the Census Circulars and Instructions. The general plan followed was to hold central meetings at which the instructions were discussed and sample schedules filled up, examined, and corrected. The latter point is one which cannot be too strongly insisted upon, and at a future Census I would recommend the issue to every superintendent, supervisor, and enumerator of a specimen book containing instructions and a few blank schedules, some two months before the time for the preliminary record arrives. The whole staff could thus be put through a practical course of training by being made to fill up entries for actual persons. On the present occasion such specimen books were supplied only to the supervising staff, but they might with advantage be given to every person to whom Census duty is assigned.

22. **The Preliminary Record.**—Except in towns, this was generally

commenced about the middle of January and completed by the beginning of February. In almost every district a rough record was first made on blank paper, and after this had been checked and corrected by the supervising agency, it was fair copied into the bound books of schedules. The district reports show the work of supervision to have been very thoroughly done. Courts and schools were closed, and it was thus possible to employ the judicial and educational establishment exclusively on Census duty. The officers of other departments were also very generally engaged in inspecting and checking the enumerator's record. That the test was well carried out there is evidence on every hand, but from one or two districts it has been reported that it was frequently not at all easy for an inspecting officer to catch the enumerator at his post, owing to his residing at a distance from the block to which he had been appointed. In most cases this could not be helped, as an enumerator from a distance had frequently to be told off to take the census of a tract where there was no one able to read and write. In such cases it was found convenient to have the Census papers kept with the village headman, as they were thus always ready for inspection and test on the visit of a supervising officer.

23. **The Final Enumeration.**—The date fixed for the final enumeration was the night of the 26th of February. In order to facilitate the task, proclamation had been issued calling upon the people to help the Census staff. They were asked to keep to their houses, to have a light burning, and to make some one stay awake till the enumerator came round. But as a rule there was no need for such proclamation. Everywhere the people appear to have been impressed with the seriousness of the matter, which for so many months had been engaging the attention of the Government officers, and of those amongst themselves who had been enlisted for the work. A general desire to be helpful was evinced, but in no respect was this more noticeable than in the anxiety most people displayed to be at their houses on the Census night. How far this may have been due to superstition it is impossible to say. Rumours there were about, in several places. As an instance the case of the Kudarmal fair in the Bilaspur district may be taken. Special arrangements had been made for the census of persons attending the fair, but these were rendered almost unnecessary by the way in which every one who could, left so as to be at his house by the night of the 26th February; the prevalent idea was that people would lose their land if they were not enumerated in their villages. It is likely also that the enumerators did their best to persuade people to be counted at their houses. That the presence of large numbers of visitors in a village would mean extra trouble on the Census night seems to have been very readily realized by the enumerating staff. For the contingency it was not always possible to provide, but that the efforts of the enumerator were not always without result, the following instance noticed by Colonel Lugard will show:—

Damoh.—Some people of the Taradehi circle, who had gone to cut the harvest in the Jubbulpore district, were driven off by the enumerators there who refused to let them stay. Many of these poor people travelled long distances to put in an appearance at their native places on the Census night.

A similar incident is reported from Chanda, where the enumerators of some of the Hyderabad villages bordering on the Ahiri Zemindari refused to let travellers cross the Pranhita until the Census was over. Such instances were probably few and far between. Generally speaking, with the exception of forest tracts, railways, and fairs, for which special measures were necessary, there was no difficulty experienced in making the final enumeration, and that the work was done so well must to a great extent be set down to the willingness of the people themselves to do everything in their power to assist the Census agency.

24. **Illiterate Enumerators.**—As at last Census there was a little difficulty in several districts with enumerators who were more than ordinarily deficient in education. For the preliminary enumeration their services had hardly been required, as in most cases the record had been prepared by the supervisor, if the enumerator was not able to write fairly well. But on the Census night, every man who could read and write, be it ever so little, had to be made use of in backward tracts. All that was required was that the enumerator should be able to read out the names written in his book. If he could not make fresh entries in a legible hand, he could make a note of some kind on a separate paper of the entries to be recorded for any new comer, and these could be written at their proper place in the enumeration book by the supervisor on the morning following the Census, after testing their accuracy as might be necessary. As ordinarily there would be very few such new comers in tracts where this device had to be resorted to, it entailed hardly any chance of mistake.

25. **The preparation of the Abstracts and Final Results.**—Every enumerator's book contained a form of abstract in which the result of the enumeration was to be posted on the morning of the 27th of February. For the preparation of this abstract, all the enumerators in a circle assembled, and in presence of the supervisor each had to add up the number of (*a*) occupied houses, (*b*) males, and (*c*) females recorded in his book. The result ascertained was not to be disclosed but kept by the supervisor, who then handed the book to another enumerator to be re-added. If the two results agreed, the figures were entered in the appropriate columns of the abstract. In case of disagreement a third addition was necessary. The totals thus arrived at were transferred by the supervisor to a circle abstract, for which printed forms had been previously supplied. Taking the circle abstract and the enumerators' books, supervisors next repaired to the Superintendent of the charge, who examined the results and compiled them into a charge summary, which he forwarded along with the books to the head-quarters of the Tehsil. Here the returns for all the charges were combined, and a Tehsil total struck which was forwarded to the Deputy Commissioner of the district. The result of the Census throughout the district being thus ascertained, the final total was communicated to the Census Superintendent at Nagpur and to the Census Commissioner at Simla simultaneously by telegraph. The above was the practical working of the scheme as generally adopted. In many cases the preparation of everything beyond the enumerators' abstracts was done at the Tehsil, as it was considered that greater accuracy would thus be attained. It may be added that large Municipalities prepared their own returns which were then forwarded direct to the District Head-Quarters ; the total for all small towns were, however, included in the sub-divisional summary in the ordinary way. Considering the difficulties, which in many districts had to be contended against, the submission of the returns was, with one or two exceptions, very promptly made. The first of the Census results to reach me were those for the Nandgaon State. Through the excellent arrangements made by the Dewan, Mr. Ramkrishna Rao, the totals for the State were worked out by midnight on March 1st, and reached me the following morning by telegram. The first district to send in its returns was Wardha, where Mr. Drysdale had his totals ready for despatch so early as the 3rd of March, three days after the Census. The Saugor district where Mr. Bhogchand, Extra Assistant Commissioner, had been throughout in charge of the operations, was only one day behind, its results reaching me by wire on the 4th. I subjoin a statement showing the dates on which the telegraphic returns were received from the different Districts and States. The variation between the figures then given and those finally worked out in the Census office is also noted.

Statement showing variation between preliminary district returns and final Census figures.

District or State.	Date on which result received.	+ where final figures are more—where final figures less.	Variation per 1,000 of the population.	Remarks.
Nandgaon	2nd March 1891	−246	1·33	Figures twice changed on account of late receipt of Railway books.
Wardha	3rd March 1891	+22	·05	
Saugor	4th March 1891	+257	·43	
Narsinghpur	5th March 1891	+635	1·73	
Makrai		+2	...	
Khairagarh		+52	·28	
Jubbulpore	6th March 1891	−1,216	1·62	Figures changed twice through late receipt of B.-N. Railway books and mistakes in East Indian Railway.
Chhindwara		−138	·33	
Rairakhol		+1	...	
Sambalpur	7th March 1891	−37	·04	Figures changed once.
Damoh		+277	·85	
Seoni		−65	·17	
Kawardha		+30	·32	
Sakti		+5	·19	
Hoshangabad	8th March 1891	+1,842	3·47	Figures once changed. Difference due to mistakes in Sohagpur Tehsil.
Sonpur		−287	1·46	
Bilaspur	10th March 1891	+7,200	6·18	Bilaspur Tehsil summary wrong.
Betul		+265	·81	
Sarangarh		−20	·24	
Nimar	11th March 1891	−13	·05	Figures once changed on account of late receipt of Rajputana-Malwa Railway books.
Chhuikhadan		+157	4·32	
Kanker	12th March 1891	−70	·84	
Raigarh		+769	4·56	
Raipur	14th March 1891	+489	·30	Figures once changed.
Patna		+2,342	7·05	
Kalahandi	15th March 1891	+302	·92	
Mandla	16th March 1891	−114	·33	
Balaghat	17th March 1891	−662	1·72	
Bhandara		−37	·04	
Nagpur		+951	1·25	
Bamra	18th March 1891	−26	·24	
Chanda	31st March 1891	−253	·36	
Bastar	1st April 1891	+44	·14	
Total Central Provinces		+12,458	·96	

The results for the remote State of Bastar were not ready till the 28th of March. The delay was to a certain extent unavoidable, as owing to the immense distances of some of the outlying parts of the State from Jagdalpur, it was almost impossible to exercise the control necessary for the prompt submission of the returns. The totals for the Chanda District were not ready till the 31st of March, Chanda thus earning the unenviable distinction of being the last district in India to submit its results. The fault lay with the Brahmapuri Tehsil staff, who throughout the operations had been invariably behindhand with the work. The totals for the Tehsils of Warora, Mul, and Sironcha had reached Chanda by the 10th of March, three weeks before those for Brahmapuri were received. The officials to blame were reported on to the Commissioner of the Division and punished for the delay.

26. **Dispatch of Books to the Census Office.**—This took place in accordance with the following instructions. "On receipt of the enumerators'

books from charge Superintendents, Tehsildars will see that they are properly arranged lengthwise and tied up by circles and charges. The charge summaries and circle abstracts should be bound together in separate files. It would be convenient if the latter are compiled according to Police station and outpost areas. A slip giving the name of the station or outpost should be inserted before each group of abstracts of circles comprising the station or outpost. On the slip should be noted the total of occupied houses, males, females, and total population for the station or outpost as ascertained from the circle, abstract figures. The books and papers arranged as noted should then be despatched direct to the Census Office at Nagpur. It should be seen that they are securely packed either in sheeting or boxes. The packing in which they arrived from the Press should, as far as possible, be made use of to save extra expense." The despatch of the books to Nagpur marked the close of the Census operations in the districts.

CHAPTER III.

SPECIAL AND SUBSIDIARY MATTERS.

27. **The Census of the Feudatory States.**—The most notable result of the present Census in the Central Provinces is the remarkable increase that has taken place in the population of the Native States. The causes of this will be discussed in another portion of the Report, but the main cause, the better administration of the States, is a matter so closely connected with the conduct of the Census operations that it may be most suitably referred to here. In 1881 the political control of the Chhatisgarh Feudatories was vested in the Deputy Commissioners of Raipur, Bilaspur, and Sambalpur. The Bastar State was politically attached to the Chanda District, and the small State of Makrai was then as now subordinate to Hoshangabad. Khairagarh of the States attached to the Raipur District, Sakti of those attached to Bilaspur, and Sarangarh and Patna of those attached to Sambalpur were under Government management, and it would appear gave little difficulty. For the remaining States the Deputy Commissioners could in 1881 make only such imperfect arrangements as were possible when the time and attention of every district official was already fully taken up with the Census work in the Khalsa. The State authorities were frequently apathetic and procrastinating, and the establishments were in most cases inefficient. In Bastar a dissension in the Raja's family brought the operations to a standstill, and though a Census was taken on the day appointed, it was admittedly of little value. Within the last ten years all this has to a great extent been changed; with the exception of Bamra and Sonpur, the States are either under direct management or the chiefs are assisted by officers of proved ability appointed by Government. Bastar and all of the Chhatisgarh Feudatories, except Kawardha and Sakti, which remain attached to Bilaspur, are under the control of a Political Agent with head-quarters at Raipur. Some advance has been made in education and the construction of the Bengal-Nagpur Railway, which at the time of the Census had been completed up to the border of the Province, has already done something to open up a part of the country. But the progress made in these latter respects has as yet been little felt, much of the immense tract covered by the Feudatories is still as difficult of access as ever, and it was only recently that "Bastar, which had hitherto been outside the pale of education, has been visited by the Inspector of Schools, and seven schools have been opened." The success which has attended the Census in the Native States is to be entirely attributed to the energy with which it has been carried out by the Chiefs and local officers and to the excellence of the arrangements they made. Mr. Goodridge, the Political Agent, to whose care and attention also a great deal of the credit for the result is due, writes to me as follows :—

"The work in connection with the Census of 1891 has I consider been well done in all the States; evidence of this is to be found in the very large increase of population in nearly every State. The Rulers and Administrators have given great attention to the subject. Indeed I fear it has engrossed too much of their time and energies, and that the administration of the Feudatories has this year been to some extent sacrificed to the needs of the Census. Some of the Administrators of the States, such as the Superintendents of Kalahandi and Patna, and the Dewan of Bastar, the late Rao Saheb Gopinath Guru, had very extensive charges, and practically none but their own subordinates to do the work. I think they deserve the greatest credit for the successful results obtained."

With these remarks I entirely concur. I would also mention the States of Bamra and Sonpur, where the Census operations were exceedingly well conducted by the Chiefs, and Sarangarh and Nandgaon by the Superintendent and Dewan in charge.

State.	Superintendent or Dewan.
Kalahandi	Mr. J. Goondiah.
Patna	Mr. T. R. Deshmukh.
Sarangarh	Mr. Raghunath Rao.
Nandgaon	Mr. Ramkrishna Rao.

28. In 1881 an abbreviated form of schedule was drawn up for use in the Native States. At the present Census the schedule in use in British districts was adopted, and the procedure was in every respect the same. The main difficulty encountered was the impossibility of finding persons capable of being employed as enumerators. In many States the work was practically done throughout by the supervisors, enumerators being only employed to assist in the final check on the Census night. A statement accompanies which gives statistics of the division of the Feudatories into Census areas and of the Census agency employed. The number of inhabitants per enumerator was above the average in 9 out of the 15 States. In 1881 there was a similar excess in 13 States. The abstract in the margin contrasts the figures for the establishments employed in 1881 and 1891 in those States in which the excess of persons per enumerator was most marked. Although what chiefly affects the accuracy of the enumeration is the completeness of the arrangements made and of the supervision exercised by the officers in charge of the Census, there can at the same time be little question that the increase in the agency, which in several cases has more than doubled, has had an appreciable effect in making the Census of 1891 more accurate than the Census of ten years ago. Of the composition of the staff employed on the present occasion it is scarcely necessary to give details. The returns received are not complete, but as might be expected they tend to show that the Census, specially in the more remote Feudatories, was chiefly taken by the State subordinates. There are few traders in those parts, and the stock of indigenous literates of any other description is small.

Statement showing the distribution of Census divisions in States.

States.	Population of State.	Number of Superintendents.	Charges: Number.	Charges: Circles per charge.	Number of Supervisors.	Circles: Number.	Circles: Blocks per circle.	Number of Enumerators.	Number of blocks.	Number per enumerator: Inhabited houses.	Number per enumerator: Inhabitants.
Makrai	18,549	3	3	4·3	13	13	6·1	79	79	47	235
Bastar	310,884	19	19	3·8	72	72	5·5	393	397	152	791
Kanker	82,379	8	2	6·0	12	12	10·5	152	126	134	542
Nandgaon	183,866	7	7	6·1	43	43	9·9	427	425	76	431
Khairagarh	181,184	6	6	8·3	50	50	11·9	594	594	57	305
Chhuikhadan	36,288	4	7	4·0	16	16	7·8	125	125	56	290
Kawardha	91,813	7	7	5·3	41	37	9·1	338	338	52	272
Sakti	25,374	1	1	11·0	11	11	9·3	102	102	42	249
Raigarh	168,525	7	7	5·3	37	37	8·5	313	313	95	538
Sarangarh	83,210	19	19	4·2	79	79	3·9	305	305	49	273
Bamra	104,367	8	8	4·6	37	37	8·8	324	324	58	322
Rairakhol	20,335	1	1	13·0	13	13	5·8	75	75	52	271
Sonpur	195,245	8	8	8·0	64	64	10·8	693	693	54	282
Patna	332,197	7	7	10·0	70	70	12·6	885	885	68	375
Kalhandi	326,295	21	21	4·5	94	94	5·3	496	496	131	658
Total	2,160,511	126	123	5·3	652	648	8·1	5,301	5,277	77	408

	1881.		1891.	
	Total strength of Census Agency.	Number of persons per enumerator.	Total strength of Census Agency.	Number of persons per enumerator.
Bastar	225	1,066	484	791
Chhuikhadan	58	701	145	290
Kanker	137	557	172	542
Sakti	56	507	114	249
Kalahandi	371	782	611	658
Raigarh	194	791	357	538
Patna	244	1,697	962	375
Sonpur	364	570	765	282

29. **Forest Tracts.**—I have elsewhere referred to the difficulties that attended the carrying out of the Census preliminaries in some of the wilder parts of the Province. What proved most troublesome was having to send strangers into such places in the rains and autumn, at a time when the jungles are noto-

riously unhealthy. On a future occasion it would, I think, be well to have all enquiries as to villages, etc., in forest tracts made during the hot weather preceding the Census. If the position and size of such settlements are known and marked on a map, blocks and circles might be devised at the head-quarters of the District, and there would be no real necessity of sending men to take up the Census work on the spot until December, when the house numbering would have to be carried out. From then until the actual enumeration, it would not be necessary to have the agency fully employed; a few good men might be required to remain on to test the correctness of the preparations made, or to accompany inspecting officers who might come round on tour. The preliminary enumeration might also be deferred until nearer the date of the Census than in ordinary tracts. The entries for forest tribes are, as a rule, so simple and uniform that there should hardly be the same need for elaborate examination of the schedules as in well settled parts, where difficulties are continually cropping up in connection with every column. There is, moreover, extremely little change in the forest population, and at the final census, but very little alteration should require to be made in the record. Given a day census, to which, in view of the stay at home proclivities of the inhabitants of these wilds, there can hardly be any objection, the amount of ground that can be covered by the enumerator should be very considerable. In this way if a few good enumerators are employed—forest officials will be available, and as at the present Census so for many years to come, it will probably be necessary to supplement these by imported men—three weeks should suffice for the whole process of enumeration. A really trustworthy official would require to be in charge of the operations in a tract dealt with in this way. But with this proviso there can, I think, be little difficulty in making the census of forest tracts a much more simple matter than it was on the present occasion. As has been already noted, a great part of the work devolved upon officials of the Forest Department. The Census frequently engrossed almost the whole of their time, and there was in one or two districts a good deal of complaint about their ordinary work being neglected in consequence. On every ground, therefore, it would be well to shorten the length of the operations in forest tracts and have the work pushed through by a few efficient men well supervised in as short a time as possible.

30. I give in the margin a statement showing the population of areas enumerated at longer periods than the night of the 26th and morning of the 27th of February, *i.e.*, of areas where the enumeration commenced either before the night of the 26th or lasted longer than noon of the 27th. A considerable number of persons in nearly every district were, no doubt, enumerated on the morning of the 27th, but as the period of synchronous enumeration was taken to extend until the forenoon following the Census night, they have not come in the return. The reports received from districts in which there is a large amount of forest area agree in pointing out that the taking of a day census in these parts can in no way affect the accuracy of the results. The people never move, and the number of strangers likely to be found in such places is practically *nil*.

District or State.	Number of persons.
Mandla	777
Hoshangabad	42,258
Chhindwara	5,864
Chanda	2,536
Balaghat	165
Bilaspur	24,795
Bastar	233,130
Raigarh	913
Rairakhol	2,051
Kalahandi	27,258
Total	339,747

31. **Municipalities.**—In Municipalities the Census was taken through the Municipal authorities, the help of such Government officials as were available being lent for purposes of supervision or direction. The arrangements made

were satisfactory, though in one or two instances there was considerable delay in having the preparatory steps carried out. It is, as a rule, more difficult to get a non-official staff to work, especially gratis, in towns than in the country, but the district reports instance little trouble in this respect. At a future Census it would be well if greater care were taken to have the area to be treated as urban marked off at the very commencement of the operations. On the present occasion no specific instructions on the subject were issued, and as a consequence in at least two cases mistakes were discovered so late in the day as the compilation of the figures for towns, which form Tables IV and V in the Imperial series. The matter will be further referred to in the first part of the Report. The only other point that requires to be noticed with regard to the Census in towns is the date for the commencement of the preliminary record. With a changing population, it is desirable that the date should be deferred so as to bring it as near the day of the Census as possible. In the smaller rural municipalities the matter is not of so much importance, but in all the larger towns from two to three weeks seems ample time to allow for the preliminary enumeration and test of the record.

32. **Military Limits.**—This presented no difficulty. Under the rules prescribed by the Census Commissioner, the Census of all purely military lines devolved upon the military authorities, while the Census of so much of the cantonment as lay beyond regimental lines or other purely military limits was taken by the Cantonment Magistrate acting under the direct orders of the civil authorities of the district. The only cantonment in these Provinces in which there is a very large non-military population is Kampti. On the night of the 26th of February, the wing of the 27th Madras Native Infantry which had been stationed at Sambalpur was on the march in the Sonpur State on its way to Cuttack. The census of the detachment and followers was taken under the supervision of the officer in command, and the books of schedules forwarded to Sambalpur and included in the returns for the cantonment there.

33. **Jails, Hospitals, etc.**—These were made into separate blocks and the census taken by the officer in charge. In Jails, the Superintendent arranged for the enumeration of all prisoners under trial, convicts, and civil prisoners, and also of all resident jail officers and their families. Prisoners were recorded in the schedules as belonging to one or other of the three classes mentioned; their former occupations were not entered. The census of persons under detention in police lock-ups was taken in the ordinary way by the enumerator in whose block the lock-up was situated.

34. **Railways.**—There are five separate lines of railway running through the Province, the Great Indian Peninsula, the East Indian, the Indian Midland, the Rajputana-Malwa, and the Bengal-Nagpur Railway; with each of these lines separate arrangements had to be made. The East Indian, the Indian Midland, and the Bengal-Nagpur Railways agreed to the census of all persons along the line of rail outside the distant signals of stations being taken by the district authorities. To this also the officials of the Rajputana-Malwa Railway at first consented, but as it had been afterwards settled that for whole of the Bombay, Baroda, and Central India system the Railway authorities should take the census between stations, the latter plan was adopted for the part of line within the Nimar District, so as to make the arrangements uniform throughout. The only line with which any difficulty was experienced was the Great Indian Peninsula Railway. The Agent's Circular No. 10, dated the 27th October 1890, mentioned as the persons to be enumerated by the Company's servants "all resident employés, their families and servants and their families, and, by special arrangements between Local Revenue authorities and the Superintendents, residents in a hut or group of huts, chiefly occupied by Railway employés between the

distant signals at each end of any station and within 200 yards of the Company's boundary, provided that such huts are more than one mile from the nearest village." The huts of work people living along the line, but outside the Railway fencing, had already almost everywhere been included in enumerator's blocks in the District Census, but as the Railway officials considered that by the departmental circular they came within their province, such huts were in many cases brought within the Railway blocks as well. The following are from the district reports :—

Hoshangabad.—"Some confusion was caused on the Great Indian Peninsula Railway owing to the absence of clear instructions as to the area to be dealt with by the Railway officials. At first it was supposed that all huts outside the Railway fencing would be enumerated by the District authorities, but at the end of October the Company's Agent issued a circular which required the Railway officials to enumerate all huts within Railway limits. This included of course all huts within the boundary stones beyond the fence, and on C class land at stations and elsewhere. In a circular No. 278, issued on 17th December, the General Traffic Manager referred to the Agent's instructions, but made it appear that they applied to huts within 200 yards of the Company's boundary, and more than a mile from the nearest village *at any point of the line*, the qualification as to distant signals being omitted. In the end I had at the last moment to arrange with the District Engineer that the Permanent-way Inspectors should travel down the line with the Supervisors through whose circles the line ran, and satisfy themselves by inspection that no hut had been included in both the Railway and the District lists."

Wardha.—"The Great Indian Peninsula Railway proceeded about the census in their own way, and all my overtures were practically treated as interference. In the end I was obliged to be content with leaving entirely to them the census within the limits of the Railway fence and of such Railway quarters outside the fence as they chose to number for their census, and I instructed the District Census Agency along the line to include all other buildings occupied by Railway servants or work people in the District Census. This necessitated a special check of the house numbering along the Railway line towards the close of the preliminary record, but in this way I secured that no such people were overlooked.

The needless irritation thus caused is to be regretted, but it is almost impossible to avoid, unless, as I should strongly recommend for the future, the enumeration of the line outside station premises be left to the District authorities. This plan worked smoothly and successfully on the Bengal-Nagpur Railway where at the present census we had most experience of its operation. At the time of the census the railway had been opened up to Sambalpur Road Station, but there were still large numbers of labourers employed on construction in places specially towards the Sambalpur end. The Sambalpur District Report mentions the steps taken for their enumeration :—

"In consultation with the Railway District Engineer the Tehsildar of Sambalpur and the Permanent-way Inspector went over the portion of the line within the district. The Tehsildar found that all the people connected with the Railway generally resided outside the railway limits, and as the residents within those limits were very few in number, it was thought more convenient to leave the censusing of the latter also to the Tehsildar. The only work then left to the Railway authorities was to take the census of the people actually travelling by rail on the Census night."

The labourers working on the line in the Bamra State were enumerated in the same way under the direction of the State officials. The Railway authorities were found willing enough to help, provided they were relieved of the control of the arrangements. In every way a great deal of trouble was saved by the management of the operations being in the hands of the District authorities. On an open line such a plan could probably not be carried out without friction arising between the Railway employés and the District staff, but the latter can, at all events, be safely left to enumerate all but Railway stations and running trains, and this rule might be universally adopted in future.

35. The Superintendent of Census, Bombay, supplied the books for the Great Indian Peninsula Railway, those for the Rajputana-Malwa Railway were got from Ajmir, and for the East Indian Railway from Allahabad. The books for the Indian Midland and Bengal-Nagpur Railways were supplied by me. When on tour I examined the preliminary record of the books along the Bengal-Nagpur Railway in company with Mr. Clark, the special officer appointed by the Company, and found it to have been carefully done. All the railways had issued full instructions based on the rules framed by the Census Commissioner as to the procedure to be followed on the census night, more particularly with regard to the enumeration of passengers travelling by rail. This, I believe, to have been well carried out. I myself visited the Nagpur Railway Station while the enumeration was in progress. Two heavy trains were leaving the station, one by the Great Indian Peninsula Railway and the other by the Bengal-Nagpur Railway. Every passenger had been censused and supplied with a traveller's ticket. To the latter the people seemed to attach as much importance as they did to their Railway passes, being apparently of the opinion that an equal penalty would attach to the loss of either. In some instances the enumeration books were not forwarded to the District authorities after the census so quickly as they might have been, and the abstracts, apparently through the instructions issued by the Companies in one or two cases overlooking this detail, were not filled up. Very clear instructions had been issued about the former, and it does not appear how any mistake arose, unless the over-centralization of the control of the Railway census had something to do with it. In the Wardha district, for example, some books of the Traffic Department census went to the office of the Traffic Superintendent at Nagpur as charge superintendent for the length of line between Bhusawal and Nagpur. They did not reach Wardha until after the despatch of the telegram, giving the results of the Census for the district. Local delivery of the books should be insisted on in future, so as to prevent any possibility of delay.

36. **Census of the Umaria Tract.**—The colliery lands at Umaria being administered by the Deputy Commissioner of Jubbulpore, the Census of the tract was carried out through him. The Census of the portion of the Katni-Bilaspur branch of the Bengal-Nagpur Railway that runs through the Rewa State was arranged for by me, under instructions from the Census Commissioner. The enumeration was effected through the Engineer in charge. The Umaria lands not being ceded in sovereignty, the Census returns for them, as well as for the railway, after being worked out in the Census Office at Nagpur, were forwarded to the Superintendent of Census, Central India, for incorporation with the figures of the Rewa State.

37. **Fairs.**—The only large fairs taking place at the time of the Census were those at Garhakota in the Saugor District and at Rajim in Raipur. The Kudarmal fair in Bilaspur assumed small proportions, as it had partly broken up before the 26th of February. For the fair at Garhakota most complete arrangements had been made by Mr. Bhogchand, the District Census Officer, but two days before the final enumeration, cholera broke out and the gathering had to be dispersed.

> "The dispersion of the fair caused great inconvenience and extra work, as special arrangements had to be made for the Census of the people who had left. Spare schedules and enumerators' books were sent by special messengers to all places where there was likely to be a large influx of people hurrying from the fair, and the work of enumeration was successfully carried out."

For the Census of the Rajim fair a strong force of officials was employed. The preliminary enumeration was begun and completed on the 25th February. All new comers on the 26th were drafted off to the appointed camping grounds, and their census taken as they arrived. At night the whole was carefully checked, the final enumeration being effected without difficulty.

38. **Travellers and wandering Gangs.**—Special arrangements for the enumeration of travellers were necessary only on the main lines of traffic, enumerators being appointed for the more frequented roads. Tickets which were to be given to travellers so as to prevent them being again censused, should another enumerator want to count them, were plentifully supplied to districts, but from what one may learn from the District Reports they were not much used. As a matter of fact, there is but little travelling by night in the cold weather. People on the move invariably put up at some recognized camping ground; these are always near a village, so that ordinarily no one remains in the open. The village Kotwars were, however, generally employed to visit any spot where by chance travellers might be found, and to bring any there might be to the village for enumeration. Gangs of Banjaras were generally asked to halt for the day preceding the Census; nowhere did their enumeration give any trouble.

39. **Officers on Tour.**—The following were the instructions issued:—

"Officers on tour should be supplied beforehand with household schedules and with a book of 16 pages. The latter they should be instructed to fill in a day or two before the Census, so as to leave only the work of correction for the Census night. On the morning of the 27th of February, the books with the household schedules stitched in and the abstract form filled up, should be forwarded to the head-quarters of the District or State where the officer may happen to be encamped. This should be done even where the head-quarters station of an officer is in a different district from that in which he is on the Census night. Officers whose tour extends over the whole Province will receive books and schedules direct from the Census Office. All others should be supplied as noted by Deputy Commissioners."

40. **Householders' schedules.**—The use of these was practically confined to Europeans and Eurasians. A few in English and Vernacular for the census of natives of India were issued to every district, but almost everywhere their use was discouraged; in many districts it was practically forbidden. There were frequent mistakes in the schedules filled by Europeans and Eurasians, all arising from the instructions printed on the reverse of the schedule not having been read. The latter were, perhaps, not succinct enough; directions were given with regard to every column, some of which certainly appear unnecessary, *e.g.*, "Sex—Enter whether male or female." I think if several of these directions were omitted so as to make the instructions not look quite so long, there would be a better chance of their being read. No advice seems necessary about how to fill up columns 1, 2, 6, 8, 9 or, if the entry of "learning" be omitted, column 12. A specimen schedule should, of course, be given.

Language.	For Europeans and Eurasians.	For Natives of India.
English	1,900	100
Urdu	...	170
Marathi*	...	400
Total	1,900	670

* Hardly any of these were issued.

41. **Separate Schedule for Christians.**—It has been proposed that the column for sect should be omitted from the ordinary schedule in future. This being the case it becomes a question whether a separate schedule containing the sect column should not be provided for all Christians. Many Native Christians could not be trusted to fill in their own entries; this would still have to be done for them. But even in their case a separate schedule would possess some advantage. At the present Census the entries for Christians, more especially with respect to columns 2 to 5, were very badly filled in by the enumerators. In the Census Office, the work of abstracting the books containing Christians for sect, race, and caste had all to be done twice over; there was scarcely a book in which corrections had not to be made. Race was entered in the

column for sect and *vice versâ* in a way that upset all one's calculations. To take an example, the return of a considerable number of persons as of "Roman" race was enough to excite suspicion until it was discovered that by "Roman" was meant "Roman Catholic," and that the entry had come in column 4 instead of column 3. If a separate schedule were supplied for Christians, this could be, to some extent, prevented. It could at once be ascertained to what households such schedules had been given and their examination by the supervising staff would thus be assured. In this way we should get at least a fair amount of accuracy. The only objection to this plan is that it would increase to some degree the complexity of the enumeration, and that by adopting it the books, in places where there are many Native Christians, would be full of loose schedules, a result which it is always well to avoid. But the fact of there being no column for sect in the ordinary schedule as well as the increased accuracy likely to be attained leads me to think that all things considered, the use of separate schedules for Christians would be an advantage.

42. **The Attitude of the People.**—The attitude of the people was generally distinctly helpful. There was, for the most part, a total indifference as to the motives of Government in taking the Census. There had been previous Censuses in 1866, 1872, and 1881, which most people could remember, and which had been followed by no evil results. Rumours, it is true, got afloat in some places, more particularly in the Native States, but generally little or no distrust was excited. Some references on the subject from the district reports are worth giving.

Damoh.—The general idea used to be that the Census was preparatory to the imposition of some tax, but on this occasion there does not appear to have been anything of the sort prevalent. It was considered rather an unprofitable fad to which all parties were willing to yield an amused indulgence.

Jubbulpore.—Even the most illiterate and unenlightened among the people are now aware that the Census means no harm, but is simply an essential part of Government work. Instances have not been wanting in which people, where houses had by some oversight been left unnumbered, had voluntarily come forward to have the omission rectified.

Mandla.—The attitude of the people towards the Census was quiet and submissive, and they afforded all assistance in their power to the District Staff and the Census Officials. An idea was, at one time, prevalent in the interior of the district that Government wanted to ascertain the names of all young girls of a marriagable age with the intention of having the whole of them kidnepped. But such fears were easily dispelled.

Hoshangabad.—The attitude of the mass of the people was one of entire indifference, coupled with a cheerful readiness to do what was required of them. Not a single case of obstruction was reported. The malguzars, as a body, took an intelligent interest in the operations and gave most loyal and efficient aid. The filling in of the schedules evoked many earnest and amusing discussions of religions, castes, and occupations, and the supervisors propounded puzzling enquiries based upon hypothetical sets of circumstances. Thus it was asked one day what entry should be made regarding the age and civil condition of a traveller arriving at a serai on the night of the Census and found by the enumerator to be both deaf and dumb.

Bilaspur.—The fact that the Census followed close upon the settlement operations in the district seems to have given rise to a rumour, which was current in the rural tracts, that all persons who were not recorded in their houses on the Census night, would have their lands recorded as waste in the settlement papers, and would lose their cultivation.

The Feudatory States.—The attitude of the people was generally one of indifference. The two last Censuses have accustomed them to the idea, and the whole thing was regarded rather as a caprice of the Sircar's than anything else. Where it was attributed to sinister motives, the object ascribed was generally an intention to impose some new kind of taxation or to raise funds for the marriage of some member of the chief's family. In Raigarh the belief was current that a certain blood-thirsty goddess had demanded a human sacrifice. To this the Sircar had demurred, and she had been eventually appeased by the Sircar agreeing that she should have only those whose names were not written in the Census books. This was evidently the ruse of some zealous enumerator. Another rumour which, probably owed its origin to the same source, was that all who were not present when called on the night of the Census would become barren.

Other ingenious explanations of the object of the Census are reported. The best one perhaps is that the Government having conquered the country of Upper Burmah were counting the people with a view to sending every tenth man, woman, and child to colonize their new possession. But the time when such stories could obtain credence seems now to have passed away, and generally no difficulty is found in getting the people to understand the objects of the Census and give what help they can to further its being taken.

43. **Legislation.**—The Census Act became law in October 1890. In this Province where non-official agency had to be so extensively employed from the very commencement of the operations, the late passing of the Act gave rise to difficulty with the staff in several districts. At a future Census the Act should be passed by July at latest, so as to enable the pressure, which it is sometimes necessary to employ to get recusant Census officers to attend to their duties, to be applied at a time when it is most required, *viz.*, at the very outset of the work. The following notification, dated 5th November 1890, under the Act was published in the *Central Provinces Gazette*:—

Dated Nagpur the 5th November 1890, No. 7029.—Under Section 2 (I) of Act XVI of 1890, the Indian Census Act, the following persons are appointed Census officers in virtue of their respective offices:—

Deputy Commissioners of Districts within their respective districts.

Secretaries to Municipal Committees within Municipal limits.

Officers in command of cantonments and Military lines, within the limits of their respective commands.

Agents and Managers of Railways, within Railway premises and adjoining areas occupied by Railway workmen.

Under Section 2 (3) of the said Act, the Chief Commissioner is pleased to delegate the power of appointing Census officers under the Act to all Deputy Commissioners, to be exercised within their respective districts; to all officers in command of cantonments and military lines, to be exercised within the limits of their respective commands; and to all Agents and Managers of Railways to be exercised within railway limits.

Under Section 6 of the said Act, Census officers are hereby empowered to ask all questions necessary to enable them to fill up the schedule in accordance with the instructions attached to it.

Under Section 9 of the said Act, the Chief Commissioner is pleased to direct that the Census schedules left by Census officers at dwelling-houses to be filled up by the occupiers, shall be filled up in accordance with the instructions printed on the back of such schedules.

Under Section 11 of the said Act, the Chief Commissioner is pleased to direct that all prosecutions under the Act shall be instituted in the Court of a Magistrate of the 1st class, provided that no such prosecution shall be instituted except with the previous sanction of the Deputy Commissioner of the district.

In most districts notifications under Section 6 of the Act were issued by Deputy Commissioners calling upon malguzars to render assistance to the Census staff. The assistance ordinarily demanded was (*a*), to furnish guides and lights to Census officers, (*b*), to arrange for supplies to Census officers for cash payment on demand, (*c*), to provide suitable accommodation for Census officers. The number of prosecutions under the Act is given in the margin. Almost all were for refusal to work, but it was only in the worst cases that an example had to be made; generally the mere fact that it provided punishment in case of refusal or

District.	Number of prosecutions.
Saugor	9
Damoh	1
Jubbulpore	2
Mandla	8
Narsinghpur	2
Hoshangabad	5
Betul	1
Chanda	1
TOTAL	29

NOTE.—There were no prosecutions under the Act in other districts. In Raipur eight persons were tried under the Indian Penal Code for assaulting Census officers.

neglect to do Census duty was sufficient. That the Act was in this way distinctly helpful as giving the Deputy Commissioners control over the large and heterogeneous establishment employed on the Census is testified to from almost every district. Its provisions are generally regarded as suitable; one district Census officer, it is true, thinks that imprisonment might be provided for such as are stubborn and desperate characters. But it is generally conceded that the existence of the Act is almost all that is wanted, the mere threat of prosecution being usually enough to deal with any case of contumacy that may arise.

CHAPTER IV.

THE PREPARATION OF THE RESULTS.

44. The Office for the preparation of the Census results was opened at Nagpur on the 4th March 1891. The building which was formerly the head-quarters of the Native Infantry stationed at Nagpur was used for the purpose; it, however, proved insufficient to hold the establishment employed when the work was its height and an adjoining building had to be rented before the whole staff could be accommodated.

45. **Receipt of Books.**—The Census books were received in the office at various dates, from the 5th of March, when those from Wardha began to arrive, up to the 13th of May, when the books from the Bastar State were received.

46. **Establishment.**—The establishment employed consisted of—

(*a*) Officials, patwaris, and non-officials deputed from the districts and States of the Province, and

(*b*) men locally enrolled at Nagpur.

(*a*.) The following gives the number of persons deputed to the office :—

	Officials.	NON-OFFICIALS.			Total.
		Patwaris.	Other non-officials.		
			On R12.	On R15.	
Deputed to Census Office	32	90	256	31	377

Most of these came to Nagpur in March and April, but after May 40 patwaris and non-officials were received chiefly in place of others who had run away. The number of non-officials and patwaris from other parts of the Province hardly at any time exceeded 300.

(*b*). Over 500 persons were at one time or another enlisted locally at Nagpur. They were paid R10 to start with, and the best men were advanced to R12 and R15 as the work went on.

47. **Attendance and Distribution of Establishment.**—The statement on the next page shows the number of non-officials (including patwaris) actually employed during each month the operations were in progress. Their distribution over the different sections is also given.

During the months of May and June 1891—the monsoon did not burst at Nagpur until 2nd July,—the amount of absenteeism was very great on account of the excessive heat, and desertions were frequent. In August 1891 a fatal case of cholera occurred among the men from Sambalpur, and half of their number ran away, throwing back the Uria work considerably, as it was difficult to replace them.

48. **Working of the Office.**—The office was, as will appear from the table given, divided into the following sections :—

1. Record-room.
2. Abstraction.
3. Preparation of test-slips.
4. Examination of test-slips.
5. Re-abstraction.
6. Tabulation.
7. Compilation.

49. **Record-room.**—In addition to the number of the assistants allowed for the ordinary work of issue and receipt of books, the record-keeper was, at the commencement of the work, given a number of men whose duty it was—

(1) to examine the books of each district and state with the supervisors' abstracts;

(2) to separate the enumerators' abstracts from the books, and

(3) to number the books serially for each charge. Working with such a large estab-

Attendance and Distribution of Non-official Establishment employed in the Census Office.

Month.	Number of working days.	Attendance. Total number of workers.	Attendance. Average number of workers per day.	Record Room. Total workers.	Record Room. Average per day.	Abstraction. Total workers.	Abstraction. Average per day.	Preparation of Test-slips. Total workers.	Preparation of Test-slips. Average per day.	Examination of Test-slips. Total workers.	Examination of Test-slips. Average per day.	Re-abstraction. Total workers.	Re-abstraction. Average per day.	Tabulation. Total workers.	Tabulation. Average per day.	Compilation. Total workers.	Compilation. Average per day.
1	2	3	4	5	6	7	8	9	10	11	12	13	14	15	16	17	18
1891, March	23	5,345	232	140	6	5,205	226	...	...	...	...	...	...	...	...	...	...
„ April	25	13,151	526	382	15	10,773	431	556	22	297	12	1,143	46	...	...	...	...
„ May	25	14,918	597	349	14	10,154	406	846	34	757	31	2,105	84	707	28	...	...
„ June	26	16,359	629	571	22	10,862	418	739	28	1,228	47	1,306	50	1,653	64	...	...
„ July	26	14,120	543	356	14	6,251	241	940	36	2,009	77	1,180	45	3,384	130	...	...
„ August	24	10,878	453	147	6	397	16	...	...	1,170	49	1,529	64	7,635	318	...	...
„ September	25	10,787	431	181	7	180	7*	...	...	885	35	889	36	8,230	329	422	7
„ October	27	10,112	375	236	9	129	5*	...	...	...	...	...	...	8,822	327	925	34
„ November	23	6,619	288	137	6	...	...	...	...	...	...	...	...	6,089	265	393	17
„ December	21	5,477	261	118	6	...	...	...	...	...	...	...	...	4,971	237	388	18
1892, January	25	5,774	231	98	4	...	...	...	...	...	...	...	...	5,226	209	450	18
„ February	25	5,357	214	93	4	...	...	...	...	...	...	...	...	4,983	199	281	11
„ March	28	4,046	144	286	10	...	...	...	...	...	...	...	...	1,804	64	1,956	70
„ April	28	1,622	58	179	7	...	...	...	...	...	...	...	...	312	11	1,131	40
„ May	27	1,348	50	187	7	...	...	...	...	...	...	...	...	...	...	1,161	43
„ June	27	1,094	40	121	4	...	...	...	...	...	...	...	...	...	...	973	36
„ July	30	952	32	57	2	...	...	...	...	...	...	...	...	...	...	895	30
„ August	26	252	10	49	2	...	...	...	...	...	...	...	...	...	...	203	8
Total	461	128,211	...	3,687	...	43,951	...	3,081	...	6,346	...	8,152	...	53,816	...	9,178	...

* These represent a few men employed in abstracting sheet VIIIB, sects of Mahomedans and Hindus.

NOTE.—To save complexity the average number of workers per day, columns 6, 8, 10, etc., is calculated on the supposition that work went on throughout the month, which does not quite represent the actual facts, *e. g.*, re-abstraction was finished on 19th September, but the average in column 14, opposite September, is calculated on 25 working days. The real measure of work done is, of course, the total number of persons employed, *i.e.*, the information given in columns 5, 7, and 9, etc. The figures in the "Total" line show the relative extent of each process of the operations. The greatest, it will be seen, was Tabulation, on account of the time taken in tabulating and totalling the Registers of Castes and Occupations.

lishment, it was found necessary to abstract the books by charges, taking no notice of circles ; arranging the books according to the latter, involved such a multiplicity of small bundles, as to cause delay and confusion.

This part of the work was not completed till June.

50. **Abstraction.**—The abstracting office was divided into two sections, in the first of which the books of the Hindi and Marathi districts were abstracted, and in the second the Uria books of Sambalpur and the Eastern States. The working sheets prescribed were*—

I.—Sex, age, religion, and civil condition.
II.—Sex, age, religion, and education.
III.—Sex, age, and occupation.
V.—Sex and parent-tongue.
VI.—Sex and birth-place.
VII.—Sex, age, caste, and infirmities.
VIIIA.—Christians, sect, race, and sex.
VIIIB.—Hindus and Mussalmans, sect and sex.
IX.—Christians, age, race and sex.
X.—Sex, religion, caste, sub-caste, and languages known by literates.

51. **Abstraction Establishment and work done.**—The table appended shows the number of men employed on the abstraction work and the work done by them.

Statement showing the original abstraction work done in the Census Office.

Total Number of entries abstracted, 12,944 805.

Working sheet.	No. of working days.	Total No. of men.	Average No. of men per day.	Average No. of entries per man per day.	When completed.
I and VII . .	119	12,270	103	1,055	
II . . .	125	6,424	51	2,016	
III . . .	115	7,990	69	1,620	July
V . . .	122	3,163	28	3,738	
VI . . .	117	3,678	31	3,520	
VIII . . .	84	1,021	12	...	October
X . . .	136	9,105	67	1,422	August

Sheets I and VII.—These were abstracted by pairs, but the abstraction of all the other sheets was done by abstractors working singly. Very many of the boys we had to employ as abstractors were exceedingly inefficient, so the rule of double working was adhered to throughout. The Uria men were especially backward in all the departments of the abstracting and tabulating work; on Sheet I they abstracted on an average 993 entries per man per day against 1,066 in the Hindi and Marathi section. The highest average attained was in the month of June, when the daily number of entries per abstractor reached 1,337, or 2,674 per pair, in the Hindi and Marathi portion of the office.

Sheet II occupied 51 men for 125 days, at the rate of 2,016 entries per man per day.

Sheet III was abstracted by 69 men in 115 days, the number of entries per man per day being 1,620, or 1,657 Hindi and Marathi and 1,431 Uria. The best work was done in May, when the average per man rose to 1,882 in the first of these sections.

Sheets V and VI were simpler to work than the other sheets ; the first occupied 28 men for 122 days, and the second 31 men for 117 days, the average number of entries per day being 3,738 in the case of Sheet V, and 3,520 in Sheet VI. In the Uria section the number of entries abstracted per day was in general one-forth less than in the Hindi or Marathi section. The language return especially was by no means easy in the case of the Eastern States on account of the great variety of aboriginal dialects in the books.

Sheet VIII.—Besides abstracting the sects of Christians, the Local Government directed sect details to be worked out for Mahomedans and for Kabirpanthis and Satnamis, these having been separately shown at the preceding Census. The work occupied 12 men for 84 days. As every book had to be examined to see whether there were persons belonging to any of these sects, the number of entries per day would be no criterion of

* The forms were generally the same as those shown at pages 63 to 70 of Vol. I of the Census Proceedings, 1891.

the work done; an abstractor might wade through 50 books without coming across a Kabirpanthi or Satnami.

Sheet X.—On this was abstracted every caste and every sub-division of caste, the use of Sheet IV prescribed by the Census Commissioner being therefore dispensed with; details of literacy by castes were also entered in Sheet X. Its working was thus by no means an easy task; it gave employment to 67 men for 136 days, at an average of 1,422 entries per man per day. Here the Uria work was much simpler, by reason of sub-divisions being seldom recorded for the Uria castes and the eastern aboriginal tribes, and the average number of entries amounted to 1,759, in June rising as high as 1,928. In the Hindi and Marathi section the average was 1,378, the highest point, 1,621, being reached in April, when the abstraction of the comparatively simple entries in the books of the hill districts was in hand.

In calculating the above averages, the number of totallers and assistant supervisors has been included in the number of abstractors, but not the number of officials employed as supervisors. The pay of the abstractors was fixed at R10, R12, or R15, as the case might be. A scale was then drawn up laying down the number of entries which each man had to do per day in order to earn full pay; if more than the stated number of entries was done, he received an efficiency allowance calculated proportionately on the excess entries, and if fewer entries were done his pay was cut accordingly. The scale was changed from time to time according as the abstractors became proficient in the work, and according to the difficulty of the books they had to deal with. This often varied very considerably and involved frequent alteration in the scale. Prescribed registers were kept by the supervisors of each working section showing the number of entries abstracted by each person, and these were at the end of the day transcribed into a general register kept by the Deputy Superintendent of the office.

52. **General remarks on Abstraction.**—The main point in the matter of abstraction was of course to get work satisfactory both in quality and amount out of the abstractors; on this I shall note below when speaking of re-abstraction. The sections in which each set of working sheets was being abstracted were kept entirely distinct and no inter-communication was allowed. The sheets prescribed were generally suitable. Those for the Hindi and Marathi work, which were printed in Bombay, were sometimes badly ruled; for instance, in Sheet I the age figures, which were written vertically down the side and against which were drawn lines on which to note the requisite entries, occasionally came in the wrong lining space, causing confusion and mistake in totalling the entries opposite them. In Sheet II equal vertical spacing was left for each religion. As by far the greatest number of entries were those of Hindus, it would be well if the first religion-space were made double the others so as to give plenty of room for all the entries that have to come under it. At a future Census I should recommend that the two parts of Sheet VII, if both are kept, should be separately abstracted; there are very few entries of infirmities, and consequently they are easily overlooked. It not infrequently happened that infirm persons were discovered in books for which no Sheet VII had been handed in; were the two parts of the sheet abstracted by different persons, these mistakes would be readily found out. I may add that the abstracting was done in the ordinary manner by making four vertical ticks and crossing them with a fifth, so that the group represented five entries. In abstracting castes it was sometimes found expedient to enter actual numbers, as in this way by comparing the book page by page with the abstraction sheet the correction of a mistake could often be easily made without having the whole book re-abstracted.

53. **Preparation of test-slips.**—The test-slip was in nearly the same form as that prescribed by the Census Commissioner in his Note N, dated 30th January 1891.* The work of entering in the test-slips the details necessary for gauging the correctness of the abstraction involved a very considerable amount of labour. At first it was supposed that it could be done by a few men, but as the work began to rapidly fall behind, a special section was opened for the purpose. Even then, however, the matter had been underestimated and the test work never got properly along side of the abstraction. This was a mistake and should be guarded against in future.

On an average 30 men were employed for 102 working days to transcribe the abstraction results on to the test-slips, the average number of books for which results were thus transcribed being 27 per man per diem. Though the test-slip work took up a great amount of time, it is of the utmost importance in securing accurate abstraction, and is well worth the trouble spent on it.

* See page 43 of Vol. II of Census Proceedings, 1892.

54. **Examination of test-slips and adjustment of errors.**—The test-slips after being filled up were passed on to a section which was opened for their examination, and which was composed of the best workers in the office. The work of finally checking the abstracted results was not completed till September. It occupied 42 men working in pairs for 151 days, the average number of books examined and adjusted being 26 per pair in each day. The following is a summary of the general rules which were issued for comparing the abstracted totals appearing in the test-slips with one another, and for making corrections in cases where such were allowable.

Sheets I, II, and III were to be compared together in point of age; if the two of them agreed and appeared otherwise correct, an adjustment of one per cent. was allowed in the age-periods of the discrepant sheet. As it was frequently difficult to make such a correction in the case of sheet I, the ordinary procedure was to send it, if disagreeing with sheets II and III, for re-abstraction. Sheets I, II, and X were to be compared for religion, and a correction of 1 per cent. made in sheet II in case of discrepancy; sheet I or X was to be re-abstracted, as adjustment of the mistake could not be properly made in their case. Sheets II and X were to be compared with regard to literacy, and if they disagreed the book was to be referred to—the education entries were generally few in number,—the mistake corrected, and the sheets passed if otherwise correct. Sheets V and VI could be compared only in respect of the total of males and females.

In every case the books of the census charge which was being checked were in the hands of the persons engaged in the work of test-slip examination, and as the examiner had always an assistant to help him, re-abstraction or comparison of a discrepant sheet with the enumeration book was frequently effected on the spot. Out of the 84,079 books of the Province, 24,396 or 29 per cent. were abstracted correctly in every item, 30,882 or 36·7 per cent. were passed in the checking section after making corrections in age-periods or the like, or on reference to the books, and 28,801 or 34·3 per cent. were ordered to be re-abstracted in one or other of the sheets. No adjustment was allowed in cases where the number of males or females disagreed in any of the sheets. At the beginning of the work many of the books had to be re-abstracted twice over, as the first re-abstraction frequently failed to bring out correct results.

55. **Re-abstraction.**—What mainly led to such a large number of books being wrong in one item or another was the great size of many of the books. The largest size of enumeration book contained 64 pages, and it was found next to impossible to get the entries for so many persons as were recorded in a book of this size abstracted correctly in every detail. When the work started, a high standard of correctness was hardly looked for, but it was thought that, as the abstractors became more accustomed to their task, matters would improve. Afterwards, when the abstraction sheets still refused to come out exactly, recourse was had to breaking up the books or at least separating from the main book the supplementary ones used along with it; but meantime a very large number of books had been abstracted in one or other of the sections, so that this plan could only be partially carried out. The reduction in the size of the books produced a very decided improvement and generally 50 per cent. of the work was found to be quite or nearly correct, or even more towards the end of the abstraction, but at the beginning hardly a single book gave exactly the same results in all the sheets. This is a matter which deserves the fullest consideration at a future Census, as more than perhaps anything else it led to difficulties at the present one. The large size books are very convenient for the record of all the persons living in an enumerator's block, but if such are again used, they might conveniently be marked off into two parts and each separately abstracted, as in this way the work of check is greatly facilitated. The sheets in which re-abstraction was chiefly necessary were, as has been noted, I and X; in the former 40·1 per cent.* of the entries were re-abstracted, and in the latter 28·8; in sheet III, 25·1 per cent. of the entries were re-abstracted, 16·2 in sheet II, 6·5 in sheet V, and 5·5 in sheet VI. The figures given do not include the partial re-abstraction or comparison of the sheets with the enumerator's books, which was done in the checking office. The Uria work always gave trouble in this connection, and much of it had to be gone over again on account of the inferior stamp of men employed. When the sheets were passed on re-abstraction, the mistakes found were entered in error-slips drawn up for the purpose and debited to the abstractors making them.

The work of re-abstraction occupied 56 men for 145 days in all the sections of the office.

* These represent the proportion of the entries re-abstracted, not of books; hence the percentage differs from that given in the last paragraph, as the books sent for re-abstraction were naturally those which contained most entries.

56. The Tabulation Registers employed were—

I.—Houses and total population.
III.—Classified list of villages and towns.
IV.—Religions.
V.—Age and religion.
VI.—Civil condition by age and religion.
VII.—Education by age and religion.
VIII.—Parent tongue.
IX.—Birth-place.
X to XIII.—Infirmities by age.
XA to XIII A.— „ by caste.
XIV.—Caste.
XVA.—Occupations of males.
XVB.— „ females.
XVI A, B, C.—Sects of Christians, Mahomedans, Kabirpanthis, Satnamis.
XVII.—Races of Christians.
XVIII.—Castes of literates.

The Registers were in the form prescribed in the Census Commissioner's Note M dated 9th October 1890. Each page consisted of 12 lines on which the entries for 12 books were tabulated. Page totals were not carried forward to the next following page, as in case of error this would have involved the correction of each page total subsequent to the place at which the error might be discovered. The page totals were separately collected and added up at the end of the Register. The Registers were made up separately for Tehsils and for all towns shown in Tables IV and V of the Imperial series.

57. Tabulation was carried on in five sections as follows:—

Section A.—Registers I to XIII A.
„ B.—Register XIV.
„ C.—Registers XV A, B.
„ D.—Register XVI.
„ E.—Register XVIII.

Register XVII was tabulated by English clerks under the direct supervision of the Deputy Superintendent. The number of men employed in these sections and the time taken to complete the work is given below.

Statement showing the Tabulation work done in the Census Office.

—	Section.	No. of working days.	Total number of men.	Average No. of men per day.	Date of Commencement.	Date of Completion.
Total number of books dealt with—84,079.	A	148	24,204	164	1st week of May, 1891 .	End of December, 1891.
	B	178	12,837	72	25th September, 1891 .	30th April, 1892.
	C	146	12,733	87	August, 1891 .	Last week of March, 1892.
	D	117	1,358	12	1st November, 1891 .	Ditto.
	E	150	2,684	18	Ditto.	30th April, 1892.

Section A. Registers I—XIII A.—The first section was opened in the first week of May, and its work was not entirely finished until December following. The work was distributed among groups of 7 men, 3½ pairs, as follows:—

1st set of 2 men prepared Registers I, IV and VII.
2nd „ 2 „ „ „ V and VI (Hindus).
3rd „ 2 „ „ „ V and VI (Other religions).
4th „ 1 man „ „ VIII—XIII A.

Register III, classified list of villages and towns, was prepared by an Assistant Supervisor under the direct superintendence of the Head Supervisor. In connection with it I may note that considerable difficulty was experienced in tracing what were properly to be considered villages, owing to want of precision in the Census papers of some districts in distinguishing between subordinate hamlets and the parent village, to which reference has already been made at paragraph 11 of the second part of the Report. A point which it is worth while to note with regard to the tabulation of Registers IV—VII, which were separately drawn up for the followers of each religion, is that for all the hill tribes, who return their religion by the tribal name, Gond, Bhil, etc., only one register should be used. At the present Census, with the intention of tabulating the enumeration entries exactly as they were abstracted, we began by keeping a separate register for persons whose religion was given as Gond, another for Korku, etc., with the result that registers tended to multiply at an alarming rate and loss of time sulted. Afterwards all the wild tribes were clubbed together in one register under the heading "Animistic" religion, and this is what should certainly be done again. T religion return, as I have shown in the first part of the Report, is not precise enough in the case of the aboriginal tribes to warrant any trouble being taken in the matter that can at all be spared. Registers VIII, Language, and IX, Birth-place, did not give much trouble except when uncommon names occurred. It was found that, by tabulating the birth-place returns exactly as they stood in the abstracted sheets, the work was unnecessarily spun out, the entries for a single book often covering pages of the Tabulation Register. The tabulation was, therefore, done by specially selected men, who first noted on the abstraction sheets in the case of, say, districts of another province, the main head, that is, the province, to which each entry belonged, and then transferred the combined figures for each such head to the Tabulation Register. Thus, if there were in a book persons returning six different districts of the North-Western Provinces, the total of these was taken and entered under the birth-place heading, North-Western Provinces, as it was only the latter which was required for publication in the final tables.

The whole work of tabulating the Registers from I to XIIIA occupied 148 men for 164 days. At this rate, the total number of books to be tabulated being 84,079, the average number of books done by each group of men per day was 24; in other words, 7 men tabulated 24 books daily in all the registers mentioned. In the Hindi and Marathi section, the average daily number of books tabulated was 27 per group; the Uria men could manage to turn out only 17. The checking and comparison of the tabulated registers was done by the official supervisors, with the assistance of non-officials specially selected from the men working in the section.

Section B. Register XIV.—This section was opened for the tabulation of the Hindi and Marathi Registers of castes on October 2nd, and its work was not completed till April 1892. On account of half the Uria contingent having left the Census Office, the tabulation of castes for the Uria books had to be done at Sambalpur, the abstraction sheets and register forms being sent there for the purpose. When the registers were returned with the tabulation work completed, they had to be totalled and compared, an operation which involved a good deal of time and labour, as the work at Sambalpur had not been very accurately done.

The tabulation of castes occupied 72 men for 178 days, and with the tabulation of occupations, was one of the most tedious operations of the Census. In Chapter X of the first part of the Report I have referred at length to the difficulties which were encountered. We at first attempted to work out full details for all the sub-divisions of castes and tribes returned at the enumeration; it was shortly seen, however, that this would involve an amount of time and labour which could not be given to the subject, but its contraction was by no means easy on account of the absence of any previous record of the castes and tribes of the Province, sufficiently comprehensive to enable it to be judged what matter might be discarded as being useless, and what might be retained as being of value.

Section C. Registers XV A—B.—As has been explained in the opening part of Chapter XI of the Report, in order to save time in re-writing lengthy names of occupations in the tabulation registers, a system of entering the latter by numbers in accordance with the Occupation Index sanctioned by the Census Commissioner was adopted. These numbers were first entered in the abstraction sheets against every occupation appearing therein, and the items regarding them thence transferred to the tabulation registers. The work of writing up the numbers in the abstraction sheets occupied 19 men for 144 days. The actual tabulation of the occupation statistics engaged 69 men for 146 days. The register was in two parts, one for males, the other for females. On an average each man could turn out only some eight books per day, so elaborate were the details required to be entered in the registers. A full account of the process is given in the Chapter on Occupation above referred to.

Sections D. and E. Registers XVI and XVIII.—These presented no special difficulty. The former register took up a good deal of time, owing to the Provincial Administration having required statistics for the Kabirpanthi and Satnami dissenting sects of Hindus to be taken out.

58. Compilation.—This was done in three sections which worked as shown in the margin. In the first, the compilation of all the Census statistics, except those of caste and occupation, was carried on and the general work of the office towards the close of the operations transacted. In the second, 19 men were employed for 139 days to arrange and compile the figures for caste, and in the third, 22 men for 105 days to prepare the tables for occupation. As has already been noticed, the figures can be looked upon only as averages; at the commencement of the compilation work many more hands were employed than at the end, when but a few specially selected men were engaged in the final arrangement of the huge tables, which stand at numbers XVI and XVII in the Imperial series.

Statement showing the work of compilation done in the Census Office.

	Number of working days.	Total number of men.	Average number of men per day.	Date of completion.
1. Compilation—General.	312	4,300	14	End of August 1892.
2. Compilation—Castes	139	2,575	19	End of July 1892.
3. Compilation—Occupations.	105	2,303	22	End of June 1892.

59. The Central Office system.—One point I wish to remark upon before closing these notes is the system of a Central Office which was adopted on the present occasion. Its advantages are the more direct supervision which can be exercised over every part of the work and the consequent promptness with which, in the conduct of operations more or less empirical, wrong methods can be adjusted and improvements carried out. Against these must be set sundry objections which are in my opinion of more weight than the advantages which I have noted. The first is the difficulty of getting good men to come from all parts of the Province to Nagpur, especially on the payment which we have to offer. There would be no such trouble about getting a fair standard of men were these to be employed at a head-quarters place in their own country. I would suggest Jubbulpore for the Jubbulpore division, Hoshangabad for the Nerbada division, Nagpur for the Nagpur division, Raipur for the Hindi districts and states of Chhatisgarh and Sambalpur for all the Uria country. The experiment of bringing Uria men to Nagpur on the present occasion must be regarded as a decided failure; at a future Census I should certainly have the Uria work done locally, whatever view be taken of the expediency of divisional offices throughout the rest of the Province. Again, though the immediate supervision of a single office can be more direct than would be the case when there are several scattered branches, it has to be remembered that a collection of some 600 or 700 untutored boys is a very unwieldy body to manage, and they can be more thoroughly controlled when they have to work in smaller batches. To this must be added the difficulty which there is in finding accommodation for such a large number of people. At the present Census, moreover, on account of the scarcity of non-officials deputed from the Hindi districts, Marathi boys had to be employed to do part of the Hindi work, with the consequence that they often mis-read the names of castes and sub-divisions entered in the enumeration books—see my remarks in Chapter X. This, a point of no small importance, will be obviated if a system of branch offices is adopted. For all these reasons I would recommend that latter course, as far as the abstraction and tabulation of the Census results are concerned.

60. Despatch of Registers to Districts.—The tabulated registers were on completion despatched to each district and state with the subjoined instructions regarding them :—

"I have the honour to advise despatch of the Census Registers of the district which are described below. In the Registers the villages are arranged according to Police Station-house and out-post circles and there is a separate set of Registers for each town and tehsil. In the beginning of Register No. I is an index showing the order in which the police circles stand; this order has been preserved throughout the series. As a rule 12 enumeration books have been tabulated on each page, and thus, except where the Registers are split up and separate parts reserved for different religions, every village occurring on a particular page of Register No. I will be found on the corresponding page of all the others. At the end of each Register has been given the correct total of the statistics it contains for the whole tehsil or town, as the case may be. In the case of castes and occupations for which such totals, on account of their complexity, could not be given, separate total Registers are supplied.

"The Registers are as follows :—

Register I contains statistics regarding (*a*) *Houses*, (*b*) *Population*—Total Male and Female. It is the one which will be most required for reference as from it the population of each village can be most readily obtained.

Register III is unimportant. It contains the villages of each tehsil classified according to size.

Register IV.—This is a useful Register, giving in detail the *Religions* of the population in detail of sex. Forest tribes, for whom the tribal name was entered in the column of religion in the enumerator's schedule, are shown accordingly as Gond, Baiga, etc.

Register V shows the *Ages* of the Population. A separate Register has been compiled for each religion. The Registers for Mahomedans, Jains, etc., contain only the books in which entries for those religions were found. Both this Register and the next will hardly be required for general reference.

Register VI.—The *Civil Condition* of the population is given in different Registers for each religion. Each Register is divided into three parts for Unmarried, Married and Widowed.

Register VII.—*Education*—shows the number of learners, literates and illiterates by certain specified age periods. There is a separate Register for each religion.

Register VIII.—*Parent Tongue.*

Register IX.—*Birth Place.*

Registers X to XIIIA relate to *Infirmities.* Nos. X to XIII show the ages of the infirm, while Nos. XA to XIIIA give detail of caste for the same.

Register XIV gives the distribution of the population by *Caste.* In this Register when all the castes of the 12 books tabulated on a page could not be contained on one page, supplementary pages have been added, each of which bears the serial number of the corresponding page in Register I with sub-numbers added.

Register XV.—*Occupation.* There is a separate Register for males—XVA, and a separate one for females—XV B. As the occupations recorded in twelve books would not all come on one page, the system of page numbering noted above for Register XIV has been followed. In the Register, in order to save time in writing out lengthy names of occupations, I have entered the latter by numbers. A complete index showing what each number signifies is supplied.

Register XVI.—*Sect*—has been prepared for (*a*) the Kabirpanthi and Satnami Sects of the Hindu religion, (*b*) for the Sects of Mahomedans and (*c*) for those of Christians.

Register XVIII sets forth the castes of all persons shown in Register VII as Literate.

"The Registers for all Municipal towns should be made over to the municipalities concerned, an agreement being taken that the Registers will be preserved in good condition until the next Census is taken, see para. (*d*) of Government of India Resolution No. $\frac{1 \text{ Census}}{12-13}$, dated 26th January 1891, appended to this Office No. 1111, dated 26th August 1891."

61. The circular letter of the Government of India referred to contained the following directions :—

"The abstraction and compilation will be carried out by Government agency, the municipality contributing funds at the rate of three months' salary of one abstracting clerk, on the average scale to be prescribed by the Provincial Superintendent of Census Operations, for every ten thousand of the population dealt with. Fractions of that total will be paid for proportionately on the same scale. Special cases in which the partial exemption of small municipalities containing less than that number of inhabitants is suggested as desirable will be considered by Local Governments.

> "The tabulated registers, when done with by the Provincial Superintendent, will in return for the assistance rendered, be made over to the municipality, provided that the municipal authority undertakes to preserve them in good order until the next general enumeration."

A similar contribution was levied from the Feudatory States. The scale fixed for the payment of three months' salary of an abstracting clerk was R12 in the case of municipalities. For the Feudatory states, in consideration of the simplicity of the generality of the entries of caste and occupation, which formed the great burden of the work in the Census Office, the rate was fixed at R12 per 30,000 of the inhabitants.

CHAPTER V.

PRINTING.

62. Printing and supply of schedules.—The schedules were printed at the Presses noted below:—

Hindi }
Uria } —Government Printing, Bengal, Calcutta.
Marathi.—Government Central Press, Bombay.
Telugu—Government Central Press, Madras.

They were supplied bound in books of three sizes, containing 16, 40 and 64 pages, respectively.

Preliminary Indents.—In order to ascertain the probable requirements of books of each size, blocks—or villages when more than one were combined in a block—were arranged in different classes according to the number of houses they contained. The number of blocks and villages in each class being thus known, the calculation of the number of books of the various sizes to be supplied was simple. What really gave trouble was the listing of villages by classes. It has already been seen that hamlets were generally enumerated apart from the main village, a separate book being allowed for each. The classifying process was in consequence a complicated one, separate note having to be taken of the number of houses in detail of hamlets. The number of books of the smallest size was further very much multiplied, a result that gave extra work in abstracting and tabulating the returns; for although it has been noticed that large books gave trouble in abstraction, it is not to be inferred that convenience is attained by having a multitude of very small ones. It will probably be always necessary to make some calculation based on the number of houses per block or village—for the sake of simplicity I have recommended that in all cases small villages should at a future census be constituted separate blocks, however many of the latter are counted by one enumerator,—but by dispensing with the separate enumeration of hamlets, this should be a matter of little difficulty.

Supply of books.—It was hoped that the book supply of the present Census would serve as an index to the requirements of the next occasion, but the district returns are in some cases not so complete as might have been desired. In almost every case, however, they will furnish a sufficient ground on which to base a preliminary indent, in accordance with which printing might be carried out. The books should reach districts by November so as to allow of distribution being made during December. By then the exact number of books required should be capable of being ascertained, and any deficiency that may be apparent can be made good. At the present Census depôts for the supply of emergent supplementary indents were maintained at Jubbulpore, Nagpur and Raipur. This might again be done, as up to the very last it is likely that demands for extra books will be received. On the present occasion the districts which chiefly offended in this way were Bhandara and Raipur, the latter running through the depôt stock and asking for many more books only a short time before the actual enumeration. At the next census the facility of getting books to the eastern part of the Province will be immensely increased owing to the opening of the Bengal-Nagpur Railway. Through communication was not

Statistics of Enumeration Books.

Language.	District.	Books supplied.				Books used.				Balance.				Remarks.
		16 pages.	40 pages.	64 pages.	Total.	16 pages.	40 pages.	64 pages.	Total.	16 pages.	40 pages.	64 pages.	Total.	
1	2	3	4	5	6	7	8	9	10	11	12	13	14	15
HINDI.	Saugor	3,515	939	1,460	5,914	2,132	875	1,384	4,391	1,383	6	76	1,523	
	Damoh	1,770	542	700	3,012	1,450	508	609	2,567	320	34	91	445	
	Jubbulpore	3,650	1,955	1,540	7,145	2,770	1,480	1,285	5,535	880	475	255	1,610	
	Mandla	3,630	590	260	4,480	3,427	532	251	4,210	203	58	9	270	
	Seoni	2,370	604	600	3,574	1,978	514	482	3,004	392	60	118	570	
	Narsinghpur	1,250	710	800	2,760	...	...	...	...	...	...	...	...	No return of books used has been given for Narsinghpur, Nimar, and Chhindwara, but the supply was nearly exhausted in all three districts.
	Hoshangabad	2,160	760	1,300	4,220	...	...	...	3,800	...	...	...	420	
	Nimar	960	330	630	1,920	...	...	...	...	...	...	...	...	
	Betul	2,150	500	450	3,100	1,900	450	356	2,706	250	50	94	394	
	Chhindwara	2,030	720	700	3,450	...	...	...	...	...	...	...	...	
	Balaghat	2,400	625	550	3,575	2,135	525	492	3,152	265	100	58	423	
	Raipur	6,210	3,140	3,240	12,590	5,270	2,536	2,820	10,626	940	604	420	1,964	
	Bilaspur	5,850	2,500	1,750	10,100	4,500	2,225	1,650	8,375	1,350	275	100	1,725	Includes books for Kawardha and Sakti.
	Sambalpur	155	90	65	310	95	50	40	185	60	40	25	125	
	Makrai	60	20	45	125	...	...	...	...	...	...	...	...	
	Bastar	2,000	700	350	3,050	...	...	...	...	...	...	...	...	
	Chinkhadan	90	60	75	225	...	...	...	...	...	...	...	...	
	Khairagarh	765	225	390	1,380	495	218	320	1,033	270	7	70	347	
	Nandgaon	310	415	360	1,085	300	410	355	1,065	10	5	5	20	
	Kanker	430	170	105	705	350	120	105	575	80	50	...	130	
	Raigarh	865	270	145	1,280	...	...	...	...	...	...	...	...	
	Sarangarh	355	235	85	675	275	156	71	502	80	79	14	173	
	Total	42,975	16,100	15,600	74,675	...	...	...	...	...	...	...	...	

Note.—The figures for books of 16 and 64 pages, given in the "Total" column, does not quite agree with that shown in the statement at paragraph 64. The difference is accounted for by a number of 16-page books having been supplied at the commencement of the operations for purposes of instruction, and some of the 64-page books having been broken up in order to supply loose leaves for the same object.

In the above it is to be remarked that the return of books used is not very reliable. In some districts, such as Saugor and Bilaspur, only the books actually used in the enumeration have been noted; in others all books employed in instructing the Census Staff or wasted and spoiled have been taken into account.

Statistics of Enumeration Books—*contd.*

Language.	Districts.	Books supplied. 16 pages.	40 pages.	64 pages.	Total.	Books used. 16 pages.	40 pages.	64 pages.	Total.	Balance. 16 pages.	40 pages.	64 pages.	Total.	Remarks.
1	2	3	4	5	6	7	8	9	10	11	12	13	14	15
MARATHI.	Nagpur	2,980	1,330	1,940	*6,250*	...	...	...	...	...	...	...	...	
	Wardha	1,500	770	1,050	*3,320*	1,126	686	951	*2,763*	374	84	99	*557*	
	Shandara	2,600	1,100	1,840	*5,540*	...	...	...	...	...	...	...	...	
	Chanda	2,630	1,150	1,650	*5,430*	...	...	...	...	...	...	...	...	
	Total	9,710*	4,350	6,480	*20,540*	...	...	...	...	...	...	...	...	* The difference between the number of 16-page books here shown and that entered at paragraph 64 is accounted for by 1,000 books having been supplied for purposes of instruction at the commencement of the operations.
URIA.	Sambalpur	3,870	1,315	1,365	*6,550*	3,320	1,030	1,180	*5,530*	550	285	185	*1,020*	
	Raigarh	220	125	100	*445*	...	...	...	...	...	...	...	...	
	Sarangarh	75	25	25	*125*	50	22	24	*96*	25	3	1	*29*	
	Bamra	965	325	180	*1,470*	820	220	140	*1,180*	145	105	40	*290*	
	Rairakhol	310	40	15	*365*	...	...	...	*295*	...	...	...	*70*	
	Sonpur	950	360	290	*1,600*	930	320	285	*1,535*	20	40	5	*65*	
	Patna	2,425	420	360	*3,205*	2,265	398	360	*3,023*	160	22	...	*182*	
	Kalahandi	3,320	595	305	*4,220*	...	...	...	...	...	...	...	...	
	Bastar	140	45	35	*220*	...	...	...	...	...	...	...	...	
	Total	12,275	3,250	2,675	*18,200*	...	...	...	...	...	...	...	...	

established until about the time of the Census in February—the line was not opened for traffic until some time later—so the Hindi books for the Chhatisgarh districts and all the Uria books had to be brought round by Bhosawal from Calcutta. This took some three weeks by goods train, and was a great source of delay and of consequent anxiety.

63. Binding and size of books.—Connected with the matter of the book supply is the question as to what is the best plan to adopt with regard to binding. There are two ways open. First, loose schedules may be supplied to districts, and may there be bound into books to suit individual blocks. The other is to have the schedules bound at the Press, in which case it becomes necessary to fix on the sizes that may be considered the most suitable for general use. By adopting the first of these methods, there is no doubt that a great deal of the difficulty about the book supply disappears. Against this, on the other hand, has to be set (1) the trouble of binding, and (2) the fact that in many cases the books would be loosely bound, and would be unfit to stand the wear and tear to which they must be subjected in passing through the hands of the abstractors. The latter is a point to which the experience of the present Census leads me to attach a good deal of importance, and it is mainly on this account that I should have books bound at the Press and not locally in districts.

Loose schedule leaves.—While on this subject, I would also record my opinion that the use of loose schedule leaves should be absolutely forbidden. Small supplementary books, say of ten pages, should be supplied in case the schedules in a main book are all filled up; the system of pasting in loose leaves is pernicious. It continually caused trouble in the abstraction office, as there was a constant tendency of such leaves to come undone, and it was frequently very difficult to replace them.

Size of books.—On what are the best sizes of books to adopt, if the latter are supplied ready bound from the Press, it is not easy to express an opinion. If the average size of a block is fixed at 60 houses, it is, I think, well to have a book which will ordinarily hold entries for the whole block. At the present Census owing to the rule that a fresh page should be taken for each house and a page left blank for every house found unoccupied, a book of 64 pages was seldom sufficient for the census of the standard block. As it is proposed to omit this rule in future, no such difficulty will arise, and entries for the standard block of sixty houses should easily be contained in a book of sixty schedules. This I should make the maximum size. For getting good work done in the abstraction office a size somewhat smaller than this, say about forty pages, is more suitable on account of the fewer entries there are to be checked in order to discover a mistake. Against this must be set the advantage of having the complete record of the average block contained in one book; this is a convenience all round and may well be adhered to. Books of intermediate sizes will also be necessary; twenty and forty pages will probably be appropriate. With these, ten-page supplementary books can be used where necessary, thus giving in an easy way combinations of thirty and fifty schedules.

64. Statistics of Enumeration Books used at the Census.—The following statement shows the number of books in each language issued from the Press for the purpose of the Census:—

Enumeration Books.

Language.	Press.	Books of 16 pages.	Books of 40 pages.	Books of 64 pages.	Loose schedule leaves.	Remarks.
1	2	3	4	5	6	7
Hindi	Calcutta	44,100	16,100	15,800	116,000	
Uria	Do.	12,275	3,250	2,675	22,500	
Marathi	Bombay	10,710	4,350	6,480	52,100	
Telugu	Madras	490	300	180	6,000	
English	Bombay	620	75	190	400	For railways and for census of Sitabuldi.
English	Calcutta	95	...	75	...	For Cantonments.
Grand Total		68,290	24,075	25,400	197,000	

District details, so far as available, are given on the foregoing pages. The number of loose schedules supplied to each district has not been separately shown, as these were generally proportionately distributed for the purpose of being used in supplementing the bound books or for use in instructing the Census staff. Of the 16-page books supplied, about 50 per cent. contained only schedule leaves, without instructions or specimen schedules. These were for the most part used as supplementary.

65. Abstraction and Tabulation Forms.—In the Central Office the following numbers of abstraction sheets and tabulation registers were printed. The Hindi work was done at the Government Central Press, Bombay, and the Uria work at the Bengal Government Press, Calcutta:—

Abstraction Sheets.

Language	Sheet No.										
	I	II	III	IV	V	VI	VII	VIII	IX	X	XII
Hindi .	110,000	105,000	130,000	80,000	110,000	110,000	80,000	40,000	1,000	105,000	1,000
Uria .	18,000	18,000	18,000	18,000	18,000	18,000	18,000	...	...	18,000	...
TOTAL .	128,000	123,000	148,000	98,000	128,000	128,000	98,000	40,000	1,000	123,000	1,000

Regarding the above, it may be noted that is was a mistake to order so many copies of Abstraction Sheet No. VII—on which details for the infirm were worked out—as when a book contained no entries of an infirmity, no Sheet VII was required to be prepared in connection with it.

Tabulation Register forms.

Register No.	Hindi.	Uria.	TOTAL.	Register No.	Hindi.	Uria.	TOTAL.
I .	6,000	1,500	*7,500*	XI A .	3,000	1,000	*4,000*
II .	500	500	*1,000*	XII .	1,500	500	*2,000*
III .	4,000	1,000	*5,000*	XII A .	3,000	1,000	*4,000*
IV .	5,500	1,500	*7,000*	XIII .	1,500	500	*2,000*
V .	25,000	7,000	*32,000*	XIII A .	3,000	1,000	*4,000*
VI .	75,000	21,000	*96,000*	XIV .	34,000	11,000	*45,000*
VII .	25,000	7,000	*32,000*	XV A .	40,000	7,000	*47,000*
VIII .	11,500	3,000	*14,500*	XV B .	37,000	7,000	*44,000*
IX .	11,500	3,000	*14,500*	XVI A* .	2,500	800	*3,300*
X .	1,500	500	*2,000*	XVI B* .	4,000	400	*4,400*
XA .	3,000	1,000	*4,000*	XVIII .	10,000	500	*10,500*
XI .	1,500	500	*2,000*				

* Hindu and Mahomedan sects.

Compilation sheets were supplied from Calcutta to the order of the Census Commissioner. In the compilation of castes and occupations, special sheets had to be printed in Nagpur, unused forms, etc., being employed for the purpose.

66. Miscellaneous forms.—Besides the forms that have been mentioned, various others were employed for various purposes in connection with the enumeration. The Block list and Circle list forms have already been referred to at paragraph 16 of the second part of the Report. For the purpose of ascertaining the results of the Census, Circle and Charge abstracts were struck off and distributed to districts, in the form prescribed in the Census Commissioner's note L, dated 18th July 1890. Two copies for each circle and charge with a surplus for wastage were allowed. Spare copies of the enumerators' abstract, as printed in the enumeration books, were also supplied, which might be used in case the original abstract was spoiled, or might be employed if a suppplementary book—which contained no abstract form—were used to census an encamping ground or for any other emergency. The numbers supplied were 22,000 in Hindi, 6,000 in Marathi, and 4,500 in Uria. Travellers' tickets were distributed in bound books of 20. The general opinion that prevailed was that little necessity existed for their employment, so that probably at a future Census their numbers might be curtailed. On the present occasion 5,500 books of tickets were supplied.

CHAPTER VI.

THE LAST.

67. Census Accounts.—A statement of the expenditure incurred at the Census is given on the next page. In the margin I append a summary of the charges under the heads prescribed by the Census Commissioner. Deductions have been shown on account of contributions realized from municipalities and Feudatory States, towards the cost of compiling the returns. The contributions from municipalities were levied in accordance with the directions contained in the Resolution of the Government of India in the Home Department (Census), No. $\frac{1}{12-23}$, dated the 26th January 1891, which has been quoted at the end of Chapter IV of the second part of the Report, and a similar charge was made upon the Feudatory States. The Enumeration charges, exclusive of those entered in Sub-head II, were in each case borne by the municipality or State concerned.

Accounts Summary.

		R
A	I.—District Charges	3,287
	II.—Schedules, etc., Printing, Paper, etc.	12,622
	Total Enumeration	*15,909*
B	III.—Abstraction, Tabulation and Compilation	80,421
	IV.—Compilation, etc., Printing	13,132
	Total Compilation, etc.	93,553
C	V.—Superintendent's Personal Charges	9,598
	VI.—Superintendent's Office	1,933
	Total Superintendence	*11,531*
	GRAND TOTAL	120,993
	Deduct—Realizations on account of sale of wastepaper, etc.	160
	NET COST	120,833
	Deduct—Contributions from Municipalities	2,476
	" " Feudatory States	2,589
	TOTAL COST TO GOVERNMENT	115,768

68. Census Expenditure in districts.—The appended statement has been prepared to show the expenditure incurred in each district on account of the taking of the Census.

Census expenditure in districts.

DISTRICTS.	1. District office establishment.	2. Contingent charges of establishment.	3. House-numbering.	4. Lights, ink, etc.	5. Remuneration of Census officers.	Freight of schedules, etc., from stations and landing-places.	TOTAL.
1	2	3	4	5	6	7	8
	R a. p.	R a. p.	R a. p.	R a. p.	R a. p.	R a. p.	R a. p.
Saugor	60 0 0	95 8 11	...	28 12 6	72 12 0	16 1 0	273 2 5
Damoh	...	43 4 0	7 6 6	43 9 6	...	25 7 0	119 11 0
Jubbulpore	...	18 4 3	...	6 13 0	...	55 9 3	80 10 6
Mandla	...	113 4 3	8 3 6	49 5 6	179 2 3	16 3 0	366 2 6
Seoni	...	21 12 0	26 0 4	31 1 6	...	16 2 0	94 15 10
Narsinghpur	...	16 10 3	...	25 0 0	...	12 5 6	53 15 9
Hoshangabad	...	4 8 0	0 12 9	2 0 0	...	13 13 0	21 1 9
Nimar	...	5 8 0	11 13 9	87 2 0	...	5 14 3	110 6 0
Betul	...	...	0 8 0	6 0 6	...	30 9 9	37 2 3
Chhindwara	...	11 6 0	...	12 7 0	...	22 7 6	46 4 6
Wardha	...	...	1 4 6	2 9 0	...	16 9 6	20 7 0
Nagpur	...	38 11 6	12 11 3	45 1 9	...	39 7 0	135 15 6
Chanda	...	86 12 11	17 9 11	189 15 11	150 14 11	60 2 9	505 8 5
Bhandara	...	1 12 0	15 0 0	...	19 0 0	29 8 6	65 4 6
Balaghat	...	5 4 0	...	10 3 6	239 0 0	20 0 3	274 7 9
Raipur	34 10 10	59 4 7	37 1 0	322 13 0	21 3 0	159 10 0	634 10 5
Bilaspur	...	60 14 3	6 8 0	36 5 4	107 1 0	36 4 6	247 1 1
Sambalpur	...	40 6 4	...	20 7 3	...	34 8 0	95 5 7
Incurred in the Census Office on account of district charges.	...	104 6 0	...	...	...	...	104 6 0
TOTAL	94 10 10	727 9 3	144 15 6	919 11 3	789 1 2	610 10 9	3,286 10 9

Accounts of the Census of 1891.

Main Head.		Sub-head.	1890-91.	1891-92.	1892-93.	Total.
1		2	3	4	5	6
			R a. p.	*R a. p.*	*R a. p.*	*R a. p.*
PART A.—ENUMERATION.	I.—District Charges.*	1. District office establishment	94 10 10	...	...	94 10 10
		2. Contingent charges of establishment	532 5 10	195 3 5	...	727 9 3
		3. House-numbering	108 4 6	36 11 0	...	144 15 6
		4. Lights, ink, etc.	864 3 9	55 7 6	...	919 11 3
		5. Remuneration of Census officers	622 0 4	167 0 10	...	789 1 2
		6. Special travelling allowances	...	...	...	...
		7. Freight of schedules, etc., from stations and landing-places	503 12 11	106 13 10	...	610 10 9
		Total I., *District Charges*	*2,725 6 2*	*561 4 7*	...	*3,286 10 9*
	II.—Enumeration Printing.	8. Paper for schedules, etc., at Press	6,320 13 4	...	...	6,320 13 4
		9. Printing and binding	3,804 10 2	...	...	3,804 10 2
		10. Despatching from Press	2,496 13 8	...	...	2,496 13 8
		Total II., *Paper and Printing, A.*	*12,622 5 2*	...	...	*12,622 5 2*
		Total, Enumeration	15,347 11 4	561 4 7	...	15,908 15 11
PART B.—ABSTRACTION AND COMPILATION.	III.—Tabulation Office.	11. Office rent	...	29 10 10	...	29 10 10
		12. Office furniture and repairs, etc.	65 7 3	213 0 3	...	278 7 6
		13. Record establishment	...	1,506 10 1	432 7 1	1,939 1 2
		14. Correspondence and accounts establishment	...	...	...	...
		15. Menial establishment	...	400 12 0	259 0 10	659 12 10
		16. Working staff, including Superintendence—*Officials*	16 1 1	6,534 4 0	2,237 0 11	8,787 6 0
		17. Working staff, clerks, *specially entertained*	...	59.203 4 11	3,729 9 0	62,932 13 11
		18. Travelling allowances to and from the Office	1,006 14 0	2,552 6 4	505 2 9	4,064 7 1
		19. Freight of schedules, etc., to office	158 7 0	574 10 9	...	733 1 9
		20. Petty stationery and contingencies	4 14 9	769 3 10	221 14 3	996 0 10
		Total III., *Tabulation Office*	*1,251 12 1*	*71,783 15 0*	*7,385 2 10*	*80,420 13 11*
	IV.—Tabulation Printing.	21. Paper for sheets, registers, and tables at Press	1,769 3 6	746 6 3	...	2,515 9 9
		22. Printing of forms, tables, and Report	936 8 6	† 2,927 1 8	5,900 0 0	9,763 10 2
		23. Freight of sheets, etc., to office	119 1 6	733 7 0	...	852 8 6
		Total IV., *Paper and Printing, B.*	*2,824 13 6*	*4,406 14 11*	*5,900 0 0*	*13,131 12 5*
		Total, Compilation	4,076 9 7	76,190 13 11	13,285 2 10	93,552 10 4
PART C.—SUPERINTENDENCE.	V.—Superintendent.	24. Provincial Superintendent's deputation allowance	2,028 13 2	2,304 0 0	1,472 0 0	5,804 13 2
		25. Pay of substitute of Superintendent	...	...	...	...
		26. Travelling allowance of Superintendent	3,013 15 0	419 10 0	360 0 0	3,793 9 0
		Total V., *Superintendent's personal charges*	*5,042 12 2*	*2,723 10 0*	*1,832 0 0*	*9,598 6 2*
	VI.—Superintendent's Office.	27. Superintendent's office establishment	103 2 7	900 8 0	339 0 0	1,342 10 7
		28. Travelling allowances for ditto	147 10 9	...	...	147 10 9
		29. Office contingencies for ditto	195 10 0	144 2 6	103 0 [illegible]	442 12 6
		30. Rent of Superintendent's office	...	...	...	...
		Total VI., *Superintendent's establishment*	*446 7 4*	*1,044 10 6*	*442 0 0*	*1,933 1 10*
		Total, Superintendence	5,489 3 6	3,768 4 6	2,274 0 0	11,531 8 0
		GRAND TOTAL	24,913 8 5	80,520 7 0	15.559 2 10	1,20,993 2 3

* Does not include charges on account of the enumeration in Municipalities and Feudatory States.
† The sum given is the amount of the Press bill; it evidently includes charges for paper, sub-head 21.

69. Incidence per thousand of the Population.—The incidence of the Census expenditure per thousand of the population under the three main divisions which have been given, is shewn below:—

	Incidence per thousand. R	a.	p.
Enumeration	1	3	8
Compilation, etc.	7	3	5
Superintendence	0	14	3
TOTAL .	9	5	4

The incidence is calculated on the total population of the Province, and takes into account the total expenditure incurred, *i.e.*, the amount shewn as net cost in the marginal statement given at para. 67.

70. Conclusion. Notices of Officers.—The only other matter to which I would refer before concluding this report is the services of the officers on whom fell the burden of the Census work in the districts. Where so much energy was shewn by all, it is scarcely possible to make distinctions, but the following were conspicuous in respect of the personal interest they took in the work and the completeness of the arrangements they made for the enumeration. Amongst Deputy Commissioners, may be mentioned, Colonel Lugard, Damoh; Colonel Hogg, Mandla; Mr. Nedham, Seoni; Mr. L. K. Laurie, Hoshangabad; Colonel Vertue, Betul; Mr. Drysdale, Wardha; and Mr. Drake-Brockman, Balaghat. The services of Mr. Crump, Assistant Commissioner, Hoshangabad, Mr. Noble, District Superintendent of Police, Chhindwara, and Mr. Gradon, Assistant Conservator of Forests, Bhandara, have been specially brought to notice in the district reports, as have also those of the following Extra Assistant Commissioners:—Mr. Bhogchand, Saugor; Mr. H. C. Bose, Jubbulpore; Mr. Mahomed Husain, Seoni; Mr. Kripashankar, Narsinghpur; Mr. Greany, Harda; Mr. Har Prasad, Nimar; Mr. K. M. Anderson, Mr. Sherlock-Hubbard, and Mr. Bapu Rao Patwardhan, Nagpur; Mr. Gulam Mustaffa, Chanda; Rai Bahadur Debi Pershad, Bhandara; Mr. Bhargo Rao, Raipur; Mr. Kashinath Rao, Bilaspur; and Mr. Devi Pershad, Sambalpur. On the good offices of the Chiefs, Superintendents, and Dewans in the Feudatory States I have already remarked at Chapter III.

I wish to further place on record the excellent services rendered by the Deputy Superintendent of the Census Office, Mr. Rambhau Meghasham, Clerk of Court in the Nerbada Division. A better man for the post could not have been found; his tact and capacity for organization were specially displayed in the early days of the work, when he had under his control a large and heterogeneous body of persons whom he kept in excellent order, and from whom he exacted a full tale of work under most trying circumstances, the hot weather lasting till July in 1891. In the subsequent operations his merits were no less conspicuous; his work was invariably conscientious and accurate, and in this respect it called forth the special approval of the Census Commissioner for India.

CENSUS OF 1891.

APPENDICES.

7. IV.—**Preparation of copies of the circle lists for the use of Charge Superintendents.**

8. V.—**Tracing of the map of each circle to be made for the use of the supervisor.**

9. VI.—**Tracing of the map of each charge to be made for the use of the Charge Superintendent.**

10. VII.—**Appointment of Supervisors and Superintendents.**—As soon as the Census circles and charges are decided on, the appointment of supervisors and Superintendents will be at once taken in hand. Each District Officer should note what the Settlement Commissioner says as to the Land Revenue establishment available for his district for Census work. Any difficulty in this respect that may be anticipated should be promptly reported on, and suggestions made for its settlement. It should be noted that Tahsildars are not to be appointed Superintendents of charges.

11. Report is also called for as to the steps each Deputy Commissioner proposes to take towards having the village lists tested. It may be explained that the mauzawar list of the villages in the circle (No. III above) and the tracing of the circle map (No. V) will be handed to each supervisor on his appointment. He will be required to go round his circle and see what changes have taken place since last Census. He will note whether new villages or hamlets have arisen or whether old ones have disappeared and make corrections accordingly. It is intended that this work should be done after May by the supervisors assisted by the patwaris if available, otherwise by the Police or kotwars. Deputy Commissioners should state what help in this respect they will be in a position to supply to the supervisors.

12. As mentioned in paragraph 10 of Book Circular No. XVI, the above arrangements are to be held to apply to Feudatory States. The Political Agent (or the Deputy Commissioner in the case of a State which is not under the Political Agent) will therefore issue orders which will ensure the carrying out, as far as possible, of all the preliminaries above noted within their areas, and will report the action taken.

30th April 1890.

Census Circular B.

The *preliminary* procedure laid down in Census Circular A, dated the 30th April, should now have been completed in all districts. The present Circular will deal with what may be called the *intermediate* stage of Census operations.

2. Appended are the English versions of five forms that are to be used. They are :—

(1) Letter of appointment for supervisors.
(2) Preliminary instructions for supervisors.
(3) Letter of appointment and preliminary instructions for enumerators.
(4) Circle List.
(5) Block List.

3. The instructions for supervisors and enumerators sufficiently explain the purpose for which the forms have been drawn up and the procedure that is to be followed. The latter is practically the same as that adopted in 1880. The following are the chief points that will have to be noted by District Officers in connection therewith.

4. The first thing to be done is the issue of letters of appointment to supervisors. These will be given to all supervisors, official as well as non-official. In the letter of appointment the name of the supervisor and of the circle to which he has been appointed will be entered. With the letter of appointment the supervisor will receive the following :—

(1). A copy of the printed instructions for supervisors, which include also those for enumerators.

In these instructions the name of the Superintendent of the charge to which the circle belongs has to be entered : as also the number borne by the circle. It may here be explained that every circle, besides bearing a name, will have a serial number assigned to it. The numbers should run for one charge only. Similarly, every block in a circle will bear a distinguishing letter, as Block B, Circle 4 of Superintendent's charge———.

(2). A tracing of the map of his circle (see paragraph 8 of Circular A, dated the 30th April).

(3). A copy of the Circle List (Form No. 4) with the list of villages (see paragraph 6 of Circular A) filled in.

It has been thought preferable to have the list of villages written into this form for supervisors. The list prepared in accordance with Circular A need not therefore be sent them. Before issuing the form to supervisors the heading and columns 1 to 3 should be carefully written up. The number as well as the name of the circle should be entered in the heading. In column 2 will be entered the name of the main village, and under it the names of sub-villages serially numbered. In column 3 will be entered the number of houses according to last Census. New villages, marked changes in the number of houses, etc., will be entered in these columns by supervisors as they go round their circles.

5. These directions should be given effect to at once, so as to enable the supervisors to begin without delay the work laid down for them in part II of the Instructions. The attention of District Officers is called to the Settlement Commissioner's note appended to Book Circular No. XVI as to the assistance which can at this period be rendered by patwaris. The first work the supervisors have to do is the testing of the list of villages supplied to them. In this the patwaris can afford material help. Again, it will probably not always be possible to at once obtain sufficient enumerators. The patwaris should in such cases be employed in preparing Block Lists and in numbering houses. The services of the patwaris are available for Census work between now and October 15th. All the procedure dealt with in the present Circular falls to be done within that time. The most should therefore be made of the opportunity offered and every possible assistance taken from patwaris.

6. The Circle List [para. 4 (3) above] sent to supervisors will be returned to the District office with corrections made in the list of villages in column 2 and any great change in the number of houses noted in column 3. The rest of the columns will have been filled up by the supervisor showing how he proposes to divide his circle and the enumerators whom he intends to appoint. The list should be carefully examined in the Deputy Commissioner's office, and any changes made in the arrangement of blocks that may be thought advisable. It should be kept in mind that in the formation of blocks too exclusive regard should not be paid to the prescribed average number of houses or residents which each may contain. Distance is an important consideration with scattered hamlets in sparsely inhabited places, and should receive attention when several such hamlets are grouped into one block. In jungle tracts it may be found necessary to have the Census taken during the day preceding the night fixed for the Census. This may also be taken into account in considering the size and distribution of blocks.

7. When checked, the circle lists will be returned to supervisors. Letters of appointment and instructions duly filled in will at the same time be supplied through the Tahsildar to the selected enumerators. The supervisors will next see that the preparation of the block lists is taken in hand. When these are prepared, they will be sent to the Deputy Commissioner for approval, along with fresh circle lists showing the exact number of houses in each village and block. The numbering of houses will not be done until after the building lists are approved. It may well be left over until after the rains, so as to save renumbering as much as possible.

8. No separate instructions will be issued to Superintendents of Census charges. They will, however, see that the instructions now issued to supervisors and enumerators are acted up to. Superintendents may receive letters of appointment from the district office in any form the rank of the receiver may indicate. It has been thought unnecessary to provide a special form for the purpose. Each Superintendent on appointment will receive for his guidance a tracing of the map of his charge, and a copy of the list of villages it contains (paras. 7 and 9, Circular A).

9. When the revised circle lists are finally approved (para. 7 above), two copies will be made of each: one for the Superintendent of charge, for each circle in his charge: and one for transmission to this office. The latter should be arranged according to Police station and out-post areas with separate indices. They should be compiled by Tahsils. Where an out-post is partly in one Tahsil and partly in another, the parts belonging to the separate Tahsils will be filed separately each in its proper Tahsil. A note to that effect should be made on the index of each part. It should be noted that but as little change as possible should be made in the circle and block lists after they are finally approved. At first it may not be possible to get sufficient supervisors and enumerators, and circles and blocks may be on a scale which will be afterwards found too large. Every effort should be made to avoid this, but it may after all be necessary to appoint

additional supervisors and enumerators. The former should be put on as assistants to the original supervisors, the circle remaining intact. Any new enumerator should be assigned a definite part of the original block, which will remain unchanged, retaining its distinguishing letter.

10. The above comprise all the preparatory arrangements for the taking of the Census. It is of the utmost importance that they should be thoroughly carried out by the middle of October at latest. Progress reports will be called for later on.

11. Public buildings, such as jails, hospitals, etc., will form separate blocks to be enumerated by the officer in charge.

12. In Municipalities, arrangements for the Census will be made through Municipal Committees as at last Census. In Cantonments, the Deputy Commissioner should act in concert with the Military authorities. The latter will be responsible for the enumeration of all persons actually living in Regimental lines. The Cantonment Magistrate, under the direction of the Deputy Commissioner, will arrange for the enumeration of all persons living outside these limits, including the residents in the Sadar Bazar and all officers not living in Regimental lines.

13. For Railways, special measures will be necessary. The Railway authorities will effect the enumeration of all persons within Railway limits on the Census night. Employés living beyond Railway limits will be enumerated in the ordinary way.

14. Special instructions on the above will be issued hereafter.

15. The issue of private enumeration schedules for house-holders should be discouraged as much as possible. Each Deputy Commissioner will decide for himself how far the concession should be granted to house-holders in his district. The issue should be restricted to the European community and natives of high rank and superior education.

20th June 1890.

Census Form No. I.

LETTER OF APPOINTMENT FOR SUPERVISOR.

FROM

THE DEPUTY COMMISSIONER, ____________

To ____________

You are hereby appointed Supervisor of ____________ Circle of ____________ Tahsil for the Census of 1891.

Deputy Commissioner.

Dated ____________ *1890.*

Census Form No. II.

PRELIMINARY INSTRUCTIONS TO SUPERVISORS.

I.—Introductory.

1. The next Census is to be taken on the night of February 26th, 1891.

2. For the purpose of the Census every district will be divided into a certain number of charges. Each charge will be under a Superintendent. The charge will be divided into circles, each under a Supervisor; and the circle into blocks, each under an enumerator.

3. The final enumeration will be done by the enumerators, each of whom will be supplied with a book called an enumeration book. Some time before the night of the Census, the enumerator will take his book and go round all the houses in his block and make entries of the inhabitants according to instructions which he will afterwards receive. This will be called the preliminary record. On the night of the Census he will again go round the houses in his block. By noting all changes that have taken place in the interval,

he will correct the entries in his book so as to make them an exact record of the inhabitants of his block on the Census night.

4. At present, however, you are concerned only with the following. The sub-division of the district into charges and circles has already been made. Each circle has now to be sub-divided into blocks and to each block an enumerator has to be appointed. A list has to be prepared for each block of the houses it contains, and to each of the latter a separate number has to be affixed. This list will be the index of the block: by it the enumerator will be guided in the work of enumeration.

5. You will have to see that all the measures mentioned in the last paragraph are carried out for the circle to which you have been appointed. The following rules are therefore furnished for your guidance.

II.—Special Instructions.

6. The circle to which you have been appointed is No.   in the charge allotted to   as Superintendent. He is the Census officer immediately superior to you. You will make any references through him.

7. You will receive with this—

(*a*) A tracing of the district map showing the boundaries of your circle.

(*b*) A list (in a prescribed form) of the villages and hamlets in your circle with the number of houses they contain according to the Census of 1881.

8. You will first go over the ground and check the correctness of this list of villages. New villages or hamlets may have sprung up since the last Census, old ones may have disappeared or names may have changed from those entered in the list given you. You will correct the list by entering in it any such additions or alterations, so as to make it an accurate record of existing villages. The number of the mauzas (column 1) must be retained. Any additional village or hamlet having a recognized name of its own will be inserted below the name of the main village in column 2 under a separate sub-number. In the case of such new villages you will enter in column 3 a rough estimate of the number of houses they contain. You should at the same time note in this column any great change there may be in the number of houses in existing villages. In such a case score out the old number and put in its place a rough estimate of what you think the number of houses now is.

9. You will now devise the most convenient sub-division of your circle into enumerators' blocks. As a rule an enumerator's block should not contain more than about 60 houses or 300 persons. Two or more small villages near together may be made into one block: or a block may contain parts of different villages or the whole of one and part of another. Any village though containing fewer than about 60 houses may be made into a separate block, if there are sufficient competent enumerators available. To each block in order you will give a distinguishing letter as A, B, C, to be entered in column 4. In column 5 you will note the probable number of houses in each block.

10. You will also select for recommendation the most reliable competent person to be appointed enumerators of each of the blocks you have thus formed. Land-holders and their agents, traders or other persons of intelligence who are people of the country and not strangers should be entrusted with the work. You will enter the name of the enumerator you propose in column 6 opposite the name of the block to which he is appointed.

11. You will then send this preliminary list through the Superintendent to the Deputy Commissioner for approval. It will be returned to you with any alterations by the Deputy Commissioner noted on it. The enumerators approved of by the Deputy Commissioner will receive through Tahsildars letters of appointment with instructions. A copy of the latter is printed below. You must master these instructions yourself and see that enumerators thoroughly understand and act up to them.

12. You will point out to each enumerator the limits of his block. You must remember that your circle area is to be divided into a number of sub-areas, each of them a block. You will thus see that the blocks take in all your circle. Village boundaries, roads or other tangible limits should be adopted as the boundaries of blocks. The enumerator must understand that he is responsible for the enumeration of all persons there may be within these limits on the Census night.

13 You will next get the enumerators to prepare block or building lists as mentioned in the enumerators' instructions printed below.

14. In the preparation of these lists you should note the following :—

(*a*). The list should contain all buildings intended for or used as human dwellings whether actually occupied at the time or not.

(*b*). By "house" is meant "the dwelling place of one or more families, with their dependents and servants, having a separate principal entrance from the public way."

NOTE.—A bungalow with servants' out-houses should be reckoned as a single house.

In Chhatisgarh and elsewhere, where there are enclosures containing separate huts or houses, the enclosure will be marked with a serial number, and the separate huts or houses with separate sub-numbers, *e.g.*, where 16 is the serial number of an enclosure containing 3 huts the numbering of the latter will be $\frac{16}{1}$, $\frac{16}{2}$, $\frac{16}{3}$.

15. You will carefully check the building lists prepared by enumerators. If it should appear advisable to transfer buildings from one block to another, you may do so in anticipation of sanction.

16. When satisfied that the building lists are correct, you will countersign and forward them to the Superintendent of the charge with a correct circle list showing the exact number of buildings in columns 3 and 5 as ascertained from the building lists.

17. When the circle list is received back with the building lists approved, you will take a copy of each building list, and retain these copies with the circle list as the record of the sanctioned sub-division of your circle and of the details of each block.

18. You will then return the original building lists to the enumerators, and see that they have numbers painted on all buildings to correspond with the building lists. You will report to the Superintendent of the charge after this is done, and forward to him after check any bills for cost of labour and paint.

19. Any demand for acceptance of gratuity in respect of any act connected with the Census is an offence punishable under the Penal Code. Be careful that nothing of the kind happens in your circle.

Census Form No. III.

LETTER OF APPOINTMENT AND PRELIMINARY INSTRUCTIONS FOR ENUMERATORS.

(*a*)—*Letter of appointment.*

FROM

THE DEPUTY COMMISSIONER, ____________________

TO

____

You are hereby appointed an enumerator for the Census of 1891.

Deputy Commissioner.

Dated

(*b*)—*Preliminary Instructions.*

1. The limits of the block to which you have been appointed enumerator will be shown you by   who is supervisor of circle   which includes your block. He is the Census officer immediately superior to you. The distinguishing letter of your block is   . The distinguishing number of the circle to which it belongs is   .

2. You will first prepare a list in a form which will be supplied of all the buildings within your block which are in human occupation, including shops, temples, mosques schools, etc. This will be called the block or building list. You must be very careful to write distinctly.

3. In filling in column 2 you will arrange buildings in the order in which it will be most convenient to visit them on the night of the Census, as nearly as may be in order of proximity in the case of streets, consecutively down one side first.

4. Encamping grounds, halting places frequented by travellers, mooring ghats for boats, and all places of likely temporary stay are to be noted in place in the building list, so as to secure their not being overlooked on the night of the Census, but numbers will only be given to actual buildings.

5. You will adopt independent numbering in the building list for your block beginning with 1. If your block include more villages or portions of more villages than one, a separate building list, commencing with the number 1, is to be prepared for each separate village or portion of separate village.

6. When your building list is complete, make it over to the circle supervisor for check, previous to its being submitted for the Deputy Commissioner's approval. When approved it will be returned to you. Preserve it carefully as the index list of your block and of the order in which you are to effect later house-hold enumeration.

7. On receiving back the building list you will proceed to have numbers corresponding to those of the building list painted with cheap material (*e.g.* geru) in a sheltered position under the eaves in front of each building. The distinguishing letter of your block and the number of the circle to which it belongs will be painted along with the number of the house, *e.g.* (2) $\frac{C}{37}$: 2 is the distinguishing letter of the circle : C the distinguishing letter of the block, and 37 the number of the house. The cost of this numbering will be paid by Government if you send in a bill with vouchers through the circle supervisor.

8. Be warned that any demand of or acceptance of gratuity in respect of any act connected with the Census is an offence punishable under the Penal Code.

Census Form No. IV.

CIRCLE LIST.

TAHSIL———.

Charge—Rajpur . . . . . Circle Deogaon—No. 2.

Superintendent—E. F. . . . . Supervisor—A. N.

Village.			Block.			Remarks.
Revenue number.	Name of village and subordinate hamlets.	No. of houses.	Letter.	No. of houses.	Name of enumerator.	
1	2	3	4	5	6	7
17	Umergaon	47	*A.*	*47*	*K. L.*	
28	Karinja	103	*B.*	*70*	*M. N.*	
	(1) Pipalgaon . . .	22	*C.*	*55*	*I. R.*	
33	Kaothal	**170*	*D.*	*60*	*M. S.*	**Estimated number of houses at present time.*
			E.	*60*	*J. Y.*	
			F.	*50*	*Q. R.*	
	(1) Sawada	20	*G.*	*45*	*K. V.*	*A new hamlet.*
	(2) *Pulgaon* . . .	*25*				

NOTE.—The form has been filled in to illustrate the procedure noted in paras. 4 (3) and 6 of the Circular. The entries in Roman character would be made in the form in the district office previous to issue to supervisors, and those in italics filled in by supervisors. In the case of populous villages care should be taken when filling in the entries in the district office to leave sufficient space between the names of villages in column 2 for entering opposite the required block details in columns 4 to 7. Four copies of this form will be used in Census work.

(1) Copy to be supplied to supervisors filled in as noted above : on this they will make proposals for the subdivision of their circles.

(2) Copy to be filled in by supervisor after the block lists are prepared, showing exact number of houses and the names of enumerators finally selected (para. 7 of Circular).

(3) Copy of No. (2) to be given to Superintendents (para. 9).

(4) Do. do. supplied to Census Office (para. 9).

Census Form No. V.

BLOCK LIST.

BLOCK LETTER———.

Village or Ward——— . . . . . Circle———.

Sub-division, hamlet, street, etc.	Houses.		Principal occupant.	Remarks.
	Serial number.	Description (dwelling house, shop, serai, etc.)		

NOTE.—This form is printed on a separate leaf of the size of the enumerator's schedule leaf. Two or more eaves stitched together will ordinarily be used for one block. When small villages are included in one block, each will have a separate block list. For this one leaf of the form will probably be found sufficient. It should be seen that enumerators write distinctly leaving a space between the entries so as to avoid all chance of confusion The lists when finally approved are to be carefully preserved, as they will be stitched into the enumerators' books, when the latter are received.

Final Instructions to Supervisors.

I.—HOUSE-NUMBERING.

1. The Census preparations set forth in the Preliminary Instructions to Supervisors have by this time been generally completed. You must now carefully examine and test the Block Lists that have been prepared, and see that the numbering of houses has been properly done. If any house is found to have been omitted or a new house is built, it should be added at the end of the Block List, a note being made in the Remarks column opposite the place where it should have come. Thus if a house has been left out between houses Nos. 34 and 35, and if 60 be the last house number on the list, the building omitted will be numbered 61, and a note to the effect that "here comes No. 61" will be made in the Remarks column after house number 34. In the enumeration book house No. 61 will be entered at its proper place between Nos. 34 and 35. When a building has been numbered which should not have received a number, it should be scored out in the Block List, a note being made in the Remarks column. The numbers for the other houses in the list will remain unaltered. In accordance with para. 11 of the Instructions for Enumerators, it will be unnecessary to separately number cattle-sheds, etc., merely because some one sleeps there for the night; such persons will be enumerated at their houses. Similarly, shops, schools, temples, etc., in which no one resides at night need not be numbered.

II.—ISSUE OF ENUMERATORS' BOOKS.

2. You will receive from the Superintendent of charge enumeration books which you will distribute to the enumerators under you. The outside label of the book will be written up as indicated. In the case of a hamlet, bearing a separate name and enumerated in a separate book, enter opposite the word "village" on the label the name of the main village, adding beneath the name of the hamlet. As statistics are required mauzawar, you should see that this is invariably done. When there are more than one book used for a single block, or for a village which forms part of a block, each book for the block or village will be numbered. The number of houses need not be entered on the docket till the preliminary record.

3. You will take receipts from enumerators for the books given them.

4. You will have a supply of loose sheets given you, which are to be carefully preserved for use in case the schedules in any enumerator's book run short. When you give loose sheets to an enumerator note the number given and date on the cover of the book.

5. You will see that a copy of the Block List is pasted in each main book unless this has already been done.

6. You must see that each enumerator understands the instructions printed in his book. Before beginning the preliminary record he must make, under your supervision, a rough draft for some complete houses in his block, so that he may thoroughly understand how the entries are to be made. This draft must be made on plain paper or on schedules specially supplied.

The enumerator must not be allowed to use his book for practising.

III.—Preliminary Record.

7. While the preliminary record is going on you must move about your circle and see that the work is being done properly.

8. When it is complete you must examine every entry for the books in your circle and correct obvious errors and omissions. You must also test as many of the entries as you can on the spot, initialling the pages so tested. When an enumerator's book has been examined, tested and passed by you, you will sign and date it on the cover.

9. The following are the matters particularly to be observed in connection with the instructions printed in the enumerator's book :—

(*a*) Para. 3. Do not use separate paging for sub-numbered buildings in an enclosure and servants' out-houses attached to a bungalow. In such cases for "house number," at the top of the schedule, enter the serial number, as 20. Begin by entering the occupants of the first sub-numbered building $\frac{20}{1}$. Then draw a line and enter the occupants of the next building $\frac{20}{2}$, and so on. The sub-numbers may be noted in place in the side of column 1.

(*b*) Rule 1.—Column 1. See that the serial number is not filled in till the final record, on 26th February. The serial number will run for each house or set of sub-numbered houses. When a house contains more families than one, be careful to see that all are enumerated. When more women than one are entered as "female" in this column, the relationship to some member of the family should be added.

(*c*) Rule 2.—Column 2. Note that if a Gond or member of a forest tribe returns himself as a Hindu, he is to be entered as such.

(*d*) Rule 4.—Column 4. Take care that the main caste or tribe is entered in this column and not a sub-division.

(*e*) Rule 7.—Column 7. Enter the number of years each person will have completed on 26th February.

(*f*) Rule 8.—Column 8. In filling up this column the enumerator should ask whether a person is or is not married and should put down whatever answer is given without further enquiry.

(*g*) Rule 11.—Column 11. Care is to be taken in filling up this column. Read carefully the paragraph relating to it in the Instructions to Enumerators.

The following distinctions should be observed in entering the occupations of persons who own or cultivate land :—

(1) A person owns land, of which he cultivates, himself or through labourers, a part or the whole : enter in column 11 the ordinary term for his ownership, as Malguzar, Mafidar, Pattidar, etc.

(2) A person owns land, all of which he lets out for cultivation to tenants, he cultivating no part himself or through labourers : in column 11, to the ordinary terms as above, add "land all let to tenants."

(3) A person has no land of his own but rents land from others for cultivation in column 11 enter the word "Cultivator."

Remember that besides asking persons what is their ordinary occupation, they should be asked whether they also own or cultivate land. If they do, both occupations are to be entered.

(*h*) Rule 12.—Column 12. Note that persons at school or college are to be entered as learning, even though they know how to read and write.

(*i*) Rule 13.—Column 13. This column is to be filled in only for those shown as literate in column 12.

(*l*) See that in every column except columns 13 and 14 an entry is made against each person. In columns 6, 8, 12, and 14 take care to see that the words used in the heading and these alone are entered.

(*m*) All the entries, corrections, etc., previous to the final record are to be made in black ink.

IV.—Final Record.

10. You must see that each enumerator is supplied with red ink, and if his book be full that he has one or two loose schedule leaves for recording extra entries, especially in large villages where travellers may be expected to stop.

11. Para. 10 of Instructions for Enumerators.—Instead of reading over all the entries made for his family, servants, etc., to the head of the house, it will ordinarily be sufficient if only the names are read over. The whole entry will, however, be struck out for persons who are not present.

12. Para. 11.—See that the enemurator understands that he is to exter as present all persons who are away from their houses for the night only. Enumerators should also be told to omit persons temporarily present in their blocks, if under this rule they will be counted at their own houses elsewhere.

13. Para. 12. When a page is full and entries have to be continued at the end of the book, add a note at the foot of the original page—"continued on page—."

14. People actually travelling on the Census night will, when enumerated, be given tickets, which they should be told to produce if any one wants to count them again.

15. On the 27th February you will assemble your enumerators and examine the new entries in their books, testing any that may appear doubtful. Then get each enumerator to work out the figures required for the abstract printed in his enumeration book. Without filling in the abstract form, pass the book to another enumerator who has not seen the results previously brought out, and get him to re-add the book. If the two totals agree the abstract form should be filled in and signed by both enumerators. You will also yourself test and sign the abstract. Where a supplementary book has been used, its total will be entered in the abstract of the main book.

16. You will then fill in the totals of the enumerators' abstracts in a Circle Abstract form which will be supplied to you. This Circle Abstract you will at once despatch to your Superintendent.

17. You will then make over the enumeration books for your circle to your Superintendent, who will give you a receipt for them once he is satisfied they are complete.

Instructions to Enumerators.

A.—The first round.—(*Preliminary Record.*)

1. Beginning from the 12th of January 1891, you will visit every house in your block to which a separate number has been affixed, in the order in which they are entered in your Block List, and enter in the schedules in your book every person residing in those houses, in the manner prescribed below.

2. You must use black ink, and write very clearly in the character you know best.

3. You must take a fresh page for each house. If there are more than eight persons in a house, you should continue the entries for that house on the next page, repeating at the top of that page the number of the house in question, with the word 'continued' after it in brackets. You must never begin the entries for a fresh house in the middle of a page, but should leave the unused lines blank.

4. If the entry for any person in any of the columns of the schedule be the same as that for the person entered on the line above, you must repeat the entry and never write the word 'ditto,' or make dots, and leave the page blank.

5. If one of the houses on the list be found unoccupied, you should write the word 'empty' after the number of that house on the top of the form.

6. You are to enter all persons who ordinarily live and take their meals from the house even though any of them may be, at the time of your visit, absent for a short time at the bazar, town, watching crops, fishing, *or even for a few days at a wedding or on a pilgrimage*, provided they are to be back at the house before the 26th February. After the residents you should enter the visitors, if any, stopping in the house, *but not such as are*

only there for a day or two, as for a wedding, etc., and will not remain there till the 26th February. In dharmshálas, serais or temples, you should enter on this occasion only those who usually live there, and not travellers, etc., stopping only a day or night or so in the building.

7. Before beginning to make these entries you must read carefully the rules for filling up each column which are printed on the next page, and also the specimen schedule on the page opposite those rules.

8. You should point out to the supervisor entries about which you are in doubt, and receive his instructions. You must have completed all the entries in your block by the 1st of February 1891.

B.—THE SECOND ROUND.—(*Final Record.*)

9. At nightfall on the 26th February 1891, you will take this book as already filled in and again visit every house in your block in order.

10. You must summon the chief member of each family residing in the house, and read over to him the entries made for his family in the schedule. You will strike out the entries for persons who are not present, and fill up the form for any person now in the house who was not there when the first visit was made, such as guests, infants newly born and others.

11. You are to consider as present all living in or taking their meals from the house, even though any of them may be out fishing or watching in the fields or at a shop, etc., for the night.

12. If there be no room left on the schedule for the fresh entries above mentioned, you must take a fresh page at the end of your book, and enter on it the house number with the word 'continued' after it, as prescribed in para. 3 above.

13. Before you start on your round, you must see that you are yourself enumerated in the house where you are stopping.

14. You must make no alteration whatever in any entry against the name of any person unless you have to strike out the entries altogether because he or she is no longer present. When you strike out a person, you must draw the line completely through all the entries following that person's name, and not merely through column 1.

15. You must use only red ink for entries and erasures made on the round on the 26th February.

16. Whilst going on this round you must visit every house marked 'empty' in your book to see whether any persons are now living there, and if so, enter their names.

17. After visiting as above all the dwelling-houses, you must go to the dharmshálas, serais, encampments and landing-places, where travellers rest for the night, and enter all particulars in the schedules for the wayfarers, boatmen, pilgrims, etc., you may find there, and strike out the entries already made against persons who are not now present. You should ascertain from the village watchmen if any wandering gang, etc., has come to pitch in your block, and if there be any such, you should go and enumerate it as above prescribed for other persons.

18. If any house-holder in your block has been given a separate schedule, you should collect it on the morning of the 27th February, and after seeing that the rules have been complied with in filling up the columns, you should stitch or pin it into your book, next to the last schedule filled by you.

19. After your book has been inspected by the supervisor, you will prepare the short abstract printed on the back of the specimen schedule in it, as directed by the supervisor, and he will not take charge of your book until he has certified it to be correct.

20. According to the Census Act every person is legally bound to furnish you with such information as is necessary for filling up the schedule; but you are forbidden to ask for any information not required for the purposes of the Census. Any enumerator detected in extorting money on any pretext connected with the Census renders himself liable to punishment under the Census Act or the Penal Code.

C.—RULES FOR FILLING UP THE SCHEDULE.

RULE 1.—Column 1 (*Serial number and name*).—Enter first the chief resident member of the family, whether male or female, then the other members of the family, and their resident servants, if any, and lastly, visitors or temporary residents. If there be any objection made to giving the name of a female, write the word 'female' in this column and fill up rest of the columns for her as usual. If an infant has not yet been named, enter the word 'infant.' The enumerator is not to insist upon any female giving her own or her husband's name.

The serial number must not be added till the final record.

RULE 2.—Column 2 (*Religion*).—Enter here the religion which each person returns, as Hindu, Mussalman, Jain, Christian, Parsi, etc. For a member of a forest tribe who does not call himself Hindu, Mussalman, or any other religion, enter the name of his tribe, as Bhil, Gond, etc.; low castes as Chamar, Mahar, etc., should be entered by the religion which they themselves return, and no dispute about it is to be raised.

RULE 3.— Column 3 (*Sect of religion*).—Enter the sect of religion followed by each person as they return it:—

As *Smârth, Vaishnav, Kabirpanthi*, etc., for Hindus; *Sunni, Shiah*, etc., for Mussalmans; and for Christians enter whether *Church of England, Roman Catholic, Presbyterian*, etc. If the sect cannot be stated, enter 'not returned' in this column, but do not leave it blank.

RULE 4.—Column 4 (*Caste, etc.*).—Enter the caste of Hindus and Jains as Brahmin, Bania, Chamar, Rajput, etc., and tribe or race for others as Pathan, Moghal, Bhil, Gond, etc. Enter Christians as European, Eurasian or Native Christian; or the caste of the latter may be entered, if recognized. Vague terms like Pardesi, Marwari, Hindustani, Madrasi, etc., must not be used.

RULE 5.—Column 5 (*Sub-division of Caste, etc.*).—If the caste has been entered in column 4, enter here its sub-division, as Kanaujia, Deshasth for Brahmins; Agarwal, Oswal for Banias. If tribe has been entered, enter its sub-division, as Pardhan, Raj Gond for Gonds. If European has been entered in column 4, enter nationality, as English, German, Irish, etc., and if Native Christian, any racial or caste sub-division that may be given, as Goanese, Madrasi, etc. If no sub-division of caste or tribe be given, repeat the entry in column 4, but do not leave the column blank.

RULE 6.—Column 6 (*Male or Female*).—Enter here each person as either *male* or *female*, even though you have written the word 'female' in column 1 already.

RULE 7.—Column 7 (*Age*).—Enter the number of years each person has completed. For infants less than one year old, enter the word 'infant.'

If a person cannot state his or her age exactly, the enumerator should ask the relations *or refer to some well-known event of local importance*, or if the person be present, make a guess at the age from the appearance. You must never insist on seeing any female who is not voluntarily produced before you.

RULE 8.—(*Marriage, etc.*)—

Children who have been married should be entered as married even though they may not have begun to actually live with their wives or husbands.

RULE 9.—Column 9 (*Parent tongue*).—Enter the language which each person returns as ordinarily spoken in the household of his parents.

RULE 10.—Column 10 (*Birth-place*).—Enter the district in which each person was born, and if the person be not born in the Central Provinces, add the name of the Province or State to the district of birth.

If the person be born out of India, enter the country, as *China, Kabul, Ceylon*. The names of villages, tehsils, etc., are not to be given.

RULE 11.—Column 11 (*Occupation or means of subsistence*) [*Read this rule very carefully, and ask the supervisor about all cases which seem doubtful to you*].—Enter here the exact occupation or means of livelihood of all males and females who do work or live on private property, such as *house-rent, pension*, etc. In the case of children and women who do no work, enter the occupation of the head of their family, or of the person who supports them, adding the word "dependent," but do not leave this column unfilled for any one, even an infant. If a person have two or more occupations, enter only the chief one, except when a person owns or cultivates land in addition to another occupation, when both should be entered.

No vague terms should be used, such as "*service*," "*Government service*," "*shop-keeping*," "*writing*," or "*labour*," etc.; but the *exact service*, the *goods sold*, the *class of writing* or *labour* must be stated. When a person's occupation is connected with agriculture, it should be stated whether the land is cultivated in person or all let to tenants; if he be an agricultural labourer, it should be stated whether he be engaged by the month or year, or is a daily field-labourer. Women who earn money by occupations independent of their husbands, such as *selling firewood, cowdung-cakes, grass*, or by *rice-pounding, weaving* or *doing house-work* for wages, should be shown under those occupations. If a person makes the articles he sells, he should be entered as "maker and seller" of them. If a person lives on alms, it should be stated whether he is a religious mendicant or an ordinary beggar. When a person is in Government, Railway, or Municipal service, the special service should be entered first, and the word Government or Municipal, etc., after, as clerk—*Government*, sweeper—*Municipal*, labourer—*Railway*.

If a person be temporarily out of employ, enter the last or ordinary occupation.

RULE 12.—Column 12 (*Instructions*).—Enter as literate persons who can read and write and are not still under instruction. Enter as learning persons who are learning to read and write at home or at school, or who have learned to read and write, but are still at school or college or learning at home. Enter as illiterate those who are not under instruction and who do not know how to both read and write, or who can read but not write, or can sign their own name but not read.

RULE 13.—Column 13 (*Language known by literate*).—Enter here the language which those shown as literate in column 12 can both read and write. Enter one language only, that best known. But if a person knows how to read and write English as well as a vernacular, enter "English" also. This column is to be left blank for those shown in column 12 as learning or illiterate.

RULE 14.—Column 14 (*Infirmities*).—If any person be blind of both eyes, or deaf and dumb from birth, or insane or suffering from corosive leprosy, enter the name of the infirmity in this column.

Do not enter those blind of one eye only, or who have become deaf and dumb after birth, or who are suffering from white leprosy only.

Specimen Schedule.

Serial number and name.	Religion.	Sect of Religion (*see* Rule 3).	Caste of Hindus and Jains, Tribe or Race of others (*see* Rule 4).	Sub-division of Caste, etc. (*see* Rule 5).	Male or Female.	Age.	Married, unmarried or widowed.	Parent tongue.	Birth District, Province or Country (*see* Rule 10).	Occupation, or means of subsistence (*see* Rule 11).	Learning, literate or illiterate.	Language known by literate (*see* Rule 13).	If any person be insane, deaf-mute from birth, totally blind or a leper, enter that person as such below.
1	2	3	4	5	6	7	8	9	10	11	12	13	14
1 Chhoti . .	Hindu .	Not returned	Mahar .	Mahar .	Female .	27	Married .	Marathi .	Wardha .	Sells wood . . .	Illiterate.	...	...
2 Punja . .	Gond .	Not returned	Gond .	Pardhan	Male .	19	Married .	Gondi .	Chanda .	Daily agricultural labourer	Illiterate.	...	...
3 Goribahu .	Jain .	Digambri .	Bania .	Parwar .	Female .	Infant	Unmarried.	Hindi .	Jubbulpore.	Saucar and owner of land all let to tenants—dependent.	Illiterate.	...	...
4 Anthony . .	Christian .	Roman Catholic.	Native Christian.	Madrasi.	Male .	35	Married .	Tamil .	Tanjore, Madras.	Butler	Literate .	Tamil, English.	...
5 Ganga . .	Hindu .	Not returned	Kurmi .	Kurmi .	Female .	43	Widowed .	Hindi .	Saugor .	Owns and cultivates land—dependent.	Illiterate.	...	...
6 Amir Hossein .	Mussulman	Shiah .	Saiad .	Saiad .	Male .	27	Married .	Urdu .	Nimar .	Clerk—Railway . .	Literate .	Urdu, English.	...
7 Raghunath .	Hindu .	Vaishnav .	Brahmin .	Deshasth	Male .	18	Married .	Marathi .	Nagpur .	Pension—dependent .	Learning	...	...
8 Rupchand .	Hindu .	Vaishnav .	Bania .	Agarwal.	Male .	60	Widowed .	Hindi .	Raipur .	Cloth-seller . . .	Literate .	Hindi .	...

Enumerator's Abstract.

(*Not to be filled up till after the Census on the 26th February 1891.*)

Station or Beat.	Block.	Occupied Houses.	Persons.		
			Males.	Females.	Total.

(Signed)

Re-added by { (*a*) Enumerator of Block . / (*b*) Enumerator of Block . } Enumerator.

Certified to have been tested, and the total found correct.

(Signed)

Compiled into Charge Summary on the of 1891. }

Supervisor.

(Signed)

Charge Superintendent.

APPENDIX B.

VILLAGES CONTAINING OVER 3,000 POPULATION.

BRITISH DISTRICTS.

A.—Villages with over 5,000 inhabitants.

District.	Village.	Population.			Hindus.	Mussalmans.	Others.	Remarks.
		1881.	1891.	Increase + or decrease —				
1	2	3	4	5	6	7	8	9
Nagpur	Kelod	4,481	5,200	+ *719*	4,674	392	134	
Chanda	Armori	5,584	5,385	— *199*	5,141	119	125	
	Chimur	4,846	5,096	+ *250*	4,536	408	152	
	Nawargáon	4,304	5,025	+ *721*	4,303	200	522	
Bhandara	Mohári	5,142	5,008	— *134*	4,647	335	26	
Raipur	Rájim	3,252	5,856	+ *2,604*	5,198	562	96	Fair held at time of Census.
Sambalpur	Jhársogra	759	5,176	+ *4,417*	4,730	354	92	Railway Station; construction of B.-N. Railway in progress at time of Census.

B.—Villages with over 3,000 and below 5,000 inhabitants.

District.	Village.	1881.	1891.	Increase + or decrease —	Hindus.	Mussalmans.	Others.	Remarks.
Saugor	Rehli	5,230	4,912	— *318*	4,229	501	182	Tehsil head-quarters and Municipality.
	Itáwa	2,177	3,982	+ *1,805*	2,878	618	486	Adjoins Bina Junction on Indian Midland Railway opened since 1881.
	Ráhatgarh	4,013	3,469	— *544*	2,424	820	225	
Damoh	Hindoria	3,788	3,843	+ *55*	3,372	354	117	
Jubbulpore	Panágar	4,915	4,457	— *458*	3,500	519	438	
	Katangi	3,505	3,869	+ *364*	2,909	714	246	
	Pátan	3,171	3,479	+ *308*	2,601	452	426	
	Umaria	2,238	3,043	+ *805*	2,898	138	7	In Sehora tehsil, not the Umaria Colliery.
Seoni	Chhapára	2,881	3,450	+ *569*	2,401	746	303	
Narsinghpur	Chhindwára	3,519	3,814	+ *295*	3,082	265	467	Municipality.
	Kareli	3,371	3,804	+ *433*	3,181	251	372	Ditto.
	Kauria	3,295	3,217	— *78*	2,918	109	190	
	Singhpur	3,130	3,134	+ *4*	2,669	315	150	
	Tendukhera	2,977	3,075	+ *98*	2,751	102	222	
Hoshangabad	Timarni	4,176	4,433	+ *257*	4,034	325	74	
	Sobhápur	4,883	4,255	— *628*	3,254	535	466	
	Sángákhera	2,957	3,419	+ *462*	3,012	141	266	
	Bábai	3,818	3,230	— *588*	2,691	342	197	Municipality.
	Pachmarhi	2,054	1,823	— *231*	1,271	493	59	Cantonment and Sanitarium.
Nimar	Sháhpur	3,812	4,142	+ *330*	3,779	274	89	
	Pandhána	2,788	3,066	+ *278*	2,449	577	40	
	Asirgarh	2,437	1,740	— *697*	968	584	188	Cantonment and fortress.

B.—Villages with over 3,000 and below 5,000 inhabitants—*continued.*

District.	Village.	Population. 1881.	1891.	Increase + or decrease —	Hindus.	Mussalmans.	Others.	Remarks.
1	2	3	4	5	6	7	8	9
Betul	Multai	3,423	3,505	+ 82	2,890	468	147	Tehsil head-quarters and Municipality.
Chhindwara	Sausar	4,311	4,707	+ 396	4,343	312	52	Ditto ditto.
	Pipla Narain	2,794	3,288	+ 494	3,033	235	20	
Wardha	Alipur	3,938	4,097	+ 159	3,755	262	80	
	Náchangáon	3,615	3,812	+ 197	3,137	368	307	
	Kárinja	3,220	3,479	+ 259	3,342	137	...	
	Selu	2,918	3,258	+ 340	3,084	145	29	
	Mándgáon	3,199	3,041	— 158	2,764	141	136	
Nagpur	Pátansáongi	4,810	4,889	+ 79	4,567	289	33	
	Belá	4,943	4,631	— 312	4,319	181	131	
	Mowár	4,054	4,581	+ 527	4,217	337	27	Municipality.
	Kátol	4,137	4,560	+ 423	4,262	202	96	Tehsil head-quarters and Municipality.
	Párseoni	4,039	4,242	+ 203	3,892	230	120	
	Bhiwápur	4,571	4,175	— 396	3,842	169	164	
	Dhápewára	3,666	3,896	+ 230	3,683	211	2	
	Beloná	3,269	3,748	+ 479	3,660	27	61	
	Kondháli	3,296	3,613	+ 317	3,119	395	99	
	Sáwargáon	3,241	3,534	+ 293	3,343	191	...	
	Kuhi	3,254	3,381	+ 127	3,204	157	20	
	Páradsinga	2,780	3,192	+ 412	3,075	56	61	
	Bori	2,849	3,162	+ 313	2,854	185	123	
	Nagardhan	2,614	3,153	+ 539	2,966	75	112	
	Gumgáon	2,712	3,081	+ 369	2,839	242	...	
Chanda	Brahmapuri	4,818	4,885	+ 67	4,370	218	297	Tehsil head-quarters.
	Sáoli	3,680	4,100	+ 420	3,920	35	145	
	Sindewáhi	4,569	3,951	— 618	3,450	68	433	
	Nágbhir	3,829	3,896	+ 67	3,342	242	312	
	Mul	3,844	3,811	— 33	3,339	101	371	Tehsil head-quarters.
	Neri	3,364	3,556	+ 192	3,220	156	180	
	Chámursi	3,480	3,468	— 12	3,172	110	186	
	Bhisi	3,257	3,154	— 103	2,882	152	120	
	Garchiroli	3,099	3,002	— 97	2,658	88	256	
Bhandara	Tirora	2,781	3,493	+ 712	3,103	306	84	Tehsil head-quarters.
	Adyál	3,092	3,436	+ 344	3,083	119	234	
	Sángarhi	3,172	3,305	+ 133	2,741	197	367	
	Dighori	2,852	3,088	+ 236	2,943	8	137	
	Gondia	1,007	2,845	+ 1,838	2,657	138	50	Railway Station; terminus of feeder road to Burha.
Balaghat	Wáráseoni	3,326	3,977	+ 651	3,494	221	262	Municipality.
	Lálbarra	3,487	3,648	+ 161	3,161	326	161	Ditto.
	Katangi	1,293	1,429	+ 136	1,195	47	187	Ditto.
Raipur	Drug	3,797	4,149	+ 352	3,607	227	315	Tehsil head-quarters.
Bilaspur	Mungeli	4,757	4,755	— 2	4,270	364	121	Ditto ditto.
	Pandaria	4,317	4,106	— 211	3,646	229	231	Zemindari chief town.
	Chámpa	3,306	3,948	+ 642	3,838	103	7	Ditto ditto.
Sambalpur	Barpáli	4,125	4,450	+ 325	4,410	40	...	Ditto ditto.
	Rampela	1,193	3,712	+ 2,519	3,358	122	232	

FEUDATORY STATES.

District.	Village.	Population. 1881.	Population. 1891.	Population. Increase + or decrease —	Hindus.	Mussalmans.	Others.	Remarks.
1	2	3	4	5	6	7	8	9
Khairagarh .	Kairágarh .	2,887	3,453	+ *566*	3,260	182	11	
Sarangarh .	Sárangarh	4,220	4,393	+ *173*	3,910	236	247	
Raigarh .	Raigarh .	4,860	4,552	— *308*	4,102	413	37	
Kalahandi .	Bhawáni-Pátna . .	3,483	3,417	— *66*	3,191	46	180	
Patna . .	Pátna .	2,053	3,714	+ *1,661*	3,240	11	463	
	Gulchitara .	...	3,427	...	2,264	...	1,163	Information for 1881 not available.
	Turla .	...	3,135	...	1,897	...	1,238	Information for 1881 not available.
	Gudár .	...	3,031	...	1,990	...	1,041	Information for 1881 not available.
	Sihini .	...	4,077	...	2,702	...	5	Information for 1881 not available.

APPENDIX C.

I.—AVERAGE NUMBER OF FEMALES TO 1,000 MALES AT EACH AGE PERIOD.

Total Population.

Age.	Saugor.	Damoh.	Jubbulpore.	Mandla.	Seoni.	Narsinghpur.	Hoshangabad.	Nimar.	Betul.	Chhindwara.	Wardha.	Nagpur.	Chanda.	Bhandara.	Balaghat.	Raipur.	Bilaspur.	Sambalpur.	Feudatory States.	Central Provinces.
1	2	3	4	5	6	7	8	9	10	11	12	13	14	15	16	17	18	19	20	21
Under 1 year . .	955	960	991	1,049	1,014	967	1,019	1,037	1,014	1,003	1,009	1,009	1,037	1,012	1,036	1,018	1,039	1,024	1,024	1,015
1 „ . .	1,037	1,041	1,086	1,115	1,081	1,079	1,085	1,095	1,039	1,093	1,065	1,048	1,117	1,086	1,054	1,112	1,083	1,052	1,073	1,080
2 years .	1,112	1,076	1,072	1,077	1,086	1,078	1,087	1,122	1,094	1,074	1,045	1,066	1,128	1,074	1,072	1,138	1,135	1,104	1,127	1,104
3 „ .	1,101	1,086	1,149	1,134	1,143	1,072	1,093	1,156	1,143	1,151	1,129	1,112	1,120	1,128	1,149	1,136	1,147	1,151	1,141	1,133
4 „ .	1,026	1,024	1,068	1,044	1,054	1,026	1,003	999	1,085	1,047	1,041	1,043	1,049	1,032	1,038	1,070	1,078	1,055	1,088	1,057
Total under 5 years	*1,049*	*1,038*	*1,077*	*1,084*	*1,078*	*1,043*	*1,055*	*1,078*	*1,081*	*1,072*	*1,055*	*1,055*	*1,090*	*1,066*	*1,072*	*1,097*	*1,100*	*1,080*	*1,096*	*1,080*
5–9 years . .	948	938	968	954	1,005	970	963	977	1,011	1,022	1,023	998	970	998	985	955	985	992	966	976
10–14 „ . .	765	779	810	816	846	777	788	821	871	864	886	858	816	849	849	834	840	856	818	828
15–19 „ . .	834	804	854	1,050	954	880	890	1,016	1,010	953	1,027	941	1,027	968	932	981	982	978	981	954
20–24 „ . .	1,062	1,094	1,072	1,187	1,199	1,190	1,127	1,123	1,155	1,206	1,228	1,154	1,199	1,214	1,108	1,237	1,224	1,209	1,187	1,178
25–29 „ . .	1,014	1,037	1,088	1,031	1,085	1,127	1,011	943	1,084	1,132	1,039	1,067	1,056	1,217	1,121	1,132	1,119	1,019	1,051	1,077
30–34 „ . .	976	1,003	1,064	926	931	999	922	857	943	977	966	1,009	962	1,022	952	984	1,001	935	937	971
35 39 „ . .	901	966	980	809	1,017	1,019	883	751	896	955	825	883	847	1,058	1,059	1,003	947	1,003	885	935
40–44 „ . .	858	924	954	841	872	912	852	852	836	905	861	956	858	908	852	894	918	863	803	877
45–49 „ . .	731	759	704	724	864	843	818	672	796	811	753	769	723	898	981	1,034	901	948	852	845
50–54 „ . .	939	936	1,029	975	984	1,045	945	846	897	1,003	879	900	921	900	928	1,020	1,025	959	916	952
55–59 „ . .	901	888	978	1,071	1,146	1,045	1,013	680	886	990	783	754	873	1,027	1,326	1,560	1,308	1,317	1,203	1,068
60 and over . .	1,147	1,186	1,361	1,409	1,292	1,333	1,314	1,034	1,088	1,256	999	1,043	1,163	1,245	1,371	1,577	1,480	1,418	1,325	1,294
Total Population .	**936**	**946**	**990**	**982**	**1,006**	**994**	**958**	**932**	**987**	**1,016**	**972**	**979**	**980**	**1,026**	**1,011**	**1,042**	**1,031**	**1,007**	**984**	**996**

APPENDIX C.

II.—AVERAGE NUMBER OF FEMALES TO 1,000 MALES AT EACH AGE PERIOD.

Animistic Religion.

Age.	Saugor.	Damoh.	Jubbulpore.	Mandla.	Seoni.	Narsinghpur.	Hoshangabad.	Betul.	Chhindwara.	Wardha.	Nagpur.	Chanda.	Bhandara.	Balaghat.	Raipur.	Bilaspur.	Sambalpur.	Bastar.	Kalahandi.	Feudatory States.	Central Provinces.
1	2	3	4	5	6	7	8	9	10	11	12	13	14	15	16	17	18	19	20	21	22
Under 1 year	888	1,021	1,009	1,046	1,025	959	1,082	1,030	996	985	910	996	1,026	1,025	1,025	1,035	968	1,081	982	1,043	1,023
1 "	1,667	1,325	1,154	1,147	1,069	1,169	1,074	1,030	1,066	1,020	1,024	1,129	1,200	1,090	1,138	1,065	1,234	1,108	1,066	1,051	1,095
2 years	1,654	1,253	1,150	1,105	1,097	1,158	1,185	1,113	1,112	1,115	1,129	1,171	1,103	1,099	1,149	1,109	1,156	1,195	1,101	1,149	1,134
3 "	1,037	1,207	1,189	1,145	1,172	1,063	1,164	1,111	1,163	1,223	1,181	1,095	1,129	1,177	1,134	1,162	1,110	1,140	1,185	1,114	1,144
4 "	995	1,046	1,145	1,053	1,076	1,174	1,033	1,117	1,071	1,044	993	1,135	1,057	1,138	1,087	1,063	1,051	1,035	1,107	1,082	1,085
Total under 5 years	*1,176*	*1,153*	*1,138*	*1,099*	*1,093*	*1,104*	*1,110*	*1,089*	*1,087*	*1,079*	*1,048*	*1,110*	*1,088*	*1,111*	*1,107*	*1,093*	*1,089*	*1,114*	*1,100*	*1,102*	*1,101*
5-9 years	1,015	958	1,011	955	1,008	1,015	993	1,022	1,019	1,131	1,020	976	994	979	943	978	1,016	940	920	958	981
10-14 "	887	801	859	839	871	867	859	944	884	862	840	823	875	821	832	865	855	802	821	823	850
15-19 "	967	886	967	1,141	1,000	955	1,037	1,029	971	1,151	1,000	1,149	1,063	998	1,018	1,036	1,010	1,174	974	1,029	1,036
20-24 "	1,225	1,440	1,220	1,276	1,332	1,330	1,285	1,260	1,275	1,526	1,353	1,205	1,259	1,201	1,247	1,282	1,171	1,342	1,080	1,195	1,250
25-29 "	1,137	1,207	1,236	1,088	1,193	1,168	1,211	1,139	1,193	1,173	1,258	1,100	1,368	1,210	1,177	1,130	1,139	970	1,109	1,061	1,145
30-34 "	898	1,140	1,118	980	969	1,095	988	936	1,040	1,091	1,102	984	1,065	968	1,031	1,076	989	962	994	980	1,007
35-39 "	864	978	1,067	809	1,065	1,105	1,032	945	1,058	850	957	843	1,146	1,127	1,016	1,016	1,032	606	729	842	951
40-44 "	845	862	915	821	866	922	805	793	900	833	838	803	866	798	914	917	753	733	696	772	836
45-49 "	812	817	764	737	928	923	950	796	809	825	772	708	968	928	1,091	969	1,000	559	793	768	845
50-54 "	740	872	889	932	939	961	956	910	986	841	806	843	913	879	1,063	961	909	790	728	836	909
55-59 "	886	725	982	1,097	1,163	1,185	1,138	964	1,197	760	865	911	1,194	1,464	1,708	1,478	1,625	781	940	1,118	1,156
60 and over	809	983	1,250	1,313	1,183	1,274	1,227	1,008	1,279	934	928	1,095	1,313	1,291	1,710	1,652	1,348	879	942	1,157	1,246
Total Animistic	**980**	**1,003**	**1,036**	**1,005**	**1,032**	**1,051**	**1,028**	**1,009**	**1,041**	**1,021**	**992**	**987**	**1,062**	**1,019**	**1,065**	**1,055**	**1,020**	**952**	**927**	**975**	**1,015**

APPENDIX C.

III.—AGE-DISTRIBUTION OF 10,000 PERSONS OF EACH SEX.

Total Population.

Age.	Saugor.		Damoh.		Jubbulpore.		Mandla.		Seoni.		Narsinghpur		Hoshangabad.		Nimar.		Betul.		Chhindwara.	
	Males.	Females.	Males.	Females.	Males.	Females.	Males.	Females.	Males.	Females.	Males.	Females.	Males.	Females.	Males.	Females.	Males.	Females.	Males.	Females.
1	2	3	4	5	6	7	8	9	10	11	12	13	14	15	16	17	18	19	20	21
Under 1 year	240	245	262	266	227	227	242	259	265	267	282	275	292	311	340	378	280	288	318	314
1 "	155	171	146	160	187	207	206	234	204	220	168	182	161	181	161	189	176	185	156	167
2 years	246	293	252	287	279	302	352	386	333	360	314	340	287	326	269	324	322	357	335	355
3 "	311	366	302	347	309	357	400	462	324	368	326	352	305	347	281	349	330	383	337	382
4 "	304	334	306	331	319	344	387	411	332	347	306	316	296	309	284	305	323	355	345	356
Total under 5 years	*1,256*	*1,409*	*1,268*	*1,391*	*1,321*	*1,437*	*1,587*	*1,752*	*1,458*	*1,562*	*1,396*	*1,465*	*1,341*	*1,476*	*1,335*	*1,545*	*1,431*	*1,568*	*1,491*	*1,574*
5—9 years	1,535	1,555	1,567	1,553	1,587	1,553	1,768	1,717	1,533	1,533	1,461	1,425	1,345	1,352	1,309	1,373	1,540	1,578	1,543	1,551
10—14 "	1,223	1,000	1,326	1,092	1,303	1,066	1,284	1,068	1,232	1,036	1,250	977	1,210	995	1,171	1,032	1,259	1,111	1,262	1,073
15—19 "	824	734	827	703	746	644	693	741	704	667	712	630	729	678	712	777	700	716	695	652
Total under 20 years	*4,838*	*4,698*	*4,988*	*4,739*	*4,957*	*4,700*	*5,332*	*5,278*	*4,927*	*4,798*	*4,819*	*4,497*	*4,625*	*4,501*	*4,527*	*4,727*	*4,930*	*4,973*	*4,991*	*4,850*
20—24 years	755	857	674	780	686	743	728	880	725	864	722	865	771	906	807	973	720	842	710	843
25—29 "	891	966	818	918	804	884	851	894	875	944	878	996	921	972	907	919	822	903	813	905
30—34 "	942	981	916	971	941	1,011	990	934	1,001	927	958	992	1,000	962	1,033	950	960	917	944	908
35—39 "	559	538	561	572	595	589	415	342	431	436	533	547	573	528	551	444	452	411	447	420
40—44 "	806	739	794	775	791	762	740	634	804	697	823	755	809	719	750	686	776	657	783	698
45—49 "	316	247	330	265	334	268	187	138	234	201	310	263	313	268	337	243	231	186	241	192
50—54 "	429	431	436	432	437	454	384	381	478	468	451	474	465	459	494	448	487	443	479	473
55—59 "	98	94	104	98	96	95	49	54	67	76	93	98	103	109	130	95	84	75	82	80
60 and over	366	449	359	450	359	494	324	465	458	589	383	513	420	576	464	515	538	593	510	631

APPENDIX C.—*continued.*

III.—AGE-DISTRIBUTION OF 10,000 PERSONS OF EACH SEX—*continued.*

Total Population.

Age.	Wardha.		Nagpur.		Chanda.		Bhandara.		Balaghat.		Raipur.		Bilaspur.		Sambalpur.		British Districts.		Feudatory States.		Total Central Provinces.	
	Males.	Females.	Males.	Females.	Males.	Females.	Males.	Females.	Males.	Females.	Males.	Females.	Males.	Females.	Males.	Females.	Males.	Females.	Males.	Females.	Males.	Females.
1	2	3	4	5	6	7	8	9	10	11	12	13	14	15	16	17	18	19	20	21	22	23
Under 1 year	302	314	285	293	259	273	303	299	295	302	309	302	304	306	304	309	286	290	275	286	284	289
1 "	174	191	166	177	204	232	203	214	199	207	242	258	232	243	186	194	194	210	216	235	198	215
2 years	285	306	277	302	312	359	360	377	335	355	345	377	330	364	286	314	310	342	312	357	311	345
3 "	257	299	263	299	320	367	351	386	331	377	400	435	395	439	343	392	337	382	395	458	347	395
4 "	258	277	259	276	339	363	349	352	326	335	348	357	324	339	332	349	322	339	343	380	325	345
Total under 5 years	*1,276*	*1,387*	*1,250*	*1,347*	*1,434*	*1,594*	*1,566*	*1,628*	*1,486*	*1,576*	*1,644*	*1,729*	*1,585*	*1,691*	*1,451*	*1,558*	*1,449*	*1,563*	*1,541*	*1,716*	*1,465*	*1,589*
5—9 years	1,283	1,350	1,321	1,343	1,548	1,532	1,574	1,530	1,566	1,527	1,783	1,633	1,776	1,697	1,630	1,606	1,578	1,546	1,738	1,705	1,605	1,572
10—14 "	1,103	1,006	1,167	1,022	1,185	987	1,142	946	1,160	975	1,086	869	1,169	953	1,381	1,174	1,203	1,001	1,241	1,032	1,209	1,006
15—19 "	631	667	653	627	596	624	575	543	615	567	638	601	684	651	827	803	691	656	741	739	699	669
Total under 20 years	*4,293*	*4,410*	*4,391*	*4,339*	*4,763*	*4,737*	*4,857*	*4,647*	*4,827*	*4,645*	*5,151*	*4,832*	*5,214*	*4,992*	*5,289*	*5,141*	*4,921*	*4,766*	*5,261*	*5,192*	*4,978*	*4,836*
20—24 years	678	857	701	826	682	834	621	735	708	777	690	819	732	868	721	866	707	833	706	852	707	836
25—29 "	846	904	794	865	847	913	764	906	839	931	809	879	841	912	902	913	840	911	838	895	839	908
30—34 "	912	907	904	931	962	944	925	921	982	925	863	814	876	850	827	768	923	904	889	845	917	894
35—39 "	657	558	523	472	483	417	465	479	453	475	548	527	559	513	518	517	526	498	548	493	530	498
40—44 "	783	694	804	785	796	698	779	690	787	664	694	595	674	600	661	567	755	674	705	576	717	658
45—49 "	400	310	329	259	278	205	292	256	238	230	240	238	243	213	250	235	279	236	230	200	271	230
50—54 "	563	509	617	568	525	494	554	486	513	471	420	411	391	389	371	353	465	446	308	342	449	429
55—59 "	184	148	147	114	102	91	106	106	77	101	73	110	65	82	91	123	95	100	67	82	90	97
60 and over	684	703	790	841	562	667	637	774	576	781	512	775	405	581	367	517	489	632	388	523	472	614

APPENDIX C.

IV.—AGE-DISTRIBUTION OF 10,000 PERSONS OF EACH SEX.

Animistic Religion.

Age.	Jubbulpore.		Mandla.		Seoni.		Narsinghpur.		Hoshangabad.		Betul.		Chhindwara.		Wardha.		Nagpur.		Chanda.	
	Males.	Females.	Males.	Females.	Males.	Females.	Males.	Females.	Males.	Females.	Males.	Females.	Males.	Females.	Males.	Females.	Males.	Females.	Males.	Females.
1	2	3	4	5	6	7	8	9	10	11	12	13	14	15	16	17	18	19	20	21
Under 1 year	214	208	231	241	240	239	246	225	243	256	264	270	288	275	296	285	265	243	232	234
1 "	234	261	214	245	217	225	176	195	190	198	190	194	164	168	196	196	157	162	213	243
2 years	306	340	364	400	339	360	303	334	304	350	345	380	344	368	290	317	271	309	316	375
3 "	342	393	429	489	338	384	333	337	339	384	375	412	358	400	268	322	254	303	365	405
4 "	378	418	417	437	365	381	310	346	352	354	381	422	381	392	281	287	285	285	362	416
Total under 5 years	*1,474*	*1,620*	*1,655*	*1,812*	*1,499*	*1,589*	*1,368*	*1,437*	*1,428*	*1,542*	*1,555*	*1,678*	*1,535*	*1,603*	*1,331*	*1,407*	*1,232*	*1,302*	*1,488*	*1,673*
5—9 years	1,750	1,709	1,859	1,767	1,621	1,583	1,509	1,457	1,500	1,448	1,678	1,700	1,654	1,618	1,273	1,412	1,374	1,414	1,601	1,583
10—14 "	1,304	1,081	1,293	1,079	1,217	1,027	1,168	964	1,211	1,011	1,283	1,200	1,285	1,090	1,133	957	1,157	980	1,160	967
15—19 "	668	624	666	756	668	647	644	585	655	660	704	718	678	633	545	615	561	566	561	653
Total under 20 years	*5,196*	*5,034*	*5,473*	*5,414*	*5,005*	*4,846*	*4,689*	*4,443*	*4,794*	*4,661*	*5,220*	*5,296*	*5,152*	*4,944*	*4,282*	*4,391*	*4,324*	*4,262*	*4,810*	*4,876*
20—24 years	591	696	689	876	672	868	670	847	689	861	672	840	679	831	552	825	555	757	713	870
25—29 "	718	856	804	870	838	969	876	975	818	964	785	886	790	905	787	904	730	926	823	917
30—34 "	903	974	949	926	1,006	944	1,002	1,044	993	954	956	886	930	928	900	962	912	1,014	963	959
35—39 "	506	523	382	308	400	413	512	538	527	529	375	352	410	417	663	552	535	516	470	402
40—44 "	828	731	756	618	834	700	939	824	891	698	772	607	807	697	862	704	929	785	815	663
45—49 "	307	226	166	122	203	183	279	245	267	247	197	155	215	167	368	297	360	280	258	185
50—54 "	474	407	381	354	497	453	541	495	477	444	442	399	473	448	610	502	661	538	508	434
55—59 "	82	77	44	48	61	69	85	96	83	92	65	62	63	72	176	131	126	110	88	82
60 and over	395	477	356	464	484	555	407	493	461	550	516	517	481	591	800	732	868	812	552	612

APPENDIX C—*continued.*

IV.—AGE-DISTRIBUTION OF 10,000 PERSONS OF EACH SEX.

Animistic Religion.

Age.	Bhandara. Males.	Bhandara. Females.	Balaghat. Males.	Balaghat. Females.	Raipur. Males.	Raipur. Females.	Bilaspur. Males.	Bilaspur. Females.	Sambalpur. Males.	Sambalpur. Females.	British Districts. Males.	British Districts. Females.	Bastar. Males.	Bastar. Females.	Chhatisgarh States. Males.	Chhatisgarh States. Females.	Uria States. Males.	Uria States. Females.	Total Central Provinces. Males.	Total Central Provinces. Females.
1	2	3	4	5	6	7	8	9	10	11	12	13	14	15	16	17	18	19	20	21
Under 1 year	260	251	270	271	297	285	275	270	338	320	258	256	169	192	217	216	260	280	251	253
1 "	185	198	190	204	228	244	216	218	314	221	202	218	200	233	317	308	175	192	205	221
2 years	322	334	319	343	343	370	334	351	407	356	329	362	327	410	334	360	281	333	323	361
3 "	336	357	332	383	387	413	397	437	183	454	363	404	409	490	411	453	386	462	371	418
4 "	349	347	329	368	346	353	346	348	417	419	363	383	389	423	360	365	336	392	361	386
Total under 5 years	*1,452*	*1,487*	*1,440*	*1,569*	*1,601*	*1,665*	*1,568*	*1,624*	*1,659*	*1,770*	*1,515*	*1,623*	*1,494*	*1,748*	*1,639*	*1,702*	*1,438*	*1,659*	*1,511*	*1,639*
5— 9 years.	1,581	1,480	1,644	1,579	1,830	1,621	1,839	1,704	1,756	1,749	1,680	1,616	1,612	1 591	1,774	1,673	1,716	1,709	1 685	1,629
10—14 "	1,112	916	1,165	939	1,110	868	1,166	956	1,382	1,158	1,210	1,011	1,118	941	1,091	914	1,310	1,112	1,211	1,014
15—19 "	529	529	563	551	600	573	629	618	796	788	632	638	657	810	631	633	790	800	654	667
Total under 20 years	*4,674*	*4,412*	*4,812*	*4,638*	*5,141*	*4,727*	*5,202*	*4,902*	*5,593*	*5,465*	*5,037*	*4,888*	*4,881*	*5,090*	*5,135*	*4,922*	*5,254*	*5,280*	*5,061*	*4,949*
20—24 "	593	703	664	782	667	782	680	826	673	772	663	818	814	1,148	678	785	665	769	673	828
25—29 "	743	956	799	949	769	851	804	860	795	887	793	906	883	900	799	865	806	906	800	903
30—34 "	972	975	994	944	867	839	837	854	747	724	937	925	903	911	880	829	881	909	925	917
35—39 "	497	536	435	481	553	528	551	531	472	478	467	451	620	434	536	519	578	523	494	463
40—44 "	877	715	855	669	734	630	753	654	215	496	808	671	702	541	744	635	778	603	794	654
45—49 "	305	278	235	214	234	239	241	221	672	211	239	203	261	153	274	227	227	197	241	201
50—54 "	580	499	534	461	425	424	455	414	356	317	477	430	343	284	416	389	381	317	454	406
55—59 "	106	119	69	99	75	121	59	83	74	117	75	85	77	63	61	94	71	82	74	85
60 and over	653	807	603	763	535	859	418	655	403	533	504	623	516	476	477	735	359	414	484	594